The Human Condition

BOOKS OF RELATED INTEREST

The Human Condition

A RHETORIC WITH THEMATIC READINGS

JOAN YOUNG GREGG
New York City Technical College
of the City University of New York

BETH M. PACHECO
New York City Technical College
of the City University of New York

WADSWORTH PUBLISHING COMPANY
Belmont, California
A Division of Wadsworth, Inc.

To Marcos and Paisley, our own college freshmen.
To Manny, Suzy, and Garfield, who saw us through the hard times.
To Ben and John.

English Editor: Angela Gantner
Production Editor: Vicki Friedberg
Managing Designer: Donna Davis
Print Buyer: Randy Hurst
Permissions Editor: Peggy Meehan
Designer: Christie Butterfield
Copy Editor: Noel Deeley
Compositor: G&S Typesetters, Inc.
Cover Design: Donna Davis
Cover Painting: Oskar Schlemmer. *Bauhaus Stairway.* 1932. Oil on canvas.
63⅞ × 45″ (162.3 × 114.3 cm). Collection, The Museum of Modern Art, New York. Gift of Philip Johnson. Photograph © 1989 The Museum of Modern Art, New York.

Printed in the United States of America   49

1 2 3 4 5 6 7 8 9 10—93 92 91 90 89

Library of Congress Cataloging-in-Publication Data

Gregg, Joan Young.
   The human condition : a rhetoric with thematic readings / Joan
Young Gregg, Beth M. Pacheco.
      p.   cm.
   Includes bibliographies.
   ISBN 0-534-09336-1
   1. English language—Rhetoric.   2. College readers.   I. Pacheco,
Beth.   II. Title.
PE1408.G8625   1989
808'.0427—dc19   88-30270
                                                                              CIP

Contents

CHAPTER THREE

Uniquely Human—The Dilemma of Love: Summarizing and Synthesizing   97

CHAPTER SEVEN

The Liberal Arts: Defining and Classifying Knowledge   325

The Written Response 572

Preface

The Human Condition: A Rhetoric with Thematic Readings is designed for use in freshman writing programs in two-year and four-year colleges. It places the freshman writing course in the context of the larger goals of a liberal education by fostering the reading, reflection, and discussion requisite for meaningful writing. The text offers a thematic approach to freshman composition based on the notion that form and content are inextricable in good writing. Each chapter focuses on some human attribute that has allowed our species to survive, progress, and create. The thematic unity of each chapter permits students to work ideas through in preparation for writing as their awareness of the complexity of issues grows through reading, analysis, and discussion. The readings have been chosen from a wide range of academic disciplines, literary genres, and historical periods. Some are familiar; some are innovative and fresh; all are provocative, thoughtful, and well written.

Freshman students have a fund of life experience; however, they often find it difficult to give meaningful shape and force to that experience in writing. Similarly, although students have rich thoughts, they are not accustomed to trying out their ideas in discussion or measuring them against a written text and modifying them in light of added knowledge. Moreover, students' ideas are rarely sufficiently developed; as inexperienced writers, they do not yet command the techniques of elaboration that practice in writing provides. In this text, through a variety of writing assignments in response to the readings, students move toward a synthesis of ideas in the composing of mature essays.

Organization of the Chapters

Each chapter of this rhetoric-reader is organized to reconstruct the writing process: thinking, reading, discussing, writing, and rewriting.

First, the theme, which provides the context for reading, discussion, and writing, is established by a photo or illustration and a brief statement for reflection. Then, The Writing Focus, a model of synthesis writing, introduces and makes a connection between the theme, the rhetorical instruction, and the reading selections. In The Writing Focus, strategies for specific modes are presented with illustrations from the readings. Concluding The Writing Focus is an Essay for Analysis, followed by an Analysis of the Essay, which examines the writer's process through annotations and commentary.

In the next section, Readings, each selection is introduced by a head-note touching on a key concept of the work. The teaching apparatus following each selection is divided into two parts. Reading and Interpreting offers a Vocabulary list and Concept Analysis questions, which invite response to the content of the selection. Thinking and Writing offers Rhetorical Technique questions, which apply the composing principles discussed in The Writing Focus to an analysis of the selection. These are followed by a Composition assignment, a springboard for writing in the rhetorical mode of the chapter. In addition, many readings include a Quickwrite assignment to stimulate the imagination and challenge the student to be inventive and even whimsical in spontaneous writing.

Each chapter concludes with The Written Response, a section with major writing assignments that draw upon both the writing instruction and the reading content. This section includes the Writing Workshop, a guided composition process that may be used collaboratively or individually; Topics for Critical Thinking and Writing, which extend the concerns discussed in the chapter into the student's world; Synthesis Questions, which call on the student to write an essay incorporating material from several of the chapter's readings; and Refining Your Essay, a composition checklist highlighting the points of writing instruction for that chapter.

Organization of the Text

The text's ten self-contained chapters are unified by the theme of the human condition. The first three chapters comprise a foundation. In Chapter 1, "The Personal Response: Writing for Self-Awareness," students read and respond to the personal expressions of others. The many exercises call on students' feelings and experiences as a stimulus for writing, which leads to the formulation of a thesis. Chapter 2, "The Human Condition: Elements of the Essay," presents stages of the writing process that follow the formulation of a thesis, including planning, subdividing ideas, and framing introductions and conclusions. Chapter 3, "Uniquely Human—The Dilemma of Love: Summarizing and Synthesizing," presents techniques for summarizing reading selections and synthesizing ideas from related works.

Chapter 4, "Nature's Book: Writing Narratives," analyzes the narrative as both an independent form of writing and as a type of illustration or support that can be incorporated into other forms of expository writing.

In Chapter 5, "Teachers and Students: Making Abstractions Concrete," students are instructed in the use of figurative language and exemplification to elaborate their points of view and to communicate their abstract ideas.

Chapter 6, "Human Accomplishment: Recording the Process," takes the process essay beyond simple listing and chronology to the more challenging demystification of a subject and the need for a controlling idea.

Chapter 7, "The Liberal Arts: Defining and Classifying Knowledge," includes selections from across the liberal arts curriculum. It provides models for instruction in two modes central to academic writing.

In Chapter 8, "When in the Course of Human Events: The Causes and Consequences of War," students read and write causal analyses of humankind's most pressing problem.

In Chapter 9, "Peers and Pairs: Human Conditions Compared and Contrasted," human personality types and institutions are the subjects of inquiry. The Writing Focus offers instruction for expressing similarities and differences between related elements.

The final chapter is Chapter 10, "Ideas and Ideals: Writing the Argumentative Essay." Its selections cover issues of conscience and belief and illustrate a wide variety of techniques for bringing others to one's point of view.

The teaching apparatus of the text draws upon the best of current approaches to writing instruction and combines them in ways that preserve their integrity. Instructors may balance several strands according to the level of their students and their own particular perspectives.

Academic writing is one aspect of the text. The elements that focus on this area are the following:

• Chapter 2, Elements of the Essay
• Chapter 3, Summarizing and Synthesizing
• Chapter 7, Defining and Classifying Knowledge
• Concept Analysis assignments
• Synthesis Questions

In addition, several of The Writing Focus sections present writing modes appropriate to the various academic disciplines so that writing becomes a tool for learning. These modes are applied in the Rhetorical Technique questions and in the Composition assignment that follows each reading.

To assist students in developing their personal voices by using writing as a process of discovery, certain portions of the text are particularly useful. The following elements focus on experiential topics, heuristics for generating ideas, and revising through multiple drafts:

• Chapter 1, Writing for Self-Awareness
• Chapter 4, Writing Narratives
• Chapter 5, Making Abstractions Concrete
• Essay for Analysis and Analysis of the Essay
• Quickwrites
• Topics for Critical Thinking and Writing
• Writing Workshop
• Refining Your Essay

In every chapter works of literature and examples of personal writing allow the student to identify with the author, offering a particularly effective content base for the process approach.

A third strand in the text allows students to gain facility in writing in the traditional rhetorical modes. The following elements emphasize the use of organizational patterns as keys to thinking, reading, and writing:

- Chapters 6 through 10
- Essay for Analysis
- Rhetorical Technique
- Composition
- Selected Topics for Critical Thinking and Writing
- Writing Workshop

Convenient access to the text is provided by the annotated Table of Contents.

Acknowledgments

We gratefully acknowledge the suggestions of the following reviewers: Lynn Beene, University of New Mexico; Gerald L. Brown, University of Pittsburgh at Johnstown; Jeffrey DeLotto, Texas Wesleyan College; Richard H. Dodge, Santa Monica College; Amy A. Doerr, State University of New York at Buffalo; Karen W. Donnelly, Pennsylvania State University; Linda D. Doran, Volunteer State Community College; Marya M. DuBose, Augusta College; Eileen B. Evans, Western Michigan University; Marjorie Ferry, Chemeketa Community College; Robert F. Geary, James Madison University; Joseph Geckle, Westmoreland County Community College; Kate Kiefer, Colorado State University; James Kinney, Virginia Commonwealth University; Ted Locker, Fresno City College; Charlotte Montandon, San Jose City College; James A. Moore, East Central University; Kae Irene Parks, Pennsylvania State University–Altoona Campus; Randall L. Popken, Tarleton State University; Suzanne M. St. Laurent, Broward Community College; and David Thomas, University of California at Riverside.

CHAPTER ONE

The Personal Response:
Writing for Self-Awareness

To be human is to wear the masks of human society: the mask of gender, the masks of the parent and the child, the mask of the worker, the masks of the oppressed and the oppressor. It takes practice to wear certain masks and courage to remove others. What social masks have you learned to wear? Which of these masks might you like to discard?

THE WRITING FOCUS

One's-self I sing, a simple separate person, . . .

Walt Whitman, "One's-Self I Sing," *Leaves of Grass*

I celebrate myself, and sing myself,
. . . .
I exist as I am, that is enough,
If no other in the world be aware I sit content,
And if each and all be aware I sit content.
. . . .

Walt Whitman, "Song of Myself," *Leaves of Grass*

To reveal his innermost thoughts and feelings, Walt Whitman stripped away the masks society assigned to him. Many of us avoid personal writing such as Whitman's, fearing that it will unmask too much of ourselves. Yet this kind of writing, which is within everyone's reach, offers unique rewards. The readings in this chapter, including diary entries, letters, autobiography, and autobiographical fiction, show that personal writing can give satisfying expression to our most striking observations, our clearest insights, our deepest feelings, and our firmest convictions.

The purpose of this chapter is neither the analysis nor the composition of completed essays. It is rather to introduce you to the first stages of the writing process: invention, focus, and thesis formulation. The readings, which vary in form from sketches of life to full-length portraits, exemplify these stages.

Invention

Writing begins with invention. With you as your own best topic, invention is what you see around you, what you see inside you. This chapter suggests ways to narrow and focus your observations and formulate theses. These activities are the earliest stages of the writing process.

Invention requires rummaging through your mental knapsack. There are several ways to do this. One is to tap your memories and ideas through freewriting.

FREEWRITING

Freewriting is the rapid, spontaneous, unstructured recording of your thoughts. The following freewriting exercises will help you warm up for the writing process. (Your instructor will provide time limits.)

1. Immediately write the first word that comes to mind when you see or hear each of the following terms:

   mask   **transparent**   **tell lies**   **a stranger**

2. Select one of the above items and freewrite about it.
3. Select one adjective from your freewriting, turn it into a noun, and freewrite about it.

BRAINSTORMING

Brainstorming is concentrating on a concept or problem and spontaneously responding to it by recording all the aspects one thinks of in note form. For example, in response to the concept *gifts* as an essay topic, the following brainstormed list was generated:

gifts in exchange for invitations

dangerous gifts—beware of Greeks bearing gifts

amounts of money

wrapping gifts

abstract gifts

artistic gifts

birthday, Christmas gifts

something-for-the-person-who-has-everything gifts

giving rather than receiving

occasions for gifts

hated getting books as gifts when young

gifts you never wanted

expensive gifts

ignoring gifts

money vs. gifts

humorous gifts

it's not the gift; it's the thought behind it

being "gifted"

memories of gifts

favorite gifts

These brainstormed items were then grouped into related clusters to provide a structure for organizing a formal essay.

1. Brainstorm one of the following items related to the theme of this chapter:

   enemies   **secrets**   **good manners**   **speeches**

2. Open a telephone book and point to any name. Write ten things that you imagine about that person. Now open the telephone book again and find another name. Describe that person as well. Brainstorm a relationship between the two people.

ASKING QUESTIONS

To explore a topic, ask questions about it such as the following:

What: What is it?
        What causes it?

What is its purpose?
What does it mean?
What does it lead to?
What is its opposite?

Who: Who is it?
Who makes it?
Who wants it?
Who needs it?

When: When did it begin?
When will it end?
When is it appropriate?

Where: Where do you find it?
Where is it from?
Where is it going?
Where does it lead?

Why: Why did it happen?
Why are you writing about it?
Why is it important?
Why are you curious about it?

How: How does it work?
How does it look?
How does it feel?
How does it affect us?
How has it changed?
How is it similar to/different from _____?

Another major source of invention is what we observe in our daily lives. Messages come to us not only through the physical senses but also from our emotions.

- sight: color, shape, size
- touch: texture—rough, smooth, hard, sharp, wet, dry, silky, fuzzy, furry, slick
- hearing: loud, discordant, shrill, low, sweet, musical, mellow, harmonious, rhythmic
- smell: faint, acrid, strong, perfumed, fetid
- taste, textures, and temperatures: chewy, slimy, hot, sweet, grainy, cold, sour, sandy, icy
- emotions: horror, happiness, scorn, contempt, boredom, fear, interest, excitement, revulsion, love, anger, disgust, maternal love, lust, passion
- motion: jumpy, jerky, smooth, rhythmic, tense, graceful

The following exercises will help you extend your ability to observe and describe.

1. Your instructor will pass an inanimate object around the class. Each student must make one original observation about it.
2. Closely observe an object such as a plant, a pet, a bicycle, or a kitchen utensil. How many colors or shades of color can you see in it? What textures do you feel? What does it smell like? How does it sound?
3. Observe the view from your classroom window for two minutes. Then, write down all the descriptive details you can remember.

KEEPING A JOURNAL

You can store your inventions, observations, memories, feelings, ideas, and responses to things read and heard in a journal. Here, you may take different approaches to recording raw material for writing. You may write at the same time each day and date your entries, or you may prefer to simply jot down ideas and images as they occur. Your entries may be brief fragments or carefully composed sentences. You need not limit yourself to what you see and hear, but you may also copy or paste in meaningful quotations or passages from your reading. You may simply log an incident or you may also record your reactions to it in a double-column journal entry. In this method, you divide your page in two, using the left-hand column for the facts of the anecdote and the right-hand column for your responses. The Quickwrite assignments in this text may also be recorded in your journal.

Focus

The writing process is stimulated by free association and unstructured observation. To produce a strong piece of writing, however, you must bring your ideas into focus. Just as a photographer selects a subject from a broad scene, eliminating some objects and shifting others around, the writer, too, must select some focal points from a mass of material. Having determined the composition of the picture, the photographer does not simply point the camera and shoot. The lens must be adjusted to bring clarity to the image and emphasize certain details. Similarly, the writer must narrow the perspective to highlight some points and subordinate others.

It is not easy to shape, or focus, raw material. But the discovery of repeated ideas, patterns, or themes is an important intermediate step in writing an essay. With practice, you will become more adept at bringing your notes, freewritings, and journal entries into focus.

The following exercises will help you learn to establish direction for ideas. (You may also apply the techniques in these exercises to unstructured writing such as you did in the section on invention.)

1. Freewrite on one of the following terms:

   enemies   secrets   good manners   gifts   speeches

   Then select a meaningful word from your freewriting. Make that word the subject of a new freewriting. Review this second freewriting to choose a second meaningful word as the subject of a third freewriting. Now skim your three successive freewritings. You will see your material coming into focus.

2. Brainstorm one of the following topics related to the theme of this chapter:

   powerless people   boredom in school   authority figures

   menial work   unhealthy friendships   manners

   Review your brainstormed list and circle the most important items. Organize the circled items into columns of related thoughts. Each column can become a part of an essay on that topic. (See Chapter 2 for a discussion of brainstorming for an outline.)

3. Refer back to brainstorming exercise 2 in the Invention section, which asked you to describe two people selected from the telephone book. Create a conflict between these two individuals and use it as the basis for a piece of writing.

4. The question-asking technique in the Invention section may also provide a focus for broad subject matter. Choosing one or two of the question types— what, who, where, when, how, why—apply these to the topic of masks.

5. A moment in the past may bring a topic into focus. How far back can you remember? Freewrite an early childhood memory. Where were you? Who was with you? What were you doing? Include sensory and emotional responses as you recall them. Make a general statement about your character or personality that is illustrated by this narrative.

Formulating a Thesis

A thesis is a controlling idea. Once you have focused your material, formulate a tentative thesis about it based on your personal observations, reflections, or experience. Your thesis statement, which may be more than one sentence, should express your topic and control its direction.

The following is an example of a controlling idea from George Orwell's *Down and Out in Paris and London* (paragraph 13 of the excerpt in this chapter):

> I calculated that one had to walk and run about fifteen miles during the day, and yet the strain of the work was more mental than physical.

The topic is the character's work as a waiter, and the controlling view is the emphasis on the mental rather than the physical strain of the job. The details that make up this section of Orwell's book support and elaborate this assertion.

No essay can treat all aspects of a topic. Therefore, limit your topic with boundaries such as time, place, culture, or socioeconomic factors. These boundaries will give your reader a more precise idea of what to expect in your essay.

Take the topic of masks, for example. The word *masks* in the first paragraph of the Writing Focus section of this chapter is limited by the phrase "masks society assigns"—that is, social masks. The reader does not expect to learn about the history of masks or about different types of theatrical masks. The topic is clearly governed by the idea of socially imposed masks. The paragraph, controlled by that idea, develops the thesis that through personal writing we can find the self hidden under our social masks.

Here are assertions from the chapter readings that serve as strong thesis statements. Use their form to create thesis statements of your own.

Example:

Anaïs Nin:

"Reading Robert's diary was my only access to the inner Robert."

Student:

Watching John compete in sports is the best way to understand his character.

C. P. Ellis:

a. "People are being used by those in control, those who have all the wealth."

b. "My father and I were very close but we didn't talk about too many intimate things."

Lord Chesterfield:

a. "Of [the] lesser talents, good-breeding is the principal and most necessary one."

George Orwell:

a. "Dirtiness is inherent in hotels and restaurants, because sound food is sacrificed to punctuality and smartness."

b. "The time between eight and half-past ten was a sort of delirium."

Consider the following statements from reading selections. Are they satisfactory thesis statements or could they be broadened or limited in some way? Select several for revision.

C. P. Ellis:

a. "My father worked in a textile mill in Durham."

b. "I loved my father."

c. "The whole world was openin' up and I was learnin' new truths that I had never learned before."

Anaïs Nin:
   a. "The first night I moved in [to my new apartment] there was a storm."
   b. "Expressing feeling is linked directly with creation."
   c. "We live in an era of destruction."
   d. "Visited the Patchens. Something baffles me here which I never experienced before."

George Orwell:
   a. "The Hôtel X was a vast, grandiose place with a classical façade, and at one side a little, dark doorway like a rat-hole, which was the service entrance."
   b. "Apart from the dirt, the *patron* swindled the customers wholeheartedly."

If you wander from your thesis statement, contradict it, or neglect to develop it, you will confuse your reader. During the writing process, however, you may decide to modify the thesis. Perhaps your thesis statement is too narrow, preventing you from including important information. Conversely, too broad a thesis statement may lead to unfocused writing. As you write, keep your thesis formulation in mind as a control on your supporting material. In your final draft, polish your thesis statement so that it firmly and precisely expresses your central point about the topic.

Finding Your Own Voice

In moving from spontaneous writing to finished essays, you need not bury all signs of yourself, the person behind the writing.

Look over your journal entries and exercises for clues to your developing writing style. Note pieces of your work that particularly please you. Analyze them for the qualities you like about them. Use questions such as these to find your own voice in your writing:

- Do you typically use long or short sentences? Or do you vary your sentence length?
- Do you favor multisyllabic words in your writing vocabulary, or are most of your content words short and plain? (For example, would you use *conceptualize* or *think about*?)
- Do you frequently use adjectives? In what way—as single words before nouns, in series?
- Is the level of your language conversational—informal vocabulary, run-on sentences, sentence fragments, contractions? Or is it more formal?
- Do you use many comparisons in your explanations and descriptions? Do

you use the vocabulary of sports, the theater, fashion, or nature in your writing?

- Are your subjects more frequently observations of the external world, narratives of events, or reflections on your feelings? Have you written more about others or about yourself?
- Have you included in your journal many quotations or paraphrases of what you have read or heard others say?
- Do you frequently incorporate dialogue into your freewriting?

Once you have made a start toward finding your own writing voice, share some of your favorite journal pieces with friends or classmates. Ask them to comment on what they most enjoy in these passages. Where does their appreciation of your style agree with or differ from your own?

Even in response to academic assignments, you can retain your personal voice. Here are some suggestions:

- Approach the academic topic from the angle of your own personal interest. Ask yourself: *What interests me in general? At what point might this topic intersect with my interests? What connection can I find to bring my interests together with the assigned topic?* Work from the familiar to the unfamiliar, the known (your own experience and perspective) to the unknown (content derived from reading, interviewing, lecture notes).
- Let the topic percolate in your head. Reflect on it for a while. Jot down notes, brainstorm it, discuss it, consider it from various angles. Let the seed of your central idea germinate.
- Then start writing to discover your message; it will become clearer as you progress. When you have control over your central idea, then give consideration to your audience and the more formal requirements of your task. You may wait to do this in your second draft.
- Don't be afraid to overwrite your first draft. Use large paper and a sharp pencil, or a typewriter or word processor to encourage your expressive flow. If you have a notion of some material you wish to include but can't quite get the phrasing right, don't worry about it. Just get it down and go back to it later. Use as many words as you need in this draft. You can condense later.
- Write on only one side of the paper for flexibility in cutting and pasting later. Use wide margins so you can make notes for your next draft. Erasing takes time, restricts the flow of ideas, and prevents you from recovering an utterance that you may want later. Instead, if you want to revise, simply draw one line through your original and run the alternative expression above, below, or alongside it.
- Be prepared to revise several times. Through continual writing practice you will learn how much of your personal voice should remain in the final draft of any particular assignment.

RICHARD WRIGHT

Black Boy

Black American novelist Richard Wright (1908–1960) suffered the hardships of neglect and poverty that he described in his autobiographical novel *Black Boy* (1945), from which the following excerpt is taken. Like many American adolescents, Wright rebelled against social conventions. His alienation, however, was threefold: he was an exuberant youth continually squashed by authoritarian adults, he was an artistic spirit at odds with a conservative religious environment, and he was a black youngster growing up in a racist world.

The school term ended. I was selected as valedictorian of my class and assigned to write a paper to be delivered at one of the public auditoriums. One morning the principal summoned me to his office.   1   Narrative begins with details of the experience

"Well, Richard Wright, here's your speech," he said with smooth bluntness and shoved a stack of stapled sheets across his desk.   2   Striking phrase

"What speech?" I asked as I picked up the papers.   3

"The speech you're to say the night of graduation," he said.   4

"But, professor, I've written my speech already," I said.   5

He laughed confidently, indulgently.   6   Precise adverbs convey character

"Listen, boy, you're going to speak to both *white* and colored people that night. What can you alone think of saying to them? You have no experience . . ."   7   Unfolding of main conflict

I burned.   8   Vivid verb recalls emotion

"I know that I'm not educated, professor," I said. "But the people are coming to hear the   9   Wright's focus students, and I won't make a speech that you've written."

He leaned back in his chair and looked at 10 me in surprise.

"You know, we've never had a boy in this 11 school like you before," he said. "You've had your way around here. Just how you managed to do it, I don't know. But, listen, take this speech and say it. I know what's best for you. You can't afford to just say *anything* before those white people that night." He paused and added mean-ingfully: "The superintendent of schools will be there; you're in a position to make a good impression on him. I've been a principal for more years than you are old, boy. I've seen many a boy and girl graduate from this school, and none of them was too proud to recite a speech I wrote for them."

Precise adverb to convey threat

I had to make up my mind quickly; I was 12 faced with a matter of principle. I wanted to graduate, but I did not want to make a public speech that was not my own.

Focus on conflict; thesis emerges: Wright's declaration of independence

"Professor, I'm going to say my own speech 13 that night," I said.

He grew angry. 14

"You're just a young, hotheaded fool," he 15 said. He toyed with a pencil and looked up at me. "Suppose you don't graduate?"

Forceful language for conflict

"But I passed my examinations," I said. 16

"Look, mister," he shot at me, "I'm the 17 man who says who passes at this school."

Metaphorical verb followed by appropriate reaction

I was so astonished that my body jerked. I 18 had gone to this school for two years and I had never suspected what kind of man the principal was; it simply had never occurred to me to wonder about him.

"Then I don't graduate," I said flatly. 19

I turned to leave. 20

"Say, you. Come here," he called. 21

I turned and faced him; he was smiling at 22 me in a remote, superior sort of way.

You know, I'm glad I talked to you," he 23 said. "I was seriously thinking of placing you in the school system, teaching. But, now, I don't think that you'll fit."

Precise adjectives convey character

He was tempting me, baiting me, this was 24
the technique that snared black young minds
into supporting the southern way of life.

Wright generalizes beyond this incident

"Look, professor, I may never get a chance 25
to go to school again," I said. "But I like to do
things right."

"What do you mean?" 26

"I've no money. I'm going to work. Now, 27
this ninth-grade diploma isn't going to help me
much in life. I'm not bitter about it; it's not
your fault. But I'm just not going to do things
this way."

"Have you talked to anybody about this?" 28
he asked me.

"No, why?" 29

"Are you sure?" 30

"This is the first I've heard of it, pro- 31
fessor," I said, amazed again.

"You haven't talked to any white people 32
about this?"

"No, sir!" 33

"I just wanted to know," he said. 34

My amazement increased; the man was 35
afraid now for his job!

"Professor, you don't understand me." I 36
smiled.

"You're just a young, hot fool," he said, 37
confident again. "Wake up, boy. Learn the world
you're living in. You're smart and I know what
you're after. I've kept closer track of you than
you think. I know your relatives. Now, if you
play safe," he smiled and winked, "I'll help you
to go to school, to college."

Forceful language

"I want to learn, professor," I told him. 38
"But there are some things I don't want to
know."

Thesis restated by
implication

"Good-bye," he said. 39

I went home, hurt but determined. I had 40
been talking to a "bought" man and he had
tried to "buy" me. I felt that I had been dealing
with something unclean. That night Griggs, a
boy who had gone through many classes with
me, came to the house.

Vivid metaphor related to
thesis

"Look, Dick, you're throwing away your 41
future here in Jackson," he said. "Go to the

principal, talk to him, take his speech and say it. I'm saying the one he wrote. So why can't you? What the hell? What can you lose?"

"No," I said. 42

"Why?" 43

"I know only a hell of a little, but my 44 speech is going to reflect that," I said.

Restatement of main conflict

"Then you're going to be blacklisted for 45 teaching jobs," he said.

"Who the hell said I was going to teach?" 46 I asked.

"God, but you've got a will," he said. 47

"It's not will. I just don't want to do things 48 that way," I said.

He left. Two days later Uncle Tom came to 49 me. I knew that the principal had called him in.

"I hear that the principal wants you to say 50 a speech which you've rejected," he said.

"Yes, sir. That's right," I said. 51

"May I read the speech you've written?" 52 he asked.

"Certainly," I said, giving him my manu- 53 script.

"And may I see the one that the principal 54 wrote?"

I gave him the principal's speech too. He 55 went to his room and read them. I sat quiet, waiting. He returned.

"The principal's speech is the better 56 speech," he said.

"I don't doubt it," I replied. "But why 57 did they ask me to write a speech if I can't deliver it?"

"Would you let me work on your speech?" 58 he asked.

"No, sir." 59

"Now, look, Richard, this is your 60 future . . ."

"Uncle Tom, I don't care to discuss this 61 with you," I said.

He stared at me, then left. The principal's 62 speech was simpler and clearer than mine, but it did not say anything; mine was cloudy, but it said what I wanted to say. What could I do? I had half a mind not to show up at the

Focus on conflict

graduation exercises. I was hating my environment more each day. As soon as school was over,
I would get a job, save money, and leave.

Recall of emotion

Griggs, who had accepted a speech written 63
by the principal, came to my house each day and
we went off into the woods to practice orating;
day in and day out we spoke to the trees, to the
creeks, frightening the birds, making the cows
in the pastures stare at us in fear. I memorized
my speech so thoroughly that I could have re-
cited it in my sleep.

Remembered scene

The news of my clash with the principal 64
had spread through the class and the students
became openly critical of me.

"Richard, you're a fool. You're throwing 65
away every chance you've got. If they had known
the kind of fool boy you are, they would never
have made you valedictorian," they said.

I gritted my teeth and kept my mouth 66
shut, but my rage was mounting by the hour.
My classmates, motivated by a desire to "save"
me, pestered me until I all but reached the
breaking point. In the end the principal had to
caution them to let me alone, for fear I would
throw up the sponge and walk out.

Focus on conflict

I had one more problem to settle before I 67
could make my speech. I was the only boy in my
class wearing short pants and I was grimly determined to leave school in long pants. Was I
not going to work? Would I not be on my own?
When my desire for long pants became known
at home, yet another storm shook the house.

Introduction of associ-
ated experience

"You're trying to go too fast," my mother 68
said.

"You're nothing but a child," Uncle Tom 69
pronounced.

"He's beside himself," Granny said. 70

Forceful expression of
conflict

I served notice that I was making my own 71
decisions from then on. I borrowed money from
Mrs. Bibbs, my employer, made a down payment on a pearl-gray suit. If I could not pay for
it, I would take the damn thing back after
graduation.

On the night of graduation I was nervous 72
and tense; I rose and faced the audience and my

speech rolled out. When my voice stopped there was some applause. <u>I did not care if they liked it or not; I was through.</u> Immediately, even before I left the platform, I tried to shunt all memory of the event from me. A few of my classmates managed to shake my hand as I pushed toward the door, seeking the street. <u>Somebody invited me to a party and I did not accept.</u> I did not want to see any of them again. I walked home, saying to myself: The hell with it! With almost seventeen years of baffled living behind me, I faced the world in 1925.

Conclusion reinforces thesis symbolically

Restatement of point of narrative: declaration of independence

---

Analysis of the Essay

THE PROCESS OF PERSONAL EXPRESSION

Invention.   Analysis of this selection reveals its source of invention as Wright's memory of an emotionally charged experience in his adolescence. The intensity of the memory fuels Wright's creative energy. By recreating dialogue, feelings, and scenes associated with the experience, he spins out his narrative, a piece of highly polished prose.

Wright uses forceful language to communicate his memory to the reader. Carefully chosen adjectives and adverbs convey the principal's threatening presence: "smooth bluntness" (2), "laughed confidently, indulgently" (6), "paused and added meaningfully" (11), "remote, superior sort of way" (22). One perfect verb captures Wright's response to the suggestion that he is incapable of writing the speech: "I burned" (8).

Wright's language captures and sustains the heated emotions of the two characters in short, forceful sentences: "Wake up, boy. Learn the world" (37).

The pitch is maintained throughout the passage as Wright bites off words to build tension just as tension had built up in him many decades before: "clash" (64), "fool" (15, 37), "throwing away your future" (41), "gritted my teeth and kept my mouth shut, but my rage was mounting" (66).

Wright's invention carries him beyond the bare bones of the narration to a vivid depiction of a scene where he and his friend Griggs "practice orating; [they] spoke to the trees, to the creeks, frightening the birds, making the cows in the pasture stare at [them] in fear." (63).

Focus.   In his memory of this incident, Wright focuses on the consequences and conflicts of his behavior. The content of his speech, the principal's speech, and the graduation ceremony itself are obscure. The most Wright reveals about the speeches is that the principal's was indeed clearer than his own. Yet Wright clings to his position and pays the emotional price: "I was hating my environment more each day. As soon as school was over, I would get a job, save money, and leave" (62). The conclusion, the graduation, is anticlimactic, yet we know that Richard Wright has passed a turning point: "The hell with it! With almost seventeen years of baffled living behind me, I faced the world in 1925" (72).

Formulating a Thesis.   Wright's thesis emerges as the event unfolds. First he becomes aware that there is a matter of conscience involved: "I was faced with a matter of principle. . . . I did not want to make a public speech that was not my own" (12). As the pressure against his decision mounts, Wright generalizes from his own specific resentment to resentment on behalf of his race against the mask that blacks must wear to support "the southern way of life" (24).

As the dialogue develops, Wright's integrity weakens the principal's authority, and Wright expresses his refusal once again: "I want to learn, professor . . . but there are some things I don't want to know" (38). Wright reflects that he has been talking to a "bought" man and he will not be bought himself, a particularly meaningful choice of words that recalls the experience of slavery.

Wright uses every confrontation as an opportunity to elaborate his thesis. To his friend Griggs, who *will* read a speech written by the principal, Richard says, "I know only a hell of a little, but my speech is going to reflect that" (44). He rebuts his uncle's remark that the principal's speech is better, and he rejects his offer of help, reflecting that although his own composition "was cloudy, it said what [he] wanted to say" (62).

The final expression of Wright's thesis is his refusal to conform to convention by his demand for long pants, a symbol of his growing maturity. His family's criticism of this demand can be interpreted on two levels. His mother says, "You're trying to go too fast" (68); his uncle, "You're nothing but a child" (69); his grandmother, "He's beside himself [insane]" (70). In these remarks we hear the speakers' anxiety over not only Richard's refusal to remain a child within the family but also, and more potentially troubling, his refusal to remain a black "boy" in a white man's world.

Richard Wright did not compose this narrative from a clearly defined thesis. As he recovers his memory through the act of writing, his ideas flow and take form through the devices of invention: dialogue, images, vivid language, a chain of recollections. The reader feels the very act of writing releasing Wright's thoughts. As student writers, your objective, like Wright's, is to enable your readers to participate with you in the discovery of your themes and feelings.

READINGS

STUDS TERKEL
American Dreams

In this excerpt from an unstructured oral history, the
speaker is a working-class white man from the rural
South who grew up in poverty and received little education. In response to the interviewer's queries about
the meaning of the "American dream," he reveals how
bitterness at failure to achieve that dream led a man to
don the literal mask of prejudice, the white pointed
hood of the Ku Klux Klan. The interviewer's questions
have stimulated Ellis's invention.

C. P. Ellis

We're in his office in Durham, North Carolina. He is the bank manager of the 1
*International Union of Operating Engineers. On the wall is a plaque: "Certificate
of Service, in recognition to C. P. Ellis for your faithful service to the city in
having served as a member of the Durham Human Relations Council. February
1977."*

At one time, he had been president (exalted cyclops) of the Durham chapter of 2
the Ku Klux Klan.

He is fifty-three years old. 3

My father worked in a textile mill in Durham. He died at forty- 4
eight years old. It was probably from cotton dust. Back then, we never
heard of brown lung. I was about seventeen years old and had a mother
and sister depending on somebody to make a livin'. It was just barely
enough insurance to cover his burial. I had to quit school and go to work.
I was about eighth grade when I quit.

My father worked hard but never had enough money to buy decent 5
clothes. When I went to school, I never seemed to have adequate clothes
to wear. I always left school late afternoon with a sense of inferiority. The
other kids had nice clothes, and I just had what Daddy could buy. I still
got some of those inferiority feelin's now that I have to overcome once in
a while.

I loved my father. He would go with me to ball games. We'd go 6
fishin' together. I was really ashamed of the way he'd dress. He would

take this money and give it to me instead of putting it on himself. I always had the feeling about somebody looking at him and makin' fun of him and makin' fun of me. I think it had to do somethin' with my life.

My father and I were very close, but we didn't talk about too many 7
intimate things. He did have a drinking problem. During the week, he would work every day, but weekend he was ready to get plastered. I can understand when a guy looks at his paycheck and looks at his bills and he's worked hard all the week, and his bills are larger than his paycheck. He'd done the best he could the entire week, and there seemed to be no hope. It's an illness thing. Finally you just say: "The heck with it. I'll just get drunk and forget it."

My father was out of work during the depression, and I remember 8
going with him to the finance company uptown, and he was turned down. That's something that's always stuck.

My father never seemed to be happy. It was a constant struggle with 9
him just like it was for me. It's very seldom I'd see him laugh. He was just tryin' to figure out what he could do from one day to the next.

After several years pumping gas at a service station, I got married. 10
We had to have children. Four. One child was born blind and retarded, which was a real additional expense to us. . . .

. . . All my life, I had to work, never a day without work, worked 11
all the overtime I could get and still could not survive financially. I began to say there's somethin' wrong with this country. I worked my butt off and just never seemed to break even.

I had some real great ideas about this great nation. (Laughs.) They 12
say to abide by the law, go to church, do right and live for the Lord, and everything'll work out. But it didn't work out. It just kept gettin' worse and worse. . . .

I really began to get bitter. I didn't know who to blame. I tried to 13
find somebody. I began to blame it on black people. I had to hate somebody. Hatin' America is hard to do because you can't see it to hate it. You gotta have somethin' to look at to hate. (Laughs.) The natural person for me to hate would be black people, because my father before me was a member of the Klan. As far as he was concerned, it was the savior of the white people. It was the only organization in the world that would take care of the white people. So I began to admire the Klan.

I got active in the Klan while I was at the service station. Every 14
Monday night, a group of men would come by and buy a Coca-Cola, go back to the car, take a few drinks, and come back and stand around talkin'. I couldn't help but wonder: Why are these dudes comin' over every Monday? They said they were with the Klan and have meetings close-by. Would I be interested? Boy, that was an opportunity I really looked forward to! To be part of somethin'. I joined the Klan and rose from member to chaplain, from chaplain to vice-president, from vice-president to president. The title is exalted cyclops.

The first night I went with the fellas, they knocked on the door and 15
gave the signal. They sent some robed Klansmen to talk to me and give
me some instructions. I was led into a large meeting room, and this was
the time of my life! It was thrilling. Here's a guy who's worked all his life
and struggled all his life to be something, and here's the moment to be
something. I will never forget it. Four robed Klansmen led me into the
hall. The lights were dim, and the only thing you could see was an illuminated cross. I knelt before the cross. I had to make certain vows and promises. We promised to uphold the purity of the white race, fight communism, and protect white womanhood.

After I had taken my oath, there was loud applause goin' throughout 16
the buildin', musta been at least four hundred people. For this little ol'
person. It was a thrilling moment for C. P. Ellis.

It disturbs me when people who do not really know what it's all 17
about are so very critical of individual Klansmen. The majority of 'em are
low-income whites, people who really don't have a part in something.
They have been shut out as well as the blacks. Some are not very well
educated either. Just like myself. We had a lot of support from doctors
and lawyers and police officers.

Maybe they've had bitter experiences in this life and they had to hate 18
somebody. So the natural person to hate would be the black person. He's
beginnin' to come up, he's beginnin' to learn to read and start votin' and
run for political office. Here are white people who are supposed to be superior to them, and we're shut out.

I can understand why people join extreme right-wing or left-wing 19
groups. They're in the same boat I was. Shut out. Deep down inside, you
want to be part of this great society. Nobody listens, so we join those
groups. . . .

This was the time when the civil rights movement was really begin- 20
nin' to peak. The blacks were beginnin' to demonstrate and picket downtown stores. I never will forget some black lady I hated with a purple
passion. Ann Atwater. Every time I'd go downtown, she'd be leadin'
a boycott. How I hated—pardon the expression, I don't use it much
now—how I hated that black nigger. (Laughs.) Big, fat, heavy woman.
She'd pull about eight demonstrations, and first thing you know they had
two, three blacks at the checkout counter. Her and I have had some pretty
close confrontations.

I felt very big, yeah. (Laughs.) We're more or less a secret organiza- 21
tion. We didn't want anybody to know who we were, and I began to do some
thinkin'. What am I hidin' for? I've never been convicted of anything in my
life. I don't have any court record. What am I, C. P. Ellis, as a citizen and a
member of the United Klansmen of America? Why can't I go to the city
council meeting and say: "This is the way we feel about the matter? We
don't want you to purchase mobile units to set in our schoolyards. We don't
want niggers in our schools."

We began to come out in the open. We would go to the meetings and 22
the blacks would be there and we'd be there. It was a confrontation every
time. I didn't hold back anything. We began to make some inroads with the
city councilmen and county commissioners. They began to call us friend.
Call us at night on the telephone: "C. P., glad you came to that meeting last
night." They didn't want integration either, but they did it secretively, in
order to get elected. They couldn't stand up openly and say it, but they were
glad somebody was sayin' it. We visited some of the city leaders in their
home and talk to 'em privately. It wasn't long before councilmen would call
me up: "The blacks are comin' up tonight and makin' outrageous demands.
How about some of you people showin' up and have a little balance? I'd get
on the telephone: "The niggers is comin' to the council meeting tonight.
Persons in the city's called me and asked us to be there."

We'd load up our cars and we'd fill up half the council chambers and 23
the blacks the other half. During these times, I carried weapons to the
meetings, outside my belt. We'd go there armed. We would wind up just
hollerin' and fussin' at each other. What happened? As a result of our
fightin' one another, the city council still had their way. They didn't want
to give up control to the blacks nor the Klan. They were usin' us.

I began to realize this later down the road. One day I was walkin' 24
downtown and a certain city council member saw me comin'. I expected
him to shake my hand because he was talkin' to me at night on the telephone. I had been in his home and visited with him. He crossed the
street. Oh shit, I began to think, somethin's wrong here. Most of 'em are
merchants or maybe an attorney, an insurance agent, people like that. As
long as they kept low-income whites and low-income blacks fightin',
they're gonna maintain control.

I began to get that feeling after I was ignored in public. I thought: 25
Bullshit, you're not gonna use me any more. That's when I began to do
some real serious thinkin'.

The same thing is happening in this country today. People are being 26
used by those in control, those who have all the wealth. I'm not espousing
communism. We got the greatest system of government in the world. But
those who have it simply don't want those who don't have it to have any
part of it. Black and white. When it comes to money, the green, the other
colors make no difference. (Laughs.)

I spent a lot of sleepless nights. I still didn't like blacks. I didn't 27
want to associate with 'em. Blacks, Jews, or Catholics. My father said:
"Don't have anything to do with 'em." I didn't until I met a black person
and talked with him, eyeball to eyeball, and met a Jewish person and
talked with him, eyeball to eyeball. I found out they're people just like
me. They cried, they cussed, they prayed, and they had desires. Just like
myself. Thank God, I got to the point where I can look beyond labels.
But at that time, my mind was closed. . . .

[He is elected to a school committee that includes black civil rights 28 activist Ann Atwater.] A Klansman and a militant black woman, co-chairmen of the school committee. It was impossible. How could I work with her? But after about two or three days, it was in our hands. We had to make it a success. This give me another sense of belongin', a sense of pride. This helped this inferiority feelin' I had. A man who has stood up publicly and said he despised black people, all of a sudden he was willin' to work with 'em. Here's a chance for a low-income white man to be somethin'. In spite of all my hatred for blacks and Jews and liberals. I accepted the job. Her and I began to reluctantly work together. (Laughs.) She had as many problems workin' with me as I had workin' with her.

One night, I called her: "Ann, you and I should have a lot of differ- 29 ences and we got 'em now. But there's somethin' laid out here before us, and if it's gonna be a success, you and I are gonna have to make it one. Can we lay aside some of these feelin's?" She said: "I'm willing if you are." I said: "Let's do it."

My old friends would call me at night: "C. P., what the hell is 30 wrong with you? You're sellin' out the white race." This begin to make me have guilt feelin's. Am I doin' right? Am I doin' wrong? Here I am all of a sudden makin' an about-face and tryin' to deal with my feelin's, my heart. My mind was beginnin' to open up. I was beginnin' to see what was right and what was wrong. I don't want the kids to fight forever.

One day, Ann and I went back to the school and we sat down. We 31 began to talk and just reflect. Ann said: "My daughter came home cryin' every day. She said her teacher was makin' fun of me in front of the other kids." I said: "Boy, the same thing happened to my kid. White liberal teacher was makin' fun of Tim Ellis's father, the Klansman, in front of other peoples. He came home cryin'." At this point—(he pauses, swallows hard, stifles a sob)—I begin to see, here we are, both people from the far ends of the fence, havin' identical problems, except hers bein' black and me bein' white. From that moment on, I tell ya, that gal and I worked together good. I began to love the girl, really. (He weeps.)

The amazing thing about it, her and I, up to that point, had cussed 32 each other, bawled each other, we hated each other. Up to that point, we didn't know each other. We didn't know we had things in common.

We worked at it, with the people who came to these meetings. They 33 talked about racism, sex education, about teachers not bein' qualified. After seven, eight nights of real intense discussion, these people, who'd never talked to each other before, all of a sudden came up with resolutions. It was really somethin', you had to be there to get the tone and feelin' of it. . . .

The whole world was openin' up, and I was learnin' new truths that I 34 had never learned before. I was beginnin' to look at a black person, shake hands with him, and see him as a human bein'. I hadn't got rid of all this stuff. I've still got a little bit of it. But somethin' was happenin' to me.

It was almost like bein' born again. It was a new life. I didn't have 35 these sleepless nights I used to have when I was active in the Klan and slippin' around at night. I could sleep at night and feel good about it. I'd rather live now than at any other time in history. It's a challenge.

Back at Duke, doin' maintenance, I'd pick up my tools, fix the com- 36 mode, unstop the drains. But this got in my blood. Things weren't right in this country, and what we done in Durham needs to be told. I was so miserable at Duke, I could hardly stand it. I'd go to work every morning just hatin' to go.

My whole life had changed. I got an eighth-grade education, and I 37 wanted to complete high school. Went to high school in the afternoons on a program called PEP—Past Employment Progress. I was about the only white in class, and the oldest. I began to read about biology. I'd take my books home at night, 'cause I was determined to get through. Sure enough, I graduated. I got the diploma at home. . . .

I tell people there's a tremendous possibility in this country to stop 38 wars, the battles, the struggles, the fights between people. People say: "That's an impossible dream. You sound like Martin Luther King." An ex-Klansman who sounds like Martin Luther King. (Laughs.) I don't think it's an impossible dream. It's happened in my life. It's happened in other people's lives in America.

I don't know what's ahead of me. I have no desire to be a big union 39 official. I want to be right out here in the field with the workers. I want to walk through their factory and shake hands with that man whose hands are dirty. I'm gonna do all that one little ol' man can do. I'm fifty-two years old, and I ain't got many years left, but I want to make the best of 'em.

When the news came over the radio that Martin Luther King was 40 assassinated, I got on the telephone and began to call other Klansmen. We just had a real party at the service station. Really rejoicin' 'cause that son of a bitch was dead. Our troubles are over with. They say the older you get, the harder it is for you to change. That's not necessarily true. Since I changed, I've set down and listened to tapes of Martin Luther King. I listen to it and tears come to my eyes 'cause I know what he's sayin' now. I know what's happenin'.

POSTSCRIPT: *The phone rings. A conversation.*
"This was a black guy who's director of Operation Breakthrough in 41 Durham. I had called his office. I'm interested in employin' some young black person who's interested in learnin' the labor movement. I want somebody who's never had an opportunity, just like myself. Just so he can read and write, that's all."

Reading and Interpreting

CONCEPT ANALYSIS

The speaker suggests that bigotry and prejudice are masks. What do they conceal?

1. Cite lines that reflect the attitudes that motivated Ellis to drift toward the Klan.
2. What specific experiences allowed him to discard his protective coverings—both the visible mask of the KKK and the invisible one of prejudice?

Thinking and Writing

RHETORICAL TECHNIQUE

1. Spontaneous speech typically moves from the specific to the general. Cite observations and explanations in Ellis's oral history that lead toward thesis statements.
2. Through free association Ellis recalls the details of past experiences. To these he adds remembered emotions and analysis. This gives the narrative its depth. Cite lines reflecting his feelings and critical commentary.
3. An interview is focused by the questions of the interviewer. What questions do you think the interviewer asked of C. P. Ellis to elicit the material of this oral history?
4. Ellis makes many challenging statements. Use techniques of invention to support or oppose one or more of the following:
   a. "Hatin' America is hard to do because you can't see it to hate it. You gotta have somethin' to look at to hate." (13)
   b. "They [the city council] were usin' us. . . . As long as they kept low-income whites and low-income blacks fightin', they're gonna maintain control." (23, 24)
   c. "Black and white. When it comes to money, the green, the other colors make no difference." (26)
   d. "An ex-Klansman who sounds like Martin Luther King. . . . I don't think it's an impossible dream." (38)

ANAÏS NIN

The Diary of Anaïs Nin

Although Anaïs Nin (1903–1977) has authored several sensitive and perceptive novels focusing on the concerns of women, she is best known for her four-volume *Diary*, which covers her life through 1971. Candid, introspective, and insightful about men and women friends and the artistic world she inhabited in Europe and the United States, Nin's *Diary* is a fascinating example of invention.

September 1940

The first night I moved in [to her new apartment in Greenwich Village,   1
New York City] there was a storm. A violent thunderstorm. I felt it was a bad omen. Is the war coming here, too? What is happening in the world is monstrous. Just as people are learning the use of gas masks, I feel I have to wear a mask of oxygen-giving dreams and work to keep alive the cells of creation as a defense against devastation. I do not want to become hard and callous as other people are doing around me. They shrug their shoulders and don another layer of indifference.

October 1940

Against hatred, power and fanaticism, systems and plans, I oppose love   2
and creation, over and over again, in spite of the insanity of the world.

We live in an era of destruction. Destruction and creation are some-   3
times balanced: great wars, great cultures. But now destruction is predominant. People die for systems that are masks for personal power and gain. Against them I close the door of a small but loving world, cells of devotion, care, work, to fight the disease and madness of the world. A small world has sometimes defeated great systems born of delusions.

Visited the Patchens. Something baffles me here which I never expe-   4
rienced before. I feel at times as if I were living in a Kafka nightmare of closed faces, silence, inexpressiveness. People do not reveal themselves, they do not seem even present. I miss the warmth and flowering which creates bridges. Patchen has nothing to say. His work . . . seems to me

like that of a sword swallower, swallowing itself, a hymn to destruction. He seems blind and deaf to others. His wife said to me: "You should not read Dostoevsky. He was a drunkard and a gambler, who beat his wife."

December 1940

[A] scene which seemed meaningful to me was one we saw in a vaudeville 5 show. A man was singing, standing next to a phonograph. Suddenly something went wrong with the machine, and then one saw that the man had not been singing but making the motion of singing by moving his lips, and that all along the song came from the phonograph record. A voice came from the machine and said: "Now you're on your own." The man had no voice. I would have started the American journey book right there. We laughed.

November 1941

Reading Robert's diary was my only access to the inner Robert [a friend]. 6 Now that he can no longer work in my studio, and has taken his papers away, he wears a mask, he is detached. He felt I was throwing him out of the nest. The human contact, by way of the diaries, broke. One cannot reach him. Outside of the diary he is brittle, he is an actor.

While I read his diary we could communicate on a level where his 7 cold rays could not reach, a level where play acting ceased. In the diary he said he was devouring me like a food. It makes him write, to read my diary. . . .

Every book I have written has brought me new friends, new realms 8 of experience, new worlds. The imagination incarnates personages who lie in the obscurest region of one's being. In writing they come to the surface, take form, body, in the reality of the book. . . . That is my essential reason for writing, not for fame, not to be celebrated after death, but to heighten and create life all around me. I cannot go into life without my books. They are my passports, my rudder, my map, my ticket. I also write because when I am writing I reach the high moment of fusion sought by the mystics, the poets, the lovers, a sense of communion with the universe.

There are passages in my books which are invitations, expectations, 9 suspenses. Anyone reading them accurately would recognize a cue and feel, I can enter her life now. This is my clue. The atmosphere is propitious. Without the writing I am timid. Through lack of audacity I cannot enter without this bridge, a portable bridge I can lay down between human beings and myself.

. . . Without my books I would often turn my back upon adven- 10 ture and become a recluse. With my books I feel I have a task. I am an explorer. I must visit the lands I am to describe. When I write the book I use the book like dynamite, to blast myself out of isolation.

January 1945

A snowstorm. I was working on *This Hunger,* when my typewriter broke 11 down. I went out into the snow with it to get it repaired. When I came back, I did not feel like writing the continuation of Djuna's life at the orphan asylum and her hunger. I felt like writing about snow. I wrote every image, every sensation, every fantasy I had experienced during my walk. The snowstorm had thrown me back into the past, into my innocent adolescence, surrounded by desires, at sixteen, intimidated, tense. I compared my adolescence with the frozen adolescence of others around me today. They all fused: snow, the frost of fear, the ice of virginity, purity, innocence, and always the sudden danger of melting. I wrote myself out. And when I was finished, I realized I had described Djuna's adolescence, and the adolescent contractions of other adolescents. I had written thirty-eight pages on the snow in women and men, on Djuna and the asylum, her hunger.

[From Nin's letter to a friend who complained he could not express 12 feeling.] Expressing feeling is linked directly with creation. My telling all to the diary helped me in this. You find yourself in a barren environment and tend to withdraw. This will be bad for you as an artist, writer, or painter. In this ability to tap the sources of feeling and imagination lies the secret of abundance. In withdrawing there is danger of sterility or withering. Try to write in your diary to keep that little flame burning. Expand, open, speak, name, describe, exclaim, paint, caricature, dance, jump in your writing. We are here as writers to say everything. Speak for your moods, make your muteness and silence eloquent. The drawings you sent are a closed face upon the world.

The defenses people build up become in themselves the trap. I think 13 what I love about the young is that they have not yet created disguises and masks.

The fear of this, which I saw happening to everyone around me, also 14 created the diary. The real Anaïs is in the diary. Even the destructive Anaïs who refuses to destroy in life. I do not harm Wilson [Edmund Wilson, renowned critic and scholar], who is for the moment a man in trouble, but I do make his portrait in the colors I do not like; the brown of philosophy, the gray ashes of scholarship, the dreary traditions.

Summer 1947

To celebrate the opening of Angelo's café [on the northern California coast] 15 we were invited to come in disguise. It was difficult to find odds and ends to make costumes out of, in the empty castle, with a wardrobe out of a valise intended for minimum necessities. There were no curtains, no draperies, no paints, no textiles. We did the best we could. I dressed John's wife: from the waist up she was a nun, in brown chiffon, with a cross on her breast. Below was the same chiffon, trailing to the floor, but without a slip underneath, so her legs could be seen in silhouette.

When we arrived, there were some costumes done by Varda which 16 were marvelous. He had dressed some of the young women as his collages. Colored paper cut-outs covered them: blue rhomboids, rose triangles, white squares, orange rectangles, purple parallelograms, green trapezoids, lavender pentagons, gold hexagons, yellow octagons.

The friendship with Varda was situated on such a level of invention, 17 counter-invention, legend and counter-legend, poetry and counter-poetry, our talks were so far out in space, that it was like two magicians ceaselessly performing for each other. We could not rest to wipe off the perspiration, or appear for one moment as human beings, hungry, cold, or restless. Magic must predominate. Varda's attitude in life was that of a Merlin, the enchanter, who must constantly enchant and seduce, fascinate and create. Young women came constantly to him, to be metamorphosed, and it was a marvelous sight to see him create a myth: rename them, reshape them, redecorate them. The Varda touch. They were no longer ordinary women. They were myths. I was a myth, even before we met, because of *Under a Glass Bell*. I possessed one of his loveliest collages. Poetry was like this masquerade of beauty, and I loved it. We all danced and flirted and paired off, and in our disguises denied our everyday selves.

Reading and Interpreting

VOCABULARY

Use your dictionary as necessary to find the meaning of the following words as used in Nin's diary:

delusions (3)   incarnate (8)   rudder (8)   propitious (9)

CONCEPT ANALYSIS

1. In several diary excerpts, Nin perceives that indifference, conventionality, or callousness are masks worn by different people. Cite the excerpts where such references occur. What are Nin's responses to these

masks? Note statements about her feelings that focus her material. Have you known people who wear these masks? Can masks such as these be removed to reveal a "real" person who is different and "better"?

2. Nin claims that creativity allows her and others to remove their masks. Refer to statements in her diary that explore this theme; comment on the basis of your own personal experience.

Quickwrite

Choose one of the following topics from this reading:

snow   selfish people   costumes   letters

Use all of the question types listed earlier in Asking Questions to extend it. Then use one question type to focus it.

Thinking and Writing

RHETORICAL TECHNIQUE

1. Nin's diary excerpts contain vivid, concrete details, but they also express broad generalizations and opinions. Select some reflections that you particularly like. What was her source for each: a specific incident? an observation? free association?

2. The last diary entry has two points of focus: the party and the person of Varda. Which would you choose to expand and why?

3. In another part of her diary, Nin explains that when she tries to transform her entries into more formal prose, the warmth and humanity get lost. For you, what are the strengths and weaknesses of spontaneous writing? Discuss your own journal writing and essay writing experience in this regard.

PHILLIP STANHOPE, FOURTH EARL OF CHESTERFIELD
Letters to His Son

Phillip Stanhope (1694–1773), the fourth Earl of Chesterfield, the embodiment of eighteenth-century English
gentility, was a popular diplomat in Ireland, a patron of
the arts, and an admired writer. Although spontaneous,
his letters focus on the virtues of compromise, control,
and tact. Unfortunately, the advice was wasted on his
son, who turned out to be a graceless, incompetent
nonentity.

No. 701

Spa, 25 July N.S. 1741

Dear Boy,

I have often told you in my former letters (and it is most certainly 1
true) that the strictest and most scrupulous honour and virtue can alone
make you esteemed and valued by mankind; that parts and learning can
alone make you admired and celebrated by them; but that the possession
of lesser talents was most absolutely necessary towards making you liked,
beloved, and sought after in private life. Of these lesser talents, good-
breeding is the principal and most necessary one, not only as it is very
important in itself; but as it adds great lustre to the more solid advantages
both of the heart and the mind. I have often touched upon good-breeding
to you before; so that this letter shall be upon the next necessary qualification to it, which is a genteel, easy manner and carriage, wholly free from
those odd tricks, ill habits, and awkwardnesses, which even very many
worthy and sensible people have in their behaviour. However trifling a
genteel manner may sound, it is of very great consequence towards pleasing in private life, especially the women; which, one time or other, you
will think worth pleasing; and I have known many a man, from his awkwardness, give people such a dislike of him at first, that all his merit could
not get the better of it afterwards. Whereas a genteel manner prepossesses
people in your favour, bends them towards you, and makes them wish to
like you. Awkwardness can proceed but from two causes; either from not
having kept good company, or from not having attended to it. As for your
keeping good company, I will take care of that; do you take care to observe
their ways and manners, and to form your own upon them. Attention is

absolutely necessary for this, as indeed it is for everything else; and a man without attention is not fit to live in the world. When an awkward fellow first comes into a room, it is highly probable that his sword gets between his legs, and throws him down, or makes him stumble at least; when he has recovered this accident, he goes and places himself in the very place of the whole room where he should not; there he soon lets his hat fall down; and, taking it up again, throws down his cane; in recovering his cane, his hat falls a second time; so that he is a quarter of an hour before he is in order again. If he drinks tea or coffee, he certainly scalds his mouth, and lets either the cup or the saucer fall, and spills the tea or coffee in his breeches. At dinner, his awkwardness distinguishes itself particularly, as he has more to do: there he holds his knife, fork, and spoon differently from other people; eats with his knife to the greater danger of his mouth, picks his teeth with his fork, and puts his spoon, which has been in his throat twenty times, into the dishes again. If he is to carve, he can never hit the joint; but, in his vain efforts to cut through the bone, scatters the sauce in everybody's face. He generally daubs himself with soup and grease, though his napkin is commonly stuck through a button-hole, and tickles his chin. When he drinks, he infallibly coughs in his glass, and besprinkles the company. Beside all this, he has strange tricks and gestures; such as snuffing up his nose, making faces, putting his fingers in his nose, or blowing it and looking afterwards in his handkerchief, so as to make the company sick. His hands are troublesome to him, when he has not something in them, and he does not know where to put them; but they are in perpetual motion between his bosom and his breeches: he does not wear his clothes, and in short does nothing, like other people. All this, I own, is not in any degree criminal; but is highly disagreeable and ridiculous in company, and ought most carefully to be avoided by whoever desires to please.

From this account of what you should not do, you may easily judge 2 what you should do; and a due attention to the manners of people of fashion, and who have seen the world, will make it habitual and familiar to you.

There is, likewise, an awkwardness of expression and words, most 3 carefully to be avoided; such as false English, bad pronunciation, old sayings, and common proverbs; which are so many proofs of having kept bad and low company. For example: if, instead of saying that tastes are different, and that every man has his own peculiar one, you should let off a proverb, and say, That what is one man's meat is another man's poison; or else, Every one as they like, as the good man said when he kissed his cow; everybody would be persuaded that you have never kept company with anybody above footmen and housemaids.

Attention will do all this; and without attention nothing is to be 4 done: want [lack] of attention, which is really want of thought, is either folly or madness. You should not only have attention to everything, but a quickness of attention, so as to observe, at once, all the people in the room; their motions, their looks, and their words; and yet without staring at them, and seeming to be an observer. This quick and unobserved observation is of infinite advantage in life, and is to be acquired with care; and, on the contrary, what is called absence, which is a thoughtlessness, and want of attention about what is doing, makes a man so like either a fool or a madman, that, for my part, I see no real difference. A fool never has thought; a madman has lost it; and an absent [inattentive] man is, for the time, without it.

Adieu! Direct your next to me, *chez* [at the house of] *Monsieur Chabért,* 5 *Banquier, à Paris;* and take care that I find the improvements I expect at my return.

No. 735

Tuesday

Dear Boy,

Good-breeding is so important an article in life, and so absolutely 6 necessary for you, if you would please, and be well received in the world, that I must give you another lecture upon it, and possibly this will not be the last neither.

I only mentioned, in my last, the general rules of common civility, 7 which whoever does not observe, will pass for a bear, and be as unwelcome as one, in company; and there is hardly anybody brutal enough not to answer when they are spoke to, or not to say, Sir, my Lord, or Madam, according to the rank of the people they speak to. But it is not enough not to be rude; you should be extremely civil, and distinguished for your good-breeding. The first principle of this good-breeding is never to say anything that you think can be disagreeable to anybody in company, but, on the contrary, you should endeavour to say what will be agreeable to them; and that in an easy and natural manner, without meaning to study for compliments. There is likewise such a thing as a civil look, and a rude look; and you should look civil, as well as be so; for if, while you are saying a civil thing, you look gruff and surly, as most English bumpkins do, nobody will be obliged to you for a civility that seemed to come so unwillingly. If you have occasion to contradict anybody, or to set them right from a mistake, it would be very brutal to say, *That is not so; I know better;* or, *you are out;* but you should say, with a civil look, *I beg your pardon, I believe you mistake;* or, *If I may take the liberty of contradicting you, I believe it is so and so;* for, though you may know a thing better than other people, yet it is very shocking to tell them so directly, without something to soften it: but remember particularly, that whatever you say or do, with ever so civil an intention, a great deal consists in the manner and the look, which must be genteel, easy, and natural, and is easier to be felt than described.

Civility is particularly due to all women; and remember, that no 8 provocation whatsoever can justify any man in not being civil to every woman; and the greatest man in England would justly be reckoned a brute, if he were not civil to the meanest woman. It is due to their sex, and is the only protection they have against the superior strength of ours; nay, even a little flattery is allowable with women; and a man may, without any meanness, tell a woman that she is either handsomer or wiser than she is. I repeat it again to you, observe the French people, and mind how easily and naturally civil their address is, and how agreeably they insinuate little civilities in their conversation. They think it so essential, that they call an honest man and a civil man by the same name, of *honnête homme;* and the Romans called civility *humanitas,* as thinking it inseparable from humanity. As nobody can instruct you in good-breeding better than your Mamma, be sure you mind all she says to you upon that subject, and depend upon it, that your reputation and success in the world will, in a great measure, depend upon the degree of good-breeding you are master of. You cannot begin too early to take that turn, in order to make it natural and habitual to you; which it is to very few Englishmen, who, neglecting it while they are young, find out too late, when they are old, how necessary it is, and then cannot get it right. There is hardly a French cook that is not better bred than most Englishmen of quality, and that cannot present himself with more ease, and a better address, in any mixed company. Remember to practise all this, and then, with the learning which I hope you will have, you may arrive at what I reckon almost the perfection of human nature, English knowledge with French good-breeding. Adieu.

Reading and Interpreting

VOCABULARY

Use your dictionary as necessary to find the meaning of the following words as used in Lord Chesterfield's letters:

scrupulous (1) genteel (1) prepossess (1) infallibly (1)

civil (7) surly (7) insinuate (8)

CONCEPT ANALYSIS

1. In Lord Chesterfield's letters to his son we hear the voice of the cultivated eighteenth-century gentleman. Do you agree with the following opinions:

a. "[To do] nothing like other people. . . . is highly disagreeable and ridiculous in company and ought most carefully to be avoided by whoever desires to please." (1)

b. " . . . false English, bad pronunciation, old sayings, and common proverbs . . . are so many proofs of having kept bad and low company." (3)

c. " . . . no provocation whatsoever can justify any man in not being civil to every woman. . . ." (8)

d. " . . . never . . . say anything that you think can be disagreeable to anybody in company. . . ." (7)

2. Would Lord Chesterfield consider "good-breeding" a mask? How do you feel about the behavior he defines as good-breeding? Is it a mask or not? To what extent do you agree with Lord Chesterfield that civility is always synonymous with honesty and humanity?

Quickwrite

In letter 701, Lord Chesterfield teaches his son indirectly by presenting a vivid and amusing catalog of what *not* to do in company. He expects his son to judge from this list what he *should* do. Borrow Lord Chesterfield's humorous writing style and focus, and compose a letter cataloging correct conduct for a classroom or for a college social function.

Thinking and Writing

RHETORICAL TECHNIQUE

1. A writer's purpose focuses his or her observations. What purposes might Chesterfield have had in writing these letters? Cite statements that give focus to each letter.

2. Lord Chesterfield appears to write spontaneously, piling up illustrative details. Are these details random, or can you detect one or more key terms around which they are organized? Explain.

3. Select your favorite details. How do these sharpen Lord Chesterfield's focus?

GEORGE ORWELL
Down and Out in Paris and London

George Orwell (1903–1950) is considered one of Britain's most important modern writers. His novels generally attack oppression and totalitarianism in any form through biting satire and spare but forceful writing. This frequently ironic excerpt illuminates Orwell's experience of poverty. The wealth of realistic and often humorous detail is given focus by the narrator's generalizations and critical observations.

The Hôtel X. was a vast, grandiose place with a classical façade, and at 1
one side a little, dark doorway like a rat-hole, which was the service entrance. I arrived at a quarter to seven in the morning. A stream of men with greasy trousers were hurrying in and being checked by a doorkeeper who sat in a tiny office. I waited, and presently the *chef du personnel,* a sort of assistant manager, arrived and began to question me. He was an Italian, with a round, pale face, haggard from overwork. He asked whether I was an experienced dishwasher, and I said that I was; he glanced at my hands and saw that I was lying, but on hearing that I was an Englishman he changed his tone and engaged me.

"We have been looking for someone to practise our English on," 2
he said. "Our clients are all Americans, and the only English we know is————" He repeated something that little boys write on the walls in London. "You may be useful. Come downstairs."

He led me down a winding staircase into a narrow passage, deep 3
underground, and so low that I had to stoop in places. It was stiflingly hot and very dark, with only dim, yellow bulbs several yards apart. There seemed to be miles of dark labyrinthine passages—actually, I suppose, a few hundred yards in all—that reminded one queerly of the lower decks of a liner; there were the same heat and cramped space and warm reek of food, and a humming, whirring noise (it came from the kitchen furnaces) just like the whir of engines. We passed doorways which let out sometimes a shouting of oaths, sometimes the red glare of a fire, once a shuddering draught from an ice chamber. As we went along, something struck me violently in the back. It was a hundred-pound block of ice, carried by a blue-aproned porter. After him came a boy with a great slab of veal on his shoulder, his cheek pressed into the damp, spongy flesh. They shoved

me aside with a cry of "*Sauve-toi,*[1] *idiot!*" and rushed on. On the wall, under one of the lights, someone had written in a very neat hand: "Sooner will you find a cloudless sky in winter, than a woman at the Hôtel X. who has her maidenhead." It seemed a queer sort of place.

One of the passages branched off into a laundry, where an old, skull- 4 faced woman gave me a blue apron and a pile of dishcloths. Then the *chef du personnel* took me to a tiny underground den—a cellar below a cellar, as it were—where there were a sink and some gas-ovens. It was too low for me to stand quite upright, and the temperature was perhaps 110 degrees Fahrenheit. The *chef du personnel* explained that my job was to fetch meals for the higher hotel employees, who fed in a small dining-room above, clean their room and wash their crockery. When he had gone, a waiter, another Italian, thrust a fierce, fuzzy head into the doorway and looked down at me.

"English, eh?" he said. "Well, I'm in charge here. If you work 5 well"—he made the motion of up-ending a bottle and sucked noisily. "If you don't"—he gave the doorpost several vigorous kicks. "To me, twisting your neck would be no more than spitting on the floor. And if there's any trouble, they'll believe me, not you. So be careful."

After this I set to work rather hurriedly. Except for about an hour, I 6 was at work from seven in the morning till a quarter past nine at night; first at washing crockery, then at scrubbing the tables and floors of the employees' dining-room, then at polishing glasses and knives, then at fetching meals, then at washing crockery again, then at fetching more meals and washing more crockery. It was easy work, and I got on well with it except when I went to the kitchen to fetch meals. The kitchen was like nothing I had ever seen or imagined—a stifling, low-ceilinged inferno of a cellar, redlit from the fires, and deafening with oaths and the clanging of pots and pans. It was so hot that all the metal-work except the stoves had to be covered with cloth. In the middle were furnaces, where twelve cooks skipped to and fro, their faces dripping sweat in spite of their white caps. Round that were counters where a mob of waiters and *plongeurs* [dishwashers] clamoured with trays. Scullions, naked to the waist, were stoking the fires and scouring huge copper saucepans with sand. Everyone seemed to be in a hurry and a rage. The head cook, a fine, scarlet man with big moustachios, stood in the middle booming continuously, "*Ça marche deux œufs brouillés! Ça marche un Chateau-briand aux pommes sautées!*"[2] except when he broke off to curse at a *plongeur*. There were three counters, and the first time I went to the kitchen I took my tray unknowingly to the wrong one. The head cook walked up to me, twisted his moustaches, and looked me up and down. Then he beckoned to the breakfast cook and pointed at me.

---

1. "Watch out; get out of the way"—Ed.
2. "Pick up two scrambled eggs! Pick up a chateaubriand steak with sautéed potatoes!"—Ed.

"Do you see *that?* That is the type of *plongeur* they send us nowadays. 7
Where do you come from, idiot? From Charenton, I suppose?" (There is a
large lunatic asylum at Charenton.)

"From England," I said. 8

"I might have known it. Well, *mon cher monsieur l'Anglais,* may I 9
inform you that you are the son of a whore? And now————the camp[3] to
the other counter, where you belong."

I got this kind of reception every time I went to the kitchen, for I 10
always made some mistake; I was expected to know the work, and was
cursed accordingly. From curiosity I counted the number of times I was
called *maquereau* during the day, and it was thirty-nine.

Our cafeterie was a murky cellar measuring twenty feet by seven by 11
eight high, and so crowded with coffee-urns, breadcutters and the like
that one could hardly move without banging against something. It was
lighted by one dim electric bulb, and four or five gas-fires that sent out a
fierce red breath. There was a thermometer there, and the temperature
never fell below 110 degrees Fahrenheit—it neared 130 at some times of
the day. At one end were five service lifts, and at the other an ice cupboard
where we stored milk and butter. When you went into the ice cupboard
you dropped a hundred degrees of temperature at a single step; it used to
remind me of the hymn about Greenland's icy mountains and India's coral
strand. Two men worked in the cafeterie besides Boris and myself. One
was Mario, a huge, excitable Italian—he was like a city policeman with
operatic gestures—and the other, a hairy, uncouth animal whom we
called the Magyar; I think he was a Transylvanian, or something even
more remote. Except the Magyar we were all big men, and at the rush
hours we collided incessantly.

The work in the cafeterie was spasmodic. We were never idle, but 12
the real work only came in bursts of two hours at a time—we called each
burst *"un coup de feu"* [a gunshot]. The first *coup de feu* came at eight, when
the guests upstairs began to wake up and demand breakfast. At eight a
sudden banging and yelling would break out all through the basement;
bells rang on all sides, blue-aproned men rushed through the passages,
our service lifts came down with a simultaneous crash, and the waiters on
all five floors began shouting Italian oaths down the shafts. I don't remember all our duties, but they included making tea, coffee and chocolate,
fetching meals from the kitchen, wines from the cellar and fruit and so
forth from the dining-room, slicing bread, making toast, rolling pats of
butter, measuring jam, opening milk-cans, counting lumps of sugar, boiling eggs, cooking porridge, pounding ice, grinding coffee—all this for
from a hundred to two hundred customers. The kitchen was thirty yards
away, and the dining-room sixty or seventy yards. Everything we sent up
in the service lifts had to be covered by a voucher, and the vouchers had to

---

3. An obscene expression—Ed.

be carefully filed, and there was trouble if even a lump of sugar was lost. Besides this, we had to supply the staff with bread and coffee, and fetch the meals for the waiters upstairs. All in all, it was a complicated job.

I calculated that one had to walk and run about fifteen miles during the day, and yet the strain of the work was more mental than physical. Nothing could be easier, on the face of it, than this stupid scullion work, but it is astonishingly hard when one is in a hurry. One has to leap to and fro between a multitude of jobs—it is like sorting a pack of cards against the clock. You are, for example, making toast, when bang! down comes a service lift with an order for tea, rolls and three different kinds of jam, and simultaneously bang! down comes another demanding scrambled eggs, coffee and grapefruit; you run to the kitchen for the eggs and to the dining-room for the fruit, going like lightning so as to be back before your toast burns, and having to remember about the tea and coffee, besides half a dozen other orders that are still pending; and at the same time some waiter is following you and making trouble about a lost bottle of soda-water, and you are arguing with him. It needs more brains than one might think. Mario said, no doubt truly, that it took a year to make a reliable cafetier [restaurant worker].

The time between eight and half-past ten was a sort of delirium. Sometimes we were going as though we had only five minutes to live; sometimes there were sudden lulls when the orders stopped and everything seemed quiet for a moment. Then we swept up the litter from the floor, threw down fresh sawdust, and swallowed gallipots of wine or coffee or water—anything, so long as it was wet. Very often we used to break off chunks of ice and suck them while we worked. The heat among the gas-fires was nauseating; we swallowed quarts of drink during the day, and after a few hours even our aprons were drenched with sweat. At times we were hopelessly behind with the work, and some of the customers would have gone without their breakfast, but Mario always pulled us through. He had worked fourteen years in the cafeterie, and he had the skill that never wastes a second between jobs. The Magyar was very stupid and I was inexperienced, and Boris was inclined to shirk, partly because of his lame leg, partly because he was ashamed of working in the cafeterie after being a waiter; but Mario was wonderful. The way he would stretch his great arms right across the cafeterie to fill a coffee-pot with one hand and boil an egg with the other, at the same time watching toast and shouting directions to the Magyar, and between whiles singing snatches from *Rigoletto,* was beyond all praise. The *patron* [boss] knew his value, and he was paid a thousand francs a month, instead of five hundred like the rest of us.

The breakfast pandemonium stopped at half-past ten. Then we scrubbed the cafeterie tables, swept the floor and polished the brasswork, and, on good mornings, went one at a time to the lavatory for a smoke. This was our slack time—only relatively slack, however, for we had only ten minutes for lunch, and we never got through it uninterrupted. The customers' luncheon hour, between twelve and two, was another period of turmoil like the breakfast hour. Most of our work was fetching meals from the kitchen, which meant constant *engueulades* [scoldings] from the cooks. By this time the cooks had sweated in front of their furnaces for four or five hours, and their tempers were all warmed up.

At two we were suddenly free men. We threw off our aprons and put 16 on our coats, hurried out of doors, and, when we had money, dived into the nearest *bistro*. It was strange, coming up into the street from those firelit cellars. The air seemed blindingly clear and cold, like arctic summer; and how sweet the petrol did smell, after the stenches of sweat and food! Sometimes we met some of our cooks and waiters in the *bistros,* and they were friendly and stood us drinks. Indoors we were their slaves, but it is an etiquette in hotel life that between hours everyone is equal, and the *engueulades* do not count. . . .

It was amusing to look round the filthy little scullery and think that 17 only a double door was between us and the dining-room. There sat the customers in all their splendour—spotless table-cloths, bowls of flowers, mirrors and gilt cornices and painted cherubim; and here, just a few feet away, we in our disgusting filth. For it really was disgusting filth. There was no time to sweep the floor till evening, and we slithered about in a compound of soapy water, lettuce-leaves, torn paper and trampled food. A dozen waiters with their coats off, showing their sweaty armpits, sat at the table mixing salads and sticking their thumbs into the cream pots. The room had a dirty, mixed smell of food and sweat. Everywhere in the cupboards, behind the piles of crockery, were squalid stores of food that the waiters had stolen. There were only two sinks, and no washing basin, and it was nothing unusual for a waiter to wash his face in the water in which clean crockery was rinsing. But the customers saw nothing of this. There were a coco-nut mat and a mirror outside the dining-room door, and the waiters used to preen themselves up and go in looking the picture of cleanliness.

It is an instructive sight to see a waiter going into a hotel dining- 18 room. As he passes the door a sudden change comes over him. The set of his shoulders alters; all the dirt and hurry and irritation have dropped off in an instant. He glides over the carpet, with a solemn priest-like air. I remember our assistant *maître d'hôtel,* a fiery Italian, pausing at the dining-room door to address an apprentice who had broken a bottle of wine. Shaking his fist above his head he yelled (luckily the door was more or less soundproof):

"*Tu me fais*———[4] Do you call yourself a waiter, you young bas- 19 tard? You a waiter! You're not fit to scrub floors in the brothel your mother came from. *Maquereau!* [Mackerel!]"

---

4. An obscene expression—Ed.

Words failing him, he turned to the door; and as he opened it he 20
delivered a final insult in the same manner as Squire Western in *Tom Jones*.

Then he entered the dining-room and sailed across it dish in hand, 21
graceful as a swan. Ten seconds later he was bowing reverently to a customer. And you could not help thinking, as you saw him bow and smile,
with that benign smile of the trained waiter, that the customer was put to
shame by having such an aristocrat to serve him. . . .

This is the good side of hotel work. In a hotel a huge and compli- 22
cated machine is kept running by an inadequate staff, because every man
has a well-defined job and does it scrupulously. But there is a weak point,
and it is this—that the job the staff are doing is not necessarily what the
customer pays for. The customer pays, as he sees it, for good service; the
employee is paid, as he sees it, for the *boulot*—meaning, as a rule, an imitation of good service. The result is that, though hotels are miracles of
punctuality, they are worse than the worst private houses in the things
that matter.

Take cleanliness, for example. The dirt in the Hôtel X., as soon as 23
one penetrated into the service quarters, was revolting. Our cafeterie had
year-old filth in all the dark corners, and the bread-bin was infested with
cockroaches. Once I suggested killing these beasts to Mario. "Why kill
the poor animals?" he said reproachfully. The others laughed when I
wanted to wash my hands before touching the butter. Yet we were clean
where we recognised cleanliness as part of the *boulot*. We scrubbed the
tables and polished the brasswork regularly, because we had orders to do
that; but we had no orders to be genuinely clean, and in any case we had
no time for it. We were simply carrying out our duties; and as our first
duty was punctuality, we saved time by being dirty.

In the kitchen the dirt was worse. It is not a figure of speech, it is a 24
mere statement of fact to say that a French cook will spit in the soup—
that is, if he is not going to drink it himself. He is an artist, but his art is
not cleanliness. To a certain extent he is even dirty because he is an artist,
for food, to look smart, needs dirty treatment. When a steak, for instance,
is brought up for the head cook's inspection, he does not handle it with a
fork. He picks it up in his fingers and slaps it down, runs his thumb
round the dish and licks it to taste the gravy, runs it round and licks
again, then steps back and contemplates the piece of meat like an artist
judging a picture, then presses it lovingly into place with his fat, pink
fingers every one of which he has licked a hundred times that morning.
When he is satisfied, he takes a cloth and wipes his fingerprints from the
dish, and hands it to the waiter. And the waiter, of course, dips *his* fingers
into the gravy—his nasty, greasy fingers which he is for ever running
through his brilliantined hair. Whenever one pays more than, say, ten
francs for a dish of meat in Paris, one may be certain that it has been fin-
gered in this manner. In very cheap restaurants it is different; there, the

same trouble is not taken over the food, and it is just forked out of the pan and flung on to a plate, without handling. Roughly speaking, the more one pays for food, the more sweat and spittle one is obliged to eat with it.

Dirtiness is inherent in hotels and restaurants, because sound food is 25 sacrificed to punctuality and smartness. The hotel employee is too busy getting food ready to remember that it is meant to be eaten. A meal is simply *"une commande"* [an order] to him, just as a man dying of cancer is simply *"a case"* to the doctor. A customer orders, for example, a piece of toast. Somebody, pressed with work in a cellar deep underground, has to prepare it. How can he stop and say to himself, "This toast is to be eaten—I must make it eatable"? All he knows is that it must look right and must be ready in three minutes. Some large drops of sweat fall from his forehead on to the toast. Why should he worry? Presently the toast falls among the filthy sawdust on the floor. Why trouble to make a new piece? It is much quicker to wipe the sawdust off. On the way upstairs the toast falls again, butter side down. Another wipe is all it needs. And so with everything. The only food at the Hôtel X. which was ever prepared cleanly was the staff's, and the *patron's*. The maxim, repeated by every-one, was: "Look out for the *patron,* and as for the clients, *s'en f——pas mal!*"[5] Everywhere in the service quarters dirt festered—a secret vein of dirt, running through the great garish hotel like the intestines through a man's body.

Apart from the dirt, the *patron* swindled the customers wholeheart- 26 edly. For the most part the materials of the food were very bad, though the cooks knew how to serve it up in style. The meat was at best ordinary, and as to the vegetables, no good housekeeper would have looked at them in the market. The cream, by a standing order, was diluted with milk. The tea and coffee were of inferior sorts, and the jam was synthetic stuff out of vast, unlabelled tins. All the cheaper wines, according to Boris, were corked *vin ordinaire.* There was a rule that employees must pay for any-thing they spoiled, and in consequence damaged things were seldom thrown away. Once the waiter on the third floor dropped a roast chicken down the shaft of our service lift, where it fell into a litter of broken bread, torn paper and so forth at the bottom. We simply wiped it with a cloth and sent it up again. Upstairs there were dirty tales of once-used sheets not being washed, but simply damped, ironed and put back on the beds. The *patron* was as mean to us as to the customers. Throughout the vast hotel there was not, for instance, such a thing as a brush and pan; one had to manage with a broom and a piece of cardboard. And the staff lavatory was worthy of Central Asia, and there was no place to wash one's hands, except the sinks used for washing crockery.

In spite of all this the Hôtel X. was one of the dozen most expensive 27

---

5. Obscene expression loosely equivalent to "To hell with them!"—Ed.

hotels in Paris, and the customers paid startling prices. The ordinary charge for a night's lodging, not including breakfast, was two hundred francs. All wine and tobacco were sold at exactly double shop prices, though of course the *patron* bought at the wholesale price. If a customer had a title, or was reputed to be a millionaire, all his charges went up automatically. One morning on the fourth floor an American who was on diet wanted only salt and hot water for his breakfast. Valenti was furious. "Jesus Christ!" he said, "what about my ten per cent.? Ten per cent. of salt and water!" And he charged twenty-five francs for the breakfast. The customer paid without a murmur.

According to Boris, the same kind of thing went on in all Paris 28 hotels, or at least in all the big, expensive ones. But I imagine that the customers at the Hôtel X. were especially easy to swindle, for they were mostly Americans, with a sprinkling of English—no French—and seemed to know nothing whatever about good food. They would stuff themselves with disgusting American "cereals," and eat marmalade at tea, and drink vermouth after dinner, and order a *poulet à la reine* [a chicken dish] at a hundred francs and then souse it in Worcester sauce. One customer, from Pittsburgh, dined every night in his bedroom on grape-nuts, scrambled eggs and cocoa. Perhaps it hardly matters whether such people are swindled or not.

Reading and Interpreting

VOCABULARY

Use your dictionary as necessary to find the meaning of the following words as used by Orwell:

grandiose (1)	labyrinthine (3)	scullions (6)	uncouth (11)
spasmodic (12)	squalid (17)	benign (21)	brilliantine (24)
festered (25)	garish (25)		

CONCEPT ANALYSIS

1. In the opening sentence of this excerpt, George Orwell contrasts two images: a grandiose place with a classical façade and a dark doorway like a rathole. Cite passages in which this theme—the difference between the mask of the institution and its behind-the-scenes reality is developed.
2. Is the narrator critical, neutral, or approving of the hotel's various masks and swindles? Support your answer with specific references to the text.

3. In describing the nasty working conditions, the narrator does not register emotional response or offer extended social commentary. How does the absence of these elements affect your reading? Cite some specific lines or passages that might have evoked emotional responses in you.

Quickwrite

Note some of Orwell's techniques for conveying rapid pace and immediacy: sentence fragments, present tense verbs, uninterrupted sequence of actions, concrete descriptions, brief dialogue. See, for example, paragraphs 12, 13, 14, 24, and 25. Use some of these techniques to record an activity in which you and/or others are pressed for time.

Thinking and Writing

RHETORICAL TECHNIQUE

1. The rapid-fire pace of the narrator's description, the humor, and the vivid characterizations of people, places, and activities lend a spontaneity and immediacy to this excerpt. Yet the writing does not ramble. Throughout, the several points of focus are signaled by general statements of observation and opinion. Underline examples of these.
2. The genius of this particular section of Orwell's autobiographical book is that it succeeds in projecting the narrator's personal voice through the use of precise action verbs and adjectives, concrete nouns for naming and describing people and places, and vivid images and explicit comparisons such as "low-ceilinged inferno" (6) and "sorting a pack of cards against the clock" (13). Cite several of the most effective descriptions in this reading.
3. Although dialogue occupies only a small portion of the writing, it is very effective in giving a personal voice to the narrative. What content has Orwell chosen to present in dialogue? What response does it generally elicit from the reader? Try turning some of the dialogue into paraphrases—that is, tell us what was said without directly quoting the speakers. How is the quality of the passage affected?

PAUL LAURENCE DUNBAR
We Wear the Mask

Without any biographical information about the poet,
see if you can determine who the "we" is in the following poem.

We wear the mask that grins and lies.
It hides our cheeks and shades our eyes,—
This debt we pay to human guile;
With torn and bleeding hearts we smile,
And mouth with myriad subtleties.   5

Why should the world be over-wise,
In counting all our tears and sighs?
Nay, let them only see us, while
        We wear the mask.

We smile, but, O great Christ, our cries   10
To thee from tortured souls arise.
We sing, but oh the clay is vile
Beneath our feet, and long the mile;
But let the world dream otherwise,
        We wear the mask!   15

Reading and Interpreting

VOCABULARY

Use your dictionary as necessary to find the meaning of the following words
as used in "We Wear the Mask":

guile (3)   myriad (5)

CONCEPT ANALYSIS

1. The author, Paul Laurence Dunbar (1872–1906), a black man, was a poet
   whose work focused on black folk themes and southern life. Does this information change your perception of the wearer of the mask? Explain.

Does the poem have universal meaning or is the theme related to black people alone?

2. Dunbar exhorts the mask wearer to retain the mask in the presence of the outside world. Why do you think he does so? What emotions does the image of the mask evoke in you?

Quickwrite

Take inventory on the topic of masks by answering the following questions. You need not share your responses.

1. Which of your masks were you wearing when you entered this class (bored, superior, naive, brash, silly, enthusiastic, confident)?
2. Why have you chosen the seat in which you are sitting? Does it serve as a mask? How?
3. Why do you wear your different masks?
4. With whom do you remove them?

Thinking and Writing

RHETORICAL TECHNIQUE

1. Dunbar's observations about the wearers of the mask are based on real life, but the details, like his thesis, are implied rather than concretely stated. In your own words, formulate a prose statement of Dunbar's central idea.
2. Reread Dunbar's poem aloud, using the third person singular instead of the first person plural (*he* or *she* instead of *we*). How does this change affect the poem's impact?

JULES HENRY
A Day at Rome High

Social anthropologist Jules Henry (1904–1969) viewed the educational process as a restrictive experience that reduces children to intellectual incompetents. He saw our school system as the means by which we preserve the masks of our cultural patterns. In this selection about Rome High, a typical midwestern high school in the 1960s, the authentic voice of the high school student is captured in the field notes of a participant-researcher. The notes offer a basis for Henry's thesis statement about American teenage culture.

[Jules Henry's introduction] Rome High is by no means entirely dedi- 1
cated to athletics and fun; it is also an institution of learning. Yet fun looms large in life at Rome High. Let us spend a day there with Lila Greene, a fourteen-year-old freshman. We start at the Researcher's meeting with Lila.

[Researcher's notes] I pick Lila up at her house. When she asks her 2
father for money he says, "What about the ten dollar bill that so mysteriously disappeared?" She smiles, shrugs her shoulders, and says, "O.K., you win." On the way to school she tells me that it was really twenty, but if he's forgotten, "that's alright with me." Lila and her brother Bill are both interested in figuring the angles.

The first class we go to is gym. Lila introduces me to her girl 3
friends—too many for me to catch the names of all of them—and to the gym teacher. Lila undresses and dresses in the shower stall in the girl's dressing room, saying that sometimes they throw girls in there to dunk them. They all like the gym teacher because they threw her in with her street clothes on and she didn't get mad.

The girls are all sharply dressed, except, of course, those who already 4
have their gym suits on. There are mirrors everywhere and the girls are preening themselves in front of them. Lila says, "Most of the girls consist of padded bras and girdles, but they're clever artists, and besides, *what else can you do?*" Lila is not wearing a girdle.

Lila tells me about three girls in this class who dislike her and when 5
I ask why, she says, "Jealous, probably. I make decent grades and have more physical ability and have fair success with boys. One of those girls, I guess, only goes out every three months. I didn't think that was possible.

The senior boys were kidding around the other day about senior girls who have never been kissed. I didn't believe it at first." I say, "Oh, it's possible," and she says, "Never? Oh, my!" She asks about my dating habits and says she goes out at least four or five times a month, and was out until 2 A.M. at the backwards dance Saturday. They went for pizza afterwards, and she paid her half of the bill because it was backwards. A couple of girls have asked her whether or not she paid.

Lila notices a boy circling the gym floor running, and says, "He's a 6 nice guy, except he has beady eyes; you can always tell by their eyes." There are NO SMOKING signs everywhere. The boys and girls are separated and do not approach one another. Girls tend to clique up. Class seems to go from ultra-chic hair styles to long mops, with no middle ground. I see two bleached blondes. This gym class contains students from all years.

Gym class is over. Back to dressing room. There *is* a prevalence of 7 padded bras and girdles here—and all of them so young! I ask, "Aren't the fellows disappointed?" and Lila says, "They don't know. Maybe some do, but most are fooled. I wear one once in awhile." One girl, a junior, looks like a high fashion model, bleached blonde.

French class. Mrs. Carling. Class is very crowded. The students get 8 their exams back. Generally the class did well. Lila signals to me that she got A. Most girls wear expensive sweaters. If I had no job I'd have a hard job meeting this standard. I wonder how the less prosperous do. Boys in class all wear slacks but run-of-the-mill shirts. No outstanding marks of wealth among them and no bizarre haircuts.

One girl in the class is Danish. Lila asked her if she spoke Danish 9 and the girl seemed disgusted at this oft-repeated question as she said, "of course." She was pale blonde, wore heavy eye-shadow, little lipstick. Class ring on chain around her neck, another on her hand. Apparently she has stripped her steady of all the tokens of love he possesses. He is hers!

The teacher is wearing a lavender wool dress, four inch spikes, rope 10 beads. She is stocky but not fat, has red hair, and wears glasses; not unattractive. Girls are segregated from boys.

The next class is Home Economics, where the room is a lovely pink 11 with tan upholstered chairs, and is luxurious and roomy compared to other rooms in the school. One wall is covered with posters I imagine the girls made. They have to do with hair, skin, weight, posture, grooming. The teacher, Miss Clements, is probably about 45 years old and is tall and bigboned. She is wearing a brown suit of good quality and glasses. Her brown hair is waved back and her lipstick is a little too bright for her age. Her rope beads may be a little frivolous but conform in general to the anticipated appearance of one in her circumstances.

Miss Clements announces that Mrs. Elphin, the special visiting 12 speaker for today, will talk to us about wool. On the wall are posters from Helena Rubinstein cosmetics about skin care, Bobbie Brooks clothing ads, a poster on Facts About Perspiration, and in one corner there is a large, three-sided wardrobe mirror, in front of which a student, with the assistance of two friends, has been primping herself since class began. She is wearing a very elaborate oriental type hair-style, piled intricately around her head, and with the help of her assistants she is combing the strays back in place. I am convinced she could not have constructed this by herself; or if she did, it must have taken her hours. She sits down before the speaker begins.

The class is getting restless. Lila passes a note: "Next is English class 13 with Mrs. Nasson. There's a tack epidemic, watch before you sit." . . .

Lila remarks by notes on other students. Eddie Strong is a tack- 14 master. Nellie Burke is smart but not goody-goody. Rob is in the second stage of imbecilic ignorance; heaven knows how he passes! Tim Aupen is very smart, gets good grades, knows what's going on and how to be legally innocent. . . .

At lunch at the cafeteria the students are separated into cliques of 15 boys and girls. The colored students sit apart from the white and they also are subdivided into all boy and all girl cliques. At our table I met the six girls Lila usually has lunch with. They are all rather plain except Pauline, whom I met in English. She is a very pretty blonde, with blue eyes. One girl gets the job of fetching and carrying the cokes and candy bars for the others. I ask Lila why and she says it's because this girl is a minister's daughter and they tell her to be a good Samaritan and set them all a good example. When I look dubious Lila laughs. Lila tells me everyone cheats in math class *because* Mr. Snider only tells you how to do the problems *after* they're due, so you don't know how to do them. Also he doesn't give enough time to do them, so they copy from the more inventive students. . . .

The teacher, Mr. Snider, is a broad-shouldered, athletic, blonde, 16 crew-cut, rugged type. Married. Dominance in his whole voice and demeanor—a little bit of beer-gut, it seems.

A note has been kicked in front of me in the most intricate manner. 17 It gets kicked along the floor, like a piece of scrap paper, to its destination.

This algebra class contains all years. There are hoods and also inno- 18 cent little freshman boys who seem less worldly than the girls of the same age. There are no *levis* in here but Elvis haircuts are showing up; there seems more attention to fashion on the part of the males. Revision: there is one pair of *levis* in here, belonging to Roger, a singularly unhandsome guy; tall. I ask Lila if he is a hood, and she says, "Um-m-m, I don't know. He goes out with girls for what he can get. I don't know him except by reputation." Teacher is now taking the class grades. Charlie Nelson is so busy trying to read over my shoulder he misses his turn and has to be called on it. He's also unhandsome. Chews gum viciously. Elvis haircut. In and out of his seat constantly. Lila tells me she will give me a story about him later that will make a "bunch of notes."

Mr. Snider is wearing a green, long-sleeved sport shirt, no tie, black 19 wool slacks, tan belt. Looks more like a sport than a teacher.

Celine to the pencil sharpener. Looks sharp today: white blouse, very 20 feminine, purple plaid full skirt, brushed wool. Nylons, black flats. Girls in here run about two-thirds for nylons, one-third for white bobby-sox and bleached tennis shoes.

Sixth hour, Mr. Johnsberg's social studies class. A girl asks if it's true 21 they're all going to Mr. Miller's class next semester. Johnsberg replies, "What does that have to do with what I'm saying?" Girl says, "Nothing—I just wanted to know." She's crestfallen. Johnsberg says, "Yes, it's true, but that doesn't make any difference." But a boy up in front says, "Yes, it does." The whole class is groaning. "We want *you,* Mr. Johnsberg." Johnsberg says gruffly, "Well, I'll miss you too. Now let's get on with it." Big bluffer, he's been touched by this. It is interesting to notice the boys are the loudest groaners in this show of affection.

Girls and boys seem to segregate themselves here as well as else- 22 where. In here, a class of all freshmen, the boys fall back on the pattern of slacks, khakis, very ordinary shirts. There is no symbolic display of wealth among them. There seem to be even three or four girls in here who aren't competing in clothing, although they are well-groomed and clean.

Lila and her friend Beatrice, who wears a clique band like Lila's, are 23 giggling. Beatrice won't believe I'm a college senior. Lila tells me most kids have told her I look 16. The top estimate so far has been 18. I show Beatrice my driver's license.

Johnsberg is wearing a gray suit and bow tie, white shirt, black 24 shoes. He makes a very nice appearance before the class. Another teacher passes through the hall wearing a sport coat, tie, slacks. Johnsberg permits all the talk to continue without a word of admonishment. The students are cheating, trading answers to the study quiz right and left, but Johnsberg doesn't seem to care.

The last bell rings and there is a mad rush to lockers and exits. Boys 25 and girls who haven't seemed to know each other all day leave the school hand-in-hand. No one loiters.

[Participant-researcher's conclusions] We have finished our day at 26 Rome High with Lila Greene, and we have come to know her as a sharp fourteen-year-old, secure in her world. She has many friends, knows everybody, and is at ease in school: there seems to be complete complementarity between Lila and her environment. She has things sized up and like so many of her fellows, she will get away with what she can. From the standpoint of *this* dimension of her existence, Rome High socializes Lila to the corrupt aspects of the adult world. Of course, this is not *all* of Rome High, but it is a significant part. . . .

[Based on the participant-researcher's notes, anthropologist Jules 27 Henry makes some generalizations.] Everyone cheats in math, says Lila, because they don't like the way the teacher makes the assignments and because he does not give the students enough time. This is another of what we may now call the *conventions of dishonesty (vide* the canons of pecuniary philosophy), the system of rationalizations by which one makes his frauds acceptable to his Self. The psychic function of these modes of thought is, of course, to defend the Self from inner aggression. Socialization to the adolescent culture thus involves an important inner gain: *adolescent culture provides its members with a system of defenses that protects the Self from attack by the voice of conscience.* Who has as much to offer them? Meanwhile . . . we must bear in mind that these children, through being taught to lie to themselves are learning how to pursue a life of decent chicanery in the adult world. Lila's assessment of Tim Aupen—that he "knows how to be legally innocent"—is culturally resonant. I do not, of course, give adolescent culture all the credit for the canons of dishonesty; this is clear, I think, from earlier discussions. What the adolescent group does is add certain thoughts of its own and lend a generalizing polish and group support to chicanery that makes it easier to absorb the finishing touches of later life. An honest adolescent life could be a crippling preliminary for many phases of contemporary culture. . . .

We have not yet exhausted the means of understanding Lila's surreptitious hand in her father's pocket. Look at the massive stimulation to raise her consumption level Lila encounters in Rome High. Consider, first, the forthright talk of Mrs. Elphin on how to spend money and enhance status. . . . 28

There, in the comparative luxury of the Home Economics room, 'mid the posters on cosmetics, dresses, and perspiration, Lila learns how to raise social status, how to avoid being linked with "dirty, untidy, cheap people," and how to be happy in an ambient world of tidy, sweet-smelling people and expensive wool! This too is acquiring an identity! What is the prettiest room in the school? The Home Ec room where Lila, a lower-middle-class girl, learns how to consume, to raise her living standard, and to move up in the social scale. This is the room that symbolizes the pressures on Lila to spend; this is where we begin to understand most clearly the compulsion to stick her hand in father's pocket when he's not looking. 29

The stimulation to spend money on clothes and grooming must be overwhelming for a normal fourteen-year-old lower-middle-class girl; and the school takes this preoccupation for granted. How could Rome High, in the center of a lower-middle-class neighborhood, be indifferent to its yearnings toward status and the high-rising living standard? How could Rome High block the glittering Id of progress? Can we expect Lila, hungering for the group, to sit against the john wall twiddling her thumbs while her peers, glorious in ultra-chic and high fashion, competitively display their cosmetic success? Those mirrors on the wall do not say who is most beautiful of all, but they do communicate to the children that the school supports their strivings toward standards of pecuniary loveliness. There is one girl who has outdistanced the field. She is the girl who, having achieved a coiffure so elaborate that she cannot manage it alone, has two others hovering around her like Nubian slaves, catching the wisps 30 of hair, and shoring up the coils that have broken loose. She might well be Lila's goal, but such opulence is costly, and it is this sort of spectacle that helps to animate the hand that slips in and out of father's pocket in the darkness of his carelessness, fuzzy-mindedness, and nonobsessive attitude toward truth.

Reading and Interpreting

VOCABULARY

Use your dictionary as necessary to understand the meaning of the following words as used in the Jules Henry selection:

preen (4) chic (6) clique (15) good Samaritan (15)
complementarity (26) conventions (27) rationalizations (27)
chicanery (27) canons (27) ambient (29) compulsion (29)

CONCEPT ANALYSIS

1. In her classes at Rome High, Lila draws lessons that were not the intended aims of instruction. State some of these unintended lessons in your own words. What are some unintended lessons from your high school education?
2. As author Jules Henry works from the researcher's notes, he too draws lessons that were not the intended aims of instruction. State some of Henry's conclusions in your own words.
3. Find examples of students and teachers at Rome High who wear masks. How have masks and the values they imply changed since the 1960s?

Quickwrite

Select one of your classes and act as a participant-researcher. Closely observe the interaction between students and the professor. Then emphasize vivid verbs and adverbs to describe what you see and hear. From your notes formulate a thesis statement about the relationship between faculty and students.

Thinking and Writing

RHETORICAL TECHNIQUE

1. The participant-researcher who accompanies Lila through her program at Rome High attempts to be objective. Her thesis, based on a great deal of concrete, detailed observations, emerges as the conclusion to her notes (paragraph 26). Underscore her thesis statement. What specific incidents in the day at Rome High support it?
2. Even factual description can convey values or attitudes through its selection of material and choice of vocabulary. Cite specific notes taken by the researcher that reflect value judgments. Are they negative or positive?

THE WRITTEN RESPONSE

Topics for Critical Thinking and Writing

1. Has a single incident or experience in your life changed it significantly or led to a heightened awareness and understanding? Discuss, with focus on the specific incident and the feelings that accompanied it. You may want to review the selections by George Orwell and Richard Wright before writing.

2. Anaïs Nin states, "The defenses people build up become in themselves the trap. I think what I love about the young is that they have not yet created disguises and masks." Use techniques of invention to explore Nin's thesis. Does your own experience support or contradict her?

3. Jules Henry writes, "An honest adolescent life could be a crippling preliminary for many phases of contemporary culture." Interpret Henry's thesis and agree or disagree in light of your own adolescence. Brainstorm and then bring the topic into focus by selecting the most significant brainstormed item for extended discussion.

4. Consider Lord Chesterfield's condemnation of "false English, bad pronunciation, old sayings, and common proverbs." Write about words or phrases that we abuse or overuse in modern American English. You can arrive at your thesis by brainstorming examples first and then formulating a thesis statement based on your material.

5. In the diary entries of Anaïs Nin and the field notes for "Rome High," the world is viewed through the eyes of a woman. Does gender give writing a special personal voice or perspective? Review your journal or freewritings. Is your gender apparent in your choice of experiences or expressions? Explain.

6. The lessons of life can be learned in the classroom, through the personal advice of others, and through experience. Which is a better teacher? Refer to two of the following authors' selections to illustrate your viewpoint: Wright, Orwell, Lord Chesterfield, and Jules Henry.

7. Develop the following thesis: *Institutions, like individuals, may wear masks.* Discuss the masks worn by some of the institutions described in this chapter: Orwell's Parisian restaurant, the Ku Klux Klan in Terkel's oral history, Jules Henry's Rome High, Richard Wright's high school.

CHAPTER TWO

The Human Condition: Elements of the Essay

*Every person born into this world represents something
new, something that never existed before, something
original and unique.*

Martin Buber, *Hasidism and Modern Man*

While affirming philosopher Martin Buber's emphasis on the originality
of every person, we are also aware that human beings share common characteristics that distinguish us from other species. What are some uniquely
human characteristics? What things about you make you an original and
unique person?

THE WRITING FOCUS

What a piece of work is a man! How noble in reason!
How infinite in faculty! In form and moving how ex-
press and admirable! In action how like an angel! In
apprehension how like a god! The beauty of the world!
The paragon of animals! . . .

William Shakespeare, *Hamlet*, act 2, scene 2

The uniqueness of the human species has been the subject of creative thinkers, writers, and artists throughout the ages. It is a natural subject for reflection and for writing.

This chapter presents the stages of writing that follow the formulation of a thesis: subdividing the topic, selecting a deductive or inductive pattern of organization, formulating subtopic statements, using transitional expressions for coherence, and, finally, framing the essay with an introduction and a conclusion. The readings highlight the physical, psychological, intellectual, spiritual, and ethical attributes that distinguish the human species from other creatures on our planet.

Planning

Writing an essay requires planning in which you envision the direction and the major elements of the completed work. You should begin your planning by considering the topic and roughly formulating a central idea. To reduce your topic to manageable size, identify the aspects or subtopics you intend to develop.

Working Up the Outline: Subdividing the Topic

There are many approaches to blocking out subdivisions of a topic or central idea. In some cases the topic itself suggests logical subdivisions. For instance, a historical tracing or process analysis lends itself to subdivision by chronological periods. Thus, in a selection in this chapter, Robert Jastrow traces the effects of the various stages of the Ice Age on the evolution of the human brain.

Other types of topics invite different approaches. For example, the topic of this chapter's Essay for Analysis is the essential distinction between human beings and other animals. The author, Lucien Maison, chooses two attributes of human development as the subdivisions for his essay: intelligence and emotion. He then breaks these divisions down into further subtopics. Intelligence has three aspects: awareness of time and space, concept formation, and the ability to combine. Emotion also includes three aspects: the need for rules, reciprocity, and giving.

The first step in outlining a broad topic is brainstorming (see Chapter 1). After you have produced a sufficient list of items, cluster those that relate to each other into two or more logical groupings. These groupings will form your major divisions. They may be further broken down into subtopics. Arrange these groups in the organization that seems most logical: chronological, from most to least important, from most to least familiar, from causes to effects, from concrete to abstract.

When you have a rough idea of the major and minor divisions of your paper and their sequence, you will be ready to construct an outline to guide your first draft. This may be a traditional topic outline using Roman and Arabic numerals, or a box outline, which is more flexible and presents a visual idea of the organization of your essay. An example of each follows the selection by Richard Leakey.

Patterns of Organization: Deductive and Inductive

The two basic patterns of organizing an essay are the deductive and the inductive. The deductive pattern begins with the thesis statement. It continually narrows the focus to more specific subtopics, applications, and examples. This pattern is very common in academic and scientific writing. It is the pattern of Richard Leakey's essay on human biology and of the essay by Robert Jastrow. Jastrow states his thesis in the opening paragraphs and first discusses the broadest, most basic reason for the rapid growth of the human brain: resourcefulness. He then narrows the focus to specific examples of human resourcefulness such as tool-making and speech.

In contrast, the inductive composition opens with details or evidence for the thesis and moves toward a thesis statement or generalization based on the particulars presented. The inductive pattern develops ideas from least to most important, works from the least familiar to the most familiar supporting details and examples, and moves from the concrete to the abstract. The inductive pattern is like a problem in addition, where specific numbers add up to the total.

Certain types of material suggest inductive ordering. It is the common method of story telling and is particularly useful for holding readers in suspense or for shocking them with unexpected assertions. Mark Twain's ironic essay, "The Lowest Animal," for example, first presents some minor human deficiencies—vulgarity and obscenity—and then works up to the thesis, a surprising criticism of qualities that are usually considered human virtues—patriotism, religion, and reason. Erich Fried's poem, "Clever Dog," is another unusual but apt application of the inductive pattern.

Formulating Subtopic Statements

Just as the thesis frames the entire essay, a subtopic statement controls each major and minor subdivision. Subtopic statements elaborate on, refine, or extend the overall thesis, but they cannot contradict or ignore it.

The process for formulating subtopic statements is similar to that for formulating thesis statements (see Chapter 1). After outlining your essay and distinguishing its various subtopics, draft subtopic statements for each of these.

In the Lancaster-Whitten article in this chapter, for example, the topic of sharing is treated deductively. The first and broadest subtopic is sharing in all primate groups; the second is sharing in specific primates—chimpanzees and human beings; the third subtopic is sharing in a particular human group, hunter-gatherers.

The first subtopic statement, for example, identifies basic primate patterns and asserts a point of view: "The most significant [primate pattern] is the relationship between young animals and adults" (9).

Techniques for Coherence

Regardless of the length or complexity of a piece of writing, a writer must establish coherence—links between its parts. The main way to do this is to repeat key concepts and terms in synonymous words and phrases. Robert Jastrow, for example, introduces his main concept with the words "accelerating growth of the human brain." Throughout the essay, he restates this concept: "explosive growth of the human brain," "better brain," "stimulated the growth of the brain," and "expanding the brain." Similarly, Lancaster and Whitten introduce their central concept, primate sharing, with the phrase "instances of food sharing among chimpanzees." In later sections of the essay, they repeat the idea with synonyms such as "shared foods," "carrying and sharing . . . food," "sharing of gathered and hunted foods," and "systems of sharing foods." Through repetition and restatement, the coherent essay keeps the reader's attention on the central idea.

There are several ways to establish coherence between paragraphs. One way is to repeat a phrase from the last sentence of one paragraph in the first sentence of the next. Another is to use an inclusive term as the link between paragraphs. An inclusive term is one that is broader than more specific terms that precede it and so includes them in its meaning. In Richard Leakey's essay, for example, paragraph 1 discusses the human face, skin, and upright posture. Paragraph 2 begins with the linking phrase, "our appearance," which incorporates face, skin, and posture.

Parallelism—the repetition of phrase structure or sentence structure—also can link related elements in a piece of writing. In Mark Twain's essay, the anti-human thesis is reinforced throughout by the repeated refrain, "Man is the only animal . . ." followed by a negative judgment of human behavior.

Another important coherence technique is the use of transitional, or signal, expressions—words and phrases that signal the relationships between ideas. The Lancaster-Whitten essay uses many such signals: to show the addition of a new idea, "*another* aspect" (16); to show a similarity, or make a comparison, "the *same* basic pattern" (12); to show a contrast, "*Although* the basic pattern" (11). Transitional signals help the reader follow the complex thoughts of mature writing. Later chapters will provide instruction on transitional expressions and coherence techniques appropriate to specific types of writing. Some commonly used transitions are:

ADDING AND LISTING

also	and
furthermore	moreover
another	in addition
finally	many
such as	various
examples are	following points
characteristics are	besides
include	to illustrate

TIME ORDER

before	while
after	later
next	earlier
soon	subsequently
following	immediately
when	the steps in
the process of	the phases in
the following procedure	conclude
begin	

COMPARISON

both	similarly
likewise	as well as
also	too
share	in common
like	same
more	less

CONTRAST

but	yet
however	still
unlike	in contrast to
on the contrary	although
even	nevertheless
while	more
less	

CAUSE

because of	the reasons for
the causes of	the effects of
due to	if
since	

EFFECT

hence	therefore
thus	consequently
result	so
outcome	accordingly

Framing the Essay

INTRODUCTION

The general purpose of an introduction is to engage the reader's interest and establish a context for reading. The readings in this chapter exemplify several kinds of introductions. One kind uses a question to introduce the central idea. The sentences that answer the question form the thesis statement or idea. An example is the introduction of Leakey's essay, which asks, "What are we?" The rest of the essay responds to that question.

A brief narrative that illustrates the central idea can also introduce an essay. Mark Twain uses this technique in "The Lowest Animal":

> In August, 1572, similar things were occurring in Paris and elsewhere in France. In this case it was Christian against Christian. The Roman Catholics, by previous concert, sprang a surprise upon the unprepared and unsuspecting Protestants, and butchered them by thousands—both sexes and all ages. This was the memorable St. Bartholomew's Day.

Another way to introduce an essay is to offer an idea and then to contradict it in the thesis statement. Look for this technique in the Lancaster-Whitten essay. The first four paragraphs present the theory that human beings are aggressive "killer apes." The authors then upset that theory in paragraph 5 with their thesis statement: "The answer lies in a distinctively human characteristic—sharing— and the evolutionary mechanism that made it possible."

In deductive essays such as those of the scientists Leakey and Jastrow, the central idea emerges in the introduction. In inductive essays such as Twain's, the introduction snowballs into a mass of details that lead to midpoint or concluding thesis statements.

CONCLUSION

The conclusion of an essay is the sum of all its parts. It is an opportunity to restate the thesis in a way that leaves a sense of completion and a lasting impression on the reader.

A traditional conclusion is a summary of the most important points in the essay. For example, the Lancaster-Whitten reading on human evolution concludes (25, 26) with a list of the evidence for the thesis—the behavioral patterns that distinguish human beings from their primate relatives—and a restatement of the thesis itself—the importance of sharing in human evolution.

Another effective conclusion is a philosophical statement or quotation that drives home the thesis. An example is the quotation from the Russian writer Dostoyevski that concludes Leakey's essay on human uniqueness: "Man needs the unfathomable and the infinite just as much as he does the small planet which he inhabits."

Some writers choose to echo the key words of the title or the introduction in their conclusion. For instance, Mark Twain concludes "The Lowest Animal" with several references to the "Higher Animals," projecting a mirror image of his title.

Conclusions may also speculate about the future. This is particularly effective in an essay on a current subject about which there are contradictory theories.

Certain phrases signal conclusions to readers. In the Leakey essay, the phrase "All the points I have mentioned" serves this function. Jastrow signals his conclusion with the word "finally." Other signals of conclusion are "in sum," "to summarize," "in conclusion," "to conclude."

Essay for Analysis

LUCIEN MAISON

The Individual and the Species

A successful essay has a logical structure that is clearly signaled. This clarity is evident in the following essay, taken from social psychologist Lucien Maison's study of "wolf children," abandoned youngsters who were not raised in a human environment. Maison examines the issue of how human culture shapes the characteristics that distinguish us from other animals, including the higher primates. Although Maison's essay is detailed and complex, its logical structure assists the reader in comprehending its ideas. Review the box outline (on the next page) of the essay before you begin to read it.

It was rash to propose a system of invariant human characteristics so long as there were still parts of the world which remained unexplored, but today this enterprise carries little such risk.   1

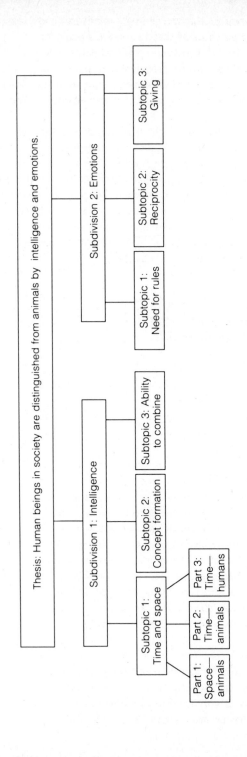

The preceding arguments have shown that there is no such thing as "human nature" in the sense that there are chemical "natures" which allow one to define a substance by its properties once and for all. Nevertheless man in society does reveal the possession of certain faculties which distinguish him unmistakably from the higher animals. We will assume for the sake of argument that it is these faculties, which man without exception has always possessed, that constitute his common inheritance. Three universal characteristics are cited by Köhler in the realm of intelligence and three by Lévi-Strauss in the emotional sphere.

Overall thesis: topic, control words

Number signals

Control words; division of essay into intelligence and emotion

Take intelligence first. When human thinking is compared with that of the inevitable chimpanzee, three characteristics stand out: man's thought is not restricted in time or space, he can think of an object by itself, and he possesses a certain combinatorial ability. Animal thought is restricted in space. An uncaged monkey finds it easy to get round an obstacle placed between him and his reward, but a caged monkey experiences great difficulty in using a stick in order to pull towards it an object placed out of its reach. In the first case success in the test depends only on the subject's motor abilities. In the second it depends on an ability to view the stick as something that will help to surmount the obstacle, as a substitute for the arm and as its spatial equivalent. Children perform this test with ease, while the most developed animal— the chimpanzee—succeeds only by chance.

2 Key term, number signal; signal of contrast; subthesis sentence: first subdivision breakdown announced: three subtopics

Key term restated; first subtopic, part 1: space

Animal thinking is restricted in time: an anthropoid can only carry out a task when confined in its own present, when, to be more precise, it is concentrating on the immediate visual field. When an animal carries out any task— particularly one involving the use of a stick— his performance is limited by what Merleau-Ponty calls "the need for visual contact." The tool, as Wallon puts it, is really only "something used on this occasion which happens to be part of the animal's immediate perceptual field."

3 Key term restated; first subtopic, part 2: time (animal thought)

Chimpanzees, he adds, cannot discriminate between different instruments. The higher animals are able to use tools as extensions of their limbs to achieve immediate aims but this ability depends very much on the original position of these intermediaries in relation to the goal. The monkey will only begin to break branches to make a stick when the bait is placed nearby. As it does so, it hesitates, stops and starts again, its whole performance halting and uncertain. Animals cannot therefore really be said to use tools at all. They have no stock of technical capital. No one has ever seen a monkey shoulder his bamboo stick and set off looking for some unknown prey.

Man's thinking, by contrast, is not confined to the present. Once he grasps the concept of unlimited time he is able to form the idea of God, to make tools with which to make other tools, and to develop a language which contains the notion of the possible and so enables him to express his wishes in words. It is no accident, no mere consequence of the monkey's impoverished phonetic range, that even those which have been carefully trained—by the Kelloggs, for example, or more recently by the Hayes—are unable to achieve the subtlety in communication which even a deaf mute displays, or the powers of expression which a small child reveals in his drawings.

The second set of findings we will cite from Köhler suggests that while men can form the concept of an object by itself, animals are incapable of abstraction in this way, and always give what they see its most obvious meaning. A chimpanzee will find it difficult to interpret a packing-case-seat as a possible packing-case-step if another chimpanzee is sitting on it. Put bluntly, the world always appears to animals as a system with definite values. Men on the other hand can distinguish objects from their immediate physical surroundings and so think of many different uses to which they may be put. Animals see objects as unambiguous things and always give them a single interpretation. Their world is an environment and never a universe.

4 Key term restated; signal of contrast; first subtopic, part 3: time (human thought)

5 Number signal

Signal of contrast; key term restated; second subtopic: concept formation

Second subtopic: concept formation

Signal of contrast

Key term restated

The last of Köhler's findings with which we shall deal indicates that animals, unlike men, have no combinatorial abilities and cannot calculate forces. An ape finds it impossible to construct a bridge out of planks and packing cases by itself, since to conceive the bridge it would have to realize that the vertical support is as important as the horizontal span. Nor can it disentangle a rope tied round a beam or remove a ring from a hook on the wall, since to be able to do this the animal would have to see the logical connection between distinct movements, which are spatially opposed but which point logically in the same direction.

If one is right in thinking that intelligence consists in the ability to solve problems whose solutions cannot be found by routine or by *a priori* methods, then, as Merleau-Ponty says, it is wrong to speak of animal intelligence in the sense with which one uses the word of humans.

The higher apes admittedly can "learn to learn." Vicki, the monkey trained by the Hayes, did, it is true, manage over the space of six years to acquire the use of three words, but one would be reluctant to call this a language, even for a complete imbecile, and it should not therefore weaken the conclusion that the animal frontier is quite clearly limited as regards intellectual ability.

In the sphere of emotion, Lévi-Strauss singles out three universal human attitudes as those which distinguish men from animals: the need for rules, the desire for reciprocity and the gesture of giving. Man, in the first place, has recourse to rules in order to escape the "intolerable burdens of arbitrariness," and he respects them simply because they are rules. Far from providing us with examples of the complete lack of order, primitive societies reveal on closer investigation the extent to which they depend on the scrupulous observation of custom and the careful attention to ritual.

In the second place, man always tries to establish contacts with other men which are governed by some sort of equivalence if not of wealth at least in his relationships. He does this

6 Number signal

Third subtopic: combinatorial abilities

Key term restated

Key term restated

7

8

9 Second subthesis sentence; second subdivision breakdown; three subtopics

Number signal for list; first subtopic: rules

10 Number signal for list; second subtopic: reciprocity

according to Lévi-Strauss (citing Susan Isaacs) because once he has realized that he is not omnipotent he tries to achieve equality with others, as it is "the lowest common multiple of all his contradictory wishes and fears."

Third and last, by making gifts man ensures that the other becomes his partner at the same time as he renders the object exchanged more valuable. The gift is an expression of his feelings of both strength and fear. The ego is flattered by the sense of power which the exchange gives him, yet his own weakness forces him to use the gift also as a way of winning the other's loyalty.

All three are in the end just different expressions of a fundamental desire for peace, and in attempting to satisfy it men devise systems of rules with which to replace the laws of the jungle. They are thus able to establish an order which is preferable at least to their destroying each other. Man's development may well have led to a chaotic profusion of different human types, but ethnological studies have cut through this apparently impenetrable thicket and revealed, beneath the manifest contradictions, the single path which man, unconsciously perhaps, attempts to follow.

What this amounts to for the purpose of our argument is that the child inherits, as its specifically human qualities, the ability to reason and the "recognition" of others. But these features, singled out in the writings of Köhler and Lévi-Strauss—and more generally in the writings of other contemporary sociologists and psychologists—are really nothing more than the defining characteristics of man in society. . . . Deprived of the society of others man becomes a monster. He cannot regress to his pre-cultural state, because such a state never existed.

11   Number signal for list; third subtopic: giving

12   Number signal to sum up subsection

13   Signal of conclusion

Synthesis and restatement of central idea

Vivid concluding image

Analysis of the Essay

THE ORGANIZING PROCESS

Subdividing the Topic.   A strong thesis statement indicates how the topic will be controlled and subdivided. In Maison's essay, the topic, distinguishing human characteristics, is controlled by the words *intelligence* and *emotional sphere* (paragraph 1); these are the two major subdivisions. Each subdivision begins with a subthesis statement, an umbrella sentence that announces the subtopics to be discussed (paragraph 2, second sentence; paragraph 9, first sentence). The first subthesis statement introduces the three-part division of intelligence into time and space concepts, abstract concept formation, and combinatorial ability. For the second division, emotion, Maison lists three uniquely human attributes: the need for rules, the desire for reciprocity, and the gesture of giving.

Formulating Subtopic Statements.   The topics introduced by the subthesis statements are detailed or further subdivided in individual paragraphs. For example, the topic of time and space concepts is discussed in paragraph 2 (introduced by the subtopic statement "Animal thought is restricted in space"), paragraph 3 (with the subtopic statement "Animal thinking is restricted in time"), and paragraph 4 ("Man's thinking, by contrast, is not confined to the present"). The subtopics of the second major subdivision, emotion, are detailed in paragraph 9 (subtopic statement: "Man . . . has recourse to rules . . ."), paragraph 10 (" . . . man always tries to establish contacts . . ."), and paragraph 11 (" . . . by making gifts . . .").

Organizing the Essay.   Maison begins his essay with the characteristic of intelligence and devotes twice as much attention to it as to emotion. The division of intelligence develops from more measurable aspects of intelligence—perceptions of time and space—to more abstract aspects. By paying more attention to intelligence, Maison provides a basis for the more complex ideas that follow. Dividing both major sections, intelligence and emotion, into three parts gives the essay a symmetry that makes it easier to understand.

Techniques for Coherence.   Maison uses several techniques to help the reader follow his thoughts. In the first division of the essay, the key concept of intelligence is repeated in such related terms as "discriminate" (3), "interpret" (5), and "see the logical connection" (6).

   In the second division, Maison uses signals of sequence to develop the three subtopics: "In the first place" (9), "In the second place" (10), and "Third and last" (11). Throughout the essay, Maison signals sequence, comparisons, contrasts, and causal relationships of his thoughts with such expressions as "The second set of findings" (5), "When human thinking is compared with" (2), "Man's thinking, by contrast" (4), and "He does this . . . because" (10).

Introduction and Conclusion.   Maison introduces the essay with an outdated theory (discussed earlier in his book) about human nature and then rebuts it with his own thesis. His conclusion logically follows from his evidence. He signals the conclusion with the expression "What this amounts to" and repeats in his last paragraph the key concepts that opened the essay. The two divisions of the essay are again mentioned: "the ability to reason" and "'recognition' of others" (another way of describing man's emotional needs). Maison closes with a vivid image that gives a visual dimension to his thesis: Without human society "man becomes a monster."

READINGS

RICHARD LEAKEY
The Human Animal

Richard Leakey, son of Louis and Mary Leakey, pioneers in the study of human origins in Africa, is himself a world-renowned paleontologist. In this excerpt from the opening chapter of his book *The Making of Mankind,* Leakey makes complex scientific material accessible through logical organization, clear subtopical divisions, and the repetition of key terms.

What are we? To the biologist we are members of a sub-species called 1 *Homo sapiens sapiens,* which represents a division of the species known as *Homo sapiens.* Every species is unique and distinct: that is part of the definition of a species. But what is particularly interesting about our species? For a start, we walk upright on our hindlegs at all times, which is an extremely unusual way of getting around for a mammal. There are also several unusual features about our head, not least of which is the very large brain it contains. A second unusual feature is our strangely flattened face with its prominent, down-turned nose. Apes and monkeys have faces that protrude forwards as a muzzle and have "squashed" noses on top of this muzzle. There are many mysteries about human evolution, and the reason for our unusually shaped nose is one of them. Another mystery is our nakedness, or rather *apparent* nakedness. Unlike the apes, we are not covered by a coat of thick hair. Human body hair is very plentiful, but it is extremely fine and short so that, for all practical purposes, we are naked. Very probably this has something to do with the second interesting feature of our body: the skin is richly covered with millions of microscopic sweat glands. The human ability to sweat is unmatched in the primate world.

So much for our appearance: what about our behaviour? Our fore- 2 limbs, being freed from helping us to get about, possess a very high degree of manipulative skill. Part of this skill lies in the anatomical structure of the hands, but the crucial element is, of course, the power of the brain. No matter how suitable the limbs are for detailed manipulation, they are useless in the absence of finely tuned instructions delivered through nerve fibres. The most obvious product of our hands and brains is technology. No other animal manipulates the world in the extensive and arbitrary way that humans do. The termites are capable of constructing intricately structured mounds which create their own "air-conditioned" environment inside. But the termites cannot choose to build a cathedral instead. Humans are unique because they have the capacity to *choose* what they do.

Communication is a vital thread of all animal life. Social insects such 3 as termites possess a system of communication that is clearly essential for their complex labours: their language is not verbal but is based upon an exchange of chemicals between individuals and on certain sorts of signalling with the body. In many animal groups, such as birds and mammals, communicating by sound is important, and the posture and movement of the body can also transmit messages. The tilting of the head, the staring or averted eyes, the arched back, the bristled hair or feathers: all are part of an extensive repertoire of animal signals. In animals that live in groups, the need to be able to communicate effectively is paramount.

For humans, body language is still very important but the voice has 4 taken over as the main channel of information-flow. Unlike any other animal, we have a spoken language which is characterized by a huge vocabulary and a complex grammatical structure. Speech is an unparalleled medium for exchanging complex information, and it is also an essential part of social interactions in that most social of all creatures, *Homo sapiens sapiens.*

All the points I have mentioned are characteristics of a very intel- 5 ligent creature, but humans are more than just intelligent. Our sense of justice, our need for aesthetic pleasure, our imaginative flights and our penetrating self-awareness, all combine to create an indefinable spirit which I believe is the "soul." Like all animals, we have to concern ourselves with the business of survival, of obtaining food and shelter, but that is not all. As Dostoevsky wrote: "Man needs the unfathomable and the infinite just as much as he does the small planet which he inhabits."

Reading and Interpreting

VOCABULARY

Use your dictionary as necessary to understand the meaning of the following words in the context of Leakey's essay:

protrude (1)   manipulative (2)   arbitrary (2)   averted (3)

repertoire (3)   paramount (3)   aesthetic (5)   unfathomable (5)

CONCEPT ANALYSIS

1. According to Leakey, how are humans physically different from other primates? What additional differences could you add to his list?
2. What are some unique human skills? According to Leakey, what physical feature(s) make these possible?
3. What are some distinctive features of human communication? Do you agree with Leakey that speech is an *essential* part of social interaction? Explain.
4. What does Leakey mean by the "soul"? Do you think his is a complete definition? Explain and elaborate.

Thinking and Writing

RHETORICAL TECHNIQUE

1. Study the box outline (on the next page) and the traditional outline (below) of Leakey's essay. What is the logic behind the sequence of divisions?

Thesis (unstated): The uniqueness of the human species lies in its physical attributes, behavior, and possession of a soul. (Answers "What are we?")

I. Physical appearance
    A. Head
        1. Large brain
        2. Flat face and down-turned nose

    B. Body
        1. Upright walking
        2. "Naked" skin
        3. Sweat glands
II. Behavior
    A. Manipulative skill
    B. Capacity to choose
    C. Communication
        1. Body language
        2. Voice
III. Soul
    A. Sense of justice
    B. Aesthetic sense
    C. Imagination
    D. Self-awareness

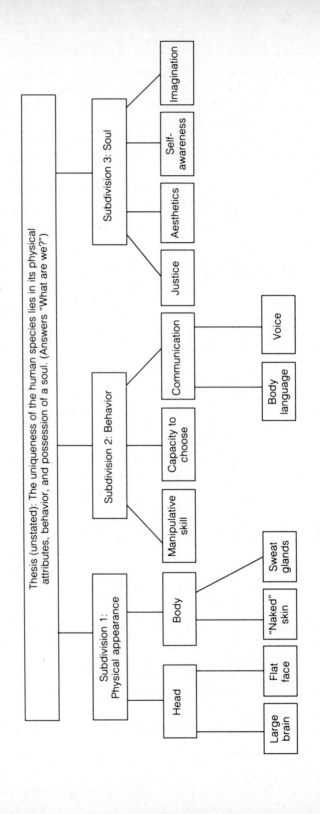

Thesis (unstated): The uniqueness of the human species lies in its physical attributes, behavior, and possession of a soul. (Answers "What are we?")

Subdivision 1: Physical appearance

Head
- Large brain
- Flat face

Body
- "Naked" skin
- Sweat glands

Subdivision 2: Behavior

Manipulative skill

Capacity to choose

Communication
- Body language
- Voice

Subdivision 3: Soul

Justice

Aesthetics

Self-awareness

Imagination

2. Leakey introduces his overall thesis by posing the question: "What are we?" State his thesis in your own words.
3. There is no subthesis sentence for the first division of Leakey's essay. Write one, and indicate where you would place it.
4. Leakey connects his divisions by a variety of devices. For example, he continually emphasizes the uniqueness of the human species by repeating related words for that idea. Find and circle these.

COMPOSITION

Leakey states that social insects perform "certain sorts of signalling with the body." Write a thesis statement in which you apply this idea to human behavior. Develop your thesis in a clearly organized essay of two or more divisions. Work up a box outline before you begin to write.

ROBERT JASTROW

Man of Wisdom

Robert Jastrow, a native New Yorker educated at Columbia University, has played a prominent role in the American space program. Jastrow's many books on astronomy and evolution include *Until the Sun Dies,* in which he explains why *Homo sapiens* has developed the largest brain of any species. In "Man of Wisdom," Jastrow begins deductively with the underlying cause of human brain development.

Starting about one million years ago, the fossil record shows an accelerat-   1
ing growth of the human brain. It expanded at first at the rate of one cubic inch[1] of additional gray matter every hundred thousand years; then the growth rate doubled; it doubled again; and finally it doubled once more. Five hundred thousand years ago the rate of growth hit its peak. At that time the brain was expanding at a phenomenal rate of ten cubic inches

---

1. One cubic inch is a heaping tablespoonful.

every hundred thousand years. No other organ in the history of life is known to have grown as fast as this.[2]

What pressures generated the explosive growth of the human brain? A change of climate that set in about two million years ago may supply part of the answer. At that time the world began its descent into a great Ice Age, the first to afflict the planet in hundreds of millions of years. The trend toward colder weather set in slowly at first, but after a million years patches of ice began to form in the north. The ice patches thickened into glaciers as more snow fell, and then the glaciers merged into great sheets of ice, as much as two miles thick. When the ice sheets reached their maximum extent, they covered two-thirds of the North American continent, all of Britain and a large part of Europe. Many mountain ranges were buried entirely. So much water was locked up on the land in the form of ice that the level of the earth's oceans dropped by three hundred feet.

These events coincided precisely with the period of most rapid expansion of the human brain. Is the coincidence significant, or is it happenstance?

The story of human migrations in the last million years provides a clue to the answer. At the beginning of the Ice Age Homo[3] lived near the equator, where the climate was mild and pleasant. Later he moved northward. From his birthplace in Africa[4] he migrated up across the Arabian peninsula and then turned to the north and west into Europe, as well as eastward into Asia.

When these early migrations took place, the ice was still confined to the lands in the far north; but eight hundred thousand years ago, when man was already established in the temperate latitudes, the ice moved southward until it covered large parts of Europe and Asia. Now, for the first time, men encountered the bone-chilling blasts of freezing winds that blew off the cakes of ice to the north. The climate in southern Europe had a Siberian harshness then, and summers were nearly as cold as European winters are today.

In those difficult times, the traits of resourcefulness and ingenuity must have been of premium value. Which individual first thought of stripping the pelt from the slaughtered beast to wrap around his shivering limbs? Only by such inventive flights of the imagination could the naked animal survive a harsh climate. In every generation, the individuals endowed with the attributes of strength, courage, and improvisation were the ones more likely to survive the rigors of the Ice Age; those who were

---

2. If the brain had continued to expand at the same rate, men would be far brainier today than they actually are. But after several hundred thousand years of very rapid growth the expansion of the brain slowed down and in the last one hundred thousand years it has not changed in size at all.

3. Latin for "man."—Ed.

4. Until recently, the consensus among anthropologists placed the origin of man in Africa. However, some recent evidence suggests that Asia may have been his birthplace.

less resourceful, and lacked the vision of their fellows, fell victims to the climate and their numbers were reduced.

The Ice Age winter was the most devastating challenge that Homo 7 had ever faced. He was naked and defenseless against the cold, as the little mammals had been defenseless against the dinosaurs one hundred million years ago. Vulnerable to the pressures of a hostile world, both animals were forced to live by their wits; and both became, in their time, the brainiest animals of the day.

The tool-making industry of early man also stimulated the growth 8 of the brain. The possession of a good brain had been one of the factors that enabled Homo to make tools at the start. But the use of tools became, in turn, a driving force toward the evolution of an even better brain. The characteristics of good memory, foresight, and innovativeness that were needed for tool-making varied in strength from one individual to another. Those who possessed them in the greatest degree were the practical heroes of their day; they were likely to survive and prosper, while the individuals who lacked them were more likely to succumb to the pressures of the environment. Again these circumstances pruned the human stock, expanding the centers of the brain in which past experiences were recorded, future actions were contemplated, and new ideas were conceived. As a result, from generation to generation the brain grew larger.

The evolution of speech may have been the most important factor of 9 all. When early man mastered the loom of language, his progress accelerated dramatically. Through the spoken word a new invention in tool-making, for example, could be communicated to everyone; in this way the innovativeness of the individual enhanced the survival prospects of his fellows, and the creative strength of one became the strength of all. More important, through language the ideas of one generation could be passed on to the next, so that each generation inherited not only the genes of its ancestors but also their collective wisdom, transmitted through the magic of speech.

A million years ago, when this magic was not yet perfected, and 10 language was a cruder art, those bands of men who possessed the new gift in the highest degree were strongly favored in the struggle for existence. But the fabric of speech is woven out of many threads. The physical attributes of a voice box, lips, and tongue were among the necessary traits; but a good brain was also essential, to frame an abstract thought or represent an object by a word.

Now the law of the survival of the fittest began to work on the popu- 11 lation of early men. Steadily, the physical apparatus for speech improved. At the same time, the centers of the brain devoted to speech grew in size and complexity, and in the course of many generations the whole brain grew with them. Once more, as with the use of tools, reciprocal forces came into play in which speech stimulated better brains, and brains improved the art of speech, and the curve of brain growth spiraled upward.

Which factor played the most important role in the evolution of human intelligence? Was it the pressure of the Ice-Age climate? Or tools? Or language? No one can tell; all worked together, through Darwin's[5] law of natural selection, to produce the dramatic increase in the size of the brain that has been recorded in the fossil record in the last million years. The brain reached its present size about one hundred thousand years ago, and its growth ceased. Man's body had been shaped into its modern form several hundred thousand years before that. Now brain and body were complete. Together they made a new and marvelous creature, charged with power, intelligence, and creative energy. His wits had been honed by the fight against hunger, cold, and the natural enemy; his form had been molded in the crucible of adversity. In the annals of anthropology his arrival is celebrated by a change in name, from Homo erectus—the Man who stands erect—to Homo sapiens—the Man of wisdom. 12

The story of man's creation nears an end. In the beginning there was light; then a dark cloud appeared, and made the sun and earth. The earth grew warmer; its body exhaled moisture and gases; water collected on the surface; soon the first molecules struggled across the threshold of life. Some survived; others perished; and the law of Darwin began its work. The pressures of the environment acted ceaselessly, and the forms of life improved. 13

The changes were imperceptible from one generation to the next. No creature was aware of its role in the larger drama; all felt only the pleasure and pain of existence; and life and death were devoid of a greater meaning. 14

But to the human observer, looking back on the history of life from the perspective of many eons, a meaning becomes evident. He sees that through the struggle against the forces of adversity, each generation molds the shapes of its descendants. Adversity and struggle lie at the root of evolutionary progress. Without adversity there is no pressure; without pressure there is no change. 15

These circumstances, so painful to the individual, create the great currents that carry life forward from the simple to the complex. Finally, man stands on the earth, more perfect than any other. Intelligent, self-aware, he alone among all creatures has the curiosity to ask: How did I come into being? What forces have created me? And, guided by his scientific knowledge, he comes to the realization that he was created by all who came before him, through their struggle against adversity. 16

---

5. English naturalist Charles Darwin (1809–1882) theorized that all species of life evolved through natural selection, a process by which individuals best suited to their environment survive, passing on their superior genetic traits to their descendants.—Ed.

Reading and Interpreting

VOCABULARY

Use your dictionary as necessary to understand the meaning of the following words in the context of Jastrow's essay:

accelerating (1)   generated (2)   coincided (3)   happenstance (3)
resourcefulness (6)   ingenuity (6)   improvisation (6)   vulnerable (7)
succumb (8)   reciprocal (11)   adversity (12)   imperceptible (14)

CONCEPT ANALYSIS

1. Jastrow asks several key questions in his essay. Underline them and make marginal notes of the answers.
2. In paragraph 8, what does the phrase "pruned the human stock" mean? In Jastrow's view, what were the "circumstances" that "pruned the human stock"? Is this a useful image for conveying his point? Explain.
3. Why does Jastrow believe that the evolution of speech may have been the most important factor in human brain development (9)?

Quickwrite

Imagine that the Ice Age is returning to our planet. What steps might you as an individual take to ensure your survival?

Thinking and Writing

RHETORICAL TECHNIQUE

1. Diagram the organization of Jastrow's essay with its principal parts.
2. Refer to your diagram of Jastrow's essay. Why do you think he arranged the divisions in this order?
3. Reference to the Ice Age and the growth of the brain are the two main threads that guide the reader through Jastrow's essay. Circle the specific expressions in each paragraph that repeat or restate these concepts.
4. Where do you think the conclusion of the essay begins? Explain.

COMPOSITION

Jastrow asserts that "adversity and struggle lie at the root of evolutionary progress." Do you believe that adversity and struggle lie at the root of an individual's progress as well? Determine your thesis. Outline your supporting ideas. Then develop your ideas in a logically organized composition.

WALT WHITMAN

I Think I Could Turn and Live with Animals

Walt Whitman (1819–1892) is considered by many to be the greatest of all American poets. In one of his best-known works, "Song of Myself," Whitman speaks as the living representation of America's democratic spirit. "I Think I Could Turn and Live with Animals," an excerpt from "Song of Myself," depicts the loss to human beings when socialization distorts the natural human condition. Each of the traits mentioned could be a subtopic in an essay on this theme.

I think I could turn and live with animals, they are so placid and self-
    contain'd,
I stand and look at them long and long.

They do not sweat and whine about their condition,
They do not lie awake in the dark and weep for their sins,
They do not make me sick discussing their duty to God,   5
Not one is dissatisfied, not one is demented with the mania of owning
    things,
Not one kneels to another, nor to his kind that lived thousands of years
    ago,
Not one is respectable or unhappy over the whole earth.

CONCEPT ANALYSIS

1. In your own words, what human behavior does the poet find disagreeable?
2. Why does Whitman include the trait of respectability (8) in his catalog of negatives?

Thinking and Writing

COMPOSITION

Brainstorm negative aspects of human behavior. Group and sequence them in an outline for a composition that catalogs human failings.

MARK TWAIN

The Lowest Animal

Mark Twain (1835–1910), born Samuel Langhorne Clemens, is best known for his masterpiece of American literature, *The Adventures of Huckleberry Finn*. Twain was also a prolific writer of short stories and essays. In all his works, as in "The Lowest Animal," Twain satirized human folly. The inductive arrangement of Twain's catalog of human defects heightens this satire.

In August, 1572, similar things were occurring in Paris and elsewhere   1
in France. In this case it was Christian against Christian. The Roman Catholics, by previous concert, sprang a surprise upon the unprepared and unsuspecting Protestants, and butchered them by thousands—both sexes and all ages. This was the memorable St. Bartholomew's Day. At

NOTE: This essay was to have been prefaced by newspaper clippings that, apparently, dealt with religious persecutions in Crete. The clippings have been lost.—Ed.

Rome the Pope and the Church gave public thanks to God when the happy news came.

During several centuries hundreds of heretics were burned at the 2 stake every year because their religious opinions were not satisfactory to the Roman Church.

In all ages the savages of all lands have made the slaughtering of 3 their neighboring brothers and the enslaving of their women and children the common business of their lives.

Hypocrisy, envy, malice, cruelty, vengefulness, seduction, rape, 4 robbery, swindling, arson, bigamy, adultery, and the oppression and humiliation of the poor and the helpless in all ways have been and still are more or less common among both the civilized and uncivilized peoples of the earth.

For many centuries "the common brotherhood of man" has been 5 urged—on Sundays—and "patriotism" on Sundays and weekdays both. Yet patriotism *contemplates the opposite of a common brotherhood.*

Woman's equality with man has never been conceded by any people, 6 ancient or modern, civilized or savage.

I have been studying the traits and dispositions of the "lower animals" (so-called), and contrasting them with the traits and dispositions of man. I find the result humiliating to me. For it obliges me to renounce my allegiance to the Darwinian theory of the Ascent of Man from the Lower Animals; since it now seems plain to me that that theory ought to be vacated in favor of a new and truer one, this new and truer one to be named the *Descent* of Man from the Higher Animals.

In proceeding toward this unpleasant conclusion I have not guessed 8 or speculated or conjectured, but have used what is commonly called the scientific method. That is to say, I have subjected every postulate that presented itself to the crucial test of actual experiment, and have adopted it or rejected it according to the result. Thus I verified and established each step of my course in its turn before advancing to the next. These experiments were made in the London Zoological Gardens, and covered many months of painstaking and fatiguing work.

Before particularizing any of the experiments, I wish to state one or 9 two things which seem to more properly belong in this place than further along. This in the interest of clearness. The massed experiments established to my satisfaction certain generalizations, to wit:

1. That the human race is of one distinct species. It exhibits slight varia- 10
   tions—in color, stature, mental caliber, and so on—due to climate,
   environment, and so forth; but it is a species by itself, and not to be
   confounded with any other.
2. That the quadrupeds are a distinct family, also. This family exhibits 11
   variations—in color, size, food preferences, and so on; but it is a family by itself.

3. That the other families—the birds, the fishes, the insects, the reptiles, 12 etc.—are more or less distinct, also. They are in the procession. They are links in the chain which stretches down from the higher animals to man at the bottom.

Some of my experiments were quite curious. In the course of my 13 reading I had come across a case where, many years ago, some hunters on our Great Plains organized a buffalo hunt for the entertainment of an English earl—that, and to provide some fresh meat for his larder. They had charming sport. They killed seventy-two of those great animals; and ate part of one of them and left the seventy-one to rot. In order to determine the difference between an anaconda and an earl—if any—I caused seven young calves to be turned into an anaconda's cage. The grateful reptile immediately crushed one of them and swallowed it, then lay back satisfied. It showed no further interest in the calves, and no disposition to harm them. I tried this experiment with other anacondas; always with the same result. The fact stood proven that the difference between an earl and an anaconda is that the earl is cruel and the anaconda isn't; and that the earl wantonly destroys what he has no use for, but the anaconda doesn't. This seemed to suggest that the anaconda was not descended from the earl. It also seemed to suggest that the earl was descended from the anaconda, and had lost a great deal in the transition.

I was aware that many men who have accumulated more millions of 14 money than they can ever use have shown a rabid hunger for more, and have not scrupled to cheat the ignorant and the helpless out of their poor servings in order to partially appease that appetite. I furnished a hundred different kinds of wild and tame animals the opportunity to accumulate vast stores of food, but none of them would do it. The squirrels and bees and certain bird made accumulations, but stopped when they had gathered a winter's supply, and could not be persuaded to add to it either honestly or by chicane. In order to bolster up a tottering reputation the ant pretended to store up supplies, but I was not deceived. I know the ant. These experiments convinced me that there is this difference between man and the higher animals: he is avaricious and miserly, they are not.

In the course of my experiments I convinced myself that among the 15 animals man is the only one that harbors insults and injuries, broods over them, waits till a chance offers, then takes revenge. The passion of revenge is unknown to the higher animals.

Roosters keep harems, but it is by consent of their concubines; 16 therefore no wrong is done. Men keep harems, but it is by brute force, privileged by atrocious laws which the other sex were allowed no hand in making. In this matter man occupies a far lower place than the rooster.

Cats are loose in their morals, but not consciously so. Man, in his 17 descent from the cat, has brought the cat's looseness with him but has left the unconsciousness behind—the saving grace which excuses the cat. The cat is innocent, man is not.

Indecency, vulgarity, obscenity—these are strictly confined to man; 18
he invented them. Among the higher animals there is no trace of them.
They hide nothing, they are not ashamed. Man, with his soiled mind,
covers himself. He will not even enter a drawing room with his breast and
back naked, so alive are he and his mates to indecent suggestion. Man is
"The Animal that Laughs." But so does the monkey, as Mr. Darwin
pointed out; and so does the Australian bird that is called the laughing
jackass. No—Man is the Animal that Blushes. He is the only one that
does it—or has occasion to.

At the head of this article we see how "three monks were burnt to 19
death" a few days ago, and a prior "put to death with atrocious cruelty."
Do we inquire into the details? No; or we should find out that the prior
was subjected to unprintable mutilations. Man—when he is a North
American Indian—gouges out his prisoner's eyes; when he is King John,
with a nephew to render untroublesome, he uses a red-hot iron; when he is
a religious zealot dealing with heretics in the Middle Ages, he skins his
captive alive and scatters salt on his back; in the first Richard's time he
shuts up a multitude of Jew families in a tower and sets fire to it; in Columbus's time he captures a family of Spanish Jews and—but *that* is not
printable; in our day in England a man is fined ten shillings for beating
his mother nearly to death with a chair, and another man is fined forty
shillings for having four pheasant eggs in his possession without being able
to satisfactorily explain how he got them. Of all the animals, man is the
only one that is cruel. He is the only one that inflicts pain for the pleasure
of doing it. It is a trait that is not known to the higher animals. The cat
plays with the frightened mouse; but she has this excuse, that she does not
know that the mouse is suffering. The cat is moderate—unhumanly moderate: she only scares the mouse, she does not hurt it; she doesn't dig
out its eyes, or tear off its skin, or drive splinters under its nails—man-
fashion; when she is done playing with it she makes a sudden meal of it
and puts it out of its trouble. Man is the Cruel Animal. He is alone in that
distinction.

The higher animals engage in individual fights, but never in orga- 20
nized masses. Man is the only animal that deals in that atrocity of atroci-
ties, War. He is the only one that gathers his brethren about him and goes
forth in cold blood and with calm pulse to exterminate his kind. He is the
only animal that for sordid wages will march out, as the Hessians did in
our Revolution, and as the boyish Prince Napoleon did in the Zulu war,
and help to slaughter strangers of his own species who have done him no
harm and with whom he has no quarrel.

Man is the only animal that robs his helpless fellow of his country— 21
takes possession of it and drives him out of it or destroys him. Man has
done this in all the ages. There is not an acre of ground on the globe that
is in possession of its rightful owner, or that has not been taken away from
owner after owner, cycle after cycle, by force and bloodshed.

Man is the only Slave. And he is the only animal who enslaves. He 22
has always been a slave in one form or another, and has always held other
slaves in bondage under him in one way or another. In our day he is always
some man's slave for wages, and does that man's work; and this slave has
other slaves under him for minor wages, and they do *his* work. The higher
animals are the only ones who exclusively do their own work and provide
their own living.

Man is the only Patriot. He sets himself apart in his own country, 23
under his own flag, and sneers at the other nations, and keeps multi-
tudinous uniformed assassins on hand at heavy expense to grab slices of
other people's countries, and keep *them* from grabbing slices of *his*. And in
the intervals between campaigns he washes the blood off his hands and
works for "the universal brotherhood of man"—with his mouth.

Man is the Religious Animal. He is the only Religious Animal. He 24
is the only animal that has the True Religion—several of them. He is the
only animal that loves his neighbor as himself, and cuts his throat if his
theology isn't straight. He has made a graveyard of the globe in trying his
honest best to smooth his brother's path to happiness and heaven. He was
at it in the time of the Caesars, he was at it in Mahomet's time, he was at
it in the time of the Inquisition, he was at it in France a couple of centuries, he was at it in England in Mary's day, he has been at it ever since he
first saw the light, he is at it today in Crete—as per the telegrams quoted
above—he will be at it somewhere else tomorrow. The higher animals
have no religion. And we are told that they are going to be left out, in the
Hereafter. I wonder why? It seems questionable taste.

Man is the Reasoning Animal. Such is the claim. I think it is open 25
to dispute. Indeed, my experiments have proven to me that he is the Un-
reasoning Animal. Note his history, as sketched above. It seems plain to
me that whatever he is, he is *not* a reasoning animal. His record is the
fantastic record of a maniac. I consider that the strongest count against his
intelligence is the fact that with that record back of him he blandly sets
himself up as the head animal of the lot: whereas by his own standards he
is the bottom one.

In truth, man is incurably foolish. Simple things which the other 26
animals easily learn, he is incapable of learning. Among my experiments
was this. In an hour I taught a cat and a dog to be friends. I put them in a
cage. In another hour I taught them to be friends with a rabbit. In the
course of two days I was able to add a fox, a goose, a squirrel and some
doves. Finally a monkey. They lived together in peace; even affectionately.

Next, in another cage I confined an Irish Catholic from Tipperary, 27
and as soon as he seemed tame I added a Scotch Presbyterian from Aber-
deen. Next a Turk from Constantinople; a Greek Christian from Crete; an
Armenian; a Methodist from the wilds of Arkansas; a Buddhist from
China; a Brahman from Benares. Finally, a Salvation Army Colonel from
Wapping. Then I stayed away two whole days. When I came back to note

results, the cage of Higher Animals was all right, but in the other there was but a chaos of gory odds and ends of turbans and fezzes and plaids and bones and flesh—not a specimen left alive. These Reasoning Animals had disagreed on a theological detail and carried the matter to a Higher Court.

One is obliged to concede that in true loftiness of character, Man 28 cannot claim to approach even the meanest of the Higher Animals. It is plain that he is constitutionally incapable of approaching that altitude; that he is constitutionally afflicted with a Defect which must make such approach forever impossible, for it is manifest that this defect is permanent in him, indestructible, ineradicable.

I find this Defect to be the *Moral Sense.* He is the only animal that 29 has it. It is the secret of his degradation. It is the quality *which enables him to do wrong.* It has no other office. It is incapable of performing any other function. It could never have been intended to perform any other. Without it, man could do no wrong. He would rise at once to the level of the Higher Animals.

Since the Moral Sense has but the one office, the one capacity—to 30 enable man to do wrong—it is plainly without value to him. It is as valueless to him as is disease. In fact, it manifestly *is* a disease. *Rabies* is bad, but it is not so bad as this disease. Rabies enables a man to do a thing which he could not do when in a healthy state: kill his neighbor with a poisonous bite. No one is the better man for having rabies. The Moral Sense enables a man to do wrong. It enables him to do wrong in a thousand ways. Rabies is an innocent disease, compared to the Moral Sense. No one, then, can be the better man for having the Moral Sense. What, now, do we find the Primal Curse to have been? Plainly what it was in the beginning: the infliction upon man of the Moral Sense; the ability to distinguish good from evil; and with it, necessarily, the ability to *do* evil; for there can be no evil act without the presence of consciousness of it in the doer of it.

And so I find that we have descended and degenerated, from some 31 far ancestor—some microscopic atom wandering at its pleasure between the mighty horizons of a drop of water perchance—insect by insect, animal by animal, reptile by reptile, down the long highway of smirchless innocence, till we have reached the bottom stage of development—namable as the Human Being. Below us—nothing. Nothing but the Frenchman.

This is only one possible stage below the Moral Sense; that is the 32 Immoral Sense. The Frenchman has it. Man is but little lower than the angels. This definitely locates him. He is between the angels and the French.

Man seems to be a rickety poor sort of a thing, any way you take 33 him; a kind of British Museum of infirmities and inferiorities. He is always undergoing repairs. A machine that was as unreliable as he is would have no market. On top of his specialty—the Moral Sense—are piled a multitude of minor infirmities; such a multitude, indeed, that one may broadly call them countless. The Higher Animals get their teeth without pain or inconvenience. Man gets his through months and months of cruel torture; and at a time of life when he is but ill able to bear it. As soon as he has got them they must all be pulled out again, for they were of no value in the first place, not worth the loss of a night's rest. The second set will answer for a while, by being reinforced occasionally with rubber or plugged up with gold; but he will never get a set which can really be depended on till a dentist makes him one. This set will be called "false" teeth—as if he had ever worn any other kind.

In a wild state—a natural state—the Higher Animals have a few 34 diseases; diseases of little consequence; the main one is old age. But man starts in as a child and lives on diseases till the end, as a regular diet. He has mumps, measles, whooping cough, croup, tonsillitis, diphtheria, scarlet fever, almost as a matter of course. Afterward, as he goes along, his life continues to be threatened at every turn: by colds, coughs, asthma, bronchitis, itch, cholera, cancer, consumption, yellow fever, bilious fever, typhus fevers, hay fever, ague, chilblains, piles, inflammation of the entrails, indigestion, toothache, earache, deafness, dumbness, blindness, influenza, chicken pox, cowpox, smallpox, liver complaint, constipation, bloody flux, warts, pimples, boils, carbuncles, abscesses, bunions, corns, tumors, fistulas, pneumonia, softening of the brain, melancholia and fifteen other kinds of insanity; dysentery, jaundice, diseases of the heart, the bones, the skin, the scalp, the spleen, the kidneys, the nerves, the brain, the blood; scrofula, paralysis, leprosy, neuralgia, palsy, fits, headache, thirteen kinds of rheumatism, forty-six of gout, and a formidable supply of gross and unprintable disorders of one sort and another. Also—but why continue the list? The mere names of the agents appointed to keep this shackly machine out of repair would hide him from sight if printed on his body in the smallest type known to the founder's art. He is but a basket of pestilent corruption provided for the support and entertainment of swarming armies of bacilli—armies commissioned to rot him and destroy him, and each army equipped with a special detail of the work. The process of waylaying him, persecuting him, rotting him, killing him, begins with his first breath, and there is no mercy, no pity, no truce till he draws his last one.

Look at the workmanship of him, in certain of its particulars. What 35 are his tonsils for? They perform no useful function; they have no value. They have no business there. They are but a trap. They have but the one office, the one industry: to provide tonsillitis and quinsy and such things for the possessor of them. And what is the vermiform appendix for? It has no value; it cannot perform any useful service. It is but an ambuscaded enemy whose sole interest in life is to lie in wait for stray grapeseeds and employ them to breed strangulated hernia. And what are the male's mammals for? For business, they are out of the question; as an ornament, they are a mistake. What is his beard for? It performs no useful function; it is a nuisance and a discomfort; all nations hate it; all nations persecute it with the razor. And because it is a nuisance and a discomfort, Nature never allows the supply of it to fall short, in any man's case, between puberty and the grave. You never see a man bald-headed on his chin. But his hair! It is a graceful ornament, it is a comfort, it is the best of all protections against certain perilous ailments, man prizes it above emeralds and rubies. And because of these things Nature puts it on, half the time, so that it won't stay. Man's sight, smell, hearing, sense of locality—how inferior they are. The condor sees a corpse at five miles; man has no telescope that can do it. The bloodhound follows a scent that is two days old. The robin hears the earthworm burrowing his course under the ground. The cat, deported in a closed basket, finds its way home again through twenty miles of country which it has never seen.

Certain functions lodged in the other sex perform in a lamentably 36 inferior way as compared with the performance of the same functions in the Higher Animals. In the human being, menstruation, gestation and parturition are terms which stand for horrors. In the Higher Animals these things are hardly even inconveniences.

For style, look at the Bengal tiger—that ideal of grace, beauty, 37 physical perfection, majesty. And then look at Man—that poor thing. He is the Animal of the Wig, the Trepanned Skull, the Ear Trumpet, the Glass Eye, the Pasteboard Nose, the Porcelain Teeth, the Silver Windpipe, the Wooden Leg—a creature that is mended and patched all over, from top to bottom. If he can't get renewals of his bric-a-brac in the next world, what will he look like?

He has just one stupendous superiority. In his intellect he is su- 38 preme. The Higher Animals cannot touch him there. It is curious, it is noteworthy, that no heaven has ever been offered him wherein his one sole superiority was provided with a chance to enjoy itself. Even when he himself has imagined a heaven, he has never made provision in it for intellectual joys. It is a striking omission. It seems a tacit confession that heavens are provided for the Higher Animals alone. This is matter for thought; and for serious thought. And it is full of a grim suggestion: that we are not as important, perhaps, as we had all along supposed we were.

Reading and Interpreting

VOCABULARY

Use your dictionary as necessary to understand the meaning of the following words as used in Twain's essay:

heretics (2)	hypocrisy (4)	conceded (6)	postulate (8)	wantonly (13)
scrupled (14)	zealot (19)	tacit (38)		

CONCEPT ANALYSIS

1. Which of Twain's paragraphs in this essay explicitly contradict the lines from Shakespeare in the Writing Focus section of this chapter? With whom do you agree more?

2. In contrast to Richard Leakey, whose essay praises humankind's "sense of justice . . . need for aesthetic pleasure . . . imaginative flights . . . and penetrating self-awareness," Mark Twain criticizes our species' moral sense. What specific points does he make about religion, patriotism, reasoning, and the moral sense?

3. In the essay's concluding paragraph, Twain confirms the point made by other writers in this chapter: The intellect of the human species is what sets us apart from other animals. Twain, however, gives us a different slant on the human intellect. In your own words, what is the central idea of the essay's last paragraph?

Quickwrite

Twain states that "Man is the Animal that Blushes. He is the only one that does it—or has occasion to." Use Twain's remark as the thesis statement for a quickwrite describing a situation in which you or someone else blushed.

Thinking and Writing

RHETORICAL TECHNIQUE

1. The contemporary supporters of the theory of human beings as "killer apes" believe that "humans, unlike their primate relatives, are innately . . . warlike. . . . [and have a] unique propensity for killing and violence . . ." (Lancaster and Whitten, paragraph 2). One hundred years before the development of this modern theory, Mark Twain communicated a similar idea in "The Lowest Animal." What are some of the specific devices he uses to make his argument convincing?

2. On the first reading, Twain's essay appears to be a spontaneous outburst with no particular order. Upon review, however, it becomes apparent that Twain has controlled his material by logically subdividing it. Reread the essay to annotate it, bracketing paragraphs that belong together under the following topic headings: introduction, "scientific experiments," catalog of moral defects, catalog of physical defects, conclusion

with thesis statement. Underscore strong assertions throughout the essay that serve as subtopic statements.

3. Review the catalog of man's moral defects. Is this argument developed inductively or deductively? Support your response with reference to the text.

    Review the catalog of man's physical defects. Is this argument inductive or deductive?

    In your opinion, are Twain's subtopics more effectively communicated by the inductive or deductive presentation? Explain.

4. Twain sequences man's moral defects as follows: indecency, vulgarity, obscenity, cruelty, slavery, patriotism, religion, and reasoning. What is ironic about this sequence? Would you eliminate or rearrange any of these traits? Would you add any?

5. One way a writer provides coherence between the elements of an essay is by repeating certain expressions almost as formulas. Cite examples where Twain uses this technique.

COMPOSITION

Robert Jastrow wrote, "Finally, man stands on the earth, more perfect than any other." After reading Mark Twain, outline a composition using one of the following introductory statements:

1. Having read Mark Twain's essay "The Lowest Animal," I disagree with Jastrow's statement. . . .
2. Despite Mark Twain's ideas in "The Lowest Animal," I agree with Jastrow that. . . .

ERICH FRIED

Clever Dog

Erich Fried is a contemporary German poet. His poem,
a single sentence divided into subordinate clauses, suggests two elements distinguishing human beings from
animals.

A dog
that dies
and that knows
that it dies

like a dog
and that can say
that it knows
that it dies
like a dog
is a man.

> ## Reading and Interpreting

CONCEPT ANALYSIS

1. What two uniquely human qualities are communicated in the poem?
2. What do you think the word *clever* means as used by the poet? Can there be a clever dog in this sense? Explain.

JANE B. LANCASTER
PHILLIP WHITTEN

Sharing in Human Evolution

In this article anthropologists Lancaster and Whitten challenge the popular theory that human beings are "naked apes." They use evidence from fossil remains and cross-cultural comparisons to argue that human beings have a disposition toward cooperation rather than toward violence and aggression. Carefully selected transitional expressions enable the reader to follow the reasoning with ease.

"There is evidence," wrote famed ethologist Konrad Lorenz in 1963, "that the first inventors of pebble tools—the African australopithecines—promptly used their weapons to kill not only game, but fellow members of their species as well. Peking Man, the Prometheus who learned to pre-

1

NOTE: References have been deleted.

serve fire, used it to roast his brothers: beside the first traces of the regular use of fire lie the . . . roasted bones of *Sinanthropus pekinensis* himself."

Thus was promulgated the view of humans as clothes-wearing "killer apes." . . . According to this view, humans, unlike their primate relatives, are innately territorial and warlike. Indeed, it is argued, this unique propensity for killing and violence is the one most responsible for our evolutionary success. 2

Proponents of the killer-ape theory make what appears at first glance to be a strong case. One does not need to look far to find evidence of human violence and destruction. In fact, however, the theory is wrong on both counts: aggression is *not* the characteristic that distinguished our early ancestors from the apes; and humans are *not* the only primates who kill their fellows. 3

Jane Goodall and her colleagues in Tanzania's Gombe Stream Reserve have observed a community of chimpanzees that split in two in 1970. By 1972 the observers noted a cooling of relations between the two groups. In 1974 several males from the original group attacked a single male from the splinter group, beating him savagely for about twenty minutes until he died. Since that time, a series of brutal gang attacks— including one in which a rock was thrown at a prostrate victim—has completely wiped out the second chimp community. 4

If aggression is not the trait that distinguished our forebears from other primates, what is? The answer lies in a distinctively human characteristic—sharing—and the evolutionary mechanism that made it possible. 5

Bipedalism

Sometime between five and ten million years ago our ancestors began to spend much of their time on the ground, walking on two legs. Long before we had developed large brains, before we had language with which to communicate, and before we could manipulate the environment to our own ends, we were bipedal. 6

Bipedalism was one of the earliest evolutionary changes that distinguished the human way of life from that of the ape. Some experts claim that hominids (the family of primates that includes human beings and our earlier fossil ancestors) first stood in order to run, or to fight, or to free their hands for using tools. But these scenarios are unlikely. The first adventurers on two legs, like toddlers learning to walk, were probably very clumsy and inefficient. Such awkwardness would be of little value in combat or in flight. Similarly, tool using by itself cannot explain the significance of bipedalism, since tools can be used as easily while sitting down as standing up. More likely the adaptive value of bipedalism lay in the social behavior that it helped bring about—cooperation and sharing. 7

Walking on the hindlimbs while clutching food to be shared with others in the forelimbs would have been an advantage to a primate group utilizing a large home range. In this context, bipedalism could evolve slowly over hundreds of thousands of years—as it undoubtedly did. Thus, rather than being violent killer apes, our ancestors—and we—can more accurately be described as *sharing* apes. . . . 8

The Basic Primate Pattern

There are few generalizations that can be made about all the higher primates. But some patterns seem to be so widespread among the Old World monkeys and apes that we can cautiously assume they must be very ancient and fundamental to the higher primate adaptation of life in social groups. The most significant of these patterns is the relationship between young animals and adults. 9

In all higher primate species, young animals spend years in physical and social dependence upon adults. This long dependence begins at birth, when the newborn first establishes a close one-to-one relationship with its mother. Unlike many other mammals, higher primates are not born into litters and hidden away in dens or nests. Instead, a single offspring is born, which for the first months of its life stays continuously in contact with its mother, clinging to her while she is moving, and resting in her arms to sleep. As Blurton-Jones has pointed out, adaptations for continuous contact with mother involve many different anatomical, physiological and behavioral systems. These range from the anatomy of the hands and feet, distribution of body fat, composition of breast milk, sleep and sucking patterns, ease of satiation, tendency to vocalize, to the need for body contact for feeling secure. 10

Although this basic pattern holds true for all the higher primates (Old World monkeys, apes, and humans), there is a striking contrast in how this continuous contact relationship between mother and infant is maintained. Among all the Old World monkeys the responsibility of maintaining the relationship rests heavily with the infant. From the moment of birth, an infant monkey must be able to cling to its mother for long periods of time while she feeds, travels, grooms, or even leaps to safety. Infants unable to maintain body contact are likely to be eliminated through accident or predation from the gene pool. Monkeys need all four limbs for locomotion; clutching a weak or sick infant to the chest while trying to hobble on three legs is difficult and leaves the pair vulnerable to predators. 11

The same basic pattern is true for the great apes—though newborn apes are less developed than monkeys and are poor at clinging for the first few weeks of life. Mother apes help their poorly coordinated infants by 12

walking on three legs and by restricting their movements and social interactions for several weeks after giving birth.

The close, continuous relationship between mother and infant gradu- 13
ally loosens as the infant is weaned and gains independence in locomotion.
Once a young monkey or ape is weaned, it has sole responsibility for feeding and drinking. If it is too weak from illness or injury to do so, it will
die before the concerned eyes of its mother. The mother will defend her
youngster, groom it, sleep with it cradled in her arms, but feeding it solid
foods is beyond her comprehension. Although isolated instances of food
sharing among chimpanzees have been observed, basically the nonhuman
primates are individual foragers. . . .

Chimpanzee and Human Behavior

The general cleverness of chimpanzees has long been known. But it was 14
not until the long-term field studies in Central Africa that particularly
humanlike aspects of chimpanzee behavior were observed. One of the
most striking of these was the wide variety of tool use by chimpanzees in
everyday life. These tools include the now-famous grass blades, vines or
sticks used to "fish" for ants and termites in their nests; leaf sponges used
to collect water, honey or wipe dirt off the body; twigs and sticks used to
investigate and probe unfamiliar objects; rough hammer stones used to
break open nuts; leafy twigs used as fly whisks; and finally sticks, stones
and vegetation used as missiles in aggressive display. Chimpanzee tool use
is similar to human in the sense that tools are an adaptive means to meet a
wide variety of problems posed by the environment.

One of the marked differences between the use of tools by humans 15
and chimpanzees is in the casualness and impermanence of the ape's tools.
Although chimpanzees make their own tools in the sense that they strip a
stick of leaves and side branches or chew up a mass of leaves for a sponge,
they do not try to keep a particularly well-made tool for future use. Chimpanzees discard their tools because it is difficult for them to carry anything
for long distances. When Goodall and her colleagues established a central
feeding station at the Gombe Stream Reserve that provided bananas for
the wild chimpanzees in the area, many came to load up a supply of bananas. They tried to carry bananas in every possible way: held in their
mouths, hands and feet, tucked under armpits and chins, even slipped
between flexed thighs and groins. Loaded up in this way, they retreated to
climb nearby trees, dropping bananas every step of the way.

Another aspect of chimpanzee behavior that has excited students of 16
human evolution is their sporadic attempts at the collective killing of
small game. Sometimes these hunts involve several adult and subadult
males who coordinate their movements to encircle the prey, some acting as

diversions while others slip close enough to dash in for the capture. Prey (usually small gazelles) are killed and eaten immediately, the participants in the hunt dividing the prey simply by tearing it to pieces. Latecomers may get a mouthful by persistent attempts to pull off a piece or by begging.

The killing and eating of meat is clearly a special event in chim- 17 panzee life. Witnesses of a kill show great interest and excitement and a clear desire for even a taste. The highly social, as opposed to nutritional, nature of chimpanzee cooperative killing and eating of prey has been noted by Geza Teleki, who observed that a dozen or more chimpanzees may take a whole day to consume an animal weighing less than 10 kg (22 lbs). The small size of game killed by primates (baboons have also been reported to hunt small mammals on occasion) is very striking. The largest prey is under 10 kg—well under the body weight of an individual hunter. Shared foods are most often minuscule scraps, more social tokens than major sources of protein.

In spite of their tool use and hunting, the behavior of modern chim- 18 panzees still fits squarely into the pattern described earlier for other primates. They are in no way quasi human. Like other monkeys and apes, they are basically individual foragers who live in long-term social groups. The infant is dependent on the mother for many years, but this relationship is based on a physical and psychological need for the mother's protection. Once weaned, young chimpanzees feed themselves. The basic diet is typical of many primates living in the tropics: vegetables, fruits and nuts, with some animal protein in the form of insects, small vertebrates and occasional small mammals. The important contrast between the feeding habits of human and nonhuman primates is not so much in what is eaten; rather it lies in whether each individual must forage for itself or whether there is a collective responsibility for gathering and sharing food between adults and young.

Modern Hunter-Gatherers

In recent years the ways of life of hunter-gatherers have attracted renewed 19 interest. Although only a few hunting-gathering groups remain in the modern world, they take on special significance when it is recalled that fully ninety-nine percent of human history was spent in the hunting-gathering stage. The peculiar demands of this life-style may well have left imprints on modern human biology and behavior.

There are certain ecological relationships and social behaviors found 20 in all known tropical hunter-gatherers, which stand out in sharp relief when contrasted with the behavior of monkeys and apes. The first of these is a diet based on a balance of plant and animal foods. This balance is highly flexible and varies according to season, geographic location and long-term cycles in food availability. Our understanding of sex roles and the ecological basis of early human societies has shifted away from an emphasis on females as camp and infant tenders and males as food providers. In the process, our concept of "man, the hunter" has been modified to "humans, the hunter-gatherers." . . .

It is informative to look at the basic material possessions of a hunting- 21 gathering woman who lives in the tropics. She must be able to carry all her possessions herself when she moves, because men are responsible for their own hunting equipment and for protecting the group. The most important items a woman possesses include a digging stick, a sling or net bag for carrying her infant, and a variety of bark and skin trays and containers for carrying and preparing food. This is all she needs to provide for her family. Significantly, none of these materials leaves a trace in the archaeological record.

The importance of carrying infants in a sling should be underscored 22 because it is a major factor in human evolutionary history. Unlike Old World monkeys and apes, human infants are unable to cling to their mothers. In fact, they are dependent on their mothers to hold them for many months. Hunting-gathering women keep their infants with them continuously during their daily foraging. They use a sling, which suspends the infant from the mother's shoulder while leaving her hands and arms free. It appears that one of the costs our species paid for evolving larger brains was a prolonged period of infant helplessness. The invention of such a simple tool as a skin sling to carry an infant may have been a crucial turning point in human history because it permitted the survival of infants born with small, immature brains and the potential for major growth after birth.

. . . The lives of hunter-gatherers differ sharply from those of other 23 primates in the tropics by virtue of one very important behavior pattern: carrying and sharing. The carrying of infants, tools, or food to be shared allowed our ancestors to shift away from individual foraging to a pattern emphasizing the sharing of gathered and hunted foods within the social group. Among the Kalahari hunter-gatherers plant foods collected by women are shared among close family members. Meat—food which comes in much larger packages—is shared in a larger network.

The success of a system of sharing foods depends on one other behav- 24 ioral innovation which sets humans off from other primates. This is the evolution of the home base, or camp. A home base need not be permanent. It can be nothing more than an agreed-upon location where members of the group can meet in order to share foods. Many monkeys and apes have favorite clumps of sleeping trees, where they often return for the night. A home base, however, is not just a location for sleeping. Rather it serves a much more important function as the site for the sharing of food among members of the social group. Like the shift from individual foraging to sharing, this represents a way novel among primates of utilizing a niche.

. . . What distinguishes our own species from our primate relatives 25 is not any innate proclivity toward violence and aggression. Rather we can accurately be described as cultural animals whose outstanding characteristics are cooperation and sharing. What separated our family from the apes was a reorganization of the relationships between the sexes and between adults and young. This shift, which favored cooperative activities, permitted early hominids to exploit a niche new to primates. The ability to exploit this new niche rested on a few, rather simple behavioral patterns. These included bipedalism, the use of tools, the division of labor between male hunters and female gatherers, a home base, and most important— cooperation and sharing.

The archaeological record, the study of modern primates, and the 26 behavior of present-day hunter-gatherers all attest to the significance of sharing in human evolution. It is the rock upon which all human culture is built; it is what makes us human.

Reading and Interpreting

VOCABULARY

Use your dictionary as necessary to understand the meaning of the following words in the context of Lancaster and Whitten's essay:

ethologist (1)	promulgated (2)	innately (2)	predation (11)
vulnerable (11)	foragers (13)	sporadic (16)	proclivity (25)

CONCEPT ANALYSIS

1. According to the essay, what is the "killer ape" theory? On what basis do Lancaster and Whitten reject this theory? What traits do they believe distinguish the human species from other primates?
2. According to Lancaster and Whitten, what is the significance of human bipedalism? Why is it presented as the first unique human trait?
3. Describe the "basic primate pattern." Despite this pattern the authors point out some important differences between the ape mother-child relationship and the human mother-child relationship. What are these? In what paragraphs do they appear?
4. The division "Modern Hunter-Gatherers" reinforces the central idea that human behavior contrasts with that of monkeys and apes. Refer to specific elements in the hunter-gatherer lifestyle that support this thesis.

RHETORICAL TECHNIQUE

1. Annotate the essay to indicate major divisions and topic statements for each.
2. The essay begins with a point of view opposing the authors' own thesis. Explain how this technique weakens or strengthens the authors' argument.
3. The authors use both the inductive and deductive methods to develop their subtopics. Where is the subtopic developed deductively? Where is it developed inductively? Which approach, the deductive or the inductive, do you find more effective? Explain your answer.
4. Complex essays require particularly clear transitional expressions to link their paragraphs. Underline these transitions in the section "Chimpanzees and Human Behavior."
5. A formal conclusion often includes references to the important subtopics in the essay. Which of this essay's major divisions are mentioned in its conclusion?

    A conclusion should also reinforce the thesis of the essay. Find key words and expressions that appear in both the introductory paragraphs and the conclusion of the essay.

COMPOSITION

According to Lancaster and Whitten, cooperation made the success of early human beings possible. Outline and then write an essay about a successful cooperative activity that you have observed in a technical, professional, academic, or social context.

THE WRITTEN RESPONSE

Writing Workshop

1. With your class consider the question "The human species: killer apes or wingless angels?" by brainstorming each of those concepts. Record all brainstormed items on the board under the appropriate topic headings.
2. Decide on the answer to the question in 1. This will be your thesis. Set aside the brainstormed group that contradicts the thesis.
3. Cluster the items that support your thesis into logical subtopics. Indicate major points and supporting details.
4. Sequence the subtopics in logical order and present them in a box outline. Begin with your thesis statement in the top box. Use the outline of the Essay for Analysis by Lucien Maison as a guide.
5. Formulate subtopic statements for the major divisions of your outline.
6. With your outline as a foundation, write a five-paragraph essay in answer to the question: "The human species: killer apes or wingless angels?"
7. Review your essay to make sure that your introduction and conclusion provide an interesting, logical frame.
8. Determine whether you have used sufficient, varied, and appropriate transitional signals. Refer to the list in the Writing Focus section of this chapter.

Topics for Critical Thinking and Writing

1. British historian Lytton Strachey has remarked, "Perhaps of all the creations of man, language is the most astonishing." Write a well-organized deductive essay in support of Strachey's thesis.
2. Haitian philosopher Jean Price Mars has stated that intelligence is "perhaps the great misfortune of human nature but it is also certainly its . . . mark of nobility." In a composition with two major divisions, elaborate on both the "misfortune" and the "nobility" that have resulted from human intelligence.
3. The uniqueness of the human species is the theme of this chapter. British scientist Julian Huxley reflects upon this theme in the following statement: "The advancement of beauty and interest, the achievement of goodness and efficacy, the enhancement of life and its variety—these are the harvest which our human uniqueness should be called upon to yield." Elaborate Huxley's statement in a composition organized into the three subtopics he suggests. Use your own ideals and ambitions as illustrations and support.

4. Which aspects of human development do you consider the most important? Select from the subtopics treated by Leakey, Jastrow, Lancaster and Whitten, and Maison in your essay.
5. Mark Twain and Walt Whitman find the human species inferior to animals. Scientists Maison and Jastrow take the opposing point of view, that human intelligence elevates our species above other animals. Write an essay in which you take sides with either Twain and Whitman or Jastrow and Maison. You may refer to their works in your essay.
6. Shame and guilt are uniquely human characteristics. Develop this thesis in an essay that incorporates references to the reading selections by Mark Twain and Walt Whitman.

Refining Your Essay

1. Review the paragraph that contains your thesis statement. Be sure that it either suggests or announces clearly the major divisions developed in the essay.
2. Check that each division contains its own topic statement. Underline this. Does each topic statement move the central idea forward? Which specific aspect of the topic does it develop?
3. Review your essay to make sure that you have presented your topics in logical order: most to least important, general to specific, most to least familiar, or the reverse.
4. Have you apportioned your space in terms of the importance of each division? A vertical box diagram of your essay based on the space allotted to each division may reveal imbalances, which can be corrected by the addition, deletion, or shifting of supporting material.
5. Can you trace a pattern of key concepts that guides your reader through the essay? Use your dictionary or thesaurus to find accurate and interesting synonyms for your key terms.
6. Have you used repeated structures or transitional expressions to alert the reader to your emphases and shifts in thought? Underline these. Examine the beginning and ending of paragraphs for links, and introduce signals for coherence as necessary.
7. Does your conclusion sum up all of your essay's major points? Have you restated your thesis and driven it home with an interesting image, quotation, or echo of your title? Have you left your reader with an idea for future thought about the topic?

CHAPTER THREE

Uniquely Human— The Dilemma of Love: Summarizing and Synthesizing

The symbolic expression of an emotion is a distinctly human characteristic, and no emotion has as many visual and verbal symbols associated with it as love. The ancient Greeks divided love into two types: *eros,* the physical, sensual, and romantic relationship that exists between two people, and *agape,* the spiritual and nurturing love of parents for their children, of siblings, and of friends. The valentine is in a sense a summary of the symbols we associate with romantic love. Identify some of these.

How do you define love? Is there some work of music, art, or literature that epitomizes love for you?

THE WRITING FOCUS

Earth's the right place for love:
I don't know where it's likely to go better.

Robert Frost, "Birches"

O, human love! thou spirit given,
On Earth, of all we hope in Heaven!

Edgar Allan Poe, "Tamerlane"

The mystery of love is unique to our species and finds expression in every genre of human communication: poetry and song; the essay, short story, and novel; drama and folktale. Love, in its infinite variety of forms, is universal, even if expressed differently in different societies and eras. As the unifying theme of this chapter, love is presented in its mythic, familial, romantic, psychological, and sexual perspectives.

Because much of your writing as a student will be based on your reading, this chapter focuses on the techniques of summarizing and synthesizing, which you will apply to the reading selections. Synthesis Questions at the end of the chapter ask you to bring together concepts about love from the various selections in support of your ideas.

Summarizing

Summarizing is the reduction of material to its essentials. It is an academic skill that is useful across the curriculum. You can summarize for a variety of purposes: reviewing lecture and discussion notes for examinations, condensing articles and reference works for library papers, recalling textbook assignments and retelling stories, plays, or films as the basis for criticism.

Reading, listening, or viewing with attention and comprehension is the foundation of summarizing. Recognizing the theme or thesis statement and the organizational elements of a work is a prerequisite for summarizing. Underlining and annotating (making marginal notes) should accompany active reading; they are a preparation for summarizing.

The length of a summary depends on the length of the original piece; the summary of a report, an essay, or an article usually should not exceed one-quarter the length of the original.

A summary concisely and accurately presents the original author's point of view through a clear paraphrase of the central idea and major points. It sets out the most important facts and illustrations in condensed but comprehensible form.

A summary usually begins with reference to the author, date, source, context, and possibly purpose of the original. It is a reduction in paragraph form, which presents the material in the order of the original. Direct quotations should be avoided except for short expressions that so aptly convey the author's view that they cannot be omitted or paraphrased. The body of the summary should not include the summarizer's interpretations, evaluations, or reactions to the material.

MAPPING A NONFICTION SELECTION

Mapping an essay, journal article, or chapter of a book is the process by which you group together related paragraphs and note their unifying topic in the margin of the text. Mapping also includes underlining key statements.

As you review a text for summarizing, underline topic statements and annotate the text by jotting down key points in the margins. Look for predominant patterns of organization, such as chronological order, comparison, contrast, and cause and effect; note these in the margin as well.

When the entire selection has been marked up, the information is transferred to a diagram, or "map," which indicates the paragraph groupings, their unifying topics, and restatements in your own words of the author's central ideas. This provides the basis for your formally written prose summary. This chapter's Essay for Analysis has been annotated and underlined. A map follows the essay.

When you have finished reading and mapping a piece you intend to summarize, state its overall thesis in your own words. This will be the introduction to your summary.

SUMMARIZING FICTION

The most frequent use of a summary of a work of fiction is to illustrate a generalization or thesis statement in an essay, library paper, examination response, or critical review. The inclusion of such illustration enriches serious writing in almost any discipline. This type of summary should relate just enough information to support the writer's assertion. The length of such summaries varies, depending on the length and complexity of the original, the length of the essay in which it is being included, and the writer's purpose for using it.

Even in miniature, however, the summary of a work of fiction should be a comprehensive restatement of the original, including reference to the following as appropriate: title, author, theme or central idea, major characters, narrative perspective, setting, and the most important incidents of plot or action.

Guide for Summarizing Fiction.   Before actually summarizing a work of fiction, you should consider the following questions and briefly note down your responses:

- What aspect of the human condition does the piece dramatize (for example, the finding of love, the rejection of love)?
- What point is the author making about this aspect of the human condition (thesis statement)?
- When and where does the action take place (social context)?
- Does the narrator play a significant role?
- Who is the major character(s)? What emotions motivate him or her?
- What is the major source of conflict: internal conflict in the major character? conflict between two or more characters? conflict between the main character(s) and the natural or social environment?
- What is the main action on which the story turns: an incident? a series of incidents? a line of thought?

After determining the main lines of the original work through the responses to these questions, consider which aspects of the piece relate most specifically to your point. As you summarize, focus on the concept you wish to illustrate so that your summary will logically fit your argument. For example, in the Essay for Analysis, Erich Fromm summarizes the story of Jonah as an apt illustration of one aspect of love: "the active concern for the life and the growth of that which we love" (9).

Frame your summary within your larger piece by appropriate transitional statements. Note how Fromm introduces his summary of the story of Jonah in paragraph 9: "This element of love has been beautifully described in the book of Jonah." Fromm concludes the summary by tying it to his definition of love as concern for life and growth: " . . . the essence of love is to 'labor' for something and 'to make something grow'. . . ."

OTHER ACADEMIC SUMMARIES

Although the term *summary* covers all reductions of material, specific kinds of summaries are associated with academic subjects.

Synopsis.   The synopsis is a general overview of material in the form of an outlined plan with headings and subheadings. The synopsis allows the major points of a subject to be taken in at a glance. A course syllabus, for example, which presents the outline of a semester's work, or the table of contents of a textbook, are synopses.

Epitome.   A summary of a work of fiction is sometimes called an epitome. Some epitomes try to convey the literary flavor of the original or include interpretive remarks by the epitomizer. The following epitome of a well-known American novelette, Edith Wharton's *Ethan Frome*, reflects the theme of this chapter. Taken from *The Oxford Companion to American Literature*, this epitome, by James D. Hart, has a vivid vocabulary and a literary style appropriate to its subject.

This grim story is told by a middle-aged engineer who pieces together the history of the inhabitants of a bleak Massachusetts farm. Zenobia (Zeena) is a whining slattern who hugs imaginary ailments to her barren breast, and spends upon quacks and patent medicines the scant substance her husband, Ethan Frome, manages to wring from the grudging earth. Her cousin, Mattie Silver, is left destitute and comes to live with them. The friendship of Ethan and Mattie arouses Zeena's jealousy and after a year Mattie is ousted to make way for a strong hired girl. On their way to the railroad station, Ethan and Mattie realize that they cannot bear to part, and when they are coasting down their favorite snow slide he purposely steers their sled into a great elm. Instead of being killed, they are crippled for life, and spend the remainder of their unhappy days on the barren farm under Zeena's surveillance.

Abstract.   An abstract is a selective condensation of the essential qualities of a nonfiction work. Using the format and terminology common to the discipline of the original, it abstracts, or draws from the original, the thesis statement, main supporting points, and conclusion in the language and organization of the original. An abstract does not contain *details* from the original; it is intended primarily to acquaint researchers with the subject of a work and the author's perspective on that subject. It is a preview that the reader can follow up by reading the whole. Dissertations, papers intended for publication or conference presentation, and bibliographies of nonfiction books frequently contain abstracts for the reader's convenience.

The following abstract of a 222-page doctoral dissertation indexed under the subject "Love" states the thesis of the original in the first two sentences of the second paragraph. Then the abstract indicates the three-part development of the thesis: " . . . three distinct elements." Transitional phrases introduce the three elements: "First, with regard to method," "Regarding content," "The final component." The abstract employs the terminology of the discipline (philosophy). Because this abstract is not the complete work, it raises questions in the reader's mind that can be answered only by reading the original. For example, what does the writer mean by "Absolute Beauty"?

Eros *and* Paideia: *Plato's Theory of Love and Learning*

Plato's theory of *eros* [erotic love] is the first attempt by Western man to highlight the intellectual and spiritual potential of love. Unlike most of his predecessors, Plato does not view *eros* as evil, but rather as a neutral force capable of either constructive or destructive application. For Plato, the key to human happiness lies in the proper management of the erotic impulse, i.e. in channeling our passions toward those things truly worth loving.

Through education we recognize that which deserves our love. It is only through *paideia* [education] that man sees the true nature of beauty, and thereby gains understanding of what is worthy of his erotic energy. This educational process contains three distinct elements. First, with regard to method, Plato emphasizes the necessity of a proper student—teacher relationship. In Plato's view, formal instruction is not conducive to learning. Consequently he prescribes a relationship of loving friendship as the ideal instructional format.

Regarding content, Plato makes good citizenship important in his educational scheme. To this end, Plato stresses the appreciation of the "beauty" of laws and institutions. Thus, the education in *eros* that Plato discusses is not an exercise in empty abstraction. The student is taught to remain engaged with and responsive to the operations of this world.

The final component is the aesthetic dimension of reason and intellect. Here, the student learns the beauty of the various sciences and comes to feel what Plato describes as a "boundless love of wisdom." Upon completing this stage, the student is ready to receive the ultimate revelation—a vision of Absolute Beauty.

Plato believes all those who successfully complete this course of study are permanently and positively altered by the experience. Unlike the majority, who stumble through life, the man who learns to enlist *eros* as an ally on behalf of *nous* [spirit] becomes a master of the art of living.

Précis. A précis is a brief statement that presents only the most essential facts or points about the subject; it does not offer evaluative or interpretive comment on the original source. The précis is commonly employed to summarize legal opinions or scientific treatises. The following précis by United States Supreme Court Justice William Brennan presents the majority opinion of the Court that an Alabama statute naming only husbands as payers of alimony is unconstitutional under the equal protection clause of the Constitution.

Orr v. *Orr, Supreme Court of the United States, 1979*

The question presented is the constitutionality of Alabama alimony statutes which provide that husbands, but not wives, may be required to pay alimony upon divorce.

On February 26, 1974, a final decree of divorce was entered, dissolving the marriage of William and Lillian Orr. That decree directed appellant, Mr. Orr, to pay appellee, Mrs. Orr, $1,240 per month in alimony. On August 19, 1976, at the hearing on Mrs. Orr's petition, Mr. Orr submitted in his defense a motion requesting that Alabama's alimony statutes be declared unconstitutional because they authorize courts to place an obligation of alimony upon husbands but never upon wives. . . . [Justice Brennan for the majority:] We now hold the Alabama statutes unconstitutional. . . .

In authorizing the imposition of alimony obligations on husbands, but not on wives, the Alabama statutory scheme "provides that different treatment be accorded . . . on the basis of . . . sex"; it thus establishes a classification subject to scrutiny under the Equal Protection Clause. The fact that the classification expressly discriminates against men rather than women does not protect it from scrutiny under the equal protection clause. . . .

[The opinion of the Alabama Court of Civil Appeals is that] the Alabama statutes were "designed" for "the wife of a broken marriage who needs financial assistance." This may be read as asserting either of two legislative objectives. One is a legislative purpose to provide help for needy spouses, using sex as a proxy for need. The other is a goal of compensating women for past discrimination during marriage, which assertedly has left them unprepared to fend for themselves in the working world following divorce. We concede, of course, that assisting spouses is a legitimate and important governmental objective. We have also recognized "[r]eduction of the disparity in economic conditions between men and women caused by the long history of discrimination against women as . . . an important governmental objective." . . .

Under the statute, individualized hearings at which the parties' relative financial circumstances are considered *already* occur. There is no reason, therefore, to use sex as a proxy for need . . . since individualized hearings can determine which women were in fact discriminated against vis-à-vis their husbands, as well as which family units defied the stereotype and left the husbands dependent on the wife.

[We find] Alabama's alimony statutes unconstitutional. . . .

Essay for Analysis

ERICH FROMM
The Theory of Love

Erich Fromm (1900–1980) came to the United States from his native Germany in 1934. Here he practiced psychoanalysis and taught in several universities. His books include *Escape from Freedom* (1941) and *The Art of Loving* (1956), from which the following excerpt is taken. Fromm is concerned with how people who live in industrialized societies can come to terms with their sense of isolation, insignificance, and doubt about the meaning of life.

Mature *love* is *union under* the condition of preserving one's integrity, one's individuality. Love
is an active power in man; a power which breaks
through the walls which separate man from his
fellow men, which unites him with others; love
makes him overcome the sense of isolation and
separateness, yet it permits him to be himself,
to retain his integrity. In love the paradox occurs
that two beings become one and yet remain two.

If we say love is an activity, we face a difficulty which lies in the ambiguous meaning of
the word "activity." By "activity," in the modern usage of the word, is usually meant an action
which brings about a change in an existing
situation by means of an expenditure of energy.
Thus a man is considered active if he does business, studies medicine, works on an endless
belt, builds a table, or is engaged in sports.
Common to all these activities is that they are
directed toward an outside goal to be achieved.
What is *not* taken into account is the *motivation*
of activity. Take for instance a man driven to in-
cessant work by a sense of deep insecurity and
loneliness; or another one driven by ambition,
or greed for money. In all these cases the person
is the slave of a passion, and his activity is in reality a "passivity" because he is driven; he is the
sufferer, not the "actor." On the other hand, a
man sitting quiet and contemplating, with no
purpose or aim except that of experiencing himself and his oneness with the world, is considered to be "passive," because he is not "doing"
anything. In reality, this attitude of concentrated meditation is the highest activity there is,
an activity of the soul, which is possible only
under the condition of inner freedom and independence. One concept of activity, the modern
one, refers to the use of energy for the achievement of external aims; the other concept of activity refers to the use of man's inherent powers,
regardless of whether any external change is
brought about. . . . Envy, jealousy, ambition,
any kind of greed are passions; love is an action,
the practice of a human power, which can be

1   Thesis statement

    Love is active power

2   Love as activity

practiced only in freedom and never as the result of a compulsion.

Love is an activity, not a passive affect; it is a "standing in," not a "falling for." In the most general way, the active character of love can be described by stating that love is primarily *giving*, not receiving.

Love = giving

What is giving? People whose main orientation is a nonproductive one feel giving as an impoverishment. Most individuals of this type therefore refuse to give. Some make a virtue out of giving in the sense of a sacrifice.

Nonproductive giving = impoverishment

For the productive character, giving has an entirely different meaning. Giving is the highest expression of potency. In the very act of giving, I experience my strength, my wealth, my power. This experience of heightened vitality and potency fills me with joy. I experience myself as overflowing, spending, alive, hence as joyous. . . . Giving is more joyous than receiving, not because it is a deprivation, but because in the act of giving lies the expression of my aliveness.

Productive giving = potency

The most important sphere of giving, however, is not that of material things, but lies in the specifically human realm. What does one person give to another? He gives of himself, of the most precious he has, he gives of his life. This does not necessarily mean that he sacrifices his life for the other—but that he gives him of that which is alive in him; he gives him of his joy, of his interest, of his understanding, of his knowledge, of his humor, of his sadness—of all expressions and manifestations of that which is alive in him. In thus giving of his life, he enriches the other person, he enhances the other's sense of aliveness by enhancing his own sense of aliveness. He does not give in order to receive; giving is in itself exquisite joy. But in giving he cannot help bringing something to life in the other person, and this which is brought to life reflects back to him; in truly giving, he cannot help receiving that which is given back to him. Giving implies to make the other person a giver

Giving of self—not sacrifice of life

also and they both share in the joy of what they have brought to life. In the act of giving something is born, and both persons involved are grateful for the life that is born for both of them. Specifically with regard to love this means: love is a power which produces love; impotence is the inability to produce love.

It is hardly necessary to stress the fact that 7 the ability to love as an act of giving depends on the character development of the person. It presupposes the attainment of a predominantly productive orientation; in this orientation the person has overcome dependency, narcissistic omnipotence, the wish to exploit others, or to hoard, and has acquired faith in his own human powers, courage to rely on his powers in the attainment of his goals. To the degree that these qualities are lacking, he is afraid of giving himself—hence of loving.

Giving—an aspect of love

Beyond the element of giving, the active 8 character of love becomes evident in the fact that it always implies certain basic elements, common to all forms of love. These are *care, responsibility, respect* and *knowledge.*

Four elements of love

That love implies *care* is most evident in a 9 mother's love for her child. No assurance of her love would strike us as sincere if we saw her lacking in care for the infant, if she neglected to feed it, to bathe it, to give it physical comfort; and we are impressed by her love if we see her caring for the child. It is not different even with the love for animals or flowers. If a woman told us that she loved flowers, and we saw that she forgot to water them, we would not believe in her "love" for flowers. *Love is the active concern for the life and the growth of that which we love.* Where this active concern is lacking, there is no love. This element of love has been beautifully described in the book of Jonah. God has told Jonah to go to Nineveh to warn its inhabitants that they will be punished unless they mend their evil ways. Jonah runs away from his mission because he is afraid that the people of Nineveh will repent and that God will forgive them. He is a man with a strong sense of order and law, but

Care = active concern—example of Jonah

without love. However, in his attempt to escape, he finds himself in the belly of a whale, symbolizing the state of isolation and imprisonment which his lack of love and solidarity has brought upon him. God saves him, and Jonah goes to Nineveh. He preaches to the inhabitants as God had told him, and the very thing he was afraid of happens. The men of Nineveh repent their sins, mend their ways, and God forgives them and decides not to destroy the city. Jonah is intensely angry and disappointed; he wanted "justice" to be done, not mercy. At last he finds some comfort in the shade of a tree which God had made to grow for him to protect him from the sun. But when God makes the tree wilt, Jonah is depressed and angrily complains to God. God answers: "Thou hast had pity on the gourd for the which thou hast not labored neither madest it grow; which came up in a night, and perished in a night. And should I not spare Nineveh, that great city, wherein are more than sixscore thousand people that cannot discern between their right hand and their left hand; and also much cattle?" God's answer to Jonah is to be understood symbolically. God explains to Jonah that the essence of love is to "labor" for something and "to make something grow," that love and labor are inseparable. One loves that for which one labors, and one labors for that which one loves.

Care and concern imply another aspect of love; that of _responsibility_. Today responsibility is often meant to denote duty, something imposed upon one from the outside. But responsibility, in its true sense, is an entirely voluntary act; it is my response to the needs, expressed or unexpressed, of another human being. To be "responsible" means to be able and ready to "respond." Jonah did not feel responsible to the inhabitants of Nineveh. He, like Cain, could ask: "Am I my brother's keeper?" The loving person responds. The life of his brother is not his brother's business alone, but his own. He feels responsible for his fellow men, as he feels responsible for himself. This responsibility, in

10

Responsibility = response to needs

the case of the mother and her infant, refers mainly to the care for physical needs. In the love between adults it refers mainly to the psychic needs of the other person.

Responsibility could easily deteriorate into 11 domination and possessiveness, were it not for a third component of love, *respect*. Respect is not fear and awe; it denotes, in accordance with the root of the word (*respicere* = to look at), the ability to see a person as he is, to be aware of his unique individuality. Respect means the concern that the other person should grow and unfold as he is. Respect, thus, implies the absence of exploitation. I want the loved person to grow and unfold for his own sake, and in his own ways, and not for the purpose of serving me. If I love the other person, I feel one with him or her, but with him *as he is,* not as I need him to be as an object for my use. It is clear that respect is possible only if *I* have achieved independence; if I can stand and walk without needing crutches, without having to dominate and exploit anyone else. Respect exists only on the basis of freedom: "l'amour est l'enfant de la liberté" as an old French song says; love is the child of freedom, never that of domination.

Respect = seeing a person as he is

To respect a person is not possible without 12 knowing him; care and responsibility would be blind if they were not guided by knowledge. Knowledge would be empty if it were not motivated by concern. There are many layers of knowledge; the knowledge which is an aspect of love is one which does not stay at the periphery, but penetrates to the core. It is possible only when I can transcend the concern for myself and see the other person in his own terms. I may know, for instance, that a person is angry, even if he does not show it overtly; but I may know him more deeply than that; then I know that he is anxious, and worried; that he feels lonely, that he feels guilty. Then I know that his anger is only the manifestation of something deeper, and I see him as anxious and embarrassed, that is, as the suffering person, rather than as the angry one.

Knowing penetrates to core of person

Knowledge has one more, and a more fundamental, relation to the problem of love. The basic need to fuse with another person so as to transcend the prison of one's separateness is closely related to another specifically human desire, that to know the "secret of man." While life in its merely biological aspects is a miracle and a secret, man in his human aspects is an unfathomable secret to himself—and to his fellow man. We know ourselves, and yet even with all the efforts we may make, we do not know ourselves. We know our fellow man, and yet we do not know him, because we are not a thing, and our fellow man is not a thing. The further we reach into the depth of our being, or someone else's being, the more the goal of knowledge eludes us. Yet we cannot help desiring to penetrate into the secret of man's soul, into the innermost nucleus which is "he." . . .

Knowing = fusion

There is one way, a desperate one, to know the secret: it is that of complete power over another person; the power which makes him do what we want, feel what we want, think what we want; which transforms him into a thing, our thing, our possession. The ultimate degree of this attempt to know lies in the extremes of sadism, the desire and ability to make a human being suffer; to torture him, to force him to betray his secret in his suffering.

Knowing for power—not love

In children we often see this path to knowledge quite overtly. The child takes something apart, breaks it up in order to know it; or it takes an animal apart; cruelly tears off the wings of a butterfly in order to know it, to force its secret. The cruelty itself is motivated by something deeper: the wish to know the secret of things and of life.

The other path to knowing "the secret" is love. Love is active penetration of the other person, in which my desire to know is stilled by union. In the act of fusion I know you, I know myself, I know everybody—and I "know" nothing. I know in the only way knowledge of that which is alive is possible for man—by experience of union—not by any knowledge our thought

Knowing "the secret" through union = love

13

14

15

16

can give. Sadism is motivated by the wish to know the secret, yet I remain as ignorant as I was before. I have torn the other being apart limb from limb, yet all I have done is to destroy him. Love is the only way of knowledge, which in the act of union answers my quest. In the act of loving, of giving myself, in the act of penetrating the other person, I find myself, I discover myself, I discover us both, I discover man.

Analysis of the Essay

THE PROCESS OF MAPPING AND SUMMARIZING

The map on the opposite page highlights the main points and support in Erich Fromm's "Theory of Love." The following summary elaborates the points highlighted in the map.

Summary: "The Theory of Love" by Erich Fromm

In the essay "The Theory of Love," psychologist Erich Fromm defines love as the active power of giving to another voluntarily, without sacrificing one's own integrity. According to Fromm, the nonproductive personality gives simply as part of an exchange; this is not love. Productive people freely give their own "aliveness" to another, requesting nothing in return. Their gift elicits a similar spirit, which is love. The author defines and illustrates elements basic to all loving situations: care, responsibility, respect, and knowledge. Care is working for what one loves. An illustration is the physical care by which a mother expresses love for her child. Responsibility is not a duty but the voluntary act of responding to the needs of another human being. Respect is appreciating others as they are, and allowing them to develop free from our control. To do this the lover must also be free of the need to dominate or exploit. Finally, knowledge of the other is the desire to go to the core of the other person's being, to understand the emotions behind the observable behavior. Wanting to know another so intensely becomes the desire to fuse with that person, to become one. Fromm states that the negative way to gain knowledge of the other is through power, rather than union, the extreme of this power being sadism. He concludes that we can never know another person as well as we do an object, but the continuing desire for this knowledge through union is love.

PARAGRAPHS	UNIFYING TOPIC	SYNTHESIS OF INFORMATION
1, 2, 3	Definition of love	Love is the active power of giving to another voluntarily, without sacrificing one's own integrity.
4, 5, 6, 7	Giving in nonproductive and productive characters; giving and love	The nonproductive, hoarding, or marketing personality gives as part of an exchange; the productive personality gives his "aliveness" to the other and calls forth the same spirit, which is love.
8	Four elements of love (intro to analysis)	Elements common to all forms of love are care, responsibility, respect, and knowledge.
9	Care	Caring is working for what one loves. An illustration is the Old Testament story of Jonah. Another is the care that expresses mother love.
10	Responsibility	Responsibility is not a duty but a voluntary act of responding to the expressed or unexpressed needs of another human being.
11	Respect	Respect is appreciating the other as he or she *is,* his or her uniqueness, and allowing him or her to develop free from our control. To do this the lover must be free of the need to dominate or exploit.
12–16	Knowledge of the other	Knowledge of the other is the desire to go to the core of the other person's being, to understand what lies beneath the surface emotions. Knowledge relates to love in that it serves our basic need to fuse with the beloved, to become one. The negative way to gain knowledge of the other is through power, the extreme of which is sadism. We can never know a person as well as we can know a thing, but the continuing desire for this knowledge through union is love.

READINGS

RUSSELL DAVIS
Love

Read and annotate for summarizing the following short
story by contemporary American writer Russell Davis
(b. 1909).

Next door to us on slightly higher ground lived the Holloways. They had   1
lived there as far back as anyone could remember. There was Sam Holloway,
a pale moon-faced bachelor who always wore a starched collar with a wrin-
kled handkerchief tucked in between it and his neck. He would start out
in the middle of every morning for downtown, and I remember how he
would come to a stop just past our fence corner where there was no shade
tree, lift his white face, eyes shut to the sun, and sneeze several times in
rapid succession before continuing on down the sidewalk.

There was Sam and there were his two gray sisters, Faith and Love,   2
both also unmarried, and that was all there was to the Holloways. There
had once been a Mrs. Holloway, the mother. My mother remembered her,
but just remembered her and that was all. There had been a Mr. Holloway
too, but that had been back before we had moved there.

Sam didn't do anything. He had worked in the carbide mill before   3
the Spanish-American War, but now he didn't do anything. He got a
small pension. He used to go down to the depot every morning and hang
around with the depot crowd. There was a more flashy, loud talking, bad
influence group who hung around the pool hall, but Sam was never one of
these. He was a mild sort, bland, untroubled. He belonged to the Odd
Fellows Lodge. They buried him. One morning he dropped dead walking
at his leisurely gait past Sheehan's Meat Market. We kids heard about it at
recess. "Hey," somebody said, "do you suppose they put him in the meat
wagon?" We all laughed and we all tried to top it. "Sure," said somebody
else, "they probably did, so he could *meet* his maker." I thought this was
pretty funny and sprung it at the supper table that night.

My mother frowned and I saw her neck stiffen. "Now that's not nice   4
at all," she said. My brother covertly held his nose with one hand and
made a pushing away gesture with the other.

My father looked thoughtful. Nodding toward the Holloway house   5
he said, "I wonder how they're fixed."

"I'm sure I don't know," said my mother, still frowning from the 6
effects of my remarks.

And that was the end of that. 7

We didn't play in the Holloway yard much, just cut across it once in 8
a while when it seemed convenient. It wasn't that the Holloways forbade
us over there, but we knew they were nervous about us, particularly at
Hallowe'en. They were, after all, just two old sisters who lived by themselves and never went out, except to funerals. At the same time it was
strange not to have a family in a house, a mother and father at least, even
if there weren't any kids left. That was the way we felt. Of course the
house itself was tall and narrow with high windows that seemed to yawn
at you, and it was so dark under the heavy elms that the lawn there had
gone mostly to moss. What grass grew was sparse and fine, like hair on a
man going bald. The place seemed so quiet always. It had once been
painted, probably gray, but now the clapboards were all darkened and the
stone steps had leaves and sticks rotting in the corners. The newest thing
about the house was their pantry window cooler that Sam had made out of
a wooden box with the sides removed and cheesecloth substituted. They
never had an ice box.

They also gained the reputation after Sam died of being very stingy. 9
Sam had done all the lawn mowing and snow shoveling. Now occasionally
they would call for my brother or me or one of the other kids in the neighborhood to come and do a chore. But we soon learned better than to respond. I shoveled them out of a two foot drift one January morning at my
mother's insistence. When I had finished, I banged the shovel on their
stone steps, then clumped up to the door and pulled the knob—not the
doorknob on the door but the glass knob at the right of the door that
operated a bell somewhere inside by means of a wire. I hauled on the knob
and let go and heard the faint sound of the bell, then nothing for a long
time, but at last I saw a movement of the curtain in the glass of the door
and an eye peeping out. Miss Faith, the plump one, opened the door just
enough to extend her gray hand and drop a rather wizened apple into my
mitten, then she closed the door and disappeared. I went home and held it
up to my mother with a sardonic expression on my face. My mother smiled
a little but then she said, "You shouldn't be hard on them, dear, I don't
think they have much money."

"Why don't they get some?" I asked. 10

My mother looked distressed. "I don't know that they have any way 11
to," she replied.

"Why don't they *get* a way, then?" I demanded. 12

My mother bit her lip. "It's not that easy, you know." 13

"Huh!" I said. 14

But then the Holloway sisters did find a way, though not a way in 15
which they were well qualified: they began to take in State wards.

First there were two girls, sisters, five and seven, who fought each 16 other all day, threw mud against the Holloway windows and finally set fire to the cellar. The fire was what decided them, Miss Faith the more talkative and friendly of the Holloways, told my mother. They were deathly afraid of fire. This was the reason they had never got electricity in their house. Gas was much safer. You know what it was and how to deal with it and need not be afraid it would draw lightning out of a thunderstorm.

Now they took in two younger children, Richard about five, and his 17 baby sister, a fat-cheeked little thing named Ola. We saw something of them because Richard was mechanically minded like us, and we helped him construct a pushcart which he would push Ola around in, getting annoyed when she failed to bother to steer, but particularly infuriated when she let the engine stop. She was supposed to keep trilling her tongue against the roof of her mouth, not only when he was pushing her, but also when the cart was standing, until he shut off the ignition switch. Richard would drive up to our cellar door where we were working inside on various projects, and come in and watch us, detaching himself angrily whenever he heard Ola running down and shouting at her not to let it stall.

But then Richard and Ola were banished by the sisters because one 18 day forty dollars disappeared from the gravy boat in the china closet. It couldn't be anybody but Richard, although Richard stoutly denied it; he said the ten dollars in his possession had been given him by a boy, a bigger boy from up the street whose name he didn't know. It wasn't until a month after the State had taken Richard and Ola away that a boy about half a mile up our street named Ham Ruther was caught sneaking out somebody's back door over on Washington Street and confessed to several such robberies, one of them the Holloway's. After this the State wouldn't give them any more wards.

They took in boarders now, but the boarders didn't stay. We didn't 19 know why until Jack Goldthwaite, the high school football coach, lived there while his wife was out West visiting her dying father. He smiled and shook his head when my mother asked him about the Holloways. "It's nothing special, just a lot of little things. Not enough to eat, of course, for one, but you can fill up on the outside. It's those small wornout hand towels, the lack of any really hot water, even the soap is always tiny; they cut it up and dole it out. And, of course, gas light. I like to read adventure stories. And well, all their chairs are uncomfortable. I suppose they can't afford better, but when you live somewhere, even temporarily, you want to live, not exist."

They had one roomer, however, who stayed several years, a Mr. Lor- 20 ing, with asthma and a slightly humped back. He was a clerk in the bank and alone in life as they were. He had a hobby. He kept bees, and there was big excitement once in a while in the neighborhood when they would swarm and get away from him. I think he died about 1926 when I was half way through high school. After that there was nobody. Certainly I didn't give the Holloway sisters much thought. I was interested in basketball, baseball, I had a paper route I traveled every afternoon and a girl over on Norcross Street who didn't believe in having only one boy friend as I believed she should. The first I knew I came home from school one afternoon in the winter and my mother was wiping tears out of her eyes because one of the Holloway sisters had died that morning. It was Faith, the more plumpish and friendly one, although she hadn't been so plump of recent years. She had become almost as thin as her sister Love, who was thin as a hatrack. My mother said Love had come over and got her and she had gone over, but there hadn't been anything she could do; Faith had been breathing her last and had died within a few minutes.

I stood still and my mouth dropped open. "You mean Miss Love 21 came out of the house?"

My mother nodded. 22

"Came over here?" 23

"Yes," said my mother. 24

"Holy Moses," I said. 25

We had never known Miss Love to venture out for anything except 26 once in a great while for a funeral, and we had never seen her out of the house alone. While Faith had gone to most of the funerals in town, Love had accompanied her only to the more obscure ones, apparently because there she would encounter fewer people.

"After all," said my mother, "her sister was dying." 27

I thought it over. "What'll she do now?" I said. 28

My mother shrugged sadly. "Live on there alone, I guess." 29

But Love didn't. The first we knew of what was happening was from 30 my father who saw the Sheriff's Sale advertised in the paper. Then a few days before the sale a taxi came to the house, deposited a woman in a business suit who went inside and came out with Love, while the taxi man brought out a high narrow ribbed trunk, and Love left. We heard soon enough where she went. The poorhouse.

I used to cut through the poorhouse grounds on my paper route. It 31 was a short cut from the end of one dead end street to another. High Street ended in the poorhouse driveway, a circular path bordered with scrub oak trees whose foliage was always gray with dust from the House of Correction Farm only a hundred yards away. I used to see Love Holloway in the window of the second floor. She had a thin, pinched up sort of face without life or expression in it, calm eyes placed surprisingly high, a long thin meaningless nose, prim lips. She was always there looking out, not apparently watching anything, just looking, staring. Once when I thought I might have caught her eye, I waved, but drew my hand down in the middle of the gesture, ashamed, wondering what her keeper or nurse, or whatever or whoever looked after her, might think of a full-grown high school boy waving. I was at a self conscious age. My love affair was not going well. A transfer from a high school in a larger town had come into Civics Class and managed to wangle himself the seat I had been trying to wangle, the one beside the girl I loved, and of course she was spoiling up to him because he was new, he was mature, he could dance, he could play the ukulele and sing, and I couldn't. I was getting nowhere fast.

On a large route like mine it was the habit of the newsdealer to hand 32 out one or two extra papers to encourage you to try to build up the route. Sometimes you could sell these singly, but more often not. One day when I was feeling particularly discouraged about my life and not in the mood for salesmanship, something made me stop at the poorhouse door and knock. The door was opened by small woman who stared at me dubiously. When I tried to hand her a paper, she shrank away.

"It's for Miss Love Holloway," I said. 33

She hesitated. 34

"It's free," I said. "Take it. It's for Miss Love Holloway." 35

I did this every day afterward. This stop, however, changed my 36 route so that it was no longer convenient to pass where I could see her in the window. Now and then I wondered about it, if she really got the paper, if she wanted it anyway, what she thought.

Then everything in my life went to pieces. The girl and her family 37 without the slightest warning moved out of town, fifty miles away. I wrote; she didn't even answer my letters. In wild desperation I dropped everything and tried to get a job for the summer as a caddy on a golf links where she had moved to, and I succeeded. This meant I would have to give up my paper route for the summer. I unloaded it without charge on the first boy I could find, and on my last trip told the woman at the poorhouse that I was leaving and the paper would come no more.

The next day was the last day of school. I was dressing for a dance to 38 which I was not taking the girl; although it was her last night in town, she was going with still another, newer boy; I was taking a spare tire girl for admission purposes—you had to bring some girl—when my mother called up the stairs to know if I'd opened my letter. I dropped my clean shirt and raced down and tore the envelope open.

Dear Sir: 39

Love wishes you to call at your earliest opportunity.

What the devil! From the poorhouse, not from the girl. 40

"Bad news?" inquired my mother. 41

"Naw, nothing," I said disgustedly and went back slowly upstairs. 42

But the next day, the dance thrust into the painful past, with noth- 43 ing better to do with my last hours in town before leaving for my summer job, I went out the road to the poorhouse and went up and knocked once more. I thought: Probably she wants me to keep bringing the paper. Well, I can't, that's all.

The same small woman opened the door. Now her eyes lit with rec- 44 ognition. "Come in," she said. Turning, she led me rather quickly up steep groaning wooden stairs, down a corridor to a room, very small, and I entered Love Holloway's room.

Its bareness shocked me. No rug on the floor, no curtain, just a 45 green window shade faded to gray, an iron bed, small table with a cardboard box on it. "Hello," I said. I think this was perhaps the only time in my life I had ever spoken to her.

She stood close beside her bed, her small highly placed eyes glitter- 46 ing, flashing a little. I thought this strange and wondered what emotion was passing through her, fear, anger—I suddenly realized there were tears in her eyes. She said nothing.

"I'm glad to see you," I said awkwardly, clutching my cap. "I'm 47 sorry I can't keep dropping you the paper, but I'm going away for the summer, and I don't know whether in the fall—" I stopped and waited for her to speak, if she would.

She didn't. Her thin mouth trembled a little. She moved now a few 48 steps. I realized suddenly that she was lame or feeble, old. Her hands trembled violently as she fumbled with the cardboard box, getting the lid off. She drew out a cheaper, cruder pair of scissors than I had ever seen and turning her head sidewise and grasping a wisp of her coarse gray old hair snipped off a lock of it, laid down the scissors and falteringly held it out to me.

"Do—do you want me to take it?" I stammered. 49

She held it, her hands trembling. 50

When I took it, she released her hold on it. "Thank you," I said a 51 little loudly, with a brief false smile. "Thank you."

She stood staring at me, her eyes still glittering with their tears. 52 After a moment I turned and saying goodbye left the room.

On my way home I had an impatient impulse to throw the lock of 53 hair away, but could not somehow. When I got home I could not even tell my mother. It was too ridiculous. She would ask why? how? I didn't want to explain. I took the lock of hair up to my room and started to put it in my padlocked tin box of souvenirs, mostly of the girl, but that didn't seem right. I put it in a seldom used pencil box at the back of the top drawer along with some cancelled stamps, a broken comb and some crayons.

Thinking and Writing

COMPOSITION

1. Use this chapter's Guide for Summarizing Fiction to make notes for a summary of "Love." Then write a summary based on your notes. Exchange and discuss your work with your classmates.

2. Revise and condense your summary for use as a reference in support of one of the following assertions from Erich Fromm's essay, "The Theory of Love":

   a. " . . . the ability to love . . . depends on the character development of the person." (7)
   b. " . . . love is a power which produces love. . . ." (6)
   c. "Giving implies to make the other person a giver also. . . ." (6)
   d. "Care and concern imply another aspect of love . . . *responsibility*." (10)

WILLIAM SHAKESPEARE
King Lear

In *King Lear* Shakespeare (1564–1616) transformed an old legend about familial relations into a powerful drama. The following selection, from act 1, scene 1, establishes the conflict central to this famous tragedy. In this scene King Lear foolishly decides to divide his kingdom among his daughters based on their expression of love for him.

Glou.   He hath been out nine years, and away he shall again. The king is coming.

Sennet.   *Enter* KING LEAR, CORNWALL, ALBANY, GONERIL, REGAN, COR-DELIA, *and* Attendants.

Lear.   Attend the lords of France and Burgundy, Gloucester.
Glou.   I shall, my liege.
                              [*Exeunt Gloucester and Edmund.*
Lear.   Meantime we shall express our darker purpose.   5
Give me the map there. Know that we have divided
In three our kingdom: and 'tis our fast intent
To shake all cares and business from our age;
Conferring them on younger strengths, while we
Unburthen'd crawl toward death. Our son of Cornwall,   10
And you, our no less loving son of Albany,
We have this hour a constant will to publish
Our daughters' several dowers, that future strife

May be prevented now. The princes, France and Burgundy
Great rivals in our youngest daughter's love,   15
Long in our court have made their amorous sojourn,
And here are to be answer'd. Tell me, my daughters,—
Since now we will divest us, both of rule,
Interest of territory, cares of state,—
Which of you shall we say doth love us most?   20
That we our largest bounty may extend
Where nature doth with merit challenge. Goneril,
Our eldest-born, speak first.
Gon.   Sir, I love you more than words can wield the matter;
Dearer than eye-sight, space, and liberty;   25
Beyond what can be valued, rich or rare;
No less than life, with grace, health, beauty, honor;
As much as child e'er loved, or father found;
A love that makes breath poor, and speech unable;
Beyond all manner of so much I love you.   30
Cor.   [*Aside*] What shall Cordelia do? Love, and be silent.
Lear.   Of all these bounds, even from this line to this,
With shadowy forests and with champains rich'd,
With plenteous rivers and wide-skirted meads,
We make thee lady: to thine and Albany's issue   35
Be this perpetual. What says our second daughter,
Our dearest Regan, wife to Cornwall? Speak.
Reg.   Sir, I am made
Of the self-same metal that my sister is,
And prize me at her worth. In my true heart   40
I find she names my very deed of love;
Only she comes too short: that I profess
Myself an enemy to all other joys,
Which the most precious square of sense possesses;
And find I am alone felicitate   45
In your dear highness' love.
Cor.   [*Aside*] Then poor Cordelia!
And yet not so; since, I am sure, my love's
More richer than my tongue.
Lear.   To thee and thine hereditary ever
Remain this ample third of our fair kingdom;   50
No less in space, validity, and pleasure,
Than that conferr'd on Goneril. Now, our joy,
Although the last, not least; to whose young love
The vines of France and milk of Burgundy
Strive to be interess'd; what can you say to draw   55
A third more opulent than your sisters? Speak.
Cor.   Nothing, my lord.

Lear.　Nothing!
Cor.　Nothing.
Lear.　Nothing will come of nothing: speak again.　　　　　　60
Cor.　Unhappy that I am, I cannot heave
My heart into my mouth: I love your majesty
According to my bond; nor more nor less.
Lear.　How, how, Cordelia! mend your speech a little,
Lest it may mar your fortunes.
Cor.　　　　　　　　　　Good my lord,　　　　　　65
You have begot me, bred me, loved me: I
Return those duties back as are right fit,
Obey you, love you, and most honor you.
Why have my sisters husbands, if they say
They love you all? Haply, when I shall wed,　　　　　　70
That lord whose hand must take my plight shall carry
Half my love with him, half my care and duty:
Sure, I shall never marry like my sisters,
To love my father all.
Lear.　But goes thy heart with this?
Cor.　　　　　　　　　　　　Ay, good my lord.　　　　　　75
Lear.　So young, and so untender?
Cor.　So young, my lord, and true.
Lear.　Let it be so; thy truth, then, be thy dower:
For, by the sacred radiance of the sun,
The mysteries of Hecate, and the night;　　　　　　80
By all the operation of the orbs
From whom we do exist, and cease to be;
Here I disclaim all my paternal care,
Propinquity and property of blood,
And as a stranger to my heart and me　　　　　　85
Hold thee, from this, for ever. The barbarous Scythian,
Or he that makes his generation messes
To gorge his appetite, shall to my bosom
Be as well neighbor'd, pitied, and relieved,
As thou my sometime daughter.　　　　　　90

Reading and Interpreting

CONCEPT ANALYSIS

1. Contrast Cordelia's expression of love to the love expressed by Lear's other daughters, Goneril and Regan. What does each stress?

2. Cordelia says that when she marries, half of her "love," "care," and "duty" will belong to her husband. How do you think that marriage affects or should affect children's love for their parents?

SUSAN M. GARFIELD
Love's Role in Marriage

This selection addresses two subjects about which most of us have fairly strong opinions—love and marriage. Written for a text on human sexuality, it traces the history of love's role in marriage beginning with the ancient Greeks and concluding with modern times.

As you read, prepare to summarize the selection. Examine how the author states and clarifies important points within one or more paragraphs. Distinguish the central and unifying ideas from their supporting details and underline the ideas.

The joining of love and marriage has not been a constant in human his-   1
tory. An overview of love's role in marriage beginning with the ancient Greeks and concluding with modern times reveals that the notion of love as a prerequisite for marriage has been a relatively recent phenomenon. The ancient Greeks perceived a schism between sexual and spiritual love. They distinguished between *eros*, carnal love associated with the sensual, physical and sexual aspects of love, and *agapé*, spiritual love which is associated with protective and altruistic feelings. *Agapé* is the non-demanding side of love, which is demonstrated, for example, in parents' love for their children and in the genuine concern that we have for the life and growth of those whom we love.

Although *eros* and *agapé* may have occurred in the ancient Greek 2
marriage, a man married primarily in order to increase his estate and to
insure its continuity by producing children. According to the Greek philosopher Demosthenes, the appropriate age for marriage was eighteen for a
woman and thirty-seven for a man; the appropriate role for a wife was "to
provide . . . legitimate children and to grow old faithfully in the interior
of the house." Greeks regarded heterosexual domestic relations as a normal part of a man's life cycle, but they did not assume that the major love
of a man's life would be his wife.

Greek culture considered women to be inferior to men; conversely, it 3
celebrated what it perceived to be the greater physical beauty of young
boys and the intellect of mature men. Apparently, the male homosexual relationship—and we do not know how prevalent such relationships
were—was that of an older man and a youth. It was believed that the
unity of *eros* and *agapé* might be realized in such relationships. The underlying assumption was that the young boy would himself grow up, in time,
marry, continue his family line, and engage in normal masculine activities. Then, at sometime in his life, he might, in turn, have a relationship
with a younger man or boy. A man's liaisons with boys and with *heterae,*
the educated and independent entertainer women of Athenian society,
were not considered threats to marriage.

Christianity, following Jewish tradition, condemned homosexuality 4
and drew a distinction between love and sex. Under the influence of the
church, sexuality was suppressed and women were idealized as nonsexual
beings. The idealization of women reached its zenith in Mariolatry, the
adoration of the Virgin Mother.

In the eleventh century courtly love, a new male-female relation- 5
ship, emerged, which combined the idealization of women with chivalry,
the knights' code of honor. Love became a novel and fashionable subject of
discussion among aristocrats, who, in their formal "courts of love," argued its merits, described its characteristics and even devised rules to
regulate lovers' behavior. Love came to mean a romantic relationship with
someone other than one's spouse. It was synonymous with desire, yearning
for what one could never entirely possess.

A liaison was formed between a knight and a lady, a woman whose 6
husband, more than likely, was away for many years fighting a crusade.
The knight pledged unselfish service to the lady. She was his source of
inspiration. He fought tournaments in her honor and praised her goodness
and beauty in song and poetry. In keeping with the Christian contempt
for sex, chastity was observed in these affairs. Occasionally, the "purity"
of the love was put to the test, when a couple slept together nude but
refrained from sexual intercourse.

The courtly love relationship developed out of the social conditions 7
of medieval life. Marriage in the Middle Ages had several clearly defined
functions: financial benefits, personal protection, procreation, but love

was not among them. Romantic love and marriage were two separate entities that fulfilled separate needs. If marriage entailed obligation, love, on the contrary, was freely extended and returned. It enabled men and women to experience feelings of tenderness for one another; it introduced gentleness and restraint into the male-female relationship, and it ensured sexual fidelity in marriage. As knighthood declined, however, so did the sexual inhibitions of romantic lovers, and love and sex began to merge, at least, outside of marriage.

The Renaissance period continued to deny the existence of love in marriage. A European nobleman may have had as many as three women in his life: a wife for representative purposes, a mistress for aesthetic conversation and a woman to fulfill his sexual needs. Yet, sometime during the Renaissance the idea that sex and romantic love could exist in marriage and that romantic love was a prelude to marriage began taking hold. Romantic love assumes that it is not necessary to have a separation between spiritual love and marital sex relations and that the latter is sanctified by the former. 8

Surprisingly, the Puritans of the seventeenth century, whom we regard in a very different light, were, in fact, appreciative of physical closeness coupled with emotional warmth. It is true that they put people in the stocks for committing what we consider minor social transgressions such as gossiping, but they also engaged in *bundling,* where sweethearts spent long cold winter nights together in bed fully clothed. A New England custom for two centuries, *bundling* afforded several practical benefits: warmth, privacy, the avoidance of a return journey in treacherous darkness. Moreover, the Puritans apparently considered sex a good and natural part of marriage. Pastor Daniel Rogers preached to his congregation, "Married love is a sweet compound of spiritual affection and carnal affection, and this blend of the two is the vital spirit and heartblood of wedlock." 9

In the eighteenth and nineteenth centuries, politics, economics and technology combined to underscore the need for stable monogamous family life. Revolutions tumbled monarchs and leveled aristocratic regimes; common folk, citizens of new democracies, could not afford various companions to meet various needs. Moreover, the industrial revolution fostered the idea that the family was a refuge, a safe harbor, from the isolation and alienation of a rapidly industrializing society. Kindness, altruism, self-sacrifice, peace, harmony: all were to be found in the ideal nineteenth-century Victorian family. 10

What happened to sex? The Victorians had large families, but sexual desire was regarded as an exclusively male phenomenon, women were supposed to be passionless, actually devoid of sexual feeling. Men sought sexual fulfillment outside of marriage, and prostitution flourished on a grand scale. A double standard of behavior was recognized: Men had far more sexual freedom than women and women were categorized as "good" and "bad." Men married the former; they had sexual relations with the latter. 11

In the twentieth century, in Western countries particularly, roman- 12 tic love has become a pre- and co-requisite for marriage. However, soaring divorce rates in recent decades may indicate that the romance requirement is having a disruptive effect on the institution of marriage itself. In explanation, psychologists suggest that we often seek in our mates those qualities which we, ourselves, lack, with a resulting personality clash that can destroy even the strongest romantic attraction. Moreover, the changing self-image of women is reflected in modern marriage. Unwilling to play traditional nurturing roles, eager to achieve career goals, outspoken about their own sexual needs, many women have concluded that marriage with or without romance is not as important a factor in their lives as it was for their mother and grandmothers.

In despair, modern romantics are experimenting with various forms 13 of marriage: open marriage; marriage by contract; homosexual marriage; group marriage; childless marriage; celibate marriage; and no marriage (living together without benefit of ceremony). The search for *eros* and *agapé,* together forever, continues.

Reading and Interpreting

VOCABULARY

Writing in an academic discipline presumes an understanding of key terms. Use a dictionary to define each of the following:

eros (1)   agapé (1)   heterosexual (2)   domestic relations (2)

heterae (3)   homosexuality (4)   Mariolatry (4)   courtly love (5)

monogamous (10)   romance (12)   celibate (13)

Thinking and Writing

COMPOSITION

Using the section Mapping a Nonfiction Selection as a guide, map "Love's Role in Marriage" and write a summary of it.

PLATO

Aristophanes' Praise of Love

The *Symposium* of Plato (ca. 428–348 B.C.) is set at a dinner party in ancient Athens, attended by such illustrious guests as the physician Eryximachus, the heroic soldier Alcibiades, the comic poet and dramatist Aristophanes, and the great philosopher and teacher Socrates. The topic chosen for discussion is love. As each person speaks according to his own experience and learning, the dialogue comes to life. This excerpt, Aristophanes' imaginative comic account of the origin of humankind and its sexual nature, is one of the most famous passages of Plato's works.

Aristophanes professed to open another vein of discourse; he had a mind   1
to praise Love in another way, unlike that either of Pausanias or Eryximachus. Mankind, he said, judging by their neglect of him, have never, as I think, at all understood the power of Love. For if they had understood him they would surely have built noble temples and altars, and offered solemn sacrifices in his honour; but this is not done, and most certainly ought to be done: since of all the gods he is the best friend of men, the helper and the healer of the ills which are the great impediment to the happiness of the race. I will try to describe his power to you, and you shall teach the rest of the world what I am teaching you. In the   10
first place, let me treat of the nature of man and what has happened to it; for the original human nature was not like the present, but different. The sexes were not two as they are now, but originally three in number; there was man, woman, and the union of the two, having a name corresponding to this double nature, which had once a real existence, but is now lost, and the word "Androgynous" is only preserved as a term of reproach. In the second place, the primeval man was round, his back and sides forming a circle; and he had four hands and four feet, one head with two faces, looking opposite ways, set on a round neck and precisely alike; also four ears, two privy members, and the remainder to correspond. He   20
could walk upright as men now do, backwards or forwards as he pleased, and he could also roll over and over at a great pace, turning on his four hands and four feet, eight in all, like tumblers going over and over with their legs in the air; this was when he wanted to run fast. Now, the sexes

were three, and such as I have described them; because the sun, moon, and earth are three; and the man was originally the child of the sun, the woman of the earth, and the man-woman of the moon, which is made up of sun and earth, and they were all round and moved round and round like their parents. Terrible was their might and strength, and the thoughts of their hearts were great, and they made an attack upon the gods; of them is told the tale of Otys and Ephialtes who, as Homer says, dared to scale heaven, and would have laid hands upon the gods. Doubt reigned in the celestial councils. Should they kill them and annihilate the race with thunderbolts, as they had done the giants, then there would be an end of the sacrifices and worship which men offered to them; but, on the other hand, the gods could not suffer their insolence to be unrestrained. At last, after a good deal of reflection, Zeus discovered a way. He said: "Methinks I have a plan which will humble their pride and improve their manners; men shall continue to exist, but I will cut them in two and then they will be diminished in strength and increased in numbers; this will have the advantage of making them more profitable to us. They shall walk upright on two legs, and if they continue insolent and will not be quiet, I will split them again and they shall hop about on a single leg." He spoke and cut men in two, like a sorb-apple which is halved for pickling, or as you might divide an egg with a hair; and as he cut them one after another, he bade Apollo give the face and the half of the neck a turn in order that the man might contemplate the section of himself: he would thus learn a lesson of humility. Apollo was also bidden to heal their wounds and compose their forms. So he gave a turn to the face and pulled the skin from the sides all over that which in our language is called the belly, like the purses which draw in, and he made one mouth at the centre, which he fastened in a knot (the same which is called the navel); he also moulded the breast and took out most of the wrinkles, much as a shoemaker might smooth leather upon a last; he left a few, however, in the region of the belly and navel, as a memorial of the primeval state. After the division the two parts of man, each desiring his other half, came together, and throwing their arms about one another, entwined in mutual embraces, longing to grow into one; they were on the point of dying from hunger and self-neglect, because they did not like to do anything apart; and when one of the halves died and the other survived, the survivor sought another mate, man or woman, as we call them,—being the sections of entire men or women—and clung to that. They were being destroyed, when Zeus in pity of them invented a new plan: he turned the parts of generation round to the front, for this had not been always their position, and they sowed the seed no longer as hitherto like grasshoppers in the ground, but in one another; and after the transposition the male generated in the female in order that by mutual embraces of man and woman they might breed, and the race might continue; or if man came to man they might be satisfied, and rest, and go their ways to the business of life: so ancient is the desire of one an- 70 other which is implanted in us, reuniting our original nature, making one of two, and healing the state of man. Each of us when separated, having one side only, like a flat fish, is but the indenture of a man, and he is always looking for his other half. Men who are a section of that double nature which was once called Androgynous are lovers of women; adulterers are generally of this breed, and also adulterous women who lust after men: the women who are a section of the woman do not care for men, but have female attachments; the female companions are of this sort. But they who are a section of the male, follow the male, and while they are young, being slices of the original man, they hang about men 80 and embrace them, and they are themselves the best of boys and youths, because they have the most manly nature. Some indeed assert that they are shameless, but this is not true; for they do not act thus from any want of shame, but because they are valiant and manly, and have a manly coun- tenance, and they embrace that which is like them. And these when they grow up become our statesmen, and these only, which is a great proof of the truth of what I am saying. When they reach manhood they are lovers of youth, and are not naturally inclined to marry or beget children,—if at all, they do so only in obedience to the law; but they are satisfied if they may be allowed to live with one another unwedded; and such a na- 90 ture is prone to love and ready to return love, always embracing that which is akin to him. And when one of them meets with his other half, the actual half of himself, whether he be a lover of youth or a lover of another sort, the pair are lost in an amazement of love and friendship and intimacy, and one will not be out of the other's sight, as I may say, even for a moment: these are the people who pass their whole lives together; yet they could not explain what they desire of one another. For the in- tense yearning which each of them has towards the other does not appear to be the desire of lover's intercourse, but of something else which the soul of either evidently desires and cannot tell, and of which she has only 100 a dark and doubtful presentiment. Suppose Hephaestus, with his instru- ments, to come to the pair who are lying side by side and to say to them, "What do you people want of one another?" they would be unable to explain. And suppose further, that when he saw their perplexity he said: "Do you desire to be wholly one; always day and night to be in one an- other's company? for if this is what you desire, I am ready to melt you into one and let you grow together, so that being two you shall become one, and while you live a common life as if you were a single man, and after your death in the world below still be one departed soul instead of two—I ask whether this is what you lovingly desire, and whether 110 you are satisfied to attain this?"—there is not a man of them who when he heard the proposal would deny or would not acknowledge that this

meeting and melting into one another, thus becoming one instead of two, was the very expression of his ancient need. And the reason is that human nature was originally one and we were a whole, and the desire and pursuit of the whole is called love. There was a time, I say, when we were one, but now because of the wickedness of mankind God has dispersed us, as the Arcadians were dispersed into villages by the Lacedaemonians. And if we are not obedient to the gods, there is a danger that we shall be split up again and go about in *basso-rilievo,* like the profile figures having only 120
half a nose which are sculptured on monuments, and that we shall be like tallies. Wherefore let us exhort all men to piety, that we may avoid evil, and obtain the good, of which Love is to us the lord and minister; and let no one oppose him—he is the enemy of the gods who opposes him. For if we are friends of the God and at peace with him we shall find our own true loves, which rarely happens in this world at present. . . .

. . . my words have a wider application—they include men and women everywhere; and I believe that if our loves were perfectly accomplished, and each one returning to his primeval nature had his original true love, then our race would be happy. And if this would be best of all, 130
the best in the next degree and under present circumstances must be the nearest approach to such an union; and that will be the attainment of a congenial love. Wherefore, if we would praise him who has given to us the benefit, we must praise the god Love, who is our greatest benefactor, both leading us in this life back to our own nature, and giving us high hopes for the future, for he promises that if we are pious, he will restore us to our original state, and heal us and make us happy and blessed. This, Eryximachus, is my discourse of love, which, although different from yours, I must beg you to leave unassailed by the shafts of your ridicule, in order that each may have his turn; each, or rather either, for 140
Agathon and Socrates are the only ones left.

Reading and Interpreting

VOCABULARY

Use your dictionary as necessary to find the meaning of these words in context.

impediment (8)	androgynous (16)	reproach (17)
primeval (17)	insolence (36)	contemplate (47)
indenture (73)	countenance (84)	prone (91)
presentiment (101)	exhort (122)	congenial (133)

CONCEPT ANALYSIS

In Aristophanes' original myth, there is a connection between the form of the first human beings and the human quest for love. Explain this connection in your own words.

Quickwrite

Aristophanes states that " . . . the desire and pursuit of the whole is called love." Given this theory that lovers are complementary parts of a perfect whole, enumerate the characteristics of an individual who is or would be your perfect "other half."

Thinking and Writing

RHETORICAL TECHNIQUE

Arrange the following topics in the order in which they are presented in Plato's original text. Then use them as an outline for summarizing the main points in Aristophanes' speech.

- Various operations performed by the command of Zeus.
- The three original sexes; their form and origin.
- The strong yet inexpressible yearning that lovers have for one another.
- Why men must honor the gods.
- Sexual nature depends on which part of an androgynous being the individual was originally severed from.
- The two halves wander about longing for one another.

KAHLIL GIBRAN

On Marriage

Kahlil Gibran (1883–1931), a Lebanese-American poet,
philosopher, and artist, is best known for his collection
of prose poems called *The Prophet*. This collection, from
which our poem is taken, is infused with mysticism and
makes shrewd observations on the world, touching on
such topics as freedom, death, and love.

Love one another, but make not a bond of love:
Let it rather be a moving sea between the shores of your souls.
Fill each other's cup, but drink not from one cup.
Give one another of your bread, but eat not from the same loaf.
Sing together and be joyous, but let each one of you be alone,   5
Even as the strings of the lute are alone,
Though they quiver with the same music.
Give your hearts, but not into each other's keeping,
For only the land of life can contain your hearts.
Stand together, yet not too near together.   10
For the pillars of the temple stand apart,
And the oak tree and the cyprus grow not in each other's shade.

Reading and Interpreting

CONCEPT ANALYSIS

Gibran encourages spouses to unite with one another but not make "a bond
of love." Which images of this harmonious but independent pairing particularly appeal to you?

Quickwrite

Write a wedding toast using Gibran's form, which employs a series of
directions, some with examples.

COMPOSITION

Paraphrase "On Marriage."

EDNA ST. VINCENT MILLAY

What Lips My Lips Have Kissed

Edna St. Vincent Millay (1892–1950) gained her reputation by voicing in her poetry the spirit of rebellious-
ness and emancipation characteristic of youth in the
1920s. In this sonnet, as in many others of her early period, Millay's female persona reveals an unconventional
attitude toward romantic love. In her later work, Millay
turned increasingly to social or political themes.

What lips my lips have kissed, and where, and why,
I have forgotten, and what arms have lain
Under my head till morning; but the rain
Is full of ghosts tonight, that tap and sigh
Upon the glass and listen for reply,   5
And in my heart there stirs a quiet pain
For unremembered lads that not again
Will turn to me at midnight with a cry.
Thus in the winter stands the lonely tree,
Nor knows what birds have vanished one by one,   10
Yet knows its boughs more silent than before:
I cannot say what loves have come and gone,
I only know that summer sang in me
A little while, that in me sings no more.

CONCEPT ANALYSIS

1. What kind of love is described in lines 1–8? What is Millay's implied definition of *love?*
2. In line 12, Millay speaks of "loves [who] have come and gone." What is the effect on you of the plural noun *loves* instead of *lovers?*

Thinking and Writing

COMPOSITION

Paraphrase the poem.

PHYLLIS ROSE

Parallel Lives:
Five Victorian Marriages

Biographer Phyllis Rose is a professor of English at Wesleyan University. In *Parallel Lives: Five Victorian Marriages* she describes the marriages of five prominent Victorians: social critic and historian Thomas Carlyle, novelists George Eliot (Mary Ann Evans) and Charles Dickens, art critic and essayist John Ruskin, and philosopher and economist John Stuart Mill. In the following excerpt, taken from the prologue to her book, Rose suggests that marriages are both literary and political in nature. The literary aspect is the portrayal, often contradictory, that each partner gives of the marriage. The political aspect is the continuing power struggle between husband and wife.

. . . this book began with a desire to tell the stories of some marriages as 1 unsentimentally as possible, with attention to the shifting tides of power between a man and a woman joined, presumably, for life. My purposes were partly feminist (since marriage is so often the context within which a woman works out her destiny, it has always been an object of feminist scrutiny) and partly, in ways I shall explain, literary.

I believe, first of all, that living is an act of creativity and that, at 2 certain moments in our lives, our creative imaginations are more conspicuously demanded than at others. At certain moments, the need to decide upon the story of our own lives becomes particularly pressing—when we choose a mate, for example, or embark upon a career. Decisions like that make sense, retroactively, of the past and project a meaning onto the future, knit past and future together, and create, suspended between the two, the present. Questions we have all asked of ourselves such as Why am I doing this? or the even more basic What am I doing? suggest the way in which living forces us to look for and forces us to find a design within the primal stew of data which is our daily experience. There is a kind of arranging and telling and choosing of detail—of narration, in short—which we must do so that one day will prepare for the next day, one week prepare for the next week. In some way we all decide when we have grown up and what event will symbolize for us that state of maturity—leaving home, getting married, becoming a parent, losing our parents, making a million, writing a book. To the extent that we impose some narrative form onto our lives, each of us in the ordinary process of living is a fitful novelist, and the biographer is a literary critic.

Marriages, or parallel lives as I have chosen to call them, hold a par- 3 ticular fascination for the biographer-critic because they set two imaginations to work constructing narratives about experience presumed to be the same for both. In using the word *parallel,* however, I hope to call attention to the gap between the narrative lines as well as to their similarity. . . .

. . . In unhappy marriages, for example, I see two versions of reality 4 rather than two people in conflict. I see a struggle for imaginative dominance going on. Happy marriages seem to me those in which the two partners agree on the scenario they are enacting, even if, as was the case with Mr. and Mrs. Mill, their own idea of their relationship is totally at variance with the facts. I speak with great trepidation about "facts" in such matters, but, speaking loosely, the facts in the Mills' case—that a woman of strong and uncomplicated will dominated a guilt-ridden man— were less important than their shared imaginative view of the facts, that their marriage fitted their shared ideal of a marriage of equals. I assume, then, as little objective truth as possible about these parallel lives, for every marriage seems to me a subjectivist fiction with two points of view often deeply in conflict, sometimes fortuitously congruent.

NOTE: Footnotes have been deleted.

That, sketchily, is the ground of my literary interest in parallel 5
lives, but there is a political dimension as well. On the basis of family life,
we form our expectations about power and powerlessness, about authority
and obedience in other spheres, and in that sense the family is, as has so
often been insisted, the building block of society. The idea of the family as
a school for civic life goes back to the ancient Romans, and feminist criticism of the family as such a school—the charge that it is a school for des-
pots and slaves—goes back at least to John Stuart Mill. . . . I cite this
tradition to locate, in part, my own position: like Mill, I believe marriage
to be the primary political experience in which most of us engage as
adults, and so I am interested in the management of power between men
and women in that microcosmic relationship. Whatever the balance,
every marriage is based upon some understanding, articulated or not,
about the relative importance, the priority of desires, between its two
partners. Marriages go bad not when love fades—love can modulate into
affection without driving two people apart—but when this understanding
about the balance of power breaks down, when the weaker member feels
exploited or the stronger feels unrewarded for his or her strength.

People who find this a chilling way to talk about one of our most 6
treasured human bonds will object that "power struggle" is a flawed circumstance into which relationships fall when love fails. (For some people
it is impossible to discuss power without adding the word *struggle*.) I
would counter by pointing out the human tendency to invoke love at moments when we want to disguise transactions involving power. Like the
aged Lear handing over his kingdom to his daughters, when we resign
power, or assume new power, we insist it is not happening and demand to
be talked to about love. Perhaps that is what love is—the momentary or
prolonged refusal to think of another person in terms of power. Like an
enzyme which blocks momentarily a normal biological process, what we
call love may inhibit the process of power negotiation—from which inhibi-
tion comes the illusion of equality so characteristic of lovers. . . . Surely, in
regard to marriage, love has received its fair share of attention, power less
than its share. . . . For every social scientist discussing the family as a
psychopolitical structure . . . for every John Stuart Mill talking about
"subjection" in marriage, how many pieties are daily uttered about love?
Who can resist the thought that love is the ideological bone thrown to
women to distract their attention from the powerlessness of their lives?
Only millions of romantics can resist it—and other millions who might
see it as the bone thrown to men to distract them from the bondage of
their lives.

In unconscious states, as we know from Freud, the mind is astonish- 7
ingly fertile and inventive in its fiction-making, but in conscious states
this is not so. The plots we choose to impose on our own lives are limited
and limiting. And in no area are they so banal and sterile as in this of love
and marriage. Nothing else being available to our imaginations, we will

filter our experience through the romantic clichés with which popular culture bombards us. And because the callowness and conventionality of the plots we impose on ourselves are a betrayal of our inner richness and complexity, we feel anxious and unhappy. . . .

Easy stories drive out hard ones. Simple paradigms prevail over complicated ones. If, within marriage, power is the ability to impose one's imaginative vision and make it prevail, then power is more easily obtained if one has a simple and widely accepted paradigm at hand. The patriarchal paradigm has long enforced men's power within marriage: a man works hard to make himself worthy of a woman; they marry; he heads the family; she serves him, working to please him and care for him, getting protection in return. This plot regularly generates its opposite, the plot of female power through weakness: the woman, somehow wounded by family life, needs to be cared for and requires an offering of guilt. . . . Neither side of the patriarchal paradigm seems to bring out the best in humanity. In regard to marriage, we need more and more complex plots. I reveal my literary bias in saying I believe we need literature, which, by allowing us to experience more fully, to imagine more fully, enables us to live more freely. In a pragmatic way, we can profit from an immersion in the nineteenth-century novel which took the various stages of marriage as its central subject.

We tend to talk informally about other people's marriages and not disparage our own talk as gossip. But gossip may be the beginning of moral inquiry, the low end of the platonic ladder which leads to better understanding. We are desperate for information about how other people live because we want to know how to live ourselves, yet we are taught to see this desire as an illegitimate form of prying. If marriage is, as Mill suggested, a political experience, then discussion of it ought to be taken as seriously as talk about national elections. Cultural pressure to avoid such talk as "gossip" ought to be resisted in a spirit of good citizenship. In that spirit, then, I offer the private lives for examination and discussion. I will try to tell these stories in such a way as to raise questions about the role of power and the nature of equality within marriage, for I assume a connection between politics and sex. In the interests of objectivity, I offer the joint lives of some Victorian men and women for whom the rules of the game were perhaps clearer than they are for us. . . .

. . . scholars in our own post-liberated age who interest themselves in innovative living arrangements are beginning to discover that people a hundred years ago may have had *more* flexibility than we do now. Lillian Faderman, for example, has described with great sympathy the nineteenth-century American practice of the "Boston marriage," a long-term monogamous relationship between two women who are otherwise unmarried. . . . The emotional and even financial advantages of such a relationship are immediately evident, whether or not—and this is something we shall never know—sex was involved. The important point is that such relationships were seen as healthy and useful. Henry James, for one, was delighted that his sister Alice had some joy in her life, in the form of her Boston marriage to Katherine Loring. But what seemed healthy and useful to the nineteenth century suddenly became "abnormal" after the impact, in the early twentieth century, of popular Freudianism. With all experience sexualized, living arrangements such as those Boston marriages could not be so easily entered upon or easily discussed; they became outlaw, suppressed, matters to hide. By the mid-1920s, it was no longer possible to mention a Boston marriage without embarrassment. By sexualizing experience, popular Freudianism had the moralistic result of limiting possibilities.

I prefer to see the sexless marriages I discuss as examples of flexi- 11 bility rather than of abnormality. Some people might say they are not really marriages because they are sexless; it's a point I'd want to argue. There must be other models of marriage—of long-term association between two people—than the very narrow one we are all familiar with, beginning with a white wedding gown, leading to children, and ending in death, or, these days increasingly often, in divorce.

Many cultural circumstances worked against the likelihood of sexual 12 satisfaction within Victorian marriages. The inflexible taboo on pre-marital sex for middle-class women meant, among other things, that it was impossible to determine sexual compatibility before marriage. The law then made the wife absolute property of her husband and sexual performance one of her duties. Imagine a young woman married to a man she finds physically repulsive. She is in the position of being raped nightly— and with the law's consent. The legendary Victorian advice about sex, "Lie back and think of England," may be seen as not entirely comical if we realize that in many cases a distaste for sex developed from a distaste for the first sexual partner and from sexual performance which was essentially forced. In addition, the absence of birth control made it impossible to separate sex from its reproductive function, so that to be sexually active meant also the discomforts of pregnancy, the pain of childbirth, and the burden of children. For men, the middle-class taboo on pre-marital sex meant sexual experience could be obtained only with prostitutes or working-class women, an early conditioning which Freud said breeds dangers in the erotic life, by encouraging a split between objects of desire and objects of respect.

We would seem to have a greater chance of happiness now. Theoreti- 13 cally, men and women can get to know each other in casual, relaxed circumstances before marrying. More young people feel free to sleep together, to live together before marriage. They do not have to wait until they are irrevocably joined to discover they are incompatible. Nor are they so irrevocably joined. If we discover, as we seem to, early and late, that despite all our opportunity to test compatibility, we have married someone with whom we are not compatible, we can disconnect ourselves and try again. Perhaps most important, women can hold jobs, earn a living, own property, thereby gaining a chance for some status in the family. Birth control is reliable and available, so women needn't be, quite so much as formerly, the slaves of children. Nor need men be so oppressed by the obligation of supporting large and expensive families. We can separate sex from reproduction; it can be purely a source of pleasure. If all this does not ensure that, cumulatively, we are happier in our domesticity than the Victorians, then perhaps we expect even more of our marriages than the Victorians did—perhaps we place too much of a burden on our personal relationships, as Christopher Lasch, among others, has suggested. . . .

We should remind ourselves, I think, of the romantic bias in Anglo- 14 American attitudes towards marriage, whether of the nineteenth or the twentieth century. Effie Ruskin, travelling in Italy, discovered how much more comfortable Continental ways of being married were than English. For the English assumed you loved your husband and were loved by him and wanted to be with him as much as possible, whereas the Europeans made no such extraordinary assumption. They knew they were making the best of a difficult situation often arranged by people other than the participants and for reasons quite apart from love, and so they gave each other considerable latitude. One hardly knows whether the Victorians suffered more from their lack of easy recourse to divorce or from the disappearance of the brisk assumptions of arranged marriages. At least when marriages were frankly arrangements of property, no one expected them to float on an unceasing love-tide, whereas we and the Victorians have been in the same boat on that romantic flood.

In general, the similarities between marriages then and now seem to 15 me greater than the differences. Then as now certain problems of adjustment, focussing usually on sex or relatives, seem typical of early stages of marriage, and others, for example absence of excitement, seem typical of later stages. In good marriages then as now shared experience forms a bond increasingly important with time, making discontents seem minor. And then as now, love also tends to walk out the door when poverty flies in the window. . . . I have been reminded continually in these Victorian marriages of marriages of friends: strong women still adopt a protective coloring of weakness as George Eliot did; earnest men with strongly egalitarian politics are still subject to domination by shrews, as John Mill was; men like Dickens still divorce in middle age the wives they have used up and outdistanced; clever women like Jane Carlyle still solace themselves for their powerlessness by mocking their husbands. Moreover, attitudes towards marriage which I would have thought outdated prove not to be. Apparently it is still possible to assume that the man is without question the more important partner in a marriage. That is, the patriarchal paradigm still prevails. Indeed, as fundamentalist religion and morality revive in contemporary America's ethical vacuum, we are likely to find ourselves fighting the nineteenth-century wars of personal morality all over again. . . .

Although I began the book with no thesis to prove, merely with a 16 feminist skepticism about marriage, a taste for the higher gossip, a distaste for the rhetoric of romantic love, and a desire to look at marriages as imaginative projections and arrangements of power, I ended with a bewildered respect for the durability of the pair, in all its variations. Perhaps predictably, I became more convinced than ever about the sterility, for men as well as women, of the patriarchal ideal of marriage and more skeptical about the chances of any particular marriage to escape its influence.

Reading and Interpreting

VOCABULARY

Use your dictionary as necessary to find the meaning of the following words in the context of Phyllis Rose's essay:

feminist (1)   retroactively (2)   biographer (2)   subjectivist (4)

fortuitously (4)   congruent (4)   invoke (6)   callowness (7)

conventionality (7)   patriarchal (8)   paradigm (8)   pragmatic (8)

innovative (10)   irrevocably (13)   latitude (14)

CONCEPT ANALYSIS

1. How does Rose distinguish between the stories of happy and unhappy marriages? How are these stories similar?
2. What is the relationship between love and power presented in paragraph 6? Underline the literary reference and the images that the author uses to explain the relationship.
3. According to Rose, where do the "plots" for our love stories come from? Why do they make us "anxious and unhappy"? What does the author suggest would help our situation? Do you agree?
4. The notion that marriage is a political experience and that the family is the training ground for civic life is the rationale for Rose's book. Review the author's reasoning in paragraph 9. Do you find it persuasive?
5. Review paragraphs 8 and 16 for the author's view of the "patriarchal paradigm." In your view, does it still influence most marriages?
6. The author makes several provocative assertions. Comment on each of the following:
   a. "Marriages go bad . . . when the balance of power breaks down." (5)

b. "[There is a] human tendency to invoke love . . . to disguise transactions involving power." (6)
c. "[There is a] romantic bias in Anglo-American attitudes towards marriage. . . ." (14)
d. " . . . discussion [about marriage] ought to be taken as seriously as talk about national elections." (9)
e. "[So-called Boston marriages] were seen as healthy and useful." (10)

Quickwrite

Select a television marriage or relationship and describe the power struggle at its center.

Thinking and Writing

RHETORICAL TECHNIQUE

1. The author states two purposes: the political and the literary. Underline sentences that achieve the transition from one purpose to the other.
2. Underline the topic sentences of paragraphs 10, 12, 13, 14, and 15. Make a marginal note of one supporting example for each.
3. In the conclusion the author sums up her major points. List these.

COMPOSITION

Summarize the major points in Rose's prologue that support her assertion that "we would seem to have a greater chance of happiness [in marriage] now" than people had one hundred years ago.

THE WRITTEN RESPONSE

Synthesizing

Every time you make connections between experiences, you engage in synthesis. Synthesis writing is the explicit process in which you connect your experiences, observations, and reading from several sources to support your ideas. Synthesizing requires, first, that you distinguish the aspects of several works that relate to the idea you are developing, and, then, that you connect these in your writing.

THE PROCESS

To begin writing a synthesis essay, roughly formulate a thesis statement in response to the given assignment. Then review your readings to select those that offer the strongest support for your point of view. Draft an outline for your essay, incorporating the selections that you will use for your synthesis.

As you draft your synthesis, use your own words to incorporate your source passages and quote only briefly. Introduce each supporting passage with its title, author, and a capsule statement of its theme to establish a context for your reference. Use only as much of your sources as is necessary to support your main idea and major points. Conversely, do not pile up generalizations or assertions that you do not illustrate with references to your sources.

Review your drafted essay to make sure that your main idea and conclusion serve as a frame for your source passages and that transitions clearly mark your movement from source to source and from general statement to example. More detailed instruction in these techniques has been presented in Chapter 2.

The following example illustrates how a writer might plan a typical synthesis assignment:

Assignment: According to Erich Fromm, love is "an active power" that "breaks through the walls" separating people from each other. Discuss Fromm's definition, using your own experience and readings from this chapter to support or refute his point of view.

Roughly formulated thesis statement: I agree with Fromm's notion that love is an active force that takes people out of isolation and unites them. Several readings in this chapter support this view.

Possible source selections from the chapter: Fromm's "Theory of Love," Davis's "Love," Garfield's "Love's Role in Marriage," Plato's "Aristophanes' Praise of Love," Gibran's "On Marriage."

Source passages:

    a. Garfield: active familial love as unifying force: Puritans, Victorians, modern Western.

    b. Gibran: images of the couple suggest connections but not dependence.

    c. Plato: myth of androgynous primeval being split in half by Zeus explains source of attraction between human beings.

Notice that the outline does not include an overall summary of each reading, but rather uses only what is needed to support the main idea. For instance, Garfield's survey of marital love covers many historical periods, but the synthesis outline refers only to the periods that viewed loving relationships as a refuge from alienation and isolation. Synthesis writing requires this kind of careful selectivity.

Synthesis Questions

1. Erich Fromm suggests that "knowledge of the other"—that is, acceptance of a person on his or her own terms—is a basis for love. Discuss this idea with reference to friendship or familial love. Support your views with your reading as well as your own experience.

2. Kahlil Gibran states that we should "love one another, but make not a bond of love." Do you believe it is possible to be in love and remain independent? Discuss with reference to your reading and your observations.

3. "O, human love! thou spirit given, / On Earth, of all we hope in Heaven!" Interpret Edgar Allan Poe's lines and illustrate your interpretation with readings from this chapter.

4. It has been said that if we didn't read about love, we would not know what it is. How have specific readings in this chapter enlarged your conception of love?

CHAPTER FOUR

Nature's Book: Writing Narratives

What interpretation of man's place in nature is reflected in the composition of this Chinese painting, "Scholar by Waterfall," by Ma Yuan?

Every culture has its own view of humankind's place in the natural world. As evidenced by the painting, non-Western, nonindustrial societies value harmony with nature rather than control of it. In contrast, Western culture emphasizes the exploitation of nature for human profit and comfort. Can you give some examples of this? Do you think Western values are changing in this regard? Explain.

THE WRITING FOCUS

In nature's infinite book of secrecy
A little I can read.

William Shakespeare, *Antony and Cleopatra*, act 1, scene 2

The subject of man in nature lends itself to the technique of narrative, telling a story. Early in human history, our ancestors told stories that recounted the day's events, explained the phenomena of the mysterious world around them, and illustrated tribal lore. Narratives permitted early people to reflect upon their existence in nature; storytelling brought them together and enhanced their humanness. The readings in this chapter are narratives that address the question of humankind's place in the natural world.

Composing Narratives

The type of composition called narration organizes events or experiences in time-linked causes and consequences. Narratives fall into two basic categories, which may overlap. One is the personal or impressionistic narrative, which has an emotional quality that the writer seeks to share with the reader. "The Open Boat," Stephen Crane's short story of four men lost at sea, for example, is a narrative infused with the emotions of both camaraderie and fear. The second type provides information about an event without the writer's personal feelings or interpretations, as in a newspaper account.

Narratives may function independently as newspaper accounts, histories, short stories, poems, or novels; or they may be included in other types of compositions to explain, illustrate, argue, or reinforce important points. A successful narrative has a clear purpose and central idea, logical sequence and coherence of events, a thoughtful selection of details, a turning point in the action, and an appropriate and consistent point of view.

DEDUCTIVE AND INDUCTIVE PATTERNS

Narratives may be developed deductively or inductively. In the first pattern, the writer begins with the thesis and follows it with a supporting narrative. An example is Rachel Carson's "The Gray Beginnings," in which a narrative of the earth's evolution illustrates the thesis that the sea played a major role in the creation of life on this planet.

In the inductive pattern, the writer plunges the reader immediately into the action. Only after some unfolding of the narrative does the thesis emerge. For example, in both his diary account and his short story, Stephen Crane wrote inductively about his shipwreck experience. His thesis about the brotherhood of men in their struggle against the adversities of nature becomes evident only toward the end of "The Open Boat."

Regardless of the position of the thesis, there must be one or more points at which meaningful change or insight occurs. In Carson's narrative, for example, the first turning point in her chronicle of millions of years occurs in paragraph 11 with a reference to the time when "the creation of life from non-life" occurred. Every narrative, no matter how brief, must have at least one of these moments of significance, which the writer shares with the reader.

In some narratives, particularly the deductive type, the thesis is explicit, that is, distinctly stated in plain language. In "The Open Boat," for example, Crane explicitly states his thesis about the spiritual kinship of men helpless before forces they cannot control: "It would be difficult to describe the subtle brotherhood of men that was here established on the seas." In other narratives such as Thurber's fable, "The Human Being and the Dinosaur," the author's main point is made implicitly—that is, it is suggested rather than openly stated.

SEQUENCE AND COHERENCE

A narrative usually relates events in chronological order. Genesis, for example, begins "in the beginning" and recounts the creation as it occurred over a period of time. Although "The Open Boat" and "The Gray Beginnings" are basically chronological narratives, both works digress from their chronology to interject either flashbacks, scenes from the past, or flash-forwards, scenes from the future.

The incidents selected for a narrative must be clearly and logically connected. A writer can achieve logical order by using appropriate verb forms and transitional expressions signifying time. For example, in "The Gray Beginnings" Rachel Carson starts a number of paragraphs with such expressions as "As soon as," "Before," and "All the while." In his diary account of the shipwreck, Crane uses transitions such as "During this time," "It was now," and "Afterward" to advance the action. Repetition also provides cohesiveness in a narration; for example, the narrator of Genesis employs the formulas "And God said" and "And the evening and the morning were the . . . day" to begin and end several sections.

SELECTION OF DETAILS

Effective storytellers purposefully choose details that are vivid and relevant to their thesis. In successive drafts, they eliminate dull, irrelevant, or repetitive details and select only those that maintain the focus of the piece. In Thurber's fable, for example, Man's foolish egotism is underscored by his pompously phrased introduction of himself to the dinosaur as "the artfully articulated architect of the future."

POINT OF VIEW

To avoid confusion, a writer must maintain a consistent point of view within a single piece. In a narrative, *point of view* means the relation of the writer to the story. The first-person narrator is a participant in the story and refers to himself or herself as "I," as in Crane's diary. The third-person narrative is a report of events that others have experienced, as is Crane's "The Open Boat."

Point of view also refers to the physical or historical perspective from which the writer views events. Carson, for example, though retelling primeval events from the distance of a modern scientist, nevertheless takes readers back in time as if they were witnessing firsthand the various phases in the birth of the sea.

The narrator's attitude toward the material must also remain consistent. For example, if Crane, who views nature as indifferent to man's suffering, were suddenly to invest it with humane and beneficient qualities, the reader would become confused and Crane's main point would be obscured.

The modern narrator, however, particularly in film, may deliberately tell the story from the perceptions of different characters, presenting the theme in a more ambiguous and challenging way.

Essay for Analysis

HENRY DAVID THOREAU
The Ant War

Henry David Thoreau (1817–1862), American philosopher and writer, chose to live apart from society for two years at Walden Pond outside Concord, Massachusetts, as an experiment in self-sufficiency. *Walden,* Thoreau's masterpiece about this experiment, explores the life of the spirit through nature. In "The Ant War," an excerpt from *Walden,* Thoreau defers his thesis until his readers have been drawn into the events of the narrative. Marginal notes call attention to particularly effective narrative elements in Thoreau's piece.

One day when I went out to my woodpile, or   1   Narrative begins with ac-
rather my pile of stumps, I observed two large   tion; time expression
ants, the one red, the other much larger, nearly

half an inch long, and black, fiercely contending with one another. Having once got hold they never let go, but struggled and wrestled and rolled on the chips incessantly. Looking farther, I was surprised to find that the chips were covered with such combatants, that it was not a *duellum* but a *bellum,* a war between two races of ants, the red always pitted against the black, and frequently two red ones to one black. The legions of these Myrmidons covered all the hills and vales in my woodyard, and the ground was already strewn with the dead and dying, both red and black. It was the only battle which I have ever witnessed, the only battlefield I ever trod while the battle was raging; internecine war; the red republicans on the one hand, and the black imperialists on the other. On every side they were engaged in deadly combat, yet without any noise that I could hear, and human soldiers never fought so resolutely. I watched a couple that were fast locked in each other's embraces, in a little sunny valley amid the chips, now at noonday prepared to fight till the sun went down, or life went out. The smaller red champion had fastened himself like a vice to his adversary's front, and through all the tumblings on that field never for an instant ceased to gnaw at one of his feelers near the root, having already caused the other to go by the board; while the stronger black one dashed him from side to side, and, as I saw on looking nearer, had already divested him of several of his members. They fought with more pertinacity than bulldogs. Neither manifested the least disposition to retreat. It was evident that their battle cry was "Conquer or die." In the meanwhile there came along a single red ant on the hillside of this valley, evidently full of excitement, who either had dispatched his foe, or had not yet taken part in the battle; probably the latter, for he had lost none of his limbs; whose mother had charged him to return with his shield or upon it. Or perchance he was some Achilles, who had nourished his wrath apart, and had now come to avenge or rescue his Patroclus. He saw this un-

Vivid adverb

Time expression

Identifying subject of narrative

Military imagery

Establishes narrator's interpretation of event

Begins to anthropomorphize ants

Vivid adjective
Ants compared to humans

Time expression

Comparison to heroes of Trojan War

equal combat from afar—for the blacks were nearly twice the size of the red—he drew near with rapid pace till he stood on his guard within half an inch of the combatants; then, watching his opportunity, he sprang upon the black warrior, and commenced his operations near the root of his right foreleg, leaving the foe to select among his own members; and so there were three united for life, as if a new kind of attraction had been invented which put all other locks and cements to shame. I should not have wondered by this time to find that they had their respective musical bands stationed on some eminent chip, and playing their national airs the while, to excite the slow and cheer the dying combatants. I was myself excited somewhat even as if they had been men. The more you think of it, the less the difference. And certainly there is not the fight recorded in Concord history, at least, if in the history of America, that will bear a moment's comparison with this, whether for the numbers engaged in it, or for the patriotism and heroism displayed. For numbers and for carnage it was an Austerlitz or Dresden. Concord Fight! Two killed on the patriots' side, and Luther Blanchard wounded! Why here every ant was a Buttrick—"Fire! for God's sake fire!"—and thousands shared the fate of Davis and Hosmer. There was not one hireling there. I have no doubt that it was a principle they fought for, as much as our ancestors, and not to avoid a three-penny tax on their tea; and the results of this battle will be as important and memorable to those whom it concerns as those of the battle of Bunker Hill, at least.

Turning point in action

Thesis suggested

Ironic comment reinforcing thesis

    I took up the chip on which the three I have particularly described were struggling, carried it into my house, and placed it under a tumbler on my window sill, in order to see the issue. Holding a microscope to the first-mentioned red ant, I saw that, though he was assiduously gnawing at the near foreleg of his enemy, having severed his remaining feeler, his own breast was all torn away, exposing what vitals he had there to the jaws of the black warrior, whose breast-

2

Focus narrows

plate was apparently too thick for him to pierce; and the dark carbuncles of the sufferer's eyes shone with ferocity such as war only could excite. They struggled half an hour longer under the tumbler, and when I looked again the black soldier had severed the heads of his foes from their bodies, and the still living heads were hanging on either side of him like ghastly trophies at his saddlebow, still apparently as firmly fastened as ever, and he was endeavoring with feeble struggles, being without feelers and with only the remnant of a leg, and I know not how many other wounds, to divest himself of them; which at length, after half an hour more, he accomplished. I raised the glass, and he went off over the window sill in that crippled state. Whether he finally survived that combat, and spent the remainder of his days in some Hôtel des Invalides, I do not know; but I thought that his industry would not be worth much thereafter. I never learned which party was victorious, nor the cause of the war; but I felt for the rest of that day as if I had had my feelings excited and harrowed by witnessing the struggle, the ferocity and carnage, of a human battle before my door.

Vivid detail

Time expression

Vivid details

Vivid adjective

Conclusion begins: reference to event

Thesis again suggested

Analysis of the Essay

The Process of Telling a Story

An Inductive Narrative.   The purpose of Thoreau's narrative is to dramatize his perception of human warfare. His subject, ants at war, might not strike most people as suitably serious for a criticism of human aggression. A close reading of the essay, however, shows that Thoreau's comparison between ant and human warfare is apt and that by using our powers of observation creatively, we may find a world of narrative to illustrate our ideas.

Since Thoreau's essay is inductive, it is not until the reader has experienced the ant battle through the writer's eyes that the thesis is suggested near the end of paragraph 1. It is not explicit, but the point is never in doubt: "The more you think of [ants like men], the less the difference." In other words, human warfare is as irrational as the ant warfare being described.

When the narrative action has ended (the victorious ant has crawled away), Thoreau's conclusion closes the essay by reinforcing the thesis, permitting the reader to reflect on the idea at the heart of the story.

Sequence and Coherence.   Thoreau narrates the events in the order in which he observes them. In paragraph 1 the emphasis is on the incidents of battle. These climax when the single red ant springs on the other two ants locked in combat and the three are "united for life." This turning point of the action generates the narrator's comparison of the ant battle with human warfare—the basis of Thoreau's implied thesis.

Another kind of sequence is followed in paragraph 2. There, Thoreau interweaves the action of the battle with his responses to it. This alternating pattern of observation and reflection is a useful one for student writers to employ in their own narratives.

The events in Thoreau's ant war are not simply listed. They are linked together so the reader can follow the action with ease. Time expressions (see marginal annotations) are one means of achieving this coherence. Another cohesive device Thoreau uses is the repetition of a sentence element: "He saw . . . he drew near . . . he stood . . . he sprang" (about the single red ant) and "I took up . . . I saw that . . . I looked again . . . I raised the glass . . ." (about his own actions). The main source of cohesiveness in any essay is the selection of words that continually remind the reader of the subject.

In almost every line, Thoreau uses a battlefield expression to highlight the horror of war: "fiercely contending," "struggled and wrestled," "the legions," "strewn with the dead and dying," "still living heads . . . like ghastly trophies." By using expressions related to the key concept throughout the essay, Thoreau keeps firm control of his composition's central idea and gives weight to his thesis. He allows no irrelevant details to obscure his point.

Point of View.   Thoreau writes this essay as a first-person observer. He opens with a broad focus on a war between two races of ants taking place all over his woodyard. In the second half of the essay, he narrows the focus, like that of a camera lens, to a close-up of three combatants on a single chip placed under a microscope. Thoreau clearly signals the shift in perspective at the beginning of paragraph 2, ensuring that the reader will not be lost by the change in point of view.

READINGS

THE OLD TESTAMENT
Genesis

Cosmologies, narratives of the creation of the world, are common to all cultures. They usually have two purposes: to explain natural phenomena in terms that human beings can understand and to celebrate the power of a creator. This cosmology (and the Hopi cosmology that follows) originated in an oral tradition. Note that time expressions clearly mark the flow of events and act as cues for following the thread of the narrative.

This excerpt from Genesis, from the King James Version of the Old Testament, places human beings in a universal scheme of nature.

In the beginning God created the heaven and the earth. And the earth was 1 without form, and void; and darkness was upon the face of the deep. And the Spirit of God moved upon the face of the waters. And God said, Let there be light: and there was light. And God saw the light, that it was good: and God divided the light from the darkness. And God called the light Day, and the darkness he called Night. And the evening and the morning were the first day.

And God said, Let there be a firmament in the midst of the waters, 2 and let it divide the waters from the waters. And God made the firmament, and divided the waters which were under the firmament from the waters which were above the firmament: and it was so. And God called the firmament Heaven. And the evening and the morning were the second day.

And God said, Let the waters under the heaven be gathered together 3 unto one place, and let the dry land appear: and it was so. And God called the dry land Earth, and the gathering together of the waters called he Seas: and God saw that it was good. And God said, Let the earth bring forth grass, the herb yielding seed, and the fruit tree yielding fruit after his kind, whose seed is in itself, upon the earth: and it was so. And the earth brought forth grass, and herb yielding seed after his kind, and the tree yielding fruit, whose seed was in itself, after his kind: and God saw that it was good. And the evening and the morning were the third day.

And God said, Let there be lights in the firmament of the heaven, to 4
divide the day from the night; and let them be for signs and for seasons,
and for days and years: And let them be for lights in the firmament of the
heaven to give light upon the earth: and it was so. And God made two
great lights; the greater light to rule the day, and the lesser light to rule
the night: he made the stars also. And God set them in the firmament
of the heaven, to give light upon the earth, and to rule over the day, and
over the night, and to divide the light from the darkness: and God saw
that it was good. And the evening and the morning were the fourth day.

And God said, Let the waters bring forth abundantly the moving 5
creature that hath life, and fowl that may fly above the earth in the open
firmament of heaven. And God created great whales, and ever living creature that moveth, which the waters brought forth abundantly after their
kind, and every winged fowl after his kind: and God saw that it was good.
And God blessed them, saying Be fruitful, and multiply, and fill the
waters in the seas, and let fowl multiply in the earth. And the evening and
the morning were the fifth day.

And God said, Let the earth bring forth the living creature after his 6
kind, cattle, and creeping thing, and beast of the earth after his kind: and
it was so. And God made the beast of the earth after his kind, and cattle
after their kind, and every thing that creepeth upon the earth after his
kind: and God saw that it was good.

And God said, Let us make man in our image, after our likeness: 7
and let them have dominion over the fish of the sea, and over the fowl of
the air, and over the cattle, and over all the earth, and over every creeping
thing that creepeth upon the earth. So God created man in his own image,
in the image of God created he him: male and female created he them.
And God blessed them, and God said unto them, Be fruitful, and multiply, and replenish the earth, and subdue it: and have dominion over the
fish of the sea, and over the fowl of the air, and over every living thing
that moveth upon the earth.

And God said, Behold, I have given you every herb bearing seed, 8
which is upon the face of all the earth, and every tree, in the which is the
fruit of a tree yielding seed: to you it shall be for meat. And to every beast
of the earth, and to every fowl of the air, and to every thing that creepeth
upon the earth, wherein there is life, I have given every green herb for
meat: and it was so. And God saw every thing that he had made, and
behold, it was very good. And the evening and the morning were the
sixth day.

Thus the heavens and the earth were finished, and all the host of 9
them. And on the seventh day God ended his work which he had made:
and he rested on the seventh day from all his work which he had made.
And God blessed the seventh day, and sanctified it: because that in it he
had rested from all his work which God created and made.

These are the generations of the heavens and of the earth when they 10
were created, in the day that the Lord God made the earth and the heavens, and every plant of the field before it was in the earth, and every herb
of the field before it grew: for the Lord God had not caused it to rain upon
the earth, and there was not a man to till the ground. But there went up a
mist from the earth, and watered the whole face of the ground. And the
Lord God formed man of the dust of the ground, and breathed into his
nostrils the breath of life; and man became a living soul.

And the Lord God planted a garden eastward in Eden: and there he 11
put the man whom he had formed. And out of the ground made the Lord
God to grow every tree that is pleasant to the sight and good for food: the
tree of life also in the midst of the garden, and the tree of knowledge of
good and evil. And a river went out of Eden to water the garden, and from
thence it was parted, and became into four heads. The name of the first is
Pison: that is it which compasseth the whole land of Havilah, where there
is gold. And the gold of that land is good: there is bdellium and the onyx
stone. And the name of the second river is Gihon: the same is it that compasseth the whole land of Ethiopia. And the name of the third river is
Hiddekel: that is it which goeth toward the east of Assyria. And the
fourth river is Euphrates. And the Lord God took the man, and put him
into the garden of Eden, to dress it and to keep it. And the Lord God
commanded the man, saying, Of every tree of the garden thou mayest
freely eat: But of the tree of the knowledge of good and evil, thou shalt not
eat of it: for in the day that thou eatest thereof thou shalt surely die.

And the Lord God said, It is not good that the man should be alone; 12
I will make him an help meet for him. And out of the ground the Lord
God formed every beast of the field, and every fowl of the air, and brought
them unto Adam, to see what he would call them; and whatsoever Adam
called every living creature, that was the name thereof. And Adam gave
names to all cattle, and to the fowl of the air, and to every beast of the
field; but for Adam there was not found an help meet for him. And the
Lord God caused a deep sleep to fall upon Adam, and he slept: and he took
one of his ribs, and closed up the flesh instead thereof. And the rib, which
the Lord God had taken from man, made he a woman, and brought her
unto the man. And Adam said, This is now bone of my bones, and flesh of
my flesh: she shall be called Woman because she was taken out of Man.
Therefore shall a man leave his father and mother and shall cleave unto his
wife; and they shall be one flesh. And they were naked, the man and his
wife, and were not ashamed.

Reading and Interpreting

VOCABULARY

Use your dictionary as necessary to find the meaning of the following words in context:

void (1)   firmament (2)   dominion (7)

CONCEPT ANALYSIS

1. List the separate elements of the physical world that God created according to Genesis. Is Genesis a complete account of the natural universe? Explain.
2. Locate the references in Genesis to the creation of human beings. Is there consistency or are there contradictions? Explain. How is the creation of human beings similar to or different from the creation of other creatures? What relationship is man given to his fellow creatures?
3. Genesis has an objective tone as it accounts for natural phenomena: "the greater light," "the lesser light," "the stars," "let the waters bring forth . . . the moving creature," "the earth brought forth . . . herb yielding seed." Yet there are also abstract and symbolic statements about nature and man that invite interpretation. Discuss some possible meanings of the following:
   a. "And God saw that it was good." (3)
   b. "And God said, "Let there be lights in the firmament of the heaven . . . for signs and for seasons. . . ."" (4)
   c. "Let us make man in our image. . . ." (7)

Quickwrite

Imagine that one of the days on which God worked according to Genesis was a holiday and God did not perform the labor of that particular day. Describe what the world would be like now without the work of the day you have selected.

RHETORICAL TECHNIQUE

1. Which pattern of relationships between events is most evident in Genesis: order of importance, chronological order, cause and effect, or comparison/contrast? Explain your answer with specific references to the text.
2. How does the narrator give authority to his narrative?
3. Two characteristics of the oral narrative are the repetition of key phrases and the explicit markings of time to facilitate the listener's comprehension of events. Cite examples in Genesis where these techniques occur.
4. Is there a turning point(s) in the events of Genesis at which meaningful change occurs? Explain.
5. The amount of space devoted to a particular event in a narrative may indicate its relative importance to the whole. Of the six days of creation in Genesis, which receives the most attention? Why do you think this is so?

A HOPI COSMOLOGY

The Creation of Mankind

The Hopi, a tribe of pueblo-dwelling Native Americans whose name means "peaceful," cultivate corn, beans, and squash atop the mesas of northern Arizona. The Hopi view of the intimate relationship between nature and human beings, implicit in this narrative, is very different from our own.

So Spider Woman gathered earth, this time of four colors, yellow, red, 1
white, and black; mixed with *tuchvala,* the liquid of her mouth; molded them; and covered them with her white-substance cape which was the creative wisdom itself. As before, she sang over them the Creation Song, and when she uncovered them these forms were human beings in the image of Sotuknang. Then she created four other beings after her own form. They were four female partners, for the first four male beings.

When Spider Woman uncovered them the forms came to life. This 2 was at the time of the dark purple light, Qoyangnuptu, the first phase of the dawn of Creation, which first reveals the mystery of man's creation.

They soon awakened and began to move, but there was still a damp- 3 ness on their foreheads and a soft spot on their heads. This was at the time of the yellow light, Sikangnuqua, the second phase of the dawn of Creation, when the breath of life entered man.

In a short time the sun appeared above the horizon, drying the 4 dampness on their foreheads and hardening the soft spot on their heads. This was the time of the red light, Talawva, the third phase of the dawn of Creation, when man, fully formed and firmed, proudly faced his Creator.

"That is the Sun," said Spider Woman. "You are meeting your Fa- 5 ther the Creator for the first time. You must always remember and observe these three phases of your Creation. The time of the three lights, the dark purple, the yellow, and the red reveal in turn the mystery, the breath of life, and warmth of love. These comprise the Creator's plan of life for you as sung over you in the Song of Creation:

SONG OF CREATION

The dark purple light rises in the north,
A yellow light rises in the east.
Then we of the flowers of the earth come forth
To receive a long life of joy.
We call ourselves the Butterfly Maidens.

Both male and female make their prayers to the east,
Make the respectful sign to the Sun our Creator.
The sounds of bells ring through the air,
Making a joyful sound throughout the land,
Their joyful echo resounding everywhere.

Humbly I ask my Father,
The perfect one, Taiowa, our Father,
The perfect one creating the beautiful life
Shown to us by the yellow light,
To give us perfect light at the time of the red light.

The perfect one laid out the perfect plan
And gave to us a long span of life,
Creating song to implant joy in life.
On this path of happiness, we the Butterfly Maidens
Carry out his wishes by greeting our Father Sun.

The song resounds back from our Creator with joy,
And we of the earth repeat it to our Creator.
At the appearing of the yellow light,
Repeats and repeats again the joyful echo,
Sounds and resounds for times to come.

The First People of the First World did not answer her; they could 6
not speak. Something had to be done. Since Spider Woman received her
power from Sotuknang, she had to call him and ask him what to do. So she
called Palongawhoya and said, "Call your Uncle. We need him at once."

Palongawhoya, the echo twin, sent out his call along the world axis 7
to the vibratory centers of the earth, which resounded his message throughout the universe. "Sotuknang, our Uncle, come at once! We need you!"

All at once, with the sound as of a mighty wind, Sotuknang ap- 8
peared in front of them. "I am here. Why do you need me so urgently?"

Spider Woman explained. "As you commanded me, I have created 9
these First People. They are fully and firmly formed; they are properly
colored; they have life; they have movement. But they cannot talk. That is
the proper thing they lack. So I want you to give them speech. Also the
wisdom and the power to reproduce, so that they may enjoy their life and
give thanks to the Creator."

So Sotuknang gave them speech, a different language to each color, 10
with respect for each other's difference. He gave them the wisdom and the
power to reproduce and multiply.

Then he said to them, "With all these I have given you this world to 11
live on and to be happy. There is only one thing I ask of you. To respect
the Creator at all times. Wisdom, harmony, and respect for the love of the
Creator who made you. May it grow and never be forgotten among you as
long as you live."

So the First People went their directions, were happy, and began to 12
multiply.

Reading and Interpreting

CONCEPT ANALYSIS

1. In this cosmology there are a number of creators. Identify each creator
   and the aspect of the universe he or she creates.
2. Here, the creator of human beings is a woman. Is her gender reflected in
   any aspect of her creation? Explain.
3. Nature is celebrated throughout this cosmology, yet there is also emphasis on qualities that are uniquely human. What aspects of humanness are
   developed in greatest detail? What role do they play in the relationship
   between man and the natural world?
4. List the stages in the creation of human beings. To what extent do these
   mirror biological birth? How are these stages similar to or different from
   those in the biblical Genesis?

Carefully observe one element of the natural world, such as a tree or flower, a thunderstorm, a house pet, or an animal in the zoo. Narrate an origin story for it, accounting for one of its prominent physical or behavioral characteristics (color, sound, movement).

Thinking and Writing

RHETORICAL TECHNIQUE

1. Unlike Genesis, the Hopi narrative includes dialogue among the Creators. How does the dialogue affect your response to the story?
2. The Hopi narrative is interrupted by the "Song of Creation." Who sings the song? What is its purpose?

RACHEL CARSON

The Gray Beginnings

Rachel Carson (1907–1964) was a biologist and writer well known for works about the sea and natural phenomena. "The Gray Beginnings" is the first chapter of her much acclaimed book, *The Sea Around Us*. Although it is commonly thought that science rests on proven, unquestioned facts, the actual basis of the scientific method is inquiry, observation, and the formulation of hypotheses, or untested theories. Aspects of the scientific method are apparent in Carson's account of the origin of the earth and its seas, yet it is primarily a narrative, incorporating story elements such as atmosphere, action, and suspense.

And the earth was without form, and void; and darkness was upon the face of the deep.

Genesis

Beginnings are apt to be shadowy, and so it is with the beginnings of that 1
great mother of life, the sea. Many people have debated how and when the
earth got its ocean, and it is not surprising that their explanations do not
always agree. For the plain and inescapable truth is that no one was there
to see, and in the absence of eyewitness accounts there is bound to be a
certain amount of disagreement. So if I tell here the story of how the
young planet Earth acquired an ocean, it must be a story pieced together
from many sources and containing whole chapters the details of which we
can only imagine. The story is founded on the testimony of the earth's
most ancient rocks, which were young when the earth was young; on other
evidence written on the face of the earth's satellite, the moon; and on hints
contained in the history of the sun and the whole universe of star-filled
space. For although no man was there to witness this cosmic birth, the
stars and the moon and the rocks were there, and, indeed, had much to do
with the fact that there is an ocean.

The events of which I write must have occurred somewhat more than 2
2 billion years ago. As nearly as science can tell, that is the approximate
age of the earth, and the ocean must be very nearly as old. It is possible
now to discover the age of the rocks that compose the crust of the earth by
measuring the rate of decay of the radioactive materials they contain. The
oldest rocks found anywhere on earth—in Manitoba—are about 2.3 billion years old. Allowing 100 million years or so for the cooling of the
earth's materials to form a rocky crust, we arrive at the supposition that
the tempestuous and violent events connected with our planet's birth occurred nearly 2½ billion years ago. But this is only a minimum estimate,
for rocks indicating an even greater age may be found at any time. . . .

The new earth, freshly torn from its parent sun, was a ball of whirl- 3
ing gases, intensely hot, rushing through the black spaces of the universe
on a path and at a speed controlled by immense forces. Gradually the ball
of flaming gases cooled. The gases began to liquefy, and Earth became a
molten mass. The materials of this mass eventually became sorted out in a
definite pattern: the heaviest in the center, the less heavy surrounding
them, and the least heavy forming the outer rim. This is the pattern
which persists today—a central sphere of molten iron, very nearly as hot
as it was 2 billion years ago, an intermediate sphere of semiplastic basalt,
and a hard outer shell, relatively quite thin and composed of solid basalt
and granite.

The outer shell of the young earth must have been a good many mil- 4
lions of years changing from the liquid to the solid state, and it is believed
that, before this change was completed, an event of the greatest importance took place—the formation of the moon. The next time you stand on
a beach at night, watching the moon's bright path across the water, and
conscious of the moon-drawn tides, remember that the moon itself may
have been born of a great tidal wave of earthly substance, torn off into
space. And remember that if the moon was formed in this fashion, the

event may have had much to do with shaping the ocean basins and the continents as we know them.

There were tides in the new earth, long before there was an ocean. In response to the pull of the sun the molten liquids of the earth's whole surface rose in tides that rolled unhindered around the globe and only gradually slackened and diminished as the earthly shell cooled, congealed, and hardened. Those who believe that the moon is a child of Earth say that during an early stage of the earth's development something happened that caused this rolling, viscid tide to gather speed and momentum and to rise to unimaginable heights. Apparently the force that created these greatest tides the earth has ever known was the force of resonance, for at this time the period of the solar tides had come to approach, then equal, the period of the free oscillation of the liquid earth. And so every sun tide was given increased momentum by the push of the earth's oscillation, and each of the twice-daily tides was larger than the one before it. Physicists have calculated that, after 500 years of such monstrous, steadily increasing tides, those on the side toward the sun became too high for stability, and a great wave was torn away and hurled into space. But immediately, of course, the newly created satellite became subject to physical laws that sent it spinning in an orbit of its own about the earth. This is what we call the moon.

There are reasons for believing that this event took place after the earth's crust had become slightly hardened, instead of during its partly liquid state. There is to this day a great scar on the surface of the globe. This scar or depression holds the Pacific Ocean. According to some geophysicists, the floor of the Pacific is composed of basalt, the substance of the earth's middle layer, while all other oceans are floored with a thin layer of granite, which makes up most of the earth's outer layer. We immediately wonder what became of the Pacific's granite covering and the most convenient assumption is that it was torn away when the moon was formed. There is supporting evidence. The mean density of the moon is much less than that of the earth (3.3 compared with 5.5), suggesting that the moon took away none of the earth's heavy iron core, but that it is composed only of the granite and some of the basalt of the outer layers.

The birth of the moon probably helped shape other regions of the world ocean besides the Pacific. When part of the crust was torn away, strains must have been set up in the remaining granite envelope. Perhaps the granite mass cracked open on the side opposite the moon scar. Perhaps, as the earth spun on its axis and rushed on its orbit through space, the cracks widened and the masses of granite began to drift apart, moving over a tarry, slowly hardening layer of basalt. Gradually the outer portions of the basalt layer became solid and the wandering continents came to rest, frozen into place with oceans between them. In spite of theories to the contrary, the weight of geologic evidence seems to be that the locations of the major ocean basins and the major continental land masses are today much the same as they have been since a very early period of the earth's history.

But this is to anticipate the story, for when the moon was born there 8 was no ocean. The gradually cooling earth was enveloped in heavy layers of cloud, which contained much of the water of the new planet. For a long time its surface was so hot that no moisture could fall without immediately being reconverted to steam. This dense, perpetually renewed cloud covering must have been thick enough that no rays of sunlight could penetrate it. And so the rough outlines of the continents and the empty ocean basins were sculptured out of the surface of the earth in darkness, in a Stygian world of heated rock and swirling clouds and gloom.

As soon as the earth's crust cooled enough, the rains began to fall. 9 Never have there been such rains since that time. They fell continuously, day and night, days passing into months, into years, into centuries. They poured into the waiting ocean basins, or, falling upon the continental masses, drained away to become sea.

That primeval ocean, growing in bulk as the rains slowly filled its 10 basins, must have been only faintly salt. But the falling rains were the symbol of the dissolution of the continents. From the moment the rains began to fall, the lands began to be worn away and carried to the sea. It is an endless, inexorable process that has never stopped—the dissolving of the rocks, the leaching out of their contained minerals, the carrying of the rock fragments and dissolved minerals to the ocean. And over the eons of time, the sea has grown ever more bitter with the salt of the continents.

In what manner the sea produced the mysterious and wonderful stuff 11 called protoplasm we cannot say. In its warm, dimly lit waters the unknown conditions of temperature and pressure and saltiness must have been the critical ones for the creation of life from non-life. At any rate they produced the result that neither the alchemists with their crucibles nor modern scientists in their laboratories have been able to achieve.

Before the first living cell was created, there may have been many 12 trials and failures. It seems probable that, within the warm saltiness of the primeval sea, certain organic substances were fashioned from carbon dioxide, sulphur, nitrogen, phosphorus, potassium, and calcium. Perhaps these were transition steps from which the complex molecules of protoplasm arose—molecules that somehow acquired the ability to reproduce themselves and begin the endless stream of life. But at present no one is wise enough to be sure.

Those first living things may have been simple microorganisms 13 rather like some of the bacteria we know today—mysterious borderline forms that were not quite plants, not quite animals, barely over the intangible line that separates the non-living from the living. It is doubtful that this first life possessed the substance chlorophyll, with which plants in sunlight transform lifeless chemicals into the living stuff of their tissues.

Little sunshine could enter their dim world, penetrating the cloud banks from which fell the endless rains. Probably the sea's first children lived on the organic substances then present in the ocean waters, or, like the iron and sulphur bacteria that exist today, lived directly on inorganic food.

All the while the cloud cover was thinning, the darkness of the nights alternated with palely illumined days, and finally the sun for the first time shone through upon the sea. By this time some of the living things that floated in the sea must have developed the magic of chlorophyll. Now they were able to take the carbon dioxide of the air and the water of the sea and of these elements, in sunlight, build the organic substances they needed. So the first true plants came into being. 14

Another group of organisms, lacking the chlorophyll but needing organic food, found they could make a way of life for themselves by devouring the plants. So the first animals arose, and from that day to this, every animal in the world has followed the habit it learned in the ancient seas and depends, directly or through complex food chains, on the plants for food and life. 15

As the years passed, and the centuries, and the millions of years, the stream of life grew more and more complex. From simple, one-celled creatures, others that were aggregations of specialized cells arose, and then creatures with organs for feeding, digesting, breathing, reproducing. Sponges grew on the rocky bottom of the sea's edge and coral animals built their habitations in warm, clear waters. Jellyfish swam and drifted in the sea. Worms evolved, and starfish, and hard-shelled creatures with many-jointed legs, the arthropods. The plants, too, progressed, from the microscopic algae to branched and curiously fruiting seaweeds that swayed with the tides and were plucked from the coastal rocks by the surf and cast adrift. 16

During all this time the continents had no life. There was little to induce living things to come ashore, forsaking their all-providing, all-embracing mother sea. The lands must have been bleak and hostile beyond the power of words to describe. Imagine a whole continent of naked rock, across which no covering mantle of green had been drawn—a continent without soil, for there were no land plants to aid in its formation and bind it to the rocks with their roots. Imagine a land of stone, a silent land, except for the sound of the rains and winds that swept across it. For there was no living voice, and no living thing moved over the surface of the rocks. 17

Meanwhile, the gradual cooling of the planet, which had first given the earth its hard granite crust, was progressing into its deeper layers; and as the interior slowly cooled and contracted, it drew away from the outer shell. This shell, accommodating itself to the shrinking sphere within it, fell into folds and wrinkles—the earth's first mountain ranges. 18

Geologists tell us that there must have been at least two periods of mountain building (often called "revolutions") in that dim period, so 19 long ago that the rocks have no record of it, so long ago that the mountains themselves have long since been worn away. Then there came a third great period of upheaval and readjustment of the earth's crust, about a billion years ago, but of all its majestic mountains the only reminders today are the Laurentian hills of eastern Canada, and a great shield of granite over the flat country around Hudson Bay.

The epochs of mountain building only served to speed up the pro- 20 cesses of erosion by which the continents were worn down and their crumbling rock and contained minerals returned to the sea. The uplifted masses of the mountains were prey to the bitter cold of the upper atmosphere and under the attacks of frost and snow and ice the rocks cracked and crumbled away. The rains beat with greater violence upon the slopes of the hills and carried away the substance of the mountains in torrential streams. There was still no plant covering to modify and resist the power of the rains.

And in the sea, life continued to evolve. The earliest forms have left 21 no fossils by which we can identify them. Probably they were soft-bodied, with no hard parts that could be preserved. Then, too, the rock layers formed in those early days have since been so altered by enormous heat and pressure, under the foldings of the earth's crust, that any fossils they might have contained would have been destroyed.

For the past 500 million years, however, the rocks have preserved 22 the fossil record. By the dawn of the Cambrian period, when the history of living things was first inscribed on rock pages, life in the sea had progressed so far that all the main groups of backboneless or invertebrate animals had been developed. But there were no animals with backbones, no insects or spiders, and still no plant or animal had been evolved that was capable of venturing onto the forbidding land. So for more than three-fourths of geologic time the continents were desolate and uninhabited, while the sea prepared the life that was later to invade them and make them habitable. Meanwhile, with violent tremblings of the earth and with the fire and smoke of roaring volcanoes, mountains rose and wore away, glaciers moved to and fro over the earth, and the sea crept over the continents and again receded.

It was not until Silurian time, some 350 million years ago, that the 23 first pioneer of land life crept out on the shore. It was an arthropod, one of the great tribe that later produced crabs and lobsters and insects. It must have been something like a modern scorpion, but, unlike some of its descendants, it never wholly severed the ties that united it to the sea. It lived a strange life, half-terrestrial, half-aquatic, something like that of the ghost crabs that speed along the beaches today, now and then dashing into the surf to moisten their gills.

Fish, tapered of body and stream-molded by the press of running 24 waters, were evolving in Silurian rivers. In times of drought, in the drying pools and lagoons, the shortage of oxygen forced them to develop swim bladders for the storage of air. One form that possessed an air-breathing lung was able to survive the dry periods by burying itself in mud, leaving a passage to the surface through which it breathed.

It is very doubtful that the animals alone would have succeeded in 25 colonizing the land, for only the plants had the power to bring about the first amelioration of its harsh conditions. They helped make soil of the crumbling rocks, they held back the soil from the rains that would have swept it away, and little by little they softened and subdued the bare rock, the lifeless desert. We know very little about the first land plants, but they must have been closely related to some of the larger seaweeds that had learned to live in the coastal shallows, developing strengthened stems and grasping, rootlike holdfasts to resist the drag and pull of the waves. Perhaps it was in some coastal lowlands, periodically drained and flooded, that some such plants found it possible to survive, though separated from the sea. This also seems to have taken place in the Silurian period.

The mountains that had been thrown up by the Laurentian revolu- 26 tion gradually wore away, and as the sediments were washed from their summits and deposited on the lowlands, great areas of the continents sank under the load. The seas crept out of their basins and spread over the lands. Life fared well and was exceedingly abundant in those shallow, sun-lit seas. But with the later retreat of the ocean water into the deeper basins, many creatures must have been left stranded in shallow, land-locked bays. Some of these animals found means to survive on land. The lakes, the shores of the rivers, and the coastal swamps of those days were the testing grounds in which plants and animals either became adapted to the new conditions or perished.

As the lands rose and the seas receded, a strange fishlike creature 27 emerged on the land, and over the thousands of years its fins became legs, and instead of gills it developed lungs. In the Devonian sandstone this first amphibian left its footprint.

On land and sea the stream of life poured on. New forms evolved; 28 some old ones declined and disappeared. On land the mosses and the ferns and the seed plants developed. The reptiles for a time dominated the earth, gigantic, grotesque, and terrifying. Birds learned to live and move in the ocean of air. The first small mammals lurked inconspicuously in hidden crannies of the earth as though in fear of the reptiles.

When they went ashore the animals that took up a land life carried 29 with them a part of the sea in their bodies, a heritage which they passed on to their children and which even today links each land animal with its origin in the ancient sea. Fish, amphibian, and reptile, warm-blooded bird and mammal—each of us carries in our veins a salty stream in which the elements sodium, potassium, and calcium are combined in almost the same proportions as in sea water. This is our inheritance from the day, untold millions of years ago, when a remote ancestor, having progressed from the one-celled to the many-celled stage, first developed a circulatory system in which the fluid was merely the water of the sea. In the same way, our lime-hardened skeletons are a heritage from the calcium-rich ocean of Cambrian time. Even the protoplasm that streams within each cell of our bodies has the chemical structure impressed upon all living matter when the first simple creatures were brought forth in the ancient sea. And as life itself began in the sea, so each of us begins his individual life in a miniature ocean within his mother's womb, and in the stages of his embryonic development repeats the steps by which his race evolved, from gill-breathing inhabitants of a water world to creatures able to live on land.

Some of the land animals later returned to the ocean. After perhaps 30 50 million years of land life, a number of reptiles entered the sea about 170 million years ago, in the Triassic period. They were huge and formidable creatures. Some had oarlike limbs by which they rowed through the water; some were web-footed, with long, serpentine necks. These grotesque monsters disappeared millions of years ago, but we remember them when we come upon a large sea turtle swimming many miles at sea, its barnacle-encrusted shell eloquent of its marine life. Much later, perhaps no more than 50 million years ago, some of the mammals, too, abandoned a land life for the ocean. Their descendants are the sea lions, seals, sea elephants, and whales of today.

Among the land mammals there was a race of creatures that took to 31 an arboreal existence. Their hands underwent remarkable development, becoming skilled in manipulating and examining objects, and along with this skill came a superior brain power that compensated for what these comparatively small mammals lacked in strength. At last, perhaps somewhere in the vast interior of Asia, they descended from the trees and became again terrestrial. The past million years have seen their transformation into beings with the body and brain and spirit of man.

Eventually man, too, found his way back to the sea. Standing on its 32 shores, he must have looked out upon it with wonder and curiosity, compounded with an unconscious recognition of his lineage. He could not physically re-enter the ocean as the seals and whales had done. But over the centuries, with all the skill and ingenuity and reasoning powers of his mind, he has sought to explore and investigate even its most remote parts, so that he might re-enter it mentally and imaginatively.

He built boats to venture out on its surface. Later he found ways to 33 descend to the shallow parts of its floor, carrying with him the air that, as a land mammal long unaccustomed to aquatic life, he needed to breathe. Moving in fascination over the deep sea he could not enter, he found ways to probe its depths, he let down nets to capture its life, he invented mechanical eyes and ears that could re-create for his senses a world long lost, but a world that, in the deepest part of his subconscious mind, he had never wholly forgotten.

And yet he has returned to his mother sea only on her own terms. 34

He cannot control or change the ocean as, in his brief tenancy of earth, he has subdued and plundered the continents. In the artificial world of his cities and towns, he often forgets the true nature of his planet and the long vistas of its history, in which the existence of the race of men has occupied a mere moment of time. The sense of all these things comes to him most clearly in the course of a long ocean voyage, when he watches day after day the receding rim of the horizon, ridged and furrowed by waves; when at night he becomes aware of the earth's rotation as the stars pass overhead; or when, alone in this world of water and sky, he feels the loneliness of his earth in space. And then, as never on land, he knows the truth that his world is a water world, a planet dominated by its covering mantle of ocean, in which the continents are but transient intrusions of land above the surface of the all-encircling sea.

Reading and Interpreting

VOCABULARY

Use your dictionary as necessary to find the meaning of the following words as used in Rachel Carson's narrative:

viscid (5)   oscillation (5)   inexorable (10)   aggregations (16)

terrestrial (23)   amphibian (27)   arboreal (31)   transient (34)

CONCEPT ANALYSIS

1. Chart the most significant events in the development of our planet and its creatures according to Carson's account. If you have read Genesis, in what ways do you see these occurrences corresponding to or contradicting the biblical account of the earth's creation?

   If you were retelling Carson's narrative in the form of Genesis, at which points would you insert the refrain "And God saw that it was good"? Explain your answer.

2. Does Carson's narrative suggest a conscious, purposeful force behind any of the natural phenomena she describes? Does she indicate differences between the creation of the human species and other species of the natural world? Cite lines in the text.

3. The principle of adaptation, the ways in which living populations modify themselves in relation to their environments so that they can survive, is a significant aspect of Carson's narrative. Which points in her account reveal the process of adaptation taking place?

4. What is the significance of the following lines in Carson's narrative:
   a. "Beginnings are apt to be shadowy. . . ." (1)

b. "unknown conditions of temperature and pressure and saltiness . . . produced the result that neither the alchemists with their crucibles nor modern scientists in their laboratories have been able to achieve." (11)
c. "When they went ashore the animals that took up a land life carried with them a part of the sea in their bodies, a heritage which . . . even today links each land animal with its origin in the ancient sea." (29)
d. "And yet [man] has returned to his mother sea only on her own terms." (34)

Thinking and Writing

RHETORICAL TECHNIQUE

1. A cause-and-effect pattern underlies Carson's narrative and gives it a scientific foundation. Cite specific examples of causal relationships in her essay.
2. In a purposeful narration, there are usually several highly significant, irrevocable turning points. Cite some of the lines in Carson's essay that indicate such turning points in the evolution of life.
3. Flashbacks and flash-forwards, interruptions of the chronological sequence, may be used for particular purposes and effects. Find instances in Carson's essay where these occur. What purposes do they serve?
4. As a scientific record of natural occurrences, Carson's account need not have used language that appeals to the senses and evokes emotion. Yet Carson does employ language that appeals to the reader in this way. For example, in paragraph 23 the opening sentence refers to the first Silurian land life as a "pioneer," a word that suggests associations beyond the scientific realm. Find other examples of such language in the essay. How does the use of nonscientific language affect your response to the essay?

COMPOSITION

Imagine that you are a creature evolving in "The Gray Beginnings." Select for yourself either an arboreal, terrestrial, aquatic, or aerial environment, and narrate an event in your life from your perspective.

JAMES THURBER

The Human Being and the Dinosaur

American humorist James Thurber's (1894–1961) comments on Western civilization ranged from mild bemusement to bitter criticism. The following satirical fable exposes our folly in believing that we have "dominion over every living thing that moveth upon the earth." It reverses the view of evolution as moving from lower, nonhuman forms to the highest form, the human being. Notice how Thurber conveys man's foolish egotism through dialogue and through mocking descriptions such as "Man strutted a little pace and flexed his muscles."

Ages ago in a wasteland of time and a wilderness of space, Man, in upper 1 case, and dinosaur, in lower, first came face to face. They stood like stones for a long while, wary and watchful, taking each other in. Something told the dinosaur that he beheld before him the coming glory and terror of the world, and in the still air of the young planet he seemed to catch the faint smell of his own inevitable doom.

"Greetings, stupid," said Man. "Behold in me the artfully articu- 2 lated architect of the future, the chosen species, the certain survivor, the indestructible one, the monarch of all you survey, and of all that everyone else surveys, for that matter. On the other hand, you are, curiously enough, for all your size a member of the inconsequent ephemera. You are one of God's moderately amusing early experiments, a frail footnote to natural history, a contraption in a museum for future Man to marvel at, an excellent example of Jehovah's jejune juvenilia."

The dinosaur sighed with a sound like thunder. 3

"Perpetuating your species," Man continued, "would be foolish and 4 futile."

"The missing link is not lost," said the dinosaur sorrowfully. "It's 5 hiding."

Man paid the doomed dinosaur no mind. "If there were no Man it 6 would be necessary to create one," said Man, "for God moves in mysterious, but inefficient, ways, and He needs help. Man will go on forever, but you will be one with the mammoth and the mastodon, for monstrosity is the behemother of extinction."

"There are worse things than being extinct," said the dinosaur 7 sourly, "and one of them is being you."

Man strutted a little pace and flexed his muscles. "You cannot even 8 commit murder," he said, "for murder requires a mind. You are capable only of dinosaurslaughter. You and your ilk are incapable of devising increasingly effective methods of destroying your own species and, at the same time, increasingly miraculous methods of keeping it extant. You will never live to know the two-party system, the multi-party system, and the one-party system. You will be gone long before I have made this the best of all possible worlds, no matter how possible all other worlds may be. In your highest state of evolution you could not develop the brain cells to prove innocent men guilty, even after their acquittal. You are all wrong in the crotch, and in the cranium, and in the cortex. But I have wasted enough time on you. I must use these fingers which God gave me, and now probably wishes He had kept for Himself, to begin writing those noble volumes about Me which will one day run to several hundred billion items, many of them about war, death, conquest, decline, fall, blood, sweat, tears, threats, warnings, boasts, hopelessness, hell, heels, and whores. There will be little enough about you and your ilk and your kith and your kin, for after all, who were you and your ilk and your kith and your kin? Good day and goodbye," said Man in conclusion. "I shall see to it that your species receives a decent burial, with some simple ceremony."

Man, as it turned out, was right. The dinosaur and his ilk and his 9 kith and his kin died not long after, still in lower case, but with a curious smile of satisfaction, or something of the sort, on their ephemeral faces.

Moral: The noblest study of mankind is Man, says Man. 10

Reading and Interpreting

VOCABULARY

Use your dictionary as necessary to find the meaning of the following words in the context of Thurber's fable:

inconsequent (2)   ephemera (2)   jejune (2)   extant (8)   cranium (8)

cortex (8)   ilk (8)

CONCEPT ANALYSIS

1. Consider the character of Man in Thurber's narrative. How does Man view his position in the natural world? Cite specific statements that illustrate your answer.

How does the dinosaur view Man?

Which character represents Thurber's point of view? Explain.

2. Irony is the use of words to mean the opposite of what they seem to say. In paragraph 8, Man calls attention to what he see as positive human traits. Actually, however, Thurber is pointing these out as human deficiencies. Give other examples of ironic statements.

3. Why did the dinosaur die with "a curious smile of satisfaction" on its face?

4. The "moral" of Thurber's fable is based on the following lines from Alexander Pope's *Essay on Man:* "Know then thyself, presume not God to scan; / The proper study of mankind is Man." What do you think Pope meant by these lines? How has Thurber changed them? What is the meaning of Thurber's added tag, "says Man"?

Quickwrite

Imagine yourself in a dialogue with a representative of an extinct species or of a species that might evolve in the future. Write a fable in which the conversation communicates a point about modern human life.

Thinking and Writing

RHETORICAL TECHNIQUE

1. The dinosaur makes only one-line responses to the extended speeches of Man. What does Thurber convey about the dinosaur by limiting his speech?

2. This narrative is largely the report of a conversation. Instead of dramatizing events, Thurber comments on the interchange by using thoughtfully selected adjectives, adverbs, and prepositional phrases, such as "said the dinosaur *sourly.*" Find other examples of these suggestive expressions and analyze their role in communicating Thurber's point of view.

3. Thurber has given his narrative the form of a fable: the action is limited to a single important incident, animal characters speak and act like human beings, and the conclusion is a brief moral rather than a fully explained thesis statement. Explain why this narrative structure has been effective for over two thousand years.

4. Which sentence in the first paragraph establishes the point of view from which the fable is told? Whose point of view is it? What shift in point of view, if any, takes place at the end of the fable? Explain.

ANAÏS NIN

Monkey

In this excerpt from *The Diary*, Anaïs Nin (see Chapter 1) selects vivid vocabulary and a wealth of concrete details to bring her narrative to life.

Someone gave me an organ-grinder's monkey they had seen in a pet shop   1
and which had appeared on the stage. He was about a foot and a half tall.
As soon as he arrived he went berserk. He leaped from curtain to curtain,
balanced on electric wires, spilled a bottle of perfume, pulled clothes
down from the hangers, scattered the sea shells, and when everyone rushed
to catch him he ran to me for refuge and in this way won my protection.

It was impossible to put him back in the cage. He was so rebellious   2
that I gave up and I locked him up in the bathroom when I went out that
evening, thinking there was little he could upset in a bathroom. But
when I returned he had opened the medicine chest, opened every bottle,
spilled their contents in the washbowl, opened the toothpaste tubes and
squeezed the paste all over the bathroom, opened the talcum and face
powder and powdered everything, unwound all the toilet paper and scattered it like serpentines all over bathtub and toilet, scattered the Kleenex.
He had smeared his face with toothpaste, emptied the laundry basket, and
when I arrived was banging on the door with the hairbrush. When I opened
the door he looked up at me innocently, climbed on my shoulder, bared his
teeth as if he were laughing, and began to look for fleas in my hair.

I tried to lure him into his cage by placing grapes at the bottom of   3
it, as he is very fond of grapes. He looked at me mockingly, slipped his
long arm through the bars, picked up the grapes without getting inside. I
had underestimated his reasoning power and the length of his arms.

He insisted that I stand by while he ate. He picked up his rice with   4
his fingers with great delicacy, cupping them around it. His nails are lac-
quered black as if covered by nail polish. I tried caresses and cajoling
words to calm him before slipping him into his cage. He responded, but
with equally coaxing gestures, pleadings, ruses. He finally let me place
him inside, but cried when I left. When I returned from the street he
received me deliriously. He uttered little cries like a bird.

He had a genius for destruction and for comedy. Someone gave him a   5
few sips of beer. He threw himself back with laughter and slapped his
stomach. He took sudden likes and dislikes to visitors and expressed them
plainly. He would take up their glass and spill it, or go up to them and
slap them.

Sunday, when I cooked pancakes and gave him a banana, he looked 6
puzzled. He fetched the telephone book, opened it, peeled the banana,
placed it between the pages and closed it. After a while he opened the
book and showed me the flattened banana, his pancake.

No matter how restless he is, if I take him into my arms he cuddles 7
tenderly and goes to sleep. But the apartment is a shambles. He opens
books, pretends to read, and then throws them on the floor. He scatters
my papers, he scatters the food on my plate, he opens all the closets, he
falls asleep on my dresses and also urinates on them. He tore the bathroom
shower curtain, destroyed all the packages of cigarettes, scratched Virginia.

He dominates the entire household. When I gave him a teaspoon of 8
beer he pretended to walk unevenly, to fall off his cage. His grin is irre-
sistible. Everyone has to laugh constantly.

One evening I left him in the cage, but not tightly locked. He got 9
out and pulled down every inch of electric wiring in the studio. He sat on
a tangle of wires, very pleased with his achievement. My typing was covered with the smoky marks of his toes on my carbon paper. He tore apart
my costume jewelry, ate the flowers in the flowerpots, hung from the tran-
som cord until he opened it and escaped to the roof.

We ached from laughing, but I could not keep him. I could not 10
work, go out, or cook without his finding something to do to divert my
attention.

It was so difficult to give him up that I asked someone to take him 11
back to the pet shop while I was out. I had become attached to him.
When I came home he was gone. I went into the bathroom. There on the
white wall were smoky imprints of his dirty paws, five clearly marked fingers, like a farewell message. I wept.

Reading and Interpreting

CONCEPT ANALYSIS

What can the reader infer about the natural behavior of monkeys in the wild
from the behavior of Nin's monkey? In what ways do the natures of wild creatures and human beings appear to differ, based on Nin's narrative?

Thinking and Writing

RHETORICAL TECHNIQUE

1. Nin's narrative about her monkey achieves focus at different points in the
   story. Identify some thesis statements that control some of the details.

2. Where is the turning point of the narrative? Cite specific lines of the narrative that prepare the reader for the turning point.
3. Note that Nin works in both the present tense for general remarks about her pet and in the past for specific events. Note the paragraphs where these tense changes occur. What is their effect on the narrative?

COMPOSITION

1. Write a narrative about a pet that has made you weep and/or laugh.
2. Nin's narrative about her monkey illustrates the general statement "He dominates the entire household." Use this statement as the controlling idea of a narrative about an individual who has a similar influence in some area of your life.

STEPHEN CRANE

Stephen Crane's Own Story

Stephen Crane's (1871–1900) literary reputation was established by his Civil War novel, *The Red Badge of Courage,* and such classic stories as "The Open Boat." Crane used unusual experiences for invention, visiting the New York slums, Mexico, Greece, and Cuba. This diary account of a shipwreck that he experienced as a war correspondent became the source for "The Open Boat."

Sleep Impossible

As darkness came upon the waters, the *Commodore* was a broad, flaming   1
path of blue and silver phosphorescence, and as her stout bow lunged at
the great black waves she threw flashing, roaring cascades to either side.
And all that was to be heard was the rhythmical and mighty pounding of
the engines. Being an inexperienced filibuster, the writer had undergone
considerable mental excitement since the starting of the ship and in consequence he had not yet been to sleep and so I went to the first mate's bunk
to indulge myself in all the physical delights of holding one's self in bed.
Every time the ship lurched I expected to be fired through a bulkhead,

and it was neither amusing nor instructive to see in the dim light a certain accursed valise aiming itself at the top of my stomach with every lurch of the vessel.

The Cook Is Hopeful

The cook was asleep on a bench in the galley. He is of a portly and noble 2 exterior, and by means of a checker board he had himself wedged on this bench in such a manner the motion of the ship would be unable to dislodge him. He woke as I entered the galley and delivered himself of some dolorous sentiments: "God," he said in the course of his observations, "I don't feel right about this ship, somehow. It strikes me that something is going to happen to us. I don't know what it is, but the old ship is going to get it in the neck, I think."

"Well, how about the men on board of her?" said I. "Are any of us 3 going to get out, prophet?"

"Yes," said the cook. "Sometimes I have these damned feelings come 4 over me, and they are always right, and it seems to me, somehow, that you and I will both get [out] and meet again somewhere, down at Coney Island, perhaps, or some place like that."

One Man Has Enough

Finding it impossible to sleep, I went back to the pilot house. An old 5 seaman, Tom Smith, from Charleston, was then at the wheel. In the darkness I could not see Tom's face, except at those times when he leaned forward to scan the compass and the dim light from the box came upon his weatherbeaten features.

"Well, Tom," said I, "how do you like filibustering?" 6

He said, "I think I am about through with it. I've been in a number 7 of these expeditions and the pay is good, but I think if I ever get back safe this time I will cut it."

I sat down in the corner of the pilot house and almost went to sleep. 8 In the meantime the captain came on duty and he was standing near me when the chief engineer rushed up the stairs and cried hurriedly to the captain that there was something wrong in the engine room. He and the captain departed swiftly.

I was drowsing there in my corner when the captain returned and, 9 going to the door of the little room directly back of the pilothouse, he cried to the Cuban leader:

"Say, can't you get those fellows to work. I can't talk their language 10
and I can't get them started. Come on and get them going."

A Whistle of Despair

Now the whistle of the *Commodore* had been turned loose, and if there ever 11
was a voice of despair and death, it was in the voice of this whistle. It had
gained a new tone. It was as if its throat was already choked by the water,
and this cry on the sea at night, with a wind blowing the spray over the
ship, and the waves roaring over the bow, and swirling white along the
decks, was to each of us probably a song of man's end.

It was now that the first mate showed a sign of losing his grip. To us 12
who were trying in all stages of competence and experience to launch the
lifeboat he raged in all terms of fiery satire and hammerlike abuse. But the
boat moved at last and swung down toward the water.

Afterward, when I went aft, I saw the captain standing, with his 13
arm in a sling, holding on to a stay with his one good hand and directing
the launching of the boat. He gave me a five-gallon jug of water to hold,
and asked me what I was going to do. I told him what I thought was
about the proper thing, and he told me then that the cook had the same
idea, and ordered me to go forward and be ready to launch the ten-
foot dinghy.

In the Ten-Foot Dinghy

I remember well that he turned then to swear at a colored stoker who was 14
prowling around, done up in life preservers until he looked like a feather
bed. I went forward with my five-gallon jug of water, and when the captain came we launched the dinghy, and they put me over the side to fend
her off from the ship with an oar.

They handed me down the water jug, and then the cook came into 15
the boat, and we sat there in the darkness, wondering why, by all our
hopes of future happiness, the captain was so long in coming over to the
side and ordering us away from the doomed ship.

The captain was waiting for the other boat to go. Finally he hailed in 16
the darkness: "Are you all right, Mr. Graines?"

The first mate answered: "All right, sir."   17

"Shove off, then," cried the captain.   18

The captain was just about to swing over the rail when a dark form 19
came forward and a voice said: "Captain, I go with you."

The captain answered: "Yes, Billy; get in."   20

Higgins Last to Leave Ship

It was Billy Higgins, the oiler. Billy dropped into the boat and a moment 21
later the captain followed, bringing with him an end of about forty yards
of lead line. The other end was attached to the rail of the ship.

As we swung back to leeward the captain said: "Boys, we will stay 22
right near the ship till she goes down."

This cheerful information, of course, filled us all with glee. The line 23
kept us headed properly into the wind, and as we rode over the monstrous
waves we saw upon each rise the swaying lights of the dying *Commodore*.

When came the gray shade of dawn, the form of the *Commodore* grew 24
slowly clear to us as our little ten-foot boat rose over each swell. She was
floating with such an air of buoyancy that we laughed when we had time,
and said "What a gag it would be on those other fellows if she didn't
sink at all."

But later we saw men aboard of her, and later still they began to 25
hail us.

Helping Their Mates

I had forgot to mention that previously we had loosened the end of the 26
lead line and dropped much further to leeward. The men on board were a
mystery to us, of course, as we had seen all the boats leave the ship. We
rowed back to the ship, but did not approach too near, because we were
four men in a ten-foot boat, and we knew that the touch of a hand on our
gunwale would assuredly swamp us.

The first mate cried out from the ship that the third boat had foun- 27
dered alongside. He cried that they had made rafts and wished us to
tow them.

The captain said, "All right." 28

Their rafts were floating astern. "Jump in!" cried the captain but 29
there was a singular and most harrowing hesitation. There were five white
men and two negroes. This scene in the gray light of morning impressed
one as would a view into some place where ghosts move slowly. These
seven men on the stern of the sinking *Commodore* were silent. Save the
words of the mate to the captain there was no talk. Here was death, but
here also was a most singular and indefinable kind of fortitude.

Four men, I remember, clambered over the railing and stood there 30
watching the cold, steely sheen of the sweeping waves.

"Jump," cried the captain again. 31

The old chief engineer first obeyed the order. He landed on the out- 32
side raft and the captain told him how to grip the raft and he obeyed as
promptly and as docilely as a scholar in riding school.

The Mate's Mad Plunge

A stoker followed him, and then the first mate threw his hands over his 33
head and plunged into the sea. He had no life belt and for my part, even
when he did this horrible thing, I somehow felt that I could see in the
expression of his hands, and in the very toss of his head, as he leaped thus
to death, that it was rage, rage, rage unspeakable that was in his heart at
the time.

And then I saw Tom Smith, the man who was going to quit fili- 34
bustering after this expedition, jump to a raft and turn his face toward us.
On board the *Commodore* three men strode, still in silence and with their
faces turned toward us. One man had his arms folded and was leaning
against the deckhouse. His feet were crossed, so that the toe of his left foot
pointed downward. There they stood gazing at us, and neither from the
deck nor from the rafts was a voice raised. Still was there this silence.

Tried to Tow the Rafts

The colored stoker on the first raft threw us a line and we began to tow. Of 35
course, we perfectly understood the absolute impossibility of any such
thing; our dinghy was within six inches of the water's edge, there was an
enormous sea running, and I knew that under the circumstances a tugboat
would have no light task in moving these rafts.

But we tried it, and would have continued to try it indefinitely, but 36
that something critical came to pass. I was at an oar and so faced the rafts.
The cook controlled the line. Suddenly the boat began to go backward and
then we saw this negro on the first raft pulling on the line hand over hand
and drawing us to him.

He had turned into a demon. He was wild—wild as a tiger. He was 37
crouched on this raft and ready to spring. Every muscle of him seemed to
be turned into an elastic spring. His eyes were almost white. His face was
the face of a lost man reaching upward, and we knew that the weight of
his hand on our gunwale doomed us.

The Commodore Sinks

The cook let go of the line. We rowed around to see if we could not get a 38
line from the chief engineer, and all this time, mind you, there were no
shrieks, no groans, but silence, silence and silence, and then the *Commodore* sank.

She lurched to windward, then swung afar back, righted and dove 39 into the sea, and the rafts were suddenly swallowed by this frightful maw of the ocean. And then by the men on the ten-foot dinghy were words said that were still not words—something far beyond words.

The lighthouse of Mosquito Inlet stuck up above the horizon like 40 the point of a pin. We turned our dinghy toward the shore.

The history of life in an open boat for thirty hours would no doubt 41 be instructive for the young, but none is to be told them now. For my part I would prefer to tell the story at once because from it would shine the splendid manhood of Captain Edward Murphy and of William Higgins, the oiler, but let suffice at this time to say that when we were swamped in the surf and making the best of our way toward the shore the captain gave orders amid the wildness of the breakers as clearly as if he had been on the quarter deck of a battleship.

John Kitchell of Daytona came running down the beach and as he 42 ran the air was filled with clothes. If he had pulled a single lever and un-dressed, even as the fire horses harness, he could not seem to me to have stripped with more speed. He dashed into the water and grabbed the cook. Then he went after the captain, but the captain sent him to me, and then it was that he saw Billy Higgins lying with his forehead on sand that was clear of the water, and he was dead.

STEPHEN CRANE

The Open Boat

In his diary Crane states that the "history of life in an open boat for thirty hours would no doubt be instructive for the young. . . ." As you read this fictionalized nar-rative, note specific incidents of significance and reflect on the lesson(s) each of these might teach about man's relationship to nature and to his fellow man.

A Tale Intended to be after the Fact:
Being the Experience of Four Men
From the Sunk Steamer *Commodore*

I

None of them knew the color of the sky. Their eyes glanced level, and 1
were fastened upon the waves that swept toward them. These waves were
of the hue of slate, save for the tops, which were of foaming white, and
all of the men knew the colors of the sea. The horizon narrowed and
widened, and dipped and rose, and at all times its edge was jagged with
waves that seemed thrust up in points like rocks.

Many a man ought to have a bath-tub larger than the boat which 2
here rode upon the sea. These waves were most wrongfully and barba-
rously abrupt and tall, and each froth-top was a problem in small-boat
navigation.

The cook squatted in the bottom, and looked with both eyes at the 3
six inches of gunwale which separated him from the ocean. His sleeves
were rolled over his fat forearms, and the two flaps of his unbuttoned
vest dangled as he bent to bail out the boat. Often he said, "Gawd! that
was a narrow clip." As he remarked it he invariably gazed eastward over
the broken sea.

The oiler, steering with one of the two oars in the boat, sometimes 4
raised himself suddenly to keep clear of water that swirled in over the
stern. It was a thin little oar, and it seemed often ready to snap.

The correspondent, pulling at the other oar, watched the waves 5
and wondered why he was there.

The injured captain, lying in the bow, was at this time buried in 6
that profound dejection and indifference which comes, temporarily at
least, to even the bravest and most enduring when, willy-nilly, the firm
fails, the army loses, the ship goes down. The mind of the master of a
vessel is rooted deep in the timbers of her, though he command for a day
or a decade; and this captain had on him the stern impression of a scene
in the grays of dawn of seven turned faces, and later a stump of a topmast
with a white ball on it, that slashed to and fro at the waves, went low
and lower, and down. Thereafter there was something strange in his
voice. Although steady, it was deep with mourning, and of a quality
beyond oration or tears.

"Keep 'er a little more south, Billie," said he. 7

"A little more south, sir," said the oiler in the stern. 8

A seat in this boat was not unlike a seat upon a bucking bronco, 9
and, by the same token a bronco is not much smaller. The craft pranced
and reared and plunged like an animal. As each wave came, and she rose
for it, she seemed like a horse making at a fence outrageously high. The
manner of her scramble over these walls of water is a mystic thing, and,
moreover, at the top of them were ordinarily these problems in white
water, the foam racing down from the summit of each wave, requiring a
new leap, and a leap from the air. Then, after scornfully bumping a crest

she would slide and race and splash down a long incline, and arrive bobbing and nodding in front of the next menace.

A singular disadvantage of the sea lies in the fact that, after successfully surmounting one wave, you discover that there is another behind it, just as important and just as nervously anxious to do something effective in the way of swamping boats. In a ten-foot dinghy one can get an idea of the resources of the sea in the line of waves that is not probable to the average experience, which is never at sea in a dinghy. As each slaty wall of water approached, it shut all else from the view of the men in the boat, and it was not difficult to imagine that this particular wave was the final outburst of the ocean, the last effort of the grim water. There was a terrible grace in the move of the waves, and they came in silence, save for the snarling of the crests. 10

In the wan light the faces of the men must have been gray. Their eyes must have glinted in strange ways as they gazed steadily astern. Viewed from a balcony, the whole thing would, doubtless, have been weirdly picturesque. But the men in the boat had no time to see it, and if they had had leisure, there were other things to occupy their minds. The sun swung steadily up the sky, and they knew it was broad day because the color of the sea changed from the slate to emerald-green streaked with amber lights, and the foam was like tumbling snow. The process of the breaking day was unknown to them. They were aware only of this effect upon the color of the waves that rolled toward them. 11

In disjointed sentences the cook and the correspondent argued as to the difference between a life-saving station and a house of refuge. The cook had said: "There's a house of refuge just north of the Mosquito Inlet Light, and as soon as they see us they'll come off in their boat and pick us up." 12

"As soon as who see us?" said the correspondent. 13

"The crew," said the cook. 14

"Houses of refuge don't have crews," said the correspondent. "As I understand them, they are only places where clothes and grub are stored for the benefit of shipwrecked people. They don't carry crews." 15

"Oh, yes, they do," said the cook. 16

"No, they don't," said the correspondent. 17

"Well, we're not there yet, anyhow," said the oiler in the stern. 18

"Well," said the cook, "perhaps it's not a house of refuge that I'm thinking of as being near Mosquito Inlet Light; perhaps it's a life-saving station." 19

"We're not there yet," said the oiler in the stern. 20

II

As the boat bounced from the top of each wave the wind tore through the   21
hair of the hatless men, and as the craft plopped her stern down again the
spray slashed past them. The crest of each of these waves was a hill, from
the top of which the men surveyed for a moment a broad, tumultuous
expanse, shining and wind-riven. It was probably splendid, it was probably glorious, this play of the free sea, wild with lights of emerald and
white and amber.

"Bully good thing it's an on-shore wind," said the cook. "If not,   22
where would we be? Wouldn't have a show."

"That's right," said the correspondent.   23

The busy oiler nodded his assent.   24

Then the captain, in the bow, chuckled in a way that expressed   25
humor, contempt, tragedy, all in one. "Do you think we've got much of
a show now, boys?" said he.

Whereupon the three were silent, save for a trifle of hemming and   26
hawing. To express any particular optimism at this time they felt to be
childish and stupid, but they all doubtless possessed this sense of the
situation in their minds. A young man thinks doggedly at such times.
On the other hand, the ethics of their condition was decidedly against
any open suggestion of hopelessness. So they were silent.

"Oh, well," said the captain, soothing his children, "we'll get   27
ashore all right."

But there was that in his tone which made them think; so the oiler   28
quoth, "Yes! if this wind holds."

The cook was bailing. "Yes! if we don't catch hell in the surf."   29

Canton-flannel gulls flew near and far. Sometimes they sat down on   30
the sea, near patches of brown seaweed that rolled over the waves with a
movement like carpets on a line in a gale. The birds sat comfortably in
groups, and they were envied by some in the dinghy, for the wrath of the
sea was no more to them than it was to a covey of prairie-chickens a
thousand miles inland. Often they came very close and stared at the men
with black, bead-like eyes. At these times they were uncanny and sinister in their unblinking scrutiny, and the men hooted angrily at them,
telling them to be gone. One came, and evidently decided to alight on
the top of the captain's head. The bird flew parallel to the boat, and did
not circle, but made short sidelong jumps in the air in chicken fashion.
His black eyes were wistfully fixed upon the captain's head. "Ugly
brute," said the oiler to the bird. "You look as if you were made with a
jack-knife." The cook and the correspondent swore darkly at the creature. The captain naturally wished to knock it away with the end of the
heavy painter, but he did not dare do it, because anything resembling an
emphatic gesture would have capsized this freighted boat; and so, with

his open hand, the captain gently and carefully waved the gull away. After it had been discouraged from the pursuit the captain breathed easier on account of his hair, and others breathed easier because the bird struck their minds at this time as being somehow gruesome and ominous.

In the meantime the oiler and the correspondent rowed; and also 31 they rowed. They sat together in the same seat, and each rowed an oar. Then the oiler took both oars; then the correspondent took both oars; then the oiler; then the correspondent. They rowed and they rowed. The very ticklish part of the business was when the time came for the reclining one in the stern to take his turn at the oars. By the very last star of truth, it is easier to steal eggs from under a hen than it was to change seats in the dinghy. First the man in the stern slid his hand along the thwart and moved with care, as if he were of Sèvres. Then the man in the rowing-seat slid his hand along the other thwart. It was all done with the most extraordinary care. As the two sidled past each other, the whole party kept watchful eyes on the coming wave, and the captain cried: "Look out, now! Steady, there!"

The brown mats of seaweed that appeared from time to time were 32 like islands, bits of earth. They were traveling, apparently, neither one way nor the other. They were, to all intents, stationary. They informed the men in the boat that it was making progress slowly toward the land.

The captain, rearing cautiously in the bow after the dinghy soared 33 on a great swell, said that he had seen the lighthouse at Mosquito Inlet. Presently the cook remarked that he had seen it. The correspondent was at the oars then, and for some reason he too wished to look at the lighthouse; but his back was toward the far shore, and the waves were important, and for some time he could not seize an opportunity to turn his head. But at last there came a wave more gentle than the others, and when at the crest of it he swiftly scoured the western horizon.

"See it?" said the captain. 34

"No," said the correspondent, slowly; "I didn't see anything." 35

"Look again," said the captain. He pointed. "It's exactly in that 36 direction."

At the top of another wave the correspondent did as he was bid, 37 and this time his eyes chanced on a small, still thing on the edge of the swaying horizon. It was precisely like the point of a pin. It took an anxious eye to find a lighthouse so tiny.

"Think we'll make it, Captain?" 38

"If this wind holds and the boat don't swamp, we can't do much 39 else," said the captain.

The little boat, lifted by each towering sea and splashed viciously 40 by the crests, made progress that in the absence of seaweed was not apparent to those in her. She seemed just a wee thing wallowing miraculously, top up, at the mercy of five oceans. Occasionally a great spread of water, like white flames, swarmed into her.

"Bail her, cook," said the captain, serenely.   41
"All right, Captain," said the cheerful cook.   42

III

It would be difficult to describe the subtle brotherhood of men that was   43
here established on the seas. No one said that it was so. No one mentioned it. But it dwelt in the boat, and each man felt it warm him. They
were a captain, an oiler, a cook, and a correspondent, and they were
friends—friends in a more curiously iron-bound degree than may be
common. The hurt captain, lying against the water-jar in the bow,
spoke always in a low voice and calmly; but he could never command a
more ready and swiftly obedient crew than the motley three of the dinghy. It was more than a mere recognition of what was best for the common safety. There was surely in it a quality that was personal and heart-
felt. And after this devotion to the commander of the boat, there was
this comradeship, that the correspondent, for instance, who had been
taught to be cynical of men, knew even at the time was the best experience of his life. But no one said that it was so. No one mentioned it.

"I wish we had a sail," remarked the captain. "We might try my   44
overcoat on the end of an oar, and give you two boys a chance to rest." So
the cook and the correspondent held the mast and spread wide the overcoat; the oiler steered; and the little boat made good way with her new
rig. Sometimes the oiler had to scull sharply to keep a sea from breaking
into the boat, but otherwise sailing was a success.

Meanwhile the lighthouse had been growing slowly larger. It had   45
now almost assumed color, and appeared like a little gray shadow on the
sky. The man at the oars could not be prevented from turning his head
rather often to try for a glimpse of this little gray shadow.

At last, from the top of each wave, the men in the tossing boat   46
could see land. Even as the lighthouse was an upright shadow on the sky,
this land seemed but a long black shadow on the sea. It certainly was
thinner than paper. "We must be about opposite New Smyrna," said the
cook, who had coasted this shore often in schooners. "Captain, by the
way, I believe they abandoned that life-saving station there about a
year ago."

"Did they?" said the captain.   47

The wind slowly died away. The cook and the correspondent were   48
not now obliged to slave in order to hold high the oar; but the waves
continued their old impetuous swooping at the dinghy, and the little
craft, no longer under way, struggled woundily over them. The oiler or
the correspondent took the oars again.

Shipwrecks are *apropos* of nothing. If men could only train for them   49 and have them occur when the men had reached pink condition, there would be less drowning at sea. Of the four in the dinghy none had slept any time worth mentioning for two days and two nights previous to embarking in the dinghy, and in the excitement of clambering about the deck of a foundering ship they had also forgotten to eat heartily.

For these reasons, and for others, neither the oiler nor the corre- 50 spondent was fond of rowing at this time. The correspondent wondered ingenuously how in the name of all that was sane could there be people who thought it amusing to row a boat. It was not an amusement; it was a diabolical punishment, and even a genius of mental aberrations could never conclude that it was anything but a horror to the muscles and a crime against the back. He mentioned to the boat in general how the amusement of rowing struck him, and the weary-faced oiler smiled in full sympathy. Previously to the foundering, by the way, the oiler had worked double watch in the engine-room of the ship.

"Take her easy now, boys," said the captain. "Don't spend your- 51 selves. If we have to run a surf you'll need all your strength, because we'll sure have to swim for it. Take your time."

Slowly the land arose from the sea. From a black line it became a 52 line of black and a line of white—trees and sand. Finally the captain said that he could make out a house on the shore. "That's the house of refuge, sure," said the cook. "They'll see us before long, and come out after us."

The distant lighthouse reared high. "The keeper ought to be able 53 to make us out now, if he's looking through a glass," said the captain. "He'll notify the life-saving people."

"None of those other boats could have got ashore to give word of 54 the wreck," said the oiler, in a low voice, "else the life-boat would be out hunting us."

Slowly and beautifully the land loomed out of the sea. The wind 55 came again. It had veered from the northeast to the southeast. Finally a new sound struck the ears of the men in the boat. It was the low thunder of the surf on the shore. "We'll never be able to make the lighthouse now," said the captain. "Swing her head a little more north, Billie."

"A little more north, sir," said the oiler. 56

Whereupon the little boat turned her nose once more down the 57 wind, and all but the oarsman watched the shore grow. Under the influence of this expansion doubt and direful apprehension were leaving the minds of the men. The management of the boat was still most absorbing, but it could not prevent a quiet cheerfulness. In an hour, perhaps, they would be ashore.

Their backbones had become thoroughly used to balancing in the 58 boat, and they now rode this wild colt of a dinghy like circus men. The correspondent thought that he had been drenched to the skin, but happening to feel in the top pocket of his coat, he found therein eight cigars. Four of them were soaked with sea-water; four were perfectly scatheless. After a search, somebody produced three dry matches; and thereupon the four waifs rode in their little boat and, with an assurance of an impending rescue shining in their eyes, puffed at the big cigars, and judged well and ill of all men. Everybody took a drink of water.

IV

"Cook," remarked the captain, "there don't seem to be any signs of life   59
about your house of refuge."

"No," replied the cook. "Funny they don't see us!"   60

A broad stretch of lowly coast lay before the eyes of the men. It was   61
of low dunes topped with dark vegetation. The roar of the surf was plain,
and sometimes they could see the white lip of a wave as it spun up the
beach. A tiny house was blocked out black upon the sky. Southward, the
slim lighthouse lifted its little gray length.

Tide, wind, and waves were swinging the dinghy northward.   62
"Funny they don't see us," said the men.

The surf's roar was here dulled, but its tone was nevertheless thun-   63
derous and mighty. As the boat swam over the great rollers the men sat
listening to this roar. "We'll swamp sure," said everybody.

It is fair to say here that there was not a life-saving station within   64
twenty miles in either direction; but the men did not know this fact, and
in consequence they made dark and opprobrious remarks concerning the
eyesight of the nation's life-savers. Four scowling men sat in the dinghy,
and surpassed records in the invention of epithets.

"Funny they don't see us."   65

The light-heartedness of a former time had completely faded. To   66
their sharpened minds it was easy to conjure pictures of all kinds of in-
competency and blindness and, indeed, cowardice. There was the shore
of the populous land, and it was bitter and bitter to them that from it
came no sign.

"Well," said the captain, ultimately, "I suppose we'll have to make   67
a try for ourselves. If we stay out here too long, we'll none of us have
strength left to swim after the boat swamps."

And so the oiler, who was at the oars, turned the boat straight for   68
the shore. There was a sudden tightening of muscles. There was some
thinking.

"If we don't all get ashore," said the captain—"if we don't all get   69
ashore, I suppose you fellows know where to send news of my finish?"

They then briefly exchanged some addresses and admonitions. As   70
for the reflections of the men, there was a great deal of rage in them. Perchance they might be formulated thus: "If I am going to be drowned—if
I am going to be drowned—if I am going to be drowned, why, in the

name of the seven mad gods who rule the sea, was I allowed to come thus far and contemplate sand and trees? Was I brought here merely to have my nose dragged away as I was about to nibble the sacred cheese of life? It is preposterous! If this old ninny-woman, Fate, cannot do better than this, she should be deprived of the management of men's fortunes. She is an old hen who knows not her intention. If she has decided to drown me, why did she not do it in the beginning, and save me all this trouble? The whole affair is absurd. . . . But no; she cannot mean to drown me. She dare not drown me. She cannot drown me. Not after all this work!" Afterward the man might have had an impulse to shake his fist at the clouds. "Just you drown me, now, and then hear what I call you!"

The billows that came at this time were more formidable. They 71 seemed always just about to break and roll over the little boat in a turmoil of foam. There was a preparatory and long growl in the speech of them. No mind unused to the sea would have concluded that the dinghy could ascend these sheer heights in time. The shore was still afar. The oiler was a wily surfman. "Boys," he said swiftly, "she won't live three minutes more, and we're too far out to swim. Shall I take her to sea again, Captain?"

"Yes; go ahead!" said the captain. 72

This oiler, by a series of quick miracles and fast and steady oars- 73 manship, turned the boat in the middle of the surf and took her safely to sea again.

There was a considerable silence as the boat bumped over the fur- 74 rowed sea to deeper water. Then somebody in gloom spoke; "Well, anyhow, they must have seen us from the shore by now."

The gulls went in slanting flight up the wind toward the gray, deso- 75 late east. A squall, marked by dingy clouds, and clouds brick-red, like smoke from a burning building, appeared from the southeast.

"What do you think of those life-saving people? Ain't they peaches?" 76

"Funny they haven't seen us." 77

"Maybe they think we're out here for sport! Maybe they think we're 78 fishin'. Maybe they think we're damned fools."

It was a long afternoon. A changed tide tried to force them south- 79 ward, but wind and wave said northward. Far ahead, where coast-line, sea, and sky formed their mighty angle, there were little dots which seemed to indicate a city on the shore.

"St. Augustine?" 80

The captain shook his head. "Too near Mosquito Inlet." 81

And the oiler rowed, and then the correspondent rowed; then the 82 oiler rowed. It was a weary business. The human back can become the seat of more aches and pains than are registered in books for the composite anatomy of a regiment. It is a limited area, but it can become the theater of innumerable muscular conflicts, tangles, wrenches, knots, and other comforts.

"Did you ever like to row, Billie?" asked the correspondent.   83

"No," said the oiler; "hang it!"   84

When one exchanged the rowing-seat for a place in the bottom of   85
the boat, he suffered a bodily depression that caused him to be careless of
everything save an obligation to wiggle one finger. There was cold sea-
water swashing to and fro in the boat, and he lay in it. His head, pil-
lowed on a thwart, was within an inch of the swirl of a wave-crest, and
sometimes a particularly obstreperous sea came inboard and drenched
him once more. But these matters did not annoy him. It is almost certain that if the boat had capsized he would have tumbled comfortably
out upon the ocean as if he felt sure that it was a great, soft mattress.

"Look! There's a man on the shore!"   86

"Where?"   87

"There! See 'im? See 'im?"   88

"Yes, sure! He's walking along."   89

"Now he's stopped. Look! He's facing us!"   90

"He's waving at us!"   91

"So he is! By thunder!"   92

"Ah, now we're all right! Now we're all right! There'll be a boat   93
out here for us in half an hour!"

"He's going on. He's running. He's going up to that house there."   94

The remote beach seemed lower than the sea, and it required a   95
searching glance to discern the little black figure. The captain saw a
floating stick, and they rowed to it. A bath towel was by some weird
chance in the boat, and tying this on the stick, the captain waved it. The
oarsman did not dare turn his head, so he was obliged to ask questions.

"What's he doing now?"   96

"He's standing still again. He's looking, I think. . . . There he   97
goes again—toward the house. . . . Now he's stopped again."

"Is he waving at us?"   98

"No, not now; he was, though."   99

"Look! There comes another man!"   100

"He's running."   101

"Look at him go, would you!"   102

"Why, he's on a bicycle. Now he's met the other man. They're both   103
waving at us. Look!"

"There comes something up the beach."   104

"What the devil is that thing?"   105

"Why, it looks like a boat."   106

"Why, certainly, it's a boat."   107

"No; it's on wheels."   108

"Yes, so it is. Well, that must be the life-boat. They drag them   109
along shore on a wagon."

"That's the life-boat, sure."   110

"No, by——, it's—it's an omnibus."   111

"I tell you it's a life-boat." 112

"It is not! It's an omnibus. I can see it plain. See? One of these big 113
hotel omnibuses."

"By thunder, you're right. It's an omnibus, sure as fate. What do 114
you suppose they are doing with an omnibus? Maybe they are going
around collecting the life-crew, hey?"

"That's it, likely. Look! There's a fellow waving a little black flag. 115
He's standing on the steps of the omnibus. There come those other two
fellows. Now they're all talking together. Look at the fellow with the
flag. Maybe he ain't waving it!"

"That ain't a flag, is it? That's his coat. Why, certainly, that's 116
his coat."

"So it is; it's his coat. He's taken it off and is waving it around his 117
head. But would you look at him swing it!"

"Oh, say, there isn't any life-saving station there. That's just a 118
winter-resort hotel omnibus that has brought over some of the boarders
to see us drown."

"What's that idiot with the coat mean? What's he signaling, 119
anyhow?"

"It looks as if he were trying to tell us to go north. There must be a 120
life-saving station up there."

"No; he thinks we're fishing. Just giving us a merry hand. See? 121
Ah, there, Willie!"

"Well, I wish I could make something out of those signals. What 122
do you suppose he means?"

"He don't mean anything; he's just playing." 123

"Well, if he'd just signal us to try the surf again, or to go to sea 124
and wait, or go north, or go south, or go to hell, there would be some
reason in it. But look at him! He just stand there and keeps his coat
revolving like a wheel. The ass!"

"There come more people." 125

"Now there's quite a mob. Look! Isn't that a boat?" 126

"Where? Oh, I see where you mean. No, that's no boat." 127

"That fellow is still waving his coat." 128

"He must think we like to see him do that. Why don't he quit it? 129
It don't mean anything."

"I don't know. I think he is trying to make us go north. It must be 130
that there's a life-saving station there somewhere."

"Say, he ain't tired yet. Look at 'im wave!" 131

"Wonder how long he can keep that up. He's been revolving his 132
coat ever since he caught sight of us. He's an idiot. Why aren't they getting men to bring a boat out? A fishing-boat—one of those big yawls—
could come out here all right. Why don't he do something?"

"Oh, it's all right now." 133

"They'll have a boat out here for us in less than no time, now that 134
they've seen us."

A faint yellow tone came into the sky over the low land. The shad- 135
ows on the sea slowly deepened. The wind bore coldness with it, and the
men began to shiver.

"Holy smoke!" said one, allowing his voice to express his impious 136
mood, "if we keep on monkeying out here! If we've got to flounder out
here all night!"

"Oh, we'll never have to stay here all night! Don't you worry. 137
They've seen us now, and it won't be long before they'll come chasing out
after us."

The shore grew dusky. The man waving a coat blended gradually 138
into this gloom, and it swallowed in the same manner the omnibus and
the group of people. The spray, when it dashed uproariously over the
side, made the voyagers shrink and swear like men who were being
branded.

"I'd like to catch the chump who waved the coat. I feel like soak- 139
ing him one, just for luck."

"Why? What did he do?" 140

"Oh, nothing, but then he seemed so damned cheerful." 141

In the meantime the oiler rowed, and then the correspondent 142
rowed, and then the oiler rowed. Gray-faced and bowed forward, they
mechanically, turn by turn, plied the leaden oars. The form of the lighthouse had vanished from the southern horizon, but finally a pale star
appeared, just lifting from the sea. The streaked saffron in the west
passed before the all-merging darkness, and the sea to the east was black.
The land had vanished, and was expressed only by the low and drear
thunder of the surf.

"If I am going to be drowned—if I am going to be drowned—if I 143
am going to be drowned, why, in the name of the seven mad gods who
rule the sea, was I allowed to come thus far and contemplate sand and
trees? Was I brought here merely to have my nose dragged away as I was
about to nibble the sacred cheese of life?"

The patient captain, drooped over the water-jar, was sometimes 144
obliged to speak to the oarsman.

"Keep her head up! Keep her head up!" 145

"Keep her head up, sir." The voices were weary and low. 146

This was surely a quiet evening. All save the oarsman lay heavily 147
and listlessly in the boat's bottom. As for him, his eyes were just capable
of noting the tall black waves that swept forward in a most sinister silence, save for an occasional subdued growl of a crest.

The cook's head was on a thwart, and he looked without interest at 148
the water under his nose. He was deep in other scenes. Finally he spoke.
"Billie," he murmured dreamfully, "what kind of pie do you like best?"

V

"Pie!" said the oiler and the correspondent, agitatedly. "Don't talk about those things, blast you!" 149

"Well," said the cook, "I was just thinking about ham sandwiches, and—" 150

A night on the sea in an open boat is a long night. As darkness settled finally, the shine of the light, lifting from the sea in the south, changed to full gold. On the northern horizon a new light appeared, a small bluish gleam on the edge of the waters. These two lights were the furniture of the world. Otherwise there was nothing but waves. 151

Two men huddled in the stern, and distances were so magnificent in the dinghy that the rower was enabled to keep his feet partly warm by thrusting them under his companions. Their legs indeed extended far under the rowing-seat until they touched the feet of the captain forward. Sometimes, despite the efforts of the tired oarsman, a wave came piling into the boat, an icy wave of the night, and the chilling water soaked them anew. They would twist their bodies for a moment and groan, and sleep the dead sleep once more, while the water in the boat gurgled about them as the craft rocked. 152

The plan of the oiler and the correspondent was for one to row until he lost the ability, and then arouse the other from his sea-water couch in the bottom of the boat. 153

The oiler plied the oars until his head drooped forward and the overpowering sleep blinded him; and he rowed yet afterward. Then he touched a man in the bottom of the boat, and called his name. "Will you spell me for a little while?" he said meekly. 154

"Sure, Billie," said the correspondent, awaking and dragging himself to a sitting position. They exchanged places carefully, and the oiler, cuddling down in the sea-water at the cook's side, seemed to go to sleep instantly. 155

The particular violence of the sea had ceased. The waves came without snarling. The obligation of the man at the oars was to keep the boat headed so that the tilt of the rollers would not capsize her, and to preserve her from filling when the crests rushed past. The black waves were silent and hard to be seen in the darkness. Often one was almost upon the boat before the oarsman was aware. 156

In a low voice the correspondent addressed the captain. He was not sure that the captain was awake, although this iron man seemed to be always awake. "Captain, shall I keep her making for that light north, sir?" 157

The same steady voice answered him. "Yes. Keep it about two points off the port bow." 158

The cook had tied a life-belt around himself in order to get even the warmth which this clumsy cork contrivance could donate, and he 159 seemed almost stove-like when a rower, whose teeth invariably chattered wildly as soon as he ceased his labor, dropped down to sleep.

The correspondent, as he rowed, looked down at the two men 160 sleeping under foot. The cook's arm was around the oiler's shoulders, and, with their fragmentary clothing and haggard faces, they were the babes of the sea—a grotesque rendering of the old babes in the wood.

Later he must have grown stupid at his work, for suddenly there 161 was a growling of water, and a crest came with a roar and a swash into the boat, and it was a wonder that it did not set the cook afloat in his life-belt. The cook continued to sleep, but the oiler sat up, blinking his eyes and shaking with the new cold.

"Oh, I'm awful sorry, Billie," said the correspondent, contritely. 162

"That's all right, old boy," said the oiler, and lay down again and 163 was asleep.

Presently it seemed that even the captain dozed, and the correspon- 164 dent thought that he was the one man afloat on all the oceans. The wind had a voice as it came over the waves, and it was sadder than the end.

There was a long, loud swishing astern of the boat, and a gleaming 165 trail of phosphorescence, like blue flame, was furrowed on the black waters. It might have been made by a monstrous knife.

Then there came a stillness, while the correspondent breathed with 166 the open mouth and looked at the sea.

Suddenly there was another swish and another long flash of bluish light, and this time it was alongside the boat, and might almost have been reached with an oar. The correspondent saw an enormous fin speed like a shadow through the water, hurling the crystalline spray and leaving the long glowing trail.

The correspondent looked over his shoulder at the captain. His face 167 was hidden, and he seemed to be asleep. He looked at the babes of the sea. They certainly were asleep. So, being bereft of sympathy, he leaned a little way to one side and swore softly into the sea.

But the thing did not then leave the vicinity of the boat. Ahead or 168 astern, on one side or the other, at intervals long or short, fled the long sparkling streak, and there was to be heard the whiroo of the dark fin. The speed and power of the thing was greatly to be admired. It cut the water like a gigantic and keen projectile.

The presence of this biding thing did not affect the man with the 169 same horror that it would if he had been a picnicker. He simply looked at the sea dully and swore in an undertone.

Nevertheless, it is true that he did not wish to be alone with the 170 thing. He wished one of his companions to awake by chance and keep him company with it. But the captain hung motionless over the water-jar, and the oiler and the cook in the bottom of the boat were plunged in slumber.

VI

"If I am going to be drowned—if I am going to be drowned—if I am 171
going to be drowned, why, in the name of the seven mad gods who rule
the sea, was I allowed come thus far and contemplate sand and trees?"

During this dismal night, it may be remarked that a man would 172
conclude that it was really the intention of the seven mad gods to drown
him, despite the abominable injustice of it. For it was certainly an abominable injustice to drown a man who had worked so hard, so hard. The
man felt it would be a crime most unnatural. Other people had drowned
at sea since galleys swarmed with painted sails, but still—

When it occurs to a man that nature does not regard him as impor- 173
tant, and that she feels she would not maim the universe by disposing of
him, he at first wishes to throw bricks at the temple, and he hates deeply
the fact that there are no bricks and no temples. Any visible expression
of nature would surely be pelleted with his jeers.

Then, if there be no tangible thing to hoot, he feels, perhaps, the 174
desire to confront a personification and indulge in pleas, bowed to one
knee, and with hands supplicant, saying, "Yes, but I love myself."

A high cold star on a winter's night is the word he feels that she 175
says to him. Thereafter he knows the pathos of his situation.

The men in the dinghy had not discussed these matters, but each 176
had, no doubt, reflected upon them in silence and according to his mind.
There was seldom any expression upon their faces save the general one of
complete weariness. Speech was devoted to the business of the boat.

To chime the notes of his emotion, a verse mysteriously entered the 177
correspondent's head. He had even forgotten that he had forgotten this
verse, but it suddenly was in his mind.

A soldier of the Legion lay dying an Algiers;
There was lack of woman's nursing, there was dearth of woman's
    tears;
But a comrade stood beside him, and he took that comrade's hand,
And he said, "I never more shall see my own, my native land."

In his childhood the correspondent had been made acquainted with 178
the fact that a soldier of the Legion lay dying in Algiers, but he had
never regarded it as important. Myriads of his school-fellows had informed him of the soldier's plight, but the dinning had naturally ended
by making him perfectly indifferent. He had never considered it his affair that a soldier of the Legion lay dying in Algiers, nor had it appeared
to him as a matter for sorrow. It was less to him than breaking of a pencil's point.

Now, however, it quaintly came to him as a human, living thing. 179
It was no longer merely a picture of a few throes in the breast of a poet,

meanwhile drinking tea and warming his feet at the grate; it was an actuality—stern, mournful, and fine.

The correspondent plainly saw the soldier. He lay on the sand with 180
his feet out straight and still. While his pale left hand was upon his chest
in an attempt to thwart the going of his life, the blood came between his
fingers. In the far Algerian distance, a city of low square forms was set
against a sky that was faint with the last sunset hues. The correspondent,
plying the oars and dreaming of the slow and slower movements of the
lips of the soldier, was moved by a profound and perfectly impersonal
comprehension. He was sorry for the soldier of the Legion who lay dying
in Algiers.

The thing which had followed the boat and waited had evidently 181
grown bored at the delay. There was no longer to be heard the slash of
the cutwater, and there was no longer the flame of the long trail. The
light in the north still glimmered, but it was apparently no nearer to the
boat. Sometimes the boom of the surf rang in the correspondent's ears,
and he turned the craft seaward then and rowed harder. Southward, some
one had evidently built a watch-fire on the beach. It was too low and too
far to be seen, but it made a shimmering, roseate reflection upon the
bluff back of it, and this could be discerned from the boat. The wind
came stronger, and sometimes a wave suddenly raged out like a mountain-
cat, and there was to be seen the sheen and sparkle of a broken crest.

The captain, in the bow, moved on his water-jar and sat erect. 182
"Pretty long night," he observed to the correspondent. He looked at the
shore. "Those life-saving people take their time."

"Did you see that shark playing around?" 183

"Yes, I saw him. He was a big fellow, all right." 184

"Wish I had known you were awake." 185

Later the correspondent spoke into the bottom of the boat. 186

"Billie!" There was a slow and gradual disentanglement. "Billie, 187
will you spell me?"

"Sure," said the oiler. 188

As soon as the correspondent touched the cold, comfortable sea- 189
water in the bottom of the boat and had huddled close to the cook's life-
belt he was deep in sleep, despite the fact that his teeth played all the
popular airs. This sleep was so good to him that it was but a moment
before he heard a voice call his name in a tone that demonstrated the last
stages of exhaustion. "Will you spell me?"

"Sure, Billie." 190

The light in the north had mysteriously vanished, but the corre- 191
spondent took his course from the wide-awake captain.

Later in the night they took the boat farther out to sea, and the 192
captain directed the cook to take one oar at the stern and keep the boat
facing the seas. He was to call out if he should hear the thunder of the

surf. This plan enabled the oiler and the correspondent to get respite together. "We'll give those boys a chance to get into shape again," said the captain. They curled down and, after a few preliminary chatterings and trembles, slept once more the dead sleep. Neither knew they had bequeathed to the cook the company of another shark, or perhaps the same shark.

As the boat caroused on the waves, spray occasionally bumped over 193 the side and gave them a fresh soaking, but this had no power to break their repose. The ominous slash of the wind and the water affected them as it would have affected mummies.

"Boys," said the cook, with the notes of every reluctance in his 194 voice, "she's drifted in pretty close. I guess one of you had better take her to sea again." The correspondent, aroused, heard the crash of the toppled crests.

As he was rowing, the captain gave him some whisky and water, 195 and this steadied the chills out of him. "If I ever get ashore and anybody shows me even a photograph of an oar—"

At last there was a short conversation. 196

"Billie! . . . Billie, will you spell me?" 197

"Sure," said the oiler. 198

VII

When the correspondent again opened his eyes, the sea and the sky were 199 each of the gray hue of the dawning. Later, carmine and gold was painted upon the waters. The morning appeared finally, in its splendor, with a sky of pure blue, and the sunlight flamed on the tips of the waves.

On the distant dunes were set many little black cottages, and a tall 200 white windmill reared above them. No man, nor dog, nor bicycle appeared on the beach. The cottages might have formed a deserted village.

The voyagers scanned the shore. A conference was held in the boat. 201 "Well," said the captain, "if no help is coming, we might better try a run through the surf right away. If we stay out here much longer we will be too weak to do anything for ourselves at all." The others silently acquiesced in this reasoning. The boat was headed for the beach. The correspondent wondered if none ever ascended the tall wind-tower, and if then they never looked seaward. This tower was a giant, standing with its back to the plight of the ants. It represented in a degree, to the correspondent, the serenity of nature amid the struggles of the individual— nature in the wind, and nature in the vision of men. She did not seem cruel to him then, nor beneficent, nor treacherous, nor wise. But she was indifferent, flatly indifferent. It is, perhaps, plausible that a man in this situation, impressed with the unconcern of the universe, should see the innumerable flaws of his life and have them taste wickedly in his mind and wish for another chance. A distinction between right and wrong seems absurdly clear to him, then, in this new ignorance of the grave-edge, and he understands that if he were given another opportunity he would mend his conduct and his words, and be better and brighter during an introduction or at a tea.

"Now, boys," said the captain, "she is going to swamp sure. All 202 we can do is to work her in as far as possible, and then when she swamps, pile out and scramble for the beach. Keep cool now, and don't jump until she swamps sure."

The oiler took the oars. Over his shoulders he scanned the surf. 203 "Captain," he said, "I think I'd better bring her about, and keep her head on to the seas, and back her in."

"All right, Billie," said the captain. "Back her in." The oiler 204 swung the boat then, and, seated in the stern, the cook and the correspondent were obliged to look over their shoulders to contemplate the lonely and indifferent shore.

The monstrous inshore rollers heaved the boat high until the men 205 were again enabled to see the white sheets of water scudding up the slanted beach. "We won't get in very close," said the captain. Each time a man could wrest his attention from the rollers, he turned his glance toward the shore, and in the expression of the eyes during this contemplation there was a singular quality. The correspondent, observing the others, knew that they were not afraid, but the full meaning of their glances was shrouded.

As for himself, he was too tired to grapple fundamentally with the 206 fact. He tried to coerce his mind into thinking of it, but the mind was dominated at this time by the muscles, and the muscles said they did not care. It merely occurred to him that if he should drown it would be a shame.

There were no hurried words, no pallor, no plain agitation. The 207 men simply looked at the shore. "Now, remember to get well clear of the boat when you jump," said the captain.

Seaward the crest of a roller suddenly fell with a thunderous crash, 208 and the long white comber came roaring down upon the boat.

"Steady now," said the captain. The men were silent. They turned 209 their eyes from the shore to the comber and waited. The boat slid up the incline, leaped at the furious top, bounced over it, and swung down the long back of the wave. Some water had been shipped, and the cook bailed it out.

But the next crest crashed also. The tumbling, boiling flood of 210 white water caught the boat and whirled it almost perpendicular. Water swarmed in from all sides. The correspondent had his hands on the gunwale at this time, and when the water entered at that place he swiftly withdrew his fingers, as if he objected to wetting them.

The little boat, drunken with this weight of water, reeled and 211
snuggled deeper into the sea.

"Bail her out, cook! Bail her out!" said the captain. 212

"All right, Captain," said the cook. 213

"Now, boys, the next one will do for us sure," said the oiler. 214
"Mind to jump clear of the boat."

The third wave moved forward, huge, furious, implacable. It fairly 215
swallowed the dinghy, and almost simultaneously the men tumbled into
the sea. A piece of life-belt had lain in the bottom of the boat, and as the
correspondent went overboard he held this to his chest with his left hand.

The January water was icy, and he reflected immediately that it was 216
colder than he had expected to find it off the coast of Florida. This appeared to his dazed mind as a fact important enough to be noted at the
time. The coldness of the water was sad; it was tragic. This fact was
somehow mixed and confused with his opinion of his own situation so
that it seemed almost a proper reason for tears. The water was cold.

When he came to the surface he was conscious of little but the 217
noisy water. Afterward he saw his companions in the sea. The oiler was
ahead in the race. He was swimming strongly and rapidly. Off to the
correspondent's left, the cook's great white and corked back bulged out
of the water; and in the rear the captain was hanging with his one good
hand to the keel of the overturned dinghy.

There is a certain immovable quality to a shore, and the correspon- 218
dent wondered at it amid the confusion of the sea.

It seemed also very attractive; but the correspondent knew that it 219
was a long journey, and he paddled leisurely. The piece of life-preserver
lay under him, and sometimes he whirled down the incline of a wave as if
he were on a hand-sled.

But finally he arrived at a place in the sea where travel was beset 220
with difficulty. He did not pause swimming to inquire what manner of
current had caught him, but there his progress ceased. The shore was set
before him like a bit of scenery on a stage, and he looked at it, and
understood with his eyes each detail of it.

As the cook passed, much farther to the left, the captain was call- 221
ing to him, "Turn over on your back, cook! Turn over on your back and
use the oar."

"All right, sir." The cook turned on his back, and, paddling with 222
an oar, went ahead as if he were a canoe.

Presently the boat also passed to the left of the correspondent, with 223
the captain clinging with one hand to the keel. He would have appeared
like a man raising himself to look over a board fence if it were not for the
extraordinary gymnastics of the boat. The correspondent marveled that
the captain could still hold to it.

They passed on nearer to shore,—the oiler, the cook, the cap- 224
tain,—and following them went the water-jar, bouncing gaily over
the seas.

The correspondent remained in the grip of this strange new enemy, 225
a current. The shore, with its white slope of sand and its green bluff,
topped with little silent cottages, was spread like a picture before him.
It was very near to him then, but he was impressed as one who, in a
gallery, looks at a scene from Brittany or Algiers.

He thought: "I am going to drown? Can it be possible? Can it be 226
possible? Can it be possible?" Perhaps an individual must consider his
own death to be the final phenomenon of nature.

But later a wave perhaps whirled him out of this small deadly cur- 227
rent, for he found suddenly that he could again make progress toward
the shore. Later still he was aware that the captain, clinging with one
hand to the keel of the dinghy, had his face turned away from the shore
and toward him, and was calling his name. "Come to the boat! Come to
the boat!"

In his struggle to reach the captain and the boat, he reflected that 228
when one gets properly wearied drowning must really be a comfortable
arrangement—a cessation of hostilities accompanied by a large degree of
relief; and he was glad of it, for the main thing in his mind for some
moments had been horror of the temporary agony; he did not wish to
be hurt.

Presently he saw a man running along the shore. He was undress- 229
ing with most remarkable speed. Coat, trousers, shirt, everything flew
magically off him.

"Come to the boat!" called the captain. 230

"All right, Captain." As the correspondent paddled, he saw the 231
captain let himself down to bottom and leave the boat. Then the correspondent performed his one little marvel of the voyage. A large wave
caught him and flung him with ease and supreme speed completely over
the boat and far beyond it. It struck him even then as an event in gymnastics and a true miracle of the sea. An overturned boat in the surf is not
a plaything to a swimming man.

The correspondent arrived in water that reached only to his waist, 232
but his condition did not enable him to stand for more than a moment.
Each wave knocked him into a heap, and the undertow pulled at him.

Then he saw the man who had been running and undressing, and 233
undressing and running, come bounding into the water. He dragged
ashore the cook, and then waded toward the captain; but the captain
waved him away and sent him to the correspondent. He was naked—
naked as a tree in winter; but a halo was about his head, and he shone
like a saint. He gave a strong pull, and a long drag, and a bully heave at
the correspondent's hand. The correspondent, schooled in the minor for-
mulae, said, "Thanks, old man." But suddenly the man cried, "What's
that?" He pointed a swift finger. The correspondent said, "Go."

In the shallows, face downward, lay the oiler. His forehead touched 234
sand that was periodically, between each wave, clear of the sea.

The correspondent did not know all that transpired afterward. 235

When he achieved safe ground he fell, striking the sand with each particular part of his body. It was as if he had dropped from a roof, but the thud was grateful to him.

It seems that instantly the beach was populated with men with 236 blankets, clothes, and flasks, and women with coffee-pots and all the remedies sacred to their minds. The welcome of the land to the men from the sea was warm and generous; but a still and dripping shape was carried slowly up the beach; the land's welcome for it could only be the . . . sinister hospitality of the grave.

When it came night, the white waves paced to and fro in the 237 moonlight, and the wind brought the sound of the great voice to the men on shore, and they felt that they could be interpreters.

Reading and Interpreting

VOCABULARY

Use your dictionary as necessary to find the meaning of the following words as used in "The Open Boat":

doggedly (26)   uncanny (30)   apropos (49)   ingenuously (50)

foundering (50)   opprobrious (64)   obstreperous (85)   myriads (178)

roseate (181)   respite (192)   implacable (215)

CONCEPT ANALYSIS

1. Many of the passages in the story suggest that human beings, unlike other creatures, are out of their element in nature. Cite images, dialogues, reflections, and occurrences that illustrate the helplessness of Crane's characters in their struggle for survival.
2. In section VI, Crane states that the correspondent "was moved by a profound and perfectly impersonal comprehension" (180). What specifically does the correspondent comprehend? In a larger sense, what has he grown to understand?
3. Whom do you view as the hero of "The Open Boat"? Explain your answer with specific references to the actions of the various characters.
4. In the last paragraph of "The Open Boat" Crane claims that the men heard the great voice of the sea and felt that they could be its interpreters. Discuss the meaning of this statement.

Like much war literature, "The Open Boat" is a story without women characters. How did the absence of women in the story strike you? How might a woman character have been introduced and how might this have changed the story?

Thinking and Writing

RHETORICAL TECHNIQUE

1. In fiction, when sympathetic characters' lives are at stake, the reader's natural wish is that they survive their plight. The uncertainty of that outcome is the primary source of suspense. What specific elements in "The Open Boat" delay the story's resolution and thereby increase the suspense? Is the story more or less successful because of these interruptions?

2. A fictional piece is never *wholly* imagined. Specify some points of Crane's diary account of the shipwreck that found their way into his short story. What are some significant omissions? Why do you think the author made these omissions?

3. Part of the challenge of "The Open Boat" is Crane's shifts of narrative viewpoint between the all-knowing storyteller looking in on the boat and the limited perspective of the four men looking out. The omniscient narrator comments that "The little boat, lifted by each towering sea and splashed viciously by the crests, made progress that in the absence of seaweed was not apparent to those in her. She seemed just a wee thing wallowing miraculously, top up, at the mercy of five oceans." From the men's point of view, however, "None of them knew the color of the sky. Their eyes glanced level, and were fastened upon the waves that swept toward them."

   Imagine that you were filming "The Open Boat." Select some passages that you would photograph from the omniscient overview and others that would reflect the vision of the men inside the boat.

COMPOSITION

Stephen Crane suggests that brotherhood and close friendship result among people who find themselves engaged in a common struggle. Narrate a personal experience that illustrates this idea. Be sure to clearly distinguish the personalities of your subjects, as Crane does, and carefully describe the nature of the struggle that unites them.

THE WRITTEN RESPONSE

Writing Workshop

The readings in this chapter suggest that nature is a teacher if human beings are willing to learn. The experiences in nature from which we learn may be as extraordinary as a shipwreck or as seemingly ordinary as the observation of ants in a backyard. The experience may be a single event or it may extend over a period of time.

1. Think of an experience in nature that was meaningful to you. Briefly note down what occurred.
2. Reflect upon the experience and write about what it meant to you. Roughly formulate this reflection into a thesis statement.
3. Note in chronological order the incidents that made up the experience. Review your notes and decide which incident was the turning point. Consider where in the sequence of incidents you want to introduce your thesis: at the beginning or in the middle of the action.
4. Draft your narrative. Then review your draft. Using the principles described in the Sequence and Coherence section of this chapter, eliminate any items that do not reinforce your central idea or move your narrative forward. Ask yourself whether the sequence of sentences accurately conveys the sequence of events that make up the experience.
5. Refine your thesis so that it clearly expresses the lesson you learned and wish to share with your reader.
6. Consider your conclusion. Does it effectively close your narrative by referring to your central idea? Review the conclusions of the various narratives in this chapter as a guide.

Topics for Critical Thinking and Writing

1. As "The Gray Beginnings" and "The Open Boat" demonstrate, colors and textures can add an important dimension to a narrative. Tell a story of an experience in nature; set the scene with colors and textures of the natural surroundings.
2. The competitiveness of life in modern industrialized society is captured in such nature images as "the rat race" or "the jungle." Formulate a thesis that embodies this idea and support your thesis with a narrative that illustrates it.

Synthesis Questions

1. In Genesis God gives man dominion over all the other creatures of the universe. How would you characterize man's relationship to the other creatures of the earth in "The Gray Beginnings," "The Open Boat," and "The Human Being and the Dinosaur"? Formulate a thesis statement that conveys your central idea on this subject and encompasses the works to which you will refer.
2. The two creation narratives (or cosmologies) belonging to an oral tradition are meant to be read aloud. The fable form used by Thurber is also an oral genre. Read these works aloud or listen to them being read. Formulate a thesis that expresses the value of reading narratives aloud and refer to these works in support of the thesis.
3. Each narrative in this chapter makes a powerful emotional appeal with its humor, suspense, tone of authority, or vivid language. Select the works that you feel are most effective. Formulate a thesis that accounts for your response and elaborate it in an essay.

Refining Your Essay

1. Locate your thesis statement and underscore it. Is it expressed clearly enough so that a reader could restate it in his or her own words?
2. Review your introduction and your conclusion to ensure that they aptly frame your narrative by leading to and reinforcing your thesis.
3. Review the events that make up your narrative essay. Eliminate the items that are repetitive or nonessential to the point of your story. Find and underscore the turning point in your narrative. Is its significance evident to your reader?
4. Read your essay aloud to check for transitional expressions such as time, example, and other directional signals. Add these where necessary to improve the flow of your narrative.
5. In one or two sentences in the margin of your draft, briefly identify your narrator. Scan your essay to ensure that you maintain a point of view consistent with the narrator you have chosen.
6. Consider the rich, eloquent language of the narratives you have read in this chapter—for example: "Stygian world of heated rock and swirling clouds and gloom" ("The Gray Beginnings"). Have you chosen expressions that vividly describe your subject? Choose three significant words or phrases in your narrative and experiment with alternatives to them.

CHAPTER FIVE

Teachers and Students: Making Abstractions Concrete

In this drawing of the top of a professor's desk, objects such as the typewriter and classical statue give concrete representation to abstract notions of academic life: knowledge, communication, and aesthetics. To illustrate a student's perspective of academic life, how would you alter the composition of the drawing? What objects would you add to or remove from the desk?

THE WRITING FOCUS

*Words, when well chosen, have so great a force in them
that a description often gives us more lively ideas than
the sight of things themselves.*

Joseph Addison, *The Spectator*

Eighteenth-century Enlightenment philosophy gave currency to the idea that at birth the human infant's mind is a *tabula rasa,* a clean slate upon which environment, and especially education, inscribe knowledge and values. Sadly, however, as some of this chapter's readings illustrate, the educational process may dampen or even stifle altogether the original enthusiasm of the child.

What is it about successful teaching that facilitates learning? Certainly, one factor is the ability of the teacher to use details and illustrations that make the message vivid and clear. When we turn to religion, the oldest form of systematized human instruction, we find that the parable, or illustrative story, the concrete embodiment of an idea, is universal. Fiction writers, seeking to evoke an emotional response to their themes, use language that calls forth associations or memories from their readers; poetry, by its very nature, speaks through imagery, thus providing the concrete details that stimulate the reader's reflection on a theme.

Making Ideas Concrete

We write to communicate ideas, which by their nature are abstract, general, and sometimes ambiguous. To write effectively, we must be concrete. Concreteness, whether in academic prose or imaginative writing, helps the reader absorb and experience the written word. Concreteness is achieved through

- vivid sensory words (words that convey sense impressions)
- figurative language (metaphor, simile, analogy, allusion)
- quotations and paraphrases of recognized authorities
- examples, cases, and illustrations
- generalizations supported by specific details

VIVID SENSORY VOCABULARY

Adjectives can be rich descriptive words. A window shade is simply a window covering. But the phrase "limp green window shade" from "A Student in Economics," a story in this chapter, helps convey the world of shabby boardinghouses where poor college students lived during the Depression. Such descriptive vocabulary creates an atmosphere that intensifies a central idea.

Writers also add color and intensity to their work with carefully chosen nouns, verbs, and adverbs. Again "A Student in Economics" supplies many examples. One character, for instance, is described as "wagg[ling] his heavy face *mournfully*"; another has "drizzled *dewlaps*," not merely folds of skin under his chin. The use of vivid vocabulary can convey color, texture, expression, sound, and taste in academic as well as creative writing. Such descriptive language is used more sparingly in academic prose, but even in scholarly writing, concrete details bring generalizations and concepts down to earth. In Sidney Painter's history of medieval universities, for example, the forceful adjective *turbulent* captures the violence of schoolmasters and students in those rude times.

FIGURATIVE LANGUAGE

Figures of speech, a type of figurative language, make comparisons between the subject under discussion and a second subject in another aspect of life. Of the two types of figures of speech, the more familiar is the simile, which states a comparison by using the linking expressions *like* or *as*. Poet Stephen Spender uses a simile to write about slum children: "children's faces / Like rootless weeds." This image suggests that the children are unattached to the community; that they have no value in the environment; that they are fragile and without resources to survive, just as weeds are shallowly rooted intruders in a garden.

A metaphor, the other figure of speech, is a *direct* comparison that suggests shared characteristics between different things. A metaphor does not employ the words *like* or *as* to signal the comparison. Metaphors may be embodied in single nouns or verbs as well as in more extended images. For example, in "A Student in Economics" the author uses the verb *whip* to describe the wind blowing across the face of the student, a metaphor that evokes the feeling of pain caused by an actual whip: slashing, stinging, smarting. Paragraph 149 contains an example of an extended image in the description of Dr. Kenshaw's "hard little eyes under craggy brows . . . moving . . . eager for a victim. . . . preying eyes."

Overused metaphors are called clichés. They no longer have the power to create mental images. An example is the expression "with flying colors," which originally referred to the raised flags of victorious armies. But repeatedly applied to victories of far less importance, the image has become stale and meaningless. Writers usually try to avoid such worn expressions, but sometimes a cliché can serve a purpose. In "A Student of Economics," for example, the shallowness of the dean is reflected when he predicts, incorrectly, that the student will succeed "with flying colors."

Another type of figurative language is the analogy, an *extended* comparison that helps clarify an unfamiliar idea by reference to something familiar. Symmetry must be maintained in the comparison; each point of the comparison must have a corresponding pair. For example, the following analogy explains tribal ritual by comparing it to an American college graduation: The stages in a tribal rite of passage—separation, instruction, and return—are mirrored in the graduation ceremony, which begins with students sitting separately from their parents and professors, continues with their receiving advice in the commencement address, and concludes with their return to society, where they embrace their well-wishers and mingle freely with them. With the familiar graduation ceremony extending the frame of reference, the reader is better able to comprehend the tribal ritual.

Allusions, references to literature, religion, and history, can function in the same way as figurative language. They heighten a reader's response to the subject by evoking conscious or unconscious associations. In our Essay for Analysis, for instance, John Ciardi illustrates his contempt for the narrowly practical college student by describing his type as "a Push-button Neanderthal." The reader who recognizes that *Neanderthal* refers to an early stage of human development "gets" the allusion and has a deeper appreciation of Ciardi's point.

QUOTATIONS AND PARAPHRASES OF AUTHORITIES

Quotations and paraphrases of the statements of experts are concrete means of support found most frequently, though not exclusively, in research writing, where they lend authority to the writer's thoughts. When used sparingly and selectively, the apt quotation or paraphrase drives home the writer's point. In the journal article "Student Learning Processes," for example, the researchers include direct quotations from students to substantiate their points. Thus a successful student's own words, "I sit in the front and look in the teacher's face like he's giving me a private lesson," buttress the researcher's view that attentiveness leads to achievement in college.

EXAMPLES, CASES, AND ILLUSTRATIONS

Effective academic writing employs concrete support—examples, case histories, and illustrations—to clarify abstract concepts. These examples may extend from a single word to a paragraph. They provide models, samples, images, and real-life instances to make generalizations and abstractions more concrete. In Painter's essay on medieval education, for instance, the author illustrates his key point that schooling for girls was considered undesirable by citing Philippe de Navarre's belief that girls should be taught to *read* for religious purposes but should not be taught to *write* because "if they knew that art, how could one be sure that they would not write love letters?"

Vignettes (brief narratives) and case histories (reports based on long-term observations of individuals) are additional means of making a writer's thesis or key concepts concrete. For example, Ciardi's opening vignette of his encounter with an unwilling student is the springboard leading to his thesis that a college education should do more than ensure employment.

As you study the Essay for Analysis and read the selections in this chapter, you will see how professional writers make generalizations and abstract ideas concrete, and you will practice fleshing out your assertions with the kinds of details that make your writing come alive for the reader.

JOHN CIARDI

Another School Year—Why?

John Ciardi (1916–1986) was an American poet, teacher, and literary critic who championed the use of modern, idiomatic language in poetry and essay. His poetic style, colloquial in diction and often satirical in tone, is apparent in this essay, which uses everyday speech and a sarcastic tone as well as the compressed images typical of his poetry. A dedicated humanist, Ciardi was a professor at Harvard and Rutgers and had firsthand experience with the type of student he so vividly portrays in this essay.

Let me tell you one of the earliest disasters in my career as a teacher. It was January of 1940 and I was fresh out of graduate school starting my first semester at the University of Kansas City. Part of the reading for the freshman English course was *Hamlet*. Part of the student body was a beanpole with hair on top who came into my class, sat down, folded his arms, and looked at me as if to say: "All right, damn you, teach me something." Two weeks later we started *Hamlet*. Three weeks later he came into my office with his hands on his hips. It is easy to put your hands on your hips if you are not carrying books, and this one was an unburdened soul. "Look," he said. "I came here to be a pharmacist. Why do I have to read this stuff?" And not having a book of his own to point to, he pointed at mine which was lying on the desk.

    New as I was to the faculty, I could have told this specimen a number of things. I could have pointed out that he had enrolled, not in a drugstore mechanics school, but in a college, and that at the end of his course he meant to reach for a scroll that read Bachelor of Science. It

Margin notes:

1   Anecdotal case as introduction.

Metaphor

Vivid vocabulary, double meaning

2   Metaphor

Analogy with other technologies

Vivid vocabulary

would not read: Qualified Pill-Grinding Technician. It would certify that he had specialized in pharmacy and had attained a certain minimum qualification, but it would further certify that he had been exposed to some of the ideas mankind has generated within its history. That is to say, he had not entered a technical training school but a university, and that in universities students enroll for both training and education.

Thesis

I could have told him all this, but it was ₃ fairly obvious he wasn't going to be around long enough for it to matter: at the rate he was going, the first marking period might reasonably be expected to blow him toward the employment agency.

Metaphor

Nevertheless, I was young and I had a high ₄ sense of duty and I tried to put it this way: "For the rest of your life," I said, "your days are going to average out to about twenty-four hours. They will be a little shorter when you are in love, and a little longer when you are out of love, but the average will tend to hold. For eight of these hours, more or less, you will be asleep, and I assume you need neither education nor training to manage to get through that third of your life.

Hyperbole

"Then for about eight hours of each work- ₅ ing day you will, I hope, be usefully employed. Assume you have gone through pharmacy school—or engineering, or aggie, or law school, or whatever—during those eight hours you will be using your professional skills. You will see to it during this third of your life that the cyanide stays out of the aspirin, that the bull doesn't jump the fence, or that your client doesn't go to the electric chair as a result of your incompetence. These are all useful pursuits, they involve skills every man must respect, and they can all bring you good basic satisfactions. Along with everything else, they will probably be what sets your table, supports your wife, and rears your children. They will be your income, and may it always suffice.

General term

Particular images representing professional skills

General term

Particular examples of various "satisfactions"

"But having finished the day's work what ₆ do you do with those other eight hours—with the other third of your life? Let's say you go home to your family. What sort of family are you raising? Will the children ever be exposed to a reasonably penetrating idea at home? We all think of ourselves as citizens of a great democracy. Democracies can exist, however, only as long as they remain intellectually alive. Will you be presiding over a family that maintains some basic contact with the great continuity of democratic intellect? Or is your family life going to be strictly penny-ante and beer on ice? Will there be a book in the house? Will there be a painting a reasonably sensitive man can look at without shuddering? Will your family be able to speak English and to talk about an idea? Will the kids ever get to hear Bach?"

That is about what I said, but this particular pest was not interested. "Look," he said, "you professors raise your kids your way; I'll take care of my own. Me, I'm out to make money."

"I hope you make a lot of it," I told him, "because you're going to be badly stuck for something to do when you're not signing checks."

Fourteen years later, I am still teaching, and I am here to tell you that the business of the college is not only to train you, but to put you in touch with what the best human minds have thought. If you have no time for Shakespeare, for a basic look at philosophy, for the continuity of the fine arts, for that lesson of man's development we call history—then you have no business being in college. You are on your way to being that new species of mechanized savage, the Push-button Neanderthal. Our colleges inevitably graduate a number of such life-forms, but it cannot be said that they went to college; rather the college went through them—without making contact.

No one gets to be a human unaided. There is not time enough in a single lifetime to invent for oneself everything one needs to know in order to be a civilized human.

Assume, for example, that you want to be a physicist. You pass the great stone halls of say, M.I.T., and there cut into the stone are the names of the master scientists. The chances are

General idea

Vivid images representing different lifestyles

Particular examples of "great continuity"

Allusion

7

Metaphor

8

Particular image of a part of life

9

Allusion

Metaphors

Metaphor

10

11

Vivid vocabulary

that few if any of you will leave your names to be cut into those stones. Yet any one of you who managed to stay awake through part of a high school course in physics knows more about physics than did many of those great makers of the past. You know more because they left you what they knew. The first course in any science is essentially a history course. You have to begin by learning what the past learned for you. Except as a man has entered the past of the race he has no function in civilization.

And as this is true of the techniques of   12
mankind, so is it true of mankind's spiritual resources. Most of these resources, both technical and spiritual, are stored in books. Books, the arts, and the techniques of science are man's peculiar accomplishment. When you have read a book, you have added to your human experience. Read Homer and your mind includes a   Allusion
piece of Homer's mind. Through books you can   Metaphor
acquire at least fragments of the mind and experience of Virgil, Dante, Shakespeare—the list is   Allusions
endless. For a great book is necessarily a gift; it   Analogy
offers you a life you have not time to live yourself, and it takes you into a world you have not time to travel in literal time. A civilized human mind is, in essence, one that contains many such lives and many such worlds. If you are too much in a hurry, or too arrogantly proud of your own limitations, to accept as a gift to your humanity some pieces of the minds of Sophocles, of Aris-   Allusions
totle, of Chaucer—and right down the scale and down the ages to Yeats, Einstein, E. B. White, and Ogden Nash—then you may be protected by the laws governing manslaughter, and you may be a voting entity, but you are neither a developed human being nor a useful citizen of a democracy.

I think it was La Rochefoucauld who said   13   Reference to authority
that most people would never fall in love if they hadn't read about it. He might have said that no one would ever manage to become human if he hadn't read about it.

I speak, I am sure, for the faculty of the   14
liberal arts college and for the faculties of the

specialized schools as well, when I say that a university has no real existence and no real purpose except as it succeeds in putting you in touch, both as specialists and as humans, with those human minds your human mind needs to include. The faculty, by its very existence, says implicitly: "We have been aided by many people, and by many books, and by the arts, in our attempt to make ourselves some sort of storehouse of human experience. We are here to make available to you, as best we can, that experience."

Metaphor

Analysis of the Essay

THE PROCESS OF MAKING IDEAS CONCRETE

Examples, Cases, and Illustrations.   Ciardi begins his essay inductively with an anecdotal case to establish a realistic context for his thesis: The proper role of the university is to provide both education and training (paragraph 2, last sentence). Throughout the essay Ciardi's abstract concepts and general statements are followed by illuminating samples, examples, and illustrations in the form of particular aspects representative of a whole. One effective use of this technique appears in paragraph 5, where the author illustrates the general term "usefully employed" with the images of the pharmacist keeping cyanide out of the aspirin, the farmer preventing the bull from jumping the fence, and the lawyer keeping his client from the electric chair. A second series of images representing a lifestyle occurs in the same paragraph: "what sets your table, supports your wife, and rears your children." In the same way, the reference to a "penny-ante and beer on ice" (6) lifestyle portrays more vividly than abstract terms the potential for emptiness in a life without education.

An interesting variation of this technique appears in paragraph 6. Here Ciardi uses a series of questions about specific details of the student's future life to convey the implied thesis of the paragraph: One should remain intellectually alive.

Vivid Vocabulary and Figurative Language.   The humor of Ciardi's vivid vocabulary and figures of speech adds to rather than detracts from the seriousness of his essay. Ciardi's basic opposition is between the nonhuman or the savage on the one hand and the educated or civilized person on the other. The discontented student of the introductory anecdote is referred to as a "specimen" (2), a "pest" (7), a "mechanized savage" (9), a "Push-button Neanderthal" (9), and a "life-form" (9). His idea of education and his degree are derided as a "drugstore-mechanics school" (2) and "Qualified Pill-Grinding Technician" (2), suggesting by analogy such occupations as an automobile mechanic's and a technician's work, which do not require university education.

Ciardi uses other analogies and metaphors to reinforce his thesis. In paragraph 12 he compares a great book to a gift to one's humanity, suggesting that books, like valued gifts, are sources of continual enrichment. Conversely, the rejection of a great book, like the rejection of a freely offered, valuable gift, would be unthinkable to a civilized person. A metaphor in the important concluding paragraph of the essay makes a comparison between university faculty and a storehouse, in the sense that both are resources for treasures that contribute to human growth and pleasure.

Allusions.   Ciardi's essay contains many allusions to writers and thinkers who represent the best of our intellectual tradition. Each allusion is intended to stimulate a response that will strengthen the reader's acceptance of Ciardi's ideas. Ciardi could have made his point here without reference to such specific figures as Bach or Shakespeare, but an appreciation of these names makes his ideas more meaningful and memorable. For this reason, allusions are worth tracing to their sources.

One particularly concrete type of allusion employed by Ciardi is the reference to authority. In paragraph 13, for instance, Ciardi applies the provocative statement about love attributed to the French essayist La Rochefoucauld to his own theme: Learning the great thoughts of the past through reading helps us to become the best kind of human beings we can.

READINGS

A SUFI TALE

The Story of Fire: How to Be Heard While Teaching

Sufis are a mystic sect of the Muslim religion. The following parable is from the wealth of Sufi tales that have been used as teaching instruments by the masters of this sect for a thousand years. A parable by definition is a story that makes an idea concrete.

Once upon a time a man was contemplating the ways in which Nature   1
operates, and he discovered, because of his concentration and application,
how fire could be made.

This man was called Nour. He decided to travel from one commu-   2
nity to another, showing people his discovery.

Nour passed the secret to many groups of people. Some took advan-   3
tage of the knowledge. Others drove him away, thinking that he must be
dangerous, before they had had time to understand how valuable this discovery could be to them. Finally, a tribe before which he demonstrated
became so panic-stricken that they set about him and killed him, being
convinced that he was a demon.

Centuries passed. The first tribe which had learned about fire re-   4
served the secret for their priests, who remained in affluence and power
while the people froze.

The second tribe forgot the art and worshipped instead the instru-   5
ments. The third worshipped a likeness of Nour himself, because it was he
who had taught them. The fourth retained the story of the making of fire
in their legends: some believed them, some did not. The fifth community
really did use fire, and this enabled them to be warmed, to cook their
food, and to manufacture all kinds of useful articles.

After many, many years, a wise man and a small band of his disciples   6
were traveling through the lands of these tribes. The disciples were
amazed at the variety of rituals which they encountered, and one and all
said to their teacher: "But all these procedures are in fact related to the
making of fire, nothing else. We should reform these people!"

The teacher said: "Very well, then. We will restart our journey. By   7 the end of it, those who survive will know the real problems and how to approach them."

When they reached the first tribe, the band was hospitably received. 8 The priests invited the travelers to attend their religious ceremony, the making of fire. When it was over, and the tribe was in a state of excitement at the event which they had witnessed, the master said: "Does anyone wish to speak?"

The first disciple said: "In the cause of Truth I feel myself constrained to say something to these people." 9

"If you will do so at your own risk, you may do so," said the master. 10

Now the disciple stepped forward in the presence of the tribal chief 11 and his priests and said: "I can perform the miracle which you take to be a special manifestation of deity. If I do so, will you accept that you have been in error for so many years?"

But the priests cried: "Seize him!" and the man was taken away, 12 never to be seen again.

The travelers went to the next territory where the second tribe were 13 worshipping the instruments of firemaking. Again a disciple volunteered to try to bring reason to the community.

With the permission of the master, he said: "I beg permission 14 to speak to you as reasonable people. You are worshipping the means whereby something may be done, not even the thing itself. Thus you are suspending the advent of its usefulness. I know the reality that lies at the basis of this ceremony."

This tribe was composed of more reasonable people. But they said to 15 the disciple: "You are welcome as a traveler and stranger in our midst. But, as a stranger, foreign to our history and customs, you cannot understand what we are doing. You make a mistake. Perhaps, even, you are trying to take away or alter our religion. We therefore decline to listen to you."

The travelers moved on. 16

When they arrived in the land of the third tribe, they found before 17 every dwelling an idol representing Nour, the original firemaker. The third disciple addressed the chiefs of the tribe:

"This idol represents a man, who represents a capacity, which can 18 be used."

"This may be so," answered the Nour-worshippers, "but the pene- 19 tration of the real secret is only for the few."

"It is only for the few who will understand, not for those who refuse 20 to face certain facts," said the third disciple.

"This is rank heresy, and from a man who does not even speak our 21 language correctly, and is not a priest ordained in our faith," muttered the priests. And he could make no headway.

The band continued their journey, and arrived in the land of the 22 fourth tribe. Now a fourth disciple stepped forward in the assembly of the people.

"The story of making fire is true, and I know how it may be done," 23 he said.

Confusion broke out within the tribe, which split into various fac- 24 tions. Some said: "This may be true, and if it is, we want to find out how to make fire." When these people were examined by the master and his followers, however, it was found that most of them were anxious to use firemaking for personal advantage, and did not realize that it was something for human progress. So deep had the distorted legends penetrated into the minds of most people that those who thought that they might in fact represent truth were often unbalanced ones, who could not have made fire even if they had been shown how.

There was another faction, who said: "Of course the legends are 25 not true. This man is just trying to fool us, to make a place for himself here."

And a further faction said: "We prefer the legends as they are, for 26 they are the very mortar of our cohesion. If we abandon them, and we find that this new interpretation is useless, what will become of our community then?"

And there were other points of view, as well. 27

So the party traveled on, until they reached the lands of the fifth 28 community, where firemaking was a commonplace, and where other preoccupations faced them.

The master said to his disciples: 29

"You have to learn how to teach, for man does not want to be 30 taught. First of all, you will have to teach people how to learn. And before that you have to teach them that there is still something to be learned. They imagine that they are ready to learn. But they want to learn what they *imagine* is to be learned, not what they have first to learn. When you have learned all this, then you can devise the way to teach. Knowledge without special capacity to teach is not the same as knowledge and capacity."

Reading and Interpreting

CONCEPT ANALYSIS

1. Recall the various tribes' responses to the teaching of the secret of fire making. Can you give past or present examples of persecution for the spreading of new ideas or information? Why do those in authority often resist the spreading of new ideas or information?

2. Why did the master's disciples fail to teach the secret of fire making to the different tribes?
3. Reread the concluding paragraph. What is the sequence of steps in successful teaching?
4. In your opinion, should the teacher or the student determine what is to be learned? Explain.
5. Describe a situation in which you were frustrated in a class because you felt you were not learning what you had expected.

Quickwrite

Select one of the tribal visits described in the Sufi tale and narrate that visit as concretely and vividly as you can. Elaborate the characters and have them express their ideas in direct quotations.

Thinking and Writing

RHETORICAL TECHNIQUE

1. As with most parables, or teaching tales, the Sufi story begins with the narrative and concludes with the lesson in the form of a moral. What might be the purpose of constructing a teaching tale in this inductive fashion?
2. The language of this story is general, abstract, and unspecific except for the name of the fire maker. In your opinion, does this vagueness of time, place, and characterization make the tale less interesting or more universal in its appeal? Explain.
3. Have you ever received instruction that used teaching stories? Was it effective? Explain your response.

SIDNEY PAINTER
Education

In this excerpt from his book *A History of the Middle Ages,* Painter describes the university in Europe between the twelfth and fourteenth centuries. He uses a wealth of realistic detail to make this unfamiliar subject vivid for the contemporary reader.

The dominant characteristic of education during the Middle Ages was its 1 essentially practical purpose. While there were scholars who loved learning for its own sake, they were exceptional and frequently felt called upon to find excuses for their intellectual curiosity. When John of Salisbury and his fellow humanists of the late twelfth century found pleasure in the beauties of pagan Latin prose, they were careful to point out that their basic purpose was to improve their Latin style for the more effective expression of the church's teachings. The general idea was that a man should have the knowledge required for his occupation; other knowledge was certainly useless and might well be dangerous. Thus Philippe de Navarre advocated teaching noble girls to read so that they could better perform their devotions, but he was vigorously opposed to having them learn to write. If they knew that art, how could one be sure that they would not write love letters? Even the extreme radical, Peter Dubois, when he suggested the foundation of an academy to give advanced education to women, intended that its alumnae should fulfill the very practical function of winning over Moslem princes by becoming their wives. Everyone had his or her proper place in society and should have the education suited to it.

Mediaeval education, therefore, cannot be described solely in terms 2 of academic institutions such as schools and universities. Every baronial household was a school for young nobles. The baron saw that the sons of his vassals and relatives who had been entrusted to him were given the training required to make them good knights. When a young man was formally dubbed a knight, he graduated from school and was ready to take his place in society. The baron's wife supervised the education of the girls and prepared them for marriage. In the towns the apprentice system of the guilds performed a similar function. The apprentices lived in the master's house and learned the trade under his supervision. The apprentice passed his final examinations when he completed his "masterpiece" and his formal admission to the guild as a master marked his graduation from school.

By far the most important educational institutions of the Middle 3
Ages were the universities. The word *universitas* meant basically "all," in a
collective sense, and could be used for any group of people cooperating for
a common end. It was freely used for the members of a guild. One finds it
applied to the barons of England and even the English people as a whole.
The universities were essentially educational guilds. In northern Europe
they were guilds of masters, while in Italy and southern Europe they were
student guilds. In both cases they were formed to protect their members
and to further their common educational interests. As masters or students
could form such cooperative organizations without specific permission
from a prince and without attracting the attention of contemporary chroniclers, no foundation date can be set for the three oldest universities, Bologna, Paris, and Oxford, and the date of the establishment of Cambridge is
most uncertain. As a rule one can only say when they received some form
of official recognition. Later universities were established by princes, and
hence their foundation dates can be easily determined.

Although the universities of Paris, Oxford, and Cambridge differed 4
in many ways, their major characteristics were essentially the same and
can be discussed in general terms. Each of the universities conducted a
long struggle to become independent of both ecclesiastical and lay authorities. As all the masters and students wore the clerical tonsure and were in
orders, they were theoretically exempt from arrest or punishment by the
secular government. Actually the heads of the universities obtained for
themselves extensive secular authority. The ways in which they attained
this end were much the same. A student would commit some offense—
tear a wine shop to pieces or rape a woman. The townsmen and their officials would try to arrest the students. Then there would be a riot, sometimes on a grand scale. On one occasion the students of Oxford were
besieged for several days by an armed mob. Since the students were also
armed, the contest was bitter and was only brought to an end by the arrival of royal troops. After a riot the university officials would appeal to
the king, and he nearly always solved the dispute by giving the head of
the university increased secular power. If the king hesitated, the university could usually rely on papal support. In the end it always won. The
chancellor of Oxford won full jurisdiction over the masters, the students,
and their servants. All quarrels over the price of food and lodging between
students and townfolk came before him. The rector of the university of
Paris also had jurisdiction over all who depended on him. In addition, he
had supervision of the guilds that supplied things specially needed by the
university, such as booksellers, ink makers, and paper sellers.

In order to be admitted to a university a student was expected to 5
prove his ability to read and write Latin, but the examinations were very
casual, and many students were poorly prepared. It was to improve this
situation that William of Wykeham founded Winchester College as a preparatory school for New College in Oxford. Once admitted, the student

started work on grammar, rhetoric, and logic. The master would take a textbook such as the *Doctrinale* of Alexander of Villa Dei, read the text, read the comments made on the text by his more noted predecessors, and then add his own comments. This process was described as "hearing" a book. At Paris, when a student had heard two books on grammar and five on logic, he became a bachelor of arts. He was then a sort of apprentice teacher and could instruct others aspiring for that degree. After hearing five books of Aristotle and some mathematical works, he was entitled to his license to teach. Five or six years of such work led to a master of arts degree. In addition to hearing books, the student was expected to read a few. At Oxford a candidate for a degree had to provide a certain number of masters to swear that he had heard and read the required works.

Although a student could embark on the curricula leading to the 6 doctor's degree in canon or civil law without first obtaining the degree of master of arts, this degree was a prerequisite for work in medicine and theology. Law was taught by the method described above—the reading of texts and commentaries by the master, who added his own comments, which he hoped would in time be used by his successors. In medicine the students heard two types of works, those on theory and those on practice. There was no actual practice in our sense and, of course, no laboratories. The most esteemed and most popular curriculum was theology, and to obtain the doctor's degree was a real achievement. A master of arts spent four years listening to lectures on the Bible and two more hearing discourses on Peter Lombard's *Sentences* to become a bachelor of divinity. He then studied six more years, which were also chiefly devoted to the Bible and the *Sentences,* to receive his license to teach theology. It usually required another year to be formally accepted as a doctor and installed in the doctor's chair. During most of these years of study the student took part in many "disputations" or public debates on points of theology. Participation in a certain number of these was required for the degree. He also as a rule had to preach a number of sermons.

Many students found it extremely difficult to meet the requirements 7 for the degrees and asked for "graces," the waiving of certain requirements. The faculties were inclined to be cooperative for a consideration such as a magnificent banquet with plenty of food and drink. Soon practically no one was meeting the requirements, and all were receiving their degrees through graces. All that was needed was residence for the proper time and money to defray the cost of the graces. This system had a serious effect on the university. No one bothered to attend lectures; and as the masters were paid by student fees, there were soon no more lectures. Thus one could obtain a degree by living in a university for a certain length of time and paying the costs. If you wanted to study and could find someone to teach you, you might learn something.

The students of the Middle Ages were not unlike those of today. 8 Some studied and some did not. Many drank and wenched. Most were in perpetual need of money. We have some of the handbooks containing model letters for the use of students. Many of these letters are examples of different excuses for obtaining money from parents, relatives, or patrons, but others show how to invite a girl to supper. As the Middle Ages was a time of violence, both masters and students were inclined to be turbulent. A German master who had slain several of his colleagues was finally dismissed for stabbing one to death in a faculty meeting. A professor at Oxford was charged with getting his students to kill a priest who had offended him. The Oxford rules forbade students to bring bows and arrows to class. Bloody riots between students and townsmen were fairly frequent. Robberies and burglaries by students were all too common. It is important to notice, however, that it was not too difficult to acquire the status of a student and that it was a tempting cloak for men who were essentially criminals. The students were exempt from the secular authorities, and the ecclesiastical courts were notoriously mild. In Paris of the fifteenth century the worst criminal section of the city lay just behind the university, and many of its inhabitants masqueraded as students.

Despite its many and obvious defects, the university performed signal services for mediaeval civilization. It supported scholars and supplied an environment conducive to learning. Most of the eminent scholars of the latter part of the Middle Ages were attached to a university. Then, the various faculties served as authorities on their respective subjects: a pope once apologized for deciding a theological point without consulting the faculty of theology at Paris. The graduates of the universities staffed the learned professions. The masters of arts who did not continue to teach in the universities became the masters of schools. The doctors of civil law either practiced in the lands where Roman law was used or became the servants of secular princes. The canon lawyers carried on the enormous business of the ecclesiastical courts. The doctorate of theology led either to a professorship or to preferment in the church. In short, it seems most unlikely that the general development of civilization that marked the later Middle Ages could have taken place without the universities.

9

FREDERICK B. ARTZ
Medieval Universities

As in the preceding reading, a detailed picture of the medieval university emerges in this selection from Frederick B. Artz's *Medieval Universities*.

"Universities," writes Haskins, "like cathedrals and parliaments, are a 1
product of the Middle Ages. Only in the twelfth and thirteenth centuries
do there emerge in the world those features of education with which we
are most familiar, all that machinery of instructions, examinations, and
academic degrees. In all these matters we are the heirs, not of Athens and
Alexandria, but of Paris and Bologna."

The university of Bologna grew out of a local law school, of which 2
there were a number in northern and central Italy. Young men interested
in the study of law began to flock to Bologna in the twelfth century. The
students organized into corporations to protect themselves against high
rents and prices; they laid down rules for their teaching and then hired
their teachers. If the professors did not live up to their regulations, they
were fined or dismissed. No professor could be absent a day, unless he
were ill or wanted to be married, though only a single day's leave was
allowed in the latter case. So much of the subject had to be covered in each
specific term of the year. No teacher could spend weeks on introduction or
bibliography or, for that matter, on autobiography. Students' organizations became a common practice in Italian, Spanish, and French universities. The teachers supported themselves primarily on the fees paid by
their students.

According to the student regulations, 3

A professor might not be absent without leave, and if he desired to
leave town he had to make a deposit to insure his return. If he failed
to secure an audience of five, he was fined as if absent. He must begin with the bell and quit within one minute after the next bell. He
was not allowed to skip a chapter in his commentary or postpone a
difficulty to the end of the hour, and he was obliged to cover the
ground systematically, so much in each specific term of the year.

C. H. Haskins,
A History of Education
During the Middle Ages

Reading and Interpreting

VOCABULARY

Use your dictionary as necessary to find the meaning of the following words
as used in the Painter reading:

humanist (1)   devotions (1)   vassals (2)   chroniclers (3)   secular (4)

papal (4)   rector (4)   defray (7)   ecclesiastical (8)

CONCEPT ANALYSIS

1. What is the original meaning of the word *universitas?* How does the meaning apply to the modern university?
2. What was the main purpose of the medieval university? How has the function of the university changed?
3. Describe the basic curriculum of the medieval university. How did the methods of instruction vary with the different curricula? Explain how different methods of instruction (lecture, group work, class discussion, lab, work internships) are used in different subjects in your college curriculum.
4. Review paragraphs 6 and 8 of the Painter excerpt and the selection from *Medieval Universities* by Frederick Artz. Which points are most surprising and shocking to you? What features of college life and types of students appear to have remained the same for 500 years? Which of the student regulations for faculty would you like to adopt?

Quickwrite

Refer to the regulations for faculty described in Artz's *Medieval Universities*. Write a set of regulations for your faculty.

Thinking and Writing

RHETORICAL TECHNIQUE

1. The Painter excerpt is an excellent example of the development of generalizations through examples and illustrations. For instance, in paragraph 1, the first sentence is the overall thesis statement. The second sentence offers an exception to the thesis statement. Sentence three provides an example of the exception, John of Salisbury and his fellow humanists.

   In paragraph 2, what specific examples drawn from medieval society support the notion that medieval education was not limited to schools and universities?
2. Because the subject of medieval life is unfamiliar, Painter is careful to make his generalizations concrete. Review paragraphs 4 and 9. What concrete examples are given to elaborate each of the following general statements?
   a. "A student would commit some offense. . . ." (4)
   b. "The rector . . . supplied things specially needed by the university." (4)

c. "The . . . graduates staffed the learned professions." (9)
3. In paragraphs 7 and 8, Painter achieves a comic effect with his deadpan delivery of the details of medieval student life; he offers some outrageous statements with no accompanying critical comment. Pick out your favorites.

COMPOSITION

Refer to paragraph 8 in Painter's writing. Compose an essay in which you vividly describe aspects of contemporary student life. Try to capture Painter's comic tone. Your thesis statement should assert that *the students of the 1980s are similar to (or not very different from) those of the Middle Ages.*

JOHN Q. EASTON
RICK GINSBERG

Student Learning Processes: How Poorly Prepared Students Succeed in College

John Easton and Rick Ginsberg are developmental educators. Their research findings are supported by the concrete details of student interviews and questionnaires.

Public concern over declining academic achievement at all levels of education has created a demand for improved teaching and learning for all students. This research paper concentrates on the effective learning processes of high-achieving community college students who have relatively low aptitudes for success in college. We have investigated in depth the learning characteristics of a sample of City Colleges of Chicago students who have achieved better than we would predict from their previous academic success and aptitude. The purpose of the study was to ascertain what common alterable attributes (Bloom, 1981) these students share. This work has centered on study habits and learning techniques that other students might acquire, rather than on traits like personality or family background that neither students nor educators can change.

Methodology

Student Selection

Our goal in selecting this sample was to obtain a group of students who 2 had done very well in college but were not necessarily high-aptitude students for whom achievement came easily. We wanted to interview students who earned high grades through diligent study rather than by virtue of high intelligence; some might call these students "overachievers." We set the following criteria for selecting the sample. Students:

- entered CCC in Fall, 1981, or Spring, 1982;
- spoke English as a native language;
- resided in Chicago;
- enrolled in four courses per semester; and
- belonged or were eligible to belong to the campus honor society.

From the list of students who met these criteria we then chose the students with relatively low reading placement test scores.

We first applied this process at Loop College, a downtown campus 3 that draws students from the entire city of Chicago. Forty-four students met the first set of criteria, and from these we chose 22 students with low reading placement test scores. We invited these students to participate in the study and interviewed 19 of them. The process was repeated on a smaller scale at two other City Colleges, both of which are distant from downtown Chicago. This sample was extended so that we could generalize our findings beyond one college. We interviewed three students at Wright College and four at Olive-Harvey College.

Student Characteristics

The following [list] describes the 26 students interviewed in this study. 4 Our experience with City Colleges students indicates that this group is representative of the population of full-time students meeting the previously listed criteria.

- Average age: 21.5 Years (S.D. = 7.7)
- Average reading placement score at college entry: 7.6 grade equivalent (Nelson-Denny Form E, comprehension plus vocabulary)
- Gender: 21 women, 5 men; Race: 21 black, 3 white, 2 Hispanic
- Living situation: 18 live with parents; 6 live with spouse, children, or others; 2 live alone
- Children: 4 have children (an average of 2.5 each)
- Work: 10 have part-time jobs (18 hours/week average); 4 looking for jobs; 12 unable or chose not to work
- Academic majors: 7 liberal arts, 6 data processing, 6 medical-related, 3 electronics, 2 business, 2 law enforcement

- Career goals: 4 data processing, 4 medical ancillary, 3 business, 3 computer programming, 3 computer/electronics technology, 2 physician, 2 teaching, 2 law enforcement

Interview Development and Interviewer Training

Staff members at the Center for the Improvement of Teaching and Learning developed the interview questions for this study, using several background sources for guidance, including previous research on effective students and their study habits, CITL research on effective teachers, personal experiences of the researchers as students and teachers, and feedback from trial interviews with City College students. . . . Our goal was to produce a set of questions that elicited meaningful responses, were unambiguous, and could be asked (and answered) in natural and appropriate language.

Two interviewers conducted all but two of the student interviews; a third staff member did the others. Since the interviewers were involved in writing and revising the questions, they were familiar with the purpose of each question. All three interviewers conducted two trial interviews with City Colleges students and reviewed these sessions with another interviewer. By the time the first regular interview took place, each interviewer had spent approximately 20 hours discussing, revising, practicing, and reviewing the interview questions.

Data Analysis

The interviewers tape-recorded the interview sessions and shortly after each session replayed the tape and summarized the data on a four-page form. The sheet provided 10 categories for these summaries: background information, financial concerns, high school background and choice of college, college, study, and work habits, in-class activities, teacher relations, personal goals, extracurricular activities, and satisfaction. The interviewers wrote the summaries using both their own descriptive language and as many direct quotes as possible.

. . . We looked through this data for categories that explained most of what the students revealed in the interviews. After revision and reconsideration we chose four major headings that described the students' study habits and techniques and a fifth category that contained personality characteristics of the students. The four categories of study techniques were not mutually exclusive; we will define and discuss these categories in the following pages.

Results

We have identified four major processes that appear to be responsible for 9 these students' academic success. *Involvement, review/restudy, selectivity,* and *planning* all characterize their learning approach. *Involvement* is participation in learning both inside and outside of the classroom; *review/restudy* is the process students utilize to study and correct both short- and long-term weaknesses; *selectivity* refers to the students' discrimination in what and how they choose to study, their choice of friends, classes and teachers; and *planning* is the conscious short- and long-term preparation students undertake to foster success in school. These processes appear to be alterable— that is, under advantageous conditions other students could be taught to apply these processes themselves. In addition to these four alterable processes, we find the excellent students to be extremely goal oriented. The remainder of this paper discusses each of the four alterable learning processes and the motivational component in detail.

Involvement

One of the most significant findings of this study is how these students 10 maintain a remarkably high level of involvement in their academic work. When involved with a subject these students pay attention, think, work through ideas and questions, and relate new concepts to previously learned ones, all in order to understand the new material as thoroughly as possible. The students vary in the intensity or degree of their involvement from time to time or place to place, yet overall they all exhibit a high degree of involvement in their academic work. For the purposes of this paper and the presentation of the findings, we distinguish between involvement in and outside the classroom.

Involvement in the Classroom   All of the students portrayed several different 11 methods and specific personalized techniques for attaining a high level of involvement in classroom learning. The typical pattern of classroom involvement includes attendance, paying attention in class, taking notes in class, and asking questions and participating in class discussions. The following paragraphs show the great variety of techniques that these students use to accomplish their classroom involvement.

Regular class attendance is an essential prerequisite to learning 12 course material and is the first step that all of these students take to become involved with their school work. "I attend all the time" is the most common response to questions concerning attendance. They understand that in order to "know what's going on," they must be physically present in the classroom to see and hear it. Attendance is not seen as important for its own sake, but rather for the opportunities that it provides for learning.

Several students mentioned that absenteeism is the single most important reason why other students do poorly in college. When the honor students do miss class (due to illness or other unavoidable reasons), they invariably ask a fellow student or the teacher for missed notes and assignments.

Being in class itself may be necessary for learning, but it is not suffi- 13 cient. While in class you must pay attention: "If you can't hear, you can't learn." As a first step for paying attention in class, the students sit in the location that they find most suitable for seeing and hearing the teacher. About two-thirds of the students prefer to sit in the front of the room where "you haven't got any choice but to sit and listen" and "you pay more attention." One woman prefers the last seat in the front row, "so people won't be on each side." These students sit in the front not only because "students in the back are too noisy," but also for more subtle and complex reasons: "I sit in the front and look in the teacher's face like he's giving me a private lesson"; "in the front the teacher even gets to know you better"; and "that is where the teachers pay attention—if they see you wandering off, they let you know!" These statements indicate that the students sit in the front to see better and increase their chances of learning and getting better grades.

Other students are able to concentrate equally well in the middle of 14 the room, but they avoid sitting close to friends "so they don't encourage me to talk." Also, they leave their newspapers on the floor so they are not tempted to read them during class. None of the students claimed a preference for the back of the classroom. To concentrate on the teacher and shut out possible distractions, the honor students sit in the middle or toward the front of the classroom.

The students focus on the instructor and class material through most 15 of the period, yet some occasionally find their minds wandering off the subject. To get back on task they tell themselves, "I need the course" or "I have time to daydream after class" or "I try to focus on the material being presented in order to maintain concentration." These self-reminders are useful ways for students to recapture attention when they become bored or distracted.

All of the students in the sample take notes during class, though 16 there is variation in the comprehensiveness of the notetaking. Some students try to write down everything the teachers say, stopping them when they talk too fast. Other students write down only the key words or key concepts, what they believe is most important, or what the teacher has told them is most important. The more selective note-takers often write in their own words rather than the teachers'. All of these students use their notes outside of class in doing homework and studying for tests.

The final commonality in the in-class behavior of these students is 17 that they ask questions when they are perplexed by the lecture or if they miss something. "I don't make problems for myself . . . if I miss something, I ask him. That's what he's there for." Although there is some slight reluctance to ask questions when they feel unprepared or believe that they will be reprimanded for not having heard an explanation, in general these students have overcome such difficulties and freely ask the teachers to repeat, clarify, or explain points that they do not understand. . . .

To summarize, the students all attend class regularly, are highly attentive in class, take notes, and ask questions and participate in discussions. Within each of these areas there is variation among students and within students from time to time or class to class. The students use different notetaking techniques and different methods of regaining lost concentration. In general, our effective students want quality time in the classroom with high concentration and minimal distractions.

Reading and Interpreting

VOCABULARY

Use your dictionary as necessary to find the meaning of the following words in context of Easton and Ginsberg's study:

feedback (5)   unambiguous (5)   alterable learning processes (9)

goal oriented (9)   motivational component (9)   commonality (17)

CONCEPT ANALYSIS

1. Why was this study conducted? Who will benefit from its publication?
2. Name the four alterable processes the researchers identified that assist poorly prepared students to succeed in college. What is the fifth characteristic of the successful student?
3. According to the study, what are some unalterable attributes?
4. Having read this article, will you alter any of your academic and/or social behavior? Explain.

Thinking and Writing

RHETORICAL TECHNIQUE

1. This article is a model of clarity because the authors introduce categories and lists within categories to make abstractions concrete. For example, in the first category under Methodology, Student Selection, they list the specific criteria for choosing the sample group. What other categories of

information appear in the article? What is the purpose of such detailed categorization?

2. Which technique for making ideas concrete is used most frequently in this article? Which are almost completely absent?

COMPOSITION

In this article the strategy of involvement in the classroom is fully developed. The other three alterable strategies are briefly defined and not elaborated. Select one of these and write an essay about it, using examples and quotations from your own academic life.

JOHN HOLT

How Children Fail

John Holt is a contemporary educational reformer who has worked as a teacher in a number of different kinds of schools. His concrete descriptions of classroom scenes in *How Children Fail* enlist the reader's support for his theories about why today's schools are failing their students.

February 26, 1961

The unbelievable incompetence of some of the kids sometimes drives me wild. They can't find anything. They have no paper or pencil when it's time for work. Their desks are a mess. They lose library books. If they do homework at home, they leave it there; if they take home material to do homework, they leave the assignment at school. They can't keep their papers in a notebook. Yet they are not stupid or incapable children; they do many things well.

Ted is an intelligent, alert, curious, humorous, and attractive boy, with a record of unbroken failure and frustration in school. He is an excellent athlete, strong, quick, and well coordinated. But his school papers are as torn, smudged, rumpled, and illegible as any I have ever seen. The other day the class was cleaning out desks, and I was "helping" him. We got about a ream of loose papers out of his desk, and I asked him to put them in the notebook. As always, when he is under tension, his face began

1

2

to get red. He squirmed and fidgeted, and began to mutter. "They won't fit, the notebook's the wrong size"—which wasn't true. Finally he assembled a thick stack of papers and began to try to jam them onto one of the rings in his notebook, not noticing that the holes in the papers were at least a half-inch from the ring. As he pushed and fumbled and muttered, I felt my blood pressure rising until, exasperated almost to rage, I said loudly, "For heaven's sake, leave it alone, do it later, I can't stand to watch any more of it!"

Thinking over this scene, and many others like it, I was suddenly 3 reminded of a movie, *A Walk in the Sun,* based on the novel by Harry Brown. It showed the adventures of a leaderless platoon of infantrymen during the first day of the invasion of Italy. At one point, while the platoon is moving through some woods, they are surprised by an enemy light tank, which, amid a good deal of confusion, they manage to ambush. When this action is over the soldiers find that their sergeant, who has been growing rapidly more anxious, and is clearly the victim of battle fatigue, has given way completely. They find him hugging the ground, shaking all over, babbling incoherently. They leave him behind, as they move inland toward their vaguely conceived objective. One of the soldiers remarks as they go that the sergeant has finally dug himself a foxhole that they can't get him out of.

It seems to me that children dig themselves similar foxholes in 4 school, that their fumbling incompetence is in many ways comparable to the psychoneurotic reactions of men who have been under too great a stress for too long. Many will reject this comparison as being wildly exaggerated and inappropriate. They are mistaken. There are very few children who do not feel, during most of the time they are in school, an amount of fear, anxiety, and tension that most adults would find intolerable. It is no coincidence at all that in many of their worst nightmares adults find themselves back in school. I was a successful student, yet now and then I have such nightmares myself. In mine I am always going to a class from which, without the slightest excuse, I have been absent for months. I know that I am hopelessly behind in the work, and that my long absence is going to get me in serious trouble, of what sort I am not sure. Yet I feel I cannot stay away any longer, I have to go.

It is bad enough to be a teacher and feel that the children in your 5 charge are using the conscious and controlled parts of their minds in ways which, in the long run and even in the short, are unprofitable, limiting, and self-defeating; to see them dutifully doing the assigned work and to be sure that they are not getting a scrap of intellectual nourishment out of it; to know that what they seem to have learned today they will have forgotten by next month, or next week, or even tomorrow.

But it is a good deal worse to feel that many children are reacting 6 to school in ways that are not under their control at all. To feel that you are helping make children less intelligent is bad enough, without having to wonder whether you may be helping to make them neurotic as well.

June 3, 1959

I've corrected and scored the final math tests. The results are not quite as dismal as last week; most people did a little better. But one exception suggests that drill is not always as helpful as most people think. Caroline took the first test after being out two weeks, during which she missed much review work. She surprised me by getting 15 out of 25. Today, after taking the other test a week ago, and after a week of further review, she got only 7 right. It looks as if she learns more when she is out of school than when she is in it.

Looking at the low gang, I feel angry and disgusted with myself for having given these tests. The good students didn't need them; the poor students, during this month or more of preparation and review, had most of whatever confidence and common sense they had picked up during the year knocked right out of them. Looking at Monica today, on the edge of tears, unable to bring herself even to try most of the problems, I felt that I had literally done her an injury.

There was a lot of room for improvement in the rather loose classes I was running last fall, but the children were doing some real thinking and learning, and were gaining confidence in their own powers. From a blind *producer* Ben was on his way to being a very solid and imaginative *thinker;* now he has fallen back into recipe-following production strategy of the worst kind. What is this test nonsense, anyway? Do people go through life taking math tests, with other people telling them to hurry? Are we trying to turn out intelligent people, or test-takers?

There must be a way to educate young children so that the great human qualities that we know are in them may be developed. But we'll never do it as long as we are obsessed with tests. At faculty meetings we talk about how to reward the *thinkers* in our classes. Who is kidding whom? No amount of rewards and satisfactions obtained in the small group thinking sessions will make up to Monica for what she felt today, faced by a final test that she knew she couldn't do and was going to fail. Pleasant experiences don't make up for painful ones. No child, once painfully burned, would agree to be burned again, however enticing the reward. For all our talk and good intentions, there is much more stick than carrot in school, and while this remains so, children are going to adopt a strategy aimed above all else at staying out of trouble. How can we foster a joyous, alert, whole-hearted participation in life, if we build all our schooling around the holiness of getting "right answers"?

Reading and Interpreting

VOCABULARY

Use your dictionary as necessary to find the meaning of the following words as used by John Holt:

neurotic (6)   literally (8)   enticing (10)

CONCEPT ANALYSIS

1. What is the central idea of Holt's February 26 entry?
2. In the June entry Holt implies the contradiction between what education is and what it could be. Based on the conclusion of this entry, what does Holt wish had happened to Caroline, Monica, and Ben on June 3?
3. State the thesis of the June entry in your own words.

Quickwrite

Write about a dream, nightmare, or memory you have had in connection with school. Try to record details as precisely as you can, making the scene vivid to the reader. Provide a thesis for the recollection either in the form of an introductory thesis statement or a concluding interpretation.

Thinking and Writing

RHETORICAL TECHNIQUE

1. The analogy between the sergeant in the film *A Walk in the Sun* and the schoolchildren whom Holt has observed is central to Holt's communication of his ideas. Cite the specific points of comparison between the two elements of the analogy. What descriptive words in the analogy are particularly effective at conveying Holt's point?
2. The organization of the June entry, like that of the February one, is inductive; details and examples build to the thesis statement. Each paragraph uses a different child to illustrate an important aspect of Holt's argument. What point does Caroline illustrate? Monica? Ben? How is the use of specific cases effective in developing Holt's thesis?

Answer Holt's question: Are our schools trying to turn out intelligent people or test takers? Make concrete references to your own school experience.

GEORGE MILBURN
A Student in Economics

George Milburn's classic short story was published in 1933, in the depths of the Great Depression. The story's theme of social and economic inequities is enhanced by figurative language and rich descriptive detail, often used with irony. There is irony implicit in the title as well: the story's hero, Charlie Wingate, is a student in economics, but poverty requires him to work day and night, thus preventing him from studying the subject.

I

All of the boys on the third floor of Mrs. Gooch's approved rooms for men had been posted to get Charlie Wingate up that afternoon. He had to go to see the Dean. Two or three of them forgot about it and two or three of them had other things to do, but Eddie Barbour liked waking people up. Eddie stuck his weasel face in at Charlie's door just as the alarm clock was giving one last feeble tap. The clock stood on the bottom of a tin washpan that was set upside-down on a wooden chair beside the bed. The alarm had made a terrific din. Eddie had heard it far down the hall. The hands showed two o'clock. Pale needles from a December sun were piercing the limp green window shade in a hundred places.

Eddie Barbour yelled, "Aw right, Charlie! Snap out of it!" He came into the chilly room and stood for a moment staring vaguely at the ridge of quilts on the sagged iron bed. The only sound was the long, regular sough of Charlie Wingate's breathing. He hadn't heard a thing. Eddie made a sudden grab for the top of the covers, stripped them back and began jouncing the sleeper by the shoulders. Charlie grunted every time the bed springs creaked, but he nuzzled his pillow and went on sleeping. Eddie went over to the study table where a large, white-enameled water pitcher stood and he came back to the bed with the water, breathing giggles. He tipped the water pitcher a little and a few drops fell on the back of Charlie's neck without waking him. Eddie sloshed the icy water up over the pitcher's mouth. A whole cupful splashed on Charlie's head. Charlie sat up quickly, batting his arms about, and Eddie Barbour whinnied with laughter.

"Arise, my lord, for the day is here," he said, going across and ceremoniously raising the crooked window shade. Charlie sat straight up among the rumpled quilts with his head cocked on one side, staring dully. He had slept with his clothes on. He sat up in bed all dressed, in a soldier's brown uniform, all but his shoes and roll puttees. | 3

"You got army today?" Eddie asked, putting the pitcher down. | 4

Charlie looked at him for a moment and blinked. Then he said in a voice stuffy with sleep, "Naw. I had army yesterday. I got army make-up today." He worked his mouth, making clopping noises. | 5

"What time you got army make-up, Charlie? When you come in from class you said get you up because you had to go see the Dean at two-thirty?" | 6

"Yeah, I do have to go see the Dean at two-thirty. But I got army make-up too. I got to make up drill cuts from three till six." All at once he flopped back down on the bed, sound asleep again. | 7

"Hey!" Eddie cried, jumping forward. "Come out of that! Wake up there, Charlie! You can't sleep no more if you got to see the Dean at two-thirty. You just about got time to make it." He jerked him back up in bed. | 8

"Screw the Dean," Charlie said; "two hours' sleep ain't enough." | 9

"Is two hours all the sleep you got last night?" | 10

"Where you get the 'last night'? I worked all night last night. I had classes till noon. Two hours' sleep was all I got today. And darn little more yesterday or the day before. When is Sunday? Sunday's the first day I'm due to get any real sleep. Two hours' sleep is not enough sleep for a man to get." | 11

He plumped his stockinged feet onto the cold floor and got up stiffly. He went over to the washstand, where he picked up his tooth brush and tooth paste and a bar of soap and slowly took his face towel down from beside the warped looking-glass. He came back to where his shoes lay and stood looking at the toilet articles in his hands as if he had forgotten what he meant to do with them. He dumped them on the bed, took the pan with the alarm clock on it and set it on the floor. Then he sat down on the chair and picked up one of the heavy army shoes, held it and felt it and studied it carefully before he put it on. He put on the other shoe with equal deliberation and stood up without lacing either of them. He took his things up from the bed and started off for the bathroom, his loose shoes clogging. Eddie Barbour followed him down the drafty hall. | 12

The creosote disinfectant that Mrs. Gooch used in her bathrooms 13
gave off a strong odor. "Dag gum bathroom smells just like a hen coop,"
Charlie said thickly as he stood in front of the whitespecked mirror
twisting his face. He wouldn't need a shave for another day. He had a
fairly good-looking face, tan and thin, with ringlets of black hair tumbling
down over his forehead. His large ears stuck straight out. He
looked at his image with dark eyes made narrow by two purplish puffs
under them, and he yawned widely.

Eddie Barbour stood leaning against the jamb of the bathroom 14
door. He said, "You ought to try and get more sleep, Charlie."

"Are you telling *me?*" Charlie said, running water in the face bowl. 15
Eddie Barbour was a freshman too.

II

Charlie Wingate came walking along University Boulevard toward the 16
campus, hunched up in his army overcoat. The raw December wind
whipped his face and made me feel wide awake. He passed a bunch of
fraternity men pitching horseshoes in the drive beside the K.A. house.
Two or three, sprucely dressed, gave him impersonal glances as he
passed. They did not speak, and he walked past self-consciously, seeing
them without looking toward them.

When he reached the business section opposite the campus he 17
turned in at the white-tiled front of The Wigwam. The noon rush was
over and Nick was not at the cash register. A few noon "dates" were still
sitting in the booths along the wall. Charlie walked straight back along
the white-tile counter and sat down on the end stool. Red Hibbert was
standing by the coffee urns reading the sports section. When Charlie sat
down Red folded his newspaper slowly and came over to wait on him.
Charlie sat with his cheeks resting on the heels of his hands.

"How's it, Chollie, old boy, old boy?" Red Hibbert said. 18

"Not bad. Give me a cup of javy without and a couple of them 19
Grandma's oatmeal cookies over there, Red. Where's Nick?"

Red scooted the plate with the cookies on it down the glassy white 20
counter top and came along with the cup of black coffee. "This is Nick's
day for Kiwanis," he said. "It looks to me like you'd stay home and get
some sleep once in a while. You're dyin' on your feet."

"I am going to get some sleep Sunday, don't you never worry. I 21
have to go see the Dean this afternoon. And I got make-up drill at three
o'clock. I've got to make up some drill cuts."

"What you got to go see the Dean about?" 22

"I don't know what about; here's all it said." Charlie reached in his 23
overcoat pocket and pulled out a jagged window envelope and a mimeo-

graphed postal card. He pushed the envelope across the counter along with the postal card. "I got that other in the morning mail too."

Red took the printed form from the Dean of Men's office out of the 24 envelope and glanced at it. Then he picked up the postal card. It was headed,

FOURTH AND FINAL NOTICE

You are hereby summoned to appear before the chairman of the Student Senate Committee on Freshman Activities, Rm 204 Student Union Bldg., not later than 4 P.M., Friday afternoon. It will be to your advantage not to ignore this summons as you have three previous ones. This is positively the last opportunity you will be given to rectify your delinquency. Should you fail to appear this time, steps will be taken to bring you.

(*signed*) Aubrey H. Carson, *Chrmn*
Com. on Frshmn Actvts.

Red waggled the postal card. "What you going to do about this?" 25

"Tear it up like I did the others, I guess. I know what they want. 26 They want to try and make me buy one of them damn' freshman caps."

"Take a tip from me, Charlie: I'd go see them. It won't hurt nothing, 27 and it might be a lot easier on you in the long run."

"Hell, what can they do?" 28

"Plenty. They could sick the Black Hoods onto you." 29

"Ah! The Black Hoods, that bunch of amateur ku kluckers!" 30

"Call 'em amateurs if you want to, Charlie, but it wasn't only but 31 last Friday night they took that little Jew-boy, Sol Lewis, out of the rooming house where I stay. It look to me like they did a pretty professional job on him. They used the buckle-end of a belt on him. They claim he was a stool pigeon for the University."

"Stool pigeon! Ah, you know that guy wasn't a stool pigeon, Red." 32

"We-ell, I'm not saying one way or the other. Anyhow, that's what 33 you're up against when you take to fooling with that Student Committee on Freshman Activities, Charlie."

"Prexy claimed in his opening address at the first of school that he 34 had put a stop to these masked frats and all this hazing."

"Yeah, he said he had; but how's he going to put a stop to the 35 Black Hoods? He can't kick out all the biggest shots in the University, can he? All the big shots on the campus are Black Hoods. Football stars and fellas like that. You won't see the President kicking guys like that out of the University."

"Maybe not, but—why, hell, that freshman cap business is noth- 36 ing but a racket. That's all it is. Damn' if I let 'em scare me into paying a dollar for a little old sleazy green cloth cap!"

"O.K., Charlie; I guess you know what you want to do." 37

"Anyway, how could I get around to see that committee before four 38 o'clock this afternoon, and see the Dean at two-thirty, and go to make-up drill from three till six? I'll be late to drill and get bawled out by the captain again. The captain's already about to flunk me for cuts. That's what's getting me down—Military. It's this Military that's getting me down."

"Jees, I don't know, Charlie; seems like I get a bigger kick out of 39 army than I do any other course I got. They sure learn you more in army than they do in anything else *in* this University."

"Yeow, you learn plenty in army, all right. But what I don't like is 40 the compulsory part. I don't think they ought to be allowed to make it compulsory for freshmen and sophomores. That's just like they had it over in Germany before they got rid of the Kaiser."

The red-haired boy gave him a startled look. He frowned heavily. 41 "Charlie," he exclaimed, "where are you getting all these radical ideas you been spouting around here lately?" Charlie peered at him. Red's face was set in earnestness.

"Why, that's not a radical idea," Charlie said, pushing back his 42 empty coffee cup. "That just a plain historical fact, that's all that is. I don't see where they got any right to make Military Training compulsory. This is supposed to be a *free* country. That compulsory stuff is what Mussle-leany and birds like that pull."

"But, Charlie, it's all for your own benefit. The University is just 43 looking out after your own interests."

"How do you figure they're looking out for *my* interests?" 44

"Well, for one thing, when the next war comes we'll all be officers, 45 us fellas that got this training in college. We'll go right into the regular army as officers. There's where we'll have the edge on guys that never did take advantage of a college education. Person'ly, when the next war comes along, I'm not hankerin' after any front-line trenches. And you know darn' well they're not going to stick their college-trained officers into frontline trenches to get shot. So there's where I figure us guys in R.O.T.C. will have a big advantage."

"Yeah, you might be right, at that, Red. But I'm not kicking 46 about R.O.T.C. It's just the compulsory part I'm kicking against."

Red perked his head and scowled impatiently. "Charlie, they *got* to 47 make it compulsory. If it wasn't compulsory, how many of the fellas would enroll in it? They have to make Military compulsory in order to give the fullest benefits. What good could they do if only a few of the fellas was taking it?"

"Anyway, I know some it's not compulsory for," Charlie said stub- 48 bornly. "Last night there was a Phi Gam pledge in here bragging about how he got out of Military. He told them at the first of school he didn't want to take Military. They told him he *had* to take it—required of all able-bodied freshmen. Couldn't get his degree without it. So he had to go buy his army shoes. Well, he got the shoe store to send the bill to his old man. His old man is one of these they call 'em pacifists. When his old man gets the bill for his kid's army shoes, maybe you think he don't get the President of this University on long distance and tell him where to head in it. And this kid didn't have to take Military, neither. His old man's a big shot lawyer in the City."

"Yeah, but you got to have pull to get away with that, Charlie." 49

"That's what I mean, Red. You can get away with plenty in this 50
University if you got the pull."

III

Charlie Wingate loped up the steps of the Administration Building, 51
hurried through the revolving doors, and walked past hissing steam radiators down the long hall to the Dean of Men's office. He was ten minutes late. Before he opened the frosted-glass door he took out a pair of amber-colored spectacles and put them on. Then he went in and handed his summons to the secretary.

"The Dean will see you in a moment," she said. "Please take a 52
chair."

Charlie sat down and gave an amber-hued glance about the outer 53
office. Three dejected freshmen, holding their green caps, were waiting with him. He recognized none of them, so he picked up a week-old copy of the *Christian Science Monitor* and started to read it. But the room was warm and he immediately went to sleep. He had his head propped back against the wall. The newspaper slipped down into his lap. His amber-colored glasses hid his eyes and no one could see that they were closed. He was awakened by the secretary shaking him. She was smiling and the freshmen were all snickering.

"Wake up and pay for your bed, fella!" one of the freshmen called, 54
and everyone laughed heartily.

"I sort of drowsed off. It's so nice and warm in here," Charlie said, 55
apologizing to the pretty secretary.

The Dean of Men got up as he entered and, with his eyes on the 56
slip bearing Charlie's name, said, "Ah, this is Charles Wingate, isn't it?" He grasped Charlie's hand as if it were an honor and pressed a button under the edge of his desk with his other hand. The secretary appeared at the door. "Miss Dunn, will you bring in Wingate's folder—Charles W-i-n-g-a-t-e. How do you like college by now, Wingate? Eyes troubling you?"

"Pretty well, sir. Yes, sir, a little. I wear these glasses." 57

The secretary came back with the folder and the Dean looked 58
through it briefly. "Well, Wingate, I suppose you're anxious to know

why I sent for you. The unpleasant truth is, Wingate, you don't seem to be doing so well in your college work. Your freshman adviser conferred with you twice about this, and this week he turned your case over to me. My purpose, of course, is to help you. Now, to be quite frank, Wingate, you're on the verge of flunking out. Less than a third of the semester remains, and you have a failing grade in English 101, conditional grades in Psychology 51 and Military Training; three hours of F and four hours of D, almost half your total number of hours. On the other hand, you have an A average in Spanish and a B in Economics 150. Wingate, how do you account for your failing English when you are an A student in Spanish?"

"To tell the truth, sir, I got behind on my written work in English, and I've never been able to catch up. And I don't really have to study Spanish. My father is a railway section foreman in my home town, and he's always had a gang of Mexicans working for him. I've been speaking Mexican ever since I was a kid. It's not the pure, what they call Castilian, Spanish, but I probably know almost as much Spanish as my professor." 59

"How about this B in Economics? That's a fairly high grade." 60

"Yes, sir. Doctor Kenshaw—he's my Ec professor—doesn't give exams. Instead he gives everyone a B until he calls for our term papers. We don't recite in his class. We just listen to him lecture. And the grade you get on your term paper is your semester grade." 61

"Ah! What you students term a pipe course, eh, Wingate?" 62

"Not exactly, sir. We have to do a lot of outside reading for the term paper. But I'm counting on keeping that B in Ec." 63

"That's fine, Wingate. But it appears to me that it's high time you were getting busy on some of these other grades, too. Why can't you dig in and pull these D's up to B's, and this F up to at least a C? You've got it in you. You made an unusually high grade on your entrance exams, your record shows. Graduated from high school with honors. What's the trouble, Wingate? Tell me!" 64

"I don't know, sir, except I work at night and—" 65

"Oh, I see it here on your enrollment card now. Where do you work?" 66

"I work nights for Nick Pappas, down at The Wigwam." 67

"How many hours a night do you work?" 68

"Ten hours, sir. From nine till seven. The Wigwam stays open all night. I eat and go to eight o'clock class when I get off." 69

"Very interesting, Wingate. But don't you suppose that it would be advisable to cut down a bit on this outside work and attend a little more closely to your college work? After all, that's what you're here for, primarily—to go to college, not work in a café." 70

"I couldn't work fewer hours and stay in school, sir. I just barely get by as it is. I get my board at The Wigwam, and I pay my room rent, 71 and I've been paying out on a suit of clothes. That leaves only about a dollar a week for all the other things I have to have."

"Wingate, shouldn't you earn more than that, working ten hours?" 72

"I get the regular, first-year-man rate, Sir. Twenty cents an hour. 73
It's set by the University. Nick takes out a dollar a day for board. Pays me five dollars a week in cash."

"Can't you arrange for a little financial support from home?" 74

"No, sir, I'm afraid I couldn't. I have two brothers and two sisters 75
at home younger than I am. It wouldn't be right for me to ask my father to send money out of what he makes."

"But surely you could get out and land something a little more 76
lucrative than this all-night restaurant job, Wingate."

"No sir. Twenty cents an hour is standard rate for working stu- 77
dents, and I haven't found anything better. Nick says he has at least thirty men on the waiting list for this job I have."

"Well, there's this about it, Wingate. The University is here, sup- 78
ported by the taxpayers of this State, for the purpose of giving the young men and women of this State educational opportunities. The University is not here for the purpose of training young men to be waiters in all-night restaurants. And, so far as I can see, that's about all you are deriving from your University career. So it occurs to me that you should make a choice: either find some way to devote more attention to your college work or drop out of school altogether. We are very loathe to encourage students who are *entirely* self-supporting. And yet, I will admit that I know any number of first-rate students who are entirely self-supporting. There's Aubrey Carson, for example. Quarterback on the football team, delegate to the Olympics, president of the Student Senate, and he's a straight A student. Aubrey Carson was telling me only last week that he hasn't had any financial assistance from home since he enrolled as a freshman. Aubrey is a fine example of the working student."

"Yes, sir; but look at the job Carson has. He works for a big to- 79
bacco company, and all he has to do is hand out Treasure Trove cigarettes to other students. The tobacco company pays him a good salary for passing out samples of their cigarettes."

"Why, Wingate, you surely must be mistaken about that. I don't 80
believe Aubrey Carson smokes. In fact, I know he doesn't smoke. He's one of the finest all-'round athletes in this country."

"No, sir; I don't say he smokes either. But that's the straight stuff 81
about his job with the cigarette company. They figure it's a good advertisement to have a popular guy like Aubrey Carson passing out Treasure Troves. Sort of an endorsement."

"All the same, Wingate, it doesn't reflect a very good attitude on 82
your part, criticizing the way one of your fellow students earns his college expenses."

"Oh, I didn't mean to criticize him, sir. I was only saying—" 83

"Yes, yes, I know; but all this is beside the point. We're here to discuss the state of your grades, Wingate. The fact is, you are on probation right now. As you must know, any student who is passing in less than half his work is automatically suspended from the University and must return to his home. Now one F more and out you'll go. Wingate. That's just being frank with you." 84

"I'd hate to have to go back home like that, sir." 85

"Well, you'd have to. If you flunk out, the University authorities are obliged to see that you return to your home immediately." 86

"I'd hate that, sir. I'd hate to go back home and have to live off my family, and that's probably what I'd have to do. I had a letter from my mother yesterday, and she says that nearly all the boys who graduated from high school with me are still there, loafing on the streets and living off their old folks. I don't like that idea. Mother's proud of me because I'm working my way through college. You know there are not many jobs to be had nowadays, sir, and I'd hate to have to go back home and loaf." 87

"It *is* a problem, I'll confess, Wingate. But what's the point in your coming to the University and working all night in a café and then flunking your class work? Moreover, your freshman adviser reports that you make a practice of sleeping in class. Is that true?" 88

"Well, yes, sir. I suppose I do drop off sometimes." 89

"Pretty impossible situation, isn't it, Wingate? Well, I've given you the best advice I can. Unless you can alter your circumstances I suggest that you withdraw from the University at once. We have six thousand other students here who need our attention, and the University has to be impartial and impersonal in dealing with these problems. Unless you can find some means to avoid flunking out I suggest withdrawing beforehand." 90

"Withdrawal would be a disgrace to me, sir. If I withdrew and went back home now, everyone at home would say that I had been expelled. You know how small towns are." 91

"Ah, now, Wingate, when you begin dealing with small-town gossip, I fear you're really getting outside my province. But I should think you'd prefer honorable withdrawal to flunking out." 92

"I believe I'll try to stick it through, sir. I'll try to remove the conditional grades, and maybe I can luck through on my finals." 93

"I hope you can, Wingate. As long as you feel that way about it, good luck to you." The Dean of Men stood up. Charlie stood up too. The Dean put out his hand and showed his teeth in a jovial smile and bore down hard on Charlie's knuckles. "I'm counting on you strong, old man," he said, encircling Charlie's shoulders with his left arm. "I know you have the stuff and that you'll come through with flying colors one of these days." 94

"Thank you, sir," Charlie said, grinning tearfully while the Dean gave his shoulder little pats. He edged toward the door as soon as the 95

Dean released him, but when he reached it he hesitated and pulled the postal card out of his pocket. "Oh, pardon me, sir, but there's something I forgot to ask you. I got this in the mail today. I've been a little bothered about what to do about it."

The Dean of Men took the mimeographed card and read it quickly. 96 "Why, I should say that you ought to go see what they want, Wingate. You shouldn't ignore things of this sort, you know. It's all a part of the normal activities of college life. No reason for antagonizing your fellow-students by ignoring a request of this kind."

"All right, sir; I'll go see them." 97

"Why, to be sure, go see them! Always keep in mind that the Uni- 98 versity is a social as well as an educational institution, Wingate."

IV

Room 204, Student Union Building, was a newly finished, rather barren 99 office that smelled dankly of lime in the fresh plaster. It was fitted with a metal desk painted to imitate painted walnut, a large brass spittoon, a square metal waste-paper basket, a green metal filing cabinet, a large bank calendar, a huge pasteboard shipping case, and Aubrey H. Carson, who had the freshman cap concession.

Charlie Wingate hesitantly opened the door and saw Aubrey H. 100 Carson tilted back in a chair, his feet on the metal walnut desk, reading a copy of *Ballyhoo*.

"Co-ome in! Co-ome in!" Aubrey Carson called loudly without 101 putting down his magazine. "All right, old timer. What's on your mind?"

Charlie held out the mimeographed card. Carson held his maga- 102 zine a moment longer before accepting the card. He shoved his hat down over one eye, turning the card, looking first at the back, then at the name on the front. "Um-m-m," he grunted. He reached over to a drawer in the filing cabinet without taking his feet down and flipped through the cards. He looked at the name on the postal card again, pulled a card out of the file, and drew his thick lips up into a rosette. He looked at the file card in silence.

"Wingate," he said at last in a severe tone, "you have been dila- 103 tory. Indeed, Wingate, I might even go so far as to say you have been remiss. At the beginning of this semester you applied for and received a refund on your student ticket fee. That signifies that you have not attended a single football game this season, and that you have no intention of honoring any of the University's athletic spectacles with your presence this season. Also, the record discloses that you did not register at the Y.M.C.A. freshman mixer. Neither did you respond to polite solicitation for a trifling monetary pledge to the Memorial Stadium Fund. And, most heinous offense of all, Wingate, we find that you have yet to pay in one dollar for your freshman cap, prescribed by your seniors and purveyed to you on a non-profit basis by the Student Committee on Freshman Activities. And yet, Wingate, I find you duly enrolled and attending classes in this here now University. Wingate, what possible excuse do you have for such gross neglect of University tradition? Speak up!"

Charlie said meekly, "Well, I work nights and it's hard for me to get here in the daytime, and I can't afford to buy a cap." 104

"What's this!" Carson exclaimed, jerking his legs down from the desk top and banging the desk with two flat hands. "Why, boy, this is treason! You mean you can't afford *not* to buy a freshman cap." 105

"No, I just came to tell you that a dollar has to go a long way with me and that I need every cent I earn to stay in school. So I wish you'd please excuse me from buying a freshman cap." 106

Carson's lean, florid face suddenly became rigid and he stuck his jaw out with his lower teeth showing and, in spite of his marcelled taffy pompadour and his creased tailored suit, he again looked very much as he did in all the sporting section photographs. "See here, Wingate," he said, hard-lipped, "You're still a freshman at this University. You'll have to wait another year before you can start saying what you will do and won't do, see? Now we've been patient with you. You've been in school here three months without putting on a freshman cap. Do you realize that over eighty-five per cent of the freshman class came in here and bought their caps before the first week of school ended? Now who do you think *you* are, Wingate—Mr. God? You're going to get you a cap, and you're going to wear it. See? No ifs, ands, or buts about it. And if you don't leave this office with a green cap on your head then I don't mind telling you that we've got ways of getting one on you before another day passes." 107

"Well, if I buy one it's going to put me in a bad hole. All the money I've got is what I saved out to pay my room rent this week." 108

"Listen, fella, if we let horsefeathers like that go here, half the freshman class wouldn't be wearing freshman caps right now. Now I've said all I'm going to to you. Do you want your green cap now or will you wait till later? That's all I want to know. I don't aim to give you any high-pressure sales talk on something that's already been decided for you. Take it or leave it." 109

Carson reached over into the large pasteboard box, groped far down in it, and brought forth a small green monkey cap. He tossed it on the desk. Charlie Wingate stuck his forefinger in his watch pocket and pulled out a small pad of three carefully folded dollar bills. He unfolded them and laid one of the desk and picked up the cap. Carson put the dollar in his pocket and stood up. 110

Charlie stood holding his cap. He scuffed the cement floor with his shoe toe and began doggedly, "The only thing is—" 111

"Aw, that's O.K., Wingate, old man," Carson said suavely, "No 112

hard feelings whatsoever." He held out a freshly opened pack of cigarettes. "Here, have a Treasure Trove on me before you go."

V

That night all the stools along the counter at The Wigwam were filled 113
when Charlie Wingate came in, still dusty from the drill field. He got
himself a set-up back of the counter and went into the kitchen. He
moved about the steam-table, dishing up his dinner. He dragged a stool
over to a zinc-covered kitchen table and sat down to eat. The kitchen
was warm and steamy and the air was thick with the odors of sour chili
grease and yellow soap melting in hot dishwater. Charlie's fork slipped
through his fingers, and he began nodding over his plate.

Fat Kruger, the night dishwasher and short-order cook, yelled, 114
"Hey, there, wake up and pay for your bed!" Charlie jerked his head up
and looked at the ponderous, good-humored cook with half-lidded eyes.
"Why'n't you try sleeping in bed once in a w'ile, Charlie?" Fat said in a
friendly tone. "You're going to kill yourself if you don't watch out, trying to go without sleep."

"Don't worry, Fat. I can take it," Charlie said. 115

Almost two hours had to pass before it would be the hour for him 116
to come on, but not time enough for him to walk back to his room and
catch a nap, so he took the book on which he had to make an outside
reading report in Economics 150 and went up to the last booth to study
until nine o'clock. He fell asleep and he did not wake up until Red Hibbert, going off, shook him and told him that it was almost time for him
to come on. He closed his book and went back to the washroom. The
acrid stench of the mothballs that Nick used to deodorize the latrine
cleared his head. He took down his apron and tied it on over his army
breeches. Then he slipped into a white coat.

The usual black-coffee addicts came dribbling in. When the tele- 117
phone rang, Charlie answered it, jotting down short orders to go. The
delivery boy came in and went out and banged off on his motorcycle with
paper bags full of "red hots" and nickel hamburgers and coffee in paper
cylinders. The Wigwam's white tile shone under the inverted alabas-
ter urns. There was a pale pink reflection in the plate-glass window as
the Neon sign outside spelled and re-spelled "Wigwam Eats. Open All
Night." A party of drunken Betas came in at ten-thirty and seated themselves noisily in the last booth. They tossed Charlie's economics book out
into the aisle with a whoop, and he came and picked it up and took their
orders in silence while they kidded him about his flap ears and the grease
on his white coat. At eleven o'clock the last whistle at the University
powerhouse blew for the closing hour, and a couple of lingering "dates"

scurried out. Finally the drunks left, after one had been sick in a corner of the booth. The delivery boy came coasting up at midnight and checked in and roared away again on his motorcycle. The long small hours began inching past.

At one o'clock Charlie finished cleaning up the drunk's mess and he 118 had cleared off the last of the tables. The Wigwam was empty, so he opened the book he must read for Ec 150. He had read a few lines when a bunch of girls from the Theta house down the street came charging in, giggling and talking in gasps and screams, their fur coats clutched over their sleeping pajamas. It was long after the closing hour, and they told Charlie to keep an eye out for the University night watchman. They took up the two back booths and they consulted The Wigwam's printed menu card without failing to read aloud the lines "Nick (Pericles) Pappas," "We Employ Student Help Exclusively," and "Please Do Not Tip. A Smile Is Our Reward" with the customary shrieks. Nearly all ordered filet mignon and French fries, which were not on the menu, but two or three ordered pecan waffles and coffee, which were. When he had served their orders Charlie went back to his book again, but the low buzz of their talk and their sudden spurts of laughter disturbed him and he could not read. At a quarter of two they began peering round corners of their booths. They asked Charlie in stage-whispers if the coast were clear.

Charlie went to the door and looked out on the street and beckoned 119 widely with his arm. They trooped out with their fur coats pulled tight, their fur-trimmed silken mules slapping their bare heels. Charlie went on back to clear away their dishes. They had left about thirty cents as a tip, all in cents and nickels. The coins were carefully imbedded in the cold steak grease and gluey syrup and putty-colored cigarette leavings on their plates. Charlie began stacking the plates without touching the money. He carried the dirty dishes back and set them through the opening in the kitchen wall. Fat Kruger came to the opening and Charlie went back to his book.

Fat called, "Hey, Charlie, you leavin' this tip again?" 120

"You're damn' right, I'm leaving it." Charlie said. "I can get along 121 without their tips. They leave it that way every time. I guess they think I'll grabble on their filthy plates to get a lousy thirty cents. It takes a woman to think up something like that."

"Charlie, you're too proud. I don't see where you can afford to be so 122 proud. The way I figure it, thirty cents is thirty cents."

"Hell, I'm not proud, Fat. I just try to keep my self-respect. When 123 those sorority sows come in and plant their tips in the dirt and grease of their plates, damn' if I'll lower myself to grub it out."

He sat down on a counter stool with the economics book before 124 him, trying to fix his mind on it. He read a page. The print became thin blurred parallels of black on the page. His eyelids kept drooping shut and he propped the muscles with his palms at his temples, trying to keep his eyes open. His head jerked forward and he caught it and began reading again. Soon his face lowered slowly through his hands and came to rest on the open book.

Fat Kruger came through the kitchen swinging door and tiptoed 125 up front. Fat stood grinning, watching Charlie sleep. Cramped over with his head on the counter, Charlie snored softly. Fat gave his head a gentle shove, and Charlie started up to catch his balance.

"For God sakes, guy, you're *dead!*" Fat howled. "Don't you never 126 get no sleep except like that?"

"What time is it?" Charlie said, yawning and arching his back. 127

"Half-past two." 128

"Jees, is that all?" 129

"Charlie, go back there and lay down on the kitchen table. I'll 130 watch the front for you. Nobody'll be coming in for a while."

As he was talking old Uncle Jim Hudson ambled in, a bundle of 131 sweaters, overcoats, and drizzled dewlaps, his black timeclock slung over one shoulder by a leather lanyard. Uncle Jim laid his long, nickled flashlight carefully on the counter and eased himself onto a stool. He ordered a cup of black coffee and in a lecherous wheeze began telling dirty stories selected from his twenty years' experience as a campus night-watchman. Fat Kruger nickered loudly after each telling, and Charlie jerked his eyes open and smiled sleepily. It was three-thirty when Uncle Jim left. Charlie opened his book again.

"Charlie, I wouldn't put my eyes out over that damn' book if I was 132 you, when you're dyin' for sleep," Fat said.

"I've got to get it read, Fat. It's my outside reading in Economics 133 and the whole semester grade depends on it. It's the hardest book to keep your mind on you ever saw. I've been reading on it for over a month and I'm only half through, and he's going to call for these reports any day now. If I flunk Ec I flunk out of school."

"Why mess with reading it? I know a guy over at the Masonic 134 Dorm who'll read it and write your report for two bucks. He writes all my English themes for me, and I'm making a straight A in English. He only charges fifty cents for short themes and two bucks for term papers. You ought to try him."

"Hell, Fat, you get five dollars a week from home. Where am I 135 going to get two dollars for hiring a guy to read this book?"

"Charlie, I just can't figure you out. You never do get any real 136 sleep. You sure must want a college education bad. It don't look to me like you would figure it's worth it."

"Oh, it's worth it! It's a big satisfaction to my folks to have me in 137 college. And where can a man without a college degree get nowadays? But I'll tell you the truth, I didn't know it was going to be like this when I came down here last Fall. I used to read *College Humor* in high school, and when fellows came home from University for the holidays, all dressed up in snappy clothes, talking about dates and football and dances, and using college slang—well, I had a notion I'd be like that when I got down here. The University publicity department sent me a little booklet showing how it was easy to work your way through college. So here I am. I haven't had a date or been to a dance or seen a football game since I enrolled. And there are plenty of others just like me. I guess I'm getting a college education, all right—but the only collegiate thing I've been able to do is go to sleep in class."

"How you get by with sleeping in class, Charlie?" 138

"I wear those colored spectacles and prop myself, and the profs 139 can't see I've got my eyes closed."

Fat waggled his heavy face mournfully. "Boy, it sure is tough when 140 a man don't get his sleep."

"Yeah, it is," Charlie said, looking down at his book again. "I'll 141 get a break pretty soon, though. I'd rather chop off a hand than to flunk out of University before I'd even finished one semester."

VI

The tardiest of the hundred students enrolled in Dr. Sylvester C. O. 142 Kenshaw's Economics 150 straggled into the lecture room and made their ways to alphabetically-assigned chairs with much scuffling and trampling of toes and mumbled apologies. Ec 150, renowned as a pipe course, was always crowded. Doctor Kenshaw was the celebrated author of seven textbooks on economics, five of which his students were required to buy each semester. Doctor Kenshaw's national reputation as an economist permitted him to be erratic about meeting his classes, but fame had never dimmed his fondness for student flattery. The only students who ever flunked Ec 150 were those who gave affront to Doctor Kenshaw by neglecting to buy his textbooks or by not laughing at his wit or by being outrageously inattentive to his lectures.

Doctor Kenshaw was late that morning. Charlie Wingate sat in his 143 chair on the back row in an agony of waiting. He had on his amber glasses and he could fall asleep as soon as Doctor Kenshaw opened his lecture. But he had to stay awake until then. There was a slow ache in the small of his back. The rest of his body was numb. He had not taken off his army shoes for twenty hours, and his feet were moist and swollen. Every time he shifted position his arms and legs were bathed in prickling fire. He kept his eyes open behind the amber lenses, watching the clock. Small noises of the classroom came to him as a low, far-off humming.

When the clock on the front wall showed nine after eleven the 144 seated class began stirring as if it were mounted on some eccentric amusement-park device. Excited whispers eddied out on the warm air of the steam-heated lecture room. "He's giving us another cut!" "He's not meeting this class today!" "He's got one more minute to make it!" "Naw; six more! You have to wait fifteen minutes on department heads."

There was a seething argument on this point, but when the clock showed fourteen minutes after eleven a bold leader sprang up and said, "Come on, everybody!" All but five or six especially conscientious students rose and milled after him toward the door. Charlie Wingate followed, thoroughly awakened by the chance of getting to bed so soon. The leader yanked the door open and Doctor Kenshaw stumbled in, all out of breath, his eyeglasses steamed, his pointed gray beard quivering, a vain little man in a greenish-black overcoat. 145

"Go back to your seats!" Doctor Kenshaw commanded sternly as soon as he could get his breath. He marched over to his lecture table and planked down his leather brief case. He took off his overcoat and began wiping the steam from his eyeglasses while the students hurried back to their chairs. "It does seem to me," he said, his voice quavering with anger, "that it would be no more than courteous for this class to await my arrival on those rare occasions when I am delayed. Day after day you come lagging into my classes, and I have always been extremely lenient in giving credit for attendance, no matter how tardy your arrival. Certainly it is no more than my privilege to ask that you wait for me occasionally." 146

A few students exchanged meaning glances. They meant, "Now we're in for it. The old boy has on one of his famous mads." 147

"Today, I believe I shall forego delivering my prepared lecture," Doctor Kenshaw went on in a more even voice, but with elaborate sarcasm, "and let *you* do the talking. Perhaps it would be meet to hear a few outside reading reports this morning. All of you doubtless are aware that these reports were due last week, although I had not expected to call for them at once. I trust that I have impressed you sufficiently with the importance of these reports. They represent to me the final result of your semester's work in this course. The grades you receive on these reports will be your grades for the semester. Let us begin forthwith. When your name is called, you will rise and read your report to the class." He opened his roll book. 148

"Mr. Abbott!" he called. Mr. Abbott stammered an excuse. Doctor Kenshaw passed coldly on to Miss Adams, making no comment. All through the A's it was the same. But with the B's an ashen, spectacled Miss Ballentyne stood up and began reading in a droning voice her report on *The Economic Consequences of the Peace*. Obviously Doctor Kenshaw was not listening to her. His hard little eyes under craggy brows were moving up one row and down the other, eager for a victim. On the back row, Charlie Wingate's propped legs had given way and he had slipped far down into his seat, fast asleep. When Doctor Kenshaw's preying eyes reached Charlie they stopped moving. Someone tittered nervously and 149 then was silent as Doctor Kenshaw jerked his head round in the direction of the noise. Miss Ballentyne droned on.

When she had finished, Doctor Kenshaw said dryly, "Very good, 150 Miss Ballentyne, very good, indeed. Er—ah—would someone be kind enough to arouse the recumbent young gentleman in the last row?"

There was a murmur of laughter while everyone turned to look at 151 Milton Weismann nudging Charlie Wingate. Doctor Kenshaw was running down the list of names in his small record book. Milton Weismann gave Charlie another stiff poke in the ribs, and Charlie sprang up quickly. Everyone laughed loudly at that.

"Mr.—ah—*Wingate,* isn't it? Mr. Wingate, your report." 152

"Pardon me, sir?" 153

"Mr. Wingate, what was the title of the book assigned to you for 154 report in this class?"

"*Theory of the Leisure Class* by Veblen, sir." 155

"Ah, then, that's the explanation. So you were assiduously engaged 156 in evolving your own theory of the leisure class. Is that right, Mr. Wingate? You have evidently concluded that Economics 150 is the leisure class."

The class rocked with laughter. Doctor Kenshaw, pleased with his 157 pun and flattered by the response to it, found it hard to keep his face straight. Suddenly he was back in good humor. "Mr. Wingate's theory is quite apparently one to which the majority of this class subscribes. Now I try to be lenient with students in this class. Surely no one could describe me as a hard taskmaster. But I resent your implication that I have been too easy-going. Now these reading reports were assigned to you last September, and you have had ample time to prepare them. I'll not call for any more of them today, but at the next session of this class I expect every one of these papers in. As for you, Mr. Wingate, if you'll see me directly after class, I'll be glad to hear any explanation or apology that you may wish to make. I want most of all to be fair. I have always given every student the benefit of the doubt until a student deliberately flouts me with his indifference. But I am capable of being quite ruthless, I assure you."

"Thank you, sir," Charlie mumbled. He suffered a slow torture, 158 trying to keep awake until the class bell rang. He rolled his hot, red-veined eyes up with drunken precision to see the clock. Fifteen minutes had to pass before the bell would ring.

When the bell rang the class arose quickly and began clumping 159 out. Several co-eds and men, politickers and apple-polishers wangling for A's, crowded about the lecture table. Doctor Kenshaw always remained behind after each class to accept their homage. But today he looked up over the heads of the eager group. He silenced their inane questions and flagrant compliments by placing his right forefinger against his thin, unsmiling lips. "Sh-h-h!" he said. The apple-polishers turned their heads in the direction of his gaze and then, giggling softly, tiptoed away. When the last had gone out, Doctor Kenshaw unscrewed his fountain pen and opened his roll book. He ran his finger down the list until he came to "Wingate, C." and in the space opposite under "Smstr Grd" he marked a precise little F.

A whiffling snore escaped Charlie Wingate in the back of the room. 160 Doctor Kenshaw looked back across the varnished chair rows with a frown of annoyance. He took his overcoat from its hanger, slipped into it, and strapped up his brief case. He jammed on his hat and strode out of the lecture room, slamming the door. The noise made a hollow echo in the empty room, but it did not disturb Charlie Wingate. He slept on behind his amber glasses.

Reading and Interpreting

VOCABULARY

Use your dictionary as necessary to find the meaning of the following words in the context of Milburn's story:

sough (2)   pacifist (48)   lucrative (76)   loathe (78)   monetary (103)
purveyed (103)   florid (107)   doggedly (111)   assiduously (156)

CONCEPT ANALYSIS

1. In this story, who fails? Does the student fail? Does the institution fail? Explain.
2. The historical context of this story is the Great Depression, a period of economic collapse and consequent social and political ferment. In this context, the author's antiestablishment bias is evident through his treatment of characters and situations.
   a. Refer to the dialogue between Red and Charlie in paragraphs 38–50. What political, social, and economic points is the author making? Does the author try to make the argument evenhanded? How do you know Charlie, not Red, represents the author's point of view?
   b. What emotions do you think the author wants the reader to feel at the end of the story? What were your emotions?
   c. What social or political action might the author wish the reader to take?
3. This story has a serious social theme—that human beings are helpless against the disinterest of powerful institutions and economic forces. The characters themselves embody this idea. What aspect of the theme does

each of the following exemplify: Fat Kruger, Red Hibbert, the girls from the Theta house and the boys from the Beta house, Doctor Kenshaw, the Dean of Men, Aubrey H. Carson?

4. The author is critical of many aspects of university life. Each aspect listed below is illustrated by a quotation from the text. Use the quote as a springboard to explore the author's view.

   a. ROTC: " . . . when the next war comes we'll all be officers, us fellas that got this training in college. . . . we'll have the edge on guys that never did take advantage of a college education. . . . And you know darn' well they're not going to stick their college-trained officers into front-line trenches to get shot. So there's where I figure us guys in R.O.T.C. will have a big advantage." (45)

   b. the institution's relationship to the individual: "We have six thousand other students here who need our attention, and the University has to be impartial and impersonal in dealing with these problems." (90)

   c. exploitation of the working class: "[The Theta girls] consulted The Wigwam's printed menu card without failing to read aloud the lines 'Nick (Pericles) Pappas,' 'We Employ Student Help Exclusively,' and 'Please Do Not Tip. A Smile Is Our Reward' with the customary shrieks." (118)

   d. institutional favoritism toward wealthier students: "And this kid didn't have to take Military, neither. His old man's a big shot lawyer in the City." "Yeah, but you got to have pull to get away with that, Charlie." "That's what I mean, Red. You can get away with plenty in this University if you got the pull." (48–50)

   e. special treatment for athletes: " . . . look at the job [Aubrey] Carson [quarterback on the football team] has. . . . The tobacco company pays him a good salary for passing out samples of their cigarettes. . . . They figure it's a good advertisement. . . . sort of an endorsement." (79, 81)

   f. snobbery: "[The Betas] tossed Charlie's economics book out into the aisle with a whoop, and he came and picked it up and took their orders in silence while they kidded him about his flap ears and the grease on his white coat." (117)

   g. laziness and cynicism of the professors: "Ec 150, renowned as a pipe course, was always crowded. . . . The only students who ever flunked Ec 150 were those who gave affront to Doctor Kenshaw by neglecting to buy his textbooks or by not laughing at his wit or by being outrageously inattentive to his lectures." (142)

   h. laziness and cynicism of the students: "Why mess with reading [your outside economics reading]? I know a guy over at the Masonic Dorm who'll read it and write your report for two bucks. He writes all my English themes for me. . . ." (134)

Describe the encounter between Charlie and his mother when Charlie returns home. Create the appropriate atmosphere and elicit the desired emotion(s) by using the techniques of elaboration: descriptive detail, vivid language, and figures of speech.

Thinking and Writing

RHETORICAL TECHNIQUE

1. The author uses vivid language, concrete details, figures of speech, and dialogue to communicate Charlie's physical deprivation and helplessness, thereby building the reader's feeling for him. Some examples: "the ridge of quilts on the sagged iron bed," "he rolled his hot, red-veined eyes up with drunken precision to see the clock." Cite other particularly effective phrases that describe Charlie, the Wigwam, and the Ec 150 class, and discuss your choices.

2. As Charlie's personal struggle intensifies, so does the reader's sympathy and frustration at his plight. His confrontations with the Dean of Men, Aubrey H. Carson, the Theta girls, and Doctor Kenshaw project the dramatic quality of a struggle between the forces of good and evil. Select one of these confrontations and discuss the various techniques by which the author makes his own feelings concrete.

COMPOSITION

How do the various students in Milburn's short story illustrate philosopher Bertrand Russell's observation that the "principle of selection [for the university] is social and hereditary, not fitness for the work"? Use concrete vocabulary and vivid images both of your own and selected from the story to make your points.

CHARLES DICKENS
Great Expectations and *David Copperfield*

Victorian novelist Charles Dickens (1812–1870) was best known in his own day as a popular writer. The public awaited installments of his serialized novels as eagerly as today's soap opera fans turn to each episode of their favorite show. Dickens, however, was more than a public entertainer. His own impoverished background, his sympathy for the downtrodden, especially children, and his ability to communicate feelings through character and situation made him an interpreter of his age. The following scenes drawn from two of Dickens's novels use figures of speech and exuberant vocabulary that enable the reader to visualize and experience both the cruel and the comical aspects of nineteenth-century English school life.

Great Expectations

Mr. Wopsle's great-aunt kept an evening school in the village; that is to 1
say, she was a ridiculous old woman of limited means and unlimited infirmity, who used to go to sleep from six to seven every evening, in the society of youth who paid twopence per week each, for the improving opportunity to seeing her do it. She rented a small cottage, and Mr. Wopsle had the room upstairs, where we students used to overhear him reading aloud in a most dignified and terrific manner, and occasionally bumping on the ceiling. There was a fiction that Mr. Wopsle "examined" the scholars, once a quarter. What he did on those occasions was to turn up his cuffs, stick up his hair, and give us Mark Antony's oration over the body of Caesar. This was always followed by Collins' Ode on the Passions, wherein I particularly venerated Mr. Wopsle as Revenge, throwing his bloodstained sword in thunder down, and taking the War-denouncing trumpet with a withering look. . . .

The Educational scheme or Course established by Mr. Wopsle's 2
great-aunt may be resolved into the following synopsis. The pupils ate apples and put straws down one another's backs, until Mr. Wopsle's great-aunt collected her energies, and made an indiscriminate totter at them

with a birch-rod. After receiving the charge with every mark of derision, the pupils formed in line and buzzingly passed a ragged book from hand to hand. The book had an alphabet in it, some figures and tables, and a little spelling—that is to say, it had had once. As soon as this volume began to circulate, Mr. Wopsle's great-aunt fell into a state of coma; arising either from sleep or a rheumatic paroxysm. The pupils then entered among themselves upon a competitive examination on the subject of Boots, with the view of ascertaining who could tread the hardest upon whose toes. This mental exercise lasted until Biddy made a rush at them and distributed three defaced Bibles (shaped as if they had been unskilfully cut off the chump-end of something), more illegibly printed at the best than any curiosities of literature I have since met with, speckled all over with ironmould, and having various specimens of the insect world smashed between their leaves. This part of the Course was usually lightened by several single combats between Biddy and refractory students. When the fights were over, Biddy gave out the number of a page, and then we all read aloud what we could—or what we couldn't—in a frightful chorus; Biddy leading with a high shrill monotonous voice, and none of us having the least notion of, or reverence for, what we were reading about. When this horrible din had lasted a certain time, it mechanically awoke Mr. Wopsle's great-aunt, who staggered at a boy fortuitously, and pulled his ears. This was understood to terminate the Course for the evening, and we emerged into the air with shrieks of intellectual victory. It is fair to remark that there was no prohibition against any pupil's entertaining himself with a slate or even with the ink (when there was any), but that it was not easy to pursue that branch of study in the winter season, on account of the little general shop in which the classes were holden—and which was also Mr. Wopsle's great-aunt's sitting-room and bedchamber—being but faintly illuminated through the agency of one lowspirited dip-candle and no snuffers.

It appeared to me that it would take time to become uncommon 3 under these circumstances: nevertheless, I resolved to try it, and that very evening Biddy entered on our special agreement, by imparting some information from her little Catalogue of Prices, under the head of moist sugar, and lending me, to copy at home, a large old English D which she had imitated from the heading of some newspaper, and which I supposed, until she told me what it was, to be a design for a buckle.

David Copperfield

A short walk brought us—I mean the master and me—to Salem House, 1 which was enclosed with a high brick wall, and looked very dull. . . .

I gazed upon the schoolroom into which he took me, as the most 2 forlorn and desolate place I had ever seen. I see it now. A long room, with three long rows of desks, and six of forms, and bristling all round with pegs for hats and slates. Scraps of old copy-books and exercises litter the dirty floor. Some silkworms' houses, made of the same materials, are scattered over the desks. Two miserable little white mice, left behind by their owner, are running up and down in a fusty castle made of pasteboard and wire, looking in all the corners with their red eyes for anything to eat. A bird, in a cage, very little bigger than himself, makes a mournful rattle now and then in hopping on his perch, two inches high, or dropping from it; but neither sings nor chirps. There is a strange unwholesome smell upon the room, like mildewed corduroys, sweet apples wanting air, and rotten books. There could not well be more ink splashed about it, if it had been roofless from its first construction, and the skies had rained, snowed, hailed, and blown ink through the varying seasons of the year.

I heard all kinds of things about the school and all belonging to it. I heard that Mr. Creakle had not preferred his claim to being a Tartar without reason; that he was the sternest and most severe of masters; that he laid about him, right and left, every day of his life, charging in among the boys like a trooper, and slashing away, unmercifully. That he knew nothing himself, but the art of slashing, being more ignorant (J. Steerforth said) than the lowest boy in the school; that he had been, a good many years ago, a small hop-dealer in the Borough, and had taken to the schooling business after being bankrupt in hops, and making away with Mrs. Creakle's money. With a good deal more of that sort, which I wondered how they knew. 3

I heard that the man with the wooden leg, whose name was Tungay, was an obstinate barbarian who had formerly assisted in the hop business, but had come into the scholastic line with Mr. Creakle, in consequence, as was supposed among the boys, of his having broken his leg in Mr. Creakle's service, and having done a deal of dishonest work for him, and knowing his secrets. I heard that with the single exception of Mr. Creakle, Tungay considered the whole establishment, masters and boys, as his natural enemies, and that the only delight of his life was to be sour and malicious. 4

I heard that Mr. Sharp and Mr. Mell were both supposed to be wretchedly paid; and that when there was hot and cold meat for dinner at Mr. Creakle's table, Mr. Sharp was always expected to say he preferred cold; which was again corroborated by J. Steerforth, the only parlor-boarder. I heard that Mr. Sharp's wig didn't fit him; and that he needn't be so "bounceable"—somebody else said "bumptious"—about it, because his own red hair was very plainly to be seen behind. 5

I heard that one boy, who was a coal-merchant's son, came as a set-off against the coal-bill, and was called on that account "Exchange or Barter"—a name selected from the arithmetic-book as expressing this arrangement. I heard that the table-beer was a robbery of parents, and the 6 pudding an imposition. I heard that Miss Creakle was regarded by the school in general as being in love with Steerforth; and I am sure, as I sat in the dark, thinking of his nice voice, and his nice face, and his easy manner, and his curling hair, I thought it very likely. I heard that Mr. Mell was not a bad sort of fellow, but hadn't a sixpence to bless himself with; and that there was no doubt that old Mrs. Mell, his mother, was as poor as Job. . . .

The rest of the half-year is a jumble in my recollection of the daily   7
strife and struggle of our lives; of the waning summer and the changing season; of the frosty mornings when we were rung out of bed, and the cold, cold smell of the dark nights when we were rung into bed again; of the evening schoolroom dimly lighted and indifferently warmed, and the morning schoolroom which was nothing but a great shivering machine; of the alternation of boiled beef with roast beef, and boiled mutton with roast mutton; of clods of bread-and-butter, dog's-eared lesson-books, cracked slates, tear-blotted copy-books, canings, rulerings, hair-cuttings, rainy Sundays, suet-puddings, and a dirty atmosphere of ink surrounding all.

Reading and Interpreting

VOCABULARY

Use your dictionary as necessary to find the meaning of the following words in context:

Great Expectations

infirmity (1)   venerated (1)   indiscriminate (2)   derision (2)
refractory (2)   din (2)   fortuitously (2)   imparting (3)

David Copperfield

corroborated (5)   bumptious (5)   imposition (6)

CONCEPT ANALYSIS

1. Dickens presents Mr. Wopsle's great-aunt's school and Mr. Creakle's Salem House as examples of Victorian education. What characteristics do the two schools have in common? What specific criticisms do these descriptions imply regarding (a) faculty qualifications, (b) curriculum, and (c) meeting the students' emotional needs?
2. Apply the following quotations to the two schools depicted by Dickens:

a. Spare the rod and spoil the child. (traditional proverb)
b. "[A] faculty, by its very existence [attempts to make itself] some sort of storehouse of human experience." (Ciardi)
c. " . . . few children . . . do not feel, during most of the time they are in school, an amount of fear, anxiety, and tension that most adults would find intolerable." (Holt)
d. "Let early education be a sort of amusement . . . you will then be better able to find out the natural bent." (Plato's *Republic*)

Quickwrite

Write a quick sketch of a disruptive incident in school that you either witnessed or participated in. Emphasize either the cruel or the comical aspects through concrete details and dialogue.

Thinking and Writing

RHETORICAL TECHNIQUE

1. In his description of Mr. Wopsle's great-aunt's school in *Great Expectations,* Dickens makes fun of the system of education. For example: "[a synopsis] of the Education scheme or Course. . . . The pupils ate apples and put straws down one another's backs . . ." (2). Cite other examples of humor. What is the source of the humor here?

2. The topic statement of paragraph 2 in the excerpt from *David Copperfield* rests upon the carefully chosen adjectives *forlorn* and *desolate.* Cite vivid images in the paragraph that give concreteness to these key adjectives. From your own experience, select images that would be as convincing as Dickens's.

3. Read aloud paragraphs 3, 4, 5, and 6 of the *David Copperfield* excerpt to appreciate the cadence, or rhythm, of the sentences. Note the repetition of "I heard that. . . ."

4. Select the character from the *David Copperfield* excerpt whom you think comes through most clearly, and underline the vivid expressions that help you visualize him or her.

5. Dickens uses metaphor, simile, and allusion in *David Copperfield* to make his writing concrete—for example: "A long room . . . *bristling* all round with pegs for hats and slates" (2). Find additional examples of figures of speech and allusions.

COMPOSITION

Think about a school that you have attended. Write a descriptive passage about it, using a variation of Dickens's pattern "I heard that. . . ." Your first line will be: "I remember (or know) all kinds of things about the school and all belonging to it."

STEPHEN SPENDER

An Elementary School Classroom in a Slum

A political radical in his youth, English poet and critic
Stephen Spender (b. 1909) drew his poetic themes from
the nineteenth-century Romantic poets, but infused his
poems with social concern. The classroom images in this
poem reveal the desolateness of the children's lives in a
far more powerful way than could a commissioner's report using educational jargon.

Far from gusty waves these children's faces.
Like rootless weeds, the hair torn round their pallor.
The tall girl with her weighed-down head.
The paper-seeming boy, with rat's eyes, the stunted unlucky heir
Of twisted bones, reciting a father's gnarled disease,   5
His lesson from his desk. At back of the dim class
One unnoted, sweet and young. His eyes live in a dream
Of squirrel's game, in tree room, other than this.

On sour cream walls, donations. Shakespeare's head,
Cloudless at dawn, civilized dome riding all cities.   10
Belled, flowery, Tyrolese valley. Open-handed map
Awarding the world its world. And yet, for these
Children, these windows, not this world, are world,
Where all their future's painted with a fog,
A narrow street sealed in with a lead sky,   15
Far far from rivers, capes, and stars of words.

Surely, Shakespeare is wicked, the map a bad example
With ships and sun and love tempting them to steal—
For lives that slyly turn in their cramped holes
From fog to endless night? On their slag heap, these children   20
Wear skins peeped through by bones and spectacles of steel
With mended glass, like bottle bits on stones.
All of their time and space are foggy slum.
So blot their maps with slums as big as doom.

Unless, governor, teacher, inspector, visitor,   25
This map becomes their window and these windows
That shut upon their lives like catacombs,
Break O break open till they break the town

And show the children to green fields, and make their world
Run azure on gold sands, and let their tongues   30
Run naked into books, the white and green leaves open
History theirs whose language is the sun.

Reading and Interpreting

VOCABULARY

Use your dictionary as necessary to find the meaning of the following words
as used in Spender's poem:

pallor (2)   slag heap (20)   catacombs (27)

CONCEPT ANALYSIS

1. Spender contrasts the free and open world of nature to that of a narrow,
   oppressive slum school. Cite specific images that portray the two contrasting environments.
2. The poem is like an inductive essay in which the concrete details and
   images lead into the author's central idea or thesis. Where do you find
   the thesis statement of the poem? How would you express it in your own
   words? How do the preceding images prepare you for Spender's critical
   viewpoint?
3. The purpose of education is to enlighten, to cast light on the dark places
   of ignorance in humankind's existence. Point to specific images of light
   and darkness that convey this school's failure to illuminate these children's existence.
4. Items in the classroom include a map of the world, a picture of Shakespeare, a poster of a flower- and steeple-dotted valley in Austria. What

educational purpose are these items intended to have? To what extent do they serve their purpose for these children? Explain, with reference to Spender's description of Shakespeare as "wicked" and the world map "a bad example."

Thinking and Writing

RHETORICAL TECHNIQUE

Spender uses concrete description and figures of speech to portray the slum school. These expressions compress many associated meanings and emotions into a few words. Explain the emotional impact of the following phrases:

a. "Like rootless weeds" (2)
b. "paper-seeming boy" (4)
c. "their future's painted with a fog,/A narrow street sealed in with a lead sky" (14–15)
d. "On their slag heap" (20)

Cite other images that have a particular visual and/or emotional force for you.

COMPOSITION

Spender might agree that in our society, school is the *last* place for education. Do you agree? Discuss this statement in terms of your own academic experience. You may refer to images from the poem as well as examples from life in support of your thesis.

THE WRITTEN RESPONSE

Writing Workshop

1. Analogies. An analogy is a comparison between elements from two different areas of life. Take school as your subject and think about communicating your ideas through an analogy. Choose one of the following corresponding areas:

the army   prison   a school gym   a gambling casino   summer camp

the theater   a museum   a family

Describe each of the following aspects of school in terms of the area you selected for the analogy:

- the function of school
- the classroom
- instructors
- student behavior
- assignments
- achievements and failures

As a guide, review John Holt's analogy of the classroom and the foxhole. Recall that he equates the "fumbling incompetence" of the schoolchild to the neurotic reactions of soldiers too long in battle: "It seems to me that children dig themselves similar foxholes [that they can't get out of] in school . . ." (4).

2. Developing Examples for a Thesis. In the first paragraph of Sidney Painter's "Education," the first sentence states the thesis, and the last sentence restates it. Between the two are a number of excellent examples. Generate a thesis on the dominant characteristic of modern education and use the same pattern to develop it.

3. Using References to Your Reading. Specific references to the ideas and philosophies of authors that you have read enhance the quality of your writing. Develop the following guide into an outline for a written theme, drawing on selections from this chapter. To lend support to your ideas, quote or paraphrase the authors of these selections.

Thesis: For most of your life you have been a student. Suppose that you now had the opportunity to be a teacher. What three selections from this chapter would influence your approach to your students and to your teaching?

    I. Introductory paragraph: statement of overall thesis and identification of selections

II. Selection 1
   A. Title, author, précis of selection
   B. Selection's influence on attitude toward students
   C. Selection's influence on teaching (methods, content, organization of class-room, other)
III. Selection 2
   A. Title, author, précis of selection
   B. Selection's influence on attitude toward students
   C. Selection's influence on teaching (methods, content, organization of class-room, other)
IV. Selection 3
   A. Title, author, précis of selection
   B. Selection's influence on attitude toward students
   C. Selection's influence on teaching (methods, content, organization of class-room, other)
V. Conclusion

Topics for Critical Thinking and Writing

1. Make a generalization about a source of learning in your life. It may be films, television, your family, the streets, or a classroom. Develop your generalization with concrete details and analogies.
2. An American ideal is that higher education should be available to everyone. John Ciardi's essay and George Milburn's short story address the question of who should go to college. In an essay of your own, respond to this question and elaborate the types of students you discuss with specific examples.
3. Review John Ciardi's essay "Another School Year—Why?" Write a personal essay in which you offer your opinion on the purpose of a college education. Discuss the extent to which your college fulfills or fails to fulfill this purpose. Use examples, anecdotes, analogies, and allusions to bring your ideas to life.
4. Several selections in this chapter deal with the effect on students of the classroom environment and the teacher's competence and personality (see Stephen Spender's poem, the Dickens excerpts, and the John Holt excerpts). Using these readings as a springboard for your imagination, design a model classroom and describe a model instructor. (You may use any educational level you wish.)

Synthesis Questions

1. In the Sufi tale "The Story of Fire," the master says that "man does not want to be taught." Use this quotation as a thesis statement and apply it to the student in Ciardi's essay, the boys in Wopsle's great-aunt's school in Dickens's *Great Expectations,* the university students described by Painter in his essay on medieval education, and yourself.
2. Schools should meet the psychological as well as the intellectual needs of their students. Spender's poem, Holt's diary, and the excerpts from Dickens explicitly or implicitly address this thesis. Review these selections and discuss how the schools described either met or failed to meet their students' psychological needs.
3. The physical environment of a schoolroom is supposed to have a positive influence on the life of a child. To what extent is this true of the classrooms described in Spender's poem, Dickens's excerpt from *David Copperfield,* and Milburn's short story?
4. Teachers and learners may have different objectives. Support this thesis by referring to your own experience and to selections in this chapter in which the objectives of teacher and student are in conflict. (You also may wish to refer to Chapter One's Essay for Analysis, in which Richard Wright describes a conflict between himself and his high school principal.)

Refining Your Essay

1. Review the descriptions in your essay. Have you used precise verbs rather than general ones to convey action? Have you chosen some vivid adjectives to give color and texture to your sentences? Are your nouns too general and abstract, or have you looked for the most specific and visual words to identify the things you are writing about? Consult a dictionary or thesaurus at least five times to sharpen the vocabulary in your final draft.
2. Review the figures of speech—similes and metaphors—that you have used in your essay. Make sure that the comparisons are appropriate. If you have not used any similes or metaphors at all, find a statement that is broad or vague, and make it concrete by introducing a comparison in the form of a figure of speech. Reflect on what your subject corresponds to in the world of nature, sports, or some other area with which you are acquainted. Your figure of speech should be clear and help convey your meaning to your reader.
3. Are there points in your essay at which your general statements could be sharpened with allusions to popular culture, religious history, or literature? Try to work in one such reference.
4. An elegant or humorous quotation or paraphrase of the remarks of an author

you have read may lend weight to your assertions. Look for places in your essay where the thesis or topic statements might profit from brief supporting references, and include one or more.

5. Apt, clear examples and illustrations are essential for clarifying your ideas. Check your idea and opinion statements. Have you followed them up with specific and concrete examples of what you mean? Have you brought your abstractions down to earth by illustrations from life?

6. Review a classmate's work, focusing on its concreteness or lack of it. Mark any assertions, claims, ideas, thesis statements, generalizations, and unspecific nouns and verbs that would benefit from revision for concreteness.

CHAPTER SIX

Human Accomplishment: Recording the Process

This scale model of an architectural student's original design represents the potential for human accomplishment. In each generation, men and women have worked with their strength, brains, and creativity to improve the human condition in uniquely human ways. Uniquely human, too, is the act of reflecting upon and recording this process of accomplishment. The record of our efforts to get things done is our guide for future generations.

What has been a real accomplishment for you? What process did you use to achieve your objectives? Did you record the process in any way? Explain.

THE WRITING FOCUS

*. . . there is {a} specific quality which distinguishes
{men and beasts} and which will admit of no dispute.
This is the faculty of self-improvement, which by the
help of circumstances gradually develops all the rest of
our faculties, and is inherent in the species. . . .*

Jean-Jacques Rousseau,
*A Discourse on the Origin
of Inequality*

Process refers to the sequence of stages or steps by which a labor is completed, a problem is solved, or a dream is realized. As creatures rooted in nature, we are properly fascinated by its processes—for example, the opening of a flower, as revealed by time-lapse photography, or the movement of the stars, as charted by a powerful telescope. In this chapter, however, human rather than natural processes are our theme. Our readings here describe endeavors undertaken by our species in its pursuit of self-improvement. The instructional focus is on the mode of written expression that analyzes and describes various processes meaningful in human existence.

Analysis, explaining a whole by examining its parts, is the foundation of process writing. The word's Greek stems, *ana* and *lyein,* literally mean an "up-loosening" in the physical sense, such as the untying of knots. In the academic world, analysis is the untangling of ideas by separating the various strands that have been woven together. Analysis shows us the relationships between the component parts of a whole. The analysis of a process both clarifies information and extends the reader's knowledge.

We can distinguish among various kinds of process analysis writing. Where the process described is a technical one, the intent is usually instructional. In its simplest form, such a process analysis provides chronological, step-by-step directions for the completion of a task. An example in this chapter is William Burroughs's "The Cut-Up Method of Brion Gysin," a piece that provides not only directions but also a sample of the procedure described.

The term *mechanical process* or *operation* is given to processes or procedures that are repeated or generalized, such as aging. In this kind of process writing, the treatment is analytic but does not offer how-to instruction, and the organization is by distinct parts or stages. Historical analysis is another kind of process writing that increases our understanding rather than giving directions. Nevertheless, like writing about a natural process or a technical method, historical process analysis traces the stages in a particular event.

Process analysis may present both information and ideas. It may include the *why* as well as the *what* and the *how* of an event. In the fire-building section of the short story "To Build a Fire," for example, Jack London gives us the character's motivation for the process: survival. London focuses, however, on the sequence of painstaking actions—the *what* and the *how*—of the process in order to build suspense, and thus interest, in his story.

The same principles govern process analysis composition whether the purpose is to deepen the reader's understanding or to provide directions.

The Controlling Idea

The controlling idea, or the thesis, focuses the process analysis paper. The Rosenthal-Jacobson essay in this chapter, for example, is controlled by the hypothesis of the self-fulfilling prophecy. The essay's purpose is to demystify the process by which teachers positively influence their students' academic performance.

The purpose and controlling idea of a process analysis dictate the selection of details, the organization of material, the extent to which the essay goes beyond simple instruction, and the writer's point of view.

Although practiced writers do not always state their thesis or their purpose explicitly, you, as a student writer, may find a clear-cut thesis statement the best way to begin. As you draft your process analysis paper, the thesis statement will serve as a focus for your material and a check against digressions.

To arrive at the controlling idea of your process paper, you must determine first what existing situation you wish to demystify or explain. You should ask yourself not only what happens in the process that leads to this situation but also how (by what means) it happens and even perhaps why (for what reasons) it happens and why it is important that your reader know about it.

Your controlling idea, for example, may be that some seemingly simple process is, in fact, more complex than it appears. This is S. J. Perelman's aim in his humorous essay about assembling toys. Or it may be that an apparently difficult process is actually easy to grasp once it has been broken down into its components, as in our selection on silk making. Or you may wish to clarify a natural process through analogy, as Shakespeare does in the soliloquy in this chapter. By focusing your process analysis and controlling the selection of relevant details, you make your paper more complex than a mere enumeration or chronology.

The conclusion of your analysis should refer again to your controlling idea and to the process—that is, the solution to your mystery.

Steps and Stages

Once you have decided on your subject, you should make a rough chronological outline of the steps in the process. In writing the first draft of the essay, you may find it easiest just to write down the various actions or steps in order, without attempting to give appropriate importance to any one detail. When you review your first draft, the steps will begin to group themselves into larger units by their relationships to each other. Clustering details in logical stages is more effective than simply listing them one after another without any such grouping. For example, in Peter Elbow's essay on writing, the various stages of the composing process are dealt with as separate sequential units.

The proportion of your essay allotted to each stage in the process depends on the importance of that stage. The more essential a stage is, the more numerous and detailed will be the steps you include in it. Depending on whether your purpose is narrowly instructive or more broadly analytic, your groups of chronologically ordered steps may include explanations and illustrations as well as the procedures involved. In general, the more instructive your purpose, the less explanation or side comment you should give, as such comment tends to distract your reader from the directions. In the silk manufacturing selection, for instance, the writer opens and closes with the controlling idea, that silk making is economically advantageous. The strictly instructional part of the piece, however, is just that—sequential details on how one goes about making silk.

Interestingly, fiction is at the same time the most analytic and least explicitly instructive of all writing. Jack London, for example, obviously did not expect the reader of our selection to build a fire. Nevertheless, he included every detail of the fire-building process, masterfully involving the reader as deeply as possible in his protagonist's agonizing experience. London's work demonstrates that details, vividly presented, can make the most ordinary activity fascinating.

Clarity and Coherence

Whether the process paper is the instructive type, giving directions, or the historical type, relating stages of an event, the writer should signal the time sequences involved to achieve clarity. You can do this by using transitional expressions such as *first, next, at the same time, subsequently,* and the like. Coherent time linkage is necessary both between details within a stage and between the stages themselves. All the writings in this chapter, including the poetic soliloquy and the short story, display this attention to coherence.

Maintaining a consistent point of view is another means of achieving clarity and coherence in your process analysis paper. If, for example, your intent is to give directions, you may address your reader directly as "you" and put your directional verbs in the imperative form, as William Burroughs does in his essay. To make poetic cut-ups, he directs, "Now *cut* the page. *You* have a new poem."

In recounting a natural process such as aging, you may use the simple present tense throughout, as Shakespeare does, to indicate that the process is always the same: "The sixth age shifts. . . ."

In writing a historical process analysis, on the other hand, you will probably use the simple past tense and the third person for past reporting and objective observation, as Orville Taylor does in his history of silk. You must consistently maintain the historical perspective, which the past tense and the third person provide, unless you have some good reason for varying it.

Finally, if you are writing for a general audience about a complex or scientific process, you should choose language suitable for that audience, as the manufacturer of the "Jiffy-Cloz" does in Perelman's "Insert Flap 'A' and Throw Away." Your language should be free of jargon, simple, and functional. If the audience is more specialized, use the technical language of the field. Whatever the topic and whatever the purpose, you should use precise and appropriate verbs for each step in the process.

Essay for Analysis

THOMAS J. PETERS
ROBERT H. WATERMAN

Close to the Customer

The Search for Excellence, from which our essay is taken, recounts how certain American firms have earned and continued their success over the years. "Close to the Customer" does not offer direct instruction to the reader; rather it analyzes how certain processes lead to desired outcomes. The authors use specific examples of processes to elaborate their thesis that business success depends on an "obsession" with the customer's needs.

Probably the most important management fundamental that is being ignored today is staying close to the customer to satisfy his needs and anticipate his wants. In too many companies, the customer has become a bloody nuisance whose unpredictable behavior damages carefully made strategic plans, whose activities mess up computer operations, and who stubbornly insists that purchased products should work.

Lew Young, Editor-in-Chief, Business Week

That a business ought to be close to its cus- 1 tomers seems a benign enough message. So the question arises, why does a chapter like this need to be written at all? The answer is that, despite all the lip service given to the market orientation these days, Lew Young and others are right: the customer is either ignored or considered a bloody nuisance.

Negative existing situation

The good news from the excellent com- 2 panies is the extent to which, and the intensity with which, the customers intrude into every nook and cranny of the business—sales, manufacturing, research, accounting. A simple message permeates the atmosphere. All business success rests on something labeled a sale, which at the least momentarily weds company and customer. A simple summary of what our research uncovered on the customer attribute is this: the excellent companies *really are* close to their customers. That's it. Other companies talk about it; the excellent companies do it.

Repetitions of key term: "customer"

Thesis: controlling idea

No existing management theory helps 3 much in explaining the role of the customer in the prototypical excellent company. At most, recent theory talks about the importance of the external environment in influencing the institution. It misses by a mile, however, the intensity of customer orientation that exists within the top performers, and that intensity seems to be one of the best kept secrets in American business.

Negative existing situation

"Mystery" of success

The case was nicely expressed by HP's 4 John Doyle (head of R&D). We were discussing sustaining business values. He said that the only posture that has a chance of surviving the ravages of time is one that is unfailingly externally focused: "The only way you're going to survive in the long haul is if everybody's out there scratching, looking for things to do to get the next product generation into the customer's premises."

In observing the excellent companies, and specifically the way they interact with customers, what we found most striking was the consistent presence of *obsession.* This characteristically occurred as a seemingly unjustifiable overcommitment to some form of quality, reliability, or service. Being customer-oriented doesn't mean that our excellent companies are slouches when it comes to technological or cost performance. But they do seem to us more driven by their direct orientation to their customers than by technology or by a desire to be the low-cost producer. Take IBM, for example. It is hardly far behind the times, but most observers will agree that it hasn't been a technology leader for decades. Its dominance rests on its commitment to service.

Service, quality, reliability are strategies aimed at loyalty and long-term revenue stream growth (and maintenance). *The point of this chapter, and a wonderful concomitant to a customer orientation, is that the winners seem to focus especially on the revenue-generation side.* The one follows the other.

Service Obsession

Although he's not a company, our favorite illustration of closeness to the customer is car salesman Joe Girard. He sold more new cars and trucks, each year, for eleven years running, than any other human being. In fact, in a typical year, Joe sold more than twice as many units as whoever was in second place. In explaining his secret of success, Joe said: "I send out over thirteen thousand cards every month."

5

Introduction of key term: "service"

Restatement of thesis: answer to the "mystery"

6   Repetition of key term

Elaboration of thesis

7   First illustrator of thesis

Existing condition "Mystery"

Why start with Joe? Because his magic is 8
the magic of IBM and many of the rest of the
excellent companies. It is simply service, overpowering service, especially after-sales service.
Joe noted, "There's one thing that I do that a lot
of salesmen don't, and that's believe the sale
really begins *after* the sale—not before. . . .
The customer ain't out the door, and my son has
made up a thank-you note." Joe would intercede
personally, a year later, with the service manager
on behalf of his customer. Meanwhile he would
keep the communications flowing:

> Joe's customers won't forget him once they
> buy a car from him; he won't let them!
> Every month throughout the year they get
> a letter from him. It arrives in a plain en-
> velope, always a different size or color. "It
> doesn't look like that junk mail which is
> thrown out before it is even opened," Joe
> confides. "And they open it up and the
> front of it reads, 'I LIKE YOU.' Inside it
> says 'Happy New Year from Joe Girard.'"
> He sends a card in February wishing the
> customers a "Happy George Washington's
> Birthday." In March it's "Happy St. Pat-
> rick's Day." They love the cards. Joe
> boasts, "You should hear the comments I
> get on them."

Out of context, Joe's 13,000 cards sounds 9
like just another sales gimmick. But like the top
companies, Joe seems genuinely *to care*. Said Joe:
"The great restaurants in the country have love
and care coming out of their kitchens . . . and
when I sell a car, my customer's gonna leave
with the same feeling that he'll get when he
walks out of a great restaurant." Joe's sense of
caring continued to shine through after the sale:
"When [the customer] comes back for service, I
fight for him all the way to get him the best. . . .
You've got to be like a doctor. Something's
wrong with his car, so feel hurt for him." Moreover, Joe has cared about every customer as an
individual. He doesn't think statistically, but

Repetition of key term

Process begins

Controlling idea of
process

Perspective is consis-
tent: simple present
tense for recounting of
operational process

Sequence of steps in the
process signaled by
holidays

Analysis of Joe's process

emphasizes that he has sold "one at a time, face-to-face, belly-to-belly." "They are not," he said, "an interruption or pain in the neck. They are my bread and butter." We introduce this section with Joe because he has acted, as well as anyone, as if the customer really does count.

Perhaps our favorite example of service overkill is *Frito-Lay*. We have been exposed to a good deal of micro-economic theory, and it sometimes appears that there is only one thing that economists are absolutely sure of after several hundred years of labor: wheat farmers in perfectly competitive markets don't have high margins. We don't have any excellent wheat farmers in our survey, but we got pretty close. Potato chips and pretzels ought to be the classic undifferentiated commodity. Like wheat farmers, potato chip manufacturers ought not to have high margins or shares. But Frito-Lay, a subsidiary of PepsiCo, sells well over $2 billion worth of potato chips and pretzels every year, owns market shares that run into the 60s and 70s in most of the country, and has margins that are the envy of the food industry. Why?

What is striking about Frito is not its brand-management system, which is solid, nor its advertising program, which is well done. What is striking is Frito's nearly 10,000-person sales force and its "99.5 percent service level." In practical terms, what does this mean? It means that Frito will do some things that in the short run clearly are uneconomic. It will spend several hundred dollars sending a truck to re-stock a store with a couple of $30 cartons of potato chips. You don't make money that way, it would seem. But the institution is filled with tales of salesmen braving extraordinary weather to deliver a box of potato chips or to help a store clean up after a hurricane or an accident. Letters about such acts pour into the Dallas headquarters. There are magic and symbolism about the service call that cannot be quantified. As we said earlier, it is a cost analyst's dream target. You can always make a case for saving money by cutting back a percentage point or two. But

Controlling idea of analysis

10 *Second illustration; repetition of key term*

Existing condition

"Mystery"

11 *Controlling idea of Frito-Lay's process*

Analysis of process without sequential steps

Technical terminology appropriate to audience

Frito management, looking at market shares and margins, won't tamper with the zeal of the sales force.

Frito simply lives for its sales force. The system succeeds because it supports the route salesman, believes in him, and makes him feel essential to its success. There are about 25,000 employees in the company. Those who are not selling live by the simple dictum, "Service to Sales." While the plant manager, to pick an example, is clearly evaluated on the traditional basis of whether or not he makes his cost budget, when the sales force is in a crunch he won't hesitate to run the plant overtime to make sure sales gets what it needs.

One of the best examples of service through people is *Walt Disney Productions*. In fact, many rate Disney and McDonald's as the two best mass service providers in America—or the world. Red Pope, a long-time Disney observer and writer, comments: "How Disney looks upon people, internally and externally, handles them, communicates with them, rewards them, is in my view the basic foundation upon which its five decades of success stand . . . I have come to observe closely and with reverence the theory and practice of selling satisfaction and serving millions of people on a daily basis successfully. It is what Disney does best."

Pope's observations on Disney are a clear validation of the Nemeroff study. For example, intense management involvement is highlighted at Disney by an annual week-long program called "cross utilization." According to Pope, this program entails Disney executives' leaving their desks and their usual business garb. They don a theme costume and head for the action. "For a full week, the boss sells tickets or popcorn, dishes ice cream or hot dogs, loads and unloads rides, parks cars, drives the monorail or the trains, and takes on any of the 100 on-stage jobs that make the entertainment parks come alive.

The service-through-people theme at Disney starts, as it does in many of the excellent companies, with a special language. There is no

12

13 Third illustration: Disney's process; repetition of key term: *service*

Controlling idea of Disney's process

14 Observer's description of Disney's training process for management

15 Repetition of key term

such thing as a worker at Disney. The employees out front are "cast members" and the personnel department is "casting." Whenever you are working with the public, you are "on stage." For example, two of Red Pope's children, aged sixteen and eighteen, were hired by Disney World in Orlando to take tickets. For this seemingly mundane job, four eight-hour days of instruction were required before they were allowed to go on stage. They learned about Guests—not lower-case "c" customers, but upper-case "G" Guests. Pope asked his children why it had taken four days to learn how to take tickets, to which they replied: "What happens if someone wants to know where the restrooms are, when the parade starts, what bus to take to get back to the campgrounds? . . . We need to know the answers and where to get the answers quickly. After all, Dad, we're on stage and help produce the Show for our Guests. Our job every minute is to help Guests enjoy the party."

Observer's description of Disney's training process for workers

People are brought into the culture early. 16 Everyone has to attend Disney University and pass "Traditions I" before going on to specialized training. Pope says:

> Traditions I is an all-day experience where the new hire gets a constant offering of Disney philosophy and operating methodology. No one is exempt from the course, from VP to entry-level part-timers. . . . Disney expects the new CM [cast member] to know something about the company, its history and success, its management style before he actually goes to work. Every person is shown how each division relates to other divisions—Operations, Resorts, Food and Beverage, Marketing, Finance, Merchandising, Entertainment, etc., and how each division "relates to the show." In other words, "Here's how all of us work together to make things happen. Here's your part in the big picture."

Analysis of the Disney process: *Why* the new hire takes Traditions I

The systems support for people on stage is 17 also dramatic. For example, there are hundreds of phones hidden in the bushes, hot lines to a central question-answering service. And the amount of effort put into the daily clean-up amazes even the most calloused outside observers. In these and scores of other ways, <u>overkill marks every aspect of Disney's approach to its customers.</u>

Whether or not they are as fanatic in their 18 service obsession as Frito, IBM, or Disney, <u>the excellent companies all seem to have very powerful service themes that pervade the institutions.</u> In fact, one of our most significant conclusions about the excellent companies is that, *whether their basic business is metal bending, high technology, or hamburgers, they have all defined themselves as service businesses.*

Inductively developed subthesis

Conclusion: restatements of thesis; solution to "mystery"

Final repetition of key term: service

Analysis of the Essay

The Process of Process Analysis

Controlling Idea.   The foundation of all process analysis is an existing situation or condition that needs to be explained or demystified to the reader. In this essay the situation is the failure of most American businesses to meet customers' needs: "the customer is either ignored or considered a bloody nuisance" (1). This assessment is reinforced in paragraph 3 with the observation that there is no current management theory to account for customer neglect. The "mystery" is the success of a few companies that do meet their customers' needs. How do they do it? What is the process?

The overall thesis, or controlling idea, of the selection that answers the question is clearly stated in paragraph 2: "the excellent companies *really are* close to their customers." It is restated in paragraph 5 near the end of the introduction: The answer to the mystery of successful companies is "orientation to their customers."

The authors illustrate their thesis with three businesses that do stay "close to the customer," each through its own individual process. The first example, auto salesman Joe Girard, maintains closeness to the customer through the process of personal contact and communication (8, 9). The second example, Frito-Lay, achieves success through the process of providing service to the customer even when it is not cost effective (11).

For the third example, Walt Disney Productions, the ideal of "service through people" is achieved through two staff training processes, one for management and one for new workers. The process for the former is based on "intense management involvement" (14). The program for workers emphasizes that "there is no such thing as a worker at Disney"; all are "cast members" in the drama of Disney (15).

Steps and Stages.   This selection provides instruction through example rather than explicit directions. Therefore, the steps and stages in the processes described are largely implied rather than enumerated. For instance, paragraph 8 mentions only three of Joe Girard's monthly reminders, but one can infer that his process of personally communicating with this customers extends through Easter, Flag Day, and the Fourth of July.

In the Frito-Lay section, the reader must infer the processes of "service overkill." Examples are given but none of the processes is elaborated.

The activities of the Disney training process are summarized, but time order is not explicitly signaled.

Despite the absence of direct process instruction, company executives, the specialized audience for Peters and Waterman's book, can find sufficient guidance about the processes of customer service to apply the concept to their own firms.

Clarity and Coherence.   The essay consistently addresses its readers in a blend of informal and technical language. Using lively quotations from persons involved in the various processes (Joe Girard, paragraphs 8, 9; Red Pope's children, 15), the authors dramatize their controlling ideas and bring the process analysis itself "close to the customer"—that is, their reader.

The authors stud their writing with repetitions of their key phrases, possibly because the book itself is intended as a "sales pitch" for management reform, and repetition is a principle of salesmanship. The key term *customer* is introduced in the first paragraph and is repeated throughout the essay. Beginning with paragraph 5, the key term *service* appears and continues to occur as a second motif of the selection (see paragraphs 6, 8, 10). The repeated reference to service in the concluding paragraph is a reinforcement of the essay's thesis—the solution to the mystery of how different kinds of firms gain and maintain their reputation for excellence.

READINGS

PETER ELBOW

Teaching Writing by Teaching Thinking

Peter Elbow, professor of English and composition theory, attempts here to demystify the process of effective
writing. First Elbow defines two apparently opposite
orders of thinking. Then he shows how a synthesis of
these two orders of thinking should underlie the writing
process.

When I celebrate freewriting and fast exploratory writing on first drafts— 1
the postponing of vigilance and control during the early stages of writing—it seems to many listeners as though I'm advocating irrationality.
Some say, "Yes, good, we all need holidays from thinking." Others say,
"Horrors! If we invite people to let down their guard, their vigilance
muscles will get flabby and they'll lose their ability to think critically."
But I insist that I'm teaching thinking.

Of course freewriting is not the only way I teach thinking through 2
writing. I also teach it by emphasizing careful, conscious, critical-minded
revision. Thus I teach two kinds of thinking. I'll call them first order and
second order thinking.

First order thinking is intuitive and creative and does not strive for 3
conscious direction or control. We use it when we get hunches or see ge-
stalts, when we sense analogies or ride on metaphors or arrange the pieces
in a collage. We use it when we write fast without censoring, and let the
words lead us to associations and intuitions we had not foreseen. Second
order thinking is conscious, directed, controlled thinking. We steer; we
scrutinize each link in the chain. Second order thinking is committed to
accuracy and strives for logic and control: we examine our premises and
assess the validity of each inference. Second order thinking is what most
people have in mind when they talk about "critical thinking."

Each kind of thinking has its own characteristic strengths and weak- 4
nesses. I like to emphasize how first order thinking often brings out
people's best and most intelligent thinking. If you want to get people to
seem dumber than they are, try asking them a hard question and then

saying, "Now think carefully." Thinking carefully means trying to think about thinking while also thinking about something else—and it often leads people to foolishness. This is one of the main reasons why normally shrewd and sensible students often write essays asserting things they do not really believe and defending them with fake reasoning they would never fall for if they were just talking thoughtfully with a friend.

If you want to get people to be remarkably insightful, on the other hand, try asking them the hard question and then saying, "Don't do any careful thinking yet, just write three or four stories or incidents that come to mind in connection with that question and then do some fast exploratory freewriting." It turns out that such unplanned narrative and descriptive exploratory writing (or speaking) will almost invariably lead the person spontaneously to formulate *conceptual* insights that are remarkably shrewd. These are fresh insights which are rooted in experience and thus they usually get around the person's prejudices, stock responses, or desires for mere consistency; they are usually shrewder than the person's long held convictions. In addition (to bring up a writer's concern) these insights are usually expressed in lively, human, and experienced language.

Finally, when someone really gets going in a sustained piece of generative writing and manages to stand out of the way and relinquish planning and control—when someone lets the words and images and ideas choose more words, images, and ideas—often a more elegant shape or organization for the material is found. . . . What is more common is that the exploratory zigzagging leads finally to a click where the writer suddenly sees, "Yes, that's the right handle for this whole issue, I couldn't find it when I just tried to think and plan."

Yet despite my fascination with the conceptual power of intuitive thinking—of what might seem to some like careless thinking—I have learned to also tell the other side of the story. That is, we are also likely to be fooled by first order thinking. In first order thinking we do not reflect on what we are doing and hence we are more likely to be steered by our assumptions, unconscious prejudices, and unexamined points of view. And often enough no shape or organization emerges at all—just randomly ordered thoughts. We cannot count on first order thinking to give us something valuable.

Thus the two kinds of thinking have opposite virtues and vices. Second order thinking is a way to check, to be more aware, to steer instead of being steered. In particular, we must not trust the fruits of intuitive and experiential first order thinking unless we have carefully assessed them with second order critical thinking. Yet we probably will not have enough interesting ideas or hypotheses to assess if we use only our assessing muscles: we need first order thinking to generate a rich array of insights. And first order thinking does not just give us more, it is faster too. Our early steps in second order thinking are often slow backwards steps into wrongheadedness. Yet this is no argument against the need for second order thinking. Indeed I suspect that the way we enlarge the penumbra of our tacit knowledge is by searching harder and further with the beam of our focal knowledge.

We are in the habit—in academe, anyway—of assuming that think- 9 ing is not thinking unless it is wholly logical or critically aware of itself at every step. But I cannot resist calling first order thinking a bona fide kind of thinking because it is a process of making sense, and putting things together. . . .

Enhancing Thinking

There is an obvious link between the writing process and these two kinds 10 of thinking. I link first order creative thinking with freewriting and first draft exploratory writing in which one defers planning, control, organiz- ing, and censoring. I link second order thinking with slow, thoughtful rewriting or revising where one constantly subjects everything to critical scrutiny. But I am not content merely to assert a link. The two writing processes enhance the two thinking processes.

It is obvious how careful revising enhances second order thinking. If 11 having any language at all (any "second signalling system") gives us more power over our thinking, it is obvious that a written language vastly in- creases that power. By writing down our thoughts we can put them aside and come back to them with renewed critical energy and a fresh point of view. We can better criticize because writing helps us achieve the peren- nially difficult task of standing outside our own thinking. Outlines are more helpful while revising than at the start of the writing process because finally there's something rich and interesting to outline. Revising is when I ask both the writer and the readers to isolate the central core of inference in a paper: What is the assertion and what premises does it rest on? . . . Since we are trying for the tricky goal of thinking about our subject and thinking about our thinking about it, putting our thoughts on paper gives us a fighting chance. But notice that what most heightens this criti- cal awareness is not so much the writing down of words in the first place, but the coming back to a text and re-seeing it from the outside (in space) instead of just hearing it from the inside (in time).

But does freewriting or uncensored, generative writing really en- 12 hance creative first order thinking? You might say that speaking is a better way to enhance creative thinking—either through creative brainstorming or through the back and forth of discussion or debate. But that only works if we have other people available, people skilled at enhancing our creative thinking. Free exploratory writing, on the other hand, though we must learn to use it, is always available. And since the goal in creative thinking is to harness intuition—to get the imagination to take the reins in its own hands—solitary writing for no audience is often more productive than speaking. Speaking is almost invariably to an audience that puts pressure on us to make sense and be able to explain inferences.

It may be argued that intuitive thinking is best enhanced by silent 13 musing; or going for a walk or sleeping on it or any of a host of other ways to push a question away from focal attention back to the preconscious. But such attempts at nonlinguistic processing often merely postpone thinking instead of being actually productive. Freewriting and exploratory writing, on the other hand, are usually productive because they exploit the autonomous generative powers of language and syntax themselves. Once you manage to get yourself writing in an exploratory but uncensored fashion, the ongoing string of language and syntax itself becomes a lively and surprising force for generation. Words call up words, ideas call up more ideas. A momentum of language and thinking develops and one learns to nurture it by keeping the pen moving. With a bit of practice, you can usually bring yourself to the place where you can stop and say, "Look at that! I've been led by this unrolling string of words to an insight or connection or structure that I could not have proposed if I were just musing or making an outline. I wasn't steering, I was being taken for a ride." In short, by using the writing process in this two sided way I am fostering opposite extremes: an improved ability to allow ourselves to be taken on rides, yet also an improved ability to assess critically the resulting views.

Practical Consequences

There is no one right way to think or write. We all know too many good 14 thinkers or writers who contradict each other and even themselves in their methods. But this notion of opposite extremes gives a constructive and specific picture of what we are looking for in good thinking and writing. Even though there are many good ways to think and write, it seems clear that excellence must involve finding *some* way to be both abundantly inventive yet toughmindedly critical. Indeed this model of conflicting goals suggests why good writers and thinkers are so varied in their techniques: if they are managing to harness opposites—in particular, opposites that tend to interfere with each other—they are doing something mysterious. Success is liable to take many forms, some of them mysterious or surprising.

As a teacher, it helps me to have these two clear goals in mind when 15 I come across a student about whom I must say, "She clearly is a smart person, but why is she so often wrong?" or, "She clearly thinks hard and carefully, but why is she so characteristically uninteresting or unproductive in her work?" I can ask of any person or performance, "Is there enough rich material to build from?" and "Is there a careful and critical enough assessment of the material?"

If I am careful to acknowledge to my students that there is really no 16 single best way to think or write and that excellence in these realms is a mystery that can be mastered in surprising ways, I can turn around and stress simplicity by harping on two practical rules.

First, since creative and critical thinking are opposite and involve 17 mental states that conflict with each other, it helps most people to learn to work on them separately moving back and forth between them. If we are trying to think creatively or write generatively, it usually hinders us if we try at the same time to think critically or to revise: it makes us reject what we are thinking before we've really worked it out—or to cross out what we've written before we've finished the sentence or paragraph and allowed something to develop. But if we hold off criticism and revising for a while we can build a safe place for generative thinking or writing. Similarly, if we devote certain times to wholehearted critical thinking, we can be more acute and powerful in our critical assessment.

One of the main things that holds us back from being as creative as 18 we could be is fear of looking silly or being wrong. That worry dissipates when we know we will soon turn to wholehearted criticism and revising and weed out what is foolish. Similarly, one of the main things that keeps us from being as critical as we could be is fear that we'll have to reject everything and be left with nothing at all. But that worry also dissipates when we know we have already generated an extremely rich set of materials to work on.

Secondly, it usually helps to start with creative thinking and explor- 19 atory writing and then engage in critical assessment and revising after- wards—after there is already lots to work on. It is not that we should necessarily try to force our writing into two self-contained steps (though I aim for this when all goes smoothly). Often I cannot finish all generating or all first order thinking before I need to do some revising or criticizing. Indeed, sometimes I can force a new burst of generativity with an inter- lude of criticizing. And it is useful to say that we are never finished with intuitive generating even when we are criticizing and revising.

I used to think that I should try to make my students good at crea- 20 tive generating before I went on to revising and being critical. But I have discovered that some students will not let go and allow themselves to be creative till after we do some hard work on critical thinking and revising. They do not feel safe relaxing their vigilance till I demonstrate that I am also teaching heightened vigilance. Sometimes, early in the semester, I ask students to rethink and revise a paper in order to prove to them that they are not stuck with what they put down in early drafts, and that care- ful critical thinking can make a big difference.

However, the fact remains that it usually hinders people to start by 21 planning, critical thinking, and making outlines. My agenda for the beginning of a semester is always to enforce generating and brainstorming and the deferral of criticism in order to build students' confidence and show them that they can quickly learn to come up with a great quantity of words and ideas. Then gradually we process to a back and forth movement between generating and criticizing. I find I help my own writing and thinking, and that of my students, by training a class to start with first order thinking and generating and take it on longer and longer rides— holding off longer and longer the transition to criticizing and logic. Back and forth, yes, but moving so that each mentality has more time to flourish before we go to its opposite.

Mutual Reinforcement

The history of our culture is often experienced as a battle between reason 22 and feeling, rationality and irrationality, logic and impulse. Because intuitive first order thinking is indissolubly mixed up with feeling, irrationality, and impulse, we end up in an adversarial situation where disciplined critical thinking and uncensored creative thinking face each other uneasily from entrenched positions. It seems as though logic and reason have just barely and only recently won the battle to be our standard for thinking and therefore advocates of reason and logic tend to criticize all relaxations of critical vigilance. Similarly, champions of creative first order thinking sometimes feel they must criticize critical thinking, if only to win some legitimacy for themselves. But this is an unfortunate historical and developmental accident. If we would see clearly the truth about thinking and writing we would see that the situation is not either/or, it's both/and: the more first order thinking, the more second order thinking, and vice versa. It's a matter of learning to work on opposites one at a time in a spirit of mutual reinforcement rather than in a spirit of fearful combat.

Reading and Interpreting

VOCABULARY

Use your dictionary as necessary to find the meaning of the following words in the context of Peter Elbow's essay:

censoring (3)   relinquish (6)   generative (6, 12, 17)   array (8)

penumbra (8)   perennially (11)   musing (13)   syntax (13)

dissipates (18)   adversarial (22)

CONCEPT ANALYSIS

1. In paragraph 4 Elbow claims that saying "Now think carefully" frequently "leads people to foolishness." Discuss this remark with reference to your own classroom experience.
2. Central to Elbow's thesis is the distinction he perceives between first-order and second-order thinking. In your own words, explain these terms as they are used in the text.
3. Why has Elbow written in defense of first-order thinking? Enumerate the values that he finds in it.
4. In his conclusion Elbow uses the metaphor of battle to describe the traditional view that creative and critical thinking are in conflict. How does he himself view the relationship between creative and critical thinking?
5. Having read Elbow's analysis of the writing process, how might you change your approach to a writing assignment?

Quickwrite

Here is a "hard question": *What is the greatest human achievement of all?* To approach the question, follow this step of Peter Elbow's writing process: "Don't do any careful thinking yet; just write [some] stories or incidents that come to mind in connection with that question and then do some fast exploratory freewriting."

Now review what you have written. Has this step led you to any "conceptual insights"? Have you surprised yourself with some fresh ideas or lively language?

Thinking and Writing

RHETORICAL TECHNIQUE

1. Elbow is writing here for teachers of composition. Although he does not explicitly present the steps in the writing process in chronological order, he does imply what they are. Make a chronological list of these steps.
2. As we said at the beginning of this chapter, analysis is the untangling of an idea by the separation and examination of its parts. Much of Elbow's article is an analysis of the relationship between the two orders of thinking. In which paragraphs does Elbow examine first-order thinking? Which paragraphs explain the relationship between the two orders of thinking?

Elbow emphasizes that careful revising enhances both first- and second-order thinking. Write a process analysis paper in which you present the benefits of your revising technique. Give your reader step-by-step directions for revising an essay.

WILLIAM S. BURROUGHS

The Cut-Up Method of Brion Gysin

William S. Burroughs (b. 1914) is an American novelist whose unorthodox writing style has focused on stories of violence and brutality. In the following selection from *The Third Mind* (1978) he explains a writing process invented by British painter Brion Gysin. Experimenting with this process in the 1960s, Burroughs found that by "cutting out" and "folding in" sentences from his own manuscript, he could achieve new images and freedom from conventional narrative forms.

At a surrealist rally in the 1920s Tristan Tzara the man from nowhere 1 proposed to create a poem on the spot by pulling words out of a hat. A riot ensued wrecked the theater. André Breton expelled Tristan Tzara from the movement and grounded the cut-ups on the Freudian couch.

In the summer of 1959 Brion Gysin painter and writer cut newspaper 2 articles into sections and rearranged the sections *at random*. "Minutes to Go" resulted from this initial cut-up experiment. "Minutes to Go" contains unedited unchanged cut-ups emerging as quite coherent and meaningful prose.

The cut-up method brings to writers the collage, which has been 3 used by painters for fifty years. And used by the moving and still camera. In fact all street shots from movie or still cameras are by the unpredictable factors of passersby and juxtaposition cut-ups. And photographers will tell you that often their best shots are accidents . . . writers will tell you the same. The best writing seems to be done almost by accident but writers until the cut-up method was made explicit—all writing is in fact cut-ups; I will return to this point—had no way to produce the accident of spontaneity. You cannot *will* spontaneity. But you can introduce the unpredictable spontaneous factor with a pair of scissors.

The method is simple. Here is one way to do it. Take a page. Like 4
this page. Now cut down the middle and across the middle. You have four
sections: 1   2   3   4 . . . one two three four. Now rearrange the
sections placing section four with section one and section two with section
three. And you have a new page. Sometimes it says much the same thing.
Sometimes something quite different—cutting up political speeches is an
interesting exercise—in any case you will find that it says something and
something quite definite. Take any poet or writer you fancy. Here, say, or
poems you have read over many times. The words have lost meaning and
life through years of repetition. Now take the poem and type out selected
passages. Fill a page with excerpts. Now cut the page. You have a new
poem. As many poems as you like. As many Shakespeare Rimbaud poems
as you like. Tristan Tzara said: "Poetry is for everyone." And André
Breton called him a cop and expelled him from the movement. Say it
again: "Poetry is for everyone." Poetry is a place and it is free to all cut
up Rimbaud and you are in Rimbaud's place. Here is a Rimbaud poem
cut up.

"Visit of memories. Only your dance and your voice house. On the 5
suburban air improbable desertions . . . all harmonic pine for strife.
"The great skies are open. Candor of vapor and tent spitting blood 6
laugh and drunken penance.
"Promenade of wine perfume opens slow bottle.   7
"The great skies are open. Supreme bugle burning flesh children 8
to mist."

Cut-ups are for everyone. Anybody can make cut-ups. It is experi- 9
mental in the sense of being *something to do*. Right here write now. Not
something to talk and argue about. Greek philosophers assumed logically
that an object twice as heavy as another object would fall twice as fast. It
did not occur to them to push the two objects off the table and see how
they fall. Cut the words and see how they fall. Shakespeare Rimbaud live
in their words. Cut the word lines and you will hear their voices. Cut-ups
often come through as code messages with special meaning for the cutter.
Table tapping? Perhaps. Certainly an improvement on the usual deplorable performance of contacted poets through a medium. Rimbaud announces himself, to be followed by some excruciatingly bad poetry. Cut
Rimbaud's words and you are assured of good poetry at least if not personal appearance.
All writing is in fact cut-ups. A collage of words read heard over- 10
heard. What else? Use of scissors renders the process explicit and subject
to extension and variation. Clear classical prose can be composed entirely
of rearranged cut-ups. Cutting and rearranging a page of written words
introduces a new dimension into writing enabling the writer to turn im-

ages in cinematic variation. Images shift sense under the scissors smell images to sound sight to sound sound to kinesthetic. This is where Rimbaud was going with his color of vowels. And his "systematic derangement of the senses." The place of mescaline hallucination: seeing colors tasting sounds smelling forms.

The cut-ups can be applied to other fields than writing. Dr. Neumann in his *Theory of Games and Economic Behavior* introduces the cut-up method of random action into game and military strategy: assume that the worst has happened and act accordingly. If your strategy is at some point determined . . . by random factor your opponent will gain no advantage from knowing your strategy since he cannot predict the move. The cut-up method could be used to advantage in processing scientific data. How many discoveries have been made by accident? We cannot produce accidents to order. The cut-ups could add new dimensions to films. Cut gambling scene in with a thousand gambling scenes all times and places. Cut back. Cut streets of the world. Cut and rearrange the word and image in films. There is no reason to accept a second-rate product when you can have the best. And the best is there for all. "Poetry is for everyone". . . 11

Now here are the preceding two paragraphs cut into four sections and rearranged: 12

ALL WRITING IS IN FACT CUT-UPS OF GAMES AND ECONOMIC BEHAVIOR OVERHEARD? WHAT ELSE? ASSUME THAT THE WORST HAS HAPPENED EXPLICIT AND SUBJECT TO STRATEGY IS AT SOME POINT CLASSICAL PROSE. CUTTING AND REARRANGING FACTOR YOUR OPPONENT WILL GAIN INTRODUCES A NEW DIMENSION YOUR STRATEGY. HOW MANY DISCOVERIES SOUND TO KINESTHETIC? WE CAN NOW PRODUCE ACCIDENT TO HIS COLOR OF VOWELS. AND NEW DIMENSION FILMS CUT THE SENSES. THE PLACE OF SAND. GAMBLING SCENES ALL TIMES COLORS TASTING SOUNDS SMELL STREETS OF THE WORLD. WHEN YOU CAN HAVE THE BEST ALL. "POETRY IS FOR EVERYONE" DR NEUMANN IN A COLLAGE OF WORDS READ HEARD INTRODUCED THE CUT-UP SCISSORS RENDERS THE PROCESS GAME AND MILITARY STRATEGY, VARIATION CLEAR AND ACT ACCORDINGLY. IF YOU POSED ENTIRELY OF REARRANGED CUT DETERMINED BY RANDOM A PAGE OF WRITTEN WORDS NO ADVANTAGE FROM KNOWING INTO WRITER PREDICT THE MOVE. THE CUT VARIATION IMAGES SHIFT SENSE ADVANTAGE IN PROCESSING TO SOUND SIGHT TO SOUND. HAVE BEEN MADE BY ACCIDENT IS WHERE RIMBAUD WAS GOING WITH ORDER THE CUT-UPS COULD "SYSTEMATIC DERANGEMENT" OF THE GAMBLING SCENE IN WITH A TEA HALLUCINATION: SEEING AND PLACES. CUT BACK. CUT FORMS. REARRANGE THE WORD AND IMAGE TO OTHER FIELDS THAN WRITING.

Reading and Interpreting

VOCABULARY

Use your dictionary as necessary to find the meaning of the following words as used by William Burroughs:

juxtaposition (3)   deplorable (9)   excruciatingly (9)   kinesthetic (10)

CONCEPT ANALYSIS

1. Review paragraph 3 of Burroughs's essay. Explain the word *collage*. Must items in a collage be related, or does bringing them together in a collage make them related? Explain.

   Can you give some examples of the use of collage techniques in writing, painting, photography, film, dance, sculpture, or music? Are the seemingly random or unconnected elements really separate from each other, or can you perceive a relationship of some kind among them? Explain with reference to your specific examples.
2. What role does Peter Elbow's notion of "thinking" play in Brion Gysin's cut-up method?

Quickwrite

Use a newspaper or magazine story to create your own text by the cut-up method. Note your impulses and insights as you engage in this creative process. What satisfaction or problems did you have using the cut-up method?

Thinking and Writing

RHETORICAL TECHNIQUE

1. In this article there are several shifts in point of view from third-person narration to second-person address (to you the reader). Indicate these with marginal notes. How does this inconsistency in point of view reflect the subject of the essay?
2. Try writing the process paragraph (4) in the third person. How does the change in person alter the material from instruction in a process to analysis of that process?

S. J. PERELMAN

Insert Flap "A" and Throw Away

American humorist S. J. Perelman's (1904–1979) irony
and facility with words have greatly influenced comedy
from the Marx brothers to "Saturday Night Live." This
essay takes the subject of process and the process of process writing to comical extremes. It entertains the reader
with insights into what happens when the process breaks
down.

One stifling summer afternoon last August, in the attic of a tiny stone   1
house in Pennsylvania, I made a most interesting discovery: the shortest,
cheapest method of inducing a nervous breakdown ever perfected. In this
technique (eventually adopted by the psychology department of Duke
University, which will adopt anything), the subject is placed in a sharply
sloping attic heated to 340°F. and given a mothproof closet known as the
Jiffy-Cloz to assemble. The Jiffy-Cloz, procurable at any department store
or neighborhood insane asylum, consists of half a dozen gigantic sheets of
red cardboard, two plywood doors, a clothes rack, and a packet of staples.
With these is included a set of instructions mimeographed in pale-violet
ink, fruity with phrases like "Pass Section F through Slot AA, taking care
not to fold tabs behind washers (see Fig. 9)." The cardboard is so processed
that as the subject struggles convulsively to force the staple through, it suddenly buckles, plunging the staple deep into his thumb. He thereupon
springs up with a dolorous cry and smites his knob (Section K) on the
rafters (RR). As a final demonic touch, the Jiffy-Cloz people cunningly
omit four of the staples necessary to finish the job, so that after indescrib-
able purgatory, the best the subject can possibly achieve is a sleazy, ca-
pricious structure which would reduce any self-respecting moth to helpless laughter. The cumulative frustration, the tropical heat, and the soft,
ghostly chuckling of the moths are calculated to unseat the strongest
mentality.

In a period of rapid technological change, however, it was inevitable   2
that a method as cumbersome as the Jiffy-Cloz would be superseded. It
was superseded at exactly nine-thirty Christmas morning by a device
called the Self-Running 10-Inch Scale-Model Delivery-Truck Kit Powered
by Magic Motor, costing twenty-nine cents. About nine on that particular
morning, I was spread-eagled on my bed, indulging in my favorite sport
of mouth-breathing, when a cork fired from a child's air gun mysteriously

lodged in my throat. The pellet proved awkward for a while, but I finally ejected it by flailing the little marksman (and his sister, for good measure) until their welkins rang, and sauntered in to breakfast. Before I could choke down a healing fruit juice, my consort, a tall, regal creature indistinguishable from Cornelia, the Mother of the Gracchi, except that her foot was entangled in a roller skate, swept in. She extended a large, unmistakable box covered with diagrams.

"Now don't start making excuses," she whined. "It's just a simple 3 cardboard toy. The directions are on the back—"

"Look, dear," I interrupted, rising hurriedly and pulling on my 4 overcoat, "it clean slipped my mind. I'm supposed to take a lesson in cross-hatching at Zim's School of Cartooning today."

"On Christmas?" she asked suspiciously. 5

"Yes, it's the only time they could fit me in," I countered glibly. 6 "This is the big week for crosshatching, you know, between Christmas and New Year's."

"Do you think you ought to go in your pajamas?" she asked. 7

"Oh, that's O.K." I smiled. "We often work in our pajamas up at 8 Zim's. Well, goodbye now. If I'm not home by Thursday, you'll find a cold snack in the safe-deposit box." My subterfuge, unluckily, went for naught, and in a trice I was sprawled on the nursery floor, surrounded by two lambkins and ninety-eight segments of the Self-Running 10-Inch Scale-Model Delivery-Truck Construction Kit.

The theory of the kit was simplicity itself, easily intelligible to Ket- 9 tering of General Motors, Professor Millikan, or any first-rate physicist. Taking as my starting point the only sentence I could comprehend, "Fold down on all lines marked 'fold down'; fold up on all lines marked 'fold up,'" I set the children to work and myself folded up with an album of views of Chili Williams. In a few moments, my skin was suffused with a delightful tingling sensation and I was ready for the second phase, lightly referred to in the directions as "Preparing the Spring Motor Unit." As nearly as I could determine after twenty minutes of mumbling, the Magic Motor ("No Electricity—No Batteries—Nothing to Wind— Motor Never Wears Out") was an accordion-pleated affair operating by torsion, attached to the axles. "It is necessary," said the text, "to cut a slight notch in each of the axles with a knife (see Fig. C). To find the exact place to cut this notch, lay one of the axles over diagram at bottom of page."

"Well, *now* we're getting someplace!" I boomed, with a false gusto 10 that deceived nobody. "Here, Buster, run in and get Daddy a knife."

"I dowanna," quavered the boy, backing away. "You always cut 11 yourself at this stage." I gave the wee fellow an indulgent pat on the head that flattened it slightly, to teach him civility, and commandeered a long, serrated bread knife from the kitchen. "Now watch me closely, children," I ordered. "We place the axle on the diagram as in Fig. C, applying a strong downward pressure on the knife handle at all times." The axle must have been a factory second, because an instant later I was in the bathroom grinding my teeth in agony and attempting to stanch the flow of blood. Ultimately, I succeeded in contriving a rough bandage and slipped back into the nursery without awaking the children's suspicions. An agreeable surprise awaited me. Displaying a mechanical aptitude clearly inherited from their sire, the rascals had put together the chassis of the delivery truck.

"Very good indeed," I complimented (naturally, one has to exagger- 12 ate praise to develop a child's self-confidence). "Let's see—what's the next step? Ah, yes. 'Lock into box shape by inserting tabs C, D, E, F, G, H, J, K, and L into slots C, D, E, F, G, H, J, K, and L. Ends of front axle should be pushed through holes A and B.'" While marshaling the indicated parts in their proper order, I emphasized to my rapt listeners the necessity of patience and perseverance. "Haste makes waste, you know," I reminded them. "Rome wasn't built in a day. Remember, your daddy isn't always going to be here to show you."

"Where *are* you going to be?" they demanded. 13

"In the movies, if I can arrange it," I snarled. Poising tabs C, D, E, 14 F, G, H, J, K, and L in one hand and the corresponding slots in the other, I essayed a union of the two, but in vain. The moment I made one set fast and tackled another, tab and slot would part company, thumbing their noses at me. Although the children were too immature to understand, I saw in a flash where the trouble lay. Some idiotic employee at the factory had punched out the wrong design, probably out of sheer spite. So that was his game, eh? I set my lips in a grim line and, throwing one hundred and fifty-seven pounds of fighting fat into the effort, pounded the component parts into a homogeneous mass.

"There," I said with a gasp, "that's close enough. Now then, who 15 wants candy? One, two, three—everybody off to the candy store!"

"We wanna finish the delivery truck!" they wailed. "Mummy, he 16 won't let us finish the delivery truck!" Threats, cajolery, bribes were of no avail. In their jungle code, a twenty-nine-cent gewgaw bulked larger than a parent's love. Realizing that I was dealing with a pair of monomaniacs, I determined to show them who was master and wildly began locking the cardboard units helter-skelter, without any regard for the directions. When sections refused to fit, I gouged them with my nails and forced them together, cackling shrilly. The side panels collapsed; with a bestial oath, I drove a safety pin through them and lashed them to the roof. I used paper clips, bobby pins, anything I could lay my hands on. My fingers fairly flew and my breath whistled in my throat. "You want a delivery truck, do you?" I panted. "All right, I'll show you!" As merciful blackness closed in, I was on my hand and knees, bunting the infernal thing along with my nose and whinnying, "Roll, confound you, roll!"

"Absolute quiet," a carefully modulated voice was saying, "and fif- 17 teen of the white tablets every four hours." I opened my eyes carefully in the darkened room. Dimly I picked out a knifelike character actor in pince-nez lenses and a morning coat folding a stethoscope into his bag. "Yes," he added thoughtfully, "if we play our cards right, this ought to be a long, expensive recovery." From far away, I could hear my wife's voice bravely trying to control her anxiety.

"What if he becomes restless, Doctor?" 18

"Get him a detective story," returned the leech. "Or better still, a 19 nice, soothing picture puzzle—something he can do with his hands."

Reading and Interpreting

CONCEPT ANALYSIS

1. Paragraph 9 of Perelman's essay begins with the ironic remark that "the kit was simplicity itself, easily intelligible to . . . any first-rate physicist." Find other examples that illustrate the complexity of this supposedly simple process.
2. In relating the process of putting the kit together, what does the author reveal about his role and the relationships in his family?

Quickwrite

Use the first paragraph of Perelman's essay as a model for your own humorous treatment of an experience in following directions.

Thinking and Writing

RHETORICAL TECHNIQUE

1. Outline the stages in the process of putting the delivery truck together.
    The steps in the process of putting the truck together are explicit in the essay. Circle the time expressions that signal the various steps. The steps in the process of the author's nervous breakdown are implicit; you must infer them. Make an outline of the stages and steps in this process. Use emotion such as hysteria, rage, panic, and paranoia for your outline headings.
2. Coherence throughout the essay is maintained by a number of devices.

First, the author repeats key motifs: pain and illness, an inflated vocabulary of battle (mock-heroic figures of speech), cheapness, and the personification of inanimate objects and kit directions as aggressive enemies. Note instances of all these motifs in the text.

Second, a tone of sarcasm is maintained throughout the essay. Indicate instances in the margin.

3. You have read earlier in the chapter that the more explanation and commentary an author includes, the less likely it is that real instruction in a process is the goal. Apply this remark to Perelman's essay.

WILLIAM SHAKESPEARE
The Seven Ages of Man

In Shakespeare's comedy *As You Like It,* Jaques, the speaker of this melancholy soliloquy on human aging, is a critic of the ways of humanity rather than a person of action. Jaques suggests here that our survival of life's various stages, rather than any particularly outstanding accomplishment, is the quintessence of human achievement.

All the world's a stage,

And all the men and women merely players:
They have their exits and their entrances;
And one man in his time plays many parts,
His acts being seven ages. At first the infant,   5
Mewling and puking in the nurse's arms.
And then the whining school-boy, with his satchel
And shining morning face, creeping like snail
Unwillingly to school. And then the lover,
Sighing like furnace, with a woeful ballad   10
Made to his mistress' eyebrow. Then a soldier,
Full of strange oaths and bearded like the pard,
Jealous in honor, sudden and quick in quarrel,
Seeking the bubble reputation
Even in the cannon's mouth. And then the justice,   15
In fair round belly with good capon lined,

With eyes severe and beard of formal cut,
Full of wise saws and modern instances;
And so he plays his part. The sixth age shifts
Into the lean and slipper'd pantaloon,   20
With spectacles on nose and pouch on side,
His youthful hose, well saved, a world too wide
For his shrunk shank; and his big manly voice,
Turning again toward childish treble, pipes
And whistles in his sound. Last scene of all,   25
That ends this strange eventful history,
Is second childishness and mere oblivion,
Sans teeth, sans eyes, sans taste, sans everything.

Reading and Interpreting

VOCABULARY

Use your dictionary as necessary to find the meaning of the following words
as used in Shakespeare's soliloquy:

mewling (6)   capon (16)   saws (18)   shank (23)

CONCEPT ANALYSIS

1. What analogy controls the soliloquy? List all the specific points of
   comparison.
2. How would you characterize Jaques's tone in his description of the seven
   ages: serious, satirical, realistic, or gently comic? Discuss Jaques's perception of the later stages of life. Is it ageist (a negative stereotype of the
   elderly) or is it realistic?
3. Why does Jaques suggest that men and women are "merely" (only) players? Do you agree that human life is as limited and restricted as he
   implies it is?

Quickwrite

Rewrite Shakespeare's soliloquy (in poetry or prose) making the subject
a woman.

RHETORICAL TECHNIQUE

1. The unfolding of the stages of life, a repeated and universal process, is signaled in "The Seven Ages of Man" by a variety of time expressions. Underscore these signals in the piece, then read the soliloquy without them and discuss the difference.
2. Shakespeare apportions a roughly equal amount of commentary to each of the seven ages. Would you reapportion the lines to give some ages more importance than others? Explain.

COMPOSITION

Use Shakespeare's seven-part division of the aging process as a basis for a composition on aging in America today.

ROBERT ROSENTHAL

LENORE JACOBSON

Pygmalion in the Classroom

Robert Rosenthal was a professor of social relations at Harvard, and Lenore Jacobson was a curriculum specialist and principal in the California school system when they collaborated on the educational research project described here. Their experiment takes its title from the Greek myth of the sculptor Pygmalion, whose love for a statue he created transforms it into a living woman. The researchers attempted to discover the process by which teachers unknowingly influence the academic performance of their students. This article is an excellent example of writing about the process of scientific investigation.

In an experiment in the San Francisco public schools two decades ago,   1
Robert Rosenthal and Lenore Jacobson explored the effect of teacher expectation on pupils' intellectual performance. At the beginning of the

school year, teachers were led to believe that specific students in their classes would show considerable academic growth during the school year. The teachers assumed that the students had been designated potential academic "spurters" on the basis of their performance on an intelligence test. The children had been selected, however, by means of a table of random numbers, which is to say, their names were picked out of a hat. Eight months later all of the children in the school were tested; those who had been singled out and brought to the attention of their teachers achieved higher scores than their classmates.

The purpose of the school experiment was to test the hypothesis of 2 the self-fulfilling prophecy. The essence of this concept is that one person's expectations of another person's behavior can become an accurate prediction of that behavior. It is possible that the prediction may be realized only in the perception of the predictor, but it is also possible that the expectation may be communicated to the other person in subtle and unintended ways and consequently influence the person's actual behavior.

In order to test for self-fulfilling prophecy in the classroom, the ex- 3 perimenters had to be sure that the teachers' expectations of the students were not based on their knowledge of the students' behavior and achievement in previous terms. Some years earlier, Robert Rosenthal had had no problem in establishing such conditions in a laboratory situation in which laboratory rats rather than students were the subjects. In one experiment, twelve psychology students were each given five perfectly ordinary laboratory rats and told to teach the rats to run a maze. Six of the students were told that their rats had been bred for maze "brightness." Six of the students were told that their rats were maze "dull."

The results of the experiment indicated that the rats believed to have 4 the higher potential proved to be the better performers. The animals believed to be dull improved for a short period of time and then their performance slackened. In fact, twenty-nine percent of the time they refused to budge from the starting position, compared to eleven percent for the allegedly bright rats.

The student experimenters made ratings of their rats and of their 5 attitudes and behavior toward them. Students who had been led to expect good performance viewed their animals as brighter, more pleasant, and more likable. They also indicated that they had been more relaxed in their handling of the animals, more gentle, friendlier, and less talkative than the experimenters who had been led to expect poor performance. The latter apparently had quite a bit to say to their animals.

Although the laboratory experiment tested the effect of both posi- 6 tive and negative expectations, in the school experiment, it was decided, on ethical grounds, to test only the proposition that favorable expectations by teachers could lead to an increase in intellectual competence. With this objective, the experiment was set up in an elementary school in the South San Francisco Unified School District.

At the beginning of the experiment in 1964, the teachers were told 7
that further validation was needed for a new kind of test designed to predict academic blooming or intellectual gain in children. In actuality they
used the "Flanagan Test of General Ability," a standardized test that was
fairly new and, therefore, unfamiliar to the teachers. They had special
covers designed for the test which bore the pompous title "Test of In-
flected Acquisition." The teachers were told that the test would be given
several times in the future and that the results would be sent to Harvard
University. In May the test was administered to the children in grades one
through five.

Before Oak School opened the following September, five children 8
in each classroom, about twenty percent of the school population, were
designated as potential academic spurters. The teachers were given the
students' names in a deliberately casual manner: the subject was brought
up at the end of the first staff meeting with the remark, "By the way, in
case you're interested in who did what in those tests we're doing for
Harvard . . .".

The experimental treatment of the children who had been chosen at 9
random involved nothing more than giving their names to their new
teachers as children who could be expected to show unusual intellectual
gains in the year ahead. The difference, then, between these children and
the remaining children who constituted the control group was entirely in
the minds of their teachers.

All children were given the same test after one semester, at the end 10
of that school year, and finally in May of the following year. The results
indicated strongly that children from whom teachers expected greater intellectual gains showed such gains. The gains, however, were not uniform
across the grades. The tests given at the end of the first year showed the
largest gains among children in the first and second grades. In the second
year the greatest gains were among the children who had been in the fifth
grade when the "spurters" were designated and who by the time of the
final test were completing sixth grade.

At the end of the academic year 1964–1965 the teachers were asked 11
to describe the classroom behavior of their pupils. The children from
whom intellectual growth was expected were described as less in need of
social approval, happier, more intellectually curious, and more interesting
than the other children. In short, the children for whom intellectual
growth was expected became more alive and autonomous intellectually, or
at least were so perceived by their teachers. These findings were particularly striking among the children in the lower grades.

An interesting contrast became apparent when teachers were asked 12
to rate the undesignated children. Many of these children had also gained
academically during the year. The more intellectually competent these
children became, the less favorably they were rated.

From these results it seemed evident to the researchers that when 13 children who are expected to gain intellectually do gain, they may benefit in other ways. As "personalities" they go up in the estimation of their teachers. The opposite appeared to be true of children who gain intellectually when improvement is not expected of them. They are viewed as showing undesirable behavior.

How is one to account for the fact that the children who were expected to gain did gain? The first answer that comes to mind is that the teachers must have spent more time with them than with the children of whom nothing was said. This hypothesis seems to be wrong, judging from some questions the researchers asked the teachers about the time they spent with their pupils. Also, if teachers had talked more to the designated children, the most likely way of investing more time in work with them, one might expect to see the largest gains in verbal intelligence. In actuality, the largest gains were in reasoning intelligence. 14

Rosenthal and Jacobson have speculated that the explanation lies in a subtler feature of the interaction of teacher and pupils. Tone of voice, facial expression, touch, and posture may be the means by which—quite unwittingly—teachers communicate their expectations to their pupils. Such communication might help the children by changing their self-concepts and, hence, their expectations of their own behavior. This is an area in which further research is clearly needed. 15

Why was the effect of teacher expectation most pronounced in the lower grades? The researchers advanced several hypotheses: Younger children may be easier to change than older ones. They are likely to have less well-established reputations in the school. It may be that they are more sensitive to the processes by which teachers communicate their expectations to pupils. 16

It is also difficult to be certain why the older children showed the better performance in the follow-up year. Perhaps the younger children, who by then had different teachers, needed continued contact with the teachers who had influenced them originally in order to maintain their improved performance. The older children, who had been harder to influence at first, may have been better able to maintain an improved performance autonomously once they had achieved it. 17

The Pygmalion experiment raised many new hypotheses. It became evident to the researchers that more attention in educational research needed to be focused on teachers to ascertain how they can effect dramatic changes in their pupils' performance. 18

CONCEPT ANALYSIS

1. What is a "self-fulfilling prophecy"? Through the scientific method, Rosenthal and Jacobson validated their hypothesis of self-fulfilling prophecy. Keeping in mind Thomas Huxley's statement that the value of a scientific hypothesis is "proportionate to the care and completeness with which its basis has been tested and verified," how confident are you in Rosenthal and Jacobson's theory of self-fulfilling prophecy?
2. The allusion to the Greek myth of Pygmalion in the title of this article implies an analogy between the Pygmalion myth and the scientific experiment described. What are the points of comparison between the myth and the experiment? Do you find the analogy helpful?

Thinking and Writing

RHETORICAL TECHNIQUE

1. In social science journals, articles usually include subtopic headings for the convenience of the reader. At what point would you introduce the following subtitles to Rosenthal and Jacobson's article: The Self-Fulfilling Prophecy, The Laboratory Experiment, The School Experiment, Teachers' Perceptions, Experimental and Control Groups, Explanations and Areas for Future Inquiry?
2. Before testing the hypothesis of self-fulfilling prophecy in the classroom, Robert Rosenthal tested it in the laboratory with rats. Informally outline either experiment, using the following labels: hypothesis, procedure (including experimental and control groups and steps), results, conclusion.

    What deduction about research follows from the experiment's conclusion?
3. What change would have to be made in Rosenthal and Jacobson's experiment to test the effect of *negative* expectations in the classroom?

COMPOSITION

1. The Rosenthal-Jacobson experiment gave evidence for a "Pygmalion effect" in the classroom. From your own experience and that of others you know, describe the process by which a particular pupil has become known or been labeled as bright or dull.

2. The researchers concluded that "more attention in educational research needed to be focused on teachers to ascertain how they can effect dramatic changes in their pupils' performance." Think about how a teacher effected a dramatic change in your self-image, either enhancing or damaging your academic performance. Discuss the process by which this change occurred.

ORVILLE TAYLOR

Silk Culture

Early nineteenth-century American educator Orville Taylor wrote the *Farmers' School Book* in an effort to reform a curriculum that he felt was irrelevant to the farm children who attended American public schools. Taylor intended this manual as a model for reading and writing as well as a source of practical information. In describing the various agricultural processes, such as silk making, his writing is clear, precise, and even eloquent.

Farmers' School Book

This book should be read in common schools in the place of the "English 1 Reader," "Columbian Orator," and other similar works. By reading the Farmers' School Book, the children will learn the business of practical life; and this is much more desirable than to read the English Reader, a book they seldom understand, and one they can put to no practical use.

The Culture of Silk

The principal articles made use of for clothing among civilized people are 2 wool, flax, cotton, and silk, all of which consisting of fine fibres, those fibres are twisted into threads, and woven into various kinds of cloth. Each of these possesses, perhaps, some peculiar advantage in quality which the others do not; but that which universally holds a most decided preference over all the others is *silk*. . . .

History of Silk

The discovery of the use of silk, and the modes of procuring and manufac- 3
turing it, was unquestionably made by the Chinese at a period of very
remote antiquity; we know nothing, therefore, of its early history, except
what we learn from them.

The account they give us is, that it was discovered in its native for- 4
ests of mulberry; and that about seven hundred years before the days
of Abraham, an emperor called Haung-to, whose name they hold in
great veneration, persuaded his wife, Si-ling-chi, to have the silkworms
gathered and domesticated, and to teach his subjects the management of
them, and use of the silk. If this account be true, the first silk grower was
an emperor.

The silk business, however, appears to have been for a long time, 5
probably for many ages, confined to a part of the Chinese dominions,
called Serica. But in process of time, garments composed of it were carried
by traders, travelling in caravans, through trackless sands and deserts to
Syria and Egypt, a journey which it took about eight or nine months to
perform.

These garments were sold to merchants, who again sold them at 6
enormous prices, and they were, no doubt, for a long period the principal
source of wealth to the last-mentioned nations.

This tedious overland carrying trade was, for a long time, chiefly 7
monopolized by the Persians, who, about three hundred and fifty years
before the Christian era, extended it to Greece, where the silk found a
prodigious demand, owing to the immense wealth of the Grecians; and
the Phoenicians also engaging in the trade, it found its way throughout
the south of Europe. But even those who brought it to Europe knew not
what it was, where it came from, nor how it was produced.

By the Romans in the third and fourth centuries it was considered an 8
article of too much extravagance to be indulged in, except by those of
immense wealth and pride. But about the fifth, and beginning of the sixth
century, it began to be a subject of inquiry among the Romans, from what
part of the world this precious article came, and what was the secret of its
production.

About this time, two monks, who had been missionaries to China, 9
returned, and brought with them the seed of the mulberry, and gave information how the silkworms were reared and fed upon the leaves, and
how those worms spun the silk. But to carry the silkworms or their eggs
out of China was forbidden on pain of death.

Still, however, in consequence of the liberal rewards offered by the 10
Emperor Justinian, these persevering individuals returned, and after a
long pilgrimage, having obtained the eggs at the risk of their lives,
brought them to the emperor concealed in a hollow cane.

The culture of silk was now engaged in by families of the highest 11 standing; but was chiefly carried on under the immediate protection of the emperor, for his own benefit; but at his death, the monopoly could be maintained no longer, and the business was entered into by individuals with great avidity; and during four hundred years the silk was distributed by the Venetian merchants throughout the west of Europe.

But in the year 1146, Roger the Norman, king of Sicily, invaded 12 Greece, and capturing a great number of silk growers and weavers, carried them to Palermo, his capitol. By the Saracens also it was carried into Spain, and it soon after found its way into Italy, where, in 1306, it was so far advanced as to yield a revenue to the state.

It now also found its way into France, and was encouraged by Louis 13 XI., and Charles VIII., and still more by Henry IV., who established it as one of the principal sources of wealth to his nation, which standing it has maintained ever since.

It began to be introduced into England a little before, and during 14 the reign of Elizabeth; and James I. endeavoured much to establish the silk culture in that kingdom. He addressed letters, written with his own hand, to the lord lieutenants of every county in the kingdom, accompanied with mulberry seeds and plants, together with a book of instructions. But though near the close of his reign he effected something towards establishing the manufacture of silk, nothing profitable was done in its production, and probably never can be in that kingdom, owing to the humidity of the atmosphere.

In the reign of George II. much was effected in improving the silk 15 manufacture by Sir Thomas Lamb, and his brothers John and Henry, and it has increased progressively to the present time. The throwsting mill, erected by the Lambs in Derby, is still standing, and is regarded with great interest, though its usefulness is much superseded by subsequent improvements.

It was probably owing to the difficulty of producing silk in England 16 that attempts were made to introduce it into the then British colonies, as early as the twentieth year of the reign of James I., who gave special instructions to the Earl of Southampton, that as he had "understood that the soil of Virginia naturally yieldeth stores of excellent mulberries, he would urge the cultivation of silk, in preference to tobacco, which bringeth with it many disorders and inconveniences."

In 1623, the colonial assembly directed mulberry trees to be planted; 17 and soon after laid a penalty of three pounds of tobacco upon every planter who should fail to plant at least ten mulberry trees for every hundred acres of land in his possession. A premium of ten thousand pounds of tobacco was offered to any person who should export two thousand pounds worth of raw silk.

These encouragements had, in a great measure, the desired effect, 18 the agriculturalists engaged spiritedly in the business, and great numbers of mulberry trees were planted. Among others, a Mr. Walker had seventy thousand trees growing in 1664. As early as 1732, at the settlement of Georgia, the lands were granted upon the express condition that one hundred white mulberry trees should be set on every ten acres of land when cleared.

In 1755, Mrs. Pinckney, a very distinguished lady of South Carolina, took with her to England a sufficient quantity of very superior silk to make three dresses. Considerable sewing silk was made in Georgia during the war of the revolution. In 1770, a filature for reeling silk was established at Philadelphia. [19]

But the silk growing and manufacturing enterprise appears to have been wholly lost sight of during the general confusion and distress which prevailed during the revolution, except in Connecticut, where it had been introduced as early as 1760, by the patriotic exertions of a Mr. Aspinwal, and where it has been continued upon a small scale ever since; but this has been chiefly confined to sewing silk. [20]

But a general awakening to a sense of the great importance of the silk growing and manufacturing interest has lately taken place, and now appears to extend through every part of the United States; and there is every reason to anticipate a most successful result. [21]

Silk Continued—Mode of Proceeding in Rearing the Worms and Producing Silk

The first step in the silk business is to procure and have in readiness an ample supply of food for the number of worms intended to be kept, which food consists chiefly of the leaves of the mulberry tree; though there are many other leaves on which they may occasionally be fed, particularly the lettuce; but it is doubtful whether anything except the mulberry leaves can be permanently depended on, either for sustaining the worms or producing silk. . . . [22]

When a sufficient number of mulberry plants have been propagated, and have grown large enough to be divested of their leaves, the next step will be to procure a small stock of eggs. This with the Chinese mulberry may be effected in a very short time, for the young trees may be multiplied by layers and cuttings from ten to a hundred fold annually; and considerable quantities of leaves may be taken from them the second year from the seedbed. [23]

When the trees have begun to put forth their leaves in the spring, the eggs of the silkmoth are placed in a warm situation (but not in the direct rays of the sun) to produce hatching, which will take place in about five or six days. [24]

When the worms are hatched, they attach themselves to the leaves of small twigs of mulberry, by which they are carried to the place where they [25] are to be fed. They are then about the twelfth part of an inch in length, and those that are healthy are generally of a black colour.

In the first stage of feeding the worm, they may be laid on tables, on 26 shelves, or even on rough boards temporarily placed for the purpose, and covered with paper, and fed with tender leaves chopped fine. In about four days, they begin to appear torpid, and cease eating, in which state they remain twenty-four or twenty-six hours, during which time they shed their skin, which is called moulting.

This operation they generally perform four times, and the interven- 27 ing times before, between, and after the moultings are called ages. The first four ages are from four to eight days each, and the fifth and last age occupies about ten days, at which time the worms attain their full size.

As the silkworms increase in size they increase also in appetite, and 28 especially during the last ages they devour large quantities of leaves. About the thirty-second day they generally cease feeding, and prepare to spin their cocoons. Little twigs, especially of oak, with the leaves on and dried, are then placed for them to climb on, when they commence spinning, and winding themselves in, and in about from four to eight days they complete their work.

The cocoons intended to be reserved for eggs are then selected, and 29 in about twelve days the moth will come out. They are then placed on papers in pairs, male and female, in a dark room; and in from twenty-four to thirty-six hours from the time of leaving the cocoon, the female moth will have laid her complement of eggs, which is generally from three to four hundred. Both the male and female die shortly after the female has done laying her eggs, and never eat after leaving the cocoons.

Those cocoons which are designed for producing silk are prepared by 30 killing, or, as it is commonly called, stifling the chrysalis, which is done by baking or steaming, or sometimes by the heat of the sun; and being thus prepared they are ready for reeling.

When the silk is to be reeled, several cocoons are placed together in 31 a vessel of hot water, in order to soften the gummy or glutinous matter which holds the fibres of the cocoon together. By stirring them round in the hot water with a kind of wisp, the ends of the fibres are collected, and the silk is reeled off with a brisk motion, each cocoon yielding a continuous fibre several hundred yards in length.

As these fibres, taken singly, would be too fine for use, several of 32 them are united together in reeling, and the glutinous substance connected with the silk connects and binds them in a single thread, of any size required. It may be reeled on any common reel, but when the business is extended, long experience has dictated a form of reels much better adapted to the purpose.

The silk thus reeled is called *raw silk,* and intended for market in 33 that state, is sold by the pound, in skeins or hanks. The ingenious Mr.

Gay of Providence has invented a plan of winding the silk from the co-coons on spools or bobbins which bids fair to be a valuable improvement.

The loose fibres which surround the cocoons previous to reeling are 34 carefully separated, and are called floss, or waste silk. Those cocoons, also, in which the chrysalis has been preserved, and others, from not being perfectly formed, and of course not susceptible of being reeled, are denominated waste silk, and when carded and spun, answer a variety of purposes.

The establishments where silk is reeled are called filatures, some of 35 which are very extensive, and the buildings appropriated to rearing and feeding silkworms are called cocooneries.

The raw silk is transferred to the manufacturer, who transforms it 36 into the elegant articles of dress and ornament we see offered for sale; in many of which great ingenuity and refined taste are displayed. But the people who produce them in foreign countries, from whence we import many millions of dollars worth every year, have no more ingenuity, and probably, in most cases, less refinement of taste, and less enterprise, than the people of our own country; and no article of silk can be imported that cannot, in a short time, be produced in this country of equal value and beauty.

The production of silk is certainly one of the most lucrative, as well 37 as pleasing and interesting employments which human industry can be engaged in. In the cultivation of the Chinese mulberry itself—the facility with which it is propagated by cuttings or layers—its peculiar tenacity of life—its beauty as a shrub, with its numerous stalks, bending with their burden of broad and shining leaves, cannot but afford pleasure to an agriculturist of any refinement of taste.

The gathering the leaves and feeding the worms give light and 38 wholesome exercise, enlivened by the anticipation of a rich reward; while the spectacle of millions of insects feeding with avidity and growing in a few days, from a scarcely visible speck to several inches in length; then almost simultaneously ceasing to eat and commencing to spin and wind themselves in a thick coat of silk, affording more than ample compensation for the food they have received; after a few days reappearing, changed to a butterfly, for no apparent purpose but to deposit the eggs for a succeeding generation, must be, to a reflecting mind, a rich subject for contemplation.

It must afford no less agreeable anticipations to the patriot, to reflect 39 that in a very few years the growing and manufacture of silk in the United States will not only afford a living, and perhaps wealth to thousands, who are now, and would otherwise remain poor and destitute, but will save to the country the immense sums which are now annually sent out of it to purchase articles which we can as well produce ourselves, and probably cheaper than those from whom we buy them.

The growth of silk is peculiarly adapted to the minds, capacities, 40 and tastes of youth of both sexes; we fondly hope, therefore, that those of that class into whose hands this little book may fall, will feel sufficiently awakened by the importance of the subject to endeavour to become more fully acquainted with it, which they can do by procuring such publications as treat of it more extensively, and perfecting the knowledge thus acquired by practice.

The best source to which we can refer our readers for a thorough 41 knowledge of the silk business is *"The Silkworm,"* a monthly periodical, published in Albany, by Mr. S. Blydenburgh, and we believe the only one in the United States, and perhaps in the world, devoted solely to the subject.

Reading and Interpreting

VOCABULARY

Use your dictionary as necessary to find the meaning of the following words as used by Orville Taylor:

procuring (3)   prodigious (7)   superseded (15)   torpid (26)

complement (29)   susceptible (34)   propagated (37)   tenacity (37)

ample (38)

CONCEPT ANALYSIS

1. This selection brings together two processes, the historical process by which silk culture was brought from China to the West and the process of silk cultivation. Why might Taylor have chosen to include the extended historical process analysis in this *practical* manual for farmers?
2. After describing the process of silk production, Taylor concludes with some reflections that encourage the cultivation of silk in the United States. Briefly list the points in support of the argument. Are you persuaded?

   Paragraph 16 indicates that in colonial times, the English king encouraged "the cultivation of silk, in preference to tobacco." Today, tobacco is the more dominant industry. Why do you think this is so?

Quickwrite

Debate the merits of synthetic versus natural fibers.

RHETORICAL TECHNIQUE

1. Make an outline in brief note form of either the historical process or the production process traced in the reading.
2. In both the historical analysis and the production description, the author guides his readers with signals of time and sequence. Underline some of these in both processes, then try alternatives and evaluate their effectiveness.
3. In the silk culture process, the various steps could be combined into sequential phases or stages of the operation. For example, paragraphs 22 through 28 deal with the mulberry tree and the feeding of silkworms. Group the remaining paragraphs under appropriate subtopic headings.

    Underline the key words that give coherence to the paragraphs that are grouped together.

COMPOSITION

Taylor describes silk making as a process that "to a reflecting mind [is] a rich subject for contemplation." Describe a process in modern technology that you feel has the same effect.

___

JACK LONDON

To Build a Fire

Jack London (1876–1916), American short story writer and novelist, has a realistic style that is unsentimental and powerful. In the following story of the Alaskan wilderness, typical of London's settings, processes occur on a number of levels. On the literal level there are the processes of getting frostbite and building a fire. On the psychological level the protagonist goes through the process of becoming aware of his own mortality. The third level is the process whereby the reader grows in understanding of the story's theme.

Day had broken cold and gray, exceedingly cold and gray, when the man 1
turned aside from the main Yukon trail and climbed the high earth bank,
where a dim and little-traveled trail led eastward through the fat spruce
timberland. It was a steep bank, and he paused for breath at the top, ex-
cusing the act to himself by looking at his watch. It was nine o'clock.
There was no sun or hint of sun, though there was not a cloud in the sky.
It was a clear day, and yet there seemed an intangible pall over the face of
things, a subtle gloom that made the day dark, and that was due to the
absence of sun. This fact did not worry the man. He was used to the lack
of sun. It had been days since he had seen the sun, and he knew that a few
more days must pass before that cheerful orb, due south, would just peep
above the skyline and dip immediately from view.

The man flung a look back along the way he had come. The Yukon 2
lay a mile wide and hidden under three feet of ice. On top of this ice were
as many feet of snow. It was all pure white, rolling in gentle undulations
where the ice jams of the freeze-up had formed. North and south, as far as
his eye could see, it was unbroken white, save for a dark hairline that
curved and twisted from around the spruce-covered island to the south,
and that curved and twisted away into the north, where it disappeared
behind another spruce-covered island. This dark hairline was the trail—
the main trail—that led south five hundred miles to the Chilcoot Pass,
Dyea, and salt water; and that led north seventy miles to Dawson, and
still on to the north a thousand miles to Nulato, and finally to St. Michael
on Bering Sea, a thousand miles and half a thousand more.

But all this—the mysterious, far-reaching hairline trail, the absence 3
of sun from the sky, the tremendous cold, and the strangeness and weird-
ness of it all—made no impression on the man. It was not because he was
long used to it. He was a newcomer in the land, a *chechaquo,* and this was
his first winter. The trouble with him was that he was without imagination. He was quick and alert in the things of life, but only in the things,
and not in the significances. Fifty degrees below zero meant eighty-odd
degrees of frost. Such fact impressed him as being cold and uncomfortable, and that was all. It did not lead him to meditate upon his frailty as a
creature of temperature, and upon man's frailty in general, able only to
live within certain narrow limits of heat and cold and from there on it did
not lead him to the conjectural field of immortality and man's place in the
universe. Fifty degrees below zero stood for a bite of frost that hurt and
that must be guarded against by the use of mittens, earflaps, warm moccasins, and thick socks. Fifty degrees below zero was to him just precisely
fifty degrees below zero. That there should be anything more to it than
that was a thought that never entered his head.

As he turned to go on, he spat speculatively. There was a sharp, ex- 4
plosive crackle that startled him. He spat again. And again, in the air,
before it could fall to the snow, the spittle crackled. He knew that at fifty
below spittle crackled on the snow, but this spittle had crackled in the air.

Undoubtedly it was colder than fifty below—how much colder he did not know. But the temperature did not matter. He was bound for the old claim on the left fork of Henderson Creek, where the boys were already. They had come over across the divide from the Indian Creek country, while he had come the roundabout way to take a look at the possibilities of getting out logs in the spring from the islands in the Yukon. He would be in to camp by six o'clock; a bit after dark, it was true, but the boys would be there, a fire would be going, and a hot supper would be ready. As for lunch, he pressed his hand against the protruding bundle under his jacket. It was also under his shirt, wrapped up in a handkerchief and lying against the naked skin. It was the only way to keep the biscuits from freezing. He smiled agreeably to himself as he thought of those biscuits, each cut open and sopped in bacon grease, and each enclosing a generous slice of fried bacon.

He plunged in among the big spruce trees. The trail was faint. A 5 foot of snow had fallen since the last sled had passed over, and he was glad he was without a sled, traveling light. In fact, he carried nothing but the lunch wrapped in the handkerchief. He was surprised, however, at the cold. It certainly was cold, he concluded, as he rubbed his numb nose and cheekbones with his mittened hand. He was a warm-whiskered man, but the hair on his face did not protect the high cheekbones and the eager nose that thrust itself aggressively into the frosty air.

At the man's heels trotted a dog, a big native husky, the proper wolf- 6 dog, gray-coated and without any visible or temperamental difference from its brother, the wild wolf. The animal was depressed by the tremendous cold. It knew that it was no time for traveling. Its instinct told it a truer tale than was told to the man by the man's judgment. In reality, it was not merely colder than fifty below zero; it was colder than sixty below, than seventy below. It was seventy-five below zero. Since the freezing point is thirty-two above zero, it meant that one hundred and seven degrees of frost obtained. The dog did not know anything about thermometers. Possibly in its brain there was no sharp consciousness of a condition of very cold such as was in the man's brain. But the brute had its instinct. It experienced a vague but menacing apprehension that subdued it and made it slink along at the man's heels, and that made it question eagerly every unwonted movement of the man, as if expecting him to go into camp or to seek shelter somewhere and build a fire. The dog had learned fire, and it wanted fire, or else to burrow under the snow and cuddle its warmth away from the air.

The frozen moisture of its breathing had settled on its fur in a fine 7 powder of frost, and especially were its jowls, muzzle, and eyelashes whitened by its crystaled breath. The man's red beard and mustache were likewise frosted, but more solidly, the deposit taking the form of ice and increasing with every warm, moist breath he exhaled. Also, the man was chewing tobacco, and the muzzle of ice held his lips so rigidly that he was unable to clear his chin when he expelled the juice. The result was that a crystal beard of the color and solidity of amber was increasing its length on his chin. If he fell down it would shatter itself, like glass, into brittle fragments. But he did not mind the appendage. It was the penalty all tobacco chewers paid in that country, and he had been out before in two cold snaps. They had not been as cold as this, he knew, but by the spirit thermometer at Sixty Mile he knew they had been registered at fifty below and at fifty-five.

He held on through the level stretch of woods for several miles, 8 crossed a wide flat of vegetation, and dropped down a bank to the frozen bed of a small stream. This was Henderson Creek, and he knew he was ten miles from the forks. He looked at his watch. It was ten o'clock. He was making four miles an hour, and he calculated that he would arrive at the forks at half-past twelve. He decided to celebrate that event by eating his lunch there.

The dog dropped in again at his heels, with a tail drooping discour- 9 agement, as the man swung along the creek bed. The furrow of the old sled trail was plainly visible, but a dozen inches of snow covered the marks of the last runners. In a month no man had come up or down that silent creek. The man held steadily on. He was not much given to thinking, and just then particularly he had nothing to think about save that he would eat lunch at the forks and that at six o'clock he would be in camp with the boys. There was nobody to talk to; and, had there been, speech would have been impossible because of the ice muzzle on his mouth. So he continued monotonously to chew tobacco and to increase the length of his amber beard.

Once in a while the thought reiterated itself that it was very cold 10 and that he had never experienced such cold. As he walked along he rubbed his cheekbones and nose with the back of his mittened hand. He did this automatically, now and again changing hands. But rub as he would, the instant he stopped his cheekbones went numb, and the following instant the end of his nose went numb. He was sure to frost his cheeks; he knew that, and experienced a pang of regret that he had not devised a nose strap of the sort Bud wore in cold snaps. Such a strap passed across the cheeks, as well, and saved them. But it didn't matter much, after all. What were frosted cheeks? A bit painful, that was all; they were never serious.

Empty as the man's mind was of thoughts, he was keenly observant, 11 and he noticed the changes in the creek, the curves and bends and timber-jams, and always he sharply noted where he placed his feet. Once, coming around a bend, he shied abruptly, like a startled horse, curved away from the place where he had been walking, and retreated several paces back along the trail. The creek, he knew, was frozen clear to the bottom—no creek could contain water in that arctic winter—but he knew also that there were springs that bubbled out from the hillsides and ran along under the snow and on top of the ice of the creek. He knew that the coldest snaps never froze these springs, and he knew likewise their danger. They were traps. They hid pools of water under the snow that might be three inches deep, or three feet. Sometimes a skin of ice half an inch thick covered them, and in turn was covered by the snow. Sometimes there were alternate layers of water and ice skin, so that when one broke through he kept on breaking through for a while, sometimes wetting himself to the waist.

That was why he had shied in such panic. He had felt the give under 12 his feet and heard the crackle of a snow-hidden ice skin. And to get his feet wet in such a temperature meant trouble and danger. At the very least it meant delay, for he would be forced to stop and build a fire, and under its protection to bare his feet while he dried his socks and moccasins. He stood and studied the creek bed and its banks, and decided that the flow of water came from the right. He reflected a while, rubbing his nose and cheeks, then skirted to the left, stepping gingerly and testing the footing for each step. Once clear of the danger, he took a fresh chew of tobacco and swung along at his four-mile gait.

In the course of the next two hours he came upon several similar 13 traps. Usually the snow above the hidden pools had a sunken, candied appearance that advertised the danger. Once again, however, he had a close call; and once, suspecting danger, he compelled the dog to go on in front. The dog did not want to go. It hung back until the man shoved it forward, and then it went quickly across the white, unbroken surface. Suddenly it broke through, floundering to one side, and got away to firmer footing. It had wet its forefeet and legs, and almost immediately the water that clung to it turned to ice. It made quick efforts to lick the ice off its legs, then dropped down in the snow and began to bite out the ice that had formed between the toes. This was a matter of instinct. To permit the ice to remain would mean sore feet. It did not know this. It merely obeyed the mysterious prompting that arose from the deep crypts of its being. But the man knew, having achieved a judgment on the subject, and he removed the mitten from his right hand and helped tear out the ice particles. He did not expose his fingers more than a minute, and was astonished at the swift numbness that smote them. It certainly was cold. He pulled on the mitten hastily, and beat the hand savagely across his chest.

At twelve o'clock the day was at its brightest. Yet the sun was too far 14 south on its winter journey to clear the horizon. The bulge of the earth intervened between it and Henderson Creek, where the man walked under a clear sky at noon and cast no shadow. At half-past twelve, to the minute, he arrived at the forks of the creek. He was pleased at the speed he had made. If he kept it up, he would certainly be with the boys by six. He unbuttoned his jacket and shirt and drew forth his lunch. The action consumed no more than a quarter of a minute, yet in that brief moment the numbness laid hold of the exposed fingers. He did not put the mitten on, but, instead, struck the fingers a dozen sharp smashes against his leg. Then he sat down on a snow-covered log to eat. The sting that followed upon the striking of his fingers against his leg ceased so quickly that he was startled. He had had no chance to take a bite of biscuit. He struck the fingers repeatedly and returned them to the mitten, baring the other hand for the purpose of eating. He tried to take a mouthful, but the ice muzzle prevented. He had forgotten to build a fire and thaw out. He chuckled at his foolishness, and as he chuckled he noted the numbness creeping into the exposed fingers. Also he noted that the stinging which had first come to his toes when he sat down was already passing away. He wondered whether the toes were warm or numb. He moved them inside the moccasins and decided that they were numb.

He pulled the mitten on hurriedly and stood up. He was a bit 15 frightened. He stamped up and down until the stinging returned into the feet. It certainly was cold, was his thought. That man from Sulphur Creek had spoken the truth when telling how cold it sometimes got in the country. And he had laughed at him at the time! That showed one must not be too sure of things. There was no mistake about it, it *was* cold. He strode up and down, stamping his feet and threshing his arms, until reassured by the returning warmth. Then he got out matches and proceeded to make a fire. From the undergrowth, where high water of the previous spring had lodged a supply of seasoned twigs, he got his firewood. Working carefully from a small beginning, he soon had a roaring fire, over which he thawed the ice from his face and in the protection of which he ate his biscuits. For the moment the cold of space was outwitted. The dog took satisfaction in the fire, stretching out close enough for warmth and far enough away to escape being singed.

When the man had finished, he filled his pipe and took his comfort- 16 able time over a smoke. Then he pulled on his mittens, settled the earflaps of his cap firmly about his ears, and took the creek trail up the left fork. The dog was disappointed and yearned back toward the fire. This man did not know cold. Possibly all the generations of his ancestry had been ignorant of cold, of real cold, of cold one hundred and seven degrees below freezing point. But the dog knew; all its ancestry knew, and it had inherited the knowledge. And it knew that it was not good to walk abroad in such fearful cold. It was the time to lie snug in a hole in the snow and wait for a curtain of cloud to be drawn across the face of outer space whence this cold came. On the other hand, there was no keen intimacy between the dog and the man. The one was the toil-slave of the other, and the only caresses it had ever received were the caresses of the whiplash and of harsh and menacing throat sounds that threatened the whiplash. So the dog made no effort to communicate its apprehension to the man. It was not concerned in the welfare of the man; it was for its own sake that it yearned back toward the fire. But the man whistled, and spoke to it with the sound of whiplashes, and the dog swung in at the man's heels and followed after.

The man took a chew of tobacco and proceeded to start a new amber 17 beard. Also, his moist breath quickly powdered with white his mustache, eyebrows, and lashes. There did not seem to be so many springs on the left fork of the Henderson, and for half an hour the man saw no signs of any. And then it happened. At a place where there were no signs, where the soft, unbroken snow seemed to advertise solidity beneath, the man broke through. It was not deep. He wet himself halfway to the knees before he floundered out to the firm crust.

He was angry, and cursed his luck aloud. He had hoped to get into 18 camp with the boys at six o'clock, and this would delay him an hour, for he would have to build a fire and dry out his foot-gear. This was imperative at that low temperature—he knew that much; and he turned aside to the bank, which he climbed. On top, tangled in the underbrush about the trunks of several small spruce trees, was a high-water deposit of dry firewood—sticks and twigs, principally, but also larger portions of seasoned branches and fine, dry, last year's grasses. He threw down several large pieces on top of the snow. This served for a foundation and prevented the young flame from drowning itself in the snow it otherwise would melt. The flame he got by touching a match to a small shred of birch-bark that he took from his pocket. This burned even more readily than paper. Placing it on the foundation, he fed the young flame with wisps of dry grass and with the tiniest dry twigs.

He worked slowly and carefully, keenly aware of his danger. Gradu- 19 ally, as the flame grew stronger, he increased the size of the twigs with which he fed it. He squatted in the snow, pulling the twigs out from their entanglement in the brush and feeding directly to the flame. He knew there must be no failure. When it is seventy-five below zero a man must not fail in his first attempt to build a fire—that is, if his feet are wet. If his feet are dry, and he fails, he can run along the trail for half a mile and restore his circulation. But the circulation of wet and freezing feet cannot be restored by running when it is seventy-five below. No matter how fast he runs, the wet feet will freeze the harder.

All this the man knew. The oldtimer on Sulphur Creek had told him 20 about it the previous fall, and now he was appreciating the advice. Already all sensation had gone out of his feet. To build the fire, he had been forced to remove his mittens, and the fingers had quickly gone numb. His pace of four miles an hour had kept his heart pumping blood to the surface of his body and to all the extremities. But the instant he stopped, the action of the pump eased down. The cold of space smote the unprotected tip of the planet, and he, being on that unprotected tip, received the full force of the blow. The blood of his body recoiled before it. The blood was alive, like the dog, and like the dog it wanted to hide away and cover itself up from the fearful cold. So long as he walked four miles an hour, he pumped that blood, willy-nilly, to the surface; but now it ebbed away and sank down into the recesses of his body. The extremities were the first to feel its absence. His wet feet froze the faster, and his exposed fingers numbed the faster, though they had not yet begun to freeze. Nose and cheeks were already freezing, while the skin of all his body chilled as it lost its blood.

But he was safe. Toes and noses and cheeks would be only touched 21 by the frost, for the fire was beginning to burn with strength. He was feeding it with twigs the size of his finger. In another minute he would be able to feed it with branches the size of his wrist, and then he could remove his wet foot-gear, and, while it dried, he could keep his naked feet warm by the fire, rubbing them at first, of course, with snow. The fire was a success. He was safe. He remembered the advice of the oldtimer on Sulphur Creek, and smiled. The oldtimer had been very serious in laying down the law that no man must travel alone in the Klondike after fifty below. Well, here he was; he had had the accident; he was alone; and he had saved himself. Those oldtimers were rather womanish, some of them, he thought. All a man had to do was to keep his head, and he was all right. Any man who was a man could travel alone. But it was surprising the rapidity with which his cheeks and nose were freezing. And he had not thought his fingers could go lifeless in so short a time. Lifeless they were, for he could scarcely make them move together to grip a twig, and they seemed remote from his body and from him. When he touched a twig he had to look and see whether or not he had hold of it. The wires were pretty well down between him and his finger-ends.

All of which counted for little. There was the fire, snapping and 22 crackling and promising life with every dancing flame. He started to untie his moccasins. They were coated with ice; the thick German socks were like sheaths of iron halfway to the knees; and the moccasin strings were like rods of steel all twisted and knotted as by some conflagration. For a moment he tugged with his numb fingers, then, realizing the folly in it, he drew his sheath knife.

But before he could cut the strings, it happened. It was his own 23 fault, or, rather, his mistake. He should not have built the fire under the spruce tree. He should have built it in the open. But it had been easier to pull the twigs from the brush and drop them directly on the fire. Now the tree under which he had done this carried a weight of snow on its boughs. No wind had blown for weeks, and each bough was fully freighted. Each time he had pulled a twig he had communicated a slight agitation to the tree—an imperceptible agitation, so far as he was concerned, but an agitation sufficient to bring about the disaster. High up in the tree one bough capsized its load of snow. This fell on the boughs beneath, capsizing them. This process continued, spreading out and involving the whole tree. It grew like an avalanche, and it descended without warning upon the man and the fire, and the fire was blotted out! Where it had burned was a mantle of fresh and disordered snow.

The man was shocked. It was as though he had just heard his own 24 sentence of death. For a moment he sat and stared at the spot where the fire had been. Then he grew very calm. Perhaps the oldtimer on Sulphur Creek was right. If he had only had a trailmate he would have been in no danger now. The trailmate could have built the fire. Well, it was up to him to build the fire over again, and this second time there must be no failure. Even if he succeeded, he would most likely lose some toes. His feet must be badly frozen by now, and there would be some time before the second fire was ready.

Such were his thoughts, but he did not sit and think them. He was 25 busy all the time they were passing through his mind. He made a new foundation for a fire, this time in the open, where no treacherous tree could blot it out. Next he gathered dry grasses and tiny twigs from the high-water flotsam. He could not bring his fingers together to pull them out, but he was able to gather them by the handful. In this way he got many rotten twigs and bits of green moss that were undesirable, but it was the best he could do. He worked methodically, even collecting an armful of the larger branches to be used later when the fire gathered strength. And all the while the dog sat and watched him, a certain yearning wistfulness in its eyes, for it looked upon him as the fire-provider, and the fire was slow in coming.

When all was ready, the man reached in his pocket for a second piece 26 of birch-bark. He knew the bark was there, and, though he could not feel it with his fingers, he could hear its crisp rustling as he fumbled for it. Try as he would, he could not clutch hold of it. And all the time, in his consciousness, was the knowledge that each instant his feet were freezing. This thought tended to put him in a panic, but he fought against it and kept calm. He pulled on his mittens with his teeth, and threshed his arms back and forth, beating his hands with all his might against his sides. He did this sitting down, and he stood up to do it; and all the while the dog sat in the snow, its wolf-brush of a tail curled around warmly over its forefeet, its sharp wolf ears pricked forward intently as it watched the man. And the man, as he beat and threshed with his arms and hands, felt a great surge of envy as he regarded the creature that was warm and secure in its natural covering.

After a time he was aware of the first far-away signals of sensation in 27 his beaten fingers. The faint tingling grew stronger till it evolved into a stinging ache that was excruciating, but which the man hailed with satisfaction. He stripped the mitten from his right hand and fetched forth the birch-bark. The exposed fingers were quickly going numb again. Next he brought out his bunch of sulphur matches. But the tremendous cold had already driven the life out of his fingers. In his effort to separate one match from the others, the whole bunch fell in the snow. He tried to pick it out of the snow, but failed. The dead fingers could neither touch nor clutch. He was very careful. He drove the thought of his freezing feet, and nose, and cheeks, out of his mind, devoting his whole soul to the matches. He watched, using the sense of vision in place of that of touch, and when he saw his fingers on each side the bunch, he closed them—that is, he willed to close them, for the wires were down, and the fingers did not obey. He pulled the mitten on the right hand, and beat it fiercely against his knee. Then, with both mittened hands, he scooped the bunch of matches, along with much snow, into his lap. Yet he was no better off.

After some manipulation he managed to get the bunch between the heels of his mittened hands. In this fashion he carried it to his mouth. The ice crackled and snapped when by a violent effort he opened his mouth. He drew the lower jaw in, curled the upper lip out of the way, and scraped the bunch with his upper teeth in order to separate a match. He succeeded in getting one, which he dropped on his lap. He was no better off. He could not pick it up. Then he devised a way. He picked it up in his teeth and scratched it on his leg. Twenty times he scratched before he succeeded in lighting it. As it flamed he held it with his teeth to the birch-bark. But the burning brimstone went up his nostrils and into his lungs, causing him to cough spasmodically. The match fell into the snow and went out.

The oldtimer on Sulphur Creek was right, he thought in the moment of controlled despair that ensued: after fifty below, a man should travel with a partner. He beat his hands, but failed in exciting any sensation. Suddenly he bared both hands, removing the mittens with his teeth. He caught the whole bunch between the heels of his hands. His arm muscles, not being frozen, enabled him to press the hand heels tightly against the matches. Then he scratched the bunch along his leg. It flared into flame, seventy sulphur matches at once! There was no wind to blow them out. He kept his head to one side to escape the strangling fumes, and held the blazing bunch to the birch-bark. As he so held it, he became aware of sensation in his hand. His flesh was burning. He could smell it. Deep down below the surface he could feel it. The sensation developed into pain that grew acute. And still he endured it, holding the flame of the matches clumsily to the bark that would not light readily because his own burning hands were in the way, absorbing most of the flame.

At last, when he could endure no more, he jerked his hands apart. The blazing matches fell sizzling into the snow, but the birch-bark was alight. He began laying dry grasses and the tiniest twigs on the flame. He could not pick and choose, for he had to lift the fuel between the heels of his hands. Small pieces of rotten wood and green moss clung to the twigs, and he bit them off as well as he could with his teeth. He cherished the flame carefully and awkwardly. It meant life, and it must not perish. The withdrawal of blood from the surface of his body now made him begin to shiver, and he grew more awkward. A large piece of green moss fell squarely on the little fire. He tried to poke it out with his fingers, but his shivering frame made him poke too far, and he disrupted the nucleus of the little fire, the burning grasses and tiny twigs separating and scattering. He tried to poke them together again, but, in spite of the tenseness of the effort, his shivering got away with him, and the twigs were hopelessly scattered. Each twig gushed a puff of smoke and went out. The fire-provider had failed. As he looked apathetically about him, his eyes chanced on the dog, sitting across the ruins of the fire from him, in the snow, making restless, hunching movements, slightly lifting one forefoot and then the other, shifting its weight back and forth on them with wistful eagerness.

The sight of the dog put a wild idea into his head. He remembered 31 the tale of the man, caught in a blizzard, who killed a steer and crawled inside the carcass, and so was saved. He would kill the dog and bury his hands in the warm body until the numbness went out of them. Then he could build another fire. He spoke to the dog, calling it to him; but in his voice was a strange note of fear that frightened the animal, who had never known the man to speak in such way before. Something was the matter, and its suspicious nature sensed danger—it knew not what danger, but somewhere, somehow, in its brain arose an apprehension of the man. It flattened its ears down at the sound of the man's voice, and its restless, hunching movements and the liftings and shiftings of its forefeet became more pronounced; but it would not come to the man. He got on his hands and knees and crawled toward the dog. This unusual posture again excited suspicion, and the animal sidled mincingly away.

The man sat up in the snow for a moment and struggled for calm- 32 ness. Then he pulled on his mittens, by means of his teeth, and got upon his feet. He glanced down at first in order to assure himself that he was really standing up, for the absence of sensation in his feet left him unrelated to the earth. His erect position in itself started to drive the webs of suspicion from the dog's mind; and when he spoke peremptorily with the sound of whiplashes in his voice, the dog rendered its customary allegiance and came to him. As it came within reaching distance, the man lost his control. His arms flashed out to the dog, and he experienced genuine surprise when he discovered that his hands could not clutch, that there was neither bend nor feeling in the fingers. He had forgotten for the moment that they were frozen and that they were freezing more and more. All this happened quickly, and before the animal could get away, he encircled its body with his arms. He sat down in the snow, and in this fashion held the dog, while it snarled and whined and struggled.

But it was all he could do, hold its body encircled in his arms and sit 33 there. He realized that he could not kill the dog. There was no way to do it. With his helpless hands he could neither draw nor hold his sheath knife nor throttle the animal. He released it, and it plunged wildly away, with tail between its legs, and still snarling. It halted forty feet away and surveyed him curiously, with ears sharply pricked forward. The man looked down at his hands in order to locate them, and found them hanging on the ends of his arms. It struck him as curious that one should have to use his eyes in order to find out where his hands were. He began threshing his arms back and forth, beating the mittened hands against his sides. He did this for five minutes, violently, and his heart pumped enough blood up to the surface to put a stop to his shivering. But no sensation was aroused in the hands. He had an impression that they hung like weights on the ends of his arms, but when he tried to run the impression down, he could not find it.

A certain fear of death, dull and oppressive, came to him. This fear 34 quickly became poignant as he realized that it was no longer a mere matter of freezing his fingers and toes, or of losing his hands and feet, but that it was a matter of life and death, with the chances against him. This threw him into a panic, and he turned and ran up the creek bed along the old dim trail. The dog joined in behind and kept up with him. He ran blindly, without intention, in fear such as he had never known in his life. Slowly, as he plowed and floundered through the snow, he began to see things again—the banks of the creek, the old timber-jams, the leafless aspens, and the sky. The running made him feel better. He did not shiver. Maybe, if he ran on, his feet would thaw out; and, anyway, if he ran far enough, he would reach the camp and the boys. Without doubt he would lose some fingers and toes and some of his face; but the boys would take care of him, and save the rest of him when he got there. And at the same time there was another thought in his mind that said he would never get to the camp and the boys; that it was too many miles away, that the freezing had too great a start on him, and that he would soon be stiff and dead. This thought he kept in the background and refused to consider. Sometimes it pushed itself forward and demanded to be heard, but he thrust it back and strove to think of other things.

It struck him as curious that he could run at all on feet so frozen that 35 he could not feel them when they struck the earth and took the weight of his body. He seemed to himself to skim along above the surface, and to have no connection with the earth. Somewhere he had once seen a winged Mercury, and he wondered if Mercury felt as he felt when skimming over the earth.

His theory of running until he reached camp and the boys had one 36 flaw in it: he lacked the endurance. Several times he stumbled, and finally he tottered, crumpled up, and fell. When he tried to rise, he failed. He must sit and rest, he decided, and next time he would merely walk and keep on going. As he sat and regained his breath, he noted that he was feeling quite warm and comfortable. He was not shivering, and it even seemed that a warm glow had come to his chest and trunk. And yet, when he touched his nose or cheeks, there was no sensation. Running would not thaw them out. Nor would it thaw out his hands and feet. Then the thought came to him that the frozen portions of his body must be extending. He tried to keep this thought down, to forget it, to think of something else; he was aware of the panicky feeling that it caused, and he was afraid of the panic. But the thought asserted itself, and persisted, until it produced a vision of his body totally frozen. This was too much, and he made another wild run along the trail. Once he slowed down to a walk, but the thought of the freezing extending itself made him run again.

And all the time the dog ran with him, at his heels. When he fell 37 down a second time, it curled its tail over its forefeet and sat in front of him, facing him, curiously eager and intent. The warmth and security of the animal angered him, and he cursed it till it flattened down its ears appeasingly. This time the shivering came more quickly upon the man. He was losing in his battle with the frost. It was creeping into his body from all sides. The thought of it drove him on, but he ran no more than a hundred feet, when he staggered and pitched headlong. It was his last panic. When he had recovered his breath and control, he sat up and entertained in his mind the conception of meeting death with dignity. However, the conception did not come to him in such terms. His idea of it was that he had been making a fool of himself, running around like a chicken with its head cut off—such was the simile that occurred to him. Well, he was bound to freeze anyway, and he might as well take it decently. With this new-found peace of mind came the first glimmerings of drowsiness. A good idea, he thought, to sleep off to death. It was like taking an anesthetic. Freezing was not so bad as people thought. There were lots worse ways to die.

He pictured the boys finding his body next day. Suddenly he found 38 himself with them, coming along the trail and looking for himself. And, still with them, he came around a turn in the trail and found himself lying in the snow. He did not belong with himself any more, for even then he was out of himself standing with the boys and looking at himself in the snow. It certainly was cold, was his thought. When he got back to the States, he could tell the folks what real cold was. He drifted on from this to a vision of the oldtimer on Sulphur Creek. He could see him quite clearly, warm and comfortable, and smoking a pipe.

"You were right, old hoss; you were right," the man mumbled to 39 the oldtimer of Sulphur Creek.

Then the man drowsed off into what seemed to him the most com- 40 fortable and satisfying sleep he had ever known. The dog sat facing him and waiting. The brief day drew to a close in a long, slow twilight. There were no signs of a fire to be made, and, besides, never in the dog's experience had it known a man to sit like that in the snow and make no fire. As the twilight drew on, its eager yearning for the fire mastered it, and with a great lifting and shifting of forefeet, it whined softly, then flattened its ears down in anticipation of being chidden by the man. But the man remained silent. Later, the dog whined loudly. And still later it crept close to the man and caught the scent of death. This made the animal bristle and back away. A little longer it delayed, howling under the stars that leaped and danced and shone brightly in the cold sky. Then it turned and trotted up the trail in the direction of the camp it knew, where were the other food-providers and fire-providers.

Reading and Interpreting

VOCABULARY

Use your dictionary as necessary to find the meaning of the following words in the context of London's story:

pall (1)   undulations (2)   apprehension (6, 31)   amber (7, 17)

reiterated (10)   shy (shied) (11, 12)   threshing (15, 33)

imperative (18)   smote (20)   extremities (20)   freighted (23)

capsizing (23)   wistfulness (25)   excruciating (27)

peremptorily (32)   chide (chidden) (40)

CONCEPT ANALYSIS

1. Early in the story, London makes the reader aware of the key flaw or limitation in the protagonist's character. He states in paragraph 3, "The trouble with him was that he was without imagination. He was quick and alert in the things of life, but only in the things, and not in the significances." What passages indicate this limitation? Which of the man's actions clearly illustrate this flaw?
2. The protagonist is described as a newcomer to the Yukon. What is his attitude toward the advice of the "oldtimers" in the community? When does he acknowledge the foolishness of his attitude?
3. The man dies; the dog survives. Why? Cite specific lines in the text to illustrate your views.

   What is the relationship between the man and the dog? What consequences does the man's treatment of the dog have for the man? Be specific in your references to the text.

Quickwrite

Jack London is able to evoke in his readers the pain that his characters experience through detailed process description. Make your reader feel your pain (a sports injury, a dental visit).

Thinking and Writing

RHETORICAL TECHNIQUE

1. The use of process in this literary work creates verisimilitude, a sense of physical reality that enables the reader to mentally experience the character's struggle and pain. For you, which of the processes described was most painful: getting frostbite (14), building the first fire (15), building the second fire (18–21), attempting to kill the dog (31–33), or freezing to death (34–37)? Which details of the process are most effective?
2. The interjection of process in a literary work creates tension and suspense by engaging the reader's attention and delaying the climax of a particular action. Read paragraphs 14 and 15. Which sentences commence and conclude the process?

    The process in paragraphs 14 and 15 could be summarized in the following statement: *He experienced numbness again in his hands and feet until he built a fire and warmed himself.* Summarize one other process in a brief statement.

    Compare your response to London's process paragraphs and your response to the summary statement. How does the narrative evoke a stronger response?

COMPOSITION

Describe in detail a political, social, or physical process that is important for the survival or the success of an individual in our society.

THE WRITTEN RESPONSE

Writing Workshop

The springboard for process analysis writing is the existence of a "mystery"—that is, a situation or condition that the writer is going to explain. The following are several mysteries about human achievement that can be explained through process analysis:

- No great thing is accomplished without some injustice being done.
- Every day, in every way, I'm getting better and better. (Emile Coué's formula for self-cure through faith)
- Science moves, but slowly, slowly, creeping on from point to point. (Alfred Lord Tennyson, "Locksley Hall")

1. Select one of these statements as a springboard for your process analysis essay.
2. Determine the type of process writing you will use: historical tracing, giving directions, describing a natural process.
3. In your introduction, ask a "how" or "what happens" question in relation to the mystery—the situation or condition you are planning to explain.
4. Formulate your thesis, which will be an assertion or generalization in response to your "how" or "what happens" question.
5. Make a rough outline of the essential steps in your process. Group the individual steps into logical stages. Note any points in the process at which you will include "side comment."
6. Write your first draft, using your outline and notes as a basis.

Topics for Critical Thinking and Writing

1. With every generation, new skills replace old ones. Use process analysis to describe one of the following:
   a. a skill that you have that your parents do not
   b. a skill that an older relative has that you do not
2. Instruct your readers in a process in physical fitness (for example, athletic training, dancing). Focus on *why* your readers should do what you are instructing them to do. Use the technical terminology appropriate to your subject.
3. Use your creative imagination to put new Disney employees through an orientation process, using the section about the Disney company in the Essay

for Analysis as a resource. Provide clear, sequential directions for the new employees to follow.

4. Describe a natural or biological process that you have observed (for example, a sunset, a pet giving birth). Give particular attention to the use of precise terminology, the repetition of key words, and linking time expressions to ease your reader's way through the various stages of the process.

Synthesis Questions

1. In your view, which selections in this chapter present the most meaningful human achievements? Your thesis statement should include a generalization that includes all the selections you will discuss. Refer to aspects of your chosen readings that provide the strongest support for your generalization.
2. Explain and comment on Peter Elbow's concept of first- and second-order thinking as the introduction to your process analysis. Apply the concept to the companies described in "Close to the Customer" and to the protagonist in London's story "To Build a Fire."
3. What *not* to do may be as important in completing a process as what to do. Discuss this concept with specific reference to the fire-building process in "To Build a Fire" and the toy assembly process described by S. J. Perelman.
4. Process instruction can do more than simply provide directions; a strong thesis statement can extend the meaning of a process analysis beyond the practical. Apply this idea to several of the readings in this chapter, referring specifically to some of the underlying values they present.
5. Both the section on the Disney corporation in the Essay for Analysis and the soliloquy from Shakespeare's *As You Like It* use analogies of the theater in their process descriptions. Explain why you think this analogy is apt and useful, using both selections to support your views.

Refining Your Essay

1. Review your thesis sentence to make sure you have been explicit about your purpose: Are you giving instructions on how to perform a process or are you analyzing a natural or historical process?
2. Review the action verbs in your instructions or descriptions to be sure they are precise and appropriate to your purpose.
3. Review your side comments. Do they enlarge your reader's understanding of particular steps or stages without becoming a distracting digression from the main point?

4. Read your process analysis aloud. Have you used sufficient and appropriate signals of coherence such as dates, times, and other expressions of chronological order? Do you repeat or use synonyms for key concepts throughout your analysis for coherence? Do you use linking words for coherence between paragraphs?

5. Review your conclusion to ensure that it contains a restatement of your central idea and a brief summary reference to your process. Have you ended with a vivid or imaginative remark that will leave a lasting impression on your reader?

CHAPTER SEVEN

The Liberal Arts: Defining and Classifying Knowledge

The liberal arts originated in the Greek concept of the nine Muses, the patron goddesses of epic poetry, love poetry, music, oratory, history, tragedy, comedy, song and dance, and astronomy. The medieval world condensed the branches of learning appropriate for free men (as opposed to slaves and serfs) into seven: grammar, logic, rhetoric, arithmetic, geometry, astronomy, and music. In the Renaissance the concept of the liberal arts was interpreted more broadly to refer to studies that offer a general rather than a vocational or specialized education.

In your college, what courses are classified as liberal arts? What relationship do they have to the Greek and medieval categories of liberal learning? How would you define their value in contrast to other courses in your curriculum?

Medieval miniature: *Philosophy Presenting the Seven Liberal Arts to Boethius*

THE WRITING FOCUS

Human knowledge is a vast body of information and ideas, which constantly increases with adversities and advancements in the human condition. Central to this knowledge are the intellectual and artistic developments that we call the liberal arts. Through the modes of definition, division, and classification, the questing human mind systematizes its learning and communicates it to others.

In Lewis Carroll's classic work *Through the Looking Glass,* Humpty Dumpty argues with Alice about the meaning of the word *glory.* "When I use a word," Humpty Dumpty states, "it means just what I choose it to mean—neither more nor less." But we, like Alice, know that contrary to Humpty Dumpty's claim, the definitions of words cannot be idiosyncratic. They must have commonly agreed upon meanings to provide a basis in language for thought and action. This is particularly true of abstract concepts in social science, art, and literature, for these terms may be ambiguous, admitting the possibility of multiple and overlapping interpretations beyond their dictionary definitions. Because these concepts may not have identical meaning for each individual, they are appropriate subjects for extended definition.

Once terms have been defined, division and classification may be used to make broad concepts and large populations manageable. Division breaks down a general subject into its separate parts. Classification groups things or ideas together on the basis of their similarities and dissociates them on the basis of their significant differences. These three modes, then, are indispensable structures for the communication of liberal learning.

Extended Definition

In a sense, learning in an academic discipline requires learning a new language. Every discipline has specialized terms that precisely define its concepts and activities. In addition, many ordinary words have specialized definitions in the context of a particular subject. The word *culture,* for example, has a different technical meaning for the student of biology than it has for the student of anthropology, and yet another meaning when we speak of a "cultured" person. Thus, in class discussion, examinations, and term papers in a specific discipline, college students must be able to state formal definitions for key terms.

A formal definition—that is, a dictionary or denotative definition—is the indispensable minimum of definition. It assumes agreement between the reader and the writer on the class, or general category, to which the object belongs and on the differentiae, the qualities that distinguish it from other members of that class. The class to which the term is assigned cannot be too broad, and the differentiae must be precise, accurate, and exhaustive. For example, to understand Havelock Ellis's discussion of dance, one of the readings in this chapter, the reader must agree to a formal definition of *dance:* a member of the class or general category of bodily movement, with the differentiae rhythm, musical accompaniment, and expression of thought and feeling.

The connotative use of a word suggests meanings beyond the denotative by adding emotional associations. For example, the word *pig* denotes a young swine of either sex. It connotes, however, filth and gluttony and is often used as a term of hostility. Fiction writers or essayists use connotative language for the purpose of evoking certain images and feelings; textbook writers, who seek to communicate factual information, rely primarily on denotative language.

A formal or denotative definition can be considered a fact that serves as the springboard for extended definition. An extended definition, which may take the form of an entire essay, elaborates a dictionary definition with such techniques as negation, etymology, descriptive language, historical tracing, illustration, narrative, comparison, contrast, division, and classification. In essays of extended definition, writers seek not merely to provide an understanding of an isolated term but to show its relationship to other aspects of the human condition.

The first step in composing an essay of extended definition is to establish a rationale. Are existing definitions inadequate? Kluckhohn, for example, begins his essay on culture by discussing meanings of the term that are inadequate because they do not apply to the discipline of anthropology.

NEGATION

Definition by negation is one way to approach extended definition of an ambiguous term. An effective way to use negative definitions is in a series that precedes your extended definition. For example, in defining *anthropology,* one could begin by showing that it is not sociology (which focuses on group interaction), psychology (which focuses on the individual), or economics (which focuses on society's production and consumption of goods and services).

DIFFERENTIAE

Another way to develop an extended definition is to use the differentiae of the term as the subtopics of your paper. You can develop each subtopic by any of the modes of support discussed in this section. Thus, if you wished to write an extended definition of *dancing,* you might take its distinguishing features—rhythm, musical accompaniment, and expressiveness—and develop each in proportion to its importance.

ETYMOLOGY

Etymology traces the development of a word from its earliest meaning through its current usage. The meanings of words evolve and change through the ages. The current meaning of a word may differ in interesting and significant ways from the original definition. For example, our word *culture* comes from the Latin word *cultus*, meaning "to worship." First used in a religious context, the word eventually broadened to mean the cultivation of crops, then the refinement of behavior through manners, and finally, the development of an aesthetic sensibility.

DESCRIPTIVE LANGUAGE, EXAMPLE, AND ILLUSTRATION

Vivid description and figures of speech aid the reader's understanding of a term by suggesting how it looks, feels, tastes, or sounds. As demonstrated in this chapter's reading selections, explaining differentiae requires the use of examples and illustrations. Essay examination questions often ask for definitions of key terms; to complete them successfully, you need apt supporting examples. Well-chosen, brief examples of the various aspects of an extended definition are central to a comprehensible and persuasive definition.

Essay questions may also require the reverse procedure; that is, you must demonstrate that a given instance or example is appropriate to a particular definition. For instance, in this chapter's Essay for Analysis, Barbara Tuchman remarks that "the primary duty of the historian is to stay within the evidence." Thus, Tuchman implies that accuracy is, or should be, a distinguishing feature of history. An essay question in a history course might require you to use this criterion to evaluate a historian's interpretation of a past event. Or you might be asked to discuss a television, literary, or film docudrama in terms of how well it stays "within the evidence."

COMPARISON AND CONTRAST

Explaining the differentiae of a term by using comparison or contrast is a common and effective technique in extended definition. For instance, in "What Use Is Poetry?" Gilbert Highet defines poetry by contrasting the language and experience of different types of poems. He suggests that some poems express "general experiences in universally acceptable words" and others "express strange and individual experiences in abstruse and sometimes unintelligible words." He exemplifies this contrast with quotations and summaries of the two types of poems.

Division and Classification

Division takes a broad subject and divides it into two or more parts, distributing the subject matter over the different sections. For example, in our selection in this chapter, Havelock Ellis divides the human arts into those that spring from inside the human person and those that are generated outside the person.

There are two ways in which classification can be used to organize material.

In the first, classification is used as a systematic sorting of populations or units of knowledge. It groups things into categories or classes based on the significant similarities or common characteristics. Here we begin with a large number of individual items that belong to a particular domain. For example, we may talk about nations or college students or poems. In order to deal with hundreds or thousands of such items, we must first establish some principle of classification. In the case of nations, for example, we might choose to group them on the basis of their economic systems. We might sort the countries of the world into groups based on the *differences* in their economic systems: capitalist, socialist, communist, and mixed. Each category includes those and only those countries whose economic systems fall within the boundaries of that category. We see this method of classification at work in Highet's essay on poetry, where the author groups poems by their primary attraction: pleasant sound, interesting story, value for memorization, and the like.

The second method breaks down a broad topic into a reasonable number of categories, and component elements are assigned to the appropriate category whose criteria it meets. For instance, in one of this chapter's readings, Serena Nanda classifies anthropology into three major categories: cultural anthropology, archeology, and physical anthropology. Linguistics, a relatively new study, is assigned to cultural anthropology because it shares the two main distinguishing characteristics of that class. It studies *learned behavior* (language) that is typical of *specific human groups*. Linguistics would not be appropriately classified under archeology or physical anthropology because these classes have different distinguishing features of content and methodology.

The assignment of a subject to an existing category primarily on the basis of superficial evidence is called pigeonholing. An extreme type of pigeonholing is stereotyping, the assignment of an oversimplified, often false set of characteristics to a group and characterization of any member of that group by those criteria.

FORMING CATEGORIES

In using classification to organize an essay or part of an essay, you must follow a clear and logical principle of categorization. Your purpose will dictate this principle and set the boundaries for your classes. In classifying students, for example, college administrations generally distinguish them by major departments or areas, such as liberal arts, business, engineering, or the like. In a personal essay on college students, however, you might wish to classify them by their reasons for attending college: intellectual, vocational, social, or athletic.

In traditional systems of scientific and technical classification, categorization accounts for every member of the population that makes up the subject. This kind of formal categorization is exemplified in this chapter's textbook excerpt by Starr and Taggart, which presents a historical survey of classification systems.

An informal or personal essay need not set up as rigorous boundaries as a scientific treatise, however. The categories in a personal essay may be imaginative or even humorous, and they need not cover every actual member of the class.

The informal essay offers many alternatives for the principle of classification. For example, Havelock Ellis classifies the different types of dancing by their function in society. Another principle of classification, however, might be that of the number of persons participating in the dance form. You might then have four categories: solo dancing, partner dancing, separated group dancing (such as square dancing), and ensemble dancing. Each individual dance with which you are familiar would be assigned to its proper category based on that principle.

Exclusivity and Completeness. Whether you are dividing a subject into a few major parts or sorting a large population into many different classes, you should follow two principles in forming the groups. The first is that the parts or classes should be mutually exclusive; categories should not overlap. If you are dividing poetry by its historic periods (romanticism, modernism), you cannot include the category epic poetry, which refers to a genre rather than a historical period.

The second guiding principle of a division or classification essay is that the proposed categories should cover the subject completely. This does not mean that you are responsible for treating each category at length, but rather that you must at least make reference to each in the introduction. For example, you may wish to introduce the subject of music by dividing it into four major areas: classical, folk, popular, and patriotic. But in your essay you may wish to focus on only one or two of these categories.

The thesis statement in your classification essay should indicate the extent to which the categories listed cover the subject. If all possible aspects of a subject do not fit under the categories named, you might introduce the subject's classification with such qualifying phrases as "divided into three *main* types" or "*basically* of four kinds." The thesis statement prepares the reader for the divisions of the essay. You must ensure that the essay's divisions do indeed correspond to whatever principle is stated.

The subtopic statement for each category should control the development of that category by naming its significant distinguishing features. You can elaborate these features by description, example, narration, comparison, or contrast. Examples of subtopic elaboration are provided in the Essay for Analysis.

The purpose of writing in the mode of classification is to illuminate a subject that lends itself to clear-cut divisions. The conclusion of a classification essay should, therefore, suggest some insights to which the classification has led. A successful essay of classification unites purpose, principle of division, and conclusion to bring order to a mass of material and to make a general body of knowledge manageable. It should help your reader see an ordinary subject, perhaps one that is taken for granted, in a new, interesting, and useful way.

BARBARA TUCHMAN

When Does History Happen?

Eminent historian Barbara Tuchman, in the preface to a collection of personal essays on history, refers to Clio, the muse of that discipline, and claims "history [is] an art, not a science." She asks why it is necessary to insist on a practical purpose for history, suggesting that it should be written and studied for its own sake "as the record of human behavior, the most fascinating subject of all."

Within three months of the Conservative party 1 crisis in Britain last October, a book by Randolph Churchill on the day-to-day history of the affair had been written and published. . . . The recent prevalence of these hot histories on publishers' lists raises the question: Should—or perhaps can—history be written while it is still smoking?

Before taking that further, I must first an- 2 swer the question: What is history? Professional historians have been exercising themselves vehemently over this query for some time. . . .

Need for a definition of history

Is history [asked E. H. Carr of Cambridge 3 University] the examination of past events or is it the past events themselves?. . . . In my innocence I had not been aware that the question posed by Mr. Carr had ever come up. I had simply assumed that history was past events existing independently, whether we examined them or not.

Author's assumed definition

I had thought that we who comment on 4 the past were extraneous to it; helpful, perhaps, to its understanding but not integral to its existence. I had supposed that the Greeks' defeat of the Persians would have given the same

Example in support of Tuchman's definition

direction to Western history whether Herodotus chronicled it or not. But that is not Mr. Carr's position. "The belief in a hard core of historical facts existing independently of the interpretation of the historian," he says, "is a preposterous fallacy but one that is very hard to eradicate."

Carr's implied definition

On first reading, this seemed to me to be preposterous nonsense. Was it some sort of recondite joke? But a thinker of such eminence must be taken seriously, and after prolonged silent arguments with Mr. Carr of which he remained happily unaware, I began to see what he was driving at. What he means, I suppose, is that past events cannot exist independently of the historian because without the historian we would know nothing about them; in short, that the unrecorded past is none other than our old friend, the tree in the primeval forest which fell where there was no one to hear the sound of the crash. If there was no ear, was there a sound?

Reference to philosophical riddle to explain Carr's statement

I refuse to be frightened by that conundrum because it asks the wrong question. The point is not whether the fall of the tree made a noise but whether it left a mark on the forest. If it left a space that let in the sun on a hitherto shade-grown species, or if it killed a dominant animal and shifted rule of the pack to one of different characteristics, or if it fell across a path of animals and caused some small change in their habitual course from which larger changes followed, then the fall made history whether anyone heard it or not.

Tuchman's implied definition—by analogy

Examples in support of her definition

I therefore declare myself a firm believer in the "preposterous fallacy" of historical facts existing independently of the historian. I think that if Domesday Book and all other records of the time had been burned, the transfer of land ownership from the Saxons to the Normans would be no less a fact of British history. Of course Domesday Book was a record, not an interpretation, and what Mr. Carr says is that historical facts do not exist independently of the *interpretation* of historians. I find this untenable. He might just as well say the Grecian Urn would not exist without Keats.

Author's definition restated

Supporting example

Carr's definition

Analogy to contradict Carr

As I see it, evidence is more important than interpretation, and facts are history whether interpreted or not. I think the influence of the receding frontier on American expansion was a phenomenon independent of Frederick Jackson Turner, who noticed it, and the role of the leisure class independent of Thorstein Veblen, and the influence of sea power upon history independent of Admiral Mahan.

. . . I am content to define history as the past events of which we have knowledge and refrain from worrying about those of which we have none—until, that is, some archeologist digs them up.

I come next to historians. Who are they: contemporaries of the event or those who come after? The answer is obviously both. Among contemporaries, first and indispensable are the more-or-less unconscious sources: letters, diaries, memoirs, autobiographies, newspapers and periodicals, business and government documents. These are historical raw material, not history. Their authors may be writing with one eye or possibly both on posterity, but that does not make them historians. To perform that function requires a view from the outside and a conscious craft.

At a slightly different level are the I-was-there recorders, usually journalists, whose accounts often contain golden nuggets of information buried in a mass of daily travelogue which the passage of time has reduced to trivia. Some of the most vivid details that went into my book *The Guns of August* came from the working press: the rag doll crushed under the wheel of a German gun carriage from Irvin Cobb, the smell of half a million unwashed bodies that hung over the invaded villages of Belgium from Will Irwin, the incident of Colonel Max Hoffmann yelling insults at the Japanese general from Frederick Palmer, who reported the Russo-Japanese War. Daily journalism, however, even when collected in book form, is, like letters and

8   Elaboration of author's definition through examples

9   Author's definition of history with distinguishing characteristics

10   Extended definition of history through classification of its recorders

Class 1: contemporary unconscious sources; examples

Principle of classification: degree to which conscious interpretation is present in the recording of postevents

11   Class 2: contemporary recorders—journalists; several examples

the rest, essentially source material rather than history.

Still contemporary but dispensable are the 12 Compilers who hurriedly assemble a book from clippings and interviews in order to capitalize on public interest when it is high. A favorite form of these hasty puddings is the overnight biography, like *The Lyndon Johnson Story,* which was in the bookstores within a few weeks of the incident that gave rise to it. The Compilers, in their treatment, supply no extra understanding and as historians are negligible.

Class 3: compilers; example

All these varieties being disposed of, there 13 remains a pure vein of conscious historians of whom, among contemporaries, there are two kinds. First, the Onlookers, who deliberately set out to chronicle an episode of their own age—a war or depression or strike or social revolution or whatever it may be—and shape it into a historical narrative with character and validity of its own. Thucydides' *Peloponnesian Wars,* on a major scale, and Theodore White's *The Making of a President,* undertaken in the same spirit though on a tiny scale in comparison, are examples.

Class 4: conscious historians

1. Onlookers; examples

Second are the Active Participants or Axe- 14 Grinders, who attempt a genuine history of events they have known, but whose accounts are inevitably weighted, sometimes subtly and imperceptibly, sometimes crudely, by the requirements of the role in which they wish themselves to appear. Josephus' *The Jewish War,* the Earl of Clarendon's *History of the Rebellion,* and Winston Churchill's *World Crisis* and *Second World War* are classics of this category. . . .

2: Active participants: examples

I found from personal experience that 15 I could not write contemporary history if I tried. . . .

When I tried to write [the last thirty years 16 of Arab-Israeli-British relationships] as history, I could not do it. Anger, disgust, and a sense of injustice can make some writers eloquent and evoke brilliant polemic, but these emotions stunted and twisted my pen. I found the tone of my concluding chapter totally different from the seventeen chapters that went before. I had suddenly walked over the line into contemporary history; I had become involved, and it showed. . . .

I am not saying that emotion should have 17 no place in history. On the contrary, I think it is an essential element of history, as it is of poetry, whose origin Wordsworth defined as "emotion recollected in tranquillity." <u>History, one might say, is emotion plus action recollected or, in the case of latter-day historians, reflected on in tranquillity after a close and honest examination of the records.</u> The primary duty of the historian is to stay within the evidence. Yet it is a curious fact that poets, limited by no such rule, have done very well with history, both of their own times and of times long gone before. . . .

Additional differentiae

Kipling had a peculiar gift for recognizing 18 history at close quarters. He wrote "Recessional" in 1897 at the time of the Queen's Diamond Jubilee when he sensed a self-glorification, a kind of hubris, in the national mood that frightened him. In *The Times* on the morning after, when people read his reminder—

> Lo, all our pomp of yesterday
>   Is one with Nineveh and Tyre!
> Judge of the Nations, spare us yet,
>   Lest we forget—lest we forget!

Supporting example

—it created a profound impression. . . . What the poets did was to convey the *feeling* of an episode or a moment of history as they sensed it. <u>The historian's task is rather to tell what happened within the discipline of the facts.</u>

Another distinguishing characteristic

<u>What his imagination is to the poet, facts 19 are to the historian.</u> His exercise of judgment comes in their selection, his art in their arrangement. His method is narrative. His subject is the story of man's past. His function is to make it known.

Analogy between poet and historian; extended definition of history— role of the historian

THE PROCESS OF DEFINING AND CLASSIFYING CONCEPTS

Review the box outline of Barbara Tuchman's "When Does History Happen?" on the facing page.

"When Does History Happen" is an informal essay of extended definition that uses examples, analogies, and classification as its means of development. First, Tuchman establishes a rationale or need for a definition of history based on her disagreement with another historian's proposed definition (paragraphs 2–5). She alludes to a philosophical problem—if a tree falls in the forest and nobody hears it, does it make a sound?—and suggests that it is not the sound but the effect of the tree's falling that is history.

Tuchman then extends her basic definition of history by classifying recorders of past events according to their conscious interpretation of the events in question. Each class presents an additional distinguishing characteristic for the definition. All of these characteristics taken together are the differentiae of her final definition of history: History is "past events existing independently" (paragraph 3) that leave a mark (paragraph 6) of which we have knowledge (paragraph 9); history is viewed from the outside (paragraph 10) and supplies extra understanding of events (paragraph 12); history is "emotion plus action recollected . . . in tranquillity" (paragraph 17) and told "within the discipline of the facts" (paragraph 18).

All Tuchman's categories of recorders and their distinguishing features are elaborated by historical references and examples, so that despite the abstractness of the subject, the reader is able to follow the author's argument.

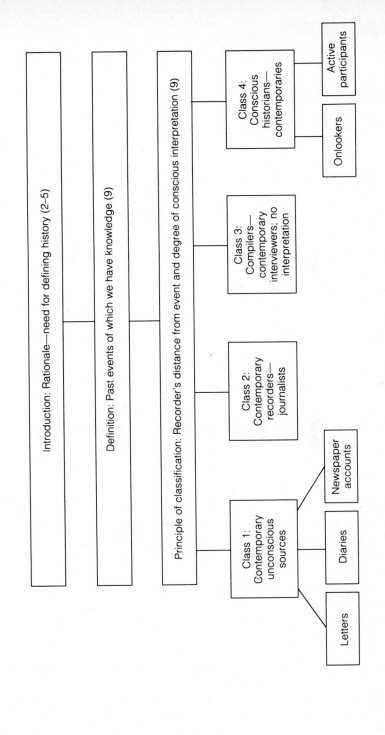

Introduction: Rationale—need for defining history (2–5)

Definition: Past events of which we have knowledge (9)

Principle of classification: Recorder's distance from event and degree of conscious interpretation (9)

Class 1: Contemporary unconscious sources

Letters

Diaries

Newspaper accounts

Class 2: Contemporary recorders—journalists

Class 3: Compilers—contemporary interviewers; no interpretation

Class 4: Conscious historians—contemporaries

Onlookers

Active participants

READINGS

JOHN HENRY NEWMAN

The Idea of a University

John Henry Newman (1801–1890), an outstanding religious thinker and essayist, delivered a lecture series at
the Catholic University of Ireland in 1882 entitled "The
Idea of a University," which drew on his own liberal
education at Oxford. He himself exemplified the "enlargement of mind" that he viewed as the result of a university education in the liberal arts. In the first passage
of our excerpt, Newman defines liberal knowledge and
its relation to education. In the second, he defines
the university by listing its aims for the individual in
society.

I

. . . Knowledge is called by the name of Science or Philosophy when it is   1
acted upon, informed, or if I may use a strong figure impregnated by Reason. . . . Knowledge, in proportion as it tends more and more to be particular, ceases to be Knowledge. It is a question whether Knowledge can
in any proper sense be predicated of the brute creation . . . it seems to me
improper to call that passive sensation, or perception of things, which
brutes seem to possess, by the name of Knowledge. When I speak of
Knowledge, I mean something intellectual, something which grasps what
it perceives through the senses; something which takes a view of things;
which sees more than the senses convey; which reasons upon what it sees,
and while it sees; which invests it with an idea. . . . The principle of real
dignity in Knowledge, its worth, its desirableness, considered irrespec-
tively of its results, is this germ within it of a scientific or a philosophical
process. This is how it comes to be an end in itself; this is why it admits of
being called Liberal. Not to know the relative disposition of things is the
state of slaves or children; to have mapped out the Universe is the boast, or
at least the ambition, of Philosophy.

Moreover, such knowledge is not a mere extrinsic or accidental ad-   2
vantage, which is ours to-day and another's to-morrow, which may be got
up from a book, and easily forgotten again, which we can command or

communicate at our pleasure, which we can borrow for the occasion, carry about in our hand, and take into the market; it is an acquired illumination, it is a habit, a personal possession, and an inward endowment. And this is the reason, why it is more correct, as well as more usual, to speak of a University as a place of education, than of instruction, though, when knowledge is concerned, instruction would at first sight have seemed the more appropriate word. We are instructed, for instance, in manual exercises, in the fine and useful arts, in trades, and in ways of business; for these are methods, which have little or no effect upon the mind itself, are contained in rules committed to memory, to tradition, or to use, and bear upon an end external to themselves. But education is a higher word; it implies an action upon our mental nature, and the formation of a character; it is something individual and permanent, and is commonly spoken of in connexion with religion and virtue. When, then, we speak of the communication of Knowledge as being Education, we thereby really imply that that Knowledge is a state or condition of mind; and since cultivation of mind is surely worth seeking for its own sake, we are thus brought once more to the conclusion, which the word "Liberal" and the word "Philosophy" have already suggested, that there is a Knowledge, which is desirable, though nothing come of it, as being of itself a treasure, and a sufficient remuneration of years of labour.

II

A university is not a birthplace of poets or of immortal authors, of founders of schools, leaders of colonies, or conquerors of nations. It does not promise a generation of Aristotles or Newtons, of Napoleons or Washingtons, of Raphaels or Shakespeares, though such miracles of nature it has before now contained within its precincts. Nor is it content on the other hand with forming the critic or the experimentalist, the economist or the engineer, though such too it includes within its scope. But a university training is the great ordinary means to a great but ordinary end; it aims at raising the intellectual tone of society, at cultivating the public mind, at purifying the national taste, at supplying true principles to popular enthusiasm and fixed aims to popular aspiration, at giving enlargement and sobriety to the ideas of the age, at facilitating the exercise of political power, and defining the intercourse of private life. It is the education which gives a man a clear conscious view of his own opinions and judgments, a truth in developing them, an eloquence in expressing them, and a force in urging them. It teaches him to see things as they are, to get right to the point, to disentangle a skein of thought, to detect what is sophistical, and to discard what is irrelevant. It prepares him to fill any post with credit, and to master any subject with facility. It shows him how to accommodate himself to others, how to throw himself into their state of mind, how to bring before them his own, how to influence them, how to come to an understanding with them, how to bear with them. He is at home in any society, he has common ground with every class; he knows when to speak and when to be silent; he is able to converse, he is able to listen; he can ask a question pertinently, and gain a lesson seasonably, when he has nothing to impart himself; he is ever ready, yet never in the way; he is a pleasant companion, and a comrade you can depend upon; he knows when to be serious and when to trifle, and he has a sure tact which enables him to trifle with gracefulness and to be serious with effect. He has the repose of mind which lives in itself, while it lives in the world, and which has resources for its happiness at home when it cannot go abroad. He has a gift which serves him in public, and supports him in retirement, without which good fortune is but vulgar, and with which failure and disappointment have a charm.

Reading and Interpreting

VOCABULARY

Use your dictionary as necessary to find the meaning of the following words as used by Newman:

predicated (1)   extrinsic (2)   endowment (2)   remuneration (2)

sophistical (2)   seasonably (2)

CONCEPT ANALYSIS

1. Newman employs lengthy sentences, parallel constructions, figurative language, and a high level of abstraction in his writing. Try to express in your own words some of his more challenging but important lines such as the following:
   a. "Knowledge, in proportion as it tends more and more to be particular, ceases to be Knowledge." (1)
   b. "Not to know the relative disposition of things is the state of slaves or children. . . ." (1)
   c. " . . . it is more correct, as well as more usual, to speak of a University as a place of education, than of instruction. . . ." (2)
   d. "[The university-educated person] has the repose of mind which lives in itself. . . ." (3)
2. Based on Newman's criteria, which of your college courses are educational? Which are instructional? Do any of your courses appear to fit into both categories? Explain.

3. According to Newman, what is the connection between a university education and a society?

What exceptions can you think of to Newman's view that educated people make a better society?

4. Newman states that "university training is the great ordinary means to a great but ordinary end." How do you interpret his use of the word *ordinary?*

5. Consider your college or university education thus far. What courses are preparing you to realize the aims of education listed by Newman?

Quickwrite

Newman asserts that a liberal university education "prepares [the student] to fill any post with credit." With your own career goals in mind, agree or disagree with this statement.

Thinking and Writing

RHETORICAL TECHNIQUE

1. Newman defines knowledge both by what it is and by what it is not and by contrasting knowledge and other types of mental activity. Write a formal definition of liberal knowledge based on Newman's criteria.

2. In defining the university, Newman lists many distinguishing characteristics. Paraphrase and synthesize these to compose a formal definition of the university.

3. To develop his definition of a university, Newman first states what it aims to do and then describes how a university-educated person acts. Which method works more effectively to communicate Newman's definition? Why does he use both methods?

COMPOSITION

Newman states that liberal knowledge is a "treasure" in that it is intrinsically valuable regardless of its practical application. Write an extended definition of the word *treasure,* and develop it with reference to aspects of your life other than education.

FRANCIS BACON
Of Studies

Sir Francis Bacon (1561–1626), Renaissance philosopher, historian, and statesman, was educated at
Cambridge and served as a political adviser to Queen
Elizabeth. In one of his chief works, *The Advancement of
Learning,* he established a three-part division of learning
in accordance with the functions of the mind. He classified history under memory, poetry under imagination,
and philosophy, in which he included the natural sciences, under reason. He emphasized the need for new
methods of instruction to advance learning. These views
are reflected in the following essay, taken from Bacon's
most important literary work, *Essays.*

Studies serve for delight, for ornament, and for ability. Their chief use for
delight is in privateness and retiring; for ornament, is in discourse; and for
ability, is in the judgment and disposition of business; for expert men can
execute, and perhaps judge of particulars, one by one; but the general
counsels, and the plots and marshalling of affairs come best from those
that are learned. To spend too much time in studies is sloth; to use them
too much for ornament is affection; to make judgment wholly by their
rules is the humour of a scholar. They perfect nature, and are perfected by
experience; for natural abilities are like natural plants, that need pruning
by study; and studies themselves do give forth directions too much at 10
large, except they be bounded in by experience. Crafty men contemn
studies, simple men admire them, and wise men use them; for they teach
not their own use; but that [which] is a wisdom without them and above
them, won by observation. Read not to contradict and confute, nor to
believe and take for granted, nor to find talk and discourse, but to weigh
and consider. Some books are to be tasted, others to be swallowed, and
some few to be chewed and digested; that is, some books are to be read
only in parts; others to be read but not curiously; and some few to be read
wholly, and with diligence and attention. Some books also may be read by
deputy, and extracts made of them by others; but that would be only in the 20
less important arguments and the meaner sort of books; else distilled books
are, like common distilled waters, flashy things. Reading maketh a full
man; conference a ready man; and writing an exact man. And, therefore, if a
man write little, he had need have a great memory; if he confer little, he had

need have a present wit; and if he read little, he had need have much cunning, to seem to know that he doth not. Histories make men wise; poets, witty; the mathematics, subtile; natural philosophy, deep; moral, grave; logic and rhetoric, able to contend: *Abeunt studia in mores!* [Studies become habits!] Nay there is no stand or impediment in the wit but may be wrought out by fit studies; like as diseases of the body may have appropriate exer- 30 cises. Bowling is good for the stone and reins [gonads and kidneys], shooting for the lungs and breast, gentle walking for the stomach, riding for the head, and the like. So if a man's wit be wandering, let him study the mathematics; for in demonstrations, if his wit be called away never so little, he must begin again. If his wit be not apt to distinguish or find differences, let him study the school-men; for they are *cymini sectores* [hair-splitters]! If he be not apt to beat over matters, and to call up one thing to prove and illustrate another, let him study the lawyers' cases. So every defect of the mind may have a special receipt.

Reading and Interpreting

VOCABULARY

Use your dictionary as necessary to find the meaning of the following words as used by Bacon:

retiring (2)   sloth (6)   confute (14)   receipt (39)

CONCEPT ANALYSIS

1. This essay is written in a compressed style; that is, Bacon uses very few words to convey a great deal of profound meaning. Parallel expressions, figures of speech, and analogies require the reader to unravel this text almost line by line to fully understand Bacon's kernels of wisdom. Select several of Bacon's statements from the following list and explain them in your own words:
   a. "[The chief use of studies] for ornament, is in discourse. . . ." (2)
   b. "[Studies] perfect nature, and are perfected by experience." (8–9)
   c. "Reading maketh a full man; conference a ready man; and writing an exact man." (22–23)
   d. "Some books are to be tasted, others to be swallowed, and some few to be chewed and digested. . . ." (16–17)
   e. " . . . logic and rhetoric [make men] able to contend. . . ." (28)
2. According to Bacon, what are the particular values of the following studies: history, poetry, mathematics, natural philosophy, moral philosophy, logic and rhetoric? Do you agree with the values Bacon assigns to each? Explain.

3. What is Bacon really saying about lawyers, mathematicians, and college professors ("school-men")?
4. Do you agree with Bacon's analysis of the relationship between studies and experience? Do you believe that one is more valuable than the other?

Quickwrite

Write a response to Bacon's statement that "crafty men contemn studies."

Thinking and Writing

RHETORICAL TECHNIQUE

1. Bacon categorizes studies by function; that is, he classifies them by what they do: "Studies serve for delight, for ornament, and for ability." Using the same principle of function, classify courses in the current curriculum of your college. Which of these functions is your chief purpose for studying?
2. Bacon classifies books into several categories. List them in your own words. Think about the books you are reading this semester. Using Bacon's criteria, to which category would you assign each book?
3. Bacon classifies studies by equating them with remedies for diseases; the proper study, he says, can cure an "impediment in the wit." What is the chief impediment to your wit? Which class of study would best "cure" you?

COMPOSITION

Reflect on Bacon's statement that "some books are to be tasted, others to be swallowed, and some few to be chewed and digested. . . ." Elaborate each of these categories, drawing examples from your own reading.

JOSÉ ORTEGA Y GASSET
Four Realities

José Ortega y Gasset (1883–1955) was a Spanish essayist and philosopher whose interest lay in defining the
ultimate reality in which all life and thought is rooted.
This essay illustrates Ortega y Gasset's concrete approach to a complicated, abstract theme.

A great man is dying. His wife is by his bedside. A doctor takes the dying   1
man's pulse. In the background two more persons are discovered: a reporter who is present for professional reasons, and a painter whom mere
chance has brought here. Wife, doctor, reporter, and painter witness one
and the same event. Nonetheless, this identical event—a man's death—
impresses each of them in a different way. So different indeed that the several aspects have hardly anything in common. What this scene means to
the wife who is all grief has so little to do with what it means to the
painter who looks on impassively that it seems doubtful whether the two
can be said to be present at the same event.

It thus becomes clear that one and the same reality may split up into   2
many diverse realities when it is beheld from different points of view. And
we cannot help asking ourselves: Which of all these realities must then be
regarded as the real and authentic one? The answer, no matter how we
decide, cannot but be arbitrary. Any preference can be founded on caprice
only. All these realities are equivalent, each being authentic for its corresponding point of view. All we can do is to classify the points of view and
to determine which among them seems, in a practical way, most normal
or most spontaneous. Thus we arrive at a conception of reality that is by
no means absolute, but at least practical and normative.

As for the points of view of the four persons present at the deathbed,   3
the clearest means of distinguishing them is by measuring one of their
dimensions, namely the emotional distance between each person and the
event they all witness. For the wife of the dying man the distance shrinks
to almost nothing. What is happening so tortures her soul and absorbs her
mind that it becomes one with her person. Or to put it inversely, the wife
is drawn into the scene, she is part of it. A thing can be seen, an event can
be observed, only when we have separated it from ourselves and it has
ceased to form a living part of our being. Thus the wife is not present at
the scene, she is in it. She does not behold it, she "lives" it.

The doctor is several degrees removed. To him this is a professional 4
case. He is not drawn into the event with the frantic and blinding anxiety
of the poor woman. However it is his bounden duty as a doctor to take a
serious interest, he carries responsibility, perhaps his professional honor is
at stake. Hence he too, albeit in a less integral and less intimate way, takes
part in the event. He is involved in it not with his heart but with the
professional portion of his self. He too "lives" the scene although with an
agitation originating not in the emotional center, but in the professional
surface, of his existence.

When we now put ourselves in the place of the reporter we realize 5
that we have traveled a long distance away from the tragic event. So far
indeed that we have lost all emotional contact with it. The reporter, like
the doctor, has been brought here for professional reasons and not out of a
spontaneous human interest. But while the doctor's profession requires
him to interfere, the reporter's requires him precisely to stay aloof; he has
to confine himself to observing. To him the event is a mere scene, a pure
spectacle on which he is expected to report in his newspaper column. He
takes no feeling part in what is happening here, he is emotionally free, an
outsider. He does not "live" the scene, he observes it. Yet he observes it
with a view to telling his readers about it. He wants to interest them, to
move them, and if possible to make them weep as though they each had
been the dying man's best friend. From his schooldays he remembers Horace's recipe: "*Si vis me flere dolendum est primum ipsi tibi*"—if you want me to
weep you must first grieve yourself.

Obedient to Horace the reporter is anxious to pretend emotion, 6
hoping that it will benefit his literary performance. If he does not "live"
the scene he at least pretends to "live" it.

The painter, in fine, completely unconcerned, does nothing but 7
keep his eyes open. What is happening here is none of his business; he is,
as it were, a hundred miles removed from it. His is a purely perceptive
attitude; indeed, he fails to perceive the event in its entirety. The tragic
inner meaning escapes his attention which is directed exclusively toward
the visual part—color values, lights, and shadows. In the painter we find
a maximum of distance and a minimum of feeling intervention.

The inevitable dullness of this analysis will, I hope, be excused if it 8
now enables us to speak in a clear and precise way of a scale of emotional
distances between ourselves and reality. In this scale, the degree of closeness is equivalent to the degree of feeling participation; the degree of remoteness, on the other hand, marks the degree to which we have freed
ourselves from the real event, thus objectifying it and turning it into a
theme of pure observation. At one end of the scale the world—persons,
things, situations—is given to us in the aspect of "lived" reality; at the
other end we see everything in the aspect of "observed" reality.

Reading and Interpreting

VOCABULARY

Use your dictionary as necessary to find the meaning of the following words in the context of Ortega y Gasset's essay:

arbitrary (2)   caprice (2)   albeit (4)

CONCEPT ANALYSIS

What is the central philosophical problem in this essay? Identify the thesis statement that responds to the problem.

Thinking and Writing

RHETORICAL TECHNIQUE

1. In Ortega y Gasset's essay, an individual's emotional distance from a dying man is the principle that distinguishes four classes of reality. List these classes.
2. Evaluate the organization and symmetry of this essay on the basis of such criteria as digressions, proportion, and clarity.
3. To which classification of reality would you assign each of the following: the dying man's son, his insurance agent, his priest, his dog, his undertaker?
4. Ortega y Gasset calls his classifactory approach to the definition of reality "practical and normative" (2), but asks to be excused for the "dullness" of his analysis (8). Do you agree? Explain.

COMPOSITION

Ortega y Gasset defines the abstract concept *reality* by describing a situation involving four different characters, each representing one aspect of the term. In a unified essay, explain an abstract concept such as *patriotism, culture, love,* or *education* in the same way.

ARCHIBALD MACLEISH

Ars Poetica

Pulitzer Prize winning American poet Archibald Mac-
Leish (1892–1982) was associated in his early career
with the symbolist poets. This accounts for his insistence in the famous poem below that poetry should be
defined not by any explicit teaching or social function
but rather by its own internal integrity.

A poem should be palpable and mute
As a globed fruit,

Dumb
As old medallions to the thumb,

Silent as the sleeve-worn stone   5
Of casement ledges where the moss has grown—

A poem should be wordless
As the flight of birds.

A poem should be motionless in time
As the moon climbs,   10

Leaving, as the moon releases
Twig by twig the night-entangled trees,

Leaving, as the moon behind the winter leaves,
Memory by memory the mind—

A poem should be motionless in time   15
As the moon climbs.

A poem should be equal to:
Not true.

For all the history of grief
An empty doorway and a maple leaf.   20

For love
The leaning grasses and two lights above the sea—

A poem should not mean
But be.

Reading and Interpreting

VOCABULARY

Use your dictionary as necessary to find the meaning of the following words as used in "Ars Poetica":

palpable (1)   medallions (4)   casement (6)

CONCEPT ANALYSIS

1. The Latin title of the poem means "the art of poetry." Why do you think the title is in Latin?
2. Lines 17 and 18 are critical to MacLeish's definition of poetry. How do you interpret them? How do they relate to the final stanza?
3. According to MacLeish, the art of poetry is its ability to communicate emotion through brief but powerful images. Do you find the images he uses to communicate grief (20) and love (22) adequate? What images would you use to communicate these emotions?

Quickwrite

Consider an abstract concept such as *revenge, lust, hatred, joy,* or *honor* and define it with several similes or images as MacLeish defines poetry in "Ars Poetica."

Thinking and Writing

RHETORICAL TECHNIQUE

MacLeish gives three general characteristics of poetry, which he then elaborates with examples. Identify the general statements. Based on these statements, write a formal definition of poetry. What distinguishing characteristics, or differentiae, would you add to this definition?

GILBERT HIGHET
What Use Is Poetry?

Like John Henry Newman a century earlier, Gilbert
Highet (b. 1906) was educated in the liberal tradition at
Oxford. A professor of classics at Columbia University,
Highet drew on his teaching experience as well as his
education to define and categorize poetry in terms of its
various functions. Highet takes a defensive posture in
this essay as he explains poetry's relevance to a techno-
logically oriented world.

Children ask lots and lots of questions, about religion, about sex, about   1
the stars. But there are some questions which they never ask: they leave
grown-ups to ask them and to answer them. Often this means that the
questions are silly: that they are questions about nonexistent problems
or questions to which the answer is obvious. Sometimes it means that
the questions *should* be asked, but that the answer is difficult or multiplex.

So, children never ask what is the good of music. They just like   2
singing and dancing, and even drumming on a low note of the piano. In
the same way, they never ask what is the use of poetry. They all enjoy
poems and songs, and very often come to like them before they can even
talk properly; but it never occurs to them that they ought to find reasons
for their enjoyment. But grown-ups do inquire about the justification of
poetry: they ask what is the point of putting words in a special order and
extracting special sound effects from them, instead of speaking plainly and
directly. And often—because they get no adequate answer, either from
the poets or from the professors—they conclude that poetry is only a set of
tricks like conjuring, or a complicated game like chess; and they turn
away from it in discouragement . . . until, perhaps, a poetic film like
Henry V shocks them into realizing something of its power; or, as they
grow older, they find that a poem learned in childhood sticks in their
mind and becomes clearer and more beautiful with age.

What is the use of poetry?   3

There must be a number of different answers to the question. Just as   4
a picture can be meant to give pleasure, or to carry a puzzle, or to convey
information, so poems are meant for many different things. We can begin
to get some of the answers if we look at the poetry that children themselves naturally enjoy, and then see how it is connected with the most famous grown-up poems.

The first pleasure of poetry is the simplest. It is the same pleasure 5
that we have in music—the pleasure of following a pattern of sound.
Everyone loves talking, and most people like what might be called dood-
ling in sound. So, if you look through the *Oxford Dictionary of Nursery
Rhymes,* you will find several tongue-twisters, like this:

Peter Piper picked a peck of pickled pepper. . . .

Now, there is a second pleasure in poetry. This is that it is some- 6
times better than prose for telling a story. It even gives authority to a story
which is illogical or incredible, or even gruesome. That is one reason children love the poem that tells of the tragic fate of Jack and Jill. There is an
interesting variant of it: the cumulative story, in which one detail is piled
up on another until the whole story has been set forth with the simple
exactitude of a primitive painting: for instance, "The House That Jack
Built," and the funeral elegy, "Who Killed Cock Robin?" . . . Another
variant is the limerick, which is simply a funny story in verse. Many a
man who would protest that he knew no poetry, and cared nothing for it,
could still recite eight or ten limericks in the right company.

In serious adult poetry there are many superb stories, including the 7
two oldest books in Western literature, the *Iliad* and the *Odyssey.* Every
good collection of poems will include some of the most dramatic tales ever
told, the English and Scottish ballads, which are still occasionally sung in
our own southern states. One of the strangest things about the stories told
as ballads is their terrible abruptness and directness. They leave out a
great deal. They give only a few details, a name or two; they draw the
outlines, harsh and black or blood-red, and they concentrate on the actions and the passions. Such is the ballad about an ambush in which a
knight was killed by his own wife's brother. It is called "The Dowie
Houms of Yarrow" (that means the sad fields beside the river Yarrow, in
the Scottish borders), and it opens immediately with the quarrel, almost
with the clash of swords. . . . That story in poetry and a few others like
"Edward, Edward"—in which a mother persuades her son to kill his own
father, and drives him mad—are absolutely unforgettable.

But besides storytelling, poetry has another use, known all over the 8
world. This is mnemonic. Put words into a pattern, and they are easier to
remember. I should never have known the lengths of the months if I had
not learned:

Thirty days hath September,
April, June, and November. . . .

This is certainly four hundred years old, for it occurs in an English manuscript dated about 1555, and there is a French poem, with the same
rhyme scheme, written three hundred years earlier. (It might be easier
to change the calendar, but mankind is by nature conservative.) On a
simpler level there are many nursery rhymes in every language which are

designed to teach children the very simplest things; for instance, counting and performing easy actions:

> One, two,
> Buckle my shoe,
> Three, four,
> Shut the door.

And even earlier, before the child can speak, he is lucky if his mother can recite the poem that goes over his five toes or fingers, one after another:

> This little pig went to market,
> This little pig stayed at home

up to the comical climax when the child is meant to squeak too, and to enjoy staying at home.

Adults also remember facts better if they are put into verse. Nearly 9 every morning I repeat to myself:

> Early to bed and early to rise
> Makes a man healthy and wealthy and wise.

And nearly every evening I change it to Thurber's parody:

> Early to rise and early to bed
> Makes a male healthy and wealthy and dead.

or occasionally to George Ade's variant:

> Early to bed and early to rise
> Will make you miss all the regular guys

This is the source of what they call didactic poetry, poetry meant to teach. The best-known example of it is the Book of Proverbs in the Bible, which ought to be translated into rhythmical prose, or even verse. The third oldest book in Greek literature, not much younger than Homer, is a farmer's handbook all set out in poetry, so that it could be learned off by heart and remembered: it is the *Works and Days* by Hesiod. To teach has long been one of the highest functions of the poet: great poetry can be written in order to carry a message of philosophical or practical truth—or sometimes an ironical counsel. . . .

There is one peculiar variation on the poem that conveys informa- 10 tion. This is the riddle poem, which tells you something—but only if you are smart enough to see through its disguise. There are some such riddles in the Bible: Samson created a good one, about the dead lion with a hive of wild bees inside it. Legend has it that Homer died of chagrin because he could not solve a rather sordid poetic puzzle. The nursery rhyme "Humpty Dumpty" was really a riddle to begin with (before Lewis Carroll and his illustrator gave it away). We are supposed to guess what was the mysterious person or thing which fell down, and then could not possibly be put together again, not even by all the king's horses and all the king's men, and nowadays by all the republic's scientific experts: the answer is an egg. There is a beautiful folk song made up of three such riddles: the cherry without a stone, the chicken without a bone, and the baby that does not cry. It is at least five hundred years old, and yet for four hundred years it was passed on from one singer to another, without ever being printed.

Again, there are some famous and splendid poems that deal with 11 mystical experience in riddling terms, phrases which have to two meanings, or three, or one concealed: these are also didactic, informative, and yet riddles. One such poem, by an American poet, deals with the paradox of God—the complete God, who includes all the appearances of the universe, both the appearance of good and the appearance of evil. This is Emerson's "Brahma." . . . [It] is a riddle which is meant not for children but for adults. There are similar riddles in the Bible sometimes equally beautiful. Such is the meditation on old age at the end of that mysterious and rather unorthodox book called *Koheleth*, or *Ecclesiastes*. . . . All [its] enigmatic and memorable phrases are descriptions of the symptoms of the last and almost the bitterest fact in life, old age. They show that it is pathetic, and yet they make it beautiful.

Such poetry is unusual. Or rather, its manner is unusual and its sub- 12 ject is a fact of common experience. It is possible for poets to speak plainly and frankly about everyday life; and that is one more of the uses of poetry—one of the best known. Poetry can express general experience: can say what many men and women have thought and felt. The benefit of this is that it actually helps ordinary people, by giving them words. Most of us are not eloquent. Most of us—especially in times of intense emotion—cannot say what we feel; often we hardly know what we feel. There, in our heart, there is the turmoil, be it love or protest or exultation or despair: it stirs us, but all our gestures and words are inadequate. As the emotion departs, we know that an opportunity was somehow missed, an opportunity of realizing a great moment to the full. It is in this field that poetry comes close to religion. Religion is one of the experiences which the ordinary man finds most difficult to compass in words. Therefore he nearly always falls back on phrases which have been composed for him by someone more gifted. Many, many thousands of times, in battles and concentration camps and hospitals, beside death beds, and even on death beds, men and women have repeated a very ancient poem only six verses long, and have found comfort in it, such as no words of their own would have brought them. It begins, "The Lord is my shepherd; I shall not want."

If we look at poetry or any of the arts from this point of view, we 13 shall gain a much greater respect for them. They are not amusements or decorations; they are aids to life. Ordinary men and women find living rather difficult. One of their chief difficulties is to apprehend their own thoughts and feelings, and to respond to them by doing the right things and saying the right sentences. It is the poets who supply the words and sentences. They too have felt as we do, but they have been able to speak, while we are dumb.

Not only that. By expressing common emotions clearly and elo- 14 quently, the poets help us to understand them in other people. It is difficult to understand—for any grown-up it is difficult to understand—what goes on in the mind of a boy or girl. Parents are often so anxious and serious that they have forgotten what it was like to be young, and vague, and romantic. It is a huge effort, rather an unpleasantly arduous effort, to think oneself back into boyhood. Yet there are several poems which will allow us to understand it, and even to enjoy the experience. . . .

This function of poetry is not the only one, but it is one of the most 15 vital; to give adequate expression to important general experiences. In 1897, when Queen Victoria celebrated her Diamond Jubilee, the Poet Laureate was that completely inadequate little fellow, Alfred Austin; but the man who wrote the poem summing up the emotions most deeply felt during the Jubilee was Rudyard Kipling. It is called "Recessional." It is a splendid poem, almost a hymn—Biblical in its phrasing and deeply prophetic in its thought. . . .

However, as you think over the poems you know, you will realize 16 that many of them seem to be quite different from this. They are not even trying to do the same thing. They do not express important general experiences in universally acceptable words. On the contrary, they express strange and individual experiences in abstruse and sometimes unintelligible words. We enjoy them not because they say what we have often thought but because they say what we should never have dreamed of thinking. If a poem like Kipling's "Recessional" or Longfellow's "Lost Youth" is close to religion, then this other kind of poetry is close to magic: its words sound like spells; its subjects are often dreams, visions, and myths.

Such are the two most famous poems by Coleridge: "The Ancient 17 Mariner" and "Kubla Khan." They are scarcely understandable. They are unbelievable. Beautiful, yes, and haunting, yes, but utterly illogical; crazy. Coleridge himself scarcely knew their sources, deep in his memory and his subconscious—sources on which a modern scholar has written a superb book. Both of them end with a mystical experience that none of us has ever had: "The Ancient Mariner" telling how, like the Wandering Jew, he must travel forever from country to country, telling his story with "strange power of speech"; and "Kubla Khan" with the poet himself creating a magical palace:

> I would build that dome in air,
> That sunny dome! those caves of ice!
> And all who heard should see them there,
> And all should cry, Beware! Beware!
> His flashing eyes, his floating hair!

Weave a circle round him thrice,
    And close your eyes with holy dread,
    For he on honey-dew hath fed,
And drunk the milk of Paradise.

Not long after those fantastic verses were written, young Keats was 18 composing a lyric, almost equally weird, which is now considered one of the finest odes in the English language. It ends with the famous words which we all know, and which few of us believe:

Beauty is truth, truth beauty,—that is all
    Ye know on earth, and all ye need to know.

It is the "Ode on a Grecian Urn"; but how many of us have ever stood, like Keats, meditating on the paintings that surround a Greek vase? and, even if we have, how many of us have thought that

Heard melodies are sweet, but those unheard
    Are sweeter?

It is a paradox. The entire ode is a paradox: not an expression of 19 ordinary life, but an extreme extension of it, almost a direct contradiction of usual experience.

Most modern poetry is like this. It tells of things almost unknown 20 to ordinary men and women, even to children. If it has power over them at all, it is because it enchants them by its strangeness. Such is the poetry of Verlaine, and Mallarmé, and Rimbaud; of the difficult and sensitive Austrian poet Rilke; in our own language, such is most of Auden's poetry, and Ezra Pound's; and what could be more unusual than most of T. S. Eliot—although he is the most famous poet writing today? Suppose we test this. Let us take something simple. Spring. What have the poets said about the first month of spring, about April? Most of them say it is charming and frail:

April, April
Laugh thy girlish laughter;
Then, the moment after,
Weep thy girlish tears!

That is Sir William Watson: turn back and see Shakespeare talking of

The uncertain glory of an April day;

turn forward, and hear Browning cry

O to be in England
Now that April's there!

and then hundreds of years earlier, see Chaucer beginning his *Canterbury Tales* with a handshake of welcome to "Aprille, with his shoures soote."

Indeed, that is what most of feel about April: it is sweet and delicate and youthful and hopeful. But T. S. Eliot begins *The Waste Land* with a grim statement which is far outside ordinary feelings:

> April is the cruellest month, breeding
> Lilacs out of the dead land, mixing
> Memory and desire, stirring
> Dull roots with spring rain.

And the entire poem, the best known of our generation, is a description of several agonizing experiences which most of us not only have never had but have not even conceived as possible. Yet there is no doubt that it is good poetry, and that it has taken a permanent place in our literature, together with other eccentric and individual visions.

But some of us do not admit it to be poetry—or rather claim that, if 21 it is so extreme and unusual, poetry is useless. This is a mistake. The universe is so vast, the universe is so various, that we owe it to ourselves to try to understand every kind of experience—both the usual and the remote, both the intelligible and the mystical. Logic is not enough. Not all the truth about the world, or about our own lives, can be set down in straightforward prose, or even in straightforward poetry. Some important truths are too subtle even to be uttered in words. A Japanese, by arranging a few flowers in a vase, or Rembrandt, by drawing a dark room with an old man sitting in it, can convey meanings which no one could ever utter in speech. So also, however extravagant a romantic poem may seem, it can tell us something about our world which we ought to know.

It is easier for us to appreciate this nowadays than it would have 22 been for our grandfathers in the nineteenth century, or for their great-grandfathers in the eighteenth century. Our lives are far less predictable; and it is far less possible to use logic alone in organizing and understanding them. Therefore there are justifications, and good ones, for reading and memorizing not only what we might call universal poetry but also strange and visionary poetry. We ourselves, at some time within the mysterious future, may well have to endure and to try to understand some experience absolutely outside our present scope; suffering of some unforeseen kind, a magnificent and somber duty, a splendid triumph, the development of some new power within us. We shall be better able to do so if we know what the poets (yes, and the musicians) have said about such enhancements and extensions of life. Many a man has lived happily until something came upon him which made him, for the first time, think of committing suicide. Such a man will be better able to understand himself and to rise above the thought if he knows the music that Rachmaninoff wrote when he, too, had such thoughts and conquered them, or if he reads the play of *Hamlet,* or if he travels through Dante's *Comedy,* which begins in utter despair and ends in the vision of love, that moves the sun and the other stars.

And even if we ourselves are not called upon to endure such ex- 23
tremes, there may be those around us, perhaps very close to us, who are
faced with situations the ordinary mind cannot assimilate: sudden wealth,
the temptations of great beauty, the gift of creation, profound sorrow, un-
merited guilt. The knowledge of what the poets have said about experiences beyond the frontiers of logic will help us at least to sympathize with
them in these experiences. Such understanding is one of the most difficult
and necessary efforts of the soul. Shelley compared the skylark, lost in the
radiance of the sun, to

> a Poet hidden
> In the light of thought,
> Singing hymns unbidden,
> Till the world is wrought
> To sympathy with hopes and fears it heeded not.

To create such sympathy is one of the deepest functions of poetry, and one
of the most bitterly needed.

Reading and Interpreting

VOCABULARY

Use your dictionary as necessary to find the meaning of the following words
as used by Highet:

justification (2)   conjuring (2)   elegy (6)   enigmatic (11)

apprehend (13)   abstruse (16)   assimilate (23)

CONCEPT ANALYSIS

1. Highet classifies poetry in terms of its uses. Why do you think he emphasizes the *uses* of poetry? What does his title imply about the value
   commonly assigned to poetry?
2. What qualities does poetry have that makes it an effective teaching tool?
3. According to Highet, what universal needs in human beings does poetry
   fulfill?
   Do you agree with Highet that the arts "are aids to life"? Explain
   with reference to your personal experience.
4. Highet describes the last type of poetry as "close to magic." What do
   poetry and magic have in common?

5. In your own words, explain Highet's statement in paragraph 21 that "Logic is not enough." Do you accept his idea that poetry can help us where logic fails?

Quickwrite

According to Highet, poetry gives ordinary people words. Select one of the following lines of poetry or choose a line from any poem you wish, and discuss how it "gives words" to an emotion, idea, or experience of yours.

- "How sharper than a serpent's tooth it is / To have a thankless child!" (Shakespeare, *King Lear*)
- "A boy's will is the wind's will, / And the thoughts of youth are long, long thoughts." (Longfellow, "My Lost Youth")
- "'Beauty is truth, truth beauty,'—that is all / Ye know on earth, and all ye need to know." (Keats, "Ode on a Grecian Urn")

Thinking and Writing

RHETORICAL TECHNIQUE

1. Highet classifies poetry into six categories by their different uses. List these. Can you think of additional functions for poetry?
2. Which two categories are explicitly contrasted by Highet? How well would an essay of division based on these two types of poetry account for the poetry with which you are familiar? Use specific poems as examples in your discussion.
3. Evaluate the sequence in which Highet presents the six functional categories of poetry. What logic appears to control his sequence of presentation?

COMPOSITION

Poetry's role or function—what poetry *does*—is Highet's principle of classification in this essay. Choose a subject such as sports, film, television, or college and discuss its functions in a classification essay.

HAVELOCK ELLIS
The Philosophy of Dancing

English physician Havelock Ellis (1859–1939) did not
practice medicine but devoted himself to literature and
the new field of psychology. Of his numerous essays and
psychological studies, the best known was *Studies in the
Psychology of Sex,* which led to criticism and abuse of Ellis
by conventional thinkers. His essay on dancing reflects
his original and even radical viewpoint, which made
him an important influence on contemporary culture.
Through his extensive and well-illustrated classification
of the functions and types of dance, Ellis demonstrates
the breadth of knowledge that is the mark of the liber-
ally educated.

I

Dancing and architecture are the two primary and essential arts. The art of   1
dancing stands as the source of all the arts that express themselves first in
the human person. The art of architecture is the beginning of all the arts
that lie outside the person. Music, acting, poetry, proceed in the one
mighty stream; sculpture, painting, all the arts of design, in the other.
There is no primary art outside these two arts, for their origin is far earlier
than man himself; and dancing came first. . . .

  The significance of dancing, in the wide sense, thus lies in the fact   2
that it is simply an intimate concrete appeal of that general rhythm which
marks all the physical and spiritual manifestations of life. Dancing is the
primitive expression alike of religion and of love,—of religion from the
earliest human times we know of, and of love from a period long anterior
to the coming of man. The art of dancing, moreover, is intimately entwined with all human traditions of war, of labor, of pleasure, of education, while some of the wisest philosophers and the most ancient civilizations have regarded the dance as the pattern in accordance with which the
moral life of man must be woven. To realize, therefore, what dancing
means for mankind,—the poignancy and the many-sidedness of its appeal,—we must survey the whole sweep of human life, both at its highest
and at its deepest moments.

II

"What do you dance?" When a man belonging to one branch of the great 3
Bantu division of mankind met a member of another, said Livingstone,
that was the question he asked. What a man danced, that was his tribe,
his social customs, his religion; for, as an anthropologist has recently put
it, "a savage does not preach his religion, he dances it."

. . . Among primitive peoples religion is so large a part of life that 4
the dance inevitably becomes of supreme religious importance. To dance
was at once both to worship and to pray. Just as we still find in our Prayer
Books that there are divine services for all the great fundamental acts of
life, for birth, for marriage, for death, as well as for the cosmic procession
of the world as marked by ecclesiastical festivals, and for the great catas-
trophes of nature, such as droughts, so also it has ever been among primitive peoples. For all the solemn occasions of life, for bridals and for funerals, for seed-time and for harvest, for war and for peace, for all these
things, there were fitting dances.

To-day we find religious people who in church pray for rain or for the 5
restoration of their friends to health. Their forefathers also desired these
things but, instead of praying for them, they danced for them the fitting
dance which tradition had handed down, and which the chief or the
medicine-man solemnly conducted. The gods themselves danced, as the
stars dance in the sky,—so at least the Mexicans, and we may be sure
many other peoples, have held,—and to dance is therefore to imitate the
gods, to work with them, perhaps to persuade them to work in the direction of our own desires. "Work for us!" is the song-refrain, expressed or
implied, of every religious dance. In the worship of solar deities in various
countries it was customary to dance around the altar, as the stars dance
around the sun. Even in Europe the popular belief that the sun dances on
Easter Sunday has perhaps scarcely yet died out. To dance is to take part in
the cosmic control of the world. Every sacred dionysian dance is an imitation of the divine dance.

All religions, and not merely those of primitive character, have been 6
at the outset, and sometimes throughout, in some measure saltatory. This
is the case all over the world. It is not more pronounced in early Christianity and among the ancient Hebrews who danced before the ark, than
among the Australian aborigines whose great *corroborees* are religious
dances conducted by the medicine-men with their sacred staves in their
hands. Every American Indian tribe seems to have had its own religious
dances, varied and elaborate, often with a richness of meaning which the
patient study of modern investigators has but slowly revealed. The Shamans
in the remote steppes of Northern Siberia have their ecstatic religious
dances, and in modern Europe the Turkish dervishes—perhaps of related
stock—still dance in their cloisters similar ecstatic dances, combined
with song and prayer, as a regular part of devotional service.

These religious dances, it may be realized, are sometimes ecstatic, 7
sometimes pantomimic. It is natural that this should be so. By each road
it is possible to penetrate toward the divine mystery of the world. The
auto-intoxication of rapturous movement brings the devotee, for a while
at least, into that self-forgetful union with the not-self which the mystic
ever seeks. Pantomimic dances, on the other hand, with their effort to
heighten natural expression and to imitate natural processes, bring the
dancers into the divine sphere of creation and enable them to assist vicari-
ously in the energy of the gods. The dance thus becomes the presentation
of a divine drama, the vital reenactment of a sacred history in which the
worshiper is enabled to play a real part. In this way ritual arises.

It is in this sphere—highly primitive as it is—of pantomimic danc- 8
ing crystallized in ritual, rather than in the sphere of ecstatic dancing, that
we may to-day in civilization witness the survivals of dance in religion.
The Divine Services of the American Indian, said Lewis Morgan, took the
form of "set dances, each with its own name, songs, steps, and costume."
At this point the early Christian worshiping the Divine Body was able to
enter into spiritual communion with the ancient Egyptian or the American Indian. They are all alike privileged to enter, each in his own way, a
sacred mystery, and to participate in the sacrifice of a heavenly Mass. . . .

. . . Genuine and not merely formalized and unrecognizable danc- 9
ing, such as the traditionalized Mass, must have been frequently introduced into Christian worship in early times. Until a few centuries ago it
remained not uncommon, and it still persists in remote corners of the
Christian world. In English cathedrals dancing went on until the fourteenth century. At Paris, Limoges, and elsewhere in France, the priests
danced in the choir at Easter up to the seventeenth century; in Roussillon
up to the eighteenth century. Roussillon is a province with Spanish traditions, and it was in Spain that religious dancing took deepest root and
flourished longest. In the cathedrals of Seville, Toledo, Valencia, and
Xeres there was formerly dancing, although it now survives only at a few
special festivals in the first. At Alaro in Majorca, also, at the present day, a
dancing company called Els Cosiers, on the festival of St. Roch, the patron saint of the place, dance in the church, in fanciful costumes, with
tambourines, up to the steps of the high altar, immediately after Mass,
and then dance out of the church. In another part of the Christian world,
in the Abyssinian Church,—an offshoot of the Eastern Church,—dancing
is said still to form a part of the worship.

Dancing, we may see throughout the world, has been so essential, so 10
fundamental a part of all vital and undegenerate religion, that whenever a
new religion appears, a religion of the spirit and not merely an anemic
religion of the intellect, we should still have to ask of it the question of
the Bantu: What do you dance?

III

Dancing is not only intimately associated with religion, it has an equally 11
intimate association with love. Here indeed the relationship is even more
primitive, for it is far older than man. Dancing, said Lucian, is as old as
love. Among insects and among birds, for instance, it may be said that
dancing is often an essential part of courtship. The male dances, sometimes in rivalry with other males, in order to charm the female; then, after
a short or long interval, the female is aroused to share his ardor and join in
the dance; the final climax of the dance is in the union of the lovers. . . .
It is indeed in this aspect that dancing has so often aroused reprobation,
from the days of early Christianity until the present, among those for
whom the dance has merely been, in the words of a seventeenth-century
writer, a series of "immodest and dissolute movements by which the
cupidity of the flesh is aroused."

But in Nature and among primitive peoples it has its value precisely 12
on this account. It is a process of courtship and, even more than that, it is
a novitiate for love, and a novitiate which was found to be an admirable
training for love. Among some peoples, indeed, as the Omahas, the same
word meant both to dance and to love. Here we are in the sphere of sexual
selection. By his beauty, his energy, his skill, the male must win the female, so impressing the image of himself on her imagination that finally
her desire is aroused to overcome her reticence. That is the task of the
male throughout nature, and in innumerable species besides man it has
been found that the school in which the task may best be learned is the
dancing school. The moths and the butterflies, the African ostrich, and
the Sumatran Argus pheasant, with their fellows innumerable, have been
the precursors of man in the strenuous school of erotic dancing, fitting
themselves for selection by the females of their choice as the most splendid
progenitors of the future race.

From this point of view of sexual selection we may better understand 13
the immense ardor with which every part of the wonderful human body
has been brought into the play of the dance. The men and women of races
spread all over the world have shown a marvelous skill and patience in
imparting rhythm and music to the most unlikely, the most rebellious
regions of the body, all wrought by desire into potent and dazzling images. To the vigorous races of Northern Europe in their cold damp climate, dancing comes naturally to be dancing of the legs, so naturally that
the English poet, as a matter of course, assumes that the dance of Salome
was a "twinkling of the feet." But on the opposite side of the world, in
Japan and notably in Java and Madagascar, dancing may be exclusively
dancing of the arms and hands, in some of the South Sea islands even of
the hands and fingers alone. Dancing may even be carried on in the seated
posture, as occurs at Fiji in a dance connected with the preparation of the
sacred drink, *ava*. In some districts of Southern Tunisia dancing, again, is

dancing of the hair, and all night long, till they perhaps fall exhausted, the marriageable girls will move their heads to the rhythm of a song, maintaining their hair in perpetual balance and sway. Elsewhere, notably in Africa, but also sometimes in Polynesia, as well as in the dances that had established themselves in ancient Rome, dancing is dancing of the body, with vibratory or rotatory movements of breasts or flanks.

IV

From the vital function of dancing in love, and its sacred function in reli- 14 gion, to dancing as an art, a profession, an amusement, may seem, at the first glance, a sudden leap. In reality the transition is gradual, and it began to be made at a very early period in diverse parts of the globe. All the matters that enter into courtship tend to fall under the sway of art; their aesthetic pleasure is a secondary reflection of their primary vital joy. Dancing could not fail to be first in manifesting this tendency. But even religious dancing swiftly exhibited the same transformation; dancing, like priesthood, became a profession, and dancers, like priests, formed a caste. This, for instance, took place in old Hawaii. The *hula* dance was a religious dance; it required a special education and an arduous training; moreover, it involved the observance of important taboos and the exercise of sacred rites; therefore it was carried out by paid performers, a professional caste.

In our modern world professional dancing as an art has become alto- 15 gether divorced from religion, and even, in any vital sense, from love; it is scarcely even possible, so far as western civilization is concerned, to trace back the tradition to either source. If we survey the development of dancing as an art in Europe, it seems to me that we have to recognize two streams of tradition which have sometimes merged, but yet remain in their ideals and their tendencies essentially distinct. I would call these traditions the Classical, which is much the more ancient and fundamental, and may be said to be of Egyptian origin, and the Romantic, which is of Italian origin, chiefly known to us as the ballet. The first is, in its pure form, solo dancing, and is based on the rhythmic beauty and expressiveness of the simple human personality when its energy is concentrated in passionate movement. The second is concerted dancing, mimetic and picturesque, wherein the individual is subordinated to the wider and variegated rhythm of the group. It may be easy to devise another classification, but this is simple and instructive enough for our purpose.

There can scarcely be a doubt that Egypt has been for many thou- 16 sands of years, as indeed it still remains, a great dancing centre, the most influential dancing-school the world has ever seen, radiating its influence south and east and north. We may perhaps even agree with the historian of the dance, who terms it "the mother-country of all civilized dancing." We are not entirely dependent on the ancient wall-pictures of Egypt for our knowledge of Egyptian skill in the art. Sacred mysteries, it is known, were danced in the temples, and queens and princesses took part in the orchestras that accompanied them. It is significant that the musical instruments still peculiarly associated with the dance were originated or developed in Egypt; the guitar is an Egyptian instrument, and its name was a hieroglyphic already used when the Pyramids were being built; the cymbal, the tambourine, triangles, and castanets, in one form or another, were all familiar to the ancient Egyptians, and with the Egyptian art of dancing they must have spread all round the shores of the Mediterranean, the great focus of our civilization, at a very early date. Even beyond the Mediterranean, at Cadiz, dancing that was essentially Egyptian in character was established, and Cadiz became the dancing-school of Spain. The Nile and Cadiz were thus the two great centres of ancient dancing, and Martial mentions them both together, for each supplied its dancers to Rome. This dancing, alike whether Egyptian or Gaditanian, was the expression of the individual dancer's body and art; the garments played but a small part in it, they were frequently transparent, and sometimes discarded altogether. It was, and it remains, simple, personal, passionate dancing; classic, therefore, in the same sense as, on the side of literature, the poetry of Catullus is classic.

Ancient Greek dancing was essentially classic dancing as here understood. On the Greek vases, as reproduced in Emmanuel's attractive book on Greek dancing and elsewhere, we find the same play of the arms, the same sideward turn, the same extreme backward extension of the body, which had long before been represented in Egyptian monuments. Many supposedly modern movements in dancing were certainly already common both to Egyptian and Greek dancing, as well as the clapping of hands to keep time, which is still an accompaniment of Spanish dancing. 17

It seems clear, however, that, on this general classic and Mediterranean basis, Greek dancing had a development so refined and so special that it exercised no influence outside Greece. Dancing became indeed the more characteristic and the most generally cultivated of Greek arts. It may well be that the Greek drama arose out of dance and song, and that the dance throughout was an essential and plastic element in it. It is said that Aeschylus developed the technique of dancing, and that Sophocles danced in his own dramas. In these developments, no doubt, Greek dancing tended to overpass the fundamental limits of classic dancing and foreshadowed the ballet. 18

The real germ of the ballet, however, is to be found in Rome, where the pantomime with its concerted and picturesque method of expressive action was developed; and Italy is the home of Romantic dancing. The same impulse which produced the pantomime, produced more than a thousand years later, in the same Italian region, the modern ballet. In 19 both cases, one is inclined to think, we may trace the influence of the same Etruscan and Tuscan race which so long has had its seat here, a race with a genius for expressive, dramatic, picturesque art. We see it on the walls of Etruscan tombs and again in pictures of Botticelli and his fellow Tuscans. The modern ballet, it is generally believed, had its origin in the spectacular pageants at the marriage of Galeazzo Visconti, Duke of Milan, in 1489. . . .

Romantic dancing, to a much greater extent than what I have called 20 classic dancing, which depends so largely on simple personal qualities, tends to be vitalized by transplantation and the absorption of new influences, provided that the essential basis of technique and tradition is preserved in the new development. Lulli in the seventeenth century brought women into the ballet; Camargo discarded the fashionable unwieldy costumes, so rendering possible all the freedom and airy grace of later dancing; Noverre elaborated plot unraveled by gesture and dance alone, and so made the ballet a complete art-form. . . .

The influence of the French school was maintained as a living force 21 into the nineteenth century, overspreading the world, by the genius of a few individual dancers. When they had gone the ballet slowly and steadily declined. As it declined as an art, so also it declined in credit and in popularity; it became scarcely respectable even to admire dancing. Thirty years ago, the few who still appreciated the art of dancing—and how few they were!—had to seek for it painfully and sometimes in strange surroundings. A recent historian of dancing, in a book published so lately as 1906, declared that "the ballet is now a thing of the past, and, with the modern change of ideas, a thing that is never likely to be resuscitated." That historian never mentioned Russian ballet, yet his book was scarcely published before the Russian ballet arrived, to scatter ridicule over his rash prophecy by raising the ballet to a pitch of perfection it can rarely have surpassed, as an expressive, emotional, even passionate form of living art.

The Russian ballet was an offshoot from the French ballet, and illus- 22 trates once more the vivifying effect of transplantation on the art of romantic dancing. The Empress Anna introduced it toward the middle of the eighteenth century, and appointed a French ballet master and a Neapolitan composer to carry it on; it reached a high degree of technical perfection during the following hundred years, on the traditional lines, and the principal dancers were all imported from Italy. It was not until recent years that this firm discipline and these ancient traditions were vitalized into an art-form of exquisite and vivid beauty by the influence of the soil in which they had slowly taken root. . . .

What we see here, in the Russian ballet as we know it to-day, is a 23 splendid and arduous technical tradition, brought at last—by the combined genius of designers, composers, and dancers—into real fusion with an environment from which during more than a century it had been held apart: Russian genius for music, Russian feeling for rhythm, Russian skill in the use of bright color, and, perhaps, above all, the Russian orgiastic temperament and the general Slav passion for folkdancing, shown in all branches of the race, Polish, Bohemian, Bulgarian and Servian. The result has been that our age sees one of the most splendid movements in the whole history of romantic dancing.

V

Dancing as an art, we may be sure, cannot die out but will always be un- 24 dergoing a re-birth. Not merely as an art but also as a social custom, it perpetually emerges afresh from the soul of the people. Less than a century ago the polka thus arose, extemporized by the Bohemian servant girl, Anna Slezakova, out of her own head for the joy of her own heart, and only rendered a permanent form, apt for world-wide popularity, by the accident that it was observed and noted down by an artist. Dancing had forever been in existence as a spontaneous custom, a social discipline. Thus it is, finally, that dancing meets us, not only as love, as religion, as art, but also as morals.

All human work, under natural conditions, is a kind of dance. In a 25 large and learned work, supported by an immense amount of evidence, Karl Bücher has argued that work differs from the dance not in kind but only in degree, since they are both essentially rhythmic. In the memory of those who have ever lived on a sailing ship—that loveliest of human creations now disappearing from the world—there will always linger the echo of the chanties which sailors sang as they hoisted the topsail yard or wound the capstan or worked the pumps. That is the type of primitive combined work, and it is indeed difficult to see how such work can be effectively accomplished without such a device for regulating the rhythmic energy of the muscles.

The dance-rhythm of work has thus acted socializingly in a parallel 26 line with the dance-rhythms of the arts, and indeed in part as their inspirer. Thus, as Bücher points out, poetic metre may be conceived as arising out of work; metre is the rhythmic stamping of feet, as in the technique of verse it is still metaphorically so called; iambics and trochees, spondees and anapests and dactyls may still be heard among blacksmiths smiting the anvil or navvies wielding their hammers in the streets. In so far as they arose out of work, music and singing and dancing are naturally a single art. . . .

It is, however, the dance itself, apart from work and apart from the 27 other arts, which, in the opinion of many to-day, has had a decisive influence in socializing, that is to say in moralizing, the human species. Work showed the necessity of harmonious rhythmic cooperation, but the dance developed that rhythmic cooperation and imparted a beneficent impetus to all human activities. . . . It is the dance that socialized man.

Thus, in the large sense, dancing has possessed peculiar value as a 28 method of national education. As civilization grew self-conscious this was realized. "One may judge of a King," according to an ancient Chinese maxim, "by the state of dancing during his reign." So also among the Greeks: it has been said that dancing and music lay at the foundation of the whole political and military as well as the religious organization of the Dorian states.

In the narrow sense, in individual education, the great importance 29 of dancing came to be realized, even at an early stage of human development, and still more in the ancient civilizations. "A good education," Plato declared in the *Laws,* the final work of his old age, "consists in knowing how to sing well and dance well." And in our own day one of the keenest and most enlightened of educators has lamented the decay of dancing. The revival of dancing, Stanley Hall declares, is imperatively needed to give poise to the nerves, schooling to the emotions, strength to the will, and to harmonize the feelings and the intellect with the body which supports them. . . .

It thus comes about that, beyond its manifold practical significance, 30 dancing has always been felt to possess also a symbolic significance. Marcus Aurelius was accustomed to regard the art of life as like the dancer's art, though that Imperial Stoic could not resist adding that in some respects it was more like the wrestler's art. In our own time, Nietzsche, from first to last, showed himself possessed by the conception of the art of life as a dance, in which the dancer achieves the rhythmic freedom and harmony of his soul beneath the shadow of a hundred Damoclean swords. The dance lies at the beginning of art, and we find it also at the end. The first creators of civilization were making the dance, and the philosopher of to-day, hovering over the dark abyss of insanity, with bleeding feet and muscles strained to the breaking-point, still seems to himself to be weaving the maze of the dance.

Reading and Interpreting

VOCABULARY

Use your dictionary as necessary to find the meaning of the following words in the context of Ellis's essay:

manifestations (2)	cosmic (4)	ecclesiastical (4)	saltatory (6)
pantomimic (7)	novitiate (12)	concerted (15)	mimetic (15)
plastic (18)	extemporized (24)		

CONCEPT ANALYSIS

1. In his classification of dance as love, what analogy does Ellis provide regarding this function of dancing? Why is this analogy effective?
2. Paragraph 13 is particularly rich in illustrative examples. In your own words, what is the central idea of that paragraph? Can you add an example from your own knowledge or experience to those given by Ellis?
3. In discussing dance as an artistic form (starting in paragraph 15), Ellis talks about two distinct traditions. What are they? How do they differ?
4. Ellis says in paragraph 20: "Romantic dancing . . . tends to be vitalized by transplantation and . . . new influences. . . ." How does he support this assertion?
5. What does Ellis mean when he asserts in paragraph 27 that dance "socialized man"?

Quickwrite

1. Ellis cites philosopher Karl Bücher as arguing that work is "essentially rhythmic." Select a job or task that you have performed and discuss its rhythm. (You may find it helpful to review George Orwell's *Down and Out in Paris and London,* starting with paragraph 12, in Chapter 1.)
2. Identify yourself by answering the question in paragraph 3, "What do you dance?" What does your dancing say about you?

Thinking and Writing

RHETORICAL TECHNIQUE

1. Ellis's basic principle of division of the arts is stated in the first paragraph. What is this principle? Can you think of any arts that are not covered by Ellis's principle?
2. Ellis's principle of classification of dance is by function, what different types of dance do. Paragraph 2 sets out the categories of dancing that the essay will develop. List these, and map the paragraphs devoted to each. Which categories does Ellis treat more extensively? Given the place of dancing in modern industrialized societies, would you have added to, omitted some of, or reapportioned Ellis's categories? Explain your response.
3. In each category, what techniques are used to extend the definition of dance: contrasting examples, figurative language, descriptive details,

etymology, historical tracing, reference to authority? Cite specific sentences to illustrate your responses.
4. Ellis suggests in paragraph 15 that "another classification" could have been used here. Can you think of another "simple and instructive" way to have divided the topic of dance as art?

COMPOSITION

1. The deductive structure of Ellis's essay is clearly evident from its introduction, paragraphs 1 and 2. Ellis narrows the broad subject of the arts through a two-part division into those internal and external to the human person and then focuses on dancing as the source of the internal arts. He clearly states the categories of dance that he will discuss.

   Choose a broad term such as *knowledge, success,* or *sport* and establish a two-part division for it. Choose one of the divisions as the focus of your essay. Using Ellis's introduction as a structural guide, compose an introduction to your essay that provides a similar overview for your audience.
2. Ellis has classified dance by its functions: religious, artistic, courtship, work, educational (socialization). Consider the dancing that you do and write an essay in which you assign it (or its different types) to one or more of Ellis's categories.

CLYDE KLUCKHOHN
The Concept of Culture

American anthropologist Clyde Kluckhohn (1905–1960) is known primarily for his studies of the Navaho people and his work in the field of culture and personality. In explaining *culture,* a term that required extended definition with the rise of the new discipline of anthropology, Kluckhohn uses numerous cross-cultural examples from his own fieldwork.

Why do the Chinese dislike milk and milk products? Why would the Japanese die willingly in a Banzai charge that seemed senseless to Americans? Why do some nations trace descent through the father, others through the mother, still others through both parents? Not because different peoples have different instincts, not because they were destined by God or Fate to different habits, not because the weather is different in China and Japan and the United States. Sometimes shrewd common sense has an answer that is close to that of the anthropologist: "because they were brought up that way." By "culture" anthropology means the total life way of a people, the social legacy the individual acquires from his group. Or culture can be regarded as that part of the environment that is the creation of man.

This technical term has a wider meaning than the "culture" of history and literature. A humble cooking pot is as much a cultural product as is a Beethoven sonata. In ordinary speech a man of culture is a man who can speak languages other than his own, who is familiar with history, literature, philosophy, or the fine arts. In some cliques that definition is still narrower. The cultured person is one who can talk about James Joyce, Scarlatti, and Picasso. To the anthropologist, however, to be human is to be cultured. There is a culture in general, and then there are the specific cultures such as Russian, American, British, Hottentot, Inca. The general abstract notion serves to remind us that we cannot explain acts solely in terms of the biological properties of the people concerned, their individual past experience, and the immediate situation. The past experience of other men in the form of culture enters into almost every event. Each specific culture constitutes a kind of blueprint for all of life's activities.

One of the interesting things about human beings is that they try to understand themselves and their own behavior. While this has been particularly true of Europeans in recent times, there is no group which has not developed a scheme or schemes to explain man's actions. To the insistent human query "why?" the most exciting illumination anthropology has to offer is that of the concept of culture. Its explanatory importance is comparable to categories such as evolution in biology, gravity in physics, disease in medicine. A good deal of human behavior can be understood, and indeed predicted, if we knew a people's design for living. Many acts are neither accidental nor due to personal peculiarities nor caused by supernatural forces nor simply mysterious. Even those of us who pride ourselves on our individualism follow most of the time a pattern not of our own making. We brush our teeth on arising. We put on pants—not a loincloth or a grass skirt. We eat three meals a day—not four or five or two. We sleep in a bed—not a hammock or on a sheep pelt. I do not have to know the individual and his life history to be able to predict these and countless other regularities, including many in the thinking process of all Americans who are not incarcerated in jails or hospitals for the insane.

To the American woman a system of plural wives seems "instinctively" abhorrent. She cannot understand how any woman can fail to be jealous and uncomfortable if she must share her husband with other women. She feels it "unnatural" to accept such a situation. On the other hand, a Koryak woman of Siberia, for example, would find it hard to understand how a woman could be so selfish and so undesirous of feminine companionship in the home as to wish to restrict her husband to one mate.

Some years ago I met in New York City a young man who did not speak a word of English and was obviously bewildered by American ways. By "blood" he was as American as you or I, for his parents had gone from Indiana to China as missionaries. Orphaned in infancy, he was reared by a Chinese family in a remote village. All who met him found him more Chinese than American. The facts of his blue eyes and light hair were less impressive than a Chinese style of gait, Chinese arm and hand movements, Chinese facial expression, and Chinese modes of thought. The biological heritage was American, but the cultural training had been Chinese. He returned to China. Another example of another kind: I once knew a trader's wife in Arizona who took a somewhat devilish interest in producing a cultural reaction. Guests who came her way were often served delicious sandwiches filled with a meat that seemed to be neither chicken nor tuna fish yet was reminiscent of both. To queries she gave no reply until each had eaten his fill. She then explained that what they had eaten was not chicken, not tuna fish, but the rich, white flesh of freshly killed rattlesnakes. The response was instantaneous—vomiting, often violent vomiting. A biological process is caught in a cultural web.

A highly intelligent teacher with long and successful experience in the public schools of Chicago was finishing her first year in an Indian school. When asked how her Navaho pupils compared in intelligence with Chicago youngsters, she replied, "Well I just don't know. Sometimes the Indians seem just as bright. At other times they just act like dumb animals. The other night we had a dance in the high school. I saw a boy who is one of the best students in my English class standing off by himself. So I took him over to a pretty girl and told them to dance. But they just stood there with their heads down. They wouldn't even say anything." I inquired if she knew whether or not they were members of the same clan. "What difference would that make?"

"How would you feel about getting into bed with your brother?" The teacher walked off in a huff, but, actually, the two cases were quite comparable in principle. To the Indian the type of bodily contact involved in our social dancing has a directly sexual connotation. The incest taboos between members of the same clan are as severe as between true brothers and sisters. The shame of the Indians at the suggestion that a clan brother and sister should dance and the indignation of the white teacher at the idea that she should share a bed with an adult brother represent equally nonrational responses, culturally standardized unreason.

All this does not mean that there is no such thing as raw human nature. The very fact that certain of the same institutions are found in all known societies indicates that at bottom all human beings are very much alike. The files of the Cross-Cultural Survey at Yale University are organized according to categories such as "marriage ceremonies," "life crisis rites," "incest taboos." At least seventy-five of these categories are represented in every single one of the hundreds of cultures analyzed. This is hardly surprising. The members of all human groups have about the same biological equipment. All men undergo the same poignant life experiences such as birth, helplessness, illness, old age, and death. The biological potentialities of the species are the blocks with which cultures are built. Some patterns of every culture crystallize around focuses provided by the inevitables of biology: the difference between the sexes, the presence of persons of different ages, the varying physical strength and skill of individuals. The facts of nature also limit culture forms. No culture provides patterns for jumping over trees or for eating iron ore.

There is thus no "either-or" between nature and that special form of nurture called culture. Culture determinism is as one-sided as biological determinism. The two factors are interdependent. Culture arises out of human nature, and its forms are restricted both by man's biology and by natural laws. It is equally true that culture channels biological processes—vomiting, weeping, fainting, sneezing, the daily habits of food intake and waste elimination. When a man eats, he is reacting to an internal "drive," namely, hunger contractions consequent upon the lowering of blood sugar, but his precise reaction to these internal stimuli cannot be predicted by physiological knowledge alone. Whether a healthy adult feels hungry twice, three times, or four times a day and the hours at which this feeling recurs is a question of culture. *What* he eats is of course limited by availability, but is also partly regulated by culture. It is a biological fact that some types of berries are poisonous; it is a cultural fact that, a few generations ago, most Americans considered tomatoes to be poisonous and refused to eat them. Such selective, discriminative use of the environment is characteristically cultural. In a still more general sense, too, the process of eating is channeled by culture. Whether a man eats to live, lives to eat, or merely eats and lives is only in part an individual matter, for there are also cultural trends. Emotions are physiological events. Certain situations will evoke fear in people from any culture. But sensations of pleasure, anger, and lust may be stimulated by cultural cues that would leave unmoved someone who has been reared in a different social tradition. . . .

It was remarked by many observers in the Japanese relocation centers that Japanese who were born and brought up in this country, especially those who were reared apart from any large colony of Japanese, resemble in behavior their white neighbors much more closely than they do their own parents who were educated in Japan.

I have said "culture channels biological processes." It is more accurate to say "the biological functioning of individuals is modified if they have been trained in certain ways and not in others." Culture is not a disembodied force. It is created and transmitted by people. However, culture, like well-known concepts of the physical sciences, is a convenient abstraction. One never sees gravity. One sees bodies falling in regular ways. One never sees an electromagnetic field. Yet certain happenings that can be seen may be given a neat abstract formulation by assuming that the electromagnetic field exists. Similarly, one never sees culture as such. What is seen are regularities in the behavior or artifacts of a group that has adhered to a common tradition. The regularities in style and technique of ancient Inca tapestries or stone axes from Melanesian islands are due to the existence of mental blueprints for the group.

Culture is a way of thinking, feeling, believing. It is the group's 12 knowledge stored up (in memories of men; in books and objects) for future use. We study the products of this "mental" activity: the overt behavior, the speech and gestures and activities of people, and the tangible results of these things such as tools, houses, cornfields, and what not. It has been customary in lists of "culture traits" to include such things as watches or lawbooks. This is a convenient way of thinking about them, but in the solution of any important problem we must remember that they, in themselves, are nothing but metals, paper, and ink. What is important is that some men know how to make them, others set a value on them, are unhappy without them, direct their activities in relation to them, or disregard them.

"Culture," then, is "a theory." But if a theory is not contradicted by 13 any relevant fact and if it helps us to understand a mass of otherwise chaotic facts, it is useful. Darwin's contribution was much less the accumulation of new knowledge than the creation of a theory which put in order data already known. An accumulation of facts, however large, is no more a science than a pile of bricks is a house. Anthropology's demonstration that the most weird set of customs has a consistency and an order is comparable to modern psychiatry's showing that there is meaning and purpose in the apparently incoherent talk of the insane. In fact, the inability of the older psychologies and philosophies to account for the strange behavior of madmen and heathens was the principal factor that forced psychiatry and anthropology to develop theories of the unconscious and of culture.

Since culture is an abstraction, it is important not to confuse culture 14 with society. A "society" refers to a group of people who interact more with each other than they do with other individuals—who cooperate with each other for the attainment of certain ends. You can see and indeed count the individuals who make up a society. A "culture" refers to the distinctive ways of life of such a group of people. Not all social events are culturally patterned. New types of circumstances arise for which no cultural solutions have as yet been devised.

A culture constitutes a storehouse of the pooled learning of the 15 group. A rabbit starts life with some innate responses. He can learn from his own experience and perhaps from observing other rabbits. A human infant is born with fewer instincts and greater plasticity. His main task is to learn the answers that persons he will never see, persons long dead, have worked out. Once he has learned the formulas supplied by the culture of his group, most of his behavior becomes almost as automatic and unthinking as if it were instinctive. There is a tremendous amount of intelligence behind the making of a radio, but not much is required to learn to turn it on.

The members of all human societies face some of the same unavoidable dilemmas posed by biology and other facts of the human situation. This is why the basic categories of all cultures are so similar. Human culture without language is unthinkable. No culture fails to provide for aesthetic expression and aesthetic delight. Every culture supplies standardized orientations toward the deeper problems, such as death. Every culture is designed to perpetuate the group and its solidarity, to meet the demands of individuals for an orderly way of life and for satisfaction of biological needs. 16

However, the variations on these basis themes are numberless. Some languages are built up out of twenty basic sounds, others out of forty. Nose plugs were considered beautiful by the predynastic Egyptians but are not by the modern French. Puberty is a biological fact. But one culture ignores it, another prescribes informal instructions about sex but no ceremony, a third has impressive rites for girls only, a fourth for boys and girls. In this culture, the first menstruation is welcomed as a happy, natural event, in that culture the atmosphere is full of dread and supernatural threat. Each culture dissects nature according to its own system of categories. The Navaho Indians apply the same word to the color of a robin's egg and to that of grass. A psychologist once assumed that this meant a difference in the sense organs, that Navahos didn't have the physiological equipment to distinguish "green" from "blue." However, when he showed them objects of the two colors and asked them if they were exactly the same colors, they looked at him with astonishment. His dream of discovering a new type of color blindness was shattered. 17

Every culture must deal with the sexual instinct. Some, however, seek to deny all sexual expression before marriage, whereas a Polynesian adolescent who was not promiscuous would be distinctly abnormal. Some cultures enforce lifelong monogamy, others, like our own, tolerate serial monogamy; in still other cultures, two or more women may be joined to one man or several men to a single woman. Homosexuality has been a permitted pattern in the Greco-Roman world, in parts of Islam, and in various primitive tribes. Large portions of the population of Tibet, and of Christendom at some places and periods, have practiced complete celibacy. To us marriage is first and foremost an arrangement between two individuals. In many more societies marriage is merely one facet of a complicated set of reciprocities, economic and otherwise, between two families or two clans. 18

The essence of the cultural process is selectivity. The selection is 19 only exceptionally conscious and rational. Cultures are like Topsy. They just grew. Once, however, a way of handling a situation becomes institutionalized, there is ordinarily great resistance to change or deviation. When we speak of "our sacred beliefs," we mean of course that they are beyond criticism and that the person who suggests modification or abandonment must be punished. No person is emotionally indifferent to his culture. Certain cultural premises may become totally out of accord with a new factual situation. Leaders may recognize this and reject the old ways in theory. Yet their emotional loyalty continues in the face of reason because of the intimate conditionings of early childhood.

A culture is learned by individuals as the result of belonging to some 20 particular group, and it constitutes that part of learned behavior which is shared with others. It is our social legacy, as contrasted with our organic heredity. It is one of the important factors which permits us to live together in an organized society, giving us ready-made solutions to our problems, helping us to predict the behavior of others, and permitting others to know what to expect of us.

Culture regulates our lives at every turn. From the moment we are 21 born until we die there is, whether we are conscious of it or not, constant pressure upon us to follow certain types of behavior that other men have created for us. Some paths we follow willingly, others we follow because we know no other way, still others we deviate from or go back to most unwillingly. Mothers of small children know how unnaturally most of this comes to us—how little regard we have, until we are "culturalized," for the "proper" place, time, and manner for certain acts such as eating, excreting, sleeping, getting dirty, and making loud noises. But by more or less adhering to a system of related designs for carrying out all the acts of living, a group of men and women feel themselves linked together by a powerful chain of sentiments. Ruth Benedict gave an almost complete definition of the concept when she said, "Culture is that which binds men together."

Reading and Interpreting

VOCABULARY

Use your dictionary as necessary to find the meaning of the following words as used by Kluckhohn:

cliques (2)   incarcerated (3)   connotation (7)   crystallize (8)

determinism (9)   physiological (9)   promiscuous (18)   celibacy (18)

reciprocities (18)

CONCEPT ANALYSIS

1. What is the purpose of the example in paragraphs 5 through 9? Where is the main idea for these paragraphs stated? How effective are Kluckhohn's illustrations in supporting his point? What are some universal categories of culture that are determined by human biology?
2. Review paragraphs 19 through 21. What is their purpose? According to Kluckhohn, is cultural behavior more rational or emotional? What aspect of our culture can you think of that is "totally out of accord with a new factual situation" (19)? Why might people continue with cultural patterns that don't fit in with reality?

Quickwrite

Some cultures are polygamous; that is, a man may have more than one wife. Other cultures are polyandrous; that is, a woman may have more than one husband. In which would you rather live? Why?

Thinking and Writing

RHETORICAL TECHNIQUE

1. Many of the definitions of *culture* in Kluckhohn's essay are metaphorical figures of speech, such as "blueprints" and "chain of sentiment." Cite other figurative definitions in the text.

    Other definitions of *culture* in the essay are literal explanations. Cite some of these. Is one type of definition more effective than the other?

    Write a formal definition of *culture* in the anthropological sense based on the information in this essay.
2. What are some of the popular meanings of the term *culture?* Why was there a need for an anthropological meaning?
3. In writing his extended definition of *culture,* Kluckhohn uses several techniques of elaboration: illustration and example, analogy, descriptive language, anecdote (brief narrative), comparison and contrast, and reference to authority. Find examples of each and assess their effectiveness.
4. Kluckhohn uses examples and anecdotes in paragraphs 4 through 7 to support the statement that "a good deal of human behavior can be understood, and indeed predicted, if we know a people's design for living." Which example or anecdote do you think is the most persuasive? Which

is the least persuasive? Reflect on your responses to these questions. To what extent do you think your answers are culturally conditioned?

5. Kluckhohn states that the Yale University Cross-Cultural Survey found at least seventy-five categories of human behavior that occur in all cultures (8). List some of these. Can you add to the examples he presents?

COMPOSITION

1. In paragraph 14, Kluckhohn defines *culture* by what it is *not*, contrasting it with *society*. Use this paragraph as a structural guide for an original paragraph in which you define an abstract term by contrasting it with a term that is similar but not synonymous (for example, *teaching* versus *training*, *information* versus *wisdom*, *law* versus *justice*).

2. Select some of the following differentiae of the term *culture* and write a paragraph of examples for each:
   a. A culture provides for "aesthetic expression and aesthetic delight."
   b. "Every culture supplies standardized orientations toward the deeper problems, such as death."
   c. "Every culture must deal with the sexual instinct."
   d. "Every culture is designed to perpetuate the group and its solidarity. . . ."
   e. "Every culture is designed . . . to meet the demands of individuals for . . . satisfaction of biological needs."

SERENA NANDA

Specialization in Anthropology

This excerpt from the opening chapter of a freshman anthropology textbook employs classification to introduce students to the relatively new and expanding body of knowledge belonging to the discipline of anthropology.

The broad range of anthropological interest has led to some specialization   1
of research and teaching. The major divisions of anthropology are cultural anthropology, archeology, and physical anthropology.

Cultural Anthropology

Cultural anthropology studies human behavior that is learned, rather than 2
genetically transmitted, and that is typical of a particular human group.
These learned and shared kinds of human behavior (including the material
results of this behavior) are called culture.

Culture is the major way in which human beings adapt to their en- 3
vironments. Cultural anthropologists attempt to understand culture in
this general sense: They study its origins, its development, and its diversity as it changes through time and among peoples. They also examine its
transmission through teaching and learning and its relation to *Homo sapiens* as a biological species. Cultural anthropologists are also interested in
particular cultures; they want to know how different societies adapt to
their environments. In its comparative perspective, cultural anthropology
attempts to discover what is specific and variable in human behavior and
what is general and uniform. Cultural anthropologists ask questions like
these: "Is religion universal?" "What kinds of family structures are found
in different societies?" They are also interested in the relationships between the different subsystems of a culture—in particular, in their cause-
and-effect relationship to cultural change. One goal of cultural anthropology is to understand how culture change works so that we can predict and
perhaps direct or control change in productive ways.

Anthropological linguistics, sometimes considered a separate sub- 4
field, may also be considered a subspeciality of cultural anthropology concerned with language. Anthropological linguists study linguistic variation,
the ways in which human languages have developed, the ways in which
they are related to one another, how language is learned, and the relationship between language and other aspects of culture. One aim of anthropological linguistics is ultimately to understand the process of thought and
the organization of the human mind as they are expressed in language.

Archeology

Anthropological archeology specializes in studying culture through mate- 5
rial remains. Most archeologists study past societies for which there are
either no written records or no writing systems that have been deciphered.
Archeology thus adds a vital time dimension to our understanding of culture and how cultures change.

The archeologist does not observe human behavior and culture di- 6
rectly but reconstructs them from material remains—pottery, tools, gar-
bage, ruins of houses and public buildings, burials, and whatever else a
society has left behind. Until about 1960, archeologists were mainly concerned with describing the artifacts, or material remains, of prehistoric
sites. They would describe the procedures they had followed and the rela-

tive frequency and locations of the artifacts, and they would compare those artifacts with similar ones in the same region. The "new archeology" redirects the interests of archeologists to new questions and research. This new archeology is interested not simply in describing prehistoric sites and artifacts but in interpreting and explaining these data in terms of what they say about the culturally patterned behavior that produced them. The new archeology is primarily interested in questions of culture process, the rate and direction of culture change.

Physical Anthropology

Physical anthropology is the study of humankind from a biological per- 7 spective. A major task of physical anthropology is to study the evolution of the human species over time and the biological processes involved in human adaptation. Paleontology is the name given to the study of tracing human evolution in the fossil record. Paleontologists study the remains of the earliest human forms, as well as those nonhuman forms that can suggest something about our own origin and development. Paleontology is a particularly fascinating subject because it tries to answer the question "Where did we come from?"

Physical anthropologists are also interested in the evolution of cul- 8 ture. In the evolution of the human species, physical and cultural evolution interacted in a complex feedback system; neither is independent of the other. The study of the complex interrelationship between physical and cultural evolution is the link between physical anthropology, cultural anthropology, and archeology.

Because early human populations were hunters and gatherers, physi- 9 cal anthropologists study contemporary foraging societies in order to fill in the fragmentary physical evidence left by early humans. In addition to studying living human groups, physical anthropologists also study living nonhuman primates (especially monkeys and apes) for clues that their chemistry, physiology, morphology (physical structure), and behavior can give us in understanding our own species. Although at one time primates were mainly studied in the artificial setting of laboratories and zoos, now much of the work of physical anthropologists involves studying these animals in the wild.

Still another major interest of physical anthropologists is the study 10 of differences among human groups that are transmitted genetically—for example, skin color, blood type, or certain kinds of diseases. In addition to the practical benefits of genetic analysis—for example, in the treatment and prevention of some harmful hereditary abnormalities— population genetics contributes to our understanding of human evolution and adaptation.

Thinking and Writing

RHETORICAL TECHNIQUE

This excerpt from an anthropology textbook is a model of classification of an academic discipline. Each division of anthropology is defined by a particular focus and methodology. Note these in outline form.

COMPOSITION

For each category of anthropology, Nanda describes what the anthropologist *does*. Using the same approach to classification, list several majors available at your college and contrast them by explaining what the student in each does rather than what the major is.

CECIE STARR

RALPH TAGGART

The Emergence of Evolutionary Thought

This excerpt from a biology textbook presents a historical overview of classification systems in biology and clearly exemplifies the technique of classification.

More than two thousand years ago, the seeds of biological inquiry were 1 taking hold among the Hellenes, a people now known as the ancient Greeks. This was a time when popular belief held that supernatural beings intervened directly in human affairs. The gods, for example, were said to cause a common ailment known as the sacred disease. Yet from a physician of the school of Hippocrates, these thoughts come down to us:

It seems to me that the disease called sacred . . . has a natural cause, just as other diseases have. Men think it divine merely because they do not understand it. But if they called everything divine that they did not understand, there would be no end of divine things! . . . If you watch these fellows treating the disease, you see them use all kinds of incantations and magic—but they are also very careful in regulating diet. Now if food makes the disease better or worse, how can they say it is the gods who do this? . . . It does not really matter whether you call such things divine or not. In Nature, all things are alike in this, in that they can be traced to preceding causes.

On the Sacred Disease (400 B.C.)

Such was the spirit of the times; such was the commitment to finding natural explanations for observable events. Into this intellectual climate, Aristotle was born.

Aristotle was a naturalist who loved the world around him, and who described it in excellent detail. He had no reference books or instruments to guide him in formulating his descriptions, for the foundation of biological science in the Western world *began* with the great thinkers of this age. Yet here was a man who was no mere collector of random bits of information. *In his descriptions we have evidence of a mind perceiving connections between observations and constructing theories for explaining the order of things.* When Aristotle began his studies, he believed (as did others) that each kind of living thing was distinct from all others. Later he began to wonder about bizarre forms that could not be readily classified. In structure or function, they so resembled other forms that their place in nature seemed blurred. (For example, to Aristotle some sponges looked like plants, but they were animals in their feeding habits.) He came to view nature as proceeding ever so gradually from lifeless matter through ever more complex forms of animal life. This view is reflected in his model of biological organization (Figure 1), the first such theoretical framework to appear in the history of biology.

In the fourteenth century, this line of thought had become transformed into a rigid view of life. A great Chain of Being was seen to extend from the lowest forms, to humans, to spiritual beings. Each kind of being, or species as it was called, was seen to have a separate, fixed place in the divine order of things. Each had remained unchanged since the time of creation, a permanent link in the chain. Scholars believed they had only to discover, name, and describe all the links, and the meaning of life would be revealed to them. Contradictory views were not encouraged; scientific inquiry had become channeled into the encyclopedic assembly of facts.

As long as the world of living things meant mostly those forms existing in Europe, the task seemed manageable. With the global explorations of the sixteenth century, however, "the world" of life expanded

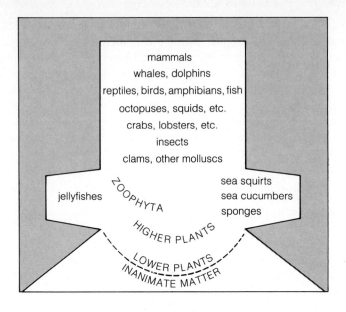

FIGURE 1 Scala Naturae—Aristotle's "ladder of life," the prototype of modern classification schemes.

enormously. Naturalists were soon overwhelmed by descriptions of thousands upon thousands of plants and animals discovered in Asia, Africa, the Pacific islands, and the New World. Some specimens appeared to be quite similar to common European forms, but some were clearly unique to different lands. How could these organisms be classified? The naturalist Thomas Moufet, in attempting to sort through the bewildering array, simply gave up and recorded such gems as this chaotic description of grasshoppers and locusts: "Some are green, some black, some blue. Some fly with one pair of wings; others with more; those that have no wings they leap; those that cannot fly or leap they walk; some have long shanks, some shorter. Some there are that sing, others are silent. . . ." It was not exactly a time of subtle distinctions.

Linnean System of Classification

The first widely accepted method of classification is attributed to Carl von   5
Linné, now known by his latinized name, Linnaeus. This man was an eighteenth-century naturalist whose enthusiasm knew no bounds. He sent ill-prepared students around the world to gather specimens of plants and animals for him, and is said to have lost a third of his collectors to the rigors of their expeditions. Although perhaps not very commendable as a

student advisor, Linnaeus did go on to develop the binomial system of nomenclature. With this system, each organism could be classified by assigning it a Latin name consisting of two parts.

For instance, *Ursus maritimus* is the scientific name for the polar 6 bear. The first name refers to the genus (plural, genera), and the first letter of the name is capitalized. Distinct but obviously similar species are grouped in the same genus. For example, other bears are *Ursus arctos,* the Alaskan brown bear, and *Ursus americanus,* the black bear. The second, uncapitalized name is the species epithet. The species epithet is never used without the full or abbreviated generic name preceding it, for it can also be the second name of a species found in an entirely different genus. The Atlantic lobster, for instance, is called *Homarus americanus.* (Hence one would not order *americanus* for dinner unless one is willing to take what one gets.)

The binomial system was the heart of a scheme that was thought to 7 mirror the patterns of links in the great Chain of Being. This classification scheme was based on perceived similarities or differences in physical features (coloration, number of legs, body size, and so forth). It eventually became structured in the manner shown in Table 1.

In retrospect, we can say that the Linnean system provided the basis 8 for the first widely accepted, shared language for naming and classifying organisms. It came at a time when ordering was desperately needed. Yet we must also say that the Linnean system reinforced the prevailing view— that species were distinctly unique *and unchanging* kinds of organisms, each locked in place in the Chain of Being. To this day, the use of rigid categories for classifying organisms works in subtle ways on our perceptions of the diversity of living things. . . .

TABLE 1   *Linnean System of Classification*

CATEGORY	INCLUDES:
Species	All organisms with distinct features that distinguish them from all other organisms
Genus	Collection of related species that share some features but are distinct from one another in some other features
Family	All closely related genera
Order	All closely related families
Class	All related orders
Phylum (or division, in botanical schemes)	All related classes
Kingdom	All related phyla; the most inclusive category of all

An Evolutionary View of Diversity

With widespread acceptance of evolutionary thought, fresh winds began 9
blowing through the rigid framework of classification systems. It was not
that the systems themselves were swept away. Such schemes were and continue to be useful ways of storing and retrieving information about the
diversity of life. The difference became one of identifying evolutionary
links between past and present species. All those cataloged species were
not necessarily exact copies of their ancestors; and their descendants might
not be exact copies of the current species form. There was an ongoing history of life here—a history of change.

Ernst Haeckel was the first to apply the emergent evolutionary the- 10
ory to classification schemes. He hypothesized that existing species could
be used as models for forms that lived long ago. From the simplest of
these forms, there evolved more specialized branchings, much as a tree
branches increasingly over time. From simple ancestral roots, evolutionary processes gave rise to different lineages specialized in form, function,
and behavior. One "family tree" of life, which Haeckel presented in 1874,
was typical of the models that were developed. In this tree, groups of organisms (phyla, classes, and some orders) were ranked hierarchically according to observed similarities and differences among existing organisms, used as models for the past.

Today, classification schemes are still based on observed characteris- 11
tics of existing organisms, but particular characteristics are now interpreted as being indicative of different lines of descent. A *genus* is now said
to include only those species related by descent from a fairly recent, common ancestral form. A *family* includes all genera related by descent from a
more remote common ancestor, and so on up to the highest (and most
inclusive) levels of classification: *phylum* and *kingdom*. A scheme that takes
into account the evolution of major lines of descent is known as a natural
system, or phylogenetic system of classification.

Constructing phylogenetic systems of classification is not easy. Over 12
time, environmental pressures and rates of evolution have not been the
same from group to group. Also, the picture of interrelationships is not
yet complete. Details must come from the fossil record, biochemistry, genetics, comparative anatomy, reproductive biology, behavior and ecology,
geology, and geography. Some information, such as parts of the fossil
record, is lost forever because of past upheavals in the earth's crust. Even
so, now that we have a better idea of where to look, and of what we are
looking for, many of the gaps are filling in fast.

Regardless of its strengths, no classification system should be viewed 13
as *the* system. As long as there are observations to be made, different
people will interpret relationships among organisms in different ways.
Some group all forms of life into two kingdoms (plants and animals).
Others group them into as many as twenty. In this book we use a modified

TABLE 2   *Classification Scheme*

KINGDOM	GENERAL CHARACTERISTICS
Monera	Single cells. Some are autotrophs (able to build own food from simple raw materials, such as carbon dioxide and water, using sunlight or other environmental energy source). Some are heterotrophs (depend on tissues, remains, or wastes of other living things for food). Cell body is prokaryotic: it has no true nucleus or other membrane-bound internal compartment. *Representatives:* archaebacteria, eubacteria (including the cyanobacteria, or blue-green algae)
Protista	Single cells. Includes autotrophs and heterotrophs. Cell body is eukaryotic: it has a true nucleus and other membrane-bound internal compartments. *Representatives:* golden algae, diatoms, amoebas, sporozoans, ciliates
Fungi	Multicelled. Heterotrophs. Most rely on digestion outside the fungal body, then absorption (they first secrete substances that break down food, then breakdown products are absorbed across the fungal cell wall). All eukaryotic. *Representatives:* slime molds, true fungi
Plantae	Multicelled. Autotrophs. With few exceptions, plants build all of their own food through photosynthesis. All eukaryotic. *Representatives:* red algae, brown algae, green algae, mosses, horsetails, lycopods, ferns, seed plants (such as cycads, ginkgo, conifers, flowering plants)
Animalia	Multicelled. Heterotrophs of varied sorts, including plant eaters, meat eaters, parasites. All eukaryotic. *Representatives:* sponges, jellyfishes, flatworms, roundworms, segmented worms, mollusks, arthropods (such as insects and lobsters), echinoderms (such as sea stars), chordates (fishes, amphibians, reptiles, birds, mammals)

version of Robert Whittaker's five-kingdom system. This version is summarized in Table 2 and sketched in Figure 2. Like other systems, it helps summarize current knowledge about life's diversity. It, too, is subject to modification as new evidence turns up.

In this model, organisms are assigned to kingdoms called the Monera, Protista, Fungi, Plantae, and Animalia. How did these kingdoms evolve? At least 3.5 billion years ago, the first cells were developing. They must have been much simpler than the one-celled bacteria found in the kingdom Monera. These bacteria have fairly complex systems for extracting energy from raw materials, and their body parts (such as cell walls) depend on systems for building some fairly complex molecules. Their ancestors were probably scavengers of simple compounds that natural geologic processes had produced. Existing bacterial lines are grouped as eubacteria and archaebacteria.

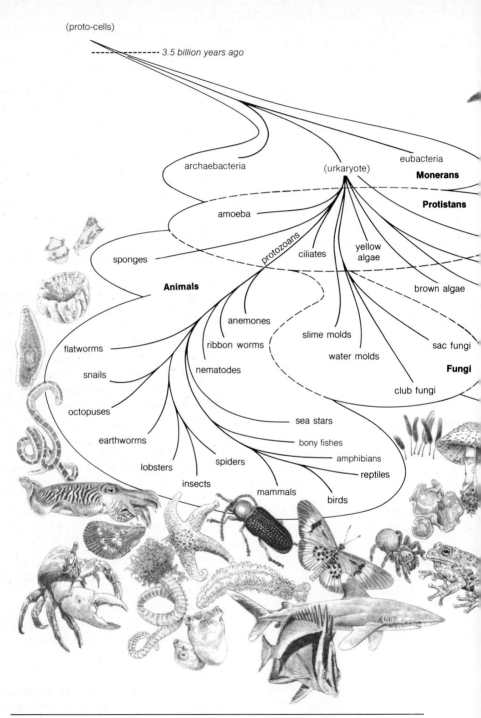

(proto-cells)

---------- 3.5 billion years ago

archaebacteria   (urkaryote)   eubacteria

Monerans

Protistans

amoeba

yellow algae

protozoans   ciliates

sponges

brown algae

Animals

anemones

slime molds

sac fungi

flatworms   ribbon worms

water molds

snails

nematodes

Fungi

octopuses

club fungi

sea stars

earthworms

bony fishes

amphibians

lobsters   spiders

reptiles

insects

mammals

birds

*FIGURE 2 Simplified diagram of the five-kingdom model for classifying life forms.
Only a few representative kinds of organisms are used to show the present scope of diver-*

algae

n algae **Plants**

mosses

seed plants

copods

ferns   conifers   flowering
                                   plants

*sity. The general pattern suggests possible routes that may have led from the origin of life
to this profusion of forms. Representatives of all kingdoms are still alive today.*

An entirely distinct bacterial line of descent (the urkaryotes) is now 15 thought to have given rise to the kingdoms Protista, Plantae, Fungi, and Animalia. Representatives of the ancestral stock have long since vanished. Today, most protistans are one-celled, like monerans. . . . However, they differ from them in significant ways. Some protistans are like plants, others like animals, some like plants *and* animals, and still others like fungi! Protistans may be living examples of the kinds of organisms that existed at a main evolutionary crossroad in the distant past. At that point, one-celled forms began evolving in ways that gave rise to multicelled plants, fungi, and animals. Multicelled organisms are grouped into these three kingdoms on the basis of their energy-acquiring strategies. Plants assemble their own energy-rich food molecules. Fungi absorb nutrients from organic matter that they have already digested outside the fungal body. Animals eat (ingest) other organisms as food.

The separate pools of life in Figure 2 are not to be viewed as one 16 flowing out of the other. *Representatives of all five kingdoms are alive today, side by side in time.* The generalized branching routes simply suggest how they might have arrived at where they are now. This is an evolutionary pattern of descent as many biologists now see it, as Darwin and Wallace might have envisioned it.

Reading and Interpreting

VOCABULARY

Use your dictionary as necessary to find the meaning of the following words as used by Starr and Taggart:

binomial (5)   nomenclature (5)   retrospect (8)   phylogenetic (11)

scavengers (14)

CONCEPT ANALYSIS

1. What was the crucial difference between the Aristotelian and the medieval approach to the study of natural science?
2. How did the age of exploration shake the medieval model of the chain of being?
3. What was Linnaeus's binomial system of nomenclature? What were its advantages and limitations?
4. Why is there no absolute classification system in biology today? What is the five-kingdom model? What are its strengths?

Quickwrite

Review naturalist Thomas Moufet's classification of grasshoppers in paragraph 4. Select a common species of living creature (cats, dogs, fish, birds, cockroaches, worms, monkeys) and write a classificatory paragraph about it from observation in Moufet's style.

Thinking and Writing

RHETORICAL TECHNIQUE

1. Define the various schemes for categorizing natural life by giving their differentiae, or distinguishing characteristics. In other words, make an outline of this reading selection based on the five major types of classification systems discussed.
2. As other readings in this text have also demonstrated, scientific writing need not be obscure or dull. Find examples of a humorous tone in this reading on biology.

COMPOSITION

Consult an encyclopedia or other appropriate reference work to learn the classification of a robin, a cockroach, an elephant, or your family pet according to the Linnean system (paragraph 6 and Table 1). Write a description based on this classification in paragraph form.

THE WRITTEN RESPONSE

Writing Workshop

1. Writing is a process of discovery. Your topic for this assignment should arise from your own desire to pursue a particular subject. Select a term or concept for extended definition from your current academic work, which may include the material in this text.
2. Research the term or concept to arrive at a working definition. Use any or all of the following resources: dictionary, textbooks, print media, reference books, lecture notes, discussion.
3. Establish a rationale—that is, a need—for your extended definition. For example, the popular understanding of the term may be too broad or the formal definition may be too narrow.
4. In an outline, block out the sections of your essay by determining the differentiae of your subject. The development of each of these distinguishing characteristics will constitute a section of your essay. Each section will have its own subthesis statement.
5. Determine your approach for elaborating each characteristic: etymology, anecdote, classification, comparison, contrast, historical tracing, example, illustration. Make a note of each method in the appropriate section of your outline.
6. Write your first draft, using your outline as a guide. Include your rationale as an introduction, your various subsections, and a conclusion, which may offer a refined version of your working definition.
7. Review your draft to sharpen and concretize the support you offer for each of your subject's distinguishing characteristics.

Topics for Critical Thinking and Writing

1. It has been said that all art carries a political message. Using a two-part division—"conform or rebel"—assign readings from this text or from your other liberal arts courses to these two messages.
2. Write an extended definition of a formal ritual in your culture (a wedding, a funeral, a graduation) to explain it to someone from another culture.
3. Many of this chapter's authors define a subject by discussing its various functions. Classify a subject (for example, college courses, sports, social organizations, social relationships) according to its various functions. Be sure that your principle of categorization is clear.

4. Complete this statement and continue with it in an essay that has a two-part division: There are two schools of thought on _____.
5. Use the following paragraph of zoological classification as a structural model for a paragraph in which you identify two items as belonging to the same group based on their similarities. You may use real or imaginary subjects.

The *classification* of types in a phylum follows:

> Because of the kinship of the grasshopper and the crayfish, scientists have placed them in the same great group, or phylum. The phylum to which they belong is called Arthropoda, which is derived from the two Greek words: "arthron," a joint, and "pous," a foot. All of the animals which have jointed, or hinged, appendages are placed in this phylum. There are also other characteristics, as we have seen, which are common to all members of this group. The phylum includes such animals as the lobster, crab, prawn, barnacle, honeybee, centipede, and spider. These animals are built on the same general plan as the grasshopper and the crayfish. All animals which possess these general characteristics belong to the phylum Arthropoda.

Charles John Pieper, Wilbur L. Beauchamp, and Orlin D. Frank,
Everyday Problems in Biology, 1932

Synthesis Questions

1. John Henry Newman suggests that liberal knowledge is a treasure in and of itself; it need not have practical application or produce tangible results. Discuss how the following works relate to Newman's position: Highet's "What Use Is Poetry?" MacLeish's "Ars Poetica," and Bacon's "Of Studies."
2. Newman states that it is improper to call the "passive sensation" of animals knowledge. Clyde Kluckhohn makes a similar distinction between animal and human mentality. Write an essay on the distinction between animal and human intelligence, either supporting or refuting the ideas of these authors.
3. Examples and illustrations make it possible to communicate the definition of an abstract term. Discuss the kind and quality of illustrative support in several of this chapter's readings.
4. Early in this chapter we said that extended definition does not just provide an understanding of an isolated term, but shows the relationship of the term to other aspects of the human condition. Apply this statement to the terms *dance, culture,* and *philosophy,* referring to the readings in this chapter.

Refining Your Essay

1. Review the introduction to your essay. If you have written an extended definition, is your rationale persuasive? Will your readers agree that an extended definition of your term will be useful? If you have written an essay of classification and/or division, does your introduction clearly state the principle on which you have organized your subject?
2. Review any formal definitions or statements of criteria for categories that you have used in your essay. Are the distinguishing characteristics precise, accurate, and exhaustive? Are they clearly separate from each other so that no overlapping occurs?
3. Do the distinguishing features or categories in your essay have a logical order and proportionate weight?
4. Have you varied your means of elaboration? Make a marginal note of how each subtopic is developed. If you have limited yourself to only one or two methods, experiment with others.
5. Does your conclusion offer an enriched understanding of the term, making reference to key points in the essay?

CHAPTER EIGHT

When in the Course of Human Events: The Causes and Consequences of War

Have there been both just and unjust wars in the past? Can you give examples? How do you distinguish them from each other? Because no major war has been fought on American soil since the Civil War (1861–1865), Americans have a different perception of the effects of war than do many other peoples. How do the effects of war differ when a country is the battlefield and when its soldiers are fighting on foreign soil?

THE WRITING FOCUS

. . . find out the cause of this effect,
Or rather say, the cause of this defect,
For this effect defective comes by cause.

William Shakespeare, *Hamlet*, act 2, scene 2

Perhaps no "effect defective" in human history has been more common and destructive to our species than the armed conflicts between peoples that we call war. *History*, as the Greeks defined it, means inquiry, and no subject has fascinated historians from the Greeks to the present as much as the subject of war. The focus of this chapter is on the causes and consequences of war.

Causal analysis, the mode of thinking and writing that traces the relationships between causes and their effects, is most appropriate to our inquiry into this subject. Only by seeking the causes of conflicts, and by examining the effects of war on human society, can we learn the lessons of the past that will help us to survive in the future.

There are two predominant forms of causal analysis. The first analyzes causes, answering the question *why* a given event has occurred or *why* a given situation exists. The second form, answering such questions as *what were the results of* a particular event or *what would happen if* a particular situation occurred, produces the essay of effect. In both types of analysis, the criterion for success is the degree to which the relationship between cause and effect is logical, clear, and supported by adequate evidence.

Types of Causes

In the mode of causal analysis, a distinction must be made among three types of causes: necessary cause, sufficient cause, and contributory cause.

A necessary cause is one that *must* be present for the event to occur, although alone and of itself, the necessary cause may not produce that effect. For example, a stockpile of nuclear arms would be a necessary cause of a nuclear war; without a supply of nuclear weapons, there could be no nuclear war. However, without the human intent to use them, the existence of nuclear arms would not result in nuclear conflict.

A cause labeled sufficient is one that by itself could produce a particular event; it is a possible but not a necessary cause. Thus, in a given context, a particular cause, although sufficient, may not apply, so the writer must be wary of attributing a particular event to the wrong cause. For instance, religious conflict is a sufficient cause of war, as demonstrated by the medieval Crusades of Christian Europe against the Islamic Middle East. Nevertheless, not all wars can be attributed to the cause of religious conflict.

CONTRIBUTORY CAUSES

In most academic writing, the analysis of events demands that we look beyond a single necessary cause to find the complex reasons for events. These reasons are called contributory causes because they combine with varying degrees of importance to make things happen.

One type of contributory cause is the ultimate or primary cause. It is worthwhile to be aware of the ultimate or primary cause of an event, but this cause may be so far distant that it is not within the scope of your essay. For example, in analyzing the contributory causes of the American Revolution, the primary cause might be viewed as the conclusion in 1763 of Europe's Seven Years' War, which encouraged Britain to use her colonial possessions as a source of revenue to pay her war debt. An essay on the causes of the American Revolution would probably make only a brief reference to this distant primary cause. Causes nearer in time and more closely linked to an event are called fundamental or underlying causes. To continue with the example of the American Revolution, we might say that one fundamental cause was Britain's economic oppression of the colonists in such legislation as the Stamp Act.

Fundamental or underlying causes often do not occur simultaneously. One may propel another sequentially in a chain, one cause leading to an effect and that effect becoming a cause for a subsequent effect. For instance, the English measures to tighten their colonial administration led to civil disorder by the colonists. This disorder in turn became a cause for more oppressive measures by the British, including the dispatch of British troops to the colonies. With the presence of British soldiers on American soil, the possibility of open warfare became a reality.

Escalating out of fundamental causes are the immediate, inciting, or overt acts that provoke events or situations. The inciting act of the American Revolution, for example, was the first gunfire at Lexington, April 18, 1775, "the shot heard round the world."

Essays focusing on effect also employ causal chains in their analyses. For instance, a reading in this chapter, Robert Penn Warren's "The Legacy of the Civil War," traces the sequential connections between the war and a multitude of economic, social, and political effects on the new American union.

Weighing the Evidence

The foundation of a cause-and-effect essay is objective evidence and logical reasoning. The evidence should open the mind to all possibilities and lead to fair conclusions. Through research and reflection the writer obtains adequate and appropriate evidence, develops logical relationships between items of evidence, and draws valid conclusions from the evidence.

In writing causal analysis, writers must avoid the error in logic known as the *post hoc* fallacy (from the Latin *post hoc, ergo propter hoc:* after this, therefore because of this), the mistake of thinking that if one event happens after another event, the first event *caused* the second. The relationship between the two occurrences may not be causative but merely chronological.

Another fallacy to avoid in causal analysis is circular reasoning: a statement of cause that simply repeats what is implied in the statement of the situation. To say, for example, that the American Revolution occurred because the colonists rebelled against their British rulers only defines the event in different words and closes off inquiry as to *why* the colonies resorted to arms.

A third type of logical problem is the false analogy, a mistaken comparison of one event with another. An analogy cannot be offered as proof of causes or effects because, by definition, it compares similar but not identical things. For example, we can speculate on the effects of a nuclear explosion based on our knowledge of a dynamite explosion, but any analogy between them is limited by the fact that dynamite and nuclear energy differ significantly.

Types of Support for Causal Analysis

Writers can use several types of support for cause-and-effect analysis. For example, scientific evidence, based on close observation of repeated physical phenomena, is central to this chapter's readings by Gregg and by Schell on the possible effects of a nuclear bomb blast. As a student, you will frequently be required to comprehend, summarize, and evaluate scientific material for cause-and-effect relationships.

A second type of evidence common to the social sciences is statistical data derived from observable social phenomena and controlled studies of human behavior. This type of evidence is open to interpretation and argument and should be carefully examined before it is accepted as support for a cause-and-effect relationship. (See "Pygmalion in the Classroom," in Chapter 6, for an example of such a controlled study.)

A third type of evidence, taken from the historical record, includes statements of fact drawn from government records, journals, letters, and newspaper accounts.

A fourth type of evidence consists of the informed views of authorities in a field. References to the works of people generally respected for their scholarship and insight will add more credibility to your causal analysis than the presentation of untested personal opinion alone. Authorities, however, differ in their views of the causes and effects of a particular event; objective historical inquiry should make room for many informed views. As a Southerner and a creative writer, for example, Robert Penn Warren has a different perspective on the Civil War than does Bruce Catton, a Northerner and a historian.

Finally, your own experience, carefully and objectively analyzed, may be appropriate in a cause-and-effect essay. However, unexamined personal responses, or simplistic overgeneralizations do not provide reasonable support for cause-and-effect analysis.

Emphasis on Effect

An essay emphasizing effect directs the reader's attention to the results of events. One type describes the actual results of past situations. A second type speculates on what might have happened if a historical event had turned out another way. For example, what would have happened if the British had won the War for Independence? In speculating on such hypothetical situations, the writer must depend more on logical thinking, analogy, and informed opinion than on facts as support. Similarly, in a third type of effect essay, predicting future results, you cannot prove that your predictions will take place, so your reasoning must be clear, logical, and based on well-documented analogous situations.

The Causal Analysis Essay

Before beginning your paper, brainstorm the causes or the effects of the situation that is your topic. Cluster causes or effects together into logical groupings: major and minor; ultimate, fundamental, and immediate; social, political, and economic.

For a paper on causes, determine the point in time at which you wish to begin. The space devoted to ultimate or far-removed causes should be small in proportion to that devoted to important contributory or immediate causes.

Next, make an outline of the various contributory causes you have listed. These will be the subsections of your paper. Within each subsection, list any causal chains that exist. Assign appropriate evidence to each subsection. You may want to rearrange your items of evidence as you reflect on your outline or after you write your first draft, as you find some subsections weaker or longer than you anticipated.

Because cause-and-effect analysis demands that your reader closely follow a complex structure of thoughts, your essay needs a strong introduction that establishes the limits of your inquiry, states your overall thesis, and indicates your organizational or reasoning pattern. You may want to inform your reader of the number of points or the major areas you will cover, as Will Durant does in the introduction of our Essay for Analysis.

In revising your first draft, focus on transitional signals that permit your reader to follow the logic of your analysis. If you are presenting a chronology of events from the historical record, you should use time expressions to clearly mark each stage. Use signal words to indicate relationships between causes and effects, reasons and results, actions and consequences. These signals include *because, because of, therefore, thus, consequently, for these reasons, since, the reason is, due to, as a result,* and so on. If your analysis includes a causal chain, signal each turn of events explicitly with such expressions as *this in turn led to, this situation caused,* and *the outcome of this was.*

Signals of intention, such as *to summarize,* are also effective devices of coherence, as exemplified in several of the selections in this chapter. Key themes should be repeated at strategic points in your essay. You can also reinforce key ideas with rhetorical questions, quotations, figures of speech, parallelisms, and interesting synonyms. If your essay is particularly long or complex, you can help the reader keep track of the analysis by providing interim summaries at the ends of sections as well as an overall summary in the conclusion.

Essay for Analysis

WILL DURANT

Why Men Fight
{The Causes of War}

Will Durant (1885–1981), American educator and historian whose first popular work, *The History of Philosophy,* was a best-seller, writes in a lucid style that incorporates many vivid examples to support his sweeping generalizations. This essay has explicit divisions, clear transitional signals, and many interesting illustrations. Since Durant is discussing the causes of war in general rather than those of a particular war, he focuses primarily on ultimate and fundamental causes rather than immediate, overt actions.

I. Perspective

In the year 1830 a French customs official unearthed, in the valley of the Somme, strange implements of flint now recognized by the learned as the weapons with which the men of the Old Stone Age made war. These stones are called *coups de poing*, or "blows of the fist," for one end was rounded to be grasped in the hand, while the other end was pointed for persuasion. With these modest tools of death, it seems, Neanderthal men from what is now Germany, and Cro-Magnon men from what is now France, fought fifty thousand years ago for the mastery of the continent, and, after a day of lusty battle, left perhaps a score of dead on the field. Twenty years ago, modern Germans and modern Frenchmen fought again, in that same valley, for that same prize, with magnificent tools of death that killed ten thousand men in a day. One art alone has made indisputable progress in history, and that is the art of war.

For five hundred centuries, two thousand generations have struggled for that terrain in a calendar of wars whose beginning is as distant as its end. Our own children rest there, some of them, lured by fear or nobility into that ancient strife. Even the sophisticated mind, accustomed to magnitude and marvels, is appalled by the panorama of historic war, from the occasional brawls and raids of normally peaceful "savages," through the sanguinary annals of Sumer, Babylonia, and Assyria, the endless fratricide of the Greek city-states, the merciful conquests of Alexander and Caesar, the brutal triumphs of Imperial Rome, the holy carnage of expanding Islam, the glorious slaughters of Genghis Khan, Tamerlane's pyramid of skulls, the destruction of Vijayanagar, the Hundred Years' War, the War of the Spanish Succession, the Seven Years' War, the English, American, French, and Russian Revolutions, the Civil Wars of England and America, the Napoleonic Wars, the War of 1812, the Crimean War, the Franco-Prussian

Marginal notes:
1 Reference to authority

Strong introduction to topic with analogies, examples, historical evidence

2 Historical evidence

Paragraph is a catalogue of examples.

War, the Spanish-American War, the Boer War, the Russo-Japanese War, the First World War, the suicide of Spain, the Sino-Japanese War, the Second World War. . . . This, in our pessimistic moments, seems to be the main and bloody current of history, beside which all the achievements of civilization, all the illumination of letters and the arts, all the tenderness of women and the courtesies of men, are but graceful incidents on the bank, helpless to change the course or character of the stream.

Suggestion of inevitability of war to be developed into thesis: human instincts as the causes of war

. . . war has always been. Will it always be? What are its causes in the nature of men and in the structure of societies? What are its effects, for good or evil, upon the soul, the species, and the state? Can it be prevented, or diminished in frequency, or in any measure controlled? Let us consider these questions as objectively as may be permitted to men and women standing on the brink of what may be the most brutal war that history has ever known.

3 Questions to elicit thesis statement

Signal of intention

Reference to reason and fact as evidence

II. *Causes*

The causes of war are psychological, biological, economic, and political—that is, they lie in the impulses of men, the competition of groups, the material needs of societies, and fluctuations of national power.

4 Thesis statement expresses four causes and organizational plan: from ultimate to more immediate causes

The basic causes are in ourselves, for the state is an enlarged picture of the soul. The five major instincts of mankind—food-getting, mating, parental love, fighting, and association—are the ultimate sources of war. Our inveterate habit of eating is the oldest and deepest cause of war. For thousands, perhaps millions, of years, men were uncertain of their food supply. Not knowing yet the bounty of the soil, they trusted to the fortunes of the hunt. Having captured prey, they tore or cut it to pieces, often on the spot, and gorged themselves to their cubic

5 Ultimate cause: psychological

Five subdivisions of psychological cause

Food: oldest of ultimate causes

capacity with the raw flesh and the hot gore; how could they tell when they might eat again? Greed is eating, or hoarding, for the future; wealth is originally a hedge against starvation; war is at first a raid for food. All vices were once virtues, indispensable in the struggle for existence; they became vices only in the degree to which social order and increasing security rendered them unnecessary for survival. Once men had to chase, to kill, to grasp, to overeat, to hoard; a hundred milleniums of insecurity bred into the race those acquisitive and possessive impulses which no laws or ideals, but only centuries of security, can mitigate or destroy.

Causal chain: food-getting → insecurity → acquisitiveness → war

The desire for mates and the love of children write half of the private history of mankind, but they have only rarely been the direct causes of war. The fighting instinct enters more obviously into the analysis, even if it operates most freely in persons above the military age. Nature develops it vigorously as an aid in getting or keeping food or mates; it arms every animal with organs of offense and defense, and lends to the physically weaker species the advantages of cunning and association. Since, by and large, those individuals and groups survived that excelled in food-getting, mate-getting, caring for children, and fighting, these instincts have been selected and intensified with every generation, and have budded into a hundred secondary forms of acquisition, venery, kindliness, and contention.

6 Second and third subdivisions

Signal of cause

Effect

As the quest for food has grown into the amassing of great fortunes, so the fighting instinct has swelled into the lust for power and the waging of war. The lust for power is in most men a wholesome stimulus to ambition and creation, but in exceptional men, dressed in great and lasting authority, it becomes a dangerous disease, an elephantiasis of the soul, which goads them on to fight a thousand battles by proxy. . . .

7 Signal of cause-effect: *as . . . so*

Lust for power → waging of war

Metaphor of illness for power

. . . Men fear solitude, and naturally seek the protection of numbers. Slowly a society develops within whose guarded frontiers men are

8 Fifth subdivision of psychological causes

free to live peaceably, to accumulate knowledge and goods, and to worship their gods. Since our self-love overflows into love of our parents and children, our homes and possessions, our habits and institutions, our wonted environment and transmitted faith, we form in time an emotional attachment for the nation and the civilization of which these are constituent parts; and when any of them is threatened, our instinct of pugnacity is aroused to the limit determined by the natural cowardice of mankind. Such patriotism is reasonable and necessary, for without it the group could not survive, and the individual could not survive without the groups. Prejudice is fatal to philosophy, but indispensable to a people. . . .

Signal of cause

Third cause: patriotic attachment to group

Put all these passions together, gather into one force the acquisitiveness, pugnacity, egoism, egotism, affection, and lust for power of a hundred million souls, and you have the psychological sources of war. It may be that these sources are not completely instinctive, not inevitably rooted in the blood; contemporary psychology is chary of instincts, and suspects that many of them are but habits formed in early years through the imitation of corrupt adults. . . .

9

Interim summary: psychological causes of war

These psychological impulses, taken in their social mass, become the biological sources of war. The group, too, as well as the individual, can be hungry or angry, ambitious or proud; the group, too, must struggle for existence, and be eliminated or survive. The protective fertility of organisms soon multiples mouths beyond the local food supply; the hunger of the parts, as in the body, becomes the hunger of the whole, and species wars against species, group against group, for lands or waters that may give more support to abounding life. Euripides, twenty-three hundred years ago, attributed the Trojan War to the rapid multiplication of the Greeks. "States that have a surplus population," said the ancient Stoic philosopher Chrysippus, "send great numbers out to colonies, and stir up wars against their neighbors." If that was the case when infanticide and Greek friendship were tolerated as means of controlling population, con-

10

Repetition of key term
Second cause of war: biological
Causal chain: desire to reproduce and increase species → overpopulation for local food supply → wars to increase land → increased birthrate to supply soldiers → increased population requires more land to feed and support population

Evidence of historical record

Signals of condition and Effect: *If . . . the results*

sider the results where statesmen encourage fertility. For then the birth rate must be raised to provide soldiers for war; war must be waged to conquer land for an expanding population; and population expands because the birth rate is so high: It is a very pinwheel of logic, bright and frail, a form of reasoning puzzlingly whimsical until we add its concealed premise—the will to power.

Group hunger begets group pugnacity, 11 and pugnacity develops in the group, as in the individual, organs of protection and attack. In the group these are called armament, and when they are powerful, they may themselves, like the boy's biceptual consciousness become a secondary source of war. On either scale some armament is necessary, for struggle is inevitable, and competition is the trade of life. The tragedy of our ideals is that we hitch them to the falling stars of equality and peace, while nature blithely bases her inescapable machinery of development upon difference and inequality of endowment and ability, upon competition and war. What chance have our ideals, nurtured in the mutual aid of the family, against that supremist court of all? Even mutual aid becomes an organ of struggle: We cooperate as individuals that we may the better compete as groups; morality and order have been developed because they strengthened the group in the inexorable competition of the world. Only when another star attacks us will the earth know internal peace; only a war of the planets can produce, for a moment, the brotherhood of man.

Causal chain: to survive, the group arms itself → armaments become a source of war: a necessary cause

Support by analogy

These psychological and biological forces 12 are the ultimate origins of human conflict. From them flow the national rivalries that generate the proximate causes of war—those economic and political causes with which superficial analysis so readily contents itself.

Interim summary

Introduction of immediate (proximate) causes of war: economic, political.

The basic economic cause is rivalry for 13 land: land to receive a designedly expanding population, land to provide material resources, land to open up new subjects to conscription and taxation. So the ancient Greeks fought their

Basic economic cause: land rivalry—three aspects

Examples from history

way through the Aegean isles to the coasts of Asia Minor and the Black Sea, and through the Mediterranean to Africa, Sicily, Italy, France, and Spain; so the English spread through the world in the last two centuries; so the Italians begin to spread today. There is, in history, a law of colonial expansion almost as explosive as any law of expansion in physics: Whenever a population fails to exploit the resources of its soil, it will sooner or later be conquered by a people able to exploit those resources, and to pour them into the commerce and uses of mankind.

These ancient provocations to conquest have been sharpened and magnified by the Industrial Revolution. To make war successfully a modern nation must be wealthy; to be wealthy it must develop industry; to maintain industry it must, in most cases, import food, fuel, and raw materials; to pay for these it must export manufactured goods; to sell these it must find foreign markets; to win these it must undersell its competitors or wage successful war. As likely as not, it will make war for any of the goods it must import, or for control of the routes by which it imports them. . . .

14 Contributory causal chain: war demands wealth → wealth demands industry → industry demands imports → paying for imports demands exports → exporting demands markets → markets demand control, often by war

The business cycle adds its own contribution to the causes of modern war. Since men are by nature unequal—some strong and some weak, some able and some (as they tell us) virtuous—it follows that in any society a majority of abilities will be possessed by a minority of men; from which it follows that sooner or later, in any society, a majority of goods will be possessed by a minority of men. But this natural concentration of wealth impedes the wide spread of purchasing power among the people; production, perpetually accelerated by invention, leaps ahead of consumption; surpluses rise and generate either depression or war. For either production must stop to let consumption catch up, or foreign markets must be found to take the surplus unbought at home. Foreign markets can be secured by underselling competitors or defeating them in war. To undersell our competitors is impracticable; our standard of living is too high for that; to lower it to the level of Japan's would

15 Second economic cause: business cycles

Logical reasoning: causal chain analyzes unequal distribution of wealth and its effects bring revolution; apparently the choice is between depression and war. But another major depression, possibly made worse through the increased displacement of costly labor by economical machines, might also bring revolution. What is left but war—or an unprecedented change in the behavior of men?

Add a few political causes, and our recipe for war will be complete. The first law of governments is self-preservation: their appetite grows by what they feed on, and they are seldom content. But further, the distribution of power among nations is always changing—through the discovery or development of new natural resources, through the rise or decline of population, through the weakening of religion, morals, and character, or through some other material, or biological, or psychological circumstance; and the nation that has become strong soon asserts itself over the nation that has become weak. Hence the impossibility of writing a peace pact that will perpetuate a *status quo;* hence the absurdity of Article X of the League of Nations Covenant; hence the failure of sanctions and the breakdown of the Treaty of Versailles. Excellent indeed is the peace treaty that does not generate a war.

These, then, are the causes of war. How natural it seems now, in the perspective of science and history; how ancient its source and how inscrutable its destiny!

Is it any wonder that peace is so often but invisible war, in which the nations rest only to fight again?

16   Fourth cause of war: political—two sources
Signal of intention: *add a few*

Signals of effects of political causes: *hence*

17   Summary

18   Conclusion with rhetorical question

Analysis of the Essay

THE PROCESS OF CAUSAL ANALYSIS

Writing in the post–World War II period, Durant selects examples of war from both the distant and the immediate past to illustrate his assertions about the causes of war.

Ultimate Causes.   Durant's introductory "Perspective" presents a sampling of the wars that have plagued our society for over two thousand generations. His thesis statement groups the causes of war into four broad categories by order of their deep-rootedness in the human condition. He treats these causes in the order in which he announces them in the thesis paragraph.

The first cause, the psychological nature of human beings, is divided into five major instincts, each of which is developed through appropriate examples. Durant indicates the importance of the food-getting instinct not only by the length and complexity of its treatment but also by its characterization as ultimate, primary, and basic (paragraph 5). The psychological bases for war are related in a causal chain to the next most deep-rooted cause of war, the biological; these two causes together form the "ultimate origins of human conflict" (paragraph 12).

Generated by these ultimate or primary causes of war are the economic and political causes, which Durant characterizes as "proximate," meaning close or immediate. The economic cause is subdivided into rivalry for land, which has three different aspects, and business cycles. Durant explains that the political causes of war have two sources: self-preservation and the changing distribution of power.

Evidence.   Durant traces the ultimate causes of war to the psychological and biological makeup of the human species. As evidence he suggests an analogy between the genetic instincts of animals and the motivations for human action. A second type of evidence, used throughout the essay, is the historical record. Durant includes not only his own citations from history but also those of writers of the past. He refers, for example, to Euripides' attribution of the Trojan War to the overpopulation of the Greeks. As a historian himself, Durant does not feel the need to refer to other authorities for insights or interpretations. He does, however, employ his own logical reasoning in the form of cause-and-effect details (paragraph 6), causal chains (5, 10, 14), and interpretation of social or economic events (15) as a significant part of his evidence.

Techniques of Coherence.   Intending to reach a broad audience, Durant pays close attention to coherence, providing his readers with signals to the content and organization of his analysis. After a strong, clear introduction enhanced by a vivid and apt illustration and a long list of examples, he announces his major subtopics—the four causes of war—and employs deductive paragraphs with unambiguous subtopic statements as he arrives at each new point. He uses restatement and interim summary to remind the reader of his key points (9, 11, 12) and signals of intention to introduce new ideas (3, 16). Throughout the essay, signals such as *since, cause,* and *hence* keep connections clear. The essay is framed by opening and closing questions.

READINGS

THOMAS JEFFERSON
The Declaration of Independence

Thomas Jefferson (1743–1826), third president of the
United States, was a delegate to the Second Continental
Congress (1775–1776), where he served as a member of
the committee to draft a declaration of independence.
Jefferson planned the document in two parts. In the pre-
amble, he restated the familiar contract theory of English Enlightenment philosopher John Locke, who had
held that governments were formed to protect the rights
of life, liberty, and property. Jefferson humanized Locke's
theory, however, by referring instead to the rights of
"life, liberty, and the pursuit of happiness." In the second part of the declaration, he listed the alleged crimes
of the British king, who, with the backing of Parliament, had violated his contract with the colonists,
thereby forfeiting all claims to their loyalty and giving
them cause for revolution.

In Congress, July 4, 1776

When in the Course of human events, it becomes necessary for one people 1
to dissolve the political bands which have connected them with another,
and to assume among the powers of the earth, the separate and equal station to which the Laws of Nature and of Nature's God entitle them, a
decent respect to the opinions of mankind requires that they should declare the causes which impel them to the separation.

We hold these truths to be self-evident, that all men are created 2
equal, that they are endowed by their Creator with certain unalienable
Rights, that among these are Life, Liberty, and the pursuit of Happiness.

That to secure these rights, Governments are instituted among 3
Men, deriving their just powers from the consent of the governed.

That whenever any Form of Government becomes destructive of 4
these ends, it is the Right of the People to alter or to abolish it, and to
institute new Government, laying its foundation on such principles and
organizing its powers in such form, as to them shall seem most likely to

effect their Safety and Happiness. Prudence, indeed, will dictate that Governments long established should not be changed for light and transient causes; and accordingly all experience hath shewn, that mankind are more disposed to suffer, while evils are sufferable, than to right themselves by abolishing the forms to which they are accustomed. But when a long train of abuses and usurpations, pursuing invariably the same Object evinces a design to reduce them under absolute Despotism, it is their right, it is their duty, to throw off such Government, and to provide new Guards for their future security.

Such has been the patient sufferance of these Colonies; and such is 5 now the necessity which constrains them to alter their former Systems of Government. The history of the present King of Great Britain is a history of repeated injuries and usurpations, all having in direct object the establishment of an absolute Tyranny over these States. To prove this, let Facts be submitted to a candid world.

He has refused his Assent to Laws, the most wholesome and neces- 6 sary for the public good.

He has forbidden his Governors to pass Laws of immediate and 7 pressing importance, unless suspended in their operation till his Assent should be obtained; and when so suspended, he has utterly neglected to attend to them.

He has refused to pass other Laws for the accommodation of large 8 districts of people, unless those people would relinquish the right of Representation in the Legislature, a right inestimable to them and formidable to tyrants only.

He has called together legislative bodies at places unusual, uncom- 9 fortable, and distant from the depository of their public Records, for the sole purpose of fatiguing them into compliance with his measures.

He has dissolved Representative Houses repeatedly, for opposing 10 with manly firmness his invasions on the rights of the people.

He has refused for a long time, after such dissolutions, to cause 11 others to be elected; whereby the Legislative powers, incapable of Annihilation, have returned to the People at large for their exercise; the State remaining in the mean time exposed to all the dangers of invasion from without, and convulsions within.

He has endeavored to prevent the population of these States; for that 12 purpose obstructing the Laws for Naturalization of Foreigners; refusing to pass others to encourage their migrations hither, and raising the conditions of new Appropriations of Lands.

He has obstructed the Administration of Justice, by refusing his As- 13 sent to Laws for establishing Judiciary powers.

He has made Judges dependent on his Will alone, for the tenure of 14 their offices, and the amount and payment of their salaries.

He has erected a multitude of New Offices, and sent hither swarms 15 of Officers to harass our people, and eat out their substance.

He has kept among us, in times of peace, Standing Armies without 16
the Consent of our legislatures.

He has affected to render the Military independent of and superior 17
to the Civil power.

He has combined with others[1] to subject us to a jurisdiction foreign 18
to our constitution, and unacknowledged by our laws; giving his Assent
to their Acts of pretended Legislation:

For Quartering large bodies of armed troops among us: 19

For protecting them, by a mock Trial, from punishment for any 20
Murders which they should commit on the Inhabitants of these States:

For cutting off our Trade with all parts of the world: 21

For imposing Taxes on us without our Consent: 22

For depriving us in many cases, of the benefits of Trial by Jury: 23

For transporting us beyond Seas to be tried for pretended offenses: 24

For abolishing the free System of English Laws in a neighboring 25
Province establishing therein an Arbitrary government, and enlarging its
Boundaries so as to render it at once an example and fit instrument for
introducing the same absolute rule into these Colonies:

For taking away our Charters, abolishing our most valuable Laws, 26
and altering fundamentally the Forms of our Governments:

For suspending our own Legislatures, and declaring themselves in- 27
vested with power to legislate for us in all cases whatsoever.

He has abdicated Government here, by declaring us out of his Pro- 28
tection and waging War against us:

He has plundered our seas, ravaged our Coasts, burnt our towns, 29
and destroyed the lives of our people.

He is at this time transporting large Armies of foreign Mercenaries 30
to compleat the works of death, desolation and tyranny, already begun
with circumstances of Cruelty & perfidy scarcely paralleled in the most
barbarous ages, and totally unworthy the Head of a civilized nation.

He has constrained our fellow Citizens taken Captive on the high 31
Seas to bear Arms against their Country, to become the executioners of
their friends and Brethren, or to fall themselves by their Hands.

He has excited domestic insurrections amongst us, and has endeav- 32
oured to bring on the inhabitants of our frontiers, the merciless Indian
Savages, whose known rule of warfare, is an undistinguished destruction
of all ages, sexes and conditions. In every stage of these Oppressions We
have Petitioned for Redress in the most humble terms: Our repeated Peti-
tions have been answered only by repeated injury. A Prince, whose character is thus marked by every act which may define a Tyrant, is unfit to be
the ruler of a free people. Nor have We been wanting in attentions to our
British brethren. We have warned them from time to time of attempts by
their legislature to extend an unwarrantable jurisdiction over us. We have

---

1. The British Parliament.

reminded them of the circumstances of our emigration and settlement here. We have appealed to their native justice and magnanimity, and we have conjured them by the ties of our common kindred to disavow these usurpations, which, would inevitably interrupt our connections and correspondence. They too have been deaf to the voice of justice and of consanguinity. We must, therefore, acquiesce in the necessity, which denounces our Separation, and hold them, as we hold the rest of mankind, Enemies in War, in Peace Friends.

We, therefore, the Representatives of the United States of America, 33 in General Congress Assembled, appealing to the Supreme Judge of the world for the rectitude of our intentions, do, in the Name and by Authority of the good People of these Colonies, solemnly publish and declare, That these United Colonies are, and of Right ought to be Free and Independent States; that they are Absolved from all Allegiance to the British Crown, and that all political connection between them and the State of Great Britain, is and ought to be totally dissolved; and that as Free and Independent States, they have full Power to levy War, conclude Peace, contract Alliances, establish Commerce, and to do all other Acts and Things which Independent States may of right do.

And for the support of this Declaration, with a firm reliance on the 34 protection of divine Providence, we mutually pledge to each other our Lives, our Fortunes and our sacred Honor.

Reading and Interpreting

VOCABULARY

Use your dictionary as necessary to find the meaning of the following words as used by Jefferson:

usurpations (4)	constrains (5)	formidable (8)	quartering (19)
arbitrary (25)	redress (32)	consanguinity (32)	rectitude (33)

CONCEPT ANALYSIS

1. What is the purpose of this document? Cite the passage that announces its intention.
2. The colonists personalize their grievances against the king as a despot. Can you give examples of modern conflicts that have focused on a particular individual as a symbol of a political philosophy or system?
3. Is it enough to change the ruler without changing the system? If King George had been more liberal toward the colonists, might they have

accepted an autonomous but not independent relationship with Britain, as did Canada and Australia? Or does the Declaration suggest other causes that would have made separation inevitable? If so, what are they?

Thinking and Writing

RHETORICAL TECHNIQUE

1. Which portion of the Declaration of Independence gives the fundamental, underlying reasons for the colonies' separation from England? What appears to be the most immediate inciting cause? Do you see any pattern in the order of causes?
2. Classify several of the causes of the colonists' declaration of independence into logical categories (for example, administrative, economic, social, legal). If you perceive causal chains, outline them. In your opinion, are there grievances that the colonists might have tolerated?
3. What form of evidence do the colonists submit to justify the dissolution of their union with England? How would you characterize that evidence: strong or weak? Explain your response.

COMPOSITION

Write an essay of effect based on the hypothetical situation that the British defeated the American colonists in the War for Independence. Include both positive and negative results. You may want to draw some analogies with the British Commonwealth nations.

ROSS K. BAKER

Why Jefferson Fainted

Ross K. Baker is a professor of political science at Rutgers University. His satire on Jefferson's Declaration of Independence gives us an insight into the power of language when it is honest and clear.

When at a given point in time in the human events cycle, the phase-out of 1
political relationships is mandated, a clear signal needs to be communicated to the world as to why we are putting independence on-line.

Truthwise, it has been apparent for some time that human resources 2
should be accorded equal treatment and that they are eligible for certain
entitlements, that among them are viability, liberty and the capability of
accessing happiness.

That, to secure this package of benefits, governments are normally 3
established, but only after adequate levels of citizen participation.

If that government begins to impact adversely on the citizens, it is 4
their right to modify the entire structure and come up with a new set of
options that will have a significant positive effect. Governments can usually hold the line when they are counterproductive or even when they tilt
toward tyranny. Citizens will typically not phase-out governments over
issues that are on the margins. But when a picture begins to emerge of a
government that wants to go forward with a program of despotism, there
is a clear mandate to terminate that government and to begin long-range
planning for the out-years.

These Colonies have engaged in flexible dialogue with the Govern- 5
ment of Great Britain, but the latest set of guidelines to emerge from London does not seem workable. The track record of the current King is one
that is chronically in a state of noncompliance. The data to support these
charges are presented below so as to facilitate the assessment of a candid world.

He has refused to facilitate credible and meaningful legislation.   6

He has forbidden his Governors to crank in crash programs unless he 7
has first interfaced with them.

His scheduling of legislative sessions is counterproductive time- 8
frame-wise.

He has refused to provide us with guidance on immigration and 9
naturalization policy.

He has assumed a low profile on funding the justice system.   10

He has caused shortfalls to occur in the salaries of judges.   11

He has authorized a proliferation of new administrative slots and 12
sent those staffers here to harass us and to over-utilize our resources.

He has upgraded troop strength without legislative input.   13

For assigning substantial numbers of British service personnel to 14
duty stations in American households;

For holding them harmless and granting them immunity from the 15
judicial process;

For capping our trade with all parts of the world;   16

For enhancing his revenues without our consent;   17

For cutting travel orders for us to offshore destinations where we 18
would be put at risk by foreign juries;

For modifying the parameters of our governmental system.   19

Military options have been prioritized and peaceful options down- 20
graded by him.

He has begun, at this point in time, to task teams of uniformed 21
third parties, operating under a consulting agreement with the Grand
Duke of Hesse-Darmstadt, for insertion into this country for the purpose
of terminating us with extreme prejudice.

The lives of Americans of all age groups have been prematurely cur- 22
tailed by members of an armed minority group deployed at his direction.

A King with such a performance record is not cost-effective as the 23
supervisor of a free people.

We generated a number of proposals and communicated them. We 24
presented the big picture to them and attempted to fine-tune our negotiations based on our common ethnicity. But they refused to monitor our
grievances and backed off from an in-depth evaluation of the outstanding
issues that divide us. Countermeasures, accordingly, should be directed
against them.

We, therefore, representatives of the States in Congress assembled, 25
appealing to the Supervisor of All Manpower, declare the termination of
all further political relationship between these Colonies and Great Britain,
to be implemented at the close of business today; that, as free and independent states, we have the full power to conduct and/or terminate military operations, maximize foreign trade and develop such other projects,
programs and activities as independent states may of a right do. And, to
come quickly to the bottom line, with a significant input in the form of
forecasts and projections from the Office of Divine Providence, we mutually pledge to each other our support services, our resource bases and our
sacred credibility.

Reading and Interpreting

VOCABULARY

Use your dictionary as necessary to find the meaning of the following words
in context:

mandated (1)   proliferation (12)   parameters (19)

CONCEPT ANALYSIS

1. Vivid, concrete language presents causes for an action more clearly than
   abstractions. Contrast the "executive summary" with the original Declaration of Independence. Consider the following pairs of items. Which
   version is more powerful? Why? Can you find other interesting contrasts
   in language?

a. Jefferson: "The history of the present King of Great Britain is a history of repeated injuries and usurpations, all having in direct object the establishment of an absolute Tyranny over these States." (5)

   Baker: "The track record of the current King is one that is chronically in a state of noncompliance." (5)

b. Jefferson: "He has erected a multitude of New Offices, and sent hither swarms of Officers to harass our people, and eat out their substance." (15)

   Baker: "He has authorized a proliferation of new administrative slots and sent those staffers here to harass us and to over-utilize our resources." (12)

c. Jefferson: "For Quartering large bodies of armed troops among us." (19)

   Baker: "For assigning substantial numbers of British service personnel to duty stations in American households." (14)

d. Jefferson: "He is at this time transporting large Armies of foreign Mercenaries to compleat the works of death, desolation and tyranny, already begun with circumstances of Cruelty & perfidy scarcely paralleled in the most barbarous ages. . . ." (30)

   Baker: "He has begun, at this point in time, to task teams of uniformed third parties, operating under a consulting agreement with the Grand Duke of Hesse-Darmstadt, for insertion into this country for the purpose of terminating us with extreme prejudice." (21)

2. Why would a modern corporate executive committee, presenting the reasons for a decisive action, use language that is verbose, imprecise, polysyllabic, timid, and full of bureaucratic jargon rather than the language of ordinary speech?

3. The language of the executive committee version is different from that of the original Declaration. Do the values expressed remain the same? Explain.

Quickwrite

Write a declaration of independence in current student slang.

BRUCE CATTON
The Civil War

American historian Bruce Catton (1899–1978) is admired by academics and general readers alike for his ability to portray complex historical events in terms of what they meant for the individuals involved. This special ability, as well as the clarity of his writing, is demonstrated in this excerpt on the sources of discord that led to the Civil War.

The American people in 1860 believed that they were the happiest and 1
luckiest people in all the world, and in a way they were right. Most of
them lived on farms or in very small towns, they lived better than their
fathers had lived, and they knew that their children would do still better.
The landscape was predominantly rural, with unending sandy roads winding leisurely across a country which was both drowsy with enjoyment of
the present and vibrant with eagerness to get into the future. The average
American then was in fact what he has been since only in legend, an independent small farmer, and in 1860—for the last time in American history—the products of the nation's farms were worth more than the output
of its factories.

This may or may not have been the end of America's golden age, but 2
it was at least the final, haunted moment of its age of innocence. Most
Americans then, difficult as the future might appear, supposed that this
or something like it would go on and on, perhaps forever. Yet infinite
change was beginning, and problems left unsolved too long would presently make the change explosive, so that the old landscape would be
blown to bits forever, with a bewildered people left to salvage what they
could. Six hundred thousand young Americans, alive when 1860 ended,
would die of this explosion in the next four years.

At bottom the coming change simply meant that the infinite fer- 3
ment of the industrial revolution was about to work its way with a tremendously energetic and restless people who had a virgin continent to
exploit. One difficulty was that two very different societies had developed
in America, one in the North and the other in the South, which would
adjust themselves to the industrial age in very different ways. Another
difficulty was that the differences between these two societies were most
infernally complicated by the existence in the South of the institution of
chattel slavery. Without slavery, the problems could probably have been

worked out by the ordinary give-and-take of politics; with slavery, they became insoluble. So in 1861 the North and the South went to war, destroying one America and beginning the building of another which is not even yet complete.

In the beginning slavery was no great problem. It had existed all across colonial America, it died out in the North simply because it did not pay, and at the turn of the century most Americans, North and South alike, considered that eventually it would go out of existence everywhere. But in 1793 Yankee Eli Whitney had invented the cotton gin—a simple device which made it possible for textile mills to use the short-staple cotton which the Southern states could grow so abundantly—and in a very short time the whole picture changed. The world just then was developing an almost limitless appetite for cotton, and in the deep South enormous quantities of cotton could be raised cheaply with slave labor. Export figures show what happened. In 1800 the United States had exported $5,000,000 worth of cotton—7 per cent of the nation's total exports. By 1810 this figure had tripled, by 1840 it had risen to $63,000,000, and by 1860 cotton exports were worth $191,000,000—57 per cent of the value of all American exports. The South had become a cotton empire, nearly four million slaves were employed, and slavery looked like an absolutely essential element in Southern prosperity.

But if slavery paid, it left men with uneasy consciences. This unease became most obvious in the North, where a man who demanded the abolition of slavery could comfort himself with the reflection that the financial loss which abolition would entail would, after all, be borne by somebody else—his neighbor to the south. In New England the fanatic William Lloyd Garrison opened a crusade, denouncing slavery as a sin and slaveowners as sinners. More effective work to organize antislavery sentiment was probably done by such Westerners as James G. Birney and Theodore Weld, but Garrison made the most noise—and, making it, helped to arouse most intense resentment in the South. Southerners liked being called sinners no better than anyone else. Also, they undeniably had a bear by the tail. By 1860 slave property was worth at least two billion dollars, and the abolitionists who insisted that this property be outlawed were not especially helpful in showing how this could be done without collapsing the whole Southern economy. In a natural reaction to all of this, Southerners closed ranks. It became first unhealthy and then impossible for anyone in the South to argue for the end of slavery; instead, the institution was increasingly justified as a positive good. Partly from economic pressure and partly in response to the shrill outcries of men like Garrison, the South bound itself to slavery.

Yet slavery (to repeat) was not the only source of discord. The two sections were very different, and they wanted different things from their national government.

In the North society was passing more rapidly than most men real- 7
ized to an industrial base. Immigrants were arriving by the tens of thousands, there were vast areas in the West to be opened, men who were
developing new industries demanded protection from cheap European imports, systems of transportation and finance were mushrooming in a fantastic manner—and, in short, this dynamic society was beginning to
clamor for all sorts of aid and protection from the Federal government at
Washington.

In the South, by contrast, society was much more static. There was 8
little immigration, there were not many cities, the factory system showed
few signs of growth, and this cotton empire which sold in the world market wanted as many cheap European imports as it could get. To please the
South, the national government must keep its hands off as many things as
possible; for many years Southerners had feared that if the North ever won
control in Washington it would pass legislation ruinous to Southern
interests.

John C. Calhoun of South Carolina had seen this first and most 9
clearly. Opposing secession, he argued that any state could protect its interests by nullifying, within its own borders, any act by the Federal government which it considered unconstitutional and oppressive. Always
aware that the North was the faster-growing section, the South foresaw
the day when the North would control the government. Then, Southerners believed, there would be legislation—a stiff high-tariff law, for instance—that would ruin the South. More and more, they developed the
theory of states' rights as a matter of self-protection.

Although there were serious differences between the sections, all of 10
them except slavery could have been settled through the democratic process. Slavery poisoned the whole situation. It was the issue that could not
be compromised, the issue that made men so angry they did not want to
compromise. It put a cutting edge on all arguments. It was not the only
cause of the Civil War, but it was unquestionably the one cause without
which the war would not have taken place. The antagonism between the
sections came finally, and tragically, to express itself through the slavery issue.

Many attempts to compromise this issue had been made. All of 11
them worked for a while; none of them lasted. Perhaps the most that can
be said is that they postponed the conflict until the nation was strong
enough—just barely so—to survive the shock of civil war.

There had been the Missouri Compromise, in 1820, when North 12
and South argued whether slavery should be permitted in the land acquired by the Louisiana Purchase. Missouri was admitted as a slave state,
but it was decreed that thereafter there should be no new slave states north
of the parallel that marked Missouri's southern boundary. Men hoped that
this would end the whole argument, although dour John Quincy Adams

wrote that he considered the debate over the compromise nothing less than "a title-page to a great, tragic volume."

Then there was the Compromise of 1850, which followed the war 13 with Mexico. . . . California was to be admitted as a free state, the territories of New Mexico and Utah were created without reference to the Wilmot Proviso, the slave trade in the District of Columbia was abolished, and a much stiffer act to govern the return of fugitive slaves was adopted. Neither North nor South was entirely happy with this program, but both sections accepted it in the hope that the slavery issue was now settled for good.

This hope promptly exploded. Probably nothing did more to create 14 anti-Southern, antislavery sentiment in the North than the Fugitive Slave Act. It had an effect precisely opposite to the intent of its backers: it aroused Northern sentiment in favor of the runaway slave, and probably caused a vast expansion in the activities of the Underground Railroad, the informal and all but unorganized system whereby Northern citizens helped Negro fugitives escape across the Canadian border. With this excitement at a high pitch, Harriet Beecher Stowe in 1852 brought out her novel *Uncle Tom's Cabin,* which sold three hundred thousand copies in its first year, won many converts to the antislavery position in the North, and, by contrast, aroused intense new resentment in the South.

On the heels of all this, in 1854 Senator Stephen A. Douglas of Illi- 15 nois introduced the fateful Kansas-Nebraska Act, which helped to put the whole controversy beyond hope of settlement. . . .

. . . When [Stephen Douglas] brought in a bill to create the ter- 16 ritories of Kansas and Nebraska he put in two special provisions. One embodied the idea of "popular sovereignty"—the concept that the people of each territory would decide for themselves, when time for statehood came, whether to permit or exclude slavery—and the other specifically repealed the Missouri Compromise. The South took the bait, the bill was passed— and the country moved a long stride nearer to war. . . .

For the Kansas-Nebraska Act raised the argument over slavery to 17 desperate new intensity. The moderates could no longer be heard; the stage was set for the extremists, the fire-eaters, the men who invited violence with violent words. Many Northerners, previously friendly to the South, now came to feel that the "slave power" was dangerously aggressive, trying not merely to defend slavery where it already existed but to extend it all across the national domain. Worse yet, Kansas was thrown open for settlement under conditions which practically guaranteed bloodshed.

Settlers from the North were grimly determined to make Kansas 18 free soil; Southern settlers were equally determined to win Kansas for slavery. . . .

Now the Supreme Court added its bit. It had before it the case of 19 Dred Scott, a Negro slave whose master, an army surgeon, had kept him for some years in Illinois and Wisconsin, where there was no slavery. Scott sued for his freedom, and in 1857 Chief Justice Roger Taney delivered the Court's opinion. That Scott's plea for freedom was denied was no particular surprise, but the grounds on which the denial was based stirred the North afresh. A Negro of slave descent, said Taney, was an inferior sort of person who could not be a citizen of any state and hence could not sue anyone; furthermore, the act by which Congress had forbidden slavery in the Northern territories was invalid because the Constitution gave slavery ironclad protection. There was no legal way in which slavery could be excluded from any territory.

The 1850's were the tormented decade in American history. Always 20 the tension mounted, and no one seemed able to provide an easement. The Panic of 1857 left a severe business depression, and Northern pressure for higher tariff rates and a homestead act became stronger than ever. The depression had hardly touched the South, since world demand for cotton was unabated, and Southern leaders became more than ever convinced that their society and their economy were sounder and stronger than anything the North could show. There would be no tariff revision, and although Congress did pass a homestead act President James Buchanan, a Pennsylvanian but a strong friend of the South, promptly vetoed it. The administration, indeed, seemed unable to do anything. It could not even make a state out of Kansas, in which territory it was clear, by now, that a strong majority opposed slavery. The rising antagonism between the sections had almost brought paralysis to the Federal government.

And then old John Brown came out of the shadows to add the final 21 touch.

With a mere handful of followers, Brown undertook, on the night of 22 October 16, 1859, to seize the Federal arsenal at Harpers Ferry and with the weapons thus obtained to start a slave insurrection in the South. He managed to get possession of an engine-house, which he held until the morning of the eighteenth; then a detachment of U.S. marines—temporarily led by Colonel Robert E. Lee of the U.S. Army—overpowered him and snuffed out his crack-brained conspiracy with bayonets and clubbed muskets. Brown was quickly tried, was convicted of treason, and early in December he was hanged. But what he had done had a most disastrous effect on men's minds. To people in the South, it seemed that Brown confirmed their worst fears: this was what the Yankee abolitionists really wanted—a servile insurrection, with unlimited bloodshed and pillage, from one end of the South to the other! The fact that some vocal persons in the North persisted in regarding Brown as a martyr simply made matters worse. After the John Brown raid the chance that the bitter sectional argument could be harmonized faded close to the vanishing point. . . .

The road led steadily downhill after this. The Republicans won the 23 election, as they were bound to do under the circumstances. Lincoln got less than a majority of the popular votes, but a solid majority in the Electoral College, and on March 4, 1861, he would become President of the United States . . . but not, it quickly developed, of all of the states. Fearing the worst, the legislature of South Carolina had remained in session until after the election had been held. Once it saw the returns it summoned a state convention, and this convention, in Charleston on December 20, voted unanimously that South Carolina should secede from the Union.

This was the final catalytic agent. It was obvious that one small state 24 could not maintain its independence; equally obvious that if South Carolina should now be forced back into the Union no one in the South ever need talk again about secession. The cotton states, accordingly, followed suit. By February, South Carolina, had been joined by Mississippi, Alabama, Georgia, Florida, Louisiana, and Texas, and on February 8 delegates from the seceding states met at Montgomery, Alabama, and set up a new nation, the Confederate States of America. A provisional constitution was adopted (to be replaced in due time by a permanent document, very much like the Constitution of the United States), and Jefferson Davis of Mississippi was elected President, with Alexander Stephens of Georgia as Vice-President. . . .

So the last chance to settle the business had gone, except for the 25 things that might happen in the minds of two men—Abraham Lincoln and Jefferson Davis. They were strangers, very unlike each other, and yet there was an odd linkage. They were born not far apart in time or space; both came from Kentucky, near the Ohio River, and one man went south to become spokesman for the planter aristocracy, while the other went north to become representative of the best the frontier Northwest could produce. In the haunted decade that had just ended, neither man had been known as a radical. Abolitionists considered Lincoln too conservative, and Southern fire-eaters like South Carolina's Robert B. Rhett felt that Davis had been cold and unenthusiastic in regard to secession.

Now these two men faced one another, figuratively, across an ever- 26 widening gulf, and between them they would say whether a nation already divided by mutual misunderstanding would be torn apart physically by war.

Reading and Interpreting

VOCABULARY

Use your dictionary as necessary to find the meaning of the following words as used by Catton:

chattel (3)   unabated (20)   catalytic (24)   figuratively (26)

CONCEPT ANALYSIS

1. What, according to Catton, were the two main causes of the Civil War? Which was the immediate inciting and necessary cause? Cite the lines that explicitly state this.
2. Discuss the role of the cotton gin in the chain of causes of the Civil War.
3. What were the several effects of the abolitionists' campaign? How did John Brown's raid become a contributory cause of the Civil War?
4. What is Catton referring to when he says in paragraph 24 that "This was the final catalytic agent"? What explanation does he give for this point?

Quickwrite

Both the Northern abolitionists and the Southern secessionists had a "cause" they were willing to fight for. Do you have such a cause? Write about either your reasons for believing in this cause or about the effects it has had on your life.

Thinking and Writing

RHETORICAL TECHNIQUE

1. Catton uses a causal chain to discuss the legislative attempts and failures at compromise as contributory causes of the Civil War. Outline this cause-and-effect chain.
2. Catton's scholarship provides a balanced view of the Northern and Southern perspectives on several points. Cite examples.
3. Catton reinforces his statement (paragraph 3) of the causes of the Civil War—slavery and sectionalism—with brief, clear topic statements, repetition of key concepts, and parallel constructions. Cite instances of his effective use of these devices of coherence.
4. Catton's style is flexible, encompassing both precise historical information and colloquial and figurative expressions. Find examples of colloquial and figurative expressions. What is their effect on his analysis?

COMPOSITION

1. Do the wounds of a civil war ever heal? In an essay discuss the effect of a contemporary or historical sectional conflict such as the "troubles" in Northern Ireland, the Vietnam and Korean wars, or the Indian-Pakistani partition.

2. Sectionalism, regional personality, and local pride may have effects in creative fields such as art, theater, music, and literature. Select one area of the United States and discuss how it has influenced a particular art form.
3. Write a personality sketch of your region of the country and discuss its causes.

ROBERT PENN WARREN

The Legacy of the Civil War

Kentucky-born poet and novelist Robert Penn Warren (b. 1905) is a writer concerned with Southern themes and characters. The moral earnestness that characterizes much of his fiction is evident in this essay, which places the Civil War in the broader perspective of national growth and the development of a new identity for the United States. His emphasis here is on the complex web of effects of the war, which he calls "the great single event of our history."

The Civil War is, for the American imagination, the great single event of our history. Without too much wrenching, it may, in fact, be said to *be* American history. Before the Civil War we had no history in the deepest and most inward sense. There was, of course, the noble vision of the Founding Fathers articulated in the Declaration and the Constitution— the dream of freedom incarnated in a more perfect union. But the Revolution did not create a nation except on paper; and too often in the following years the vision of the Founding Fathers, which men had suffered and died to validate, became merely a daydream of easy and automatic victories, a vulgar delusion of manifest destiny, a conviction of being a people divinely chosen to live on milk and honey at small expense. 1

The vision had not been finally submitted to the test of history. There was little awareness of the cost of having a history. The anguished scrutiny of the meaning of the vision in experience had not become a national reality. It became a reality, and we became a nation only with the Civil War. 2

The Civil War is our only "felt" history—history lived in the na- 3 tional imagination. This is not to say that the War is always, and by all men, felt in the same way. Quite the contrary. But this fact is an index to the very complexity, depth, and fundamental significance of the event. It is an overwhelming and vital image of human, and national, experience. . . .

A second clear and objective fact is that the Civil War abolished 4 slavery, even if it did little or nothing to abolish racism; and in so doing removed the most obvious, if perhaps not the most important, impediment to union. However we may assess the importance of slavery in the tissue of "causes" of the Civil War—in relation to secession, the mounting Southern debt to the North, economic rivalry, Southern fear of encirclement, Northern ambitions, and cultural collisions—slavery looms up mountainously and cannot be talked away. It was certainly a necessary cause, to use the old textbook phrase, and provided the occasion for all the mutual vilification, rancor, self-righteousness, pride, spite, guilt, and general exacerbation of feeling that was the natural atmosphere of the event, the climate in which the War grew. With slavery out of the way, a new feeling about union was possible. . . .

The new nation came not merely from a military victory. It came 5 from many circumstances created or intensified by the War. The War enormously stimulated technology and productivity. Actually, it catapulted America from what had been in considerable part an agrarian, handicraft society into the society of Big Technology and Big Business. "Parallel with the waste and sorrows of war," as Allan Nevins puts it, "ran a stimulation of individual initiative, a challenge to large-scale planning, and an encouragement of co-operative effort, which in combination with new agencies for developing natural resources amounted to a great release of creative energy." The old sprawling, loosely knit country disappeared into the nation of Big Organization.

It is true that historians can debate the question whether, in the 6 long run and in the long perspective, war—even wars of that old preatomic age—can stimulate creativity and production. And it is true that there had been a surge of technological development in the decade or so before 1861, followed, some maintain, by an actual decline in inventiveness during the War. But the question is not how many new inventions were made but how the existing ones were used. The little device of the "jig," which, back in 1798, had enabled Eli Whitney to make firearms with interchangeable parts led now to the great mass-production factories of the Civil War—factories used not merely for firearms but for all sorts of products. The Civil War demanded the great American industrial plant, and the industrial plant changed American society.

To take one trivial fact, the ready-made clothing industry was an 7 offshoot of the mass production of blue uniforms—and would not this standardization of fashion, after the sartorial whim, confusion, fantasy and individualism of an earlier time, have some effect on man's relation to man? But to leap from the trivial to the grand, the War prepared the way for the winning of the West. Before the War a transcontinental railroad was already being planned, and execution was being delayed primarily by debate about the route to take, a debate which in itself sprang from, and contributed something to, the intersectional acrimony. After the War, debate did not long delay action. But the War did more than remove impediment to this scheme. It released enormous energies, new drives and know-how for the sudden and massive occupation of the continent. And for the great adventure there was a new cutting edge of profit.

Not only the industrial plant but the economic context in which industry could thrive came out of the War. The Morril tariff of 1861 actually preceded the firing on Sumter, but it was the mark of Republican victory and an omen of what was to come; and no session of Congress for the next four years failed to raise the tariff. Even more importantly came the establishment of a national banking system in place of the patchwork of state banks, and the issuing of national greenbacks to rationalize the crazy currency system of the state-bank notes. The new system, plus government subsidy, honed the cutting edge of profit. "The fact is that people have the money and they are looking around to see what to do with it," said the New York magnate William E. Dodge in a speech in Baltimore in 1865. At last, he said, there was indigenous capital to "develop the natural interests of the country." And he added, enraptured: "The mind staggers as we begin to contemplate the future." . . .   8

Not only New York bookkeeping but Washington bookkeeping was a new force for union. The war had cost money. Hamilton's dream of a national debt to insure national stability was realized, by issuing the bonds so efficiently peddled by Jay Cooke, to a degree astronomically beyond Hamilton's rosiest expectations. For one thing, this debt meant a new tax relation of the citizen to the Federal government, including the new income tax; the citizen had a new and poignant sense of the reality of Washington. But the great hand that took could also give, and with pensions and subsidies, the iron dome of the Capitol took on a new luster in the eyes of millions of citizens.   9

Furthermore, the War meant that Americans saw America. The farm boy of Ohio, the trapper of Minnesota, and the pimp of the Mackerelville section of New York City saw Richmond and Mobile. They not only saw America, they saw each other, and together shot it out with some Scot of the Valley of Virginia or ducked hardware hurled by a Louisiana Jew who might be a lieutenant of artillery, CSA. By the War, not only Virginia and Louisiana were claimed for the union. Ohio and Minnesota were, in fact, claimed too—claimed so effectively that for generations the memory of the Bloody Shirt and the GAR would prompt many a Middle-western farmer to vote almost automatically against his own interests.   10

But let us leave the Southerner and his War, and return to the more general effects of the War on American life. It formed, for example, the American concept of war, and since the day when Grant tried his bold   11 maneuver in the Wilderness and Lee hit him, military thinking at Washington has focused as much on problems of supply, transport, matériel, and attrition, as it ever did on problems of slashing tactics and grand strategy.

Furthermore, on land and sea, the Civil War was a war waged under 12 new conditions and in a new economic, technological, political and moral context. The rules in the textbooks did not help very much. The man whose mind could leap beyond the book was apt to win. It was a war fought, on both sides, with the experimental intelligence, the experimental imagination, not only in the arena of lethal contact, but in the very speculations about the nature of war. Out of the Civil War came the concept of total war, the key to Northern Victory. . . .

Union, the abolition of slavery, the explosion of the westward expan- 13 sion, Big Business and Big Technology, style in war, philosophy, and politics—we can see the effects of the Civil War in all of these things. In a sense they all add up to the creation of the world power that America is today. Between 1861 and 1865 America learned how to mobilize, equip, and deploy enormous military forces—and learned the will and confidence to do so. For most importantly, America emerged with a confirmed sense of destiny, the old sense of destiny confirmed by a new sense of military and economic competence. The Civil War was the secret school for 1917–18 and 1941–45. Neither the Kaiser nor the Führer had read the right history book of the United States.

Perhaps we ourselves shall not have read the right history book if we 14 think we can stop here and complacently cast our accounts with the past. Every victory has a price tag; every gain entails a loss, not merely the price of effort and blood to achieve the victory but the rejection, or destruction, of values which are incommensurable with the particular victory. All victories carry with them something of the irony of the fairy story of the three wishes; and even if we willingly settle for our victory we should, if we are wise, recognize that, as William James in "Pragmatism and Religion" puts it, "something permanently drastic and bitter always remains at the bottom of the cup."

With the War the old America, with all its virtues and defects, was 15 dead. With the War the new America, with its promise of realizing the vision inherited from the old America, was born. But it was born, too, with those problems and paradoxes which Herman Melville, during the War, could already envisage when he wrote that the wind of History "spins *against* the way it drives," and that with success, "power unanointed" may come to corrupt us,

And the Iron Dome,
Stronger for stress and strain
Fling her huge shadow athwart the main;
But the Founders' dream shall flee.

The War made us a new nation, and our problem, because of the 16
very size and power of that new nation and the nobility of the promise
which it inherits, remains that of finding in our time and in our new
terms a way to recover and reinterpret the "Founders' dream." Is it possible for the individual, in the great modern industrial state, to retain
some sense of responsibility? Is it possible for him to remain an individual? Is it possible, in the midst of all the forces making for standardization
and anonymity, for society to avoid cultural starvation—to retain, and
even develop, cultural pluralism and individual variety, and foster both
social and individual integrity? Can we avoid, in its deep and more destructive manifestations, the tyranny of the majority, and at the same time
keep a fruitful respect for the common will? We sense that one way, however modest, to undertake this mandatory task of our time is to contemplate the Civil War itself, that mystic cloud from which emerged our
modernity.

Reading and Interpreting

VOCABULARY

Use your dictionary as necessary to find the meaning of the following words
as used by Warren:

vulgar (1)   sartorial (7)   acrimony (7)   honed (8)   indigenous (8)

incommensurable (14)   unanointed (15)   mandatory (16)

CONCEPT ANALYSIS

1. Review the essay and list, in your own words, the various effects of the
   Civil War that Warren presents.
2. The exuberant tone of this essay indicates a justification for the Civil
   War. What particularly negative issue does Warren neglect to develop in
   his discussion of the effects of the war on America?
3. In the introduction and conclusion to his essay, Warren emphasizes the
   importance of the Civil War in shaping the "new America." How was
   the "new America" different from the old? What does Warren imply or
   state are some problems of the "new America"?

Robert Penn Warren writes: "Every victory has a price tag." Discuss a personal conflict in which you won a victory but paid a price.

Thinking and Writing

RHETORICAL TECHNIQUE

1. What types of evidence does Warren present for the various effects of the Civil War?
2. Can you design a causal chain based on this essay that leads from the Civil War to the "new nation"?
3. Outline the causal chain Warren employs to discuss the Civil War debt.
4. Like Bruce Catton, Warren uses forceful topic statements, parallel constructions, repetitions of key words, and interim summaries to bring coherence to his analysis. Find instances of these.
5. Reread paragraphs 7 through 10. With a pencil, cross out the following expressions:
   - paragraph 7: "to take one trivial fact"; "But to leap from the trivial to the grand"; "But" (third from last sentence); "And" (last sentence)
   - paragraph 8: "Not only . . . but" (substitute *and* for *but*); "Even more importantly"; "And" (last sentence)
   - paragraph 9: "Not only . . . but" (substitute *and* for *but*); "But" (last sentence)
   - paragraph 10: "Furthermore"

   Now read the paragraphs again, and after comparing the two versions, discuss the effect of these transitional signals.

COMPOSITION

In paragraph 10, Warren suggests that in some instances patriotism or local pride may cause people to act against their own best interests. Write a causal analysis of a political situation to which this principle applies.

JOHN McCRAE
In Flanders Fields

The effect of war is death. World War I, the first war in which modern technology such as the tank, the submarine, aerial bombing, and poison gas were used, accounted for an unprecedented loss of millions of young men. The visual image opening Canadian John McCrae's poem became an emblem of the war's death toll. Contrast this poem with the poem by Wilfred Owen, which follows.

In Flanders fields the poppies blow
Between the crosses, row on row,
    That mark our place; and in the sky
    The larks, still bravely singing, fly
Scarce heard amid the guns below.   5

We are the Dead. Short days ago
We lived, felt dawn, saw sunset glow,
    Loved and were loved, and now we lie
    In Flanders fields.

Take up our quarrel with the foe: 10
To you from failing hands we throw
    The torch; be yours to hold it high.
    If ye break faith with us who die
We shall not sleep, though poppies grow
    In Flanders fields.   15

WILFRED OWEN

Dulce et Decorum Est

English poet Wilfred Owen (1893–1918), who was
killed in World War I, counters McCrae's sentiments in
this realistic depiction of the effects of a poison gas attack with its ironic use of the Latin proverb and suggests
that uncritical patriotism may be a contributory cause
of war.

Bent double, like old beggars under sacks,
Knock-kneed, coughing like hags, we cursed through sludge,
Till on the haunting flares we turned our backs
And towards our distant rest began to trudge,
Men marched asleep. Many had lost their boots   5
But limped on, blood-shod. All went lame; all blind;
Drunk with fatigue; deaf even to the hoots
Of gas shells dropping softly behind.

Gas! GAS! Quick, boys!—An ecstasy of fumbling
Fitting the clumsy helmets just in time;   10
But someone still was yelling out and stumbling,
And flound'ring like a man in fire or lime . . .
Dim, through the misty panes and thick green light,
As under a green sea, I saw him drowning.

In all my dreams, before my helpless sight,   15
He plunges at me, guttering, choking, drowning.

If in some smothering dreams you too could pace
Behind the wagon that we flung him in,
And watch the white eyes writhing in his face,
His hanging face, like a devil's sick of sin;   20
If you could hear, at every jolt, the blood
Come gargling from the froth-corrupted lungs,
Obscene as cancer, bitter as the cud
Of vile, incurable sores on innocent tongues,—
My friend, you would not tell with such high zest   25
To children ardent for some desperate glory,
The old Lie: Dulce et decorum est
Pro patria mori. *

---

*It is sweet and fitting to die for one's country.

Reading and Interpreting

CONCEPT ANALYSIS

1. "In Flanders Fields" is written from the perspective of soldiers who have died in the war. How does this contrast with the first-person point of view in "Dulce et Decorum Est"? What is the message from the grave in this poem? What effect is it intended to have on the living?
2. Wilfred Owen's war poetry received acclaim only after World War I. Why do you think this was so? Should poems like "Dulce et Decorum Est" receive public attention during wartime? Discuss.
3. During the Vietnam War, television brought the reality of armed conflict into American homes with the same intensity as conveyed in Owen's poem. How did this exposure affect the American people and influence American policy?

Thinking and Writing

RHETORICAL TECHNIQUE

1. Does McCrae's poem affect the emotions or the intellect? Support your response with specific lines. What effect do you think this poem has had as war propaganda?
2. What has Owen concluded is a chief cause of war? Do you agree?
3. Contrast the action, language, realism, and message about the effects of war in Owen's poem to those in McCrae's poem. Cite graphic images from Owen's poem to support your response.

A. M. ROSENTHAL

No News from Auschwitz

The hostility of Germany's Third Reich (1934–1945) against the Jews was a conscious aspect of policy, the effects of which were calculated to exterminate an entire people. The Holocaust must be considered in a different light from the usual effects of war on a civilian population in that the war against the Jews was not a means to an end, but rather an end in itself. *New York Times* executive editor Abraham Rosenthal wrote this article as a correspondent in Warsaw, Poland, in 1958.

Brzezinka, Poland—The most terrible thing of all, somehow, was that at   1
Brzezinka the sun was bright and warm, the rows of graceful poplars were lovely to look upon and on the grass near the gates children played.

It all seemed frighteningly wrong, as in a nightmare, that at Brze-   2
zinka the sun should ever shine or that there should be light and greenness and the sound of young laughter. It would be fitting if at Brzezinka the sun never shone and the grass withered, because this is a place of unutterable terror.

And yet, every day, from all over the world, people come to Brze-   3
zinka, quite possibly the most grisly tourist center on earth. They come for a variety of reasons—to see if it could really have been true, to remind themselves not to forget, to pay homage to the dead by the simple act of looking upon their place of suffering.

Brzezinka is a couple of miles from the better-known southern Pol-   4
ish town of Oswiecim. Oswiecim has about 12,000 inhabitants, is situated about 171 miles from Warsaw and lies in a damp, marshy area at the eastern end of the pass called the Moravian Gate. Brzezinka and Oswiecim together formed part of that minutely organized factory of torture and death that the Nazis called Konzentrationslager Auschwitz.

By now, fourteen years after the last batch of prisoners was herded   5
naked into the gas chambers by dogs and guards, the story of Auschwitz has been told a great many times. Some of the inmates have written of those memories of which sane men cannot conceive. Rudolf Franz Ferdinand Hoess, the superintendent of the camp, before he was executed wrote his detailed memoirs of mass exterminations and the experiments on living bodies. Four million people died here, the Poles say.

And so there is no news to report about Auschwitz. There is merely 6
the compulsion to write something about it, a compulsion that grows out
of a restless feeling that to have visited Auschwitz and then turned away
without having said or written anything would somehow be a most grievous act of discourtesy to those who died here.

Brzezinka and Oswiecim are very quiet places now; the screams can 7
no longer be heard. The tourist walks silently, quickly at first to get it
over with and then, as his mind peoples the barracks and the chambers
and the dungeons and flogging posts, he walks draggingly. The guide
does not say much either, because there is nothing much for him to say
after he has pointed.

For every visitor, there is one particular bit of horror that he knows 8
he will never forget. For some it is seeing the rebuilt gas chamber at Oswiecim and being told that this is the "small one." For others it is the fact
that at Brzezinka, in the ruins of the gas chambers and the crematoria the
Germans blew up when they retreated, there are daisies growing.

There are visitors who gaze blankly at the gas chambers and the fur- 9
naces because their minds simply cannot encompass them, but stand shivering before the great mounds of human hair behind the plate-glass window
or the piles of babies' shoes or the brick cells where men sentenced to
death by suffocation were walled up.

One visitor opened his mouth in a silent scream simply at the sight 10
of boxes—great stretches of three-tiered wooden boxes in the women's
barracks. They were about six feet wide, about three feet high, and into
them from five to ten prisoners were shoved for the night. The guide
walks quickly through the barracks. Nothing more to see here.

A brick building where sterilization experiments were carried out on 11
women prisoners. The guide tries the door—it's locked. The visitor is
grateful that he does not have to go in, and then flushes with shame.

A long corridor where rows of faces stare from the walls. Thousands of 12
pictures, the photographs of prisoners. They are all dead now, the men and
women who stood before the cameras, and they all knew they were to die.

They all stare blank-faced, but one picture, in the middle of a row, 13
seizes the eye and wrenches the mind. A girl, 22 years old, plumply
pretty, blond. She is smiling gently, as at a sweet, treasured thought.
What was the thought that passed through her young mind and is now
her memorial on the wall of the dead at Auschwitz?

Into the suffocation dungeons the visitor is taken for a moment and 14
feels himself strangling. Another visitor goes in, stumbles out and crosses
herself. There is no place to pray at Auschwitz.

The visitors look pleadingly at each other and say to the guide, 15
"Enough."

There is nothing new to report about Auschwitz. It was a sunny day 16
and the trees were green and at the gates the children played.

CONCEPT ANALYSIS

1. Why did Rosenthal write this essay?
2. Why do tourists choose to visit Auschwitz?
3. In paragraph 6 the author writes, "And so there is no news to report about Auschwitz." How does this line differ from the title in meaning?

Quickwrite

If you had the opportunity, would you choose to visit Auschwitz? Why or why not?

Thinking and Writing

RHETORICAL TECHNIQUE

Rosenthal creates the effect of Auschwitz on those who lived and died there through the responses of the tourists. Cite some of these.

COMPOSITION

Visit a place with a past, and by describing your own responses to it, recreate for your reader a sense of its effects on those who were a part of it. To help the reader feel those effects, make your details precise and graphic.

DAVID W. GREGG
Beyond Star Wars: Protection in Time

Gregg's purpose in writing the book from which this chapter on the effects of a nuclear bombing is excerpted is to reopen for public debate the issue of a United States civil defense. As a scientist who has worked on various issues of national security for many years, Gregg employs scientific data and theoretical hypotheses as the basis for his outline of the effects that would result from a nuclear attack.

Nuclear Blast Characteristics and Expedient Protective Measures

Even though the destructive power of these weapons is frightening, they 1
have definite limitations and can be defended against by taking the appropriate actions. However, without taking such actions, it is true that an unprotected society has little chance of surviving even a modest nuclear attack.

This chapter first addresses the effects of a simple nuclear explosion 2
with a power of one megaton, exploded 7,000 feet above ground level. This was chosen as a reference example since it is believed that a majority of the Soviet warheads are approximately this size. And, for this warhead, a 7,000 foot high airburst would maximize the radius of destruction for surface buildings, a likely Soviet military objective. Then, the consequences of a multiple warhead attack are considered. . . .

The explosive power and altitude of detonation chosen need not be 3
exact for the discussion to be meaningful since the effects will be relatively insensitive to warhead size and altitude of detonation. The kill radius increases only with the square root of warhead power. Thus a weapon four times more powerful will have a kill radius only twice as large. And, the basic principles of protection will remain unchanged.

There are five major effects of a nuclear explosion: blast, thermal 4
flash, prompt radiation, fallout radiation, and the electromagnetic pulse. All of these effects take place simultaneously, but it would be hopeless to attempt to gain an understanding of their impact without first evaluating them separately. Thus, for clarity, each effect, and its specific lethal mechanism, is discussed as an isolated phenomenon. Then, the effects are combined to show the overall lethality of the explosion.

The Blast Wave and High-Velocity Winds

Most of the material damage caused by a nuclear explosion at moderate 5 altitude is due to the blast wave and high velocity winds accompanying it. The blast wave starts out at an extremely high pressure near the nuclear explosion, and then diminishes fairly quickly with distance. Also, associated with the blast wave are short-duration (lasting one or two seconds), high-velocity winds that can cause further damage. Close to ground zero (the point on the surface directly under the explosion), people and buildings will have a difficult time surviving. However, the further away they are, the better chance they have. And, beyond a particular distance, the blast wave and winds will have diminished to a point where there is no damage.

Specifically, there are four potentially lethal injury mechanisms associated with the blast wave and winds: 6

1. lung damage from the blast wave,
2. injuries from collapsing buildings,
3. injuries from flying debris, and
4. injuries from being thrown around bodily.

Thermal "Flash" Radiation—Fire and Smoke Hazards

One of the important differences between a nuclear weapon and conventional high-explosives is the large proportion of energy released in a nuclear explosion as thermal radiation. Because of the very high temperatures associated with nuclear explosions as much as 35 to 40% of their total energy is released in the thermal "flash" (with a spectral distribution very similar to that of the sun), which can ignite fires many miles from ground zero. Such fires can be lethal, especially if they are ignited in collapsed buildings where people are trapped, and thus this effect warrants careful evaluation. 7

Thermal "Flash" Radiation—Direct Tissue Burn Hazard

The thermal flash from a nuclear weapon, if looked at directly, can burn 8 the retina and cause blindness at almost any distance from which it can be seen. However, this can be easily avoided by not looking at it. Even if you are looking in the direction of the flash when it occurs, it develops slowly enough (over several seconds) to allow you to blink or turn your head in time, which you will probably do instinctively. Thus, this type of injury is not likely to be an important factor.

The primary burn hazard associated with the thermal flash will 9 be skin burns. The probability for such flash burns of different severity is . . . a function of distance from ground zero for our one-megaton explosion. . . .

Prompt Nuclear Radiation

One of the special features of a nuclear explosion is the emission of nuclear 10 radiation, which is quite different from thermal radiation. It consists of gamma rays, neutrons, beta particles, and alpha particles. Most of the neutrons and part of the gamma radiation are emitted in the first few seconds after the explosion and are called the prompt nuclear radiation. This is to be distinguished from fallout radiation which is emitted over a much longer time from fission products. The ranges of alpha and beta particles are quite short, and neutrons account for less than 10% of the gamma radiation dose at the surface. Therefore, only prompt gamma radiation needs to be considered. . . .

It can be seen that for people in exposed locations, moving from 0.9 11 mile to 1.1 miles from ground zero (0.2 mile) can change their survival rate from about 10% to roughly 90%. Likewise, moving from 0.75 mile to 1.15 miles (0.4 mile) can change the survival rate from 0 to 100%. Thus, moving relatively small distances away from ground zero (distances that can be covered on foot in from 10 to 30 minutes) can dramatically improve the survival rate from prompt nuclear radiation. . . .

Radioactive Fallout Hazard

After surviving the initial effects of the nuclear explosion, the next task 12 will be to survive the radioactive fallout. This residual nuclear radiation arises mainly from the weapon debris.

However, fallout becomes a serious hazard only when the fireball 13 touches the ground and engulfs a great deal of surface material. Surface material then provides the bulk of the mass of the particulate matter that causes the radioactive weapon debris to filter out of the atmosphere onto the surface of the ground.

If the explosion is so high that the fireball does not touch the ground, 14 the radioactive residues of the weapon condense into very small particles (with diameters in the range of from 0.01 to 20 micrometers). Because of their small size, they will take so long to deposit on the surface that by the time they do they will be widely dispersed by the winds and will have decayed to a much lower level of specific radioactivity. Because of this, fallout is usually considered to be an unimportant hazard for airbursts. Thus, for our reference one-megaton explosion at 7,000 feet, there will be little fallout hazard. . . .

Electromagnetic Pulse

A nuclear explosion will generate a very intense electromagnetic pulse 15 that presents no direct hazard to individuals, but which tends to destroy electrical equipment. The radius for potential damage from this effect is essentially the entire country. High-technology equipment will be particularly vulnerable. . . .

Nuclear Winter

Recently, a number of scientists have been studying the potential effect 16 that a massive nuclear exchange would have on the overall climate of the earth. . . . It has been calculated that dust and smoke (from fires) would be produced in such quantities and would be injected so high in the atmosphere that it would block out significant amounts of sunlight for many months.

This would produce a "nuclear winter" with characteristic winter 17 temperatures occurring even in the middle of the summer. Such temperature drops could have a devastating effect on that year's crop, and perhaps on several years' crops, if enough seed stock were to be destroyed. Human populations at great distances might then starve to death, regardless of who actually absorbed the nuclear attack.

This concept has been invoked as a possible deterrent argument, 18 which says that if the Russians ever did initiate a massive attack on us, they would also destroy themselves in the process, thus making nuclear war impossible (assuming they believe it also). The nuclear winter concept would then serve as an important deterrent.

This is an interesting argument if true, and it therefore needs careful 19 evaluation. . . .

To evaluate this, estimating calculations may be useful, but experi- 20 mental evidence is supremely essential due to the complexity of atmospheric effects. Large volcanic eruptions are the only natural phenomena in recorded history that are massive enough to begin to simulate such an effect, and thus are our only source of experimental evidence that could help us evaluate the validity of the concept.

Supporting the "nuclear winter" concept was the explosive eruption 21 of the Indonesian volcano, Tambora, in 1815. This event was responsible for the "year without a summer" in parts of North America and elsewhere. . . . Snow fell in New England in the middle of the summer, and there was considerable crop damage. Another (less radical) global cooling was recorded after the 1883 eruption of Krakatau in the same region. In both cases, the climate returned almost to normal by the following year.

Global coolings have not always resulted from massive volcanic 22 eruptions. An equally dramatic heating effect has also been recorded. . . . According to records kept in Europe, the 1783 eruption of Laki volcano in Iceland resulted in a dramatic warming effect. The eruption began June 8, 1783, and lasted eight months. Estimates indicate that the eruption covered approximately 220 square miles with lava and threw volcanic ash into the stratosphere. The ash spread across Europe to Siberia, and to Africa and North America. This resulted in a dramatic rise in temperature in Europe. There was massive crop damage, and a resulting famine. But, in this case, it was apparently due to the sulfurous gases and a heating, not a cooling effect. Again, the climate returned essentially to normal within a year after the eruptions subsided, and the affected societies survived.

These natural events suggest that large injections of dust and smoke 23 into the atmosphere will certainly cause global climatic changes. However, the recovery processes appear to have an effective time scale of less than a year, perhaps no more than a few months.

Thus, the measured recovery times associated with the volcanic 24 eruptions, less than one year, should be reasonable representations of what would be expected for recovery from a massive nuclear attack. . . .

I thus conclude that we could definitely expect global climatic 25 changes from a massive nuclear attack, but we can not predict with certainty whether it would produce a nuclear winter or a nuclear summer.

Reading and Interpreting

VOCABULARY

Use your dictionary as necessary to find the meaning of the following words as used by David Gregg:

spectral (7)   particulate (13)

CONCEPT ANALYSIS

1. Gregg's purpose in writing his book is to demonstrate that an adequate civil defense system would make it less likely for nuclear attack to occur because the effects would be less disastrous. How is his purpose reflected in his assumptions in paragraphs 2, 12, and 14? How is his purpose related to his focus on the local, immediate effects of a nuclear explosion?
2. What evidence does Gregg provide to minimize the nuclear winter concept? What strength or weakness do you perceive in his evidence?

Quickwrite

If civil defense shelters were available to you in the event of a nuclear bombing, who and what would you take with you?

Thinking and Writing

RHETORICAL TECHNIQUE

As a scientist writing for lay persons, Gregg presents his material in a clear and well-organized manner. What techniques does he use to communicate his message?

COMPOSITION

Preparation for a situation can prevent or minimize its effects. Elaborate this idea with illustrations from your own experience.

JONATHAN SCHELL

The Republic of Insects and Grass

The title of this excerpt suggests the global effects of a nuclear holocaust envisioned by many of America's most respected scientific thinkers. Schell cites numerous research studies on the possible effect of nuclear bombing. He acknowledges that there is *solid* evidence for only the local, primary effects. Predictions of secondary and global effects are speculative, based on analogy and theoretical calculations. However, they must be taken seriously because of their implications for our species and our total environment.

If we had no knowledge at all of the likely consequences of a holocaust   1 for the earth, there would, of course, be no basis whatever for judgment. However, given the extent of what there is to know about the earth, it is no contradiction to say that while our ignorance is vast and, in a certain sense, irremediable (although, at the same time, the amount that we can and certainly will find out is also probably measureless), our knowledge is also vast, and that what we know is extremely alarming. Since in a global holocaust even the so-called local effects of the explosions may cover the whole land mass of the Northern Hemisphere, they may have secondary consequences that are truly global. The destruction of estuarine life throughout the Northern Hemisphere and the radioactive poisoning of the local waters could cause general harm to life in the oceans. Ecological collapse on the land in large parts of the Northern Hemisphere could have large consequences for the climate of the earth as a whole. Loss of vegetation, for example, increases the surface reflectivity of the earth, and this has a cooling effect on the atmosphere. In heavily irradiated zones, the mutation of plant pathogens might create virulent strains that could, in the words of the 1975 N.A.S. report, "produce disease epidemics that would spread globally." The irradiated northern half of the earth would in general become a huge radioecological laboratory, in which many species would be driven to extinction, others would flourish and possibly invade unharmed parts of the earth, and still others would evolve into new and unpredictable forms.

But more important by far, in all probability, than the global after-effects of the local destruction would be the direct global effects, the most important of which is ozone loss. The concentration of ozone in the earth's atmosphere is very small—not more than ten parts by weight per million parts of air. Yet the ozone layer has a critical importance to life on earth, because it protects the earth's surface from the harmful ultraviolet radiation in sunlight, which would otherwise be "lethal to unprotected organisms as we now know them," to quote Dr. Martyn M. Caldwell, a leading authority on the biological effects of ultraviolet radiation, in a recent article of his in *BioScience* titled, "Plant Life and Ultraviolet Radiation: Some Perspective in the History of the Earth's UV Climate." I have already mentioned Glasstone's remark that without the absorption of solar ultraviolet radiation by the ozone "life as currently known could not exist except possibly in the ocean." The 1975 N.A.S. report states, "As biologists, geologists, and other students of evolution recognize, the development of an oxygen-rich atmosphere, with its *ozone layer, was a precondition to the development of multicelled plants and animals, and all life forms on land have evolved under this shield*" (italics in the original). B. W. Boville, of the Canadian Atmospheric Environment Service, has written that the ozone layer is "a crucial element to climate and to the existence of all life on earth." Dr. Fred Iklé, who served as the director of the Arms Control and Disarmament Agency under Presidents Nixon and Ford, and now serves as Under Secretary of Defense for Policy under President Reagan, has stated that severe reduction of the ozone layer through nuclear explosions could "shatter the ecological structure that permits man to remain alive on this planet." And a paper delivered at a United Nations-sponsored scientific conference in March, 1977, states, "The whole biological world, so dependent on micro-organisms, may, if doses [of ultraviolet radiation] increase, be in serious trouble." . . .

If the formation of the ozone layer was one of the necessary preconditions for the "dramatic appearance" of life on land, then the question naturally arises whether heavy depletion of the ozone, by nuclear explosions or any other cause, might not bring about a dramatic disappearance of life, including human life, from the land. . . . But that question, having been raised, is one of those which cannot be answered with confidence, given the present state of our knowledge of the workings of the earth. Even the estimates of ozone loss that would be brought about by holocausts of different sizes are highly uncertain (in calculating some of these figures, the National Academy of Sciences found the largest computers insufficient)—as is made clear in the 1975 N.A.S. report, which found that the explosion of ten thousand megatons of nuclear weapons would increase the amount of nitric oxide in the stratosphere to something between five and fifty times the normal amount (a tenfold uncertainty is characteristic of calculations in this field), that it would (as has been mentioned) reduce the ozone layer in the Northern Hemisphere, where the report assumes that the explosions would occur, by anything from thirty to seventy per cent, and that it would reduce it in the Southern Hemisphere by anything from twenty to forty per cent. . . .

The extent of the biological damage that would be done by various 4 increases in ultraviolet radiation is, if anything, even less well known than what the increases caused by nuclear detonations might be, but the available information suggests that the damage to the whole ecosphere would be severe. One reason is that certain wavelengths of ultraviolet that are known to be particularly harmful biologically would be disproportionately increased by ozone reduction. Moreover, the cause of the biological damage—increased ultraviolet radiation—would be similar everywhere, but the effects would be different for each of the earth's species and ecosystems. And the effects of those effects, spreading outward indefinitely through the interconnected web of life, are not within the realm of the calculable. However, it is known with certainty that ultraviolet radiation is harmful or fatal to living things. In fact, precisely because of its abiotic qualities ultraviolet light has long been in use as a sterilizing agent in medical and other scientific work. The most comprehensive study of ultraviolet's effects which has been done so far is the Department of Transportation's Climatic Impact Assessment Program report "Impacts of Climatic Change on the Biosphere." It states that "excessive UV-B radiation"—the part of the ultraviolet spectrum which would be significantly increased by ozone depletion—"is a decidedly detrimental factor for most organisms, including man," and continues, "Even current levels of solar UV-B irradiance can be linked with phenomena such as increased mutation rates, delay of cell divisions, depression of photosynthesis in phytoplankton, skin cancer in humans, eye cancer in certain cattle, and lethality of many lower organisms, such as aquatic invertebrates and bacteria."

Research concerning the effects of UV-B irradiance on specific orga- 5 nisms—and especially on organisms in their natural habitats—has been slight, and in a recent conversation Dr. Caldwell, who was chairman of the scientific panel that produced the Climatic Impact Assessment Program report, told me that not enough experiments have been done for anyone to generalize with confidence about the ultimate fate of living things subjected to increased ultraviolet radiation. From the experiments that have been done, however, it is known that, among mammals, human beings are especially vulnerable, because of their lack of body hair. . . . Of much greater seriousness, though, would be the temporary loss of sight through photophthalmia, or snow blindness, which can be contracted by exposure to heightened ultraviolet radiation and may last for several days after each exposure. Photophthalmia is, in the words of the 1975 N.A.S. report, "disabling and painful"; also, "there are no immune groups," and "there is no adaptation." One can avoid photophthalmia by wearing goggles whenever one goes outside, but so far the world has made no provision for each person on earth to have a pair of goggles in case the ozone is depleted. However, if the higher estimates of depletion turn out to be correct, people will not be able to stay outdoors very long anyway. At these levels, "incapacitating" sunburn would occur in several minutes; if the reduction of the ozone reached the seventy per cent maximum that the report assigns to the Northern Hemisphere, the time could be ten minutes. Moreover, the report states that in the months immediately following the attack ozone depletion could be even higher than seventy per cent. "We have no simple way," the report observes, "to estimate the magnitude of short-term depletion." The ten-minute rule is not one that the strategists of "recovery" after a nuclear attack usually figure into their calculations. If high levels of ultraviolet radiation occur, then anyone who crawls out of his shelter after radiation from fallout has declined to tolerable levels will have to crawl back in immediately. In the meantime, though, people would not have been able to go out to produce food, and they would starve. A further possible harmful consequence—in itself a potential human and ecological catastrophe of global proportions—is that increased ultraviolet light would raise the amounts of Vitamin D in the skin of mammals and birds to toxic levels. But the experimentation necessary to determine whether or not this sweeping catastrophe would occur has not been done. The 1975 N.A.S. report observes, alarmingly but inconclusively, "We do not know whether man and other vertebrate animals could tolerate an increased Vitamin D synthesis that might result from a large and rapid increase in [ultraviolet] exposure." The report "urgently" recommends further study of the question. . . .

Sight and smell permit animals to find their way in the environment and to fulfill the roles mapped out for them by nature, and the loss of sight would throw the environment into disarray as billions of blinded beasts, insects, and birds began to stumble through the world. The disorientation of insects would be fateful not only for them but for plant life, much of which depends on insects for pollination and other processes essential to survival. Ultraviolet light is, in fact, known to play a role in many activities of insects, including phototaxis, celestial navigation, and sex identification, and an increase in ultraviolet light would no doubt impair these capacities. But plant life would in any case be under direct assault from increased ultraviolet radiation. While confident generalization about the fate of plants has to be ruled out, experiments that have been performed with crops show that while some are quite resistant, others, including tomatoes, beans, peas, and onions, would be killed or "severely scalded," according to the N.A.S. report. Because ultraviolet radiation breaks down DNA, which regulates reproduction, and because it also represses photosynthesis, which is the chief metabolic process of plants, the direct effect of increased ultraviolet radiation on plant life is likely to be widespread and serious. And because many species, the N.A.S. report states, "survive at an upper limit of tolerance," any increase in ultraviolet radiation is "a threat to the survival of certain species and accordingly to entire ecosystems." The global damage to plants and the global damage to the insects are synergistic: the damage to the insects damages the plants, which in turn, damage the insects again, in a chain of effects whose outcome is unforeseeable. On the question of the harm to the insects that would be caused by the harm to the rest of the ecosphere, Ting H. Hsiao, a professor of entomology at Utah State University, has written in the Climatic Impact Assessment Program report, "Since insects are important in the world's ecosystems, any changes in other components of the ecosystem could have an impact on insect populations. Ultraviolet radiation is a physical factor that directly influences all biotic components of the ecosystem. . . . A change in abiotic factors, such as temperature, rainfall, or wind, associated with elevated ultraviolet radiation could profoundly affect behavior, biology, population structure, dispersal, and migration of insects." Dr. Hsiao's observations about insects and the ecosphere can, in fact, be generalized to include all global effects of a holocaust, for there are few that do not have potentially large consequences for the character and severity of all the others.

The web of life in the oceans, perhaps more than any other part of the environment, is vulnerable to damage from increased ultraviolet radiation. John Calkins, of the Department of Radiation Medicine of the University of Kentucky, and D. Stuart Nachtwey, a professor of radiation biology at Oregon State University, remark in the Climatic Impact Assessment Program report that the experimentation that has been done so far, though it is inadequate, suggests that "many aquatic micro-organisms and invertebrates have little reserve capacity to cope with surface levels of solar UV-B." The organisms at greatest risk are the unicellular organisms that lie at the base of the marine food chain, and thus ultimately sustain the higher creatures in the oceans. Since the removal of an organism from the food chain can eliminate all the organisms above it in the chain, the loss of even part of the chain's base could have huge consequences. Once again, quantitative judgments are not possible, but such experiments as have been carried out make the danger clear. In the early nineteen-seventies, researchers discovered that even normal levels of UV-B radiation are harmful or fatal to many aquatic organisms if they are not permitted to descend deeper into the water or otherwise shield themselves from exposure. The finding is important, because it means that the question to be asked about increased UV-B radiation is not whether it would be biologically harmful but whether the intensity would be great enough to overpower the mechanisms of defense that organisms have built up over billions of years of evolution to deal with normal levels of ultraviolet radiation. . . . If a change in the environment occurs slowly, an organism may prove able to adapt, but a holocaust would bring a sudden change, and the usefulness of adaptation would be greatly reduced. . . .

A second global consequence of ozone reduction would be climatic change. The earth's climate, like the ecosphere as a whole, the 1975 N.A.S. report reminds us, is "holocoenotic"; in other words, it is a whole in which "any action influencing a single part of the system can be expected to have an effect on all other parts of the system." As is hardly surprising, the totality of those effects is unknown even for a single major climatic disturbance, and the N.A.S. report notes that "no adequate climatic models exist that would permit prediction of the nature and degree of climatic changes that might result from a large-scale nuclear event." Of the three large components of the earth's surface—land, sea, and air—the air is probably the most changeable. The parts of this delicately balanced whole include, among many others, the chemical composition of both the troposphere and the stratosphere; the temperature levels of the atmosphere and the degree of moisture at all altitudes; the temperature and reflectivity of the earth's surface; the circulatory patterns of the air; the circulatory patterns of the ocean currents; and the degree of retention of the earth's reflected warmth by the atmosphere, in the so-called greenhouse effect. Each of these parts could be disturbed by a holocaust, and the disturbance of any one could disturb many or all of the others. According to present thinking, a depletion of the ozone layer would simultaneously act to warm the surface of the earth, by permitting more solar radiation to reach it, and act to cool it, by reducing the layer's capacity to radiate back to earth the heat reflected from the earth's surface. But, according to the N.A.S. report, the cooling at the surface of the earth, which might last for several years, is expected to exceed the warming by, at most, an amount estimated (very tentatively, considering that "no adequate climatic models exist") at approximately one degree Fahrenheit. Temperature change at the surface, however, may be less important than temperature change elsewhere in the atmosphere. For example, cooling of the upper troposphere and of the lower stratosphere "is likely to be much larger" than cooling at the surface, and may cause alterations in the cloud cover, which would, in turn, influence the climate. This whole subject, however, is one of the many subjects that remain relatively unexplored. It is estimated that dust and smoke lofted by the explosions would add to the cooling by another degree Fahrenheit. Temperatures on earth can fluctuate tens of degrees in a single day, yet the net reduction of a couple of degrees in the temperature of the entire surface of the earth after a holocaust would be of great consequence. For example, it could cut the biological productivity of deciduous forests by as much as twenty per cent, shift the monsoons in Asia in a way that could be ruinous for both agriculture and ecosystems, and eliminate all wheat-growing in Canada. The N.A.S. report also mentions that climatic change identified as "dramatic" and "major," but not otherwise specified, "cannot be ruled out," and adds that although the change is likely to last only a few years, the possibility exists that it "may not be reversible." Greater reductions would, of course, have larger consequences. Another global consequence of the injection of oxides of nitrogen into the stratosphere by nuclear explosions would be pollution of the environment as these gases fell back into the troposphere. Nitrogen dioxide, for example, is one of the most harmful components of the smog that afflicts many modern cities, such as Los Angeles. It reacts with hydrocarbons present in the air above these cities, actually causing in the process some ozone formation. While ozone in the stratosphere is beneficial to human beings, ozone near ground level is not. It has been found not only to increase respiratory problems among human beings but to be harmful to some plant life. The formation of nitrogen dioxide, accordingly, is still another global effect of a holocaust whose consequences are not calculable. In addition, nitrogen dioxide is responsible in polluted cities for turning the sky brown, and after a holocaust it might happen that the sky of the whole earth would turn from blue to brown for as long as the pollution lasted (perhaps several years).

Reading and Interpreting

VOCABULARY

Use your dictionary as necessary to find the meaning of the following words as used by Schell:

estuarine (1) pathogens (1) depletion (3) abiotic (4) phototaxis (6)
celestial (6) synergistic (6) troposphere (8) stratosphere (8)
deciduous forests (8)

CONCEPT ANALYSIS

1. With reference to paragraph 1, distinguish between the local and the global effects of a nuclear holocaust.

2. What does Schell believe to be the most important global effect of a nuclear holocaust? What is the explanation for its significance?
3. What is the current known effect of excessive UV-B radiation on life? What are some of the predicted biological effects of UV-B in the event of a nuclear explosion?
4. What explanation does Schell give for his statement that the "web of life in the ocean, perhaps more than any other part of the environment, is vulnerable. . . ."? (7)
5. Discuss some of the predicted effects on the climate of ozone reduction. What would be some of the specific effects of a "net reduction of a couple of degrees in the temperature of the entire surface of the earth"? (8)
6. What would be a third global consequence of a nuclear holocaust?

Thinking and Writing

RHETORICAL TECHNIQUE

1. What chain of cause and effect does Schell present to illustrate the assertion of the National Academy of Sciences that "any increase in ultraviolet radiation is a 'threat to the survival of certain species and accordingly to entire ecosystems'"? (6)
2. The scientific evidence in this essay is complex. Therefore, the paragraphs are longer than usual in order to complete each train of thought. Nevertheless, the author's skillful use of signals of intention and transitional expressions maintains coherence. Select two paragraphs that exemplify Schell's skillful use of these devices.

COMPOSITION

1. Schell discusses both short-term and long-term effects of a nuclear explosion. Describe a current political situation and discuss its potential short-term and long-term effects.
2. Describe an action that has environmental impact, such as the building of a dam, the draining of a swamp, or the elimination of a pest, and, using a causal chain, discuss its effects on the ecosystem.

Will Durant

Why Men Fight {The Effects of War}

This companion piece to Durant's essay on the causes of war exhibits the same clarity of organization, coherence, and readability as the other. In the earlier piece Durant focused on the general causes of war rather than on the causes of particular wars. Similarly, here he treats the general effects of war rather than the effects of particular wars. Durant presents the effects of war in the same order as he did the causes: psychological, biological, economic, and political. The development of each effect is consistent: first, he offers a positive effect, or one which appears positive, and then he delineates the negative effect at greater length. Throughout, he uses devices of coherence such as restatement of key concepts, transitional expressions, and parallel structures.

III. *Effects*

Consider briefly the effects of war. We think of these too often, too seldom the causes. A <u>reminding summary</u> will suffice.

    There are <u>psychological effects.</u> A certain <u>exaltation of spirit</u> may come to a country embarked upon what it believes to be a just war; the mind and heart of the <u>people are unified,</u> hyphens drop out, and the <u>diverse elements of the population</u> are more closely fused into a homogeneous nation. The citizens acquire habits of <u>order and discipline,</u> of courage and tenacity; if they are not destroyed, they are made stronger. <u>Against these gains</u> there is the silent <u>gloom of parents and children bereaved,</u> the <u>disorders of</u>

1   Signal of intention
      Signal of organization

2   First effect:
      psychological
      Positive effects

      Signal of intention: negative psychological effects

demobilization, the demoralization of men, new-trained to habits of violence, promiscuity, and deceit.

For a time there is a revulsion against war: pacifism flourishes so long as the evils of war are fresh in the memory; generous men like the Abbé of St. Pierre and Immanuel Kant and Woodrow Wilson offer plans for perpetual peace, and many humane resolutions are made. But as a fresh generation grows up, pacifism subsides; aged reminiscence idealizes the past, and the young are ready to believe that war is 99 per cent glory and only 1 per cent diarrhea. War loses some of its terrors; to give one's life for one's country is again sweet and beautiful; and to die in bed becomes a shameful fate reserved for noncombatants and generals.

Biologically, war reduces the pressure of population upon the means of subsistence— which is an academic way of saying that some millions of people have been killed. Probably as a result of this, the birth rate has, before our Malthusian days, risen after war; and for some unknown reason, the ratio of male to female births has increased. Dysgenic and eugenic processes go on side by side. The strong and brave go to meet their deaths; the weak remain, and the timid return, to multiply their kind. Pugnacity and brutality are diminished by the superior death rate of the pugnacious and the brutal, both in war and in peace. But usually the finer, more cultured and artistic societies are crushed out, or dominated, by the cruder and more warlike groups: Athens by Sparta, Greece by Macedonia and Rome, T'ang China by the Tatars, Sung China by the Mongols, Gupta India by the Huns, Rome by the barbarians, Renaissance Italy by France, France by Germany, Samurai Japan by the United States. History is a war between war and art, as life is a war between life and death; life and art are always defeated, and always reborn.

To most participating nations, a modern war brings complex economic results. Science and industry are occasionally advanced by re-

---

3   Cause-effect chain: from pacifism to idealization of war

4   Second effect: biological
Positive effect

Signal of effect

Parallel structures
Antonyms mark contrast

Negative biological effects

Evidence of historical record

Interpretation of historical record

5   Third effect: economic; positive economic effect

Parallel structure

searches derived from the stimulus and energy of war. Life and property are destroyed; vast sums are consumed in armament; impossible debts accumulate. Repudiation in some form becomes inevitable; currencies are depreciated or annulled, inflation relieves debtor governments and individuals, savings and investments are wiped out, and men patiently begin to save and lend again. Overexpansion in war is followed by a major depression in peace. International trade is disrupted by intensified nationalism, exalted tariffs, and the desire to develop at home all industries requisite in war. The vanquished are enslaved physically, as in antiquity, financially and by due process of law today. The victorious masses gain little except in self-conceit; the ruling minority among the victors may gain much in conquered lands, markets, spheres of influence, supplies, and taxable population. . . .

Negative economic effects in cause-effect chain

Parallel structure

Contrasting effects

Politically, war may bring, to the conquered, revolution; to the victors, a strengthened government, the domination of the exchequer by returning soldiers, and the transformation of good generals into bad statesmen.

6 Fourth effect: positive political
Parallel structure
Negative effects

The methods and institutions that won the war tend to spread abroad and to replace the methods and institutions that lost. The pride of triumph and the appetite for spoils encourage further war, until men and materials are thrown recklessly into the lap of Mars, and the victor, like Assyria and Rome, destroys itself with its victories.

7

Causal chain leads to further war

THE WRITTEN RESPONSE

Writing Workshop

1. Reflect upon a current political situation—local, national, or international—that has the potential for open conflict or has erupted into open conflict.
2. For your essay, decide whether you will analyze the causes of this situation or its effects. (You may devote one paragraph to the other aspect either in your introduction or as a part of your summary at the end of your essay.)
3. Brainstorm the causes or effects of the situation you have chosen. Cluster the items into logical groups (for example, as Durant does, psychological, biological, economic, political; by order of importance; by chronological order; by types of causes: necessary, contributory, fundamental, immediate).
4. Decide on and note the type of evidence you will use to support each of your cause or effect groupings: statistics, the historical record, research studies, logical reasoning, scholarship of authorities, personal experience, observations.
5. Write an introduction in which you clearly state your thesis and indicate your organizational plan and the sequence of your groupings. You may wish to introduce your thesis with a question.
6. Write a conclusion that briefly but clearly summarizes your analysis of causes or effects.
7. After your first draft, review your essay for coherence: Do your introduction and conclusion both state the same thesis? Have you used cause-and-effect signals and other transitions, interim summaries, and the repetition of key words to help the reader follow your ideas? Try to devise a title that states your main idea in an interesting way.

Topics for Critical Thinking and Writing

1. Will Durant states that conflict in "the social mass" is a reflection of conflicts on the personal and psychological level. Individuals may be in conflict with their families, their communities, their employers, their government, their peers, or even themselves. Discuss a conflict in your personal experience, emphasizing either its causes or its effects.
2. Write an essay of effect based on one of the following hypothetical situations:

a. the colonists establishing the United States as a monarchy rather than a democratic republic

b. the Confederacy succeeding in establishing itself as an independent nation

3. Advertising and the popular media, like politicians, tend to romanticize the causes of war and sanitize its effects. Discuss one or more books, films, television programs, or advertisements illustrating this assertion.

4. Review Will Durant's Essay for Analysis on the causes of war, with special attention to his causal chains. Write an essay about conflict in general (for example, conflict between generations, conflict between cultural groups) or a specific conflict (the fighting in Northern Ireland or the Middle East, racial conflict in South Africa); employ one or more causal chains in the essay.

5. Will Durant is writing about war in general throughout history, and Robert Penn Warren is writing about a war that occurred one hundred years ago. Which specific points in their analyses apply to current or potential armed conflicts?

Synthesis Questions

1. Categorize and discuss the reading selections in this chapter as hopeful or pessimistic about the human condition.

2. Slavery as a cause of the Civil War is treated differently by Bruce Catton and Robert Penn Warren. In a deductive essay, express your own views regarding slavery as a cause of the Civil War. Incorporate the views of these writers.

3. The Declaration of Independence figures in the selection by Robert Penn Warren. How does he use that document to support his thesis? Write an essay in which you elaborate the concept that the Declaration of Independence lives on, using Warren's work as an example.

4. How has your position on nuclear arms control been affected by the essays "Beyond Star Wars" and "The Republic of Insects and Grass"? Write an essay in which you synthesize these two works to support your point of view.

5. Irony and understatement are common to many of the selections in this chapter. This suggests that the enormity of war cannot be conveyed by intellectual analysis and detailed physical description alone. Discuss the impact on you of the ironic and understated tone of several of this chapter's selections, including Wilfred Owen's poem.

6. The following editorial on recent developments in college curriculum design proposes several objectives for a program of peace and conflict studies. Select from the readings in this chapter the works that you would find most meaningful in such a program. Discuss how these works would help meet each objective stated in the editorial.

MICHAEL T. KLARE
Studying How to Wage Peace

This fall, many college students entered classes in a new and burgeoning academic field: peace and conflict studies. While the intensity of anti-nuclear protest appears to have subsided, student interest in academic studies of war and peace is on the rise. Fully one-third of the freshman class at Hampshire College—120 students—signed up for an introductory course I'm co-teaching on "War, Revolution and Peace."

Although no accurate tally of these programs is available, teachers report that about 250 U.S. colleges and universities now have some courses or a major in this area, and that many more are considering the introduction of such programs in the years ahead. No single academic designation unites all of these programs—all, however, generally involve considerations of the global arms race and the various methods and proposals that have been advanced for controlling it.

Typically, an introductory course in this field—such as Smith College's "Peace and War in the Nuclear Age"—is taught by a team of faculty members including a physicist, historian, political scientist, psychologist, economist and perhaps a teacher of ethics or religion. Some institutions, however, have begun offering degree programs in this field and there is a growing—if cautious—trend toward viewing peace and conflict studies as an independent field of inquiry.

Supporters of this trend perceive three major objectives for these programs:

- First, to educate students about the basic "facts of life" of survival in the Nuclear Age. Given that American citizens and policymakers are being asked to make decisions on more and more complex issues of weapons procurement, military strategy and arms control negotiations, such instruction is viewed by many educators as a fundamental responsibility of colleges and universities.
- Second, to develop a body of theory and data to support a full-fledged program of academic research in peace and conflict studies. This effort reflects the belief of many (if not all) in the field that the study of war and peace phenomena has not been adequately pursued within the existing academic structures, and that an independent effort—drawing upon many disciplines—is needed to give this critical topic attention it deserves.
- Third, and perhaps most important, to marshal the creative energies of academia for the search for new approaches to peace and world security. Although many individual professors and university-affiliated research institutes have long been active in the study of modern warfare, academia, as an institution, has not played a conspicuous role in developing strategies for the prevention of nuclear war. Yet there is a widespread belief

that prevailing strategies for war prevention—notably deterrence based on massive arsenals of nuclear weapons along with agreements of the SALT I and II variety—cannot guarantee immunity to global nuclear annihilation.

Only a new and far-ranging investigation, it is thought, can lead to new solutions to this most critical of all human dilemmas.

No one believes that American colleges and universities will produce instant remedies to the 40-year-old predicament of nuclear weapons. But there is a growing sense, in at least some quarters, that some promising new directions for research and analysis have been opened up. Exemplifying this effort is the publication last summer of "Hawks, Doves and Owls," a book by three Harvard professors (the "owls" of the book's title) advocating a new approach to superpower "crisis control" that would reduce the risk of accidental or inadvertent nuclear war. At other colleges and universities, many professors are looking anew at the teachings of anthropology, sociology, economics, psychology and history for new insights that could be brought to bear on the nuclear dilemma.

Perhaps it is Polyannish to think that college students and professors can find dramatic new alternatives to the policies developed by several generations of American leaders. Many of us believe, however, that a truly exhaustive search for new solutions has never really been attempted, and that the growth of peace studies programs at American colleges and universities offers a singular opportunity to undertake such a search while there is still time to avert a catastrophe.

7. Nazi Germany defended the extermination of the Jews (and Socialists, Communists, and gypsies) on economic and political grounds independent of moral considerations. Can you give examples of current governmental policies—ours or others'—that present economic and political rationales for immoral actions against civilians?
8. Select one of the following quotations and write a cause or effect analysis that supports it:
   a. "The war is just which is necessary." (Machiavelli, *The Prince*)
   b. "An unjust peace is better than a just war." (Cicero, *Ad Atticum*)

Refining Your Essay

1. Review your introduction. Have you clearly indicated whether you will focus on causes or effects?
2. Are related causes or effects grouped together logically? See if you can verbally express your pattern of organization—that is, your subtopics and the logic of their sequence.

3. If you have asked questions in your introduction or at other points in your essay, make sure you provide relevant and complete answers.
4. Do you use various types of evidence? Brief narratives, anecdotes, character sketches, and quotations are lively follow-ups to documentary evidence. Include some of these.
5. Examine your verbs to ensure they are consistent in tense with the time of your topic. For example, if you are examining the *potential* effects of a current situation, your verbs should be primarily in the future and conditional tenses.
6. Circle all your transitional signals. What function does each have? Check their appropriateness by consulting a dictionary or reference work on usage. (For example, is there a difference in meaning and usage between *in contrast* and *on the other hand*?)

CHAPTER NINE

Peers and Pairs: Human Conditions Compared and Contrasted

The balletic pas de deux is an aesthetic image of comparison and contrast. Although both the male and the female dancer must be agile, strong, and graceful, the role of the male dancer emphasizes power and stability while the role of his female partner emphasizes lightness and delicacy.

THE WRITING FOCUS

*There is one radical distinction between different
minds . . . that some minds are stronger and apter to
mark the difference of things, others to mark their
resemblances.*

Francis Bacon, *Novum Organum I*

Aristotle called the ability to see similarities between unlike things and differences between similar things a mark of genius. Your instructors will, at the very least, consider your ability to compare and contrast elements a mark of intelligence. Both in academic and in professional life you will be called on for comparative and contrastive analyses of ideas, situations, and individuals.

The comparison or contrast essay sets out related elements of a subject and reveals how they are similar or different in significant ways. Comparison encompasses both the similarities and the differences between elements. When similarities predominate, the term *comparison* is used. When the focus is on differences, the term *contrast* is used. These modes challenge writers to scrutinize a subject from many perspectives and to juxtapose related elements in a way that provides new insights.

Purpose and Subject

In addition to highlighting likenesses and differences between related elements, writers use the comparison-and-contrast mode to indicate the superiority of one element to another, to explain the unfamiliar by comparing it to something familiar, or to examine a subject in different time periods. Comparison or contrast (or both) can be used to structure a complete essay, or these modes can be incorporated in other types of essays to explain an aspect of a central idea.

ELEMENTS OF THE SUBJECT

For a successful comparison or contrast essay, the elements chosen for comparison must be sufficiently alike to make their similarities or differences significant. For instance, in an essay in this chapter, "On Friendship," Margaret Mead and Rhoda Metraux concentrate on the concept of adult friendship, contrasting the elements of American, French, British, and German friendship. The topic of children's friendship in contrast to adult friendship would have been inappropriate in the essay, as children's friendship is outside the class—adult friendship—established for the comparison.

The extremes of a subject make good elements for a comparison or contrast because they make us aware of the full spectrum of possibilities. For example, in our Essay for Analysis, Gilbert Highet provocatively enlarges the concept of personal freedom through his depiction of two widely divergent human types: Diogenes, the destitute philosopher, and Alexander the Great, the philosopher-king.

Any subject presents a variety of elements for comparison or contrast, depending on where your interest and purpose lie. You could explore architecture, for example, by comparing two buildings that are beautiful in different ways, by contrasting a beautiful building and an ugly building, by comparing the functionalism of one building and that of another, or by contrasting the architectural features of buildings of two different eras.

In choosing elements for your comparison or contrast, you must look for those that have some significant commonality. For example, if you were asked to compare two fictional or historical characters, you would search for characters who are logically related to each other in some important ways. There would be little purpose, for example, in comparing Pinocchio and Hamlet, as they appear in different literary genres, develop in entirely different ways, and were meant to appeal to very different audiences. A comparison of Lucinda Matlock and George Gray, two characters from *Spoon River Anthology* by Edgar Lee Masters, however, would produce a rich essay. These two fictional people lived in the same era in the same American small town, and the styles in which they are presented are significantly similar. Yet their outlooks on life diverged widely, suggesting a strong thesis statement expressing the contrast between them and indicating that this polarity is generally representative of people in real life.

Formulating a Working Thesis

Writing a comparison or contrast essay that is more than a mere list of similarities or differences requires careful planning. Once you have established your subject and determined the elements for comparison, thoughtful reflection about them will help you formulate a working thesis statement that will give shape and meaning to your essay. The more thoroughly you know the elements you are comparing, the easier it will be to generate a working thesis about them. A close reading of the two poems "Lucinda Matlock" and "George Gray" suggests a thesis statement such as the following: *Lucinda Matlock and George Gray lived ordinary lives in an ordinary town, but they drew very different lessons from life.*

Establishing Points of Comparison and/or Contrast

Your next step is to establish the points on which you will examine the elements for similarities and/or differences. You should select points that both your elements share, develop each point in roughly equal proportion, and treat the points in the same order for each element to achieve symmetry and balance in your essay.

Brainstorming and other techniques for invention (see Chapter 1) will help you generate a multitude of points of comparison or contrast. Begin with observable, concrete details about each of your elements, jotting them down as they occur to you. Deeper reflection will yield more intangible or abstract qualities. Group related items together, then combine, modify, and eliminate items to form major groupings. These will be the points of comparison or contrast you will discuss. See the following grid as a guide.

In an essay of comparison, you can introduce the elements of your topic by conceding that some differences exist between them. In an essay of contrast, you can introduce the subject with a statement of some basic commonalities. Thus, for example, in one of our readings Bruce Catton introduces his contrasting elements, Civil War generals Grant and Lee, by mentioning their shared qualities: "These men were bringing the Civil War to its virtual finish. . . . two strong men . . . (2, 3). Such introductions clearly indicate the relationship between the elements and the direction your essay will take.

In the body of your essay you should limit your points of comparison or contrast to those that most strongly support your thesis. As in any type of essay, you must support these points with details and examples.

A PRELIMINARY GRID OUTLINE

A preliminary grid will allow you to view your elements and points of comparison clearly. The following example is based on Highet's "Diogenes and Alexander":

Subject: Personal freedom

Elements: Diogenes, destitute philosopher; Alexander, philosopher-king

Commonalities: Ancient Greeks who possessed personal freedom

Working thesis: Although Diogenes and Alexander lived at opposite ends of the social spectrum, they both illustrated the quality of personal freedom in the highest degree.

	ELEMENT A: DIOGENES	ELEMENT B: ALEXANDER
Contrasting Point 1: Material Possessions	Almost none	Infinite wealth
Contrasting Point 2: Social Philosophy	Unconventional, no respect for rank; no manners, respected only life of the spirit	Highest rank, educated, well-traveled, chivalrous
Contrasting Point 3: Power	None except influence of his teaching	Absolute authority

Following the construction of your grid, you can add details and examples, as shown here:

	ELEMENT A: DIOGENES	ELEMENT B: ALEXANDER
Contrasting Point 1: Material Possessions	Almost none: home in a cask; begged food; single blanket	Infinite wealth: royal robes, servants
Contrasting Point 2: Social Philosophy	Unconventional, no respect for rank; no manners, respected only life of the spirit	Highest rank; educated by Aristotle; traveled to East to learn wisdom; chivalrous
Contrasting Point 3: Power	None except influence of his teaching; wise sayings a model for students	Absolute authority: king, emperor, commander in chief

Patterns of Organization

The two basic patterns of organization for a comparison or contrast essay are the block pattern and the alternating pattern. In the block pattern you move *vertically* down your grid outline, covering every point about your first element before moving on to the same points for the second element. To continue with our example, Highet discusses Diogenes completely in the first ten paragraphs before turning to Alexander in subsequent paragraphs. A paragraph of transition links the two contrasted elements. A summary paragraph concludes the essay, uniting the two characters in a statement of the theme of personal freedom.

In the alternating pattern, the point rather than the element is the focus of each paragraph. Each point is examined with regard to the two elements of contrast or comparison. For this method, you work *horizontally* across your grid, discussing each point by weaving back and forth between elements A and B. An example of the alternating pattern is David Riesman's contrast of Churchill and Roosevelt in paragraph 14 of "Images of Power."

There are advantages to both the block and the alternating patterns of organization. The block pattern is less complicated. You group together all the points about one element, make a clear-cut transition, and then group together the same points about your second element. This method permits your reader to concentrate on each element separately.

The alternating method is more complex and demanding. You must make immediate comparisons between your elements in regard to each point, and you must use a transitional signal each time you shift from one element to the other. This method permits your reader to focus on the similarities and/or differences between your elements. It may be a preferable pattern in essays where there are numerous points under consideration.

Transitions

Transitions play a major role in achieving clarity in the modes of comparison and contrast. In the block pattern, transition between contrasting elements is usually achieved through one or more linking paragraphs. Typically, these paragraphs contain a summarizing reference to the first element and an introductory reference to the second. They should also include a reference to the thesis that controls your essay.

In the alternating pattern, you need to use transitional signals, such as *on the other hand, in contrast to, similarly,* and *both,* as you move your discussion from one element to the other within the same paragraph.

Whether you use the block or alternating method, transitional expressions play an important part in the introduction of your essay, where you introduce the elements you are comparing, and in the conclusion, where you summarize the central idea brought out in the comparison.

GILBERT HIGHET

Diogenes and Alexander

Classicist Highet's contrastive essay brings to life two figures from ancient Greece through vivid description and anecdote. Diogenes, the beggar-philosopher, and Alexander the Great, who at the age of 30 wept because he had no more worlds to conquer, are the two contrasting elements. Though they represent extremes of the human condition, Highet has found a commonality in their personal freedom.

Before you read, find the current meaning of the word *cynicism,* and as you read, compare it to its original meaning as a philosophical creed.

Lying on the bare earth, shoeless, bearded, half-naked, he looked like a beggar or a lunatic. He was one, but not the other. He had opened his eyes with the sun at dawn, scratched, done his business like a dog at the roadside, washed at the public fountain, begged a piece of breakfast bread and a few olives, eaten them squatting on the ground, and washed them down with a few handfuls of water scooped from the spring. (Long ago he had owned a rough wooden cup, but he threw it away when he saw a boy drinking out of his hollowed hands.) Having no work to go to and no family to provide for, he was free. As the market place filled up with shoppers and merchants and gossipers and sharpers and slaves and foreigners, he had strolled through it for an hour or two. Everybody knew him, or knew of him. They would throw sharp questions at him and get sharper answers. Sometimes they threw jeers, and got jibes; sometimes bits of food, and got scant thanks; sometimes a mischievous pebble, and got a shower of stones and

Annotations (right margin):

1 — Block pattern begins with Diogenes

Striking introduction of first element

Inductive development

Point 1: material possessions

abuse. They were not quite sure whether he was mad or not. He knew they were mad, all mad, each in a different way; they amused him. Now he was back at his home.

Point 2: social philosophy

It was not a house, not even a squatter's hut. He thought everybody lived far too elaborately, expensively, anxiously. What good is a house? No one needs privacy: natural acts are not shameful; we all do the same things, and need not hide them. No one needs beds and chairs and such furniture. The animals live healthy lives and sleep on the ground. All we require, since nature did not dress us properly, is one garment to keep us warm, and some shelter from rain and wind. So he had one blanket—to dress him in the daytime and cover him at night—and he slept in a cask. His name was Diogenes. He was the founder of the creed called Cynicism (the word means "doggishness"); he spent much of his life in the rich, lazy, corrupt Greek city of Corinth, mocking and satirizing its people, and occasionally converting one of them.

2 Contrast between how he is perceived and how he perceives others

His home was not a barrel made of wood: too expensive. It was a storage jar made of earthenware, something like a modern fuel tank—no doubt discarded because a break had made it useless. He was not the first to inhabit such a thing: the refugees driven into Athens by the Spartan invasion had been forced to sleep in casks. But he was the first who ever did so by choice, out of principle.

Diogenes was not a degenerate or a maniac. He was a philosopher who wrote plays and poems and essays expounding his doctrine; he talked to those who cared to listen; he had pupils who admired him. But he taught chiefly by example. All should live naturally, he said, for what is natural is normal and cannot possibly be evil or shameful. Live without conventions, which are artificial and false; escape complexities and superfluities and extravagances, only so can you live a free life. The rich man believes he possesses his big house with its many rooms and its elaborate furniture, his pictures and his expensive clothes, his horses and his servants and his

4 Point 3: the source of his political power; the influence of his teaching

bank accounts. He does not. He depends on them, he worries about them, he spends most of his life's energy looking after them; the thought of losing them makes him sick with anxiety. They possess him. He is their slave. In order to procure a quantity of false, perishable goods he has sold the only true, lasting good, his own independence.

There have been many men who grew tired of human society with its complications, and went away to live simply—on a small farm, in a quiet village, in a hermit's cave, or in the darkness of anonymity. Not so Diogenes. He was not a recluse, or a stylite, or a beatnik. He was a missionary. His life's aim was clear to him: it was "to restamp the currency." (He and his father had once been convicted for counterfeiting, long before he turned to philosophy, and this phrase was Diogenes' bold, unembarrassed joke on the subject.) To restamp the currency: to take the clean metal of human life, to erase the old false conventional markings, and to imprint it with its true values.

The other great philosophers of the fourth century before Christ taught mainly their own private pupils. In the shady groves and cool sanctuaries of the Academy, Plato discoursed to a chosen few on the unreality of this contingent existence. Aristotle, among the books and instruments and specimens and archives and research-workers of his Lyceum, pursued investigations and gave lectures that were rightly named *esoteric* "for those within the walls." But for Diogenes, laboratory and specimens and lecture halls and pupils were all to be found in a crowd of ordinary people. Therefore he chose to live in Athens or in the rich city of Corinth, where travelers from all over the Mediterranean world constantly came and went. And, by design, he publicly behaved in such ways as to show people what real life was. He would constantly take up their spiritual coin, ring it on a stone, and laugh at its false superscription.

He thought most people were only half-alive, most men only half-men. At bright

5   Signal of contrast

6   Contrast: Diogenes and other philosophers

      Signal of contrast

7   Anecdotes develop points of contrast

noonday he walked through the market place carrying a lighted lamp and inspecting the face of everyone he met. They asked him why. Diogenes answered, "I am trying to find a *man*."

To a gentleman whose servant was putting on his shoes for him, Diogenes said, "You won't be really happy until he wipes your nose for you: that will come after you lose the use of your hands." 8

Once there was a war scare so serious that it stirred even the lazy, profit-happy Corinthians. They began to drill, clean their weapons, and rebuild their neglected fortifications. Diogenes took his old cask and began to roll it up and down, back and forward. "When you are all so busy," he said, "I felt I ought to do *something!*" 9

And so he lived—like a dog, some said, because he cared nothing for privacy and other human conventions, and because he showed his teeth and barked at those whom he disliked. Now he was lying in the sunlight, as contented as a dog on the warm ground, happier (he himself used to boast) than the Shah of Persia. Although he knew he was going to have an important visitor, he would not move. 10

Signal of transition to second element

The little square began to fill with people. Page boys elegantly dressed, spearmen speaking a rough foreign dialect, discreet secretaries, hard-browed officers, suave diplomats, they all gradually formed a circle centered on Diogenes. He looked them over, as a sober man looks at a crowd of tottering drunks, and shook his head. He knew who they were. They were the attendants of the conqueror of Greece, the servants of Alexander, the Macedonian king, who was visiting his newly subdued realm. 11

Transitional paragraph between contrasting elements: Diogenes and Alexander

Only twenty, Alexander was far older and wiser than his years. Like all Macedonians he loved drinking, but he could usually handle it; and toward women he was nobly restrained and chivalrous. Like all Macedonians he loved fighting; he was a magnificent commander, but he was not merely a military automaton. He could think. At thirteen he had become a pupil of the greatest mind in Greece, Aristotle. No exact rec- 12

Block pattern: Alexander
Points: social philosophy; source of political power

ord of his schooling survives. It is clear, though, that Aristotle took the passionate, half-barbarous boy and gave him the best of Greek culture. He taught Alexander poetry: the young prince slept with the *Iliad* under his pillow and longed to emulate Achilles, who brought the mighty power of Asia to ruin. He taught him philosophy, in particular the shapes and uses of political power: a few years later Alexander was to create a supranational empire that was not merely a power system but a vehicle for the exchange of Greek and Middle Eastern cultures.

Aristotle taught him the principles of scientific research: during his invasion of the Persian domains Alexander took with him a large corps of scientists, and shipped hundreds of zoological specimens back to Greece for study. Indeed, it was from Aristotle that Alexander learned to seek out everything strange which might be instructive. Jugglers and stunt artists and virtuosos of the absurd he dismissed with a shrug; but on reaching India he was to spend hours discussing the problems of life and death with naked Hindu mystics, and later to see one demonstrate Yoga self-command by burning himself impassively to death. 13

Now, Alexander was in Corinth to take command of the League of Greek States which, after conquering them, his father Philip had created as a disguise for the New Macedonian Order. He was welcomed and honored and flattered. He was the man of the hour, of the century: he was unanimously appointed commander-in-chief of a new expedition against old, rich, corrupt Asia. Nearly everyone crowded to Corinth in order to congratulate him, to seek employment with him, even simply to see him: soldiers and statesmen, artists and merchants, poets and philosophers. He received their compliments graciously. Only Diogenes, although he lived in Corinth, did not visit the new monarch. With that generosity which Aristotle had taught him was a quality of the truly magnanimous man, Alexander determined to call upon Diogenes. Surely Dio-genes, the God-born, would acknowledge 14

Signal of contrast

Anecdote of contrast begins

the conqueror's power by some gift of hoarded wisdom.

With his handsome face, his fiery glance, his strong supple body, his purple and gold cloak and his air of destiny, he moved through the parting crowd, toward the Dog's kennel. When a king approaches, all rise in respect. Diogenes did not rise, he merely sat up on one elbow. When a monarch enters a precinct, all greet him with a bow or an acclamation. Diogenes said nothing. ¹⁵

15 Alternating pattern between elements illustrates points: material possessions, power

There was a silence. Some years later Alexander speared his best friend to the wall, for objecting to the exaggerated honors paid to His Majesty; but now he was still young and civil. He spoke first, with a kindly greeting. Looking at the poor broken cask, the single ragged garment, and the rough figure lying on the ground, he said: "Is there anything I can do for you, Diogenes?" ¹⁶

16 Anecdote of contrast continues

"Yes," said the Dog, "Stand to one side. You're blocking the sunlight." ¹⁷

There was silence, not the ominous silence preceding a burst of fury, but a hush of amazement. Slowly, Alexander turned away. A titter broke out from the elegant Greeks, who were already beginning to make jokes about the Cur that looked at the King. The Macedonian officers, after deciding that Diogenes was not worth the trouble of kicking, were starting to guffaw and nudge one another. Alexander was still silent. To those nearest him he said quietly, "If I were not Alexander, I should be Diogenes." They took it as a paradox, designed to close the awkward little scene with a polite curtain line. But Alexander meant it. He understood Cynicism as the others could not. Later he took one of Diogenes' pupils with him to India as a philosophical interpreter (it was he who spoke to the naked *saddhus*). He was what Diogenes called himself, a *cosmopolitēs*, "citizen of the world." Like Diogenes, he admired the heroic figure of Hercules, the mighty conqueror who labors to help mankind while all others toil and sweat ¹⁸

18

Signal of contrast

only for themselves. He knew that of all men
then alive in the world only Alexander the conqueror and Diogenes the beggar were truly free.

Thesis: commonality of
the contrastive elements

Analysis of the Essay

THE PROCESS OF EXPRESSING SIMILARITIES AND DIFFERENCES

Gilbert Highet's inductive essay uses the block pattern to take the reader to his
implied thesis that only the king and the person who rejects the kingdom are truly
free. He begins with a striking image of the beggar Diogenes, which shocks the
reader into attention. Paragraphs 1 through 10 elaborate the following points
about Diogenes: his material possessions, social philosophy, and political power.
The points overlap in different paragraphs, but their general sequence is from the
concrete details of Diogenes' existence to the more abstract concepts of his social behavior, philosophy, and influence as a teacher. Certain paragraphs, however, treat one point exclusively. For example, paragraphs 4, 5, and 6, are devoted
exclusively to his philosophy and teaching style.

Because this essay is more of a narrative than a formal analysis, Highet does
not treat the points of comparison for each element systematically. Less space is
devoted to Alexander than to Diogenes, and the points are not elaborated with as
much detail. However, the three major points of contrast are covered for both
men. Alexander's material wealth is communicated with a brief reference to his
"purple and gold cloak." His philosophy is described at greater length in paragraphs 12 and 13. Finally, several paragraphs illuminate the quality of his political power.

Paragraph 11 introduces Alexander, thereby marking the transition between
the two elements. It encapsulates the polarity between Diogenes, the Cynic, who
has only disdain for the riches of the world, and Alexander, who is the embodiment of these riches. Then several paragraphs in the block pattern present Alexander to the reader.

Highet repeats key concepts and uses signal words to link ideas within and
between paragraphs. He uses many signals of opposition because he is contrasting Diogenes not only to Alexander but also to conventional people, to other philosophers, and to the lunatic he appears to be. The opening of the essay is a clear example: Diogenes "looked like a beggar or a lunatic. He was one, but not the other."

The concluding paragraph brings the two elements together, signaling their
commonality with the word *like* and stating that "of all men . . . only Alexander . . . and Diogenes . . . were truly free."

READINGS

BRUCE CATTON

Grant and Lee: A Study in Contrasts

Historian Bruce Catton's *A Stillness at Appomattox* (1953)
won both the Pulitzer Prize and the National Book
Award (1954). This excerpt contrasts the opposing military leaders of the Civil War both as individuals and as
embodiments of dissimilar values and aspirations.

When Ulysses S. Grant and Robert E. Lee met in the parlor of a modest   1
house at Appomattox Court House, Virginia, on April 9, 1865, to work
out the terms of the surrender of Lee's Army of Northern Virginia, a great
chapter in American life came to a close, and a great new chapter began.

These men were bringing the Civil War to its virtual finish. To be   2
sure, other armies had yet to surrender, and for a few days the fugitive
Confederate government would struggle desperately and vainly, trying to
find some way to go on living now that its chief support was gone. But in
effect it was all over when Grant and Lee signed the papers. And the little
room where they wrote out the terms was the scene of one of the poignant,
dramatic contrasts in American history.

They were two strong men, these oddly different generals, and they   3
represented the strengths of two conflicting currents that, through them,
had come into final collision.

Back of Robert E. Lee was the notion that the old aristocratic con-   4
cept might somehow survive and be dominant in American life.

Lee was tidewater Virginia, and in his background were family, cul-   5
ture, and tradition . . . the age of chivalry transplanted to a New World
which was making its own legends and its own myths. He embodied a
way of life that had come down through the age of knighthood and the
English country squire. America was a land that was beginning all over
again, dedicated to nothing much more complicated than the rather hazy
belief that all men had equal rights and should have an equal chance in the
world. In such a land Lee stood for the feeling that it was somehow of
advantage to human society to have a pronounced inequality in the social
structure. There should be a leisure class, backed by ownership of land; in
turn, society itself should be keyed to the land as the chief source of

wealth and influence. It would bring forth (according to this ideal) a class of men with a strong sense of obligation to the community; men who lived not to gain advantage for themselves, but to meet the solemn obligations which had been laid on them by the very fact that they were privileged. From them the country would get its leadership; to them it could look for the higher values—of thought, of conduct, of personal deportment—to give it strength and virtue.

Lee embodied the noblest elements of this aristocratic ideal. Through him, the landed nobility justified itself. For four years, the Southern states had fought a desperate war to uphold the ideals for which Lee stood. In the end, it almost seemed as if the Confederacy fought for Lee; as if he himself was the Confederacy . . . the best thing that the way of life for which the Confederacy stood could ever have to offer. He had passed into legend before Appomattox. Thousands of tired, underfed, poorly clothed Confederate soldiers, long since past the simple enthusiasm of the early days of the struggle, somehow considered Lee the symbol of everything for which they had been willing to die. . . . 6

Grant fought with tenacity for the broader concept of society. He fought so because everything he lived by was tied to growth, expansion, and a constantly widening horizon. What he lived by would survive or fall with the nation itself. He could not possibly stand by unmoved in the face of an attempt to destroy the Union. He would combat it with everything he had, because he could only see it as an effort to cut the ground out from under his feet. 7

So Grant and Lee were in complete contrast, representing two diametrically opposed elements in American life. Grant was the modern man emerging; beyond him, ready to come on the stage, was the great age of steel and machinery, of crowded cities and a restless burgeoning vitality. Lee might have ridden down from the old age of chivalry, lance in hand, silken banner fluttering over his head. Each man was the perfect champion of his cause, drawing both his strengths and his weaknesses from the people he led. 8

Yet it was not all contrast, after all. Different as they were—in background, in personality, in underlying aspiration—these two great soldiers had much in common. Under everything else, they were marvelous fighters. Furthermore, their fighting qualities were really very much alike. 9

Each man had, to begin with, the great virtue of utter tenacity and fidelity. Grant fought his way down the Mississippi Valley in spite of acute personal discouragement and profound military handicaps. Lee hung on in the trenches at Petersburg after hope itself had died. In each man there was an indomitable quality . . . the born fighter's refusal to give up as long as he can still remain on his feet and lift his two fists. 10

Daring and resourcefulness they had, too; the ability to think faster 11 and move faster than the enemy. These were the qualities which gave Lee the dazzling campaigns of Second Manassas and Chancellorsville and won Vicksburg for Grant.

Lastly, and perhaps greatest of all, there was the ability, at the end, 12 to turn quickly from war to peace once the fighting was over. Out of the way these two men behaved at Appomattox came the possibility of a peace of reconciliation. It was a possibility not wholly realized, in the years to come, but which did, in the end, help the two sections to become one nation again . . . after a war whose bitterness might have seemed to make such a reunion wholly impossible. No part of either man's life became him more than the part he played in this brief meeting in the McLean house at Appomattox. Their behavior there put all succeeding generations of Americans in their debt. Two great Americans, Grant and Lee—very different, yet under everything very much alike. Their encounter at Appomattox was one of the great moments of American history.

Reading and Interpreting

VOCABULARY

Use your dictionary as necessary to find the meaning of the following words as used by Bruce Catton:

pronounced (5)   deportment (5)   tenacity (7)   diametrically (8)
burgeoning (8)

CONCEPT ANALYSIS

1. What are the two specific points or bases of commonality between the two generals? What other qualities do they share?
2. Is Catton's primary aim to contrast the two men or the two philosophies that they embody? Discuss the philosophy that each man represents.

Quickwrite

Catton characterizes both Grant and Lee as having an "indomitable quality . . . the born fighter's refusal to give up as long as he can still remain on his feet and lift his two fists." Write a description of such an individual whom you know. Include a brief anecdote to illustrate this indomitability.

Thinking and Writing

RHETORICAL TECHNIQUE

1. To what extent is this essay organized in the block and alternating patterns? Map the essay by labeling the paragraphs either block, alternating, or transitional.
2. In paragraphs 5 and 8 Catton uses the metaphor of a medieval knight to describe Lee. Compose a metaphor for Grant that would heighten the comparison.

COMPOSITION

1. Select two people whom you know or know about, and write a brief contrastive study beginning with a statement of similarities. Use paragraphs 9 through 12 in Catton's essay as a model for your conclusion.
2. Choose two public figures who represent diametrically opposed philosophies. Using Catton's essay as a model, write a contrastive essay about them.

EDGAR LEE MASTERS

Lucinda Matlock and *George Gray*

Edgar Lee Masters's (1869–1950) American masterpiece *Spoon River Anthology* is a book of free verse epitaphs that dramatize the inner lives of people buried in the cemetery of Spoon River, a fictional midwestern town. Lucinda Matlock's and George Gray's poetic statements are representative of Masters' realistic portrayals of universal themes.

Lucinda Matlock

I went to the dances at Chandlerville,
And played snap-out at Winchester,
One time we changed partners,
Driving home in the moonlight of middle June,
And then I found Davis.   5
We were married and lived together for seventy years.
Enjoying, working, raising the twelve children,
Eight of whom we lost
Ere I had reached the age of sixty.
I spun, I wove, I kept the house, I nursed the sick.   10
I made the garden, and for holiday
Rambled over the fields where sang the larks.
And by Spoon River gathering many a shell
And a flower and medicinal weed—
Shouting to the wooded hills, singing to the green valleys.   15
At ninety six I had lived enough, that is all,
And passed to a sweet repose.
What is this I hear of sorrow and weariness,
Anger, discontent, and drooping hopes?
Degenerate sons and daughters,   20
Life is too strong for you—
It takes life to love life.

George Gray

I have studied many times
The marble which was chiseled for me—
A boat with a furled sail at rest in a harbor.
In truth it pictures not my destination
But my life.   5
For love was offered me, and I shrank from its disillusionment;
Sorrow knocked at my door, but I was afraid;
Ambition called to me, but I dreaded the chances,
Yet all the while I hungered for meaning in my life
And now I know that we must lift the sail   10
And catch the winds of destiny
Wherever they drive the boat.
To put meaning in one's life may end in madness,
But life without meaning is the torture
Of restlessness and vague desire—   15
It is a boat longing for the sea and yet afraid.

Reading and Interpreting

VOCABULARY

Use your dictionary as necessary to find the meaning of the following words:

degenerate ("Lucinda Matlock," 20).   furled ("George Gray," 3)

CONCEPT ANALYSIS

1. What statement does each character make about a worthwhile life?
2. Why does Lucinda Matlock criticize the current generation? Lucinda Matlock's life suggests that hardships produce strong character. Do you agree or disagree? Discuss, applying your view to your own as well as earlier generations.
3. The image of a boat with a furled sail at rest in the harbor is an appropriate emblem for George Gray's life. What might be an appropriate image for Lucinda Matlock's life?

Quickwrite

Create an image that is emblematic of your life. Explain its aptness.

Thinking and Writing

RHETORICAL TECHNIQUE

"George Gray" is a study in the contrast between this character's feelings and his actions. Which lines explicitly express this contrast?

COMPOSITION

Write a sketch contrasting Lucinda Matlock and George Gray in terms of their feelings about life and the content of their lives. Use the alternating pattern of organization.

GEORGE FREDRICKSON

A Closer Parallel: Southern Blacks and Cape Coloreds

George Fredrickson subtitles *White Supremacy,* his work on racial relationships, *A Comparative Study in American and South African History.* Black Americans form one element of the study. The South African element includes two different groups: native black peoples, who are segregated in "homelands," and Cape Coloreds, an ethnic group of mixed racial origins, who form a minority in the South African population. It is with this latter group that Fredrickson finds the "closer parallel" to American blacks in the following essay.

If the situations and historical experiences of the Afro-American minority   1
and the black South African majority differ in some fundamental ways, there is another important racial group in South Africa that has had a changing relationship with the dominant whites that more closely parallels the "strange career of Jim Crow" in the South. The history of the Cape Coloreds since the era of emancipation is comparable to that of southern blacks in that it involved an early movement toward equality followed by a rise or extension of segregation and disfranchisement culminating in full legalization of a separate and inferior status. More than the contrast with "native segregation," such a comparison can shed light on some of the circumstances likely to promote the emergence of legalized caste distinctions based exclusively and unambiguously on racial criteria. The cultural divergence between whites and those Africans who maintained strong ties with a traditional culture—a factor that complicates any effort to see the European-African confrontation as purely or simply a race struggle—is not an element here, any more than it was a central and defining feature of black-white relations in the South.

The common or analogous elements of the Afro-American and Cape   2
Colored experiences are numerous. Both groups are descended to a large extent from slaves or quasi-slaves rather than from indigenous groups that were conquered and allotted reservations under conditions that permitted them to retain substantial elements of their traditional culture. . . . Both are of racially mixed origin, although there is a difference of degree. Studies of gene frequency among contemporary Afro-American population

samples give a wide range of results for the apparent percentage of white admixture, but the best estimates are between 4 and 11 percent for southern blacks and 19 to 26 percent for nonsouthern. Uncalculated and indeterminate are the effects of black-Indian intermixture. . . . Hence Afro-Americans, while far from being purely African in descent, are predominantly so. Cape Coloreds, according to one recent study, are more clearly tri-racial in origin; indeed "the Cape Colored population in Cape Town . . . are constituted by approximately equal proportions of European, Asian, and Southern African genes." . . .

Moving from the realm of genetic intermixture to that of cultural 3 adaptation, one finds that both southern blacks and Cape Coloreds have been profoundly influenced by white or European culture—an inevitable result of two or three centuries of close interaction with the dominant group. It is not accurate to say that they have undergone total cultural assimilation; for Afro-Americans have adapted some of their African heritage to American conditions to create a distinct and vital subculture of their own, and certain elements among the Cape Coloreds, most notably the Muslim community known as the Cape Malays, have retained living ties to a non-European tradition. . . . But in comparison to most indigenous Africans or American Indians, they have become substantially "Western" in their cultural orientations. Both groups, for example, are predominantly Christian and speak no languages other than those also spoken by whites.

They also represent similar proportions of the total population of the 4 nations in which they reside—about 10 percent or slightly more in recent decades. Another striking demographic similarity is revealed by comparing their numbers relative to the whites in South Africa as a whole and in the American South during the segregation era. In both cases, these racial minorities are about one-half as numerous as the whites. The western Cape, where most of the Coloreds have remained concentrated, can be likened to the deep South or the cotton belt before the Great Migration. Here one is dealing with something close to demographic parity between whites and Afro-Americans or Coloreds. . . .

Of greatest significance for our purposes, however, are the compa- 5 rable historical experiences of emancipation from thralldom, being granted equality under the law and access to the suffrage, and then losing most of these rights as the result of an upsurge of white supremacy. What happened to Afro-Americans in the period 1890–1910 was not fully experienced by Cape Coloreds until the 1940s and 50s, but in both instances there was a prior history of partial or customary segregation and an erosion of political and civil rights that anticipated formal and complete disfranchisement and the legalization of separate and unequal treatment in virtually every aspect of social activity.

Of course the profound differences in the larger national and so- 6 cial context must be borne in mind in making the comparison. As a denigrated minority in an overwhelmingly white nation, Afro-Americans became the major scapegoat for majority prejudices and served as the lowest-ranking reference group for the society as a whole. As a minority within a society with a larger white minority and a black majority, Cape Coloreds have sometimes been in a position to enjoy the relative advantage of intermediate or buffer status, which has shielded them from some of the racial hostility vented on Afro-Americans. Where blacks have been the main object of white antagonism in the United States, it is the Africans and not the Coloreds who have been most feared by Europeans in South Africa. Hence the status and situation of the Coloreds have been determined as much by how whites perceived their role in African-white relations as by the intrinsic character of their own relationship with the dominant racial group.

Reading and Interpreting

VOCABULARY

Use your dictionary as necessary to find the meaning of the following words in context:

indigenous (2)   parity (4)   thralldom (5)   intrinsic (6)

CONCEPT ANALYSIS

1. To analyze this essay, complete the following grid with Fredrickson's points of comparison:

POINTS	ELEMENT A:	ELEMENT B:
1:		
2:		
3:		
4:		
5:		

2. State the fundamental contrast(s) between the two comparative elements in this essay.

Quickwrite

Fredrickson points out that black Americans have served as the "major scapegoat for majority prejudices. . . ." Discuss the concept of "scapegoating." Today, which group(s) do you feel are placed in the position of scapegoats?

Thinking and Writing

RHETORICAL TECHNIQUE

1. Is this essay inductively or deductively developed? Support your response by underlining the thesis statement.
2. Because Fredrickson's essay uses the alternating pattern of organization, signal words are very important. Underline the signals for comparison used in paragraphs 1 through 5. Select several sentences and paraphrase them, using alternative expressions.

COMPOSITION

Fredrickson's essay focuses on the similarity between two groups that might appear quite different to the superficial observer. Select two seemingly different groups in American society (from work, the university, or the community), and write a short essay emphasizing their similarities.

GEORGE ORWELL

Down and Out in Paris and London

In this excerpt from his fictionalized autobiography, Orwell makes trenchant observations about the hierarchy of a hotel restaurant staff. He concludes that waiters don't become socialists. Can you follow his reasoning?

This gives some idea of the elaborate caste system existing in a hotel. Our 1
staff, amounting to about a hundred and ten, had their prestige graded as
accurately as that of soldiers, and a cook or waiter was as much above a
plongeur as a captain above a private. Highest of all came the manager,
who could sack anybody, even the cooks. We never saw the *patron,* and all
we knew of him was that his meals had to be prepared more carefully than
that of the customers; all the discipline of the hotel depended on the manager. He was a conscientious man, and always on the lookout for slack-
ness, but we were too clever for him. A system of service bells ran through
the hotel, and the whole staff used these for signalling to one another. A
long ring and a short ring, followed by two more long rings, meant that
the manager was coming, and when we heard it we took care to look busy.

Below the manager came the *maître d'hôtel.* He did not serve at 2
table, unless to a lord or someone of that kind, but directed the other
waiters and helped with the catering. His tips, and his bonus from the
champagne companies (it was two francs for each cork he returned to
them), came to two hundred francs a day. He was in a position quite apart
from the rest of the staff, and took his meals in a private room, with silver
on the table and two apprentices in clean white jackets to serve him. A
little below the head waiter came the head cook, drawing about five thousand francs a month; he dined in the kitchen, but at a separate table, and
one of the apprentice cooks waited on him. Then came the *chef du personnel;* he drew only fifteen hundred francs a month, but he wore a black coat
and did no manual work, and he could sack *plongeurs* and fine waiters.
Then came the other cooks, drawing anything between three thousand
and seven hundred and fifty francs a month; then the waiters, making
about seventy francs a day in tips, besides a small retaining fee; then the
laundresses and sewing women; then the apprentice waiters, who received
no tips, but were paid seven hundred and fifty francs a month; then the
plongeurs, also at seven hundred and fifty francs; then the chambermaids,
at five or six hundred francs a month; and lastly the cafetiers, at five hundred a month. We of the cafeterie were the very dregs of the hotel, despised and *tutoied* by everyone.

There were various others—the office employees, called generally 3
couriers, the storekeeper, the cellarman, some porters and pages, the ice
man, the bakers, the night-watchman, the doorkeeper. Different jobs were
done by different races. The office employees and the cooks and sewing-
women were French, the waiters Italians and Germans (there is hardly
such a thing as a French waiter in Paris), the *plongeurs* of every race in
Europe, beside Arabs and negroes. French was the lingua franca, even the
Italians speaking it to one another.

All the departments had their special perquisites. In all Paris hotels 4
it is the custom to sell the broken bread to bakers for eight sous a pound,
and the kitchen scraps to pigkeepers for a trifle, and to divide the proceeds

of this among the *plongeurs*. There was much pilfering, too. The waiters all stole food—in fact, I seldom saw a waiter trouble to eat the rations provided for him by the hotel—and the cooks did it on a larger scale in the kitchen, and we in the cafeterie swilled illicit tea and coffee. The cellarman stole brandy. By a rule of the hotel the waiters were not allowed to keep stores of spirits, but had to go to the cellarman for each drink as it was ordered. As the cellarman poured out the drinks he would set aside perhaps a teaspoonful from each glass, and he amassed quantities in this way. He would sell you the stolen brandy for five sous a swig if he thought he could trust you. . . .

What keeps a hotel going is the fact that the employees take a genu- 5 ine pride in their work, beastly and silly though it is. If a man idles, the others soon find him out, and conspire against him to get him sacked. Cooks, waiters and *plongeurs* differ greatly in outlook, but they are all alike in being proud of their efficiency.

Undoubtedly the most workmanlike class, and the least servile, are 6 the cooks. They do not earn quite so much as waiters, but their prestige is higher and their employment steadier. The cook does not look upon himself as a servant, but as a skilled workman; he is generally called "*un ouvrier*," which a waiter never is. He knows his power—knows that he alone makes or mars a restaurant, and that if he is five minutes late everything is out of gear. He despises the whole noncooking staff, and makes it a point of honour to insult everyone below the head waiter. And he takes a genuine artistic pride in his work, which demands very great skill. It is not the cooking that is so difficult, but the doing everything to time. Between breakfast and luncheon the head cook at the Hôtel X. would receive orders for several hundred dishes, all to be served at different times; he cooked few of them himself, but he gave instructions about all of them and inspected them before they were sent up. His memory was wonderful. The vouchers were pinned on a board, but the head cook seldom looked at them; everything was stored in his mind, and exactly to the minute, as each dish fell due, he would call out, "*Faites marcher une côtelette de veau*" (or whatever it was) unfailingly. He was an insufferable bully, but he was also an artist. It is for their punctuality, and not for any superiority in technique, that men cooks are preferred to women.

The waiter's outlook is quite different. He too is proud in a way of 7 his skill, but his skill is chiefly in being servile. His work gives him the mentality, not of a workman, but of a snob. He lives perpetually in sight of rich people, stands at their tables, listens to their conversation, sucks up to them with smiles and discreet little jokes. He has the pleasure of spending money by proxy. Moreover, there is always the chance that he may become rich himself, for, though most waiters die poor, they have long runs of luck occasionally. At some cafés on the Grand Boulevard there is so much money to be made that the waiters actually pay the *patron* for their employment. The result is that between constantly seeing money, and hoping to get it, the waiter comes to identify himself to some extent with his employers. He will take pains to serve a meal in style, because he feels that he is participating in the meal himself.

I remember Valenti telling me of some banquet at Nice at which he 8 had once served, and of how it cost two hundred thousand francs and was talked of for months afterwards. "It was splendid, *mon p'tit, mais magnifique!* Jesus Christ! The champagne, the silver, the orchids—I have never seen anything like them, and I have seen some things. Ah, it was glorious!"

"But," I said, "you were only there to wait?" 9

"Oh, of course. But still, it was splendid." 10

The moral is, never be sorry for a waiter. Sometimes when you sit in 11 a restaurant, still stuffing yourself half an hour after closing time, you feel that the tired waiter at your side must surely be despising you. But he is not. He is not thinking as he looks at you, "What an overfed lout"; he is thinking, "One day, when I have saved enough money, I shall be able to imitate that man." He is ministering to a kind of pleasure he thoroughly understands and admires. And that is why waiters are seldom Socialists, have no effective trade union, and will work twelve hours a day—they work fifteen hours, seven days a week, in many cafés. They are snobs, and they find the servile nature of their work rather congenial.

The *plongeurs*, again, have a different outlook. Theirs is a job which 12 offers no prospects, is intensely exhausting, and at the same time has not a trace of skill or interest; the sort of job that would always be done by women if women were strong enough. All that is required of them is to be constantly on the run, and to put up with long hours and a stuffy atmosphere. They have no way of escaping from this life, for they cannot save a penny from their wages, and working from sixty to a hundred hours a week leaves them no time to train for anything else. The best they can hope for is to find a slightly softer job as night-watchman or lavatory attendant.

And yet the *plongeurs*, low as they are, also have a kind of pride. It is 13 the pride of the drudge—the man who is equal to no matter what quantity of work. At that level, the mere power to go on working like an ox is about the only virtue attainable. *Débrouillard* is what every *plongeur* wants to be called. A *débrouillard* is a man who, even when he is told to do the impossible, will *se débrouiller*—get it done somehow. One of the kitchen *plongeurs* at the Hôtel X., a German, was well known as a *débrouillard*. One night an English lord came to the hotel, and the waiters were in despair, for the lord had asked for peaches, and there were none in stock; it was late at night, and the shops would be shut. "Leave it to me," said the German. He went out, and in ten minutes he was back with four peaches. He had gone into a neighbouring restaurant and stolen them. That is what is meant by a *débrouillard*. The English lord paid for the peaches at twenty francs each.

Mario, who was in charge of the cafeterie, had the typical drudge 14
mentality. All he thought of was getting through the "*boulot*" and he defied you to give him too much of it. Fourteen years underground had left
him with about as much natural laziness as a piston rod. "*Faut être dur,*"[1]
he used to say when anyone complained. You will often hear *plongeurs*
boast, "*Je suis dur*"[2]—as though they were soldiers, not male charwomen.

Thus everyone in the hotel had his sense of honour, and when the 15
press of work came we were all ready for a grand concerted effort to get
through it. The constant war between the different departments also made
for efficiency, for everyone clung to his own privileges and tried to stop the
others idling and pilfering.

Reading and Interpreting

VOCABULARY

Use your dictionary as necessary to find the meaning of the following words
as used by Orwell:

caste (1)   perquisites (4)   illicit (4)   proxy (7)

CONCEPT ANALYSIS

1. Whom do you think Orwell admires? despises? Explain your responses
   with reference to the text.
2. Can Orwell's points about the hotel staff be generalized to the human
   condition? Discuss.

---

1. "You've got to be tough."—Ed.
2. "I'm tough."—Ed.

Complete the following contrastive structures from Orwell's essay with items from any aspect of life or with individuals you know:

1. _____ and _____ differ greatly in _____ , but they are alike in _____ . (5)

2. _____ was an insufferable _____ , but he [she] was also an _____ . (6)

3. It is for their _____ , and not for any _____ , that _____ are preferred to _____ . (6)

4. And yet the _____ , low as they are, also have a kind of _____ . (13)

5. There were various others— _____ , _____ , _____ . Different _____ were done by different _____ . (3)

6. Our _____ had their prestige graded as accurately as that of soldiers. Highest of all came _____ . Below [these] came the _____ . A little below came _____ . Then came the other _____ ; then the _____ ; then the _____ ; and lastly the _____ . [These] were the dregs. (1–2)

Use one of your completed statements as a controlling idea for a quickwrite.

Thinking and Writing

RHETORICAL TECHNIQUE

1. What word in the first paragraph of this deductive essay suggests the principle of contrast that will govern the essay? Which phrase indicates the commonality among the elements?

2. Review paragraphs 2, 3, and 4, and list the point of comparison that controls each.

3. What is the point of comparison that controls the essay from paragraph 6 onward?

4. What pattern of organization predominates from paragraph 5 onward— block or alternating? Underline the signals of transition.

COMPOSITION

Analyze the composition of one of the following: your family, the staff at your job, a summer camp group, your dormitory group, your social or athletic club. Write an essay of comparison or contrast about your elements, beginning with a clear thesis statement of their commonality.

MARGARET MEAD
RHODA METRAUX

On Friendship

Distinguished American anthropologist Margaret Mead (1901–1978) brought popular recognition to her field with her ethnographic studies of South Seas cultures and her many books, including *Coming of Age in Samoa*. Anthropologist Rhoda Metraux (b. 1914), Mead's collaborator on the following article, has done fieldwork in many countries, including Haiti, Mexico, Argentina, and New Guinea. Here Mead and Metraux apply a cross-cultural perspective to the value of friendship in contemporary Western societies.

Few Americans stay put for a lifetime. We move from town to city to 1 suburb, from high school to college in a different state, from a job in one region to a better job elsewhere, from the home where we raise our children to the home where we plan to live in retirement. With each move we are forever making new friends, who become part of our new life at that time.

For many of us the summer is a special time for forming new friend- 2 ships. Today millions of Americans vacation abroad, and they go not only to see new sights but also—in those places where they do not feel too strange—with the hope of meeting new people. No one really expects a vacation trip to produce a close friend. But surely the beginning of a friendship is possible? Surely in every country people value friendship?

They do. The difficulty when strangers from two countries meet is 3 not a lack of appreciation of friendship, but different expectations about what constitutes friendship and how it comes into being. In those European countries that Americans are most likely to visit, friendship is quite sharply distinguished from other, more casual relations, and is differently related to family life. For a Frenchman, a German or an Englishman friendship is usually more particularized and carries a heavier burden of commitment.

But as we use the word, "friend" can be applied to a wide range of 4 relationships—to someone one has known for a few weeks in a new place, to a close business associate, to a childhood playmate, to a man or woman, to a trusted confidant. There are real differences among these relations for Americans—a friendship may be superficial, casual, situational or deep and enduring. But to a European, who sees only our surface behavior, the differences are not clear.

As they see it, people known and accepted temporarily, casually, 5 flow in and out of Americans' homes with little ceremony and often with little personal commitment. They may be parents of the children's friends, house guests of neighbors, members of a committee, business associates from another town or even another country. Coming as a guest into an American home, the European visitor finds no visible landmarks. The atmosphere is relaxed. Most people, old and young, are called by first names.

Who, then, is a friend? 6

Even simple translation from one language to another is difficult. 7 "You see," a Frenchman explains, "if I were to say to you in France, 'This is my good friend,' that person would not be as close to me as someone about whom I said only, 'This is my friend.' Anyone about whom I have to say *more* is really less."

In France, as in many European countries, friends generally are of 8 the same sex, and friendship is seen as basically a relationship between men. Frenchwomen laugh at the idea that "women can't be friends," but they also admit sometimes that for women "it's a different thing." And many French people doubt the possibility of a friendship between a man and a woman. There is also the kind of relationship within a group—men and women who have worked together for a long time, who may be very close, sharing great loyalty and warmth of feeling. They may call one another *copains*—a word that in English becomes "friends" but has more the feeling of "pals" or "buddies." In French eyes this is not friendship, although two members of such a group may well be friends.

For the French, friendship is a one-to-one relationship that demands 9 a keen awareness of the other person's intellect, temperament and particular interests. A friend is someone who draws out your own best qualities, with whom you sparkle and become more of whatever the friendship draws upon. Your political philosophy assumes more depth, appreciation of a play becomes sharper, taste in food or wine is accentuated, enjoyment of a sport is intensified.

And French friendships are compartmentalized. A man may play 10
chess with a friend for thirty years without knowing his political opinions,
or he may talk politics with him for as long a time without knowing about
his personal life. Different friends fill different niches in each person's life.
These friendships are not made part of family life. A friend is not expected
to spend evenings being nice to children or courteous to a deaf grandmother. These duties, also serious and enjoined, are primarily for relatives. Men who are friends may meet in a café. Intellectual friends may
meet in larger groups for evenings of conversation. Working people may
meet at the little *bistro* where they drink and talk, far from the family.
Marriage does not affect such friendships; wives do not have to be taken
into account.

In the past in France, friendships of this kind seldom were open to 11
any but intellectual women. Since most women's lives centered on their
homes, their warmest relations with other women often went back to their
girlhood. The special relationship of friendship is based on what the
French value most—on the mind, on compatibility of outlook, on vivid
awareness of some chosen area of life.

Friendship heightens the sense of each person's individuality. Other 12
relationships commanding as great loyalty and devotion have a different
meaning. In World War II the first resistance groups formed in Paris were
built on the foundation of *les copains*. But significantly, as time went on
these little groups, whose lives rested in one another's hands, called themselves "families." Where each had a total responsibility for all, it was
kinship ties that provided the model. And even today such ties, crossing
every line of class and personal interest, remain binding on the survivors
of these small, secret bands.

In Germany, in contrast with France, friendship is much more articu- 13
lately a matter of feeling. Adolescents, boys and girls, form deeply senti-
mental attachments, walk and talk together—not so much to polish their
wits as to share their hopes and fears and dreams, to form a common front
against the world of school and family and to join in a kind of mutual
discovery of each other's and their own inner life. Within the family, the
closest relationship over a lifetime is between brothers and sisters. Outside
the family, men and women find in their closest friends of the same sex the
devotion of a sister, the loyalty of a brother. Appropriately, in Germany
friends usually are brought into the family. Children call their father's
and mother's friends "uncle" and "aunt." Between French friends, who
have chosen each other for the congeniality of their point of view, lively
disagreement and sharpness of argument are the breath of life. But for
Germans, whose friendships are based on mutuality of feeling, deep disagreement on any subject that matters to both is regarded as a tragedy.
Like ties of kinship, ties of friendship are meant to be irrevocably binding.
Young Germans who come to the United States have great difficulty in

establishing such friendships with Americans. We view friendship more tentatively, subject to changes in intensity as people move, change their jobs, marry, or discover new interests.

English friendships follow still a different pattern. Their basis is 14 shared activity. Activities at different stages of life may be of very different kinds—discovering a common interest in school, serving together in the armed forces, taking part in a foreign mission, staying in the same country house during a crisis. In the midst of the activity, whatever it may be, people fall into step—sometimes two men or two women, sometimes two couples, sometimes three people—and find that they walk or play a game or tell stories or serve on a tiresome and exacting committee with the same easy anticipation of what each will do day by day or in some critical situation. Americans who have made English friends comment that, even years later, "you can take up just where you left off." Meeting after a long interval, friends are like a couple who begin to dance again when the orchestra strikes up after a pause. English friendships are formed outside the family circle, but they are not, as in Germany, contrapuntal to the family nor are they, as in France, separated from the family. And a break in an English friendship comes not necessarily as a result of some irreconcilable difference of viewpoint or feeling but instead as a result of misjudgment, where one friend seriously misjudges how the other will think or feel or act, so that suddenly they are out of step.

What, then, is friendship? Looking at these different styles, includ- 15 ing our own, each of which is related to a whole way of life, are there common elements? There is the recognition that friendship, in contrast with kinship, invokes freedom of choice. A friend is someone who chooses and is chosen. Related to this is the sense each friend gives the other of being a special individual, on whatever grounds this recognition is based. And between friends there is inevitably a kind of equality of give-and-take. These similarities make the bridge between societies possible, and the American's characteristic openness to different styles of relationship makes it possible for him to find new friends abroad with whom he feels at home.

Reading and Interpreting

VOCABULARY

Use your dictionary as necessary to find the meaning of the following words as used by Mead and Metraux:

particularized (3)   compartmentalized (10)   enjoined (10)

articulately (13)   irrevocably (13)

CONCEPT ANALYSIS

1. Express the thesis of this essay in your own words. Where is the thesis explicitly stated in the essay?
2. Write brief phrases about each element to complete the following grid as an outline of the essay. (Not every point may apply to each of the contrasting elements.) Why did the authors choose these elements?

POINTS	AMERICANS	FRENCH	GERMANS	ENGLISH
1: Length of time	Brief to lifelong			
2: Degree of intimacy				
3: Basis of companion-ship				
4: Sex-linked friendship				

Thinking and Writing

RHETORICAL TECHNIQUE

1. This essay's introduction (paragraphs 1 through 6) is particularly clear in providing a preview of its contents. What essential information does the reader find there?

    What signals of contrast are used in the introduction to present the different elements that the essay will discuss?
2. Is this essay primarily organized in the block or the alternating pattern? Which paragraphs depart from the primary pattern?

    What expressions of contrast occur in the body of the essay as transitions between the different elements?
3. Evaluate the concluding paragraph: how well does it answer the questions raised in the introduction? Refer to specific lines in the text in your response.
4. Friendship among the French is given lengthier treatment than the other types of friendship. Underline the key expressions that link together the paragraphs about the French.

    Does the order of the elements in this essay surprise you? Would you have sequenced them differently?

COMPOSITION

1. In an essay, compare or contrast family relationships to friendship. Illustrate your remarks with references to specific individuals.
2. Select a universal human value or activity such as courtship, education, a wedding, or a birth. Explore your topic with regard to three comparative or contrastive elements—for example, different regions, different relatives or friends, or different social or economic groups. Use the block pattern of organization in the Mead-Metraux essay as your guide.

DAVID RIESMAN
Images of Power

In this classic study American sociologist David Riesman (b. 1909) introduces the terms *tradition-directed, inner-directed,* and *other-directed* to categorize three social types. The tradition-directed character is found primarily in unchanging agricultural societies, where long-established patterns of living dominate the lives of individuals. The inner-directed character is most typical in societies where there is opportunity for personal mobility and rapid accumulation of capital and where technological development and expansion of production are taking place. The greater choice offered by these societies demands people with greater initiative to cope with new problems. The successful inner-directed person can live without strict and explicit traditions, depending on his or her own sense of achievement and worth as motivation toward goals.

The other-directed individual, emerging in recent times, may be most clearly seen in the highly industrialized, bureaucratic society of middle-class, urban America. This is a society in which the problems demanding management involve other people rather than the material environment. The other-directed individual is primarily motivated by the desire for the approval of others; he or she is more comfortable with a philosophy of abundance and consumption than of scarcity and production. It is the inner-directed and the other-directed types that Riesman contrasts in the following essay.

In the United States the more opulent citizens
take great care not to stand aloof from the people;
on the contrary, they constantly keep on easy
terms with the lower classes; they listen to them,
they speak to them every day. They know that the
rich in democracies always stand in need of the
poor, and that in democratic times you attach a
poor man to you more by your manner than by
benefits conferred.

Alexis de Tocqueville, Democracy in America

There has been in the last fifty years* a change in the configuration of 1
power in America, in which a single hierarchy with a ruling class at its
head has been replaced by a number of "veto groups" among which power
is dispersed. This change has many complex roots and complex consequences, including the change in political mood from moralizing to tolerance. A clear-cut power structure helped to create the clarity of goals of
the inner-directed; an amorphous power structure helps to create the con-
sumer orientation of the other-directed.

The Leaders and the Led

There have been two periods in American history in which a sharply de- 2
fined ruling class emerged. . . . [One was] after the Civil War, when the
captains of industry emerged as a ruling class. During their hegemony the
images and the actualities of power in America coincided more closely
than I think they do today.

Captains of Industry and Captains of Consumption
. . . the election of 1896 appears as an historical watershed: the high 3
point of oligarchic rule. . . . there were groups that had a clear picture of
themselves and of their interests; they responded to the election in an
inner-directed way. . . .

Certainly, the victorious leaders—McKinley, Hanna, and Morgan 4
in their several bailiwicks—were not aware of ambiguity. The success of
their electoral bid is less important to us than the mood of their undertak-
ing, which was one of conscious leadership, directed by conscious class
considerations. This self-conscious leadership took support from the close
connection, to which I have already called attention, between politics and

---

*Since 1900—Ed.

work. The world of work was the great world; politics was an extension that could either facilitate work or sabotage it. While bankers and Grangers had different notions as to what work politics should do and what leave undone, they agreed as to the primacy of the production side of life.

Of course, the political sphere was not devoid of entertainment for 5 the inner-directed man: with its opportunity for cracker-barrel argument, beer drinking, and shirt-sleeved good-fellowship by torchlight, it had its occasional uses as a "downward" escape from the dignities of work and the propertied existence. But the great difference from today is that the leaders went into politics to do a job—primarily to assure the conquest of American resources—rather than to seek a responsive audience. As Rockefeller sold his oil more by force or cheapness than by brand, so the late nineteenth-century political leader sold his wares (votes or decisions) to the highest bidder. Either cash or morality might bid—but not "good will" as such.

This situation and these inner-directed motivations gave a clarity to 6 the political and social scene in 1896 that it does not appear to have had in Tocqueville's day and has not had since. The bullet that killed McKinley marked the end of the days of explicit class leadership. Muckraking and savage political cartooning—arts that depend on clarity of line—continued for a time and of course have not quite vanished yet. But as the old-time religion depended on a clear image of heaven and hell and clear judgments of good and evil, so the old-time politics depended on a clear class structure and the clear and easily moralized judgments of good and bad that flow from it. It depended, too, and I cannot emphasize the point too much, on an agreement between leaders and led that the work sphere of life was dominant. And because the goals were clear, the obvious job of the leader was to lead; of the led, to follow. Their political cooperation, like their cooperation in industry and agriculture, was based on mutual interests, whether directly moralized or not, rather than on mutual preferences and likings.

What I have said must be taken as an "ideal-typical" political portrait of the age, useful by way of contrast to our own times. Actually, the 7 changes are, as always, changes in emphasis and degree, and the portrait would be seriously overdrawn if the reader should conclude that no emotional moods, no cravings for charisma and glamor, eddied about the relations between leaders and led. These relations were not built entirely out of sober moralizing and well-understood economic interests, but occasionally, as Veblen described matters, the Captain of Industry served to provide the underlying population with personages to admire "to the greater spiritual comfort of all parties concerned."

Ruling-class theories, applied to contemporary America, seem to be 8 spectral survivals of this earlier time. The captain of industry no longer runs business, no longer runs politics, and no longer provides legitimate "spiritual comfort." Here and there, it is true, there are survivals. In the booming Southwest, Texas still produces men like Glen McCarthy, and California produced an old-style lion of the jungle in A. P. Giannini (who was, significantly enough, from a family which lacked the opportunity to educate him for the newer business motivations). Yet even these types are touched by traits that were not nearly so evident in the earlier captains of industry who fascinated Veblen as Lucifer fascinated Milton. Like Henry Kaiser, they depend much more than did the older magnificoes on public opinion and, as a corollary to public opinion, on the attitude of government. To this end they tend to exploit their personalities, or allow them to be exploited, in a way that makes the elder Rockefeller's Ivy Lee stunt of dime-giving seem as remote as the Fuggers.

Much more than their pre-World War I predecessors, then, these 9 surviving captains stay within the limits as well as the possibilities of the economy of the glad hand. If they enter politics they do so because it is a sport or obligation for the rich; or simply because they are tied in with government at every step in their ramifying enterprises. These latter-day captains neither see themselves nor are recognized as political leaders who, by their presence and by what they stand for, clarify and thereby moralize politics. The elder Morgan and his friends thought it was up to them to stop Bryan and to stop the depression of 1907. No one has taken their place.

In the focus of public attention the old captains of industry have 10 been replaced by an entirely new type: the Captains of Nonindustry, of Consumption and Leisure. Surveys of content in the mass media show a shift in the kinds of information about business and political leaders that audiences ask for. . . . In an earlier day the audience was given a story of the hero's work-minded rise to success. Today, the ladder climbing is taken for granted or is seen in terms of "the breaks," and the hero's tastes in dress, food, women, and recreation are emphasized—these are, as we have seen, the frontiers on which the reader can himself compete, while he cannot imagine himself in the work role of the president of the United States or the head of a big company.

What is more, there is a shift in such biographies from an accent on 11 business leaders to an accent on "leaders" in consumption. Proportionately, actors, artists, entertainers, get more space than they used to, and the heroes of the office, hustings, and factory get less. These consumers of the surplus product may, in Veblen's terms, provide "spiritual comfort" by their very skill in consumption. The glamor of such heroes of consumption may reside in their incompetence in the skills of businesslike performance and, as we have seen, in some cases their wholly personal "sincerity" may do duty in place of more objective artistic criteria.

But, of course, these captains of consumption are not leaders. They 12 are still only personalities, employed to adorn movements, not to lead them. Yet the actual leaders have much in common with them.

For an illustration we can turn to a recent American leader—un- 13 doubtedly a leader—who shared many characteristics of the artist and entertainer: Franklin D. Roosevelt. We are accustomed to thinking of him as a man of great power. Yet his role in leading the country into war was very different from that of McKinley or even of Wilson. Think of McKinley pacing the floor of his study, deciding whether or not to ask for a declaration of war on Spain—when he already knew that Spain would capitulate. McKinley felt it was up to him; so did Wilson. Roosevelt felt he could only maneuver within very narrow limits, limits which came close to leaving the decision to the enemy.

Again, if we compare his activities during the war years with those of Churchill, we can see important differences. Churchill led the British in something like the old-time sense of an explicit relation between the leader and the followers. That he led, moreover, as a moralizing leader and not, despite his great personal charm, as a "personality," appeared in the readiness of the electorate to follow him in war and to dispense with him in peace: they were work-minded rather than consumption-minded about him. Roosevelt on the other hand remained throughout the war, as before, a powerful though tolerant persuader, even conniver and stimulator, of changes in public opinion that he followed with deep concern at all times. Churchill exploited his indignation, Roosevelt his charm. 14

The obviously real differences in the military situation of Britain and the United States during this period are not sufficient to explain these differences in the mood and method of leadership. Much more important than the wartime differences between the two countries are the differing shifts in political pattern during the last half century. America in the 90's could be led politically and morally. Since then we have entered a social and political phase in which power is dispersed among veto groups. These groups are too many and diverse to be led by moralizing; what they want is too various to be moralized and too intangible to be bought off for cash alone; and what is called political leadership consists, as we could see in Roosevelt's case, in the tolerant ability to manipulate coalitions. 15

This means that the men who, at an earlier historical period, were political leaders are now busy with the other-directed occupation of studying the feedback from all the others—their constituencies, their correspondents, and friends and enemies within influential pressure groups. The revolution in communications makes this attention possible in ways that were not available to the equally assiduous client-cultivator of an earlier day, who could buy a few editors if he wanted favorable things said. And those who were once the followers have learned the arts of lobbying and publicity. The roll call of nineteenth- and early twentieth-century leaders contains many men who refused to follow their flock: Gladstone and Cleveland, Robert Peel and John Stuart Mill (as M.P.), Woodrow Wilson and Winston Churchill. Even today the need to impose unpopular courses brings to the fore inner-directed types: Cripps, for instance, in 16

England; Stimson and Robert Patterson in this country. Of course, political figures in all ages have been dependent on their following, and opportunism and manipulation are not a twentieth-century discovery. The inner-directed leader, however, was quite conscious of discrepancies between his views and those of others; if he shifted his course, it was still *his* course. Moreover, since he was ambitious, he might well prefer later fame to momentary warmth of response; in any event he did not need to have everybody love him, but only those who mattered for his fortunes.

In his autobiography, John Stuart Mill tells the following story: 17

> In the pamphlet, "Thoughts on Parliamentary Reform," I had said, rather bluntly, that the working classes, though differing from those of some other countries, in being ashamed of lying, are yet generally liars. This passage some opponent got printed in a placard which was handed to me at a meeting, chiefly composed of the working classes, and I was asked whether I had written and published it. I at once answered "I did." Scarcely were these two words out of my mouth, when vehement applause resounded through the whole meeting.

It is interesting to compare this incident with the practices of certain 18 American public figures who not only would not think of saying anything that might offend an audience but who frequently depart from a prepared text, carefully designed to please a wide audience, in order to mollify the smaller face-to-face group before whom the speech happens to be delivered.

The old-time captain of industry was also a captain of consumption: 19 what standards were set, were set by him. He was also a captain of politics. The new captain of consumption who has usurped his place in the public eye is limited severely to the sphere of consumption—which itself has of course greatly expanded. Today, the personalities from the leisure world, no matter how much loved, lack the strength and the situation for leadership. If a movie star of today tries to put across a political message, in or out of films, he finds himself vulnerable to all sorts of pressures. The movie producer is no more powerful. The Catholics, the Methodists, the organized morticians, the state department, the southerners, the Jews, the doctors, all put their pressure on the vehicle that is being prepared for mass distribution. Piety or decency protects some minority groups that have no lobbies. The movie maker acts as a broker among these veto groups in a situation much too intricate to encourage his taking a firm, moralizing stance. At best, he or someone in his organization may sneak a moral and political message into the film as Roosevelt or someone in his organization sneaked over an appointment or a new coordinating agency. The message, the appointment, the agency—none of them could get very far in the Alice in Wonderland croquet game of the veto groups.

Reading and Interpreting

VOCABULARY

Use your dictionary as necessary to find the meaning of the following words as used by Riesman:

amorphous (1)   watershed (3)   oligarchic (3)   spectral (8)

ramifying (9)   assiduous (16)   mollify (18)   usurped (19)

CONCEPT ANALYSIS

1. Briefly summarize the characteristics of inner-directed leadership (see paragraphs 4–6). What comparison does Riesman make between the religion and the politics of the inner-directed era?
2. What are the characteristics of the new type of leaders: "the Captains of Nonindustry" (10)?
3. In paragraphs 13–15 Riesman offers Roosevelt and Churchill as examples. What concept does each of them exemplify?
4. Discuss the degree of dependence on their followers that characterizes the inner-directed versus the other-directed leader. What purpose does the quotation from John Stuart Mill's autobiography (17) serve in this regard?
5. Summary paragraph 19 addresses the concepts of leadership and power. In addition to contrasting the old and new leaders, what does it say about leadership and power in modern society? With whom does power lie?

Quickwrite

Reread Alexis de Tocqueville's quotation that introduces this selection. Apply it to the contemporary world of politics, entertainment, education, or fashion. Are you describing primarily an inner-directed or an other-directed society?

RHETORICAL TECHNIQUE

1. In this deductive essay, the first paragraph establishes the elements of contrast. What are they?

    Is the essay developed primarily in the block or alternating pattern? Note any paragraphs that are exceptions to the basic pattern.
2. The transitional paragraphs in this essay describe transitional figures of power in American life. Identify these paragraphs and underscore the signals of comparison and contrast. Study paragraphs 13 and 14 for their effective use of signals of comparison and contrast. Try substituting alternative signals to see if they work as well.
3. This essay contrasts its elements in terms of such points as moral authority, production and consumption, manipulation of others, class structure, public image of political leaders, and feedback from the electorate. Choose the three points you feel are most significant in distinguishing between inner-directed and other-directed types of leadership, and construct a grid outline to summarize Riesman's argument.

COMPOSITION

1. Select two prominent figures in American life (politics, entertainment, sports, the arts)—one inner-directed, one other-directed. Using paragraphs 12–14 of the essay as a general guide, develop an essay of contrast about your two elements.
2. Riesman distinguishes between the inner-directed emphasis on the work ethic and production and the other-directed focus on leisure and consumption. Write a contrastive essay on this distinction, using yourself as one element and a relative, friend, or employer as the other.

STEPHEN LEACOCK

Oxford as I See It

Canadian mathematics professor Stephen Leacock
(1869–1944) was one of the most intriguing comic
writers of the English-speaking world. Like Dickens and
Twain, with whom he is often compared, he presents a
complex point of view that is not easily comprehended
by the casual reader. Look carefully for the irony in this
essay, which contrasts traditional Oxford education with
a modern American postsecondary learning experience.
Is Leacock making fun of the English or the American
university system?

My private station being that of a university professor, I was naturally 1
deeply interested in the system of education in England. I was therefore
led to make a special visit to Oxford and to submit the place to a searching
scrutiny. Arriving one afternoon at four o'clock, I stayed at the Mitre
Hotel and did not leave until eleven o'clock next morning. The whole of
this time, except for one hour spent in addressing the undergraduates, was
devoted to a close and eager study of the great university. When I add to
this that I had already visited Oxford in 1907 and spent a Sunday at All
Souls with Colonel L. S. Amery, it will be seen at once that my views on
Oxford are based upon observations extending over fourteen years. . . .

On the strength of this basis of experience I am prepared to make the 2
following positive and emphatic statements. Oxford is a notable university. It has a great past. It is at present the greatest university in the
world; and it is quite possible that it has a great future. Oxford trains
scholars of the real type better than any other place in the world. Its methods are antiquated. It despises science. Its lectures are rotten. It has professors who never teach and students who never learn. It has no order, no
arrangement, no system. Its curriculum is unintelligible. It has no president. It has no state legislature to tell it how to teach, and yet—it gets
there. Whether we like it or not, Oxford gives something to its students,
a life and a mode of thought which in America as yet we can emulate but
not equal. . . .

These singular results achieved at Oxford are all the more surprising 3
when one considers the distressing conditions under which the students
work. The lack of an adequate building fund compels them to go on working in the same old buildings which they have had for centuries. The

buildings at Brasenose had not been renewed since the year 1525. In New College and Magdalen the students are still housed in the old buildings erected in the sixteenth century. At Christ Church I was shown a kitchen which had been built at the expense of Cardinal Wolsey in 1527. Incredible though it may seem, they have no other place to cook in than this and are compelled to use it to-day. On the day when I saw this kitchen, four cooks were busy roasting an ox whole for the students' lunch: this, at least, is what I presumed they were doing from the size of the fire-place used: but it may not have been an ox, perhaps it was a cow. On a huge table, twelve feet by six and made of slabs of wood five inches thick, two other cooks were rolling out a game pie. I estimated it as measuring three feet across. In this rude way, unchanged since the time of Henry VIII, the unhappy Oxford students are fed. I could not help contrasting it with the cosy little boarding-houses on Cottage Grove Avenue where I used to eat when I was a student at Chicago, or the charming little basement dining-rooms of the students' boarding-houses in Toronto. But then, of course, Henry VIII never lived in Toronto.

The same lack of a building fund necessitates the Oxford students 4 living in the identical old boarding-houses they had in the sixteenth and seventeenth centuries. Technically they are called 'quadrangles,' 'closes,' and 'rooms'; but I am so broken in to the usage of my student days that I can't help calling them boarding-houses. In many of these the old stairway has been worn down by the feet of ten generations of students; the windows have little latticed panes; there are old names carved here and there upon the stone, and a thick growth of ivy covers the walls. The boarding-house at St. John's dates from 1509, the one at Christ Church from the same period. A few hundred thousand pounds would suffice to replace these old buildings with neat steel and brick structures like the normal school at Schenectady, N.Y., or the Peel Street High School at Montreal. But nothing is done. A movement was, indeed, attempted last autumn towards removing the ivy from the walls, but the result was unsatisfactory and they are putting it back. Anyone could have told them beforehand that the mere removal of the ivy would not brighten Oxford up, unless at the same time one cleared the stones of the old inscriptions, put in steel fire-escapes, and, in fact, brought the boarding-houses up to date.

But Henry VIII being dead, nothing was done. Yet, in spite of its 5 dilapidated buildings and its lack of fire-escapes, ventilation, sanitation, and up-to-date kitchen facilities, I persist in my assertion that I believe that Oxford, in its way, is the greatest university in the world. I am aware that this is an extreme statement and needs explanation. Oxford is much smaller in numbers, for example, than the State University of Minnesota, and is much poorer. It has, or had till yesterday, fewer students than the University of Toronto. To mention Oxford beside the 26,000 students of Columbia University sounds ridiculous. In point of money, the $39,000,000 endowment of the University of Chicago, the $35,000,000 of Columbia, and the $43,000,000 of Harvard seem to leave Oxford nowhere. Yet the peculiar thing is that it is not nowhere. By some queer process of its own it seems to get there every time. It was therefore of the very greatest interest to me, as a profound scholar, to try to investigate just how this peculiar excellence of Oxford arises.

It has hardly been due to anything in the curriculum or programme 6 of studies. Indeed, to anyone accustomed to the best models of a university curriculum as it flourishes in the United States and Canada, the programme of studies is frankly quite laughable. There is less Applied Science in the place than would be found with us in a theological college. Hardly a single professor at Oxford would recognise a dynamo if he met it in broad daylight. The Oxford student learns nothing of chemistry, physics, heat, plumbing, electric wiring, gasfitting, or the use of a blowtorch. Any American college student can run a motor-car, take a gasoline engine to pieces, fix a washer on a kitchen tap, mend a broken electric bell, and give an expert opinion on what has gone wrong with the furnace. It is these things, indeed, which stamp him as a college man and occasion a very pardonable pride in the minds of his parents. But in all these things the Oxford student is the merest amateur.

This is bad enough. But, after all, one might say, this is only the 7 mechanical side of education. True; but one searches in vain in the Oxford curriculum for any adequate recognition of the higher and more cultured studies. Strange though it seems to us on this side of the Atlantic, there are no courses at Oxford in Housekeeping, or in Salesmanship, or in Advertising, or on Comparative Religion, or on the influence of the press. There are no lectures whatever on Human Behaviour, on Altruism, on Egotism, or on the Play of Wild Animals. Apparently, the Oxford student does not learn these things. This cuts him off from a great deal of the larger culture of our side of the Atlantic. "What are you studying this year?" I once asked a fourth-year student at one of our great colleges. "I am electing Salesmanship and Religion," he answered. Here was a young man whose training was destined inevitably to turn him into a moral business man: either that or nothing. At Oxford, Salesmanship is not taught, and Religion takes the feeble form of the New Testament. The more one looks at these things the more amazing it becomes that Oxford can produce any results at all.

The effect of the comparison is heightened by the peculiar position 8 occupied at Oxford by the professor's lectures. In the colleges of Canada and the United States the lectures are supposed to be a really necessary and useful part of the student's training. Again and again I have heard the graduates of my own college assert that they had got as much, or nearly as much, out of the lectures at college as out of athletics or the Greek Letter Society or the Banjo and Mandolin Club. In short, with us the lectures form a real part of the college life. At Oxford it is not so. The lectures, I understand, are given and may even be taken. But they are quite worthless and are not supposed to have anything much to do with the development of the student's mind. "The lectures here," said a Canadian student to me, "are punk." I appealed to another student to know if this was so. "I don't know whether I'd call them exactly punk," he answered, "but they're certainly rotten." Other judgments were that the lectures were of no importance; that nobody took them; that they don't matter; that you can take them if you like; that they do you no harm.

It appears, further, that the professors themselves are not keen on 9 their lectures. If the lectures are called for they give them; if not, the professor's feelings are not hurt. He merely waits and rests his brain until in some later year the students call for his lectures. There are men at Oxford who have rested their brains this way for over thirty years: the accumulated brain power thus dammed up is said to be colossal.

I understand that the key to this mystery is found in the operations 10 of the person called the tutor. It is from him, or rather with him, that the students learn all that they know; one and all are agreed on that. Yet it is a little odd to know just how he does it. "We go over to his rooms," said one student, "and he just lights a pipe and talks to us." "We sit round with him," said another, "and he simply smokes and goes over our exercises with us." From this and other evidence I gather that what an Oxford tutor does is to get a little group of students together and smoke at them. Men who have been systematically smoked at for four years turn into ripe scholars. If anybody doubts this, let him go to Oxford and he can see the thing actually in operation. A well-smoked man speaks and write English with a grace that can be acquired in no other way.

In what was said above, I seem to have been directing criticism 11 against the Oxford professors as such; but I have no intention of doing so. For the Oxford professor and his whole manner of being I have nothing but a profound respect. There is, indeed, the greatest difference between the modern up-to-date American idea of a professor and the English type. But even with us in older days, the bygone time when such people as Henry Wadsworth Longfellow were professors, one found the English idea: a professor was supposed to be a venerable kind of person, with snow-white whiskers reaching to his stomach. He was expected to moon around the campus oblivious of the world around him. If you nodded to him he failed to see you. Of money he knew nothing; of business far less. He was, as his trustees were proud to say of him, "a child."

On the other hand, he contained within him a reservoir of learning 12 of such depth as to be practically bottomless. None of this learning was supposed to be of any material or commercial benefit to anybody. Its use was in saving the soul and enlarging the mind.

At the head of such a group of professors was one whose beard was 13 even whiter and longer, whose absence of mind was even still greater, and whose knowledge of money, business, and practical affairs was below zero. Him they made the president.

All this is changed in America. A university professor is now a busy, 14
hustling person, approximating as closely to a business man as he can do
it. It is on the business man that he models himself. He has a little place
that he calls his "office," with a typewriter machine and a stenographer.
Here he sits and dictates letters, beginning after the best business models,
"In *re* yours of the eighth ult., would say, etc. etc." He writes these letters
to students, to his fellow-professors, to the president—indeed, to any
people who will let him write to them. The number of letters that he
writes each month is duly counted and set to his credit. If he writes
enough he will get a reputation as an "executive," and big things may
happen to him. He may even be asked to step out of the college and take a
post as an "executive" in a soap company or an advertising firm. The man,
in short, is a "hustler," and "advertiser" whose highest aim is to be a
"live-wire." If he is not, he will presently be dismissed, or, to use the
business term, be "let go," by a board of trustees who are themselves hus-
tlers and live-wires. As to the professor's soul, he no longer needs to think
of it, as it has been handed over along with all the others to a Board of
Censors.

The American professor deals with his students according to his 15
lights. It is his business to chase them along over a prescribed ground at a
prescribed pace like a flock of sheep. They all go humping together over
the hurdles with the professor chasing them with a set of "tests" and "recitations," "marks" and "attendances," the whole apparatus obviously copied
from the time-clock of the business man's factory. This process is what is
called "showing results." The pace set is necessarily that of the slowest,
and thus results in what I have heard Mr. Edward Beatty describe as the
"convoy system of education."

In my own opinion, reached after fifty-two years of profound reflec- 16
tion, this system contains in itself the seeds of destruction. It puts a premium on dullness and a penalty on genius. It circumscribes that attitude
of mind which is the real spirit of learning. If we persist in it we shall
presently find that true learning will fly away from our universities and
will take rest wherever some individual and inquiring mind can mark out
its path for itself.

Now, the principal reason why I am led to admire Oxford is that the 17
place is little touched as yet by the measuring of "results" and by this
passion for visible and provable "efficiency." The whole system at Oxford
is such as to put a premium on genius and to let mediocrity and dullness
go their way. On the dull student Oxford, after a proper lapse of time,
confers a degree which means nothing more than that he lived and breathed
at Oxford and kept out of jail. This for many students is as much as society can expect. But for the gifted student Oxford offers great opportunities. There is no question of his hanging back till the last sheep has
jumped over the fence. He need wait for no one. He may move forward as
fast as he likes, following the bent of his genius. If he has in him any

ability beyond that of the common herd, his tutor, interested in his studies, will smoke at him until he kindles him into a flame. For the tutor's soul is not harassed by herding dull students, with dismissal hanging by a thread over his head in the class-room. The American professor has not time to be interested in a clever student. He has time to be interested in his "department," his letter-writing, his executive work, and his organizing ability and his hope of promotion to a soap factory. But with that his mind is exhausted. The student of genius merely means to him a student who gives no trouble, who passes all his "tests," and is present at all his "recitations." Such a student also, if he can be trained to be a hustler and an advertiser, will undoubtedly "make good." But beyond that the professor does not think of him. The everlasting principle of equality has inserted itself in a place where it has no right to be, and where inequality is the breath of life.

American or Canadian college trustees would be horrified at the notion of professors who apparently do no work, give few or no lectures, and draw their pay merely for existing. Yet these are really the only kind of professors worth having—I mean, men who can be trusted with a vague general mission in life, with a salary guaranteed at least till their death, and a sphere of duties entrusted solely to their own conscience and the promptings of their own desires. Such men are rare, but a single one of them, when found, is worth ten "executives" and a dozen "organizers." 18

The excellence of Oxford, then, as I see it, lies in the peculiar vagueness of the organization of its work. It starts from the assumption that the professor is a really learned man whose sole interest lies in his own sphere; and that a student, or at least the only student with whom the university cares to reckon seriously, is a young man who desires to know. This is an ancient mediaeval attitude long since buried in more up-to-date places under successive strata of compulsory education, state teaching, the democratization of knowledge and the substitution of the shadow for the substance, and the casket for the gem. No doubt, in newer places, the thing has got to be so. Higher education in America flourishes chiefly as a qualification for entrance into a money-making profession, and not as a thing in itself. But in Oxford one can still see the surviving outline of a nobler type of structure and a higher inspiration. 19

Viewing the situation as a whole, I am led, then, to the conclusion that there must be something in the life of Oxford itself that makes for higher learning. Smoked at by his tutor, fed in Henry VIII's kitchen, and sleeping in a tangle of ivy, the student evidently gets something not easily obtained in America. And the more I reflect on the matter the more I am convinced that it is the sleeping in the ivy that does it. How different it is from student life as I remember it! . . . 20

The real thing for the student is the life and environment that surrounds him. All that he really learns he learns, in a sense, by the active operation of his own intellect and not as the passive recipient of lectures. 21

And for this active operation what he really needs most is the continued and intimate contact with his fellows. Students must live together and eat together, talk and smoke together. Experience shows that that is how their minds really grow. And they must live together in a rational and comfortable way. They must eat in a big dining-room or hall, with oak beams across the ceiling, and the stained glass in the windows, and with a shield or tablet here or there upon the wall, to remind them between times of the men who went before them and left a name worthy of the memory of the college. If a student is to get from his college what it ought to give him, rooms in college, with the life in common that they bring, are his absolute right. A university that fails to give it to him is cheating him.

If I were founding a university—and I say it with all the seriousness 22 of which I am capable—I would found first a smoking room; then when I had a little more money in hand I would build rooms; then after that, or more probably with it, a decent reading room and a library. After that, if I still had money over that I couldn't use, I would hire a professor and get some textbooks.

Reading and Interpreting

VOCABULARY

Use your dictionary as necessary to find the meaning of the following words in the context of Leacock's essay:

emulate (2)   latticed (4)   altruism (7)   oblivious (11)

premium (16)   casket (19)

CONCEPT ANALYSIS

1. Leacock communicates many of his points through irony; therefore, many of his statements cannot be taken literally. This is evident in paragraph 1, where he states that he only visited Oxford for a short time. Does the essay support this claim?
2. The two elements being contrasted are Oxford education and American and Canadian university education. The points Leacock has selected as the bases of his comparison are summarized in paragraph 2. What is the thesis statement?
   Some of Leacock's statements in paragraph 2 appear illogical. Can you explain them in terms of the thesis?
3. Do you feel that Leacock's portrayal of the American college student in paragraphs 6 and 7 is accurate and fair? Explain.

4. Leacock truly admires Oxford and the education it offers, yet he characterizes it in negative ways. What does he really mean when he says "distressing conditions under which the students work" (3), a "laughable" program of studies (6), professors who "rest their brains" until their lectures are called for (9), and students who are "smoked at" by their tutors (10)?

   Conversely, Leacock uses positive expressions to describe American and Canadian university education. Find examples and explain what you think he really means.

Quickwrite

After reading Leacock's description, would Oxford have been the university of your choice?

Thinking and Writing

RHETORICAL TECHNIQUE

1. Leacock introduces the reader to Oxford through the block pattern. What is the effect on his subject? Then Leacock uses both block and alternating patterns in the remainder of the essay. Label paragraphs 6 onward either block, alternating, or a combination of both. What effect does the alternating pattern have on his subject?
2. Underline the transitional expressions that contrast Leacock's two elements both within the alternating paragraphs and between paragraphs.

COMPOSITION

Select two educational institutions on the elementary, high school, or college level. Write a contrastive essay making reference to Leacock's points of comparison: physical facilities, course of study, faculty background and interests, teaching techniques, values.

STRINGFELLOW BARR

The Civilization of the Dialogue

Stringfellow Barr (b. 1897), a distinguished American
scholar known for his introduction of a Great Books curriculum, believes that the study of the classics is an important preparation for modern life. In this excerpt from
The Three Worlds of Man, he offers Socratic dialogue as a
means of testing our opinions for their truth or falsity.

What is the nature of the dialectic that Socrates prescribed as the final   1
preparation of his Guardians if they would rule wisely and that he himself
practiced while offering his prescription? It is fundamentally a kind of argument between two persons, but it is a kind rarely heard in Athens in his
day and perhaps even more rarely in twentieth-century America. Most arguments then and now tend to be what Socrates called eristic. Now, the
word eristic is derived from *eris,* the Greek word for strife. In eristic both
sides are trying to win. In dialectic, both sides argue hard but not to win.
They have a common goal: to find the true answer to the problem. For
both sides may start off with a false or incomplete opinion. We may look
to a sport like tennis to see the difference. Two men may play a tennis
match in which each contestant is even more anxious to win than to play
good tennis. Two other men may play, with each man trying to put up the
best game possible, regardless of who wins. There is a quality of sports-
manship in this second way of playing. There is a quality of professional-
ism in the first way, whether money changes hands or not. In the first
match only one player can achieve his purpose—a victorious score. In the
second match both sides can achieve their common purpose—tennis playing of high quality. The first match has the quality of eristic but it has no
common purpose. The second has the quality of Socratic dialectic and has
a very high common purpose—good play.

The analogy between ways of arguing and ways of playing tennis is   2
not yet exhausted. It takes at least two persons to play either game. Moreover, both kinds of tennis and both kinds of argument must be rigorously,
not sloppily, scored. Again, if either side plays or argues eristically, defeat
is likely to be bitter, since the defeated player gains nothing that he
wants. Again, an eristic player is likely to assume that his opponent's
goal, like his own, is the eristic goal, even if in actual fact his opponent is
playing dialectically. Similarly, if the true dialectician seems to enough of

his opponents to have won eristic victories from them he may find the silver cup he wins brimful of hemlock; he may, like Socrates, be ordered to drink it. When Socrates drank hemlock in his prison cell, no doubt many of those he had appeared to triumph over felt that at last they had triumphed over Socrates. Had he not met the greatest defeat of all—death? But Plato's *Crito* and *Phaedo* show Socrates still playing his game of dialectic in his prison cell with whatever friends came to call. His goal remained unchanged: the joint pursuit of truth through the dialectical destruction of those false and inadequately examined and deeply cherished opinions which men hold as truth itself. And when he won the cup of hemlock, he willingly drained it, hoping to gain entrance to some place where he could play his game of dialectic with great players who had lived in Hellas long before and had preceded him to that other place.

If we read Plato's *Dialogues* and listen to Socrates himself practice 3 dialectic, we observe that his preferred method is to ask short questions and to encourage short answers. This cross-examination tests his opponent's opinion somewhat as a laboratory scientist tests his own or another's hypothesis. But over and over again in the *Dialogues* the person questioned grows violent, raises his voice, and substitutes for the short answer the long, vague, rhetorical speech. As signs multiply that his opinion is about to be refuted, and out of his own mouth at that, he fears personal disgrace. This confusion between refutation and disgrace is perhaps reflected by the Greek word *elenchos*, which, depending on its gender, means either refutation or disgrace. The basic trouble, of course, is that Socrates' sparring partner views the encounter in terms of eristic and fears defeat. But for Socrates the testing of the opinion is the goal, and it is not important who happens to be the opinion's advocate. If the opinion fails, it will be logic, not Socrates, which condemns it.

Reading and Interpreting

VOCABULARY

Use your dictionary as necessary to find the meaning of the following words as used by Barr:

dialectic (1)   rhetorical (3)   refutation (3)

CONCEPT ANALYSIS

1. Barr's subject is argument. What are the two elements of his comparison? Underline the sentence(s) that defines each element and expresses the contrast. What do you see as the major point of contrast?

2. Comment on Barr's analogy between arguing and tennis playing. Do you think it is an effective analogy? Explain.

Think about an argument you have engaged in recently. Did you argue to convince someone of your "truth" or to find the truth? Explain.
3. According to Barr, what are the different meanings of *defeat* in the dialectical and eristic methods? How may the eristic "player" misinterpret his dialectical opponent's aim? How does Barr apply this to the case of Socrates? Why was disgrace impossible for Socrates?

Quickwrite

Write about your participating in a sport or game. Characterize your aims as dialectical, eristic, or a combination of the two. Include your feelings about victory and defeat.

Thinking and Writing

RHETORICAL TECHNIQUE

1. Does Barr use the block or the alternating method of organization to explore his subject? Support your answer with references to the text.
2. Signals of contrast between the elements are used sparingly in the first paragraph. Underline them. Where else might you insert signals of contrast such as *on the one hand . . . on the other hand, in contrast, however,* or *but?*

Barr's second paragraph, which extends the analogy between a game of tennis and argumentation, uses signal expressions more consistently. Underline them. Is Barr's focus in this paragraph on comparison or contrast? Refer to the text in your response.

COMPOSITION

1. Barr's distinction between two types of argument is extended by his analogy to a game of tennis. Write an essay in which you contrast two elements (for example, two teaching methods, two ways of raising children, two types of artistic expression), and use an analogy from a familiar activity to illustrate your distinctions.
2. Summarize the two sides of a current political, social, economic, or scientific issue in a grid outline. Then write an essay of contrast in the alternating, point-by-point method.

THE WRITTEN RESPONSE

Writing Workshop

1. Your subject will be two people, either fictional, historical, or known to you personally. List several pairs of people who have a logical connection with each other (for example, two relatives, two American political leaders, two entertainers, two characters from the same fictional work, or two characters from different fictional works by the same author).

2. From your list select one pair in which the people are clear opposites in some significant way (for example, behavior, philosophy, social role). These will be the two elements of your contrastive essay. For example, you might select the two American presidents John F. Kennedy and Jimmy Carter as contrasting political leaders.

3. Drawing on another realm of life (such as nature, sports, food), think of a pair of opposites that captures the essence of the two elements you selected in the preceding step. For example, from the world of nature you might think of the peacock and the sparrow and use them to represent the contrasting personalities of Kennedy and Carter.

4. Use these two items in an analogy about your two elements. This analogy will form the basis of your thesis statement and help provide the structure of your contrastive essay. Thus, for an essay about Kennedy and Carter, we might formulate the following working thesis statement: *In their political styles, two of America's midcentury Democratic presidents, John F. Kennedy and Jimmy Carter, were as different from each other as the splendid peacock is from the humble sparrow.*

5. With your thesis statement in mind, brainstorm the points of contrast between your two elements. Modify, eliminate, and cluster points until you have three strong points to develop in your essay.

6. Fill in the slots of the following grid with the contrastive points that you will develop in the body of your essay. For example, to contrast Kennedy and Carter, you might select such points as their regional character, their physical presence, and their media image.

	ELEMENT A	ELEMENT B
Point 1:		
Point 2:		
Point 3:		

7. With your grid filled in, determine whether you want to develop your essay with a block or an alternating pattern. For the block pattern, describe all the points about element A first. Write a transitional paragraph, and then write about all the same points for element B. In other words, you will be moving *vertically* down the grid.

   For the alternating pattern, you will be moving *horizontally* across the grid, contrasting the first point about element A with the same point about element B before moving on to the second point in the next paragraph.

8. Compose a first draft of your essay. If you are using the block pattern, pay particular attention to the transitional paragraph linking the two elements. If you are using the alternating method, review your main paragraphs for precise signal expressions of contrast between the two elements.

9. In writing and revising your first draft, incorporate references to your analogy about the two elements at appropriate points. For example, in discussing Kennedy's physical presence, one might compare his glamorous appeal to the public to the excitement generated by the appearance of a strutting peacock in a public park.

10. Be sure your concluding paragraph does three things: refers to the commonalities of the two elements to make comparison of them meaningful, briefly summarizes the significant contrasting points, and makes reference to the analogy that has controlled the essay.

   The following sentence might provide a satisfactory conclusion for our hypothetical essay about John F. Kennedy and Jimmy Carter: *Just as the peacock and the sparrow have their particular values in the scheme of nature, there is room for the contrasting styles of a Kennedy and a Carter in American politics.*

Topics for Critical Thinking and Writing

1. David Riesman mentions various groups—"the Catholics, the Methodists, the organized morticians, the state department, the southerners, the Jews, the doctors"—as sources of political influence in America. Select a controversial issue and write an essay about it, presenting the contrasting perspectives of at least two such special interest groups.

2. Compare representatives of two different generations with regard to each of the following values: competitiveness, conformity, and consumption.

3. In an essay, compare or contrast one of the following pairs: same-sex and opposite-sex friendships, familial love and romantic love, love for a child and love for a parent, love of God and brotherhood.

4. Contrast the female and male perspectives on life, using three major points of comparison.

5. David Riesman and George Fredrickson trace the effect of time on particular social groups, contrasting earlier and later populations. In a tracing of your

own life, emphasize the similarities or differences between your character in childhood and your character as an adult.

Synthesis Questions

1. The principle of change in the American character is the subject of the readings by David Riesman and Bruce Catton. Choose one aspect of American character and discuss it with reference to the works of these two authors.
2. Several of our readings present contrastive outlooks on life. In an essay, state your personal philosophy of life and use the readings to illustrate your points.
3. George Orwell, Stephen Leacock, David Riesman, and Gilbert Highet challenge the reader on the value of making money. Write a five-paragraph essay in which you discuss three of these writers' viewpoints on the profit motive.
4. Gilbert Highet and Stringfellow Barr suggest that individuals may take different paths to similar goals. Elaborate this thesis with reference to their readings.

Refining Your Essay

1. Have you chosen suitable elements for your essay? Do these elements share one or more significant commonalities? Make a marginal note in your draft at the point where you have stated the commonality. Is it clearly and precisely expressed?
2. Are you sure your points support your thesis? Have you chosen only the most significant and interesting points for comparison and/or contrast?
3. Is the order of your points logical: least to most important, chronological, general to specific? Have you treated the points for each element in the same order?
4. If you have used the block method of organization, be sure that your paragraph of transition refers to both your elements. Have you restated your central idea in regard to the second element? Underline the sentence that makes this transition and check it for clarity.
5. With the alternating method, have you used signals that clearly guide your reader back and forth between your elements?
6. Can you think of an analogy that includes comparative elements appropriate to your subject? If so, review your essay, particularly its introduction and conclusion, for places at which you might use this analogy.
7. Does your concluding paragraph make an evaluative statement that brings your elements together?

CHAPTER TEN

Ideas and Ideals: Writing the Argumentative Essay

Demonstrations for ideals have been an American tradition since the Boston Tea Party. In this photo, protesters against apartheid in South Africa march with the support of organized labor. For which of your ideas and ideals would you take to the streets in peaceful protest?

THE WRITING FOCUS

*We may convince others by our arguments, but we can
persuade them only by their own.*

Joseph Joubert, *Pensées*

With the theme of ideas and ideals, we enter the highest plane of the human condition. Human beings want to communicate their thoughts and beliefs. Not only do we want to share our ideas but we also want to convince people of their value and possibly even to persuade them to take action on behalf of our beliefs. The argumentative essay gives you the opportunity to take a stand.

An argument presents an idea and offers logic—that is, a chain of valid reasoning—to support or refute it. Persuasion is a form of argument that may include logic but relies more on emotion to convince its audience. Persuasion brings argument beyond the abstract to motivate the reader to action.

There are different types of argumentative and persuasive essays. A writer may wish to interpret a work of art or a social phenomenon, going beyond simple description or explanation into the mode of argument. This type of essay seeks to raise people's consciousness regarding complex and controversial subjects. Examples in this chapter are Bartolomeo Vanzetti's advocacy of universal brotherhood and Martin Luther King's dream of bringing blacks into the mainstream of American social and economic life.

A more common purpose of argumentative and persuasive essays is to defend our own or attack others' positions or values. Our readings from Edmund Burke's and Thomas Paine's essays in favor of American independence are classics of this type.

Approaches to Argument

Although most argumentative essays blend a variety of approaches, we can distinguish three main types. One is the traditional deductive essay, in which the introduction establishes the issue and states the thesis. The writer develops his or her points using facts, illustrations, and other kinds of support. After establishing the case, the writer often concludes by refuting anticipated opposing arguments.

A second approach to argumentation is the dialectical argument. Here the writer formulates and supports one thesis and then develops an opposing thesis, or antithesis. The issue is resolved in the synthesis, a compromise position between the two extremes. An example of this approach is Burke's essay, which, in its complete form, expresses a desire for British-colonial union but rejects force as a means of maintaining it and finally offers the compromise of a relaxed but still binding relationship.

A third approach is the point-counterpoint argument. The writer first states, analyzes, and refutes the arguments of the opposition and then advances his or her own counterpoints.

Arguments can be organized in the block or alternating methods. In the block method all anticipated opposing points are listed together. Then each is refuted one after another. Colin Turnbull uses block organization in his essay on capital punishment. An example of the alternating approach is Burke's argument against Britain's use of force in the American colonies; Burke rebuts each opposition point as he presents it.

Constructing Your Argument

Identifying a controversial issue and brainstorming its opposing sides are your first steps in composing an argumentative essay. From your brainstorming you will make two lists. The first will contain as many specific points as you can think of that support your opinion. The second will include arguments you anticipate on the other side.

The next step is to review each list, combining repeated or overlapping points and clustering the remaining items into logical groupings. These will become the subtopics—the points in your argument.

Now you must decide on your approach. Will you develop your essay by attacking the opposition's arguments and then presenting your own stance—point-counterpoint? Will you first state and support your own thesis and then attack the opposition—the deductive method? Or will you give consideration to both sides and arrive at a compromise position—the dialectical approach?

Whatever the organization of your essay, you must sequence your points logically—for example, from most to least familiar, from most to least important, or chronologically. Colin Turnbull's essay, as an illustration, arranges its points against capital punishment from the most to least familiar.

If your subject or point of view is not familiar, or if your point of view is controversial or unpopular, you may want to engage your audience by beginning with facts or indisputable observations. For example, if you took the generally unpopular view that personality-altering drugs should be legalized, you might begin with the startling fact that annual deaths related to tobacco use outnumber deaths from substance abuse by one thousand to one. As you build audience acceptance of your introductory statements, you can then link them step by step to the broader ideas or assertions that are central to your thesis.

To help your reader follow your points, you can make the order of their importance known by such signal expressions as *one reason, a reason of great importance,* or *equally important.*

Introductions and Conclusions

Most introductions of argumentative and persuasive essays are developed inductively; that is, they lead from concrete facts or illustrations to the writer's thesis. The inductive opening is intended to clarify the issue, engage the reader's attention, and invite acceptance of the thesis. Writers accomplish these goals in several ways. In our Essay for Analysis, Clarence Darrow clarifies the issue by defining two opposing beliefs, agnosticism and Christianity, in the beginning of his essay.

Other writers use a provocative fact, anecdote, or image in the introduction, to dramatize the central issue of their argument. Jonathan Swift's "A Modest Proposal," for example, begins with a shocking image of child beggars in the streets of Dublin. This sets the stage for both ironic and genuine solutions to the problem of Irish poverty.

A statement of personal integrity and objectivity toward the subject, the presentation of a philosophical rationale, and an explanation of the writer's methodology are other means of introducing a thesis in the argumentative or persuasive essay.

The conclusion of your essay may also be the place to state your objectivity regarding the issue. In addition, your conclusion may contain a judgment, prediction, or warning about the future based on the acceptance or rejection of your thesis. One of this chapter's readings, Edward Markham's poem about the oppression of the European peasantry, ends with such a warning.

Logical Reasoning

Within your essay, logic, or the process of correct reasoning, must govern the connections between your ideas.

Of first importance to any argument is the premise, the underlying truth on which the thesis is based. The premise of your argument may be implied or openly stated, but it must consist of "common ground"—ideas that your audience accepts without contest. When an audience does not accept the arguer's premise, then the logical proofs that follow will carry little weight, and the audience will not accept the thesis.

The Declaration of Independence (see Chapter 8), for example, begins with this premise: "We hold these truths to be self-evident, that all men are created equal, that they are endowed by their Creator with certain unalienable rights, that among these are life, liberty, and the pursuit of happiness." If this premise had not been accepted by the colonists, then the chain of reasons developed in the Declaration would have been neither logical nor convincing.

The Declaration builds on its premise through the process of logic known as syllogistic reasoning. Syllogisms connect statements so that if two or more are agreed to be true, a further statement based on the first two must also be true.

Thus, the Declaration follows up its first premise with a second: "That to secure these rights, governments are instituted among men, deriving their just powers from the consent of the governed." This premise, like the first, is offered as self-evident. A third statement, a conclusion following from the two premises, announces "that whenever any form of government becomes destructive of these ends, it is the right of the people to alter or to abolish it." If the audience has accepted the premises, then the conclusion follows logically. After thus establishing a logical basis for its argument in favor of separation, the Declaration of Independence cites specific instances of British oppression as supporting evidence.

The success of an argumentative essay depends on the validity, truth, and completeness of its claims and evidence. *Validity* refers to the consistency of statements with each other; if one idea is based on another, the first idea cannot be false nor can the two ideas contradict each other. *Truth* refers to the correspondence between statements and facts or experience. If an arguer's claim runs counter to what others recognize as true in their physical or psychological worlds, then the claim must either be explained or abandoned as false. *Completeness* refers to the comprehensiveness an argument must have to be convincing. If a chain of logic leaves out vital points or examines them from only one perspective, the audience may reach a conclusion different from that of the arguer or may consider the conclusion still open to debate.

LOGICAL FALLACIES

Certain ways of thinking that weaken an argument are known as logical fallacies:

1. A *sweeping generalization* is a statement that attributes a characteristic to all members of a given class. Using words such as *all* or *every* or implying these words, sweeping generalizations are absolute assertions such as "Women are not strong enough to do men's jobs." You can avoid this fallacy by qualifying your assertions with such expressions as *some* or *many* or with restrictive phrases of time or place.
2. A *non sequitur* (Latin for "it does not follow") is a statement that makes no sense because it does not relate logically to the statement or statements that preceded it. An example of a non sequitur is that one should vote for a particular candidate for political office because he has the support of many sports celebrities. The non sequitur is that having friends with athletic talent has no logical connection to political judgment.
3. The *post hoc ergo propter hoc* fallacy (Latin for "after this, therefore because of this") mistakenly links two events in a cause-effect relationship simply because one follows the other in time. (See Chapter 8 for further discussion of causal relationships.)
4. An *oversimplification* is a partial answer to a complicated problem. For example, saying "Love it or leave it" to someone publicly protesting some aspect of American policy is an oversimplified response to dissent in a free society.

5. A *false dilemma* limits a field of several alternatives on an issue to an either-or situation. For example, when a politician suggests that murderers must be executed or decent people will not be able to walk the streets in safety, the politician is ignoring the alternatives to capital punishment.

6. *Begging the question* is to proceed from an assumption or premise as if it were a proven fact and use it as the basis for an argument. A spokesperson against pornography who began by saying "Everyone knows that pornographic material incites sexual violence; therefore, we should ban such material from distribution through stores and the mail" would be begging the question. The fact is that no direct link between pornography and sexual violence has been established to the satisfaction of all researchers.

7. The *ad hominem* argument (Latin for "to the man") personalizes an issue by attacking the character of an opponent rather than the opponent's position on the issue. A characterization of Edmund Burke and his supporters as cowards for taking a position against England's going to war with the American colonists would be an ad hominem argument.

Persuasive Techniques

Because persuasion is meant not simply to convince but to *convert* readers and to impel them to a course of action, the persuasive essay incorporates devices generally not found in the essay of argumentation. Logic does have a place in the persuasive essay, but there is greater reliance on opinion and appeals to emotion. Connotative, or suggestive, language, figures of speech, and symbols play a legitimate role in persuasive writing. Rhetorical questions, which invite a response desired by the writer, are also commonly used as a means of bringing the audience to the writer's side. There are many examples of these in Darrow's essay on agnosticism.

Martin Luther King's speech "I Have a Dream" exemplifies persuasion at its best. King makes use of all the effective techniques of persuasion. For instance, he uses highly suggestive phrases such as "flames of withering injustice" to make vivid the damage done by oppression, and he employs the Emancipation Proclamation as a symbol to which all Americans can respond positively. In describing America's unpaid debt to its black citizens through metaphors such as a "bad check" and a "promissory note," King appeals to one of America's most cherished images of itself, that of a nation that pays its dues and gives a square deal to every hardworking individual.

In composing a persuasive essay, the writer must not distort the truth to achieve an aim. Propaganda, writing to promote (or oppose) a cause or an institution, often simplifies issues and uses exaggerated, inflammatory language to manipulate people. Readers and writers alike must beware of the devices of the propagandist:

1. *Name calling* is to attach negative labels to causes or individuals to discredit them (this technique is a form of the ad hominem argument).
2. *Glittering generalities* are overgeneralizations using terms that excite emotions. Depending on your politics, the same person may be called a "freedom fighter" or a "terrorist." Such glittering generalities stifle critical thought.
3. *Appealing to illegitimate authority* is to cite individuals who are not experts on the issue but who have achieved celebrity in other, unrelated fields. Using a prominent athlete or entertainer to support a political cause typifies this type of appeal.
4. The *bandwagon* device is based on the idea that people feel most comfortable when they are in the majority on a position. A bandwagon appeal attempts to convince people that everyone believes or is doing what the persuader is advocating. Thus, television evangelists often inflate the numbers of their viewers to persuade members of the audience to "jump on the bandwagon" and contribute to the cause.

Essay for Analysis

CLARENCE DARROW

Why I Am an Agnostic

Clarence Darrow (1857–1938), One of America's best-known trial lawyers, played an important role in many controversial political, labor, and criminal cases. Darrow was unsuccessful in his defense of biology teacher John Scopes, tried for teaching evolutionary theory in a Tennessee school. But his argument that open inquiry is essential to education is as relevant today as it was three generations ago.

The following essay was originally delivered as a talk at a symposium on religion, in which Darrow's fellow speakers articulated the creeds of the Jewish, Protestant, and Catholic faiths. Darrow uses a combination of logical reasoning and persuasive techniques to support his argument.

An agnostic is a doubter. The word is generally applied to those who doubt the verity of accepted religious creeds of faiths. Everyone is an agnostic as to the beliefs or creeds they do not accept. Catholics are agnostic to the Protestant creeds, and the Protestants are agnostic to the Catholic creed. Anyone who thinks is an agnostic about something, otherwise he must believe that he is possessed of all knowledge. And the proper place for such a person is in the madhouse or the home for the feeble-minded. In a popular way, in the western world, an agnostic is one who doubts or disbelieves the main tenets of the Christian faith.

1   Definition: *agnostic*

Establishment of common ground

I would say that belief in at least three tenets is necessary to the faith of a Christian: a belief in God, a belief in immortality, and a belief in a supernatural book. Various Christian sects require much more, but it is difficult to imagine that one could be a Christian, under any intelligent meaning of the word, with less. Yet there are some people who claim to be Christians who do not accept the literal interpretation of all the Bible, and who give more credence to some portions of the book than to others.

2   Definition: *Christian*

I am an agnostic as to the question of God. I think that it is impossible for the human mind to believe in an object or thing unless it can form a mental picture of such object or thing. Since man ceased to worship openly an anthropomorphic God and talked vaguely and not intelligently about some force in the universe, higher than man, that is responsible for the existence of man and the universe, he cannot be said to believe in God. One cannot believe in a force excepting as a force that pervades matter and is not an individual entity. To believe in a thing, an image of the thing must be stamped on the mind. If one is asked if he believes in such an animal as a camel, there immediately arises in his mind an image of the camel. This image has come from experience or knowledge of the animal gathered in some way or other. No such image comes, or can come, with the idea of a God who is described as a force. . . .

3   Thesis statement

To say that God made the universe gives us no explanation of the beginning of things. If we are told that God made the universe, the question immediately arises: Who made God? Did he always exist, or was there some power back of that? Did he create matter out of nothing, or is his existence co-extensive with matter? The problem is still there. What is the origin of it all? If, on the other hand, one says that the universe was not made by God, that it always existed, he has the same difficulty to confront. To say that the universe was here last year, or millions of years ago, does not explain its origin. This is still a mystery. As to the question of the origin of things, man can only wonder and doubt and guess.

As to the existence of the soul, all people may either believe or disbelieve. Everyone knows the origin of the human being. They know that it came from a single cell in the body of the mother, and that the cell was one out of ten thousand in the mother's body. Before gestation the cell must have been fertilized by a spermatozoön from the body of the father. This was one out of perhaps a billion spermatozoa that was the capacity of the father. When the cell is fertilized a chemical process begins. The cell divides and multiplies and increases into millions of cells, and finally a child is born. Cells die and are born during the life of the individual until they finally drop apart, and this is death.

If there is a soul, what is it, and where did it come from, and where does it go? Can anyone who is guided by his reason possibly imagine a soul independent of a body, or the place of its residence, or the character of it, or anything concerning it? If man is justified in any belief or disbelief on any subject, he is warranted in the disbelief in a soul. Not one scrap of evidence exists to prove any such impossible thing.

Many Christians base the belief of a soul and God upon the Bible. Strictly speaking, there is no such book. To make the Bible, sixty-six books are bound into one volume. These books are written by many people at different

4 — Refuting opposition beliefs
First point: against God's creation of universe
Support by logical reasoning

5 — Second point: against existence of the soul

Support by facts (scientific data)

6 — Rhetorical questions

7 — Third point: against "truth" of the Bible

times, and no one knows the time or the identity of any author. Some of the books were written by several authors at various times. These books contain all sorts of contradictory concepts of life and morals and the origin of things. Between the first and the last nearly a thousand years intervened, a longer time than has passed since the discovery of America by Columbus.

Support by facts

When I was a boy the theologians used to assert that the proof of the divine inspiration of the Bible rested on miracles and prophecies. But a miracle means a violation of a natural law, and there can be no proof imagined that could be sufficient to show the violation of a natural law; even though proof seemed to show violation, it would only show that we were not acquainted with all natural laws. One believes in the truthfulness of a man because of his long experience with the man, and because the man has always told a consistent story. But no man has told so consistent a story as nature. . . .

8   Fourth point: against miracles

Primitive and even civilized people have grown so accustomed to believing in miracles that they often attribute the simplest manifestations of nature to agencies of which they know nothing. They do this when the belief is utterly inconsistent with knowledge and logic. They believe in old miracles and new ones. Preachers pray for rain, knowing full well that no such prayer was ever answered. When a politician is sick, they pray for God to cure him, and the politician almost invariably dies. The modern clergyman who prays for rain and for the health of the politician is no more intelligent in this matter than the primitive man who saw a separate miracle in the rising and setting of the sun, in the birth of an individual, in the growth of a plant, in the stroke of lightning, in the flood, in every manifestation of nature and life. . . .

9

Refutation of opposition by analogy

Can any rational person believe that the Bible is anything but a human document? We now know pretty well where the various books came from, and about when they were written. We know that they were written by human be-

10   Return to third point: against Bible as truth

ings who had no knowledge of science, little knowledge of life, and were influenced by the barbarous morality of primitive times, and were grossly ignorant of most things that men know today. For instance, Genesis says that God made the earth, and he made the sun to light the day and the moon to light the night, and in one clause disposes of the stars by saying that "he made the stars also." This was plainly written by someone who had no conception of the stars. Man, by the aid of his telescope, has looked out into the heavens and found stars whose diameter is as great as the distance between the earth and the sun. We know that the universe is filled with stars and suns and planets and systems. Every new telescope looking further into the heavens only discovers more and more worlds and suns and systems in the endless reaches of space. The men who wrote Genesis believed, of course, that this tiny speck of mud that we call the earth was the center of the universe, the only world in space, and made for man, who was the only being worth considering. These men believed that the stars were only a little way above the earth, and were set in the firmament for man to look at, and for nothing else. Everyone today knows that this conception is not true.

Support by facts

The origin of the human race is not as 11 blind a subject as it once was. Let alone God creating Adam out of hand, from the dust of the earth, does anyone believe that Eve was made from Adam's rib—that the snake walked and spoke in the Garden of Eden—that he tempted Eve to persuade Adam to eat an apple, and that it is on that account that the whole human race was doomed to hell—that for four thousand years there was no chance for any human to be saved, though none of them had anything whatever to do with the temptation; and that finally men were saved only through God's son dying for them, and that unless human beings believed this silly, impossible and wicked story they were doomed to hell? Can anyone with intelligence really believe that a child born today

Rhetorical questions to refute belief in Bible

should be doomed because the snake tempted Eve and Eve tempted Adam? To believe that is not God-worship: it is devil-worship.

Can anyone call this scheme of creation and damnation moral? It defies every principle of morality, as man conceives morality. Can anyone believe today that the whole world was destroyed by flood, save only Noah and his family and a male and female of each species of animal that entered the Ark? There are almost a million species of insects alone. How did Noah match these up and make sure of getting male and female to reproduce life in the world after the flood had spent its force? And why should all the lower animals have been destroyed? Were they included in the sinning of man? This is a story which could not beguile a fairly bright child of five years of age today.

Do intelligent people believe that the various languages spoken by man on earth came from the confusion of tongues at the Tower of Babel, some four thousand years ago? Human languages were dispersed all over the face of the earth long before that time. Evidences of civilizations are in existence now that were old long before the date that romancers fix for the building of the Tower, and even before the date claimed for the flood.

Do Christians believe that Joshua made the sun stand still, so that the day could be lengthened, that a battle might be finished? What kind of person wrote that story, and what did he know about astronomy? It is perfectly plain that the author thought that the earth was the center of the universe and stood still in the heavens, and that the sun either went around it or was pulled across its path each day, and that the stopping of the sun would lengthen the day. We know now that had the sun stopped when Joshua commanded it, and had it stood still until now, it would not have lengthened the day. We know that the day is determined by the rotation of the earth upon its axis, and not by the movement of the sun. Everyone knows that this

Name calling
Rhetorical questions

12

13

14

Refutation of Bible by facts

story simply is not true, and not many even pretend to believe the childish fable.

What of the tale of Balaam's ass speaking 15 to him, probably in Hebrew? Is it true, or is it fable? Many asses have spoken, and doubtless some in Hebrew, but they have not been that breed of asses. Is salvation to depend on a belief in a belief in a monstrosity like this?

False dilemma

Above all the rest, would any human being 16 today believe that a child was born without a father? Yet this story was not at all unreasonable in the ancient world; at least three or four miraculous births are recorded in the Bible, including John the Baptist and Samson. Immaculate conceptions were common in the Roman world at the time and at the place where Christianity really had its nativity. Women were taken to the temples to be inoculated of Gods that their sons might be heroes, which meant, generally, wholesale butchers. Julius Caesar was a miraculous conception—indeed, they were common all over the world. How many miraculous-birth stories is a Christian now expected to believe?

Persuasive techniques: rhetorical questions

The reasons for agnosticism are abundant 17 and compelling. Fantastic and foolish and impossible consequences are freely claimed for the belief in religion. All the civilization of any period is put down as a result of religion. All the cruelty and error and ignorance of the period has no relation to religion. The truth is that the origin of what we call civilization is not due to religion but to skepticism. So long as men accepted miracles without question, so long as they believed in original sin and the road to salvation, so long as they believed in a hell where man would be kept for eternity on account of Eve, there was no reason whatever for civilization: life was short, and eternity was long, and the business of life was preparation for eternity.

Signals of argument for agnosticism

When every event was a miracle, when 18 there was no order or system or law, there was no occasion for studying any subject, or being interested in anything excepting a religion which took care of the soul. As man doubted the

Support for thesis (logical reasoning)

primitive conceptions about religion, and no longer accepted the literal, miraculous teachings of ancient books, he set himself to understand nature. We no longer cure disease by casting out devils. Since that time, men have studied the human body, have built hospitals and treated illness in a scientific way. Science is responsible for the building of railroads and bridges, of steamships, of telegraph lines, of cities, towns, large buildings and small, plumbing and sanitation, of the food supply, and the countless thousands of useful things that we now deem necessary to life. Without skepticism and doubt, none of these things could have been given to the world.

The fear of God is not the beginning of 19 wisdom. The fear of God is the death of wisdom. Skepticism and doubt lead to study and investigation, and investigation is the beginning of wisdom.

The modern world is the child of doubt 20 and inquiry, as the ancient world was the child of fear and faith.

Conclusion: warning

Analysis of the Essay

THE PROCESS OF TAKING A STAND

Clarence Darrow's argument for agnosticism begins with a definition of the term *agnostic* both in its usual sense as one who doubts religious belief in general and in an unusual sense as one who doubts all religions excepts one's own. Darrow indulges in the propagandistic device of name calling, saying that anyone who is not an agnostic about something is either insane or feebleminded. Thus, somewhat provocatively, he establishes the common ground for his argument.

Type of Argument. Darrow argues deductively, expressing his thesis statement in paragraph 3. He takes up the bases of the opposite viewpoint one by one and discredits them through statements of fact, logical reasoning, and ridicule. For example, he attacks the biblical account of God's creation of the human species by asking rhetorical questions and implying there is only one answer—a negative—to his inquiries (paragraph 11). He supports his argument against the existence of the soul with scientific facts as well as rhetorical questions (5, 6). He argues against the Bible as truth and against the occurrence of miracles, using logical reasoning as well as scientific facts (7–10).

The order in which Darrow presents and demolishes the arguments of the opposition is, logically, from the most essential to the least essential, for if he can shake his listener's faith in the existence of God, then skepticism about the soul, the Bible, and miracles will come more easily.

In presenting his own argument, Darrow again relies on a deductive pattern. He asserts his thesis that civilization came about through skepticism rather than religion in paragraph 17, clearly signalling his argument: "The reasons for agnosticism . . ." and "The truth is. . . ." His strongest arguments are built on historical facts, logical reasoning, and concrete illustrations. He concludes with a parallel construction in which images of the modern world and the ancient world are contrasted, encapsulating his views in a memorable form.

Techniques of Persuasion.   As a successful trial lawyer, Darrow was practiced in the techniques of logical argumentation and persuasion. In this essay he uses a number of persuasive techniques, including some devices of the propagandist such as name calling. In paragraph 15 he forces a false dilemma on his audience, offering only a choice between the Bible's fable of Balaam's talking donkey and agnosticism, when in fact there is a host of religious creeds that don't involve a "monstrosity like this." In paragraphs 11 through 16 he uses an ad hominem argument, attacking the believer along with the belief, by asking a series of rhetorical questions ridiculing the intelligence and morality of those who believe biblical stories.

One of Darrow's cleverest techniques of persuasion is the manner in which he turns Christian beliefs against themselves. He makes such beliefs as the story of Adam and Eve or the birth of Jesus to a virgin appear so silly that no educated person could assent to them. In paragraph 11 he argues that belief in the story of Adam and Eve and the snake in the Garden of Eden is devil worship, another example of name calling. In paragraph 16, Darrow links the miraculous births of Julius Caesar and other Roman heroes, whom he characterizes as "wholesale butchers" to the miraculous births mentioned in the Bible. He ironically implies a similarity between pagan beliefs, which Christianity rejected, and the beliefs of Christianity itself.

Thus, by establishing an apparent common ground about the beliefs of Christianity to which all Christians would assent, and then by demolishing those beliefs as absurd to any intelligent person, Darrow forcefully (if not necessarily successfully) argued his views on this most controversial subject of his day.

READINGS

COLIN TURNBULL

Death by Decree: An Anthropological Approach to Capital Punishment

Anthropologist Colin Turnbull is well known for his sympathetic portrayals of the tribal peoples of Africa in such popular works as *The Lonely African* and *The Forest People*. Three years as an instructor of anthropology in the Virginia State Penitentiary enabled Turnbull to bring personal experience as well as the methodology of his discipline to his argument against capital punishment.

Anthropologists, particularly when in the field, try to be as detached as possible, eschewing value judgments, looking at social institutions in their context. Sometimes I think they become too detached and lose sight of their own social values and responsibilities. Sometimes I think they become detached from humanity itself. Yet anthropology is as much a humanity as a science, if not more so. If we are dealing exclusively with society as a system of interrelated social institutions, then we can achieve a greater legitimate measure of detachment, and indeed we should. But we are also dealing with human beings and with human values, and we have to recognize that human emotions and the need for their expression are powerful forces in shaping the structure of any society. To be truly holistic, which is one of our claims, we must be subjective as well as objective in our quest for truth and meaning. It is not always a comfortable quest, least of all when dealing with an issue such as capital punishment.

In all societies and all legal systems, and certainly in our own, persons are distinguished from things. To persons we attribute inalienable human rights. The institution of slavery was justified, even by Christian moralists, by the simple denial of that basic tenet. We classified one group of persons as things and from that moment on had no moral obligation to them as humans. Joseph Towles, a black American anthropologist, who has some experience of what it is to be treated as a thing, recently pointed out to me the similarity of the process as applied to slaves and as applied to prisoners, particularly those on death row today. He was thinking not only of the deprivation suffered by, and the injury done to, the slaves but also of the deprivation and injury experienced by the masters. (It is now recognized that the institution of slavery eroded the most basic human values throughout the system, brutalizing and dehumanizing both slave and master.) As an anthropologist, he was seeking a structural comparison that would at least explain, although not necessarily justify, the brutalization and dehumanization that take place on death row, recognizing that the tragedy is as great for those in authority as for those subject to it and that, as with slavery, the effects permeate society throughout, threatening our very understanding of the word humanity.

One frequently heard argument is that those on death row are not 3 human. They are often referred to as savages, beasts, subhuman, beyond redemption, animals. The word *animal* is of particular significance to the anthropologist who knows that in many "primitive" societies this is the word used most often to distinguish people from "nonpeople," or "the others." Exactly the same concept of exclusivity underlies racism, religious factionalism, economic warfare, political chauvinism, and other similar characteristics that exist in our modern society, however much we wish it were otherwise.

We cannot avoid recognizing that this concept permeates our society 4 just as strongly as the belief that to classify persons as things is wrong. Why then do we legitimize it in our prison system? Look at the process for a moment if you deny it is so. On entry into prison, a prisoner's name is taken away from him. He is bathed; often his hair is cut. He is disinfected, given a prison uniform, and deprived of contact with the outside world, the world of the living. It is a ritual death of his entire being as a human, comparable in remarkable detail to initiation rituals in which children who are candidates for adulthood are similarly separated from their earlier existence, from family and friends. Their names are taken from them, and they are ritually cleansed and given new uniforms appropriate to their limbo state, until they are ready for induction as the reborn, the final rite being a ritual of rebirth into adulthood. On death row, however, the process is reversed. The candidate enters as a man, is systematically separated from all that manhood is, and placed in limbo until the moment of induction into his new status, death. To the structuralist, the process makes sense. As a humanist, however much I may despise a man who commits murder, I am still bothered about taking away his humanity. Taking his life is bothersome enough; taking his humanity not only seems logically unjustified (unless we can show that he has *no* human qualities) but far more important, it legalizes the dangerous concept that under certain circumstances—those convenient to society—we may classify certain groups of persons as things and treat them accordingly. Disposable things.

However, let us set about finding the reason for this concept through 5 an examination of the process.

My research has only begun; like all fieldwork it is intensely involv- 6
ing: at times it depresses; at times it inspires. As a humanist I am as much
concerned with the families of murder victims, with the lives of the prison
officials, with those who pass sentence and those who implement it, as
with the lives of the condemned men and women, their families, and the
life of society at large. This is not an argument for or against capital punishment. It is an attempt to understand and to provoke the kinds of questions we all ought to be trying to answer. Field research spreads like a
weed, and like a weed it occasionally blossoms into flower. Let me give an
example so that you can see what I mean.

In the field I enter an African village, and in my notebook I hastily 7
sketch an outline of the village—the disposition of houses and meeting
places. Later I supplement these sketches with information about who
lives where. I have no idea what the significance will be. I only know that,
more likely than not, it will be significant.

So my first visit to death row produced a sketch of a dark, cramped, 8
unventilated basement. There was one corridor, with the ten cells facing
each other. Directly behind them was the chamber housing the electric
chair. Such light as there was came from an inadequate supply of electricity; ironically, across one end of the corridor ran a huge thick cable carrying an ample supply to the chair.

The next death row I saw was light and airy, up on the second floor. 9
There were some ninety cells (my notes would tell me exactly, but that is
close enough for the moment), in two double rows, each back to back, so
that each cell looked out only on a heavily barred and empty corridor and
through that to the sunny skies of the world beyond. The electric chair
was on the ground level, where another, smaller double row of cells, similarly back to back, housed men within one week of execution. At the
time, these cells were empty; the second floor was full.

A third was similar in most respects to the second example, except 10
that beyond the empty corridor there were no windows letting in a flood
of sunlight; instead yet another heavily barred corridor was patrolled by
armed guards, and behind that was a high wall topped by windows that
let in some diffused daylight. And there was no large waiting area way
down below (this was the top floor), just two tiny cells, barely large
enough for a cot, in which the condemned spent their last night prior to
taking the short walk to the gas chamber a few feet away. But there was
another, more curious difference in the last instance: up on the top floor
each empty corridor was spaced with television sets, one to every three
cells, and each cell had a control.

These sketches corresponded to my initial sketches of an African vil- 11
lage. I began to look for significance and instantly I was drawn in several
different directions, which is why it is impossible to do more than begin
to tell the story in such a short account. The significance lay not just with
the obvious difference in the quality of living conditions: the amount of

fresh air, the adequacy of natural light, the sanitation, and the degree of isolation (the back-to-back cells each had a buttress that projected about three feet beyond the inner cell door, so that from one cell you could not even see the outstretched arm of the person next door). The architecture and furnishings also had to do with security and, in this connection, inmate morale, as well as with the antiquity of the building, which gave little leeway to prison authorities who might have wished for a different design, different living conditions.

A connection was made in my mind between security and morale. I 12 began to look, for instance, at the varied functions of television. For those prisoners who were not semicatatonic, that is, those who were not lying on the cold floor of their cell staring at me with unblinking eyes but not seeing, not moving a muscle as I tried to engage their attention, television provided entertainment and relaxation. But the TV sets also served a much less obvious function; they bound inmates who could not even see each other into social units, within which there was cooperation, caring, and understanding. Each unit came to its own agreement as to which shows to watch and when. These units were rather like sublineages; the lineage as a whole manifests itself during exercise periods when half of one row at a time is taken to the roof for exercise. The television also served to anesthetize, as indeed it does in our living rooms. It drained the energy and sapped the will to think. It thus functioned (which is not to say that it was necessarily installed for this purpose) to take away the will to live. A man about to die surely has something better to do with his time than watch "I Love Lucy." For this very reason, a number of inmates refused television.

The small basement death row, with cells facing each other, with all 13 its disadvantages (it is one of the oldest buildings in the country still in use as a penitentiary) at least afforded the possibility of continual visual communication, but for many years the men were forbidden to talk above a whisper in an attempt to minimize any interaction. It had the disadvantage of being in such proximity to the death chamber that the sound and smell of death was ever present, whereas in other prisons the men were removed from that, at least until the final week or day. . . .

The first step in classical anthropological observation and analysis is 14 descriptive ethnography—to observe and describe without academic or personal prejudice. This is where anthropologists demand of themselves an objectivity that is as complete and free of value judgments as possible. This is also where our holistic concept is important, for since we are unencumbered by theoretical considerations at this stage, we have no preconceptions as to what might be significant or insignificant—we observe and note everything around us, however trivial it might seem at the time, for we are interested in the total social system, not just one part of it.

In this case, although I am concerned with capital punishment as an 15 institution and its interrelationships with other institutions. I am also concerned with the value system within which it operates and therefore interested in opinions, which are value statements, regarding it. As an observer then, without initial judgment concerning capital punishment itself, I look at: (1) the common arguments *for* capital punishment; (2) the common arguments *against* capital punishment; (3) the nature of capital punishment.

Only then am I in a position to assess and interpret the role of the institution in our society and determine just how far it affects the lives of every one of us in that society. 16

THE ARGUMENTS FOR CAPITAL PUNISHMENT

1. It is a deterrent
2. It prevents recurrence
3. It is a moral duty
4. It is more economical than life imprisonment
5. It is kinder than life imprisonment
6. Those sentenced to death are only the worst offenders and are beyond rehabilitation
7. Those sentenced to death are beyond humanity and therefore deserve no consideration as such (a counterargument to "cruel and unusual punishment")
8. "We don't know what else to do, and we have to do something," an argument first stated to me by a prominent judge who, as a lawyer, had successfully won the restoration of the death penalty in one state, yet was willing to concede all arguments except this one.

THE ARGUMENTS AGAINST CAPITAL PUNISHMENT

1. It is not a deterrent. Here again it is necessary to stress that the best-informed opinion within the legal system is, at best, divided, since the argument is as impossible of proof as it is of disproof. Every murder committed where subject to the death penalty is positive proof that in that case the penalty was *not* a deterrent. Clifton Duffy, who as warden of San Quentin witnessed ninety executions and dealt with many of the most hardened criminals in the country, said of the death penalty, "It is not a deterrent to crime. . . . I have yet to meet the man who let the thought of the gas chamber stop him from committing murder." Hard data support this view. There has been a slightly higher murder rate in some states having a death penalty. The abolition or introduction of the penalty does not make *any* significant difference in the rate of commission of capital crimes; in any case, such fluctuation can only be assessed in relationship to other considerations as well, such as a changing social context. The only valid rational verdict on deterrence, then, is "not proved." 17
2. It does not necessarily prevent recurrence. The only validity of the 18

"prevention" argument for the death penalty is that in killing a murderer we prevent the possibility of that one man murdering again. Of the more than four hundred men and women on death row at this moment or of the thousands executed in this country recently (about four thousand in the last forty years) few had committed more than one murder or showed evidence they were likely to do so. The great majority were crimes of the passion of a single moment, and although such people need to be restrained, confinement would do that as well as execution and would seem more appropriate.

3. It is not a moral duty. Those who try to justify capital punishment on 19 moral grounds can only cite ancient Hebraic law ("Eye for eye. . . .") which, in itself, is susceptible to different interpretations and was in any case applicable in a totally different context some two thousand years ago. Further, the major churches have argued strongly *against* capital punishment. The significant discrepancy between church leadership and the extent to which it is followed by nominal adherents has to be explained, and the explanation is probably that the churches, no more than other anti-capital punishment bodies, have failed to come up with an effective alternative or even with effective arguments other than a direct moral commitment.

4. It is not more economical, necessarily, to execute a criminal than to 20 keep him in confinement for life. The cost to the state of a capital offense trial and of all the subsequent appeals is exorbitant, as is the added cost of maintaining a prisoner on death row for what might be many years of appeal. Summary execution would of course reduce that cost and would add something to the possibility of the penalty acting as a deterrent, but is unacceptable under our present concept of justice and due process. For those unwilling to accept that anyone in authority would consider mere economics in an issue of such gravity, I cite the recent case where the warden of a state penitentiary asked for legalization of lethal injection as a means of execution because it would cost only one dollar per head. Against that kind of thinking there is no refutation.

5. It is not "kinder" than keeping a man in prison for life unless prison 21 conditions are admittedly inhumane. In any case, it is inconsistent to invoke "kindness" in this one respect, yet ignore it when it comes to consideration of the extreme deprivation, physical and psychological, under which prisoners live on death row. There might be an argument for giving a choice, but that would be legalizing suicide in the same sense that execution legalizes murder.

6. It has been clearly demonstrated and confirmed by prison officials that 22 those sentenced to die are not beyond rehabilitation. Faced with this extreme crisis, many prisoners often reflect on life and sociality in a way they might never have done otherwise. In cases where such men have had their sentence commuted they sometimes become model

prisoners and form a constructive and stable element of the general prison population. It is almost as though, by accident, we have discovered the secret of rehabilitation, in rather a drastic way. Such data might be of the greatest significance in the wider area of prison reform and rehabilitation. Murderers and other prisoners I have talked with frequently express a deep frustration at being denied the possibility of making effective atonement. Punishment alone is not atonement.

7. The experience of prison wardens alone demonstrates that convicted murderers may, at least, have human potential. That is a negative way of stating the issue, which is of much greater significance. I refer to the concept of justice found in most primitive societies, where an offender is judged not only for that offense but also for his positive attributes. Even a murderer, after all, might be a good father, an admirable husband, a cooperative and productive craftsman, and a devoutly religious person. In executing that part of him that is "bad" we also execute the good. Even if that had to be so, then should we not continue to grant the condemned person the right to be treated as a human being until the moment of his death, and give him the opportunity to prepare for and meet his death with the decency and dignity our law demands for all human beings? 23

8. We may not know what else to do, but there is no way that we can demonstrate that nothing else can be done. We have examples of alternatives even within our own country, let alone in foreign countries that have completely abandoned the death penalty. We cannot declare that an equally effective solution to murder is impossible, since one cannot logically deny the existence of that which is not known. If successful alternatives have been found in other societies and if we value the sanctity of all human life, even that of humans who have committed crimes, then we are logically bound to search for such alternatives. Regrettably, it is both easier and cheaper not to do so, and this places in question whether our stated human values are any longer valid. Such a quest for an alternative is within our intellectual ability and our financial capability; it is merely a matter of choice and will. 24

While the above constitute refutations of arguments in support of capital punishment, opponents of capital punishment have two irrefutable arguments. The first is the possibility of mistake. We know that innocent victims have been executed; fortunately, others condemned to death have been found innocent prior to execution. And we have to face the very real possibility that other mistakes have never been discovered because following execution, the incentive for costly investigation to prove innocence is largely gone; in nearly all instances the cases of those who maintained their innocence until the moment of death are dropped at that time. 25

The other irrefutable argument against capital punishment is the existence of two prime factors—caprice and selectivity—that effectively determine who shall die and who shall not. Let me cite three of the most obvious demonstrations of this process at work. The proportion of black 26

Americans on death row is totally inconsistent not only with their numbers in relation to the total population but with the numbers of all convicted murderers, black or white. Furthermore, although more than half the murder victims in the United States are black, Dr. Riedel, of the University of Pennsylvania, has shown that in 87 percent of the cases where the death penalty was given, the victim was white. And there is virtually a total absence of persons of any wealth, even moderate, on death row. The penalty clearly selects poor and black, those least able to afford the expert defense such a charge necessitates and whose guilt is most likely to be accepted without protest by the general public. Finally the death penalty discriminates heavily against males. Few women have faced a capital charge, and fewer still have been executed.

There is more—so much more—but this has to be enough. What 27 sense does capital punishment make? It exists in this particular form and therefore, the anthropologist says it is likely to have reason, to make sense, somehow to be necessary for the survival of our society. Perhaps so, but I refuse to admit there is no alternative, for that would be to admit there is an end to humanity. I think back to the final reasoning of the judge who successfully fought to have the death penalty reinstated: What else can we do?

There *is* a desperate situation. Murder seems to have almost become 28 a pastime. We all want to feel safe on the streets, safe in our homes. We are not in authority, so we have the right to demand of those who are that "something be done." I have just described what they do. The deliberate taking of human life is sensational, perhaps the most dramatic act that can be performed.

All other considerations aside, our system is supremely inefficient. 29 We are only accomplishing the disposal of a number of human beings, many of whom are perfectly good people who may have, in a moment of passion, committed a single crime; some may even be totally innocent. We do this in a way that is singularly barbaric, enormously expensive to the public at large, and more particularly, detrimental to the mental and physical health of all those involved. And while we do all this in the name of society at large, the focus is kept firmly on the individual crime and the individual criminal, who is disposed of without any opportunity for atonement. If the entire process were more public; indeed if judge and jurors were compelled to participate in the execution, and if their attention as well as the attention and concern of the rest of society were focused on the need for goodness in society instead of the mere sordid destruction of one individual, then perhaps something might be accomplished by capital punishment.

But if we were that concerned with the well-being of society, there 30 would be little or no need for capital punishment in the first place. Meanwhile it persists merely to provide the public with the illusion that something is being done.

VOCABULARY

Use your dictionary as necessary to find the meaning of the following words in the context of Turnbull's essay:

eschewing (1)   holistic (1)   chauvinism (3)   limbo (4)   disposition (7)

catatonic (12)   anesthetize (12)   fluctuation (17)   discrepancy (19)

summary (20)   atonement (22)   irrefutable (25)   caprice (26)

CONCEPT ANALYSIS

1. According to Turnbull, why and how is dehumanization legitimized in our prison system? What role do prison architecture and furnishings play in this dehumanization?
2. Cite some paragraphs where Turnbull applies the methodology of anthropology to the issue of capital punishment.
3. Select three of Turnbull's points against capital punishment and assess them for their persuasiveness.
4. Paraphrase Turnbull's two additional "irrefutable" arguments against capital punishment. Do you agree with him that these two points make capital punishment unacceptable? Discuss.

Quickwrite

Write about an incident in which you experienced or witnessed the process of dehumanization.

Thinking and Writing

RHETORICAL TECHNIQUE

1. What importance does Turnbull's lengthy introduction (paragraphs 1–15) play in his argument? Would the essay have been more or less effective without it?
2. Which argumentative approach does Turnbull take: deductive, dialectical, or point-counterpoint? Explain your response with specific reference to the organization of the essay.
3. What supporting techniques does Turnbull use for his arguments

against capital punishment: facts, logical reasoning, appeals to authority, emotional language? Give examples of each technique that you find in the essay.

4. Do you find any logical fallacies in Turnbull's essay? Explain.

5. Turnbull presents only one sentence for each argument supporting capital punishment. He presents one paragraph for each of his counterpoints. Does this treatment affect your response to his argument? Explain.

COMPOSITION

1. Using Turnbull's technique of listing and refuting opposition arguments, write an essay on one of the following topics: a peacetime military draft, the legalization of abortion, the legalization of prostitution. Make reference to the issue of dehumanization at some point in your argument.

2. If you support capital punishment, write an essay in which you counter Turnbull's arguments. Use the structure of Turnbull's essay as a guide, presenting his arguments against capital punishment first and your refutation of them afterward.

SIDNEY LENS
Hold That Line

Sidney Lens is editor of *The Progressive,* a magazine that reflects the ideas and ideals of the Progressive Party founded in 1912 by Wisconsin Senator Robert La Follette. Traditionally, the magazine advocates reform in America's political, social, and economic policies.

Time was when working men and women, liberals and radicals of all persuasions, held one rule sacred and inviolable: Never cross a picket line. It wasn't a precept that required discussion or debate. It made no difference which union was on strike, or what it was demanding. Good people didn't cross picket lines. Ever.

Once we learned that rule, we stayed with it. Our politics might have changed, or we might have drifted away from activism, but the picket line remained sacrosanct. Honoring a picket line was a matter of principle, and the principle was absolute and immutable.

Not long ago, I asked a wealthy friend why he continues to respect 3 picket lines that are clearly at odds with his class interests. "I don't know," he replied. "I guess it's because I was brought up that way. My father was a member of the Amalgamated Clothing Workers. . . ."

That's how it was with many millions of us. We or our parents or our 4 grandparents had taken part in the needle-trade strikes, the steel and coal battles, the hard-rock mine struggles, the sit-down strikes in the auto and rubber industries, the bitter confrontation with police or national guardsmen in Minneapolis, Toledo, San Francisco. And even if we or our families were not directly involved, we had heard and read about pickets being beaten, jailed, sometimes killed. Honoring a picket line was the least we could do.

It still is. Observing the rule never to cross a labor picket line is, it 5 seems to me, as important now as it was a couple of generations ago—a minimal show of solidarity with those who are struggling to achieve a better life or a better world. And the rule should allow no exceptions; our observance must be uniform, not selective. It's a matter of principle, of social philosophy. Whether we admire a particular union or a particular strike is beside the point; the *cause* is just and deserves our support.

During the years of protest against U.S. military involvement in 6 Vietnam, I once arranged a television appearance for a young woman, a dedicated peace activist. At the entrance to the station, we encountered a picket line of striking technicians. "Too bad," I said to my young friend. "This is one TV show we'll have to miss." And I started to walk away.

But she refused to leave with me. "Like hell I'll miss this show," she 7 said. "Those union bastards are our enemies." She cited a recent incident: In New York City, a group of construction workers—hard hats—had assaulted antiwar demonstrators. "Why should I care about them?" she asked.

I argued that the tactics the Government was using against us in the 8 peace movement—arrests, injunctions, official and unofficial violence— had been used for generations against the labor movement. I tried to instill in her a sense of solidarity, a feeling for human beings who were also underdogs, who were also attempting to right societal wrongs. It was all in vain. She walked through the picket line and taped the broadcast.

I'm sure many other young people, in and out of the peace move- 9 ment, would not have followed her example. But it seems to me that in recent years I have met many more who wouldn't think twice about crossing a union picket line. The old rule seems to have lost much of its force. Why?

Prosperity is one factor, I suppose. Many workers now earn middle- 10 class or even upper-class incomes. When a $15-an-hour construction worker or a $75,000-a-year airline pilot goes on strike, a $4-an-hour clerk is more likely to be jealous than sympathetic. It was different in the 1920s and 1930s, the years of economic stagnation and open-shop repression, when we were all in the same leaky boat.

The waves of European immigrants also helped promote and protect 11 the sanctity of the picket line. There were strong traditions of working-class solidarity among many of the newcomers—particularly the Jews, Germans, and Irish. Children brought up in such homes learned early in life to stay on this side of the picket line.

What mattered most, however, was a sense of solidarity within the 12 house of labor itself and a moral vision that friends and sympathizers could readily embrace. Both the sense of solidarity and the moral vision have fallen on hard times lately. It isn't easy to work up much comradely fervor for Jackie Presser of the Teamsters, who earns more than half a million dollars a year and is an admitted informer for the FBI. It isn't easy to make common cause with striking airline pilots who didn't hesitate to cross the picket lines of flight attendants and machinists when *they* were out on strike.

From my own years in the labor movement, I can recall a dozen oc- 13 casions when I had to plead with union leaders to respect our picket lines. Such support was not always forthcoming—we lost three or four strikes because other unions wouldn't back us—and when it was, personal friendship or union politics often played a greater role than working-class solidarity.

In the late 1940s, I headed a drive by two national unions to orga- 14 nize a Chicago retail chain that included ten large stores. The workers responded enthusiastically, and soon we were ready to file an application with the National Labor Relations Board for a union certification election. At that point, however, the employer fired more than 100 of our most active recruits, leaving us no choice but to strike.

The two national unions were conservative bastions of the American 15 Federation of Labor with close ties to the Teamsters, so we were confident we could shut down the stores and compel management to rehire the dismissed union activists. It didn't work out that way; after respecting our picket lines for three-and-a-half hours, the Teamsters called to say they would have to go through. Without the Teamsters' support, our strike soon collapsed. The chain remains unorganized to this day, and tens of thousands of other retail workers who would have benefited from our struggle remain outside the ranks of union labor.

Some unions fail to respect a picket line because they are led by busi- 16 ness unionists who have no concept of working-class solidarity. Some unions have been intimidated by the threat of civil lawsuit, or fear criminal prosecution for observing a picket line. The Taft-Hartley Act's ban on "secondary boycotts" has been particularly effective. During the recent strike of Greyhound bus drivers, one major national union contributed $50,000 to the drivers' strike fund but directed its members to cross the picket line and service the buses in accord with their contract. In the 1930s, contract or no contract, this union would have honored the picket line.

In the western United States, Phelps Dodge copper miners on strike 17 for many months receive regular pledges of support and occasional cash contributions from other unions. But union members across the country continue to handle products made from Phelps Dodge's scab copper; to do anything else might mean costly lawsuits or even imprisonment of labor leaders. In an earlier era, union officers would have taken their chances. Today, most unions are prudent: stingy with their treasuries, protective of their investments, and obsessed with their officials' job security.

And the rest of us—liberals, radicals—have become ever so careful, 18 too, weighing the issues, choosing which causes we will support and which we will ignore or undermine, deciding "objectively," as if there were an impartial measure to determine whether, in any particular instance, the rich or the poor are "in the right."

The vanishing sanctity of the picket line is as valid an indicator as 19 any of our political disarray and decay. We'll have a functioning movement when the old rule is in full force again: Never cross a picket line.

Reading and Interpreting

VOCABULARY

Use your dictionary as necessary to find the meaning of the following words as used by Sidney Lens:

sacrosanct (2)   immutable (2)   bastions (15)

CONCEPT ANALYSIS

1. What are some of the reasons Lens offers for the traditional honoring of the picket line by "working men and women, liberals and radicals of all persuasions"? What political philosophy does not share the common ground of this group and is, therefore, not addressed in Lens's essay?
2. What reasons does Lens give for the fact that crossing a union picket line today is more common than it was in the past?
3. What is Lens's thesis? Where is it stated and restated? What is his rationale?
4. Do you find Lens's analysis of the labor movement balanced or biased? Explain your response with reference to the text.
   For you, do Lens's negative comments about labor unions invalidate his thesis, or are you persuaded by it?

5. Do you agree with Lens's conclusion that the "vanishing sanctity of the picket line" is a "valid . . . indicator . . . of our political disarray and decay"? What other conclusions could you draw from Lens's statement of the arguments on both sides of the issue?

Quickwrite

Lens bases a great deal of his argument on the notion of class solidarity. In your opinion, what are the criteria that determine class? With which class do you identify? Describe your class in terms of your criteria.

Thinking and Writing

RHETORICAL TECHNIQUE

1. Lens's essay has a dialectical structure in that his thesis grows out of a respectful argument on both sides of the issue. Do you find this method of argument effective, or does it weaken the argument and leave you confused?
2. Three times in his essay, Lens provides a brief anecdote to support a particular point of view. What point is Lens making with each? How effective are they?
3. What is the order of importance of Lens's reasons for the decreasing sanctity of the picket line? Underline the transitional expressions that signal this order.

COMPOSITION

1. The laws affecting the right to strike of public employees (for example, teachers and police officers) are stricter than those affecting labor in the private sector. Argue the issue of whether public employees should be permitted to strike.
2. Certain industries, such as agriculture and the garment industry, hire great numbers of nonunion workers. Some people call this exploitation of workers; others call it an opportunity for workers to survive. Argue one side of this issue, emphasizing the logic of your position. Anticipate and rebut one or more arguments of the opposition.

EDMUND BURKE
The American Love of Freedom

Edmund Burke (1729–1797), British political writer
and statesman, championed many reforms while retaining confidence in political, social, and religious institutions. He opposed rebellion and force as a means for re-
solving problems. Burke argued in Parliament for wiser
treatment of the American colonies, asserting that although in theory Britain had a constitutional right to
tax them, this policy was potentially harmful. His clearly
reasoned prose reflects the balance and moderation of his
message.

. . . America, gentlemen say, is a noble object—it is an object well 1
worth fighting for. Certainly it is, if fighting a people be the best way of
gaining them. Gentlemen in this respect will be led to their choice of
means by their complexions and their habits. Those who understand the
military art will of course have some predilection for it. Those who wield
the thunder of the state may have more confidence in the efficacy of arms.
But I confess, possibly for want of this knowledge, my opinion is much
more in favor of prudent management than of force; considering force not
as an odious, but a feeble instrument for preserving a people so numerous,
so active, so growing, so spirited as this, in a profitable and subordinate
connection with us.

First, Sir, permit me to observe, that the use of force alone is but 2
temporary. It may subdue for a moment; but it does not remove the necessity of subduing again; and a nation is not governed which is perpetually
to be conquered.

My next objection is its *uncertainty*. Terror is not always the effect of 3
force, and an armament is not a victory. If you do not succeed, you are
without resource: for, conciliation failing, force remains; but force failing,
no further hope of reconciliation is left. Power and authority are sometimes bought by kindness; but they can never be begged as alms by an
impoverished and defeated violence.

A further objection to force is that you *impair the object* by your very 4
endeavors to preserve it. The thing you fought for is not the thing which
you recover, but depreciated, sunk, wasted, and consumed in the contest.
Nothing less will content me than *whole America*. I do not choose to consume its strength along with our own; because in all parts it is the British

strength that I consume. I do not choose to be caught by a foreign enemy at the end of this exhausting conflict, and still less in the midst of it. I may escape, but I can make no insurance against such an event. Let me add that I do not choose wholly to break the American spirit; because it is the spirit that has made the country.

Lastly, we have no sort of *experience* in favor of force as an instrument 5 in the rule of our colonies. Their growth and their utility has been owing to methods altogether different. Our ancient indulgence has been said to be pursued to a fault. It may be so; but we know, if feeling is evidence, that our fault was more tolerable than our attempt to mend it, and our sin far more salutary than our penitence.

These, Sir, are my reasons for not entertaining that high opinion of 6 untried force by which many gentlemen, for whose sentiments in other particulars I have great respect, seem to be so greatly captivated. But there is still behind a third consideration concerning this object, which serves to determine my opinion on the sort of policy which ought to be pursued in the management of America, even more than its population and its commerce: I mean its *temper and character.*

In this character of the Americans a love of freedom is the pre- 7 dominating feature which marks and distinguishes the whole: and as an ardent is always a jealous affection, your colonies become suspicious, restive, and untractable whenever they see the least attempt to wrest from them by force, or shuffle from them by chicane, what they think the only advantage worth living for. This fierce spirit of liberty is stronger in the English colonies, probably, than in any other people of the earth, and this from a great variety of powerful causes; which, to understand the true temper of their minds, and the direction which this spirit takes, it will not be amiss to lay open somewhat more largely.

First, the people of the colonies are descendants of Englishmen. En- 8 gland, Sir, is a nation which still, I hope, respects, and formerly adored, her freedom. The colonists emigrated from you when this part of your character was most predominant; and they took this bias and direction the moment they parted from your hands. They are therefore not only devoted to liberty, but to liberty according to English ideas and on English principles. Abstract liberty, like other mere abstractions, is not to be found. Liberty inheres in some sensible object; and every nation has formed to itself some favorite point, which by way of eminence becomes the criterion of their happiness. It happened, you know, Sir, that the great contests for freedom in this country were from the earliest times chiefly upon the question of taxing. . . . On this point of taxes the ablest pens and most eloquent tongues have been exercised, the greatest spirits have acted and suffered. . . . They took infinite pains to inculcate, as a fundamental principle, that in all monarchies the people must in effect themselves, mediately or immediately, possess the power of granting their own money, or no shadow of liberty could subsist. The colonies draw from you, as with their lifeblood, these ideas and principles. . . . I do not say whether they were right or wrong in applying your general arguments to their own case. It is not easy, indeed, to make a monopoly of theorems and corollaries. The fact is that they did thus apply those general arguments; and your mode of governing them, whether through lenity or indolence, through wisdom or mistake, confirmed them in the imagination that they, as well as you, had an interest in these common principles. . . .

If anything were wanting to this necessary operation of the form of 9 government, religion would have given it a complete effect. Religion, always a principle of energy, in this new people is no way worn out or impaired; and their mode of professing it is also one main cause of this free spirit. The people are Protestants, and of that kind which is the most adverse to all implicit submission of mind and opinion. This is a persuasion not only favorable to liberty, but built upon it. I do not think, Sir, that the reason of this averseness in the dissenting churches from all that looks like absolute government is so much to be sought in their religious tenets as in their history. Everyone knows that the Roman Catholic religion is at least coeval with most of the governments where it prevails, that it has generally gone hand in hand with them, and received great favor and every kind of support from authority. The Church of England, too, was formed from her cradle under the nursing care of regular government. But the dissenting interests have sprung up in direct opposition to all the ordinary powers of the world, and could justify that opposition only on a strong claim to natural liberty. Their very existence depended on the powerful and unremitted assertion of that claim. All Protestantism, even the most cold and passive, is a sort of dissent. But the religion most prevalent in our northern colonies is a refinement on the principle of resistance: it is the dissidence of dissent, and the protestantism of the Protestant religion. This religion, under a variety of denominations agreeing in nothing but in the communion of the spirit of liberty, is predominant in most of the northern provinces, where the Church of England, notwithstanding its legal rights, is in reality no more than a sort of private sect, not composing, most probably, the tenth of the people. The colonists left England when this spirit was high, and in the emigrants was the highest of all; and even that stream of foreigners which has been constantly flowing into these colonies has, for the greatest part, been composed of dissenters from the establishments of their several countries, and have brought with them a temper and character far from alien to that of the people with whom they mixed.

Sir, I can perceive, by their manner, that some gentlemen object to 10 the latitude of this description, because in the southern colonies the Church of England forms a large body, and has a regular establishment. It is certainly true. There is, however, a circumstance attending these colonies which, in my opinion, fully counterbalances this difference and makes the spirit of liberty still more high and haughty than in those to the northward. It is that in Virginia and the Carolinas they have a vast multitude of slaves. Where this is the case in any part of the world, those who are free are by far the most proud and jealous of their freedom. Freedom is to them not only an enjoyment, but a kind of rank and privilege. Not seeing there that freedom, as in countries where it is a common blessing, and as broad and general as the air, may be united with much abject toil, with great misery, with all the exterior of servitude, liberty looks, amongst them, like something that is more noble and liberal. I do not mean, Sir, to commend the superior morality of this sentiment, which has at least as much pride as virtue in it; but I cannot alter the nature of man. The fact is so; and these people of the southern colonies are much more strongly, and with a higher and more stubborn spirit, attached to liberty, than those to the northward. Such were all the ancient commonwealths; such were our Gothic ancestors; such in our days were the Poles; and such will be all masters of slaves, who are not slaves themselves. . . .

Permit me, Sir, to add another circumstance in our colonies which 11 contributes no mean part towards the growth and effect of this untractable spirit: I mean their education. In no country, perhaps, in the world is the law so general a study. The profession itself is numerous and powerful, and in most provinces it takes the lead. The greater number of the deputies sent to the Congress were lawyers. But all who read, and most do read, endeavor to obtain some smattering in that science. . . . This study renders men acute, inquisitive, dexterous, prompt in attack, ready in defense, full of resources. In other countries, the people, more simple, and of a less mercurial cast, judge of an ill principle in government only by an actual grievance; here they anticipate the evil, and judge of the pressure of the grievance by the badness of the principle. They augur misgovernment at a distance, and snuff the approach of tyranny in every tainted breeze.

The last cause of this disobedient spirit in the colonies is hardly less 12 powerful than the rest, as it is not merely moral, but laid deep in the natural constitution of things. Three thousand miles of ocean lie between you and them. No contrivance can prevent the effect of this distance in weakening government. Seas roll, and months pass, between the order and the execution; and the want of a speedy explanation of a single point is enough to defeat a whole system. You have, indeed, winged ministers of vengeance, who carry your bolts in their pounces to the remotest verge of the sea; but there a power steps in that limits the arrogance of raging passions and furious elements, and says, "So far shalt thou go, and no farther." Who are you that should fret and rage, and bite the chains of nature? Nothing worse happens to you than does to all nations who have extensive empire; and it happens in all the forms into which empire can be thrown. In large bodies, the circulation of power must be less vigorous at the extremities. Nature has said it. The Turk cannot govern Egypt, and Arabia, and Kurdistan, as he governs Thrace; nor has he the same dominion in Crimea and Algiers which he has at Brusa and Smyrna. Despotism itself is obliged to truck and huckster. The Sultan gets such obedience as he can. He governs with a loose rein that he may govern at all; and the whole of the force and vigor of his authority in his center is derived from a prudent relaxation in all his borders. Spain, in her provinces, is perhaps not so well obeyed as you are in yours. She complies, too; she submits; she watches times. This is the immutable condition, the eternal law, of extensive and detached empire.

Then, Sir, from these six capital sources, of descent, of form of government, of religion in the northern provinces, of manners in the southern, of education, of the remoteness of situation from the first mover of government—from all these causes a fierce spirit of liberty has grown up. It has grown with the growth of the people in your colonies, and increased with the increase of their wealth: a spirit that, unhappily meeting with an exercise of power in England, which, however lawful, is not reconcilable to any ideas of liberty, much less with theirs, has kindled this flame that is ready to consume us.

Reading and Interpreting

VOCABULARY

Use your dictionary as necessary to find the meaning of the following words as used by Burke:

efficacy (1)	prudent (1, 12)	odious (1)	depreciated (4)	salutary (5)
ardent (7)	untractable (7, 11)	chicane (7)	inheres (8)	eminence (8)
inculcate (8)	mediately (8)	lenity (8)	averseness (9)	latitude (10)
mercurial (11)	augur (11)	truck and huckster (12)		immutable (12)

CONCEPT ANALYSIS

1. In your own words, state Burke's arguments against the use of force in dealing with the colonies. Do you find any of these arguments relevant to current American foreign policy? Can you apply any of these arguments to recent or current United States involvement with foreign countries? Discuss.
2. In your opinion, to what degree do the attributes of the American temper and character described by Burke exist today? Discuss.
3. According to Burke, how do Roman Catholicism and the Church of England differ from American Protestantism? What is the significance of the following statement in terms of Burke's argument about the American character: "All Protestantism, even the most cold and passive, is a

sort of dissent. But the religion most prevalent in our northern colonies is a refinement on the principle of resistance: it is the dissidence of dissent, and the protestantism of the Protestant religion" (9)?

4. According to Burke, liberty is more highly valued in states where slavery exists. How does Burke explain this? Do you agree?

5. Burke states in paragraph 12 that there is an "immutable condition, [an] eternal law, of extensive and detached empire." What is this condition or law? Does geography have the same effect on imperialism today as it did in Burke's time? Illustrate your response with reference to specific political situations.

6. In Burke's view, what does education have to do with the American character?

Quickwrite

The irony of Britain's conflict with her colonies is that the colonies had inherited their love of liberty from England herself. Consider what qualities you have inherited from your parents that make it difficult for them to deal with you.

Thinking and Writing

RHETORICAL TECHNIQUE

1. Make a box outline of Burke's essay, including the thesis statement, his dismissal of the opposition's arguments, his transition between the opposition's arguments and his own, his support for his own position, and his conclusion.

2. Despite the profundity of Burke's argument, it is clear and easy to follow. Why is this so? Underline words or expressions that are effective in assisting the audience to follow Burke's logic.

3. What type of support plays the biggest role in Burke's argument: facts, examples, logical reasoning, appeals to authority, or persuasive techniques such as emotional language and rhetorical questions? Can you find any logical fallacies or devices of propaganda in Burke's essay?

4. Focus on the language in one of Burke's arguments. Cite phrases that you find particularly memorable.

COMPOSITION

1. Select a current political conflict and argue either for or against the use of force to resolve it. Your essay should include a rebuttal of the opposing point of view.
2. Describe the "temper and character" of American youth. Based on your description, argue for or against the imposition of age-related regulations such as a minimum drinking age, college dormitory rules, and dress codes.

THOMAS PAINE

Common Sense

Thomas Paine (1737–1809), political theorist and writer, immigrated to the American colonies from England in 1774. As editor of *Pennsylvania Magazine,* he called for social reform, denouncing such aristocratic customs as inherited titles and exclusionary rights to employment. Years ahead of his time, Paine championed causes that others ignored or were ignorant of, including women's rights and abolition of slavery. He wrote persuasively in favor of old-age pensions and humane treatment of animals. In America's first best-seller, the pamphlet *Common Sense,* Paine used reason and dramatic language to convince readers that the colonies had outgrown any need for English control and should be given independence.

In the following pages I offer nothing more than simple facts, plain arguments, and common sense; and have no other preliminaries to settle with the reader, than that he will divest himself of prejudice and prepossession, and suffer his reason and his feelings to determine for themselves; that he will put on, or rather that he will not put off, the true character of a man, and generously enlarge his views beyond the present day. . . . 1

The Sun never shone on a cause of greater worth. 'Tis not the affair of a city, a county, a province, or a kingdom, but of a continent—of at least one eighth part of the habitable globe. 'Tis not the concern of a day, a year, or an age; posterity are virtually involved in the contest, and will be 2 more or less affected even to the end of time, by the proceedings now. Now is the seed-time of continental union, faith and honour. The least fracture now will be like a name engraved with the point of a pin on the tender rind of a young oak; the wound will enlarge with the tree, and posterity read it in full grown characters. . . .

I have heard it asserted by some, that as America has flourished un- 3 der her former connection with Great Britain, the same connection is necessary towards her future happiness, and will always have the same effect. Nothing can be more fallacious than this kind of argument. We may as well assert that because a child has thrived upon milk, that it is never to have meat, or that the first twenty years of our lives is to become a precedent for the next twenty. But even this is admitting more than is true, for I answer roundly, that America would have flourished as much, and probably much more, had no European power taken any notice of her. The commerce by which she hath enriched herself are the necessaries of life, and will always have a market while eating is the custom of Europe.

But she has protected us, say some. That she hath engrossed us is 4 true, and defended the continent at our expense as well as her own is admitted; and she would have defended Turkey from the same motives, *viz.* for the sake of trade and dominion. . . .

But Britain is the parent country, say some. Then the more shame 5 upon her conduct. Even brutes do not devour their young, nor savages make war upon their families; wherefore the assertion, if true, turns to her reproach; but it happens not to be true, or only partly so, and the phrase *parent* or *mother country* hath been jesuitically adopted by the King and his parasites, with a low papistical design of gaining an unfair bias on the credulous weakness of our minds.

Europe, and not England, is the parent country of America. This 6 New World hath been the asylum for the persecuted lovers of civil and religious liberty from *every part* of Europe. Hither have they fled, not from the tender embraces of the mother, but from the cruelty of the monster; and it is so far true of England, that the same tyranny which drove the first emigrants from home, pursues their descendants still. . . .

It is repugnant to reason, to the universal order of things, to all ex- 7 amples from former ages, to suppose that this continent can long remain subject to any external power. The most sanguine in Britain doth not think so. The utmost stretch of human wisdom cannot, at this time, compass a plan, short of separation, which can promise the continent even a year's security. Reconciliation is *now* a fallacious dream. Nature hath deserted the connection, and art cannot supply her place. For, as Milton wisely expresses, "never can true reconcilement grow where wounds of deadly hate have pierced so deep." . . .

Small islands not capable of protecting themselves are the proper ob- 8 jects for government to take under their care; but there is something very absurd in supposing a continent to be perpetually governed by an island.

In no instance hath nature made the satellite larger than its primary planet; and as England and America . . . reverse the common order of nature, it is evident that they belong to different systems. England to Europe—America to itself.

I am not induced by motives of pride, party, or resentment to es- 9
pouse the doctrine of separation and independence; I am clearly, positively, and conscientiously persuaded that it is the true interest of this continent to be so; that every thing short of *that* is mere patchwork, that it can afford no lasting felicity,—that it is leaving the sword to our children, and shrinking back at a time when a little more, a little further, would have rendered this continent the glory of the earth. . . .

But where, say some, is the King of America? I'll tell you, friend, 10
He reigns above, and doth not make havoc of mankind like the royal brute of Great Britain. Yet that we may not appear to be defective even in earthly honours, let a day be solemnly set apart for proclaiming the charter; let it be brought forth placed on the Divine Law, the Word of God; let a crown be placed thereon, by which the world may know, that so far as we approve of monarchy, that in America *the law is king*.

For as in absolute governments the king is law, so in free countries 11
the law ought to be king; and there ought to be no other. But lest any ill use should afterwards arise, let the Crown at the conclusion of the ceremony be demolished, and scattered among the people whose right it is.

A government of our own is our natural right: and when a man seri- 12
ously reflects on the precariousness of human affairs, he will become convinced, that it is infinitely wiser and safer, to form a constitution of our own in a cool deliberate manner, while we have it in our power, than to trust such an interesting event to time and chance.

Ye that tell us of harmony and reconciliation, can ye restore to us the 13
time that is past? Can ye give to prostitution its former innocence? Neither can ye reconcile Britain and America. The last cord is now broken; the people of England are presenting addresses against us. There are injuries which nature cannot forgive; she would cease to be nature if she did. As well can the lover forgive a ravisher of his mistress, as the continent forgive the murders of Britain. The Almighty hath implanted in us these unextinguishable feelings for good and wise purposes. They are the guardians of His image in our hearts. They distinguish us from the herd of common animals. The social compact would dissolve, and justice be extirpated from the earth, or have only a casual existence, were we callous to the touches of affection. The robber and the murderer would often escape unpunished, did not the injuries which our tempers sustain, provoke us into justice.

O! ye that love mankind! Ye that dare oppose not only the tyranny 14
but the tyrant, stand forth! Every spot of the old world is overrun with oppression. Freedom hath been hunted round the globe. Asia and Africa

have long expelled her, Europe regards her like a stranger, and England hath given her warning to depart. O! receive the fugitive, and prepare in time an asylum for mankind.

Reading and Interpreting

VOCABULARY

Use your dictionary as necessary to find the meaning of the following words as used by Paine:

prepossession (1)   engrossed (4)   jesuitically (5)   sanguine (7)
precariousness (12)

CONCEPT ANALYSIS

1. Review paragraphs 4–6. What premise is Paine attacking here? What arguments does he use to demolish it?
2. How does Paine anticipate and refute his opponents' argument that American needs a monarch?
     What use does Paine make of God as an "authority" for the American point of view?
3. List Paine's arguments for American independence and evaluate the logic of each.

Quickwrite

Write an argument advocating or opposing a monarchical form of government.

Thinking and Writing

RHETORICAL TECHNIQUE

1. Which approach to argument does Paine use: the deductive, the dialectical, or the point-counterpoint?
     Paine clearly signals the anticipated arguments of his opponents. Un-

derline the expressions he uses to mark these points. Why do you think he was so careful to employ these signals?

2. The essay employs both logic and emotional appeals. Cite examples of each technique. Do you perceive a pattern in the use of logical argument and persuasion? A contrast between the introduction and the conclusion?

3. Perhaps because of his reputation as a radical, Paine takes care to present himself and his argument as reasonable. Cite instances in the essay where this tone is evident.

4. Paine uses many analogies in his characterization of the relationship between Great Britain and the colonies. Cite several of them. What specific associations or emotions would each analogy arouse in the American audience?

COMPOSITION

1. Write an argument against independence for the colonies, using both common sense and appeals to the emotions, as Paine does.

2. In paragraph 2 Paine stresses the urgency of independence with the word *now*. He uses the analogy of a name carved in a tree to illustrate that current actions have crucial future consequences. Write for or against a pending government decision (either local or national) that you feel will have crucial consequences.

EDWIN MARKHAM
The Man with the Hoe

Edwin Markham (1852–1940), an American poet, grew up in California, where he taught school. The following well-known poem was inspired by French artist Jean-François Millet's painting of peasants laboring in the fields. Both the painting and the poem protest the exploitation and degradation of workers.

(Written after seeing Millet's world-famous painting)

Bowed by the weight of centuries he leans
Upon his hoe and gazes on the ground,
The emptiness of ages in his face,

And on his back the burden of the world.
Who made him dead to rapture and despair,   5
A thing that grieves not and that never hopes,
Stolid and stunned, a brother to the ox?
Who loosened and let down this brutal jaw?
Whose was the hand that slanted back this brow?
Whose breath blew out the light within this brain?   10

Is this the Thing the Lord God made and gave
To have dominion over sea and land;
To trace the stars and search the heavens for power;
To feel the passion of Eternity?
Is this the dream He dreamed who shaped the suns   15
And marked their ways upon the ancient deep?
Down all the caverns of Hell to their last gulf
There is no shape more terrible than this—
More tongued with censure of the world's blind greed—
More filled with signs and portents for the soul—   20
More packt with danger to the universe.

What gulfs between him and the seraphim!
Slave of the wheel of labor, what to him
Are Plato and the swing of Pleiades?
What the long reaches of the peaks of song,   25
The rift of dawn, the reddening of the rose?
Through this dread shape the suffering ages look;
Time's tragedy is in that aching stoop;
Through this dread shape humanity betrayed,
Plundered, profaned, and disinherited,   30
Cries protest to the Judges of the World,
A protest that is also prophecy.

O masters, lords and rulers in all lands,
Is this the handiwork you give to God,
This monstrous thing distorted and soul-quenched?   35
How will you ever straighten up this shape;
Touch it again with immortality;
Give back the upward looking and the light;
Rebuild in it the music and the dream;
Make right the immemorial infamies,   40
Perfidious wrongs, immedicable woes?

O masters, lords and rulers in all lands,
How will the Future reckon with this man?
How answer his brute question in that hour
When whirlwinds of rebellion shake all shores?   45
How will it be with kingdoms and with kings—

With those who shaped him to the thing he is—
When this dumb terror shall rise to judge the world,
After the silence of centuries?

Reading and Interpreting

VOCABULARY

Use your dictionary as necessary to find the meaning of the following words
in the context of Markham's poem:

stolid (7)   Pleiades (24)   perfidious (41)

CONCEPT ANALYSIS

1. In this poem of social protest Markham's portrayal of the oppressed peasant is conveyed through highly emotional language and figures of
   speech. Cite some examples.
2. Whom does Markham hold responsible for the condition of the peasant?
   Cite lines that support your response.
      What prophecy and warning does Markham give in this poem?
3. Why does Markham characterize the debased figure of the peasant as
   "humanity betrayed" (29)? What is the betrayal? Which lines suggest
   another, potentially higher kind of human being?

Thinking and Writing

RHETORICAL TECHNIQUE

1. The issue of Markham's poem is the dehumanized condition of the peasantry. Who is his audience? What does he wish to persuade his audience
   to feel and to do?
      What are some of the techniques of persuasion he employs? In your
   view, is the poem an example of honest persuasion or does it use mis-
   leading propaganda devices? Explain.
2. Markham develops his argument through a series of rhetorical questions.
   How effective is this technique?
3. Markham's introductory and concluding stanzas incorporate standard
   techniques of argument and persuasion. What is the implied premise of
   the first stanza? What is Markham's purpose in the conclusion?

COMPOSITION

Write an essay to persuade an audience that a particular segment of our society is oppressed. Offer suggestions to reverse this condition. Include a warning for the future if the problem is not solved.

MARTIN LUTHER KING, JR.
I Have a Dream

Minister and civil rights leader Martin Luther King, Jr. (1929–1968), was profoundly influenced by Mahatma Gandhi's doctrine of passive resistance. King's consistently nonviolent approach to the struggle against racial discrimination in America earned him the Nobel Peace Prize. "I Have a Dream," delivered to 250,000 participants in the 1963 march on Washington, a civil rights protest demonstration, is considered his finest oration. Its fiery figurative language and use of repetition as a device of persuasion owe much to the rhetorical style of the black church.

Five score years ago, a great American, in whose symbolic shadow we 1 stand today, signed the Emancipation Proclamation. This momentous decree came as a great beacon of light and of hope to millions of Negro slaves who had been seared in the flames of withering injustice. It came as a joyous daybreak to end the long night of their captivity.

But one hundred years later, the Negro still is not free. One hundred 2 years later, the life of the Negro is still sadly crippled by the manacles of segregation and the chains of discrimination.

One hundred years later, the Negro lives on a lonely island of pov- 3 erty in the midst of a vast ocean of material prosperity. One hundred years later, the Negro is still languished in the corners of American society and finds himself an exile in his own land. So we have come here today to dramatize a shameful condition.

In a sense we have come to our nation's capital to cash a check. When 4 the architects of our republic wrote the magnificent words of the Constitution and the Declaration of Independence, they were signing a promissory note to which every American was to fall heir. This note was a promise that all men, yes, black men as well as white men, would be granted the inalienable rights of life, liberty, and the pursuit of happiness.

It is obvious today that America has defaulted on this promissory 5 note insofar as her citizens of color are concerned. Instead of honoring this sacred obligation, America has given the Negro people a bad check, which has come back marked "insufficient funds."

But we refuse to believe that the bank of justice is bankrupt. We 6 refuse to believe that there are insufficient funds in the great vaults of opportunity of this nation. So we have come to cash this check—a check that will give us upon demand the riches of freedom and the security of justice.

We have also come to this hallowed spot to remind America of the 7 fierce urgency of now. This is no time to engage in the luxury of cooling off or to take the tranquilizing drug of gradualism. Now is the time to make real the promises of democracy. Now is the time to rise from the dark and desolate valley of segregation to the sunlit path of racial justice. Now is the time to lift our nation from the quicksands of racial injustice to the solid rock of brotherhood. Now is the time to make justice a reality for all of God's children.

It would be fatal for the nation to overlook the urgency of the move- 8 ment and to underestimate the determination of the Negro. This sweltering summer of the Negro's legitimate discontent will not pass until there is an invigorating autumn of freedom and equality. 1963 is not an end but a beginning. Those who hope that the Negro needed to blow off steam and will now be content will have a rude awakening if the nation returns to business as usual.

There will be neither rest nor tranquility in America until the Negro 9 is granted his citizenship rights. The whirlwinds of revolt will continue to shake the foundations of our nation until the bright day of justice emerges.

But there is something that I must say to my people who stand on 10 the warm threshold which leads into the palace of justice. In the process of gaining our rightful place we must not be guilty of wrongful deeds.

Let us not seek to satisfy our thirst for freedom by drinking from the 11 cup of bitterness and hatred. We must forever conduct our struggle on the high plane of dignity and discipline. We must not allow our creative protest to degenerate into physical violence. Again and again we must rise to the majestic heights of meeting physical force with soul force.

The marvelous new militancy which has engulfed the Negro com- 12 munity must not lead us to a distrust of all white people, for many of our white brothers, as evidenced by their presence here today, have come to realize that their destiny is tied up with our destiny and they have come to realize that their freedom is inextricably bound to our freedom. This offense we share mounted to storm the battlements of injustice must be carried forth by a bi-racial army. We cannot walk alone.

And as we walk, we must make the pledge that we shall always 13 march ahead. We cannot turn back. There are those who are asking the devotees of civil rights, "When will you be satisfied?" We can never be satisfied as long as the Negro is the victim of the unspeakable horrors of police brutality.

We can never be satisfied as long as our bodies, heavy with the fa- 14 tigue of travel, cannot gain lodging in the motels of the highways and the hotels of the cities. We cannot be satisfied as long as the Negro's basic mobility is from a smaller ghetto to a larger one.

We can never be satisfied as long as our children are stripped of their 15 selfhood and robbed of their dignity by signs stating "for whites only." We cannot be satisfied as long as a Negro in Mississippi cannot vote and a Negro in New York believes he has nothing for which to vote. No, we are not satisfied, and we will not be satisfied until justice rolls down like waters and righteousness like a mighty stream.

I am not unmindful that some of you have come here out of excessive 16 trials and tribulation. Some of you have come fresh from narrow jail cells. Some of you have come from areas where your quest for freedom left you battered by the storms of persecution and staggered by the winds of police brutality. You have been the veterans of creative suffering. Continue to work with the faith that unearned suffering is redemptive.

Go back to Mississippi; go back to Alabama; go back to South Caro- 17 lina; go back to Georgia; go back to Louisiana; go back to the slums and ghettos of the Northern cities, knowing that somehow this situation can, and will be changed. Let us not wallow in the valley of despair.

So I say to you, my friends, that even though we must face the diffi- 18 culties of today and tomorrow, I still have a dream. It is a dream deeply rooted in the American dream that one day this nation will rise up and live out the true meaning of its creed—we hold these truths to be self-evident, that all men are created equal.

I have a dream that one day on the red hills of Georgia, sons of for- 19 mer slaves and sons of former slave-owners will be able to sit down together at the table of brotherhood.

I have a dream that one day, even the state of Mississippi, a state 20 sweltering with the heat of injustice, sweltering with the heat of oppression, will be transformed into an oasis of freedom and justice.

I have a dream my four little children will one day live in a nation 21 where they will not be judged by the color of their skin but by the content of their character. I have a dream today!

I have a dream that one day, down in Alabama, with its vicious rac- 22 ists, with its governor having his lips dripping with the words of interposition and nullification, that one day, right there in Alabama, little black boys and black girls will be able to join hands with little white boys and white girls as sisters and brothers. I have a dream today!

I have a dream that one day every valley shall be exalted, every hill 23 and mountain shall be made low, the rough places shall be made plain, and the crooked places shall be made straight and the glory of the Lord will be revealed and all flesh shall see it together.

This is our hope. This is the faith that I go back to the South with. 24

With this faith we will be able to hew out of the mountain of despair 25 a stone of hope. With this faith we will be able to transform the jangling discords of our nation into a beautiful symphony of brotherhood.

With this faith we will be able to work together, to pray together, to 26 struggle together, to go to jail together, to stand up for freedom together, knowing that we will be free one day. This will be the day when all of God's children will be able to sing with new meaning—"my country 'tis of thee; sweet land of liberty; of thee I sing; land where my fathers died, land of the pilgrim's pride; from every mountain side, let freedom ring"— and if America is to be a great nation, this must become true.

So let freedom ring from the prodigious hilltops of New Hampshire. 27

Let freedom ring from the mighty mountains of New York. 28

Let freedom ring from the heightening Alleghenies of Pennsylvania. 29

Let freedom ring from the snow-capped Rockies of Colorado. 30

Let freedom ring from the curvaceous slopes of California. 31

But not only that. 32

Let freedom ring from Stone Mountain of Georgia. 33

Let freedom ring from Lookout Mountain of Tennessee. 34

Let freedom ring from every hill and molehill of Mississippi, from 35 every mountainside, let freedom ring.

And when we allow freedom to ring, when we let it ring from every 36 village and hamlet, from every state and city, we will be able to speed up that day when all of God's children—black men and white men, Jews and Gentiles, Catholics and Protestants—will be able to join hands and to sing in the words of the old Negro spiritual, "Free at last, free at last; thank God Almighty, we are free at last."

Reading and Interpreting

VOCABULARY

Use your dictionary as necessary to find the meaning of the following words as used by King:

languished (3)   promissory note (4)   redemptive (16)   prodigious (27)

CONCEPT ANALYSIS

1. King won the Nobel Peace Prize for a lifetime of dedication to brotherhood. Cite specific portions of the speech that illustrate King's commitment to this idea.

2. King was a follower of Mahatma Gandhi's and Henry David Thoreau's philosophies of nonviolent civil disobedience. Find specific examples of his commitment to this ideal.
3. What, in your view and in your own words, is Martin Luther King's dream?

How does the last paragraph of his speech relate to philosopher Herbert Spencer's remark that "no one can be perfectly free till all are free"?

Quickwrite

The speech we have just read was Martin Luther King's dream. What is your dream?

Thinking and Writing

RHETORICAL TECHNIQUE

1. Discuss King's audience in terms of those sympathetic and those unsympathetic to his views. What are the messages to each in the speech?
2. King's persuasive speech relies heavily on figurative language, including images of light and darkness, of heights and depths, of commerce and battle. The speech also makes allusions to Christianity, American historical documents, and well-known American songs. List several examples of each. Why is each of these devices relevant and effective in terms of King's audience and his purpose?
3. Read aloud paragraph 7. Note its use of the word *now* and its repetition of the phrase "Now is the time." What response does this paragraph evoke in you? Find other examples of parallel construction and repetition of phrases. How does this technique affect your response to the content of the speech?
4. King's introduction and conclusion both focus on the idea of freedom and both make strong emotional appeals. Underline words and images that link the introduction to the conclusion and evoke an emotional response.

COMPOSITION

Choose an issue of religious, ethical, or philosophical importance to you. Imagine an audience of the "unconverted" and write as persuasively as you can to bring them to your point of view. Try using some of King's techniques of imagery and repetition.

BARTOLOMEO VANZETTI
My Intellectual Life and Creed

Bartolomeo Vanzetti and Nicola Sacco, Italian immigrants, were arrested and tried for the murder of a shoe
company paymaster in Massachusetts in 1920. Both
men were anarchists; when they were convicted and sentenced to death, many believed that the conviction was
based on anti-Italian and antiradical sentiment. The
execution of Sacco and Vanzetti on August 22, 1927,
was preceded by worldwide sympathy demonstrations.
To this day, many regard them as martyrs. In the following chapter from his autobiography, Vanzetti writes
forcefully about the evolution of his political vision.

1 I want to retrace my steps in memory for a while. I have given the physical
facts of my story. The deeper, truer story is not in the outward circumstances of a man's life, but in his inner growth, in mind and soul, and
universal consciousness.

2 I went to school from the age of six to the age of thirteen. I loved
study with a real passion. During the three years passed in Cavour I had
the good luck to be near a certain learned person. With his help I read all
the publications that came in my hands. My superior was a subscriber to a
Catholic periodical in Genoa. I thought that lucky, because I was then a
fervent Catholic.

3 In Turin I had no companions except fellow workers, young store
clerks and laborers. My fellow workers declared themselves socialists and
made fun of my religious streak, calling me a hypocrite and bigot. One
day it led to a fist fight with one of them. . . . So real was the effect of the
environment that I, too, soon commenced to love socialism without knowing it, or believing myself a socialist.

4 All things considered, the stage of evolution of those people was beneficent for me and improved me greatly. The principles of humanism and
equality of rights began to make a breach in my heart.

5 In the last days of my stay in the land of my birth I learned much
from Dr. Francis, the chemist Scrimaglio and the veterinarian Bo. Already
I began to understand that the plague which besets humanity most cruelly
is ignorance and the degeneracy of natural sentiments. My religion soon
needed no temples, altars and formal prayers. God became for me a perfect
spiritual Being, devoid of any human attributes. Although my father told

me often that religion was necessary in order to hold in check human passions, and to console the human being in tribulation, I felt in my own heart the yea and nay of things. In this state of mind I crossed the ocean.

Arrived in America, I underwent all the sufferings, the disillusions 6 and the privations that come inevitably to one who lands at the age of twenty, ignorant of life, and something of a dreamer. Here I saw all the brutalities of life, all the injustice, the corruption in which humanity struggles tragically.

But despite everything I succeeded in fortifying myself physically 7 and intellectually. Here I studied the works of Peter Kropotkin, Gorki, Merlino, Malatesta, Reclus. I read Marx's *Capital,* and the works of Leone di Labriola, the political *Testament* of Carlo Pisacane, Mazzini's *Duties of Man,* and many other writings of social import. Here I read the journals of every socialist, patriotic and religious faction. Here I studied the Bible, *The Life of Jesus* (Renan), and *Jesus Christ Has Never Existed* by Miselbo. Here I read Greek and Roman history, the story of the United States, of the French Revolution and of the Italian Revolution. I studied Darwin and Spencer, Laplace and Flammarion. I returned to the *Divine Comedy* and to *Jerusalem Liberated.* I re-read Leopardi and wept with him. I read the works of Hugo, of Leo Tolstoi, of Zola, of Cantu, the poetry of Giusti, Guerrini, Rapisardi and Carducci.

Do not believe me, my dear reader, a prodigy of science; that would 8 be a mistake. My fundamental instruction was too incomplete, my mental powers insufficient, to assimilate all this vast material. Then it must be remembered that I studied while doing hard work all day, and without any congenial accommodations. Ah, how many nights I sat over some volume by a flickering gas jet, far into the morning hours! Barely had I laid my head on the pillow when the whistle sounded and back I went to the factory or the stone pits.

But I brought to the studies a cruel, continuous and inexorable ob- 9 servation of men, animals and plants—of everything, in a word, that surrounds man. The Book of Life: that is the Book of Books! All the others merely teach how to read this one. The honest books, I mean; the dishonest ones have an opposite purpose.

Meditation over this great book determined my actions and my 10 principles. I denied that "Every man for himself and God for all!" I championed the weak, the poor, the oppressed, the simple and the persecuted. I admired heroism, strength and sacrifice when directed towards the triumph of justice. I understood that in the name of God, of Law, of the Patria, of Liberty, of the purest mental abstractions, of the highest human ideals, are perpetrated and will continue to be perpetrated, the most ferocious crimes; until the day when by the acquisition of light it will no longer be possible for the few, in the name of God, to do wrong to the many.

I understood that man cannot trample with immunity upon the un- 11 written laws that govern his life, he cannot violate the ties that bind him to the universe. I understood that the mountains, the seas, the rivers called "natural boundaries" were formed before man, by a complexity of physical and chemical processes, and not for the purpose of *dividing peoples*.

I grasped the concept of fraternity, of universal love. I maintained 12 that whosoever benefits or hurts a man, benefits or hurts the whole species. I sought my liberty in the liberty of all; my happiness in the happiness of all. I realized that the equity of deeds, of rights and of duties, is the only moral basis upon which could be erected a just human society. I earned my bread by the honest sweat of my brow. I have not a drop of blood on my hands, nor on my conscience.

I understood that the supreme goal of life is happiness. That the 13 eternal and immutable bases of human happiness are health, peace of conscience, the satisfaction of animal needs, and a sincere faith. I understood that every individual had two I's, the real and the ideal, that the second is the source of all progress, and that whatever wants to make the first seem equal to the second is in bad faith. The difference in any one person between his two egos is always the same, because whether in perfection or in degeneration, they keep the same distance between them.

I understood that man is never sufficiently modest towards himself 14 and that true wisdom is in tolerance.

I wanted a roof for every family, bread for every mouth, education 15 for every heart, the light for every intellect.

I am convinced that human history has not yet begun; that we find 16 ourselves in the last period of the prehistoric. I see with the eyes of my soul how the sky is suffused with the rays of the new millennium.

I maintain that liberty of conscience is as inalienable as life. I sought 17 with all my power to direct the human spirit to the good of all. I know from experience that rights and privileges are still won and maintained by force, until humanity shall have perfected itself.

In the real history of future humanity—classes and privileges, the 18 antagonisms of interest between man and man abolished—progress and change will be determined by intelligence and the common convenience.

If we and the generation which our women carry under their bosoms 19 do not arrive *nearer* to that goal, we shall not have obtained anything real, and humanity will continue to be more miserable and unhappy.

I am and shall be until the last instant (unless I should discover that 20 I am in error) an anarchist-communist, because I believe that communism is the most humane form of social contract, because I know that only with liberty can man rise, become noble, and complete.

Now? At the age of thirty-three—the age of Christ and, according 21 to certain learned alienists, the age of offenders generally—I am scheduled for prison and for death. Yet, were I to recommence the "journey of life," I should tread the same road, seeking, however, to lessen the sum of my sins and errors and to multiply that of my good deeds.

I send to my comrades, to my friends, to all good men my fraternal 22
embrace, love and fervent greetings!

Reading and Interpreting

VOCABULARY

Use your dictionary as necessary to find the meaning of the following words
as used by Vanzetti:

hypocrite (3)   bigot (3)   breach (4)   prodigy (8)   immunity (11)

millennium (16)

CONCEPT ANALYSIS

1. Trace the stages in Vanzetti's evolution from a "fervent Catholic" to an
   "anarchist-communist."
2. Books were crucial to Vanzetti's "inner growth." Review paragraph 9, in
   which he distinguishes among "The Book of Life," "honest books," and
   "dishonest ones." Explain these contrasts.
3. Do you agree with Vanzetti's definition of the "bases of human happiness" as expressed in paragraph 13? Do you agree with his ordering of
   these elements?
4. Compare paragraph 17 of this essay to paragraph 11 of Martin Luther
   King's "I Have a Dream" speech. Whose point of view on the use of
   force is more persuasive?

Quickwrite

Write your response to the author's statement in paragraph 16 that human civilization is in the "last period of the prehistoric."

Thinking and Writing

RHETORICAL TECHNIQUE

1. What are Vanzetti's primary techniques of persuasion: images, references
   to authority, symbols, repetition of phrases? Find examples that support
   your opinion. Where do you find logical reasoning in this essay?

2. Review the second part of the essay beginning with paragraph 11. Which elements of Vanzetti's creed appeal to you most? Which do you reject?

COMPOSITION

1. Write a persuasive essay in which you draw a relationship between your intellectual life (education, reading, informed discussion) and your philosophical and ethical beliefs.
2. In your own view, what is the supreme goal of life? Write a persuasive essay that elaborates your view. Appeal to your reader on both emotional and logical grounds.

JONATHAN SWIFT
A Modest Proposal

Jonathan Swift (1667–1745), Anglo-Irish churchman and writer, is best known for his sociopolitical satire *Gulliver's Travels*. Swift often disguises his biting arguments for social reform as the presentation of a fictionalized author whose deadpan delivery of morally outrageous ideas provokes the reader to indignation or anger. The following essay is a classic example of Swift's satirical method of argumentation and persuasion and his forceful, energetic prose.

It is a melancholy object to those who walk through this great town or travel in the country, when they see the streets, the roads, and cabin-doors crowded with beggars of the female sex, followed by three, four, or six children, all in rags, and importuning every passenger for an alms. These mothers instead of being able to work for their honest livelihood, are forced to employ all their time in strolling to beg sustenance for their helpless infants, who, as they grow up, either turn thieves for want of work, or leave their dear native country, to fight for the Pretender in Spain, or sell themselves to the Barbadoes. 1

I think it is agreed by all parties, that this prodigious number of children in the arms, or on the backs, or at the heels of their mothers, and 2 frequently of their fathers, is in the present deplorable state of the kingdom a very great additional grievance; and therefore whoever could find out a fair, cheap, and easy method of making these children sound and useful members of the common-wealth, would deserve so well of the public as to have his statue set up for a preserver of the nation.

But my intention is very far from being confined to provide only for 3 the children of professed beggars; it is of a much greater extent, and shall take in the whole number of infants at a certain age, who are born of parents in effect as little able to support them, as those who demand our charity in the streets.

As to my own part, having turned my thoughts, for many years, 4 upon this important subject, and maturely weighed the several schemes of other projectors, I have always found them grossly mistaken in their computation. It is true, a child just dropt from its dam, may be supported by her milk for a solar year with little other nourishment, at most not above the value of two shillings, which the mother may certainly get, or the value in scraps, by her lawful occupation of begging; and it is exactly at one year old that I propose to provide for them in such a manner, as, instead of being a charge upon their parents, or the parish, or wanting food and raiment for the rest of their lives, they shall, on the contrary, contribute to the feeding and partly to the clothing of many thousands.

There is likewise another great advantage in my scheme, that it will 5 prevent those voluntary abortions, and that horrid practice of women murdering their bastard children, alas! too frequent among us—sacrificing the poor innocent babes, I doubt, more to avoid the expense than the shame—which would move tears and pity in the most savage and inhuman breast.

The number of souls in this kingdom being usually reckoned one 6 million and a half, of these I calculate there may be about two hundred thousand couples whose wives are breeders; from which number I subtract thirty thousand couples, who are able to maintain their own children, although I apprehend there cannot be so many, under the present distresses of the kingdom; but this being granted, there will remain an hundred and seventy thousand breeders. I again subtract fifty thousand, for those women who miscarry, or whose children die by accident or disease within the year. There only remain an hundred and twenty thousand children of poor parents annually born: The question therefore is, How this number shall be reared, and provided for? which, as I have already said, under the present situation of affairs, is utterly impossible by all the methods hitherto proposed; for we can neither employ them in handicraft or agriculture; we neither build houses (I mean in the country) nor cultivate land: They can very seldom pick up a livelihood by stealing till they arrive at six years old, except where they are of towardly parts, although, I confess, they learn the rudiments much earlier, during which time they can however be properly looked upon only as probationers; as I have been informed by a principal gentleman in the county of Cavan, who protested to me, that he never knew above one or two instances under the age of six, even in a part of the kingdom so renowned for the quickest proficiency in that art.

I am assured by our merchants, that a boy or a girl before twelve 7 years old, is no saleable commodity, and even when they come to this age, they will not yield above three pounds, or three pounds and half a crown at most, on the exchange; which cannot turn to account either to the parents or kingdom, the charge of nutriment and rags having been at least four times that value.

I shall now therefore humbly propose my own thoughts, which I 8 hope will not be liable to the least objection.

I have been assured by a very knowing American of my acquaintance 9 in London, that a young healthy child well nursed is at a year old a most delicious, nourishing, and wholesome food, whether stewed, roasted, baked, or boiled; and I make no doubt that it will equally serve in a fricassee, or ragout.

I do therefore humbly offer it to publick consideration, that of the 10 hundred and twenty thousand children, already computed, twenty thousand may be reserved for breed, whereof only one fourth part to be males; which is more than we allow to sheep, black cattle, or swine; and my reason is that these children are seldom the fruits of marriage, a circumstance not much regarded by our savages; therefore one male will be sufficient to serve four females. That the remaining hundred thousand may, at a year old, be offered in the sale to the persons of quality and fortune through the kingdom; always advising the mother to let them suck plentifully in the last month, so as to render them plump and fat for a good table. A child will make two dishes at an entertainment for friends; and when the family dines alone, the fore or hind quarter will make a reasonable dish, and seasoned with a little pepper or salt will be very good boiled on the fourth day, especially in winter.

I have reckoned upon a medium that a child just born will weigh 12 11 pounds, and in a solar year, if tolerably nursed, increaseth to 28 pounds.

I grant this food will be somewhat dear, and therefore very proper 12 for landlords, who, as they have already devoured most of the parents, seem to have the best title to the children.

Infants' flesh will be in season throughout the year, but more plen- 13 tiful in March, and a little before and after; for we are told by a grave author, an eminent French physician, that fish being a prolific diet, there are more children born in Roman Catholic countries about nine months after Lent than at any other season; therefore, reckoning a year after Lent, the markets will be more glutted than usual, because the number of popish infants is at least three to one in this kingdom: and therefore it will have one other collateral advantage, by lessening the number of papists among us.

I have already computed the charge of nursing a beggar's child (in 14 which list I reckon all cottagers, laborers, and four-fifths of the farmers) to be about two shillings per annum, rags included; and I believe no gentleman would repine to give ten shillings for the carcass of a good fat child, which, as I have said, will make four dishes of excellent nutritive meat, when he hath only some particular friend or his own family to dine with him. Thus the squire will learn to be a good landlord, and grow popular among his tenants; the mother will have eight shillings net profit, and be fit for work till she produces another child.

Those who are more thrifty (as I must confess the times require) may 15 flay the carcass, the skin of which artificially dressed will make admirable gloves for ladies, and summer boots for fine gentlemen.

As to our city of Dublin, shambles [a slaughterhouse] may be ap- 16 pointed for this purpose in the most convenient parts of it, and butchers we may be assured will not be wanting; although I rather recommend buying the children alive and dressing them hot from the knife, as we do roasting pigs.

A very worthy person, a true lover of his country, and whose virtues 17 I highly esteem, was lately pleased in discoursing on this matter to offer a refinement upon my scheme. He said that many gentlemen of this kingdom, having of late destroyed their deer, he conceived that the want of venison might be well supplied by the bodies of young lads and maidens, not exceeding fourteen years of age nor under twelve; so great a number of both sexes in every country being now ready to starve for want of work and service; and these to be disposed of by their parents if alive, or otherwise by their nearest relations. But with due deference to so excellent a friend, and so deserving a patriot, I cannot be altogether in his sentiments; for as to the males, my American acquaintance assured me from frequent experience, that their flesh was generally tough and lean, like that of our schoolboys, by continual exercise, and their taste disagreeable, and to fatten them would not answer the charge. Then as to the females, it would, I think with humble submission, be a loss to the publick, because they soon would become breeders themselves: And besides it is not improbable that some scrupulous people might be apt to censure such a practice (although indeed very unjustly) as a little bordering upon cruelty, which, I confess, hath always been with me the strongest objection against any project, how well soever intended.

But in order to justify my friend, he confessed that this expedient 18 was put into his head by the famous Psalmanazar, a native of the island Formosa, who came from thence to London, above twenty years ago, and in conversation told my friend, that in his country when any young person happened to be put to death, the executioner sold the carcass to persons of quality, as a prime dainty, and that, in his time, the body of a plump girl of fifteen who was crucified for an attempt to poison the Emperor was sold to his Imperial Majesty's prime minister of state, and other great mandarins of the court, the joints from the gibbet, at four hundred crowns.

Neither indeed can I doubt that if the same use were made of several plump young girls of this town, who, without one single groat to their fortunes, cannot stir abroad without a chair, and appear at a play-house and assemblies in foreign fineries which they never will pay for, the kingdom would not be the worse.

Some persons of a desponding spirit are in great concern about the vast number of poor people, who are aged, diseased, or maimed, and I have been desired to employ my thoughts what course may be taken, to ease the nation of so grievous an encumbrance. But I am not in the least pain upon that matter, because it is very well known, that they are every day dying, and rotting, by cold, and famine, and filth, and vermin, as fast as can be reasonably expected. And as to the younger labourers, they are now in almost as hopeful a condition. They cannot get work, and consequently pine away for want of nourishment, to a degree, that if at any time they are accidentally hired to common labour, they have not strength to perform it, and thus the country and themselves are happily delivered from the evils to come. [19]

I have too long digressed, and therefore shall return to my subject. I think the advantages by the proposal which I have made are obvious and many, as well as of the highest importance. [20]

For *first,* as I have already observed, it would greatly lessen the number of papists, with whom we are yearly over-run, being the principal breeders of the nation, as well as our most dangerous enemies, and who stay at home on purpose with a design to deliver the kingdom to the Pretender, hoping to take their advantage by the absence of so many good Protestants, who have chosen rather to leave their country, than stay at home, and pay tithes against their conscience to an Episcopal curate. [21]

Secondly, the poorer tenants will have something valuable of their own, which by law may be made liable to distress and help to pay their landlord's rent, their corn and cattle being already seized, and money a thing unknown. [22]

Thirdly, whereas the maintenance of an hundred thousand children, from two years old and upward, cannot be computed at less than ten shillings apiece per annum, the nation's stock will be thereby increased fifty thousand pounds per annum, besides the profit of a new dish introduced to the tables of all gentlemen of fortune in the kingdom who have any refinement in taste. And the money will circulate among ourselves, the goods being entirely of our own growth and manufacture. [23]

Fourthly, the constant breeders, beside the gain of eight shillings sterling per annum by the sale of their children, will be rid of the charge of maintaining them after the first year. [24]

Fifthly, this food would likewise bring great custom to taverns, where the vintners will certainly be so prudent as to procure the best receipts for dressing it to perfection, and consequently have their houses frequented by all the fine gentlemen who justly value themselves upon their [25] knowledge in good eating; and a skillful cook, who understands how to oblige his guests, will contrive to make it as expensive as they please.

Sixthly, this would be a great inducement to marriage, which all 26 wise nations have either encouraged by rewards or enforced by laws and penalties. It would increase the care and tenderness of mothers toward their children, when they were sure of a settlement for life to the poor babes, provided in some sort by the public, to their annual profit instead of expense. We should soon see an honest emulation among the married women, which of them could bring the fattest child to the market. Men would become as fond of their wives during the time of their pregnancy as they are now of their mares in foal, their cows in calf, their sows when they are ready to farrow; nor offer to beat or kick them (as is too frequent a practice) for fear of a miscarriage.

Many other advantages might be enumerated. For instance, the ad- 27 dition of some thousand carcasses in our exportation of barreled beef, the propagation of swine's flesh, and improvement in the art of making good bacon, so much wanted among us by the great destruction of pigs, too frequent at our tables; which are no way comparable in taste or magnificence to a well-grown, fat, yearling child, which roasted whole will make a considerable figure at a lord mayor's feast or any other public entertainment. But this and many others I omit, being studious of brevity.

Supposing that one thousand families in this city would be constant 28 customers for infants' flesh, besides others who might have it at merry meetings, particularly at weddings and christenings, I compute that Dublin would take off annually about twenty thousand carcasses; and the rest of the kingdom (where probably they will be sold somewhat cheaper) the remaining eighty thousand.

I can think of no one objection that will possibly be raised against 29 this proposal, unless it should be urged that the number of people will be thereby much lessened in the kingdom. This I freely own, and 'twas indeed one principal design in offering it to the world. I desire the reader will observe that I calculate my remedy for this one individual kingdom of Ireland, and for no other that ever was, is, or, I think, ever can be upon earth. Therefore let no man talk to me of other expedients: of taxing our absentees at five shillings a pound: of using neither clothes, nor household furniture, except what is of our own growth and manufacture: of utterly rejecting the materials and instruments that promote foreign luxury: of curing the expensiveness of pride, vanity, idleness, and gaming in our women: of introducing a vein of parsimony, prudence and temperance: of learning to love our country, where in we differ even from Laplanders, and the inhabitants of Topinamboo; of quitting our animosities, and factions, nor act any longer like the Jews, who were murdering one another at the very moment their city was taken: of being a little cautious not to sell our country and consciences for nothing: of teaching landlords to have at least one degree of mercy towards their tenants. Lastly, of putting a spirit of honesty, industry, and skill into our shop-keepers, who, if a resolution could now be taken to buy only our native goods, would immediately unite to cheat and exact upon us in the price, the measure, and the goodness, nor could ever yet be brought to make one fair proposal of just dealing though often and earnestly invited to it.

Therefore I repeat, let no man talk to me of these and the like expedients, till he hath at least some glimpse of hope, that there will ever be some hearty and sincere attempt to put them in practice. 30

But as to my self, having been wearied out for many years with offering vain, idle, visionary thoughts, and at length utterly despairing of success, I fortunately fell upon this proposal, which as it is wholly new, so it hath something solid and real, of no expense and little trouble, full in our own power, and whereby we can incur no danger in disobliging England. For this kind of commodity will not bear exportation, the flesh being of too tender a consistence, to admit a long continuance in salt, although perhaps I could name a country, which would be glad to eat up our whole nation without it. 31

After all, I am not so violently bent upon my own opinion, as to reject any offer, proposed by wise men, which shall be found equally innocent, cheap, easy, and effectual. But before something of that kind shall be advanced in contradiction to my scheme, and offering a better, I desire the author or authors, will be pleased maturely to consider two points. *First,* as things now stand, how they will be able to find food and raiment for a hundred thousand useless mouths and backs. And *secondly,* there being a round million of creatures in human figure throughout this kingdom, whose whole subsistence put into a common stock would leave them in debt two millions of pounds sterling, adding those who are beggars by profession, to the bulk of farmers, cottagers and labourers, with their wives and children, who are beggars in effect; I desire those politicians, who dislike my overture, and may perhaps be so bold to attempt an answer, that they will first ask the parents of these mortals, whether they would not at this day think it a great happiness to have been sold for food at a year old, in the manner I prescribe, and thereby have avoided such a perpetual scene of misfortunes as they have since gone through, by the oppression of landlords, the impossibility of paying rent without money or trade, the want of common sustenance, with neither house nor clothes to cover them from the inclemencies of the weather, and the most inevitable prospect of entailing the like or greater miseries upon their breed for ever. 32

I profess, in the sincerity of my heart, that I have not the least personal interest in endeavoring to promote this necessary work, having no other motive than the public good of my country, by advancing our trade, providing for infants, relieving the poor, and giving some pleasure to the rich. I have no children by which I can propose to get a single penny; the youngest being nine years old, and my wife past child-bearing. 33

Reading and Interpreting

VOCABULARY

Use your dictionary as necessary to find the meaning of the following words as used by Swift:

importuning (1)   prodigious (2)   rudiments (6)   papists (13)

repine (14)   deference (17)   scrupulous (17)   expedient (18, 29, 30)

gibbet (18)   encumbrance (19)   pine away (19)   digressed (20)

tithes (21)   procure (25)   emulation (26)   propagation (27)

parsimony (29)   animosities (29)   disobliging (31)   overture (32)

entailing (32)

CONCEPT ANALYSIS

1. What do you infer were the conditions in Ireland that motivated Swift to write this essay? (See particularly paragraphs 19, 29, and 32.)
2. State in your own words Swift's "modest proposal." As Swift elaborates its details, what are your feelings about it?
3. One of the ways people make cruelty acceptable is to dehumanize its victims. Find images and analogies that dehumanize the Irish poor in Swift's essay.
4. We know Swift's stated proposal. In your own words what are his real proposals for remedying Ireland's ills? Evaluate them in light of Swift's description of Ireland.

   Can you think of similar socioeconomic conditions in other historical periods, including the present? To what extent would Swift's real proposals be applicable in such situations?
5. Swift's title establishes the essay's ironic nature: Statements have double meanings and imply the opposite of what they appear to say. Explain the real meaning of Swift's title and some of the following quotations:
   a. " . . . whoever could find out a fair, cheap, and easy method of making these children sound and useful members of the commonwealth, would deserve so well of the public as to have his statue set up for a preserver of the nation" (2).
   b. "I grant this food [year-old babies] will be somewhat dear, and therefore very proper for landlords, who, as they have already devoured most of the parents, seem to have the best title to the children" (12).
   c. "And as to the younger labourers, they are now in almost as hopeful a condition [as the poor people, who are aged, diseased, or maimed]" (19).
   d. "[The modest proposal] would increase the care and tenderness of mothers toward their children . . ." (26).

e. "[There would be] constant customers for infants' flesh . . . at merry meetings, particularly at weddings and christenings . . ." (28).

f. " . . . having been wearied out for many years with offering vain, idle, visionary thoughts . . . I fortunately fell upon this proposal, which . . . hath something solid and real, of no expense and little trouble, full in our own power, and whereby we can incur no danger in disobliging England" (31).

Quickwrite

What "modest proposal" can you suggest to prevent children in the United States from becoming a burden to their parents or their country?

Thinking and Writing

RHETORICAL TECHNIQUE

1. In which paragraph(s) does Swift establish the common ground of his argument? What expressions signal this?

2. Review Swift's introduction to his proposal (paragraphs 1–9). Is this introduction deductive or inductive? What is his purpose in choosing this pattern?

3. What are Swift's chief types of support for his "modest proposal": facts, examples, logical reasoning, reference to authority, emotional language? Refer to specific lines in the text in your response.

   Why are these techniques particularly effective in light of Swift's purpose?

4. Which of the different types of argument does Swift use to advance his proposal: deductive, dialectical, point-counterpoint?

   Label the parts of the essay: introduction, statement of thesis, logical proofs, refutation of opposing arguments, conclusion.

   Note paragraphs 4, 17, and 18. How would you distinguish between the content of these paragraphs and the content of paragraph 29?

5. At various points in the essay, Swift presents the advantages of his scheme. Categorize these advantages in terms of whom they benefit. Underline the words and expressions that signal the advantages.

6. The conclusion of an argumentative essay restates the thesis, reaffirms the correctness of the writer's logic, and may include a prediction related to the issue. Review Swift's conclusion (paragraphs 31–33) to identify these elements. What other purpose does Swift's conclusion appear to serve?

COMPOSITION

1. Write a serious proposal for remedying one of the following social ills: homelessness, unemployment, discrimination against women, crime in the streets, racism, or street begging. Follow Swift's deductive approach to argumentation.
2. Write an ironic "modest proposal" to remedy one of the following problems: traffic congestion, smoking in public places, noise pollution, litter, failing grades. Conclude with a paragraph modeled after Swift's paragraph 29, beginning with the sentence "Therefore let no man talk to me of other expedients," and listing a number of real alternative solutions to your stated problem.

THE WRITTEN RESPONSE

Writing Workshop

The objective of this assignment is to write an argumentative essay in the block point-counterpoint approach.

1. Choose an arguable issue, one in which two opposing sides are clearly defined. (Such issues in this chapter include capital punishment, the independence of the American colonies, and religious versus agnostic beliefs.)
2. Collaboratively or individually, brainstorm opposition points and your own points on the issue.
3. Formulate a working thesis for your point of view on the issue and complete the following chart, which will provide the structure for the development of your essay:

AUDIENCE	ISSUE (PROBLEM)	THESIS (SOLUTION)	ANTICIPATED OPPOSING POINTS	YOUR COUNTERPOINTS	ADDITIONAL POINTS

4. Begin your first draft with an introduction that leads to a statement of your thesis. Open your essay with a provocative image or anecdote, a definition of terms, or a statement of your objectivity.
5. Refer to your chart to present the opposition's points. Then in block form, refute each point with your own counterpoint.
6. Strengthen your argument by adding any further points of your own.
7. Conclude with a prediction or warning about the consequences if your thesis goes unheeded.

Topics for Critical Thinking and Writing

1. Thomas Paine wrote that the American colonies needed no monarch because in America "the law is king." Two hundred years later, can we still claim that the law is king in the United States? Support your viewpoint with arguments based on fact, logical reasoning, and examples.
2. Media appeals on the following issues have become familiar:
   a. not wearing fur coats
   b. not driving while drunk
   c. not smoking
   d. not having sexual relations without protection
   Imagine that you have five hundred words of media time or space to make a persuasive appeal on one of these issues. Write the copy.
3. Reflect on what you know of labor unions through personal experience or the experience of others close to you. Compose an argument about the role labor unions should play in American life. Using the dialectical approach, discuss both the positive and negative aspects of labor unions. In your conclusion, summarize both sides of the issue and state your synthesis, or compromise position. (You may wish to review Sidney Lens's essay "Hold That Line.")
4. Select one of the issues raised in this chapter. Write a letter to your congressional representatives in which you urge that they initiate legislation related to the issue. Use techniques of argumentation and persuasion in your letter.
5. Identify a condition or policy at your college that you believe should be changed. Write a letter to your college president advocating this change. Use logical reasoning and personal examples as your primary means of support for your thesis.
6. Figurative language plays an important part in persuasive writing. For example, Martin Luther King uses a metaphor of a bad check and Thomas Paine uses a metaphor of an unnatural parent. Select an issue for persuasive writing. Create a metaphor, simile, or analogy that represents your thesis, and develop the essay by extending this comparison throughout.
7. Using the deductive or dialectical approach to argumentation, weigh the strengths and weaknesses of each of the media—newspapers, radio, television—as a forum for the debate of complex ideas and ideals.
8. Select any issue about which you have strong feelings, and write an argumentative essay in which you advance the opposing point of view.

Synthesis Questions

1. Several writers in this chapter express or imply the idea that no one is free until all are free. Interpret and argue this notion with reference to the readings by Edmund Burke, Bartolomeo Vanzetti, Martin Luther King, and Colin Turnbull.
2. A pivotal idea in several selections in this chapter is the value of open inquiry. Think of the place of open inquiry in your own education, and discuss this idea with reference to the readings by Clarence Darrow, Colin Turnbull, and Bartolomeo Vanzetti.
3. It is crucial in argumentation for the writer or speaker to establish sincerity and credibility. Select three authors from this chapter and discuss their techniques and their effectiveness in creating a believable and persuasive voice.
4. In the argumentative or persuasive essay, predictions or warnings about the future play an important part in convincing the audience of the author's viewpoint. Review the readings by Markham, Swift, and King. In a synthesis essay, paraphrase their warnings and comment on their relevance for contemporary society.

Refining Your Essay

1. Examine your premise. Have you established common ground with your audience?
2. Review your chains of logical reasoning. Do they link ideas correctly or have you left out steps? Can you spot any logical fallacies?
3. Where might you strengthen your argument with more facts or concrete examples?
4. Have you adequately and accurately represented the opposition viewpoint?
5. Circle your key words and phrases. Are they clearly defined to avoid ambiguity?
6. Can you make your argument clearer by employing additional signal expressions?
7. Review your introduction and conclusion. Have you established your credibility and objectivity? Have you left your audience with a sense of impending doom if your arguments are ignored?

ACKNOWLEDGMENTS

Chapter Opening Illustrations

Chapter 1: Wadsworth Publishing Company.

Chapter 2: Photos courtesy Joan Young Gregg (top left), Serena Nanda (top right), John Gregg (bottom left), United Nations (bottom right).

Chapter 3: From the Collection of The Boston Children's Museum.

Chapter 4: From the Collection of The Metropolitan Museum of Art.

Chapter 5: Drawing by Marcos Pacheco. Photo by Jerry Sieser.

Chapter 6: Model and photo by Claudia Prose.

Chapter 7: From the Collection of The Pierpont Morgan Library.

Chapter 8: Photo courtesy YIVO Institute for Jewish Research.

Chapter 9: Scene from the New York City Ballet's *Nutcracker*. Photo © Martha Swope 1986.

Chapter 10: Photo from the ILGWU magazine *Justice* courtesy International Ladies' Garment Workers Union.

Text Selections

Ross K. Baker: "Why Jefferson Fainted" is from *The New York Times*, July 4, 1984. Copyright © 1984 by The New York Times Company. Used with permission of The New York Times Company.

Stringfellow Barr: "The Civilization of the Dialogue" is from *The Three Worlds of Man* (Columbia: University of Missouri Press, 1963).

William S. Burroughs: "The Cut-Up Method of Brion Gysin" is from *The Third Mind*. Copyright © The Estate of Brion Gysin 1978. Used with permission of the agent, Wylie, Aitken & Stone, Inc., New York.

Rachel Carson: "The Gray Beginnings" is from *The Sea Around Us*, Revised Edition, pp. 1–15. Copyright © 1950, 1951, 1961 by Rachel L. Carson; renewed 1979 by Roger Christie. Used with permission of Oxford University Press, Inc., New York.

Bruce Catton: "The Civil War" is from *The Civil War*, pp. 3–21. © 1960 American Heritage Inc. Used with permission of American Heritage Inc., New York, from *The American Heritage Picture History of the Civil War* by Bruce Catton. "Grant and Lee: A Study in Contrasts" is from Earl Schenck Miers, editor, *The American Story*, 1956. Used with permission of The United States Capitol Historical Society, Washington, D.C.

John Ciardi: "Another School Year— Why?" is from *Rutgers Alumni Monthly*, November 1954, pp. 2–3.

Clarence Darrow: "Why I Am an Agnostic" was originally presented at a symposium on religion, 1929.

Russell Davis: "Love" is used with permission of Russell Davis, Lakewood, New Jersey. Russell F. Davis has published numerous short stories and three novels for young adults.

Paul Laurence Dunbar: "We Wear the Mask" is from *The Complete Poems of Paul Laurence Dunbar*, 1980. Used with permission of Dodd, Mead & Company, Inc., New York.

Will Durant: "Why Men Fight [The Causes of War]" and "Why Men Fight [The Effects of War]" are from *The Saturday Evening Post*. Copyright 1937 The Curtis Publishing Co. Used with permission of The Saturday Evening Post Society, a division of the Benjamin Franklin Literary & Medical Society, Indianapolis, Indiana.

John Q. Easton and Rick Ginsberg: "Student Learning Processes: How Poorly Prepared Students Succeed in College" is from *Research and Teaching in Developmental Education*, Vol. 1, Issue 1, 1985, pp. 12–37. Used with permission of the editor, Rita Pollard, Niagara University, and the authors, John Q. Easton, Chicago Public Schools, and Rick Ginsberg, University of South Carolina at Columbia.

Peter Elbow: "Teaching Writing by Teaching Thinking" is from *Change,* September, 1983. Copyright © 1983. Published by Heldref Publications, 4000 Albemarle Street, N.W., Washington, D.C. 20016. Used with permission of the Helen Dwight Reid Educational Foundation.

Havelock Ellis: "The Philosophy of Dancing" is from *The Dance of Life,* 1923. Used with permission of Professor François Lafitte, copyright owner and executor of the Havelock Ellis literary estate in Birmingham, England.

George Fredrickson: "A Closer Parallel: Southern Blacks and Cape Coloreds" is from *White Supremacy: A Comparative Study in American and South African History.* © 1981 by Oxford University Press, Inc. Used with permission of Oxford University Press, Inc., New York.

Erich Fried: "Clever Dog" is from *Eternal Life* by Hans Kung. Translation © 1984 by William Collins Sons & Company, Ltd. and Doubleday, a division of the Bantam, Doubleday, Dell Publishing Group, Inc. Used with permission of Doubleday, a division of the Bantam, Doubleday, Dell Publishing Group, Inc., New York.

Erich Fromm: "The Theory of Love" is from *The Art of Loving.* Copyright © 1956 by Erich Fromm. Used with permission of Harper & Row, Publishers, Inc., New York.

Kahlil Gibran: "On Marriage" is from *The Prophet,* pp. 15–16. Copyright 1923 by Kahlil Gibran and renewed 1951 by Administrators C.T.A. of the Estate of Kahlil Gibran and Mary G. Gibran. Used with permission of Alfred A. Knopf, Inc., New York.

David W. Gregg: "Beyond Star Wars: Protection in Time" is used with permission of David W. Gregg, Moraga, California.

Jules Henry: "A Day at Rome High" is from *Culture Against Man,* pp. 194–208. Copyright © 1963 by Random House, Inc. Used with permission of Random House, Inc., New York.

Gilbert Highet: "Diogenes and Alexander" is from *Horizon,* March 1963. © 1963. Used with permission of American Heritage, a division of Forbes Inc., New York. "What Use Is Poetry?" is from *A Clerk of Oxenford,* Copyright © 1954 by Gilbert Highet. Used with permission of the agent, Curtis Brown, Ltd., New York.

John Holt: "How Children Fail" is from *How Children Fail,* Revised Edition. Copyright © 1964, 1982 by John Holt. Used with permission of Delacorte Press/Seymour Lawrence, New York.

Robert Jastrow: "Man of Wisdom" is from *Until the Sun Dies,* pp. 119–123. Copyright © 1977 by Robert Jastrow. Used with permission of W. W. Norton & Company, Inc., New York.

Martin Luther King, Jr.: "I Have a Dream." Copyright © 1963 by Martin Luther King, Jr. Used with permission of the agent, Joan Daves, New York.

Michael T. Klare: "Studying How to Wage Peace" is from *Newsday,* November 19, 1986. Used with permission of Michael T. Klare, Director and Associate Professor, Five College Program in Peace & World Security Studies, based at Hampshire College, Amherst, Massachusetts.

Clyde Kluckhohn: "The Concept of Culture" is from *Mirror for Man* (Tucson: University of Arizona Press, 1985). Used with permission of George E. Taylor, Seattle, Washington.

Jane B. Lancaster and Phillip Whitten: "Sharing in Human Evolution" is used with permission of Jane B. Lancaster, University of New Mexico at Albuquerque, and Phillip Whitten, Marblehead, Massachusetts.

Stephen Leacock: "Oxford as I See It" is from *My Discovery of England.* Copyright 1922 by Dodd, Mead & Company, Inc. Copyright renewed 1949 by George Leacock. Used with permission of Dodd, Mead & Company, Inc., New York.

Richard Leakey: "The Human Animal" is from *The Making of Mankind.* Used with permission of Rainbird Publishing Group Ltd., London.

Sidney Lens: "Hold That Line" is from *The Progressive,* January 1986. Copyright © 1985 The Progressive, Inc. Used with permission of The Progressive, Inc., Madison, Wisconsin.

Archibald MacLeish: "Ars Poetica" is from *New and Collected Poems: 1917–1982.*

Robert Rosenthal and Lenore Jacobson: "Pygmalion in the Classroom" is adapted from *Pygmalion in the Classroom*, pp. 102–105. Copyright © 1968 by Holt, Rinehart and Winston, Inc. Used with permission of Holt, Rinehart and Winston, Inc., Orlando, Florida.

Jonathan Schell: "The Republic of Insects and Grass" is from *The Fate of the Earth*. Copyright © 1982 by Jonathan Schell. Used with permission of Alfred A. Knopf, Inc., New York.

Stephen Spender: "An Elementary School Classroom in a Slum" is from *Selected Poems*. Copyright 1942 and renewed 1970 by Stephen Spender. Used with permission of Random House, Inc., New York, and Faber and Faber Ltd., London.

Cecie Starr and Ralph Taggart: "The Emergence of Evolutionary Thought" is from *Biology*, Third Edition, pp. 25–27 and 33–36. © 1984 by Wadsworth, Inc. "Aristotle's 'Ladder of Life'" (Figure 1) is from *Biology*, Fourth Edition, p. 23. © 1987 by Wadsworth, Inc. Both used with permission of Wadsworth Publishing Company, Belmont, California.

Studs Terkel: "American Dreams" is from *American Dreams: Lost and Found*. Copyright © 1980 by Studs Terkel. Used with permission of Pantheon Books, a division of Random House, Inc., New York.

James Thurber: "The Human Being and the Dinosaur" is from *Fables for Our Time*, published by Harper & Row. Copr. © 1940 James Thurber. Copr. © 1968 Helen Thurber. Used with permission of Rosemary A. Thurber, South Haven, Michigan.

Barbara Tuchman: "When Does History Happen?" is from *The New York Times Book Review*, March 8, 1964. Copyright © 1964 by Barbara Tuchman. Used with permission of the agents for the author, Russell and Volkening, Inc., New York.

Colin Turnbull: "Death by Decree: An Anthropological Approach to Capital Punishment" is from *Natural History Magazine*, May 1978. Used with permission of the author and the author's agents, Scott Meredith Literary Agency, Inc., New York.

Mark Twain: "The Lowest Animal" is from *Letters from the Earth*, edited by Bernard DeVoto. Copyright © 1962 by the Mark Twain Co. Copyright 1942 by The President and Fellows of Harvard College. Used with permission of Harper & Row, Publishers, Inc., New York.

Robert Penn Warren: "The Legacy of the Civil War" is from *The Legacy of the Civil War*, pp. 3–16. Copyright © 1961 by Robert Penn Warren. Used with permission of Random House, Inc., New York.

Richard Wright: "Black Boy" is an excerpt from *Black Boy*, Chapter 8. Copyright 1937, 1942, 1944, 1945 by Richard Wright. Used with permission of Harper & Row, Publishers, Inc., New York.